HARCOURT BRACE & COMPANY

Orlando Atlanta Austin Boston San Francisco Chicago Dallas New York
Toronto London

Printed in the United States of America
ISBN 0-15-301866-6
8 9 10   048   97

▪ ACKNOWLEDGMENTS ▪

Some computer lessons in this book are based on AppleWorks® by Claris Corporation. © 1989
by Claris Corporation. All rights reserved. Claris is a registered trademark of Claris Corporation.
AppleWorks is a registered trademark of Apple Computer, Inc. licensed to Claris Corporation.
Apple is a registered trademark of Apple Computer, Inc.

Logo lessons in this book present the Terrapin Logo version. Terrapin is a registered trademark of
Terrapin Software, Inc.

See page H33 for photo and art credits.

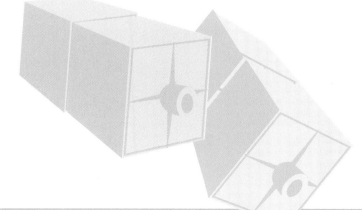

∎AUTHORS∎

Grace M. Burton
Professor, Department of Curricular Studies
University of North Carolina at Wilmington
Wilmington, North Carolina

Jerome D. Kaplan
Professor of Education
Seton Hall University
South Orange, New Jersey

Martha H. Hopkins
Associate Professor
University of Central Florida
Orlando, Florida

Leonard Kennedy
Professor Emeritus
California State University at Sacramento
Sacramento, California

Howard C. Johnson
Chair, Mathematics Education
Professor of Mathematics and Mathematics Education
Syracuse University
Syracuse, New York

Karen A. Schultz
Professor, Mathematics Education
Georgia State University
Atlanta, Georgia

∎SENIOR EDITORIAL ADVISORS∎

Francis (Skip) Fennell
Professor of Education
Western Maryland College
Westminster, Maryland

Evan M. Maletsky
Professor of Mathematics
Montclair State College
Upper Montclair, New Jersey

∎ADVISORS∎

Janet S. Abbott
Curriculum Coordinator
Chula Vista Elementary School District
Chula Vista, California

Michael C. Hynes
Professor
University of Central Florida
Orlando, Florida

Sid Rachlin
Mathematics Education Coordinator
East Carolina University
Greenville, North Carolina

Don S. Balka
Professor
Saint Mary's College
Notre Dame, Indiana

Marsha W. Lilly
Mathematics Coordinator, K–12
Alief Independent School District
Alief, Texas

Kay Sammons
Supervisor of Mathematics - Elementary
Howard County School District
Ellicott City, Maryland

George W. Bright
Professor of Mathematics Education
The University of North Carolina at
  Greensboro
Greensboro, North Carolina

Douglas McLeod
Professor of Mathematics
San Diego State University
San Diego, California

Dorothy S. Strong
Manager, Mathematics Support
Chicago Public Schools
Chicago, Illinois

∎MULTICULTURAL ADVISORS∎

Pat A. Browne
Director, African Centered Multicultural
  Education
Indianapolis Public Schools
Indianapolis, Indiana

Asa G. Hilliard III
Fuller E. Callaway Professor of Urban
  Education
Georgia State University
Atlanta, Georgia

Young Pai
Chairman, Div. of Social-Philosophical
  Foundations of Education
University of Missouri
Kansas City, Missouri

Gilbert Cuevas
Professor of Education
University of Miami
Coral Gables, Florida

Genevieve M. Knight
Professor of Mathematics
Coppin State College
Baltimore, Maryland

Susan Cashman Paterniti
School Board Member
Port Charlotte, Florida

CONTENTS

2 Adding and Subtracting Whole Numbers and Decimals

5 Dividing Whole Numbers by 1-Digit Numbers

6 Dividing Whole Numbers by 2-Digit Numbers

7 Statistics and Graphing

8 Multiplying and Dividing Decimals

9 Number Theory and Fractions

12 Perimeter, Area, and Volume

THEME: Carpentry   386

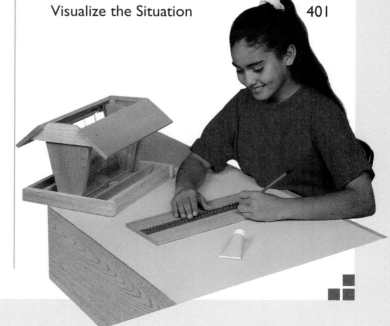

13 Ratio, Percent, and Probability

Welcome to MATHEMATICS PLUS

Mathematics is an important part of your daily life. You use it at school, at home, and everywhere you go!

As you learn mathematics this year, look in your book for M.C. Lion. M.C. will give you hints for solving problems and tips for studying math.

This year you are going to use ideas you have already learned in interesting, new ways. You will learn more about solving problems. You will use the calculator and the computer as problem-solving tools. You will learn more about decimals and fractions. You will learn more about the perimeter and area of plane shapes and about the volume of solid shapes. You will work with very large and very small numbers. You will learn to do mental math and to estimate—so you can use numbers quickly to solve problems every day!

Math is fun! You will work in groups to share what you are learning. You will have fun solving the puzzles and problems in the **Math Fun Magazine** at the back of this book.

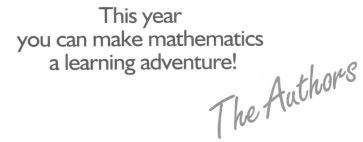

This year
you can make mathematics
a learning adventure!

The Authors

How Do You Use Math Every Day?

People use math to help them do many things. Here are some of the things you do in which you use math.

shop	weigh
count	measure
share	save
build	cook
travel	tell time
compare	keep score
estimate	predict

Look at these pictures. Talk about how math is being used. Think of some ways you have used math to help you. Share your ideas with a classmate.

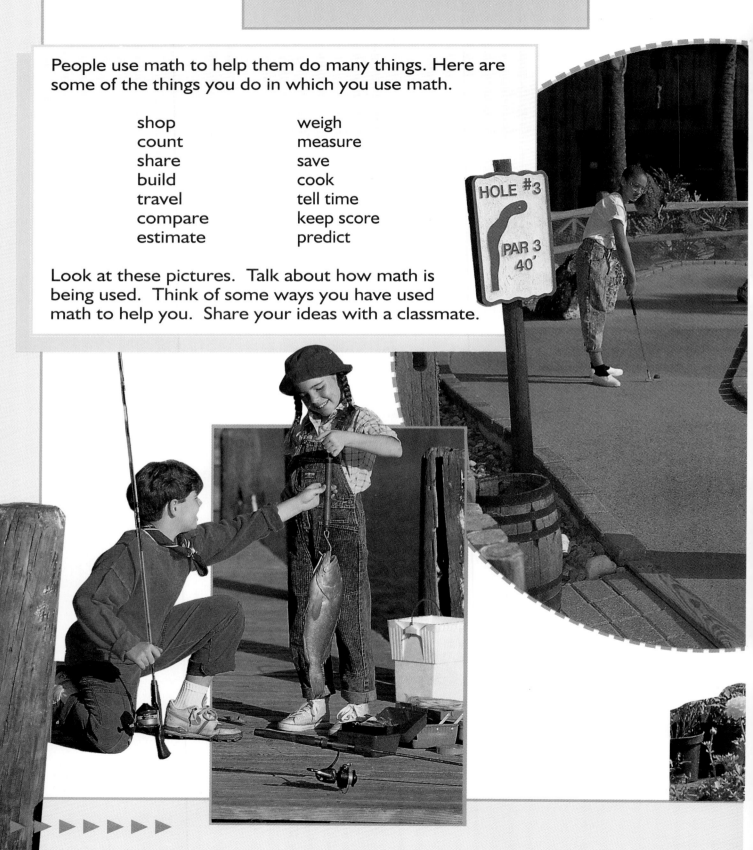

How Will You Solve Problems?

You use math every day to solve problems. In this book you will learn how to solve problems by asking yourself questions. These questions will help you

- UNDERSTAND the problem.
- PLAN a solution.
- SOLVE the problem.
- LOOK BACK and check your solution.

Will has a problem to solve. Read his problem slowly and carefully.

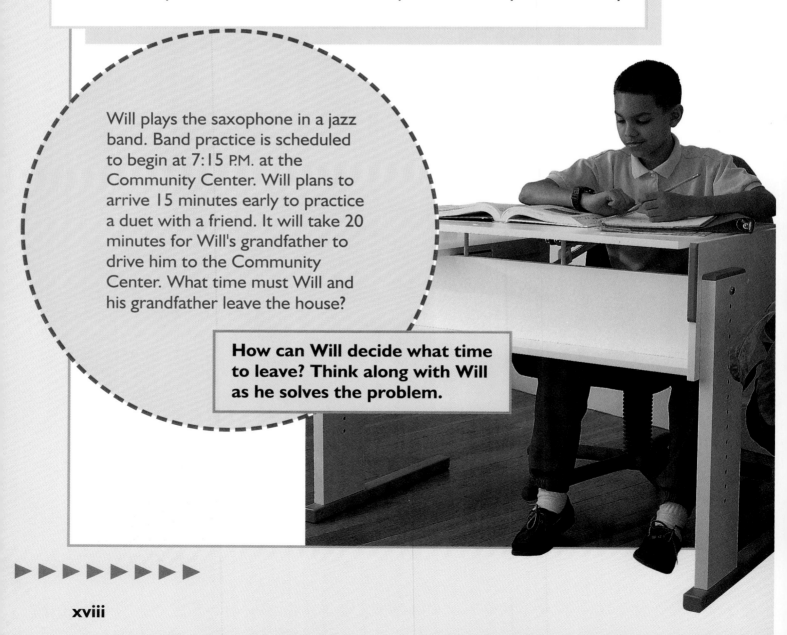

Will plays the saxophone in a jazz band. Band practice is scheduled to begin at 7:15 P.M. at the Community Center. Will plans to arrive 15 minutes early to practice a duet with a friend. It will take 20 minutes for Will's grandfather to drive him to the Community Center. What time must Will and his grandfather leave the house?

How can Will decide what time to leave? Think along with Will as he solves the problem.

Understand the Problem

First, Will must UNDERSTAND the problem.

He restates the problem to himself. He wants to be sure he knows what the problem is about. Then he asks himself these questions.

What must I find?
I must find the time when I should leave the house so I can meet my friend before band practice and be on time for practice.

What facts do I have?
Band practice starts at 7:15 P.M. I need to meet my friend 15 minutes before practice. It takes 20 minutes to drive to the Community Center.

How would you restate Will's problem in your own words?

Then, Will must PLAN how to solve his problem.

He thinks about the ways he solves problems. He chooses one of these strategies.

- Draw a picture
- Make a model
- Work backward
- Guess and check
- Act out the problem
- Write a number sentence

Then he makes a plan by asking himself this question.

How can I solve the problem? Since I know when practice starts, I can work backward from that time to find the time I must leave the house.

What other plan could Will have made?

▶ ▶ ▶ ▶ ▶ ▶ ▶ ▶ ▶

Solve the Problem

Next, Will must SOLVE the problem.

He must decide how to solve the problem. He must choose the method of computation he will use to find the answer.

PAPER AND PENCIL

MENTAL MATH

CALCULATOR

MANIPULATIVES

I can use paper and pencil to find the answer.

 I can draw a clockface and work backward from 7:15 to find the time I should leave the house.

20 min. — 15 min. Start at 7:15.

Go back 15 minutes.

Go back 20 minutes.

So, I must leave the house at 6:40.

Why do you think Will worked backward to find the time? What method would you choose?

Look Back

Last, Will can LOOK BACK and check whether his answer is correct.

He thinks about a way to check his answer. He thinks about whether his solution answers the question.

He asks himself these questions.

How can I check my answer? I can add the number of minutes I will practice with my friend and the number of minutes it takes to drive to the Community Center. I can then count back the total number of minutes from 7:15.

15 min + 20 min = 35 min
35 minutes before 7:15 is 6:40.

Does my solution answer the question? Since I found when I need to leave the house to arrive at band practice on time, my solution answers the question.

How else could Will check his answer?

Will solved his problem. He used math to help him get to band practice on time.

In Mathematics Plus you will learn to be a problem solver!

▶ ▶ ▶ ▶ ▶ ▶ ▶ ▶

How Will You Learn Math?

In Mathematics Plus you will learn math in different ways. All of the ways to learn involve *thinking*.

You will learn math by

- working with a group.
- modeling problems, using objects and diagrams.
- listening to your teacher and your classmates.
- talking about math ideas.
- writing about math ideas.
- recording the meanings of new words.
- choosing problem-solving strategies.
- making decisions about how to solve problems.
- using math in school, at home, and everywhere.

WORKING TOGETHER

- Listen carefully to other people's ideas.
- Encourage others to share their ideas.
- Discuss ideas in a friendly way.
- Plan how your group is going to share the work.

PLACE VALUE
WHOLE NUMBERS AND DECIMALS

Did you know . . .

. . . that in 1833 Benjamin H. Day started the *New York Sun,* the first of many successful newspapers, and charged $0.01 per copy?

TALK ABOUT IT

The number of United States newspapers peaked in 1909, when the country had about 2,600 different daily newspapers. Today the country has about 1,700 different daily newspapers. What conclusions can you draw about the number of newspapers in 1909 and the number of newspapers today?

BOSTON

★★   *★★*

GAZETTE

5¢

Home Delivery
30c/Week

NEWS!!

nday, August 6, 1893

ne 25, No. 37
ges

BOSTON

★★   *★★*

GAZETTE

5¢

Home Delivery
30c/Week

NEWS!!

Monday, August 6, 1893

Volume 25, No. 37
16 Pages

BOSTON

★★   *★★*

GAZETTE

5¢

Home Delivery
30c/Week

NEWS!!

RAILROAD
RATES
NTRIBUTE
BUSINESS
PANIC

Doctor's Horse Runs Amuck In Courtroom

Doctor Matling's horse, Toby, took
matters into his own hands last Thursday.

At 2:30 in the afternoon the horse with empty buggy attached,
climbed the courthouse steps and entered one of the
court rooms greatly disturbing its occupants.

A Rare Event!

World's Fair In Chicago

EDISON RECEIVES PATENT

CHILD LABOR MUST CEASE

EXPLORING

Place Value of Whole Numbers

Building Understanding

One way that number values can be shown is with base-ten blocks. If you let the unit represent 1, you can make the following chart.

Thousands	Hundreds	Tens	Ones
cube	flat	long	unit

TALK ABOUT IT

- Show the block that represents 10×1.

- Show the block that represents 10×10.

- Show the block that represents 10×100.

Use the base-ten blocks to explore place-value ideas.

A. What relationship do you see between the two base-ten blocks in each pair?

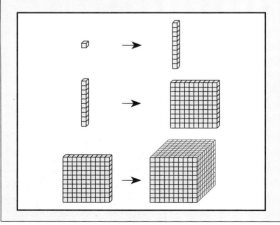

B. What relationship does this function table show? What is the rule?

X	?
1	10
10	100
100	1,000
1,000	?

C. As you move from the right to the left, what is the relationship between place-value positions in the place-value chart?

Thousands	Hundreds	Tens	Ones

2

Making the Connection

This chart shows the value of 1 in different place-value positions.
The factors complete a multiplication sentence for each value.

Thousands			Ones			
Hundreds	Tens	Ones	Hundreds	Tens	Ones	
					1	
				1	0	$= 10 \times 1$
			1	0	0	$= 10 \times 10$
		1 ,	0	0	0	$= 10 \times 10 \times 10$
	1	0 ,	0	0	0	$= 10 \times 10 \times 10 \times 10$
1	0	0 ,	0	0	0	$= 10 \times 10 \times 10 \times 10 \times 10$

You can use **exponents** to express numbers.

exponent
$$10^4$$
base

4 is the exponent. It shows how many times the base is a factor multiplied by itself.

10 is the base.

Read: ten to the fourth power

So, $10^4 = 10 \times 10 \times 10 \times 10 = 10,000$.
power of 10   factors   value

1. What base-ten block represents 10^3?

2. How many times greater is 10^3 than 10^2?

3. How is the number of zeros in a number related to the exponent for its power of ten?

4. Use the place-value chart to write each value from 10 through 100,000 by using an exponent. Example: $10 = 10^1$.

Checking Understanding

Complete.

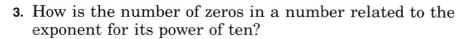

5. $10 \times \blacksquare = 100$ 6. $10^2 = \blacksquare$ 7. $10^{\blacksquare} = 100,000$

	Number Name	Number	Multiplication	Power of Ten
8.	ten	$\blacksquare$	10×1	10^1
9.	hundred	100	10×10	$\blacksquare$
10.	thousand	1,000	$\blacksquare$	10^3
11.	_?_	10,000	$10 \times 10 \times 10 \times 10$	10^4
12.	hundred thousand	100,000	$10 \times 10 \times 10 \times 10 \times 10$	$\blacksquare$

PLACE VALUE
to Hundred Thousands

The news media cover many athletic events in stadiums. This table shows the number of seats in some stadiums in the United States.

Seating Capacity in Stadiums	
Stadium	Number of Seats
Pontiac Silverdome	80,638
Rose Bowl	106,721
Astrodome	50,599

You can use the place-value chart to name the value of each digit in 106,721.

Thousands			Ones		
Hundreds	Tens	Ones	Hundreds	Tens	Ones
1	0	6	7	2	1

$$1 \times 1 = 1$$
$$2 \times 10 = 20$$
$$7 \times 100 = 700$$
$$6 \times 1,000 = 6,000$$
$$0 \times 10,000 = 0$$
$$1 \times 100,000 = 100,000$$

A number can be expressed in different ways.

Standard Form: 106,721
Expanded Form:

$$100,000 + 0 + 6,000 + 700 + 20 + 1$$
$$(1 \times 100,000) + (0 \times 10,000) + (6 \times 1,000) + (7 \times 100) + (2 \times 10) + (1 \times 1)$$
$$(1 \times 10^5) + (0 \times 10^4) + (6 \times 10^3) + (7 \times 10^2) + (2 \times 10^1) + (1 \times 10^0)$$

Word Form: one hundred six thousand, seven hundred twenty-one

Check for Understanding

Write two other forms for each number.

1. $40,000 + 7,000 + 600 + 10 + 3$

2. 361,401

Write the value of each underlined digit.

3. 2_9_,416

4. 98,_5_40

5. 380,2_5_6

6. _2_02,439

Practice

Write two other forms for each number.

7. 18,960   **8.** 68,582   **9.** 124,379   **10.** 207,503

11. one hundred fifteen thousand, four hundred eighty-seven

12. three hundred fifty-one thousand, five hundred twelve

13. 200,000 + 80,000 + 4,000 + 600 + 70 + 3

14. 400,000 + 6,000 + 10

> I can change the standard form into expanded form and word form.

Write the value of each underlined digit.

15. 6,7<u>9</u>5   **16.** <u>9</u>03   **17.** 1<u>6</u>,098   **18.** <u>7</u>60,439

19. 5<u>1</u>7,034   **20.** 80<u>7</u>,213   **21.** 32,<u>7</u>16   **22.** 1,00<u>6</u>

Mixed Applications

Write in two different forms.

23. I am a number greater than 99,999 but less than 100,001. What am I?

24. I am a number less than 150,000 but greater than 149,998. What am I?

SOCIAL STUDIES CONNECTION

Roman numerals can be found on clock faces, pages of books, and cornerstones. Where have you seen Roman numerals?

I	II	III	IV	V	VI	VII	VIII	IX	X	L	C
1	2	3	4	5	6	7	8	9	10	50	100

To find the value of a Roman numeral, add when the symbols are alike or when they decrease in value from left to right.

XVII = 10 + 5 + 1 + 1, or 17   CLXI = 100 + 50 + 10 + 1, or 161

Subtract when the value of a symbol is less than the value of the symbol to its right.

In the number CIX, C = 100, I is less than X, so IX = 10 − 1, or 9. So, CIX = 100 + 9, or 109.

Write the Roman numerals in standard form.

25. XVI   **26.** XXIII   **27.** XC   **28.** VL

Describe how the expanded form helps you understand the value of a number.

WRAP UP...

PLACE VALUE
to Hundred Millions

People throughout the world like to follow sports. Cricket is a popular sport in England and Australia as well as in many other countries. After a recent match between England and Australia, about 12,000,000 people read newspaper accounts of the match.

Use the place-value chart to help you read this number.

Millions			Thousands			Ones		
Hundreds	Tens	Ones	Hundreds	Tens	Ones	Hundreds	Tens	Ones
	1	2,	0	0	0,	0	0	0

← periods

Large numbers are separated into **periods,** each containing three place-value positions. Commas separate the periods and show where to use the period name.

Standard Form: 12,000,000

Expanded Form:

10,000,000 + 2,000,000
$(1 \times 10{,}000{,}000)$ + $(2 \times 1{,}000{,}000)$
(1×10^7) + (2×10^6)

Word Form: twelve million

Talk About It

Look at this number.   44,444,444

▶ How does the value of the digit 4 change as you look from right to left?

▶ How can you use a calculator to change the number to 54,444,444?

Check for Understanding

Use the number 784,251,060 for Exercises 1–4.

1. Write the value of the digit 8.

2. Write the word form of the number.

3. Name the period that includes the digits 251.

4. Name the place-value position of the digit 7.

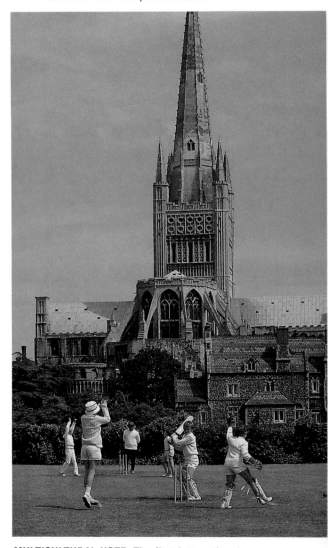

MULTICULTURAL NOTE: The first international cricket match was played between England and Australia in 1877.

Practice

Write the value of each underlined digit.

5. 1,98<u>2</u>,435
6. <u>8</u>,759,635
7. 75,<u>9</u>27,643

8. 49<u>3</u>,850,969
9. 790,2<u>6</u>3,485
10. <u>1</u>52,065,468

Write two other forms for each number.

11. 932,400
12. 8,210,100
13. 853,425,756

14. 100,000,000 + 50,000,000 + 400,000 + 20,000 + 5,000 + 700

15. 500,000,000 + 3,000,000 + 200,000 + 70,000 + 6,000 + 400

16. forty million, nine hundred thousand, five hundred eight

17. one hundred three million, six hundred eighty-five

18. two hundred thirty-five million, three thousand, ten

Mixed Applications

19. In a recent year, 50,241,840 homes had cable television. If 5 million more homes were added to this number, what would be the total number of homes with cable television?

20. A top television show was viewed in about fifty million homes. Write in two different forms the number that is one million less than fifty million.

EVERYDAY MATH CONNECTION

You can use the short word form to write a large number. First, write the digits in each period. Then, write the name of each period. It is not necessary to write the word form for the ones period.

Standard Form: 321,506,974
Short Word Form: 321 million, 506 thousand, 974

250 MILLION...

Write the short word form.

21. 250,725,697
22. 801,048,500
23. 900,000,050

Why is it important to remember the name of each period in a large number?

WRAP UP...

COMPARING AND ORDERING
Whole Numbers

Mr. Lucci turned a spinner five times and called out one digit each time. Sara and Ben each tried to write the greater number.

Sara ⟨1⟩⟨2⟩,⟨6⟩⟨7⟩⟨3⟩   Ben ⟨1⟩⟨2⟩,⟨7⟩⟨6⟩⟨3⟩

- How can you tell who wrote the greater number?

You can compare numbers by comparing the digits in each place-value position.

<	is less than
>	is greater than
=	is equal to

Compare 12,673 and 12,763. Start at the left. Check each place until the digits are different.

Step 1	**Step 2**	**Step 3**
Compare the ten thousands.	Compare the thousands.	Compare the hundreds.
12,673	12,673	12,673
↓ same number of ten thousands	↓ same number of thousands	↓ 7 > 6
12,763	12,763	12,763

Since 12,763 > 12,673, Ben wrote the greater number.

You can order numbers by comparing them in the same way.
Order from greatest to least. 34,267; 35,764; 32,876

Step 1	**Step 2**	**Step 3**	**Step 4**
Compare the ten thousands.	Compare the thousands.	Order the digits.	Order the numbers.
34,267	34,267		
↓	↓		35,764
35,764 same number of ten thousands	35,764	5 > 4 > 2	34,267
↓	↓		32,876
32,876	32,876		

Talk About It

▶ Why do you start at the left to compare the digits?

▶ How could you order 34,267; 35,764; and 32,876 from least to greatest?

▶ How is comparing 13,425 and 7,289 different from the comparison above?

Check for Understanding

Name the place-value position where the numbers differ.

1. 1,200; 1,500

2. 15,750; 15,740

3. 125,200; 120,500

Write whether the numbers are in order from *least to greatest* or from *greatest to least*.

4. 1,250; 1,500; 12,000

5. 18,525; 18,250; 1,850

6. 49,672; 49,762; 49,768

Practice

Write <, >, or = for ●.

7. 1,467 ● 1,376

8. 42,347 ● 42,437

9. 5,416,367 ● 5,416,367

Order from least to greatest.

10. 1,928; 1,856; 2,414

11. 26,430; 25,478; 26,413

12. 360,030; 306,600; 300,060

Order from greatest to least.

13. 4,645; 6,765; 6,583

14. 12,680; 13,200; 13,039

15. 458,608; 567,806; 485,304

Mixed Applications

Use the table to answer Exercises 16–18.

Network TV Program Viewing	
Evening Programs	**Number of Households**
Informational program	10,350,000
General drama	11,020,000
Suspense and mystery	13,040,000
Situation comedy	15,920,000
Feature film	14,580,000
Adventure	8,770,000

16. Which programs are viewed by the most households? the fewest households?

17. Which programs are viewed by fewer than 12,000,000 households?

18. **Making Decisions**   Which two kinds of TV programs would you choose to advertise a new product? Why?

How do you use place-value ideas when you compare numbers?

ESTIMATE
by Rounding Whole Numbers

A newspaper office reports a circulation of 36,475 newspapers. To the nearest ten thousand, about how many newspapers are circulated?

You can estimate 36,475 by rounding to the nearest ten thousand. You can use a number line to help you.

36,475

Notice that 36,475 is closer to 40,000 than to 30,000. So, about 40,000 newspapers are circulated.

To round a number, look at the digit to the right of the place to which you are rounding.

If that digit is less than 5, the digit being rounded remains the same. | If that digit is 5 or more, the digit being rounded increases by 1.

Examples

A. Round 36,475 to the nearest thousand.

digit to be rounded ⟶ 4 < 5

3**6**,475
↓
3**6**,000

So, the thousands digit remains the same.

B. Round 36,475 to the nearest hundred.

digit to be rounded ⟶ 7 > 5

36,**4**75
↓
36,**5**00

So, the hundreds digit increases by 1.

C. Round 36,475 to the nearest ten.

digit to be rounded ⟶ 5 = 5

36,4**7**5
↓
36,4**8**0

So, the tens digit increases by 1.

Talk About It

▶ Why would the newspaper want to round its circulation to the nearest ten thousand rather than to the nearest thousand?

▶ What happens when you round 18,967 to the nearest hundred?

Check for Understanding

Round to the nearest thousand.

1. 2,816   2. 13,465   3. 238,716   4. 46,528

Round to the nearest hundred.

5. 3,621   6. 945   7. 20,835   8. 175,984

Practice

Round to the nearest ten.

9. 423   **10.** 549   **11.** 495   **12.** 834   **13.** 1,287

Round to the nearest hundred.

14. 874   **15.** 416   **16.** 764   **17.** 4,398   **18.** 1,952

Round to the nearest thousand.

19. 3,267   **20.** 8,090   **21.** 9,900   **22.** 15,123   **23.** 68,500

Round to the nearest ten thousand.

24. 37,205   **25.** 58,936   **26.** 324,520   **27.** 845,625

Round to the nearest hundred thousand.

28. 483,267   **29.** 678,090   **30.** 449,300   **31.** 12,786,500

Round to the nearest million.

32. 35,458,936   **33.** 20,843,267   **34.** 135,984,600

Mixed Applications

Use the table for Exercises 35–36.

35. Which kind of magazine has a circulation of about 5,000,000?

36. Round to the nearest million, and write about how many more news magazines are sold than travel magazines.

Circulation of Magazines	
Kinds of Magazines	**Number Circulated**
News magazine	5,748,324
Sports magazine	4,928,165
Food magazine	1,875,692
Travel magazine	1,379,685

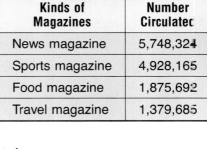

37. Number Sense The number 149 is the greatest three-digit number that can be rounded to 100. What is the greatest four-digit number that can be rounded to 1,000?

38. Number Sense The number 50 is the least two-digit number that can be rounded to 100. What is the least three-digit number that can be rounded to 1,000?

In what kinds of situations are rounded numbers more useful than exact numbers?

More Practice, Lesson 1.5, page H35

PROBLEM SOLVING

STRATEGY • Make a Table

An ecologist has been studying fish near a coral reef. He wants to find out which of four species of fish was most affected by an oil spill. He has a list of the number of fish he observed in the area before and after the oil spill. Which species of fish was most affected by the oil spill?

Information, or **data,** about problems in the environment is often given in the news.

▶ **UNDERSTAND**

What is the problem about?

What does the ecologist want to find out?

▶ **PLAN**

How can the ecologist display his data?

First, he can make a table to organize the data. Then, he can compare the data.

▶ **SOLVE**

How will you carry out the plan?

Make a table of the data; then compare the fish counted before and after the spill.

Live Fish Counted		
Species of Fish	**Before Spill**	**After Spill**
Angelfish	238	58
Clownfish	434	391
Shark	9	9
Squirrel fish	168	159

← Name the table.

← Label the columns.

Fill in the data.

So, the species of fish most affected by the oil spill was the angelfish.

▶ **LOOK BACK**

How does the table help you find the answer?

WHAT IF... ... the ecologist had counted 500 angelfish before the spill? Would he be more worried or less worried about them?

Apply

Make a table and answer the questions.

Cats Are Top Dog

Coretta and her classmates gathered information about pets belonging to students. They found that the kindergarten students had 34 dogs, 41 cats, 23 tropical fish, 8 birds, and 6 hamsters. The first graders had 31 dogs, 27 tropical fish, 8 hamsters, 7 birds, and 38 cats.

A Day at the Beach

Three boys counted shells they saw at the beach. In the morning Bert counted 43 shells, Hank counted 52 shells, and Jerome counted 65 shells. That evening Bert counted 48 shells, Hank counted 37 shells, and Jerome counted 46 shells.

(1) Which kind of pet is owned by the most students?

(2) Which group of students owns more dogs?

(3) Do the first graders own more birds or more hamsters?

(4) Who counted the most shells in the morning?

(5) Did Bert count more shells in the morning or in the evening?

Mixed Applications ➡ **STRATEGIES** Make a Table • Act It Out • Make a Drawing

Choose a strategy and solve.

Use the following information for Exercises 6–7.

Central School had a reading contest. The students from Room A read 20 books the first week, 35 books the second, and 27 books the third. The students from Room B read 27 books the first week, 30 books the second, and 35 books the third.

(6) Which class read the most books the first week?

(7) Which week did Room A students read more books than Room B students?

(8) Steven, David, Maria, Jon, and Chris sit in the same row in math class. Maria sits in front of Steven, and Jon sits four seats in front of Chris. David sits behind Steven. Who sits directly behind Jon?

(9) Each side of a square patio is 10 feet long. Starting at one corner, there is a plant every 2 feet around the border of the patio. How many plants are around the patio?

More Practice, Lesson 1.6, page H35

REVIEW AND MAINTENANCE

Make a table to answer each question.

Remember to name the table, label the columns, and fill in the data.

1. Tommy, Teresa, and David are collecting photos from magazines for a project. Before lunch Tommy found 10 photos, Teresa found 13, and David found 18. After lunch Teresa found 14 photos, Tommy found 12, and David found 8. Who found the most photos?

2. Sheila delivers newspapers on Mondays, Wednesdays, and Fridays. On Monday and Friday mornings, she delivers to 35 homes. On Wednesday mornings, she delivers to 30 homes. On Monday and Wednesday afternoons, she delivers to 25 homes. On which day does Sheila deliver the most papers?

Write two other forms for each number.

3. 18,960

4. 12,000,008

5. 30,000,000 + 80,000 + 4,000 + 50 + 8

6. one hundred fifteen thousand, four hundred eighty-seven

Name the place-value position where the numbers differ.

7. 13,574; 23,574

8. 17,524; 17,324

Write in order from least to greatest.

9. 4,568; 5,658; 5,458; 4,856

10. 1,250,000; 1,050,000; 1,025,000; 1,005,000

Round to the nearest million.

11. 153,849,400

Round to the nearest thousand.

12. 472,135

Round to the nearest ten thousand.

13. 85,473

Round to the nearest hundred.

14. 1,894

Complete.

15. $10 \times \blacksquare \times 10 = 1,000$

16. $10^6 = \blacksquare$

17. $10 \times 10 \times 10 \times 10 = \blacksquare$

18. $100 = 10^{\blacksquare}$

ASIA

Philippines

Draw Conclusions

You can use a table to help you analyze and compare data. You can **draw conclusions** from data that has been collected.

The following table gives some information about several major volcanoes.

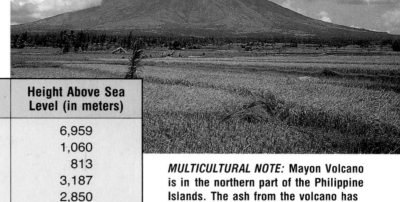

Name	Location	Height Above Sea Level (in meters)
Aconcagua	Argentina	6,959
El Chichón	Mexico	1,060
Krakatoa	Indonesia	813
Lassen Peak	United States	3,187
Mount Tambora	Indonesia	2,850
Paricutín	Mexico	2,808
Vesuvius	Italy	1,277

MULTICULTURAL NOTE: Mayon Volcano is in the northern part of the Philippine Islands. The ash from the volcano has greatly improved the fertility of the soil.

Work Together

Using the data in the table above, answer the following questions.

1. List the three tallest volcanoes, from the highest to the lowest.

2. What is the difference in meters between the highest and lowest volcanoes?

3. Which volcano is higher, El Chichón or Vesuvius?

4. Compare the difference in height between Vesuvius and El Chichón and the difference between El Chichón and Krakatoa. Which difference is greater?

5. Write your own problem based on the table. Exchange with a partner and solve.

EXPLORING

Place Value of Decimals

Building Understanding

Decimal numbers and fractions can be modeled on decimal squares.

This square represents a whole, or 1.	The whole is divided into 10 equal parts. One part is shaded.	The whole is divided into 100 equal parts. One part is shaded.
Read: one **Write:** 1 or 1.0	**Read:** one tenth **Write:** $\frac{1}{10}$ or 0.1	**Read:** one hundredth **Write:** $\frac{1}{100}$ or 0.01

Decimal numbers can be modeled using money.

dollar (100 cents)	dime (10 cents)	penny (1 cent)

$1.00	$0.10	$0.01

Decimal numbers can be modeled using a meterstick.

meter (100 centimeters)	decimeter (10 centimeters)	centimeter

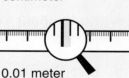

1.0 meter	0.1 meter	0.01 meter

TALK ABOUT IT

- How is the whole represented in decimal squares, money, and metric units? the tenth? the hundredth?

- How many pennies equal a dime? dimes equal a dollar?

- How many centimeters equal a decimeter? decimeters equal a meter?

- What pattern do you observe in all three models?

Making the Connection

As with whole numbers, decimal numbers can be shown on a place-value chart.

Hundreds	Tens	Ones	.	Tenths	Hundredths	
1	0	0	.			= 100
	1	0	.			= 10
		1	.			= 1
		0	.	1		= 0.1 or $\frac{1}{10}$
		0	.	0	1	= 0.01 or $\frac{1}{100}$

↑ decimal point

TALK ABOUT IT

• What is the purpose of the decimal point?

• Is 0.01 greater than or less than 0.1? Explain.

• Is 0.1 greater than or less than 1? Explain.

• What happens to the value of the 1 as it moves to the right on the place-value chart?

Checking Understanding

Write the amount as a decimal form of the whole unit.

1. 3 dimes

2. 3 decimeters

3. 3 tenths

4. 7 pennies

5. 7 centimeters

6. 7 hundredths

Complete.

7. 10 cents = ▨

8. 1 penny = ▨

9. ▨ = 100 pennies

10. 1 decimeter = ▨ meter

11. ▨ dimes = 1 dollar

12. 1 meter = ▨ centimeters

13. 1 dime = ▨ pennies

14. 1 dollar = ▨ pennies

15. 1 centimeter = ▨ meter

 Use a calculator. Write in order the keys you can use to change the given numbers.

16. 6.78 to 6.08

17. 12.06 to 12.46

DECIMALS
Tenths and Hundredths

Decimals are used to name parts of a whole. You can use base-ten blocks to help you read and write decimals for 10 or 100 equal parts of a whole.

Tens	Ones	Tenths	Hundredths
cube	flat	long	unit
ten 10.0	one 1.0	one tenth 0.1	one hundredth 0.01

If you let the flat represent 1, you can make this chart.

You can use a place-value chart to find the value of each digit.

Tens	Ones	Tenths	Hundredths
3	4	6	5
			5 × 0.01 5 hundredths = 0.05
		6 × 0.1 6 tenths = 0.6	
	4 × 1 = 4.0 4 ones = 4.0		
3 × 10 = 30.0 3 tens = 30.0			

Standard Form: 34.65
Expanded Form: 30 + 4 + 0.6 + 0.05 = 34.65
Word Form: thirty-four and sixty-five hundredths

- How does a calculator display four tenths? fifty-two hundredths?

- Why do you use the word *and* to name the decimal point?

Check for Understanding

1.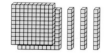

2.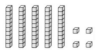

3.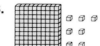

Write the value of each underlined digit as a decimal and a fraction.

4. 0.<u>2</u>   **5.** <u>1</u>8.37   **6.** 0.7<u>8</u>   **7.** 41.<u>0</u>3   **8.** <u>1</u>00.05

Practice

Draw the base-ten blocks used to show each decimal number.

9. 0.7   **10.** 0.82   **11.** 2.9   **12.** 3.75

Copy and complete the table.

Word Form	Fraction Form	Decimal Form
13. three tenths	$\frac{3}{10}$	■
14. __?__	$\frac{15}{100}$	0.15
15. seven hundredths	■	0.07
16. four and nine tenths	$4\frac{9}{10}$	■
17. __?__	$82\frac{49}{100}$	82.49
18. thirty hundredths	■	0.30

$5.20

$0.50

$2.95

Look at the pictures to solve Exercises 19–20.

19. The price of which item has the digit 5 in the hundredths place?

20. The price of which item has the digit 2 in the tenths place?

Mixed Applications

21. Paper speeds through a printing press at a rate of three-tenths kilometer per minute. If a new printing press could print one-tenth kilometer more paper per minute, what would the new rate be?

22. What is the number that has the digit 8 in the hundredths place and the digit 6 in the ones and tenths places? Write this number in decimal form and in word form.

MIXED REVIEW

Write <, >, or = for ●.

1. 57 ● 65   **2.** 760 ● 758   **3.** 4,500 ● 4,500   **4.** 12,432 ● 10,891   **5.** 9,280 ● 19,280

Round to the nearest ten thousand.

6. 57,416   **7.** 82,620   **8.** 128,307   **9.** 923,415

How are decimals like fractions? **WRAP** UP...

DECIMALS
Thousandths

This computer screen is made up of 1,000 small squares. What part of the screen is one square?

Word Form: one thousandth

Decimal Form: 0.001

There are 12 squares shaded in blue. What part of the screen are the 12 squares?

Word Form: twelve thousandths

Decimal Form: 0.012

There are 135 squares shaded in red. How much of the whole screen are the 135 squares?

Word Form: one hundred thirty-five thousandths

Decimal Form: 0.135

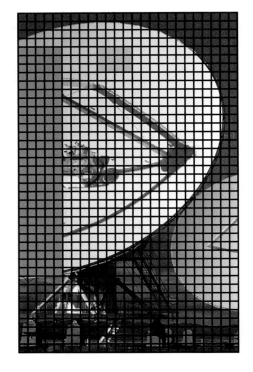

You can use the place-value chart to write 6.327 in expanded form.

Ones	Tenths	Hundredths	Thousandths
6 .	3	2	7
			7 × 0.001 7 thousandths = 0.007
		2 × 0.01 2 hundredths = 0.02	
	3 × 0.1 3 tenths = 0.3		
6 × 1 6 ones = 6.0			

Expanded Form: 6 + 0.3 + 0.02 + 0.007 = 6.327

Word Form: six and three hundred twenty-seven thousandths

Talk About It

▶ For numbers less than one, what does the zero written before the decimal point mean?

▶ How many times greater is hundredths than thousandths?

Check for Understanding

Write two other forms for each number.

1. fifty-three thousandths
2. two and four thousandths
3. four hundred seventeen thousandths

Write the value of each underlined digit.

4. 6.4̲59
5. 0.95̲2
6. 1.486̲
7. 0.1̲25
8. 6.058̲

Practice

Write in standard form.

9. five hundred sixteen thousandths
10. two hundred thirty-one thousandths
11. seven and four hundredths
12. five and five thousandths
13. six and fifteen hundredths
14. nine thousandths

Write the place-value position of each underlined digit.

15. 0.3̲1
16. 1.21̲9
17. 0.47̲
18. 0.748̲
19. 5.1̲06
20. 5̲.608
21. 3.409̲
22. 0.007̲
23. 9.7̲83
24. 4̲.859

Mixed Applications

Use the standard form for Exercises 25–26.

25. A record store sold 1,000 tapes one week. Of that number, 85 were country music tapes and 13 were classical music tapes. What part of the total sales were country music tapes and what part were classical music tapes?

26. One thousand people were asked to name their favorite radio station. The most popular station had 535 votes. What part of the people surveyed did not name the most popular station?

What would have to happen to the hundredths block to show thousandths?

WRAP
UP...

PLACE VALUE
from Thousands to Thousandths

A science magazine reports that the Concorde, built by the English and the French, can travel 2,125.348 kilometers per hour.

You can use a place-value chart to show the value of each digit in 2,125.348. The value of each place-value position in a decimal is 10 times greater than the value of the place to its right.

Thousands	Hundreds	Tens	Ones	Tenths	Hundredths	Thousandths
1 × 1,000	1 × 100	1 × 10	1 × 1	1 × 0.1	1 × 0.01	1 × 0.001
2 ,	1	2	5 .	3	4	8

MULTICULTURAL NOTE: The Concorde is a supersonic transport plane. It can fly through the air at 1,550 mph with more than 100 passengers.

Standard Form: 2,125.348

Expanded Form: 2,000 + 100 + 20 + 5 + 0.3 + 0.04 + 0.008

Word Form: two thousand, one hundred twenty-five *and* three hundred forty-eight thousandths

The whole-number part of the number is 2,125. The decimal part is 0.348. A decimal point separates the whole-number part from the decimal part, or the part less than 1.

Talk About It

Look at this number.   6,425.421

▶ Write the value of the digit 2 in both place-value positions. Explain how they are different.

▶ How many times greater is 4 hundreds than 4 tenths? Explain.

Check for Understanding

Use the number 3,910.246 for Exercises 1–4.

1. Write the value of the digit 9.

2. Write the word form of the number.

3. Name the place-value position of the zero.

4. What place-value position is 10 times greater than tens?

Practice

Write in standard form.

5. five thousand, one hundred forty-two and ninety-one hundredths

6. eighty-two and three hundred seven thousandths

7. six thousand and seven hundredths

8. one thousand, two hundred and two hundred fifteen thousandths

Write the place-value position of each underlined digit.

9. 36.4<u>7</u>

10. 98.30<u>2</u>

11. 103.<u>5</u>

12. <u>9</u>,008.409

13. <u>2</u>5.43

14. <u>7</u>40.56

Write the value of the digit 4 in each number.

15. 46.39

16. 506.402

17. 358.047

18. 4.906

19. 428.72

20. 4,013.8

Mixed Applications

21. Jan lives 35.6 miles from the radio station. Raul lives one-tenth mile farther away. How far does Raul live from the radio station?

22. A radio commercial is timed at 15.2 seconds. Another commercial is two-tenths second longer. How long is this commercial?

23. Write a decimal number using the digits 9, 8, 7, 6, 5, and 4. It must have a 9 in the tenths place, 6 ones, 8 tens, and 7 hundreds. The digit 4 is a whole number. The number is less than 5,000.

24. What number has a 9 in the thousands and thousandths places, a 7 in the hundreds and hundredths places, a 5 in the tens and tenths places, and a 3 in the ones place?

PATTERNS AND RELATIONSHIPS

Write the next three numbers for each pattern.

25. 0.2, 0.4, 0.6, ■, ■, ■

26. 0.03, 0.06, 0.09, ■, ■, ■

27. 0.25, 0.20, 0.15, ■, ■, ■

28. 0.498, 0.499, 0.500, ■, ■, ■

How can you compare the thousands place to the thousandths place?

WRAP UP...

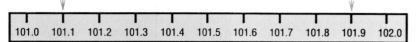

COMPARING AND ORDERING
Decimals

Suppose you turn on the radio with the dial set at FM 102.0. Which station is closer to the 102.0 setting, 101.1 or 101.9?

You can use a number line to compare decimals.

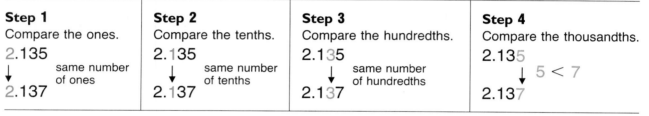

The number 101.9 is to the right of 101.1. This means 101.9 is greater than 101.1. So, 101.9 is closer to 102.0.

Compare 2.135 and 2.137.

Step 1	Step 2	Step 3	Step 4
Compare the ones.	Compare the tenths.	Compare the hundredths.	Compare the thousandths.
2.135 ↓ same number of ones 2.137	2.135 ↓ same number of tenths 2.137	2.135 ↓ same number of hundredths 2.137	2.135 ↓ 5 < 7 2.137

So, 2.135 < 2.137.

You can order decimals by comparing them in the same way. Order from least to greatest. 5.46, 5.39, 5.20

Step 1	Step 2	Step 3	Step 4
Compare the ones.	Compare the tenths.	Order the digits.	Order the numbers.
5.46 ↓ 5.39 same number of ones ↓ 5.20	5.46 ↓ 5.39 ↓ 5.20	2 < 3 < 4	5.20 5.39 5.46

• Order the numbers from greatest to least.

Check for Understanding

Name the place-value position where the numbers differ.

1. 1.26; 1.06
2. 12.14; 12.41
3. 129.023; 129.025

Order from greatest to least.

4. 2.09, 2.01, 2.15
5. 57.18, 56.99, 57.81, 57.80
6. 97.62, 97.26, 99.78, 100.26

Connection, pages 462–463

Practice

Write <, >, or = for ●.

7. 36.49 ● 36.46

8. 742.45 ● 742.54

9. 1.02 ● 1.020

10. 0.610 ● 0.600

11. 0.080 ● 0.008

12. 0.73 ● 0.70

13. 0.05 ● 0.50

14. 35.350 ● 35.35

15. 438.563 ● 438.536

Order from least to greatest.

16. 3.26, 3.19, 3.07, 3.70

17. 9.345, 93.450, 9.354, 93.540

18. 24.051, 42.015, 24.060, 24.560

19. 396.78, 39.78, 39.87, 396.87

Order from greatest to least.

20. 12.50, 12.40, 12.54, 12.45

21. 0.70, 0.77, 7.70, 7.07

22. 32.050, 32.150, 32.155, 32.515

23. 234.627, 243.625, 243.007, 234.067

In which number of each pair does the digit 6 have the greater value?

24. 26.7 or 62.7

25. 208.6 or 218.16

26. 5.06 or 5.65

27. 3.136 or 0.06

28. 6.02 or 0.16

29. 16.15 or 162.7

30. 51.6 or 37.26

31. 23.96 or 5.306

Mixed Applications

Use the table for Exercises 32–33.

32. According to the radio store's price list, which radios cost less than $9.00?

33. Which radio costs more than the portable radio but less than the clock radio?

34. Jim's favorite radio station is between 105.5 and 106.0. What is a good estimate for the station number?

Radio Store Price List	
Portable radio	$8.99
Radio headset	$9.05
AM radio	$8.89
Clock radio	$9.93

How is comparing and ordering decimal fractions like comparing and ordering whole numbers?

ESTIMATE
by Rounding Decimals

Newspaper ads can vary in size from less than 2.5 centimeters in length to a full page. Suppose Sally wants to place three ads with the lengths given in the table. Estimate each length to the nearest centimeter.

Newspaper Ads	
Display Ad	**Length (in cm)**
Car	12.3
Grocery	12.5
Tire	12.7

A number line can help you estimate decimals by rounding to the nearest whole number.

```
12          Car    Grocery    Tire          13
├──┼──┼──┼──┼──┼──┼──┼──┼──┼──┼──►
12.0 12.1 12.2 12.3 12.4 12.5 12.6 12.7 12.8 12.9 13.0
```

Car ad: 12.3 is closer to 12, so it is rounded to 12 centimeters.

Grocery ad: 12.5 is halfway between 12 and 13, so it is rounded to the next larger number, or 13 centimeters.

Tire ad: 12.7 is closer to 13, so it is rounded to 13 centimeters.

You can use the rules for rounding whole numbers to round decimals.

Examples

A. Round 3.572 to the nearest whole number.

digit to be rounded → 3.572   5 = 5

↓
4

So, the ones digit increases by 1.

B. Round 3.572 to the nearest tenth.

digit to be rounded → 3.572   7 > 5

↓
3.6

So, the tenths digit increases by 1.

C. Round 3.572 to the nearest hundredth.

digit to be rounded → 3.572   2 < 5

↓
3.57

So, the hundredths digit remains the same.

Talk About It

▶ Why are the digits to the right of the rounding place dropped?

▶ The price of gasoline at a pump may appear as $1.239. Why is the total amount rounded to the nearest cent?

Check for Understanding

Round to the nearest whole number.

1. 18.4   **2.** 26.3   **3.** 3.9   **4.** 7.05

Round to the nearest tenth and the nearest hundredth.

5. 5.387   **6.** 14.876   **7.** 1.072   **8.** 29.708

Idea Bank, page 465, Exercise 14

Practice

Round to the nearest tenth.

9. 84.07   **10.** 89.93   **11.** 0.98   **12.** 0.32

13. 103.506   **14.** 165.094   **15.** 2,045.055   **16.** 1,390.039

Round to the nearest hundredth.

17. 0.934   **18.** 7.783   **19.** 37.839   **20.** 45.005

21. 0.014   **22.** 0.996   **23.** 93.097   **24.** 198.894

Round to the nearest dollar.

25. $2.93   **26.** $11.67   **27.** $0.98

28. $4.02   **29.** $32.39   **30.** $199.49

Round to the nearest whole number.

31. 3.75   **32.** 87.42   **33.** 18.9

34. 42.09   **35.** 100.54   **36.** 99.99

Mixed Applications

37. Number Sense Write a number that can be rounded to 0.65 using the digits 4, 6, and 8.

38. Number Sense If a number is rounded to 5.55, what digits could be in the thousandths place in 5.54 ?

MIXED REVIEW

Write <, >, or = for ●.

1. 0.20 ● 0.02   **2.** 4.238 ● 4.230   **3.** 12.85 ● 12.85   **4.** 5.2 ● 8.5

Write the word name for each decimal number.

5. 0.045   **6.** 0.98   **7.** 1.123   **8.** 205.106

What place-value position do you look at when you want to round to the nearest dollar? the nearest dime?

PROBLEM SOLVING

Choose a Strategy

Leigh Anne has less than $5 to spend on supplies. She has 1 more dime than nickels, 1 less quarter than nickels, and the same number of dollars as dimes. If she has 2 nickels, what coins and bills does she have?

Understand
Plan
Solve
Look Back

Sometimes you can use different strategies to solve the same problem.

Strategy: Make a Model

Beginning with the 2 nickels, you can use play money and the clues given in the problem to make a model.

 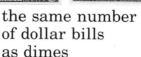

2 nickels	1 more dime than nickels (2 + 1 = 3)	1 less quarter than nickels (2 − 1 = 1)	the same number of dollar bills as dimes (3) = $3.00
(2) = $0.10	(3) = $0.30	(1) = $0.25	

Strategy: Make a Diagram or Drawing

Nickels	Dimes	Quarters	Dollars
5¢ 5¢	10¢ 10¢ 10¢	25¢	1$ 1$ 1$

Start with the 2 nickels. Then complete the diagram with the rest of the clues.

So, Leigh Anne has 3 one-dollar bills, 1 quarter, 3 dimes, and 2 nickels, or a total of $3.65.

WHAT IF... ... Leigh Anne has 1 nickel to start with? How many coins and bills does she have?

Mixed Applications ⟩ **STRATEGIES**

Make a Table • Act It Out
• Make a Diagram or Drawing
• Make a Model

Choose a strategy and solve.

1 Vince sold school newspapers. He collected $2.50 in coins. If he had 3 nickels, twice as many dimes as nickels, and the rest in quarters, how many of each coin did he have?

2 The school reporter wanted to list the starting lineup of five swimmers. She remembered that Kim was in the first lane. If Jane was between Mary and Renee, and Mary was next to Kim, in which lane was Carol?

Use the following information to solve Exercises 3–4.

Suzanne is reporting the scores from the gymnastics competition. She knows the Longwood team had a total score of 38.275 on the vault and 42.750 on the floor exercise. Westridge had a total team score of 38.450 on the vault and 42.655 on the floor exercise.

3 Which team had a higher total score for the floor exercise?

4 Which team scored higher than 38.30 on the vault?

Use the following information to solve Exercises 5–6.

It was reported that one gymnast scored 7.90 on the vault. A second gymnast scored 0.50 of a point higher. A third gymnast scored 0.20 of a point higher than the second.

5 What was the highest score for the vault?

6 Suppose another gymnast scored 0.05 of a point higher than the first. What would that gymnast's score be?

WRITER'S CORNER

7 Choose two decimal numbers that could represent scores or times in an athletic event. Write a short article for a school newspaper, using these two numbers.

Vocabulary Check

Choose a word or words from the box to complete each sentence.

data
decimal
expanded form
exponents
million
number line
period
rounded
standard form
thousandths

1. You can use _?_ to express numbers as powers of ten. *(page 3)*

2. The usual way of writing a number is called the _?_ . *(page 4)*

3. The number 200,000 + 30,000 + 100 + 60 + 9 is written in _?_ . *(page 4)*

4. Each group of three digits in the number 738,109,869 is called a(n) _?_ . *(page 6)*

5. The value of the 9 in the number 9,480,321 is nine _?_ . *(page 6)*

6. A _?_ can be used to help you round whole numbers and decimals. *(pages 10, 26)*

7. The number 23,492 can be _?_ to 23,500. *(page 10)*

8. Another name for information is _?_ . *(page 12)*

9. Seven tenths can be written in _?_ form as 0.7. *(page 16)*

10. The value of the 6 in the number 4,325.026 is six _?_ . *(page 20)*

> If you do not remember a definition, look at the page listed in the chapter.

Concept Check

Write in standard form. *(pages 4, 18)*

11. five thousand, six hundred twelve

12. fourteen and thirty-two hundredths

Complete. *(page 16)*

13. 20 cents = ■

14. 2 meters = ■ centimeters

Write the value of each underlined digit. *(pages 4, 6, 18)*

15. 75<u>5</u>,096

16. 90.7<u>5</u>

17. <u>2</u>,800,750

18. 4,638.<u>4</u>5

Complete. *(page 3)*

19. $100 = 10 \times 10 = 10^{■}$

20. $10^3 = 10 \times 10 \times 10 = ■$

Skill Check

Use commas to separate periods. *(page 6)*

21. 18346
22. 609352
23. 4258691
24. 97459132

Write $<$, $>$, or $=$ for ●. *(pages 8, 24)*

25. 4,586 ● 5,311
26. 89,247 ● 9,246
27. 456,000 ● 456,000

28. 0.6 ● 0.6
29. 31.021 ● 3.102
30. 0.37 ● 0.73

Write in order from least to greatest. *(pages 8, 24)*

31. 2,415; 2,400; 2,410
32. 6,070; 15,707; 6,000; 15,600

33. 0.123, 1.23, 0.12, 1.234
34. 14.6, 14.060, 14.63, 14.36

Round to the nearest ten thousand. *(page 10)*

35. 43,927
36. 839,124
37. 1,653,109
38. 1,075,400

Round to the nearest tenth and hundredth. *(page 26)*

39. 0.937
40. 6.921
41. 9.546
42. 0.899

Problem-Solving Check

Solve. *(pages 12, 28)*

43. A farmer has 28 meters of fence. He wants to enclose a rectangular piece of land that is 8 meters long and 6 meters wide. If fence posts are placed 4 meters apart on the long side and 3 meters apart on the short side, how many posts will he need?

44. Last month our veterinarian treated 112 dogs, 75 cats, and 15 hamsters. This month she treated 76 dogs, 89 cats, and 2 hamsters. Make a table for the set of data. Which kind of animal did she treat the most often during the past two months?

45. Chang asked 20 fourth graders and 20 fifth graders about their favorite fruits. Of the fourth graders, 9 chose apples, 5 chose pears, and 6 chose oranges. Of the fifth graders, 13 chose apples, 4 chose pears, and 3 chose oranges. Which fruits did more fourth graders than fifth graders like?

46. Mike's goal was to run the 200-meter race in less than one minute. The first day he recorded his time as 60.12 seconds. The next day his time was 0.05 second faster. The third day his time was 0.08 second faster than the second day. Did Mike reach his goal? (HINT: When he runs faster, he takes less time.)

1. Use a place-value chart to read the number 123,034.303 and identify the value of each 3 in the number. Show how you do this.

2. Use a number line to help you order these numbers from least to greatest: 75.1, 76.2, 75.8. Show how you do this.

3. Use a number line to help you round 6,329 to the nearest thousand. Show how you do this.

4. Read Exercise 9 on page 13. Follow the steps on the Problem-Solving Think Along worksheet to show how to solve this problem.

A place-value chart helps me identify the value of each digit in a number.

Write About It

5. What is something you discovered about place value that you didn't know before studying this chapter?

6. How is place value of whole numbers like place value of decimals? How is it different?

TEAMWORK Project

Make an Advertisement for a Product

A high fee paid for a 30-second television commercial was $1,500,000. Costs of advertising vary a great deal depending on the product being advertised and the media used. With your teammates, research and analyze data about various advertising media. Decide what product you want to advertise and which media would be best to use.

Decide Talk about how you can use an encyclopedia and books from the library to compare advertising costs for television, radio, and newspapers.

Do Work with your teammates. Use a reference book to find costs for a 30-second radio commercial, a 30-second television commercial, and a 1-page newspaper display advertisement. You may wish to call a local television station, radio station, or newspaper for the information. Record the information in a table.

Share Show your table. Describe the difference in cost of using different media for advertising.

TALK ABOUT IT

a. How can you use your table to compare the cost of advertising in a magazine?

b. Describe everyday situations in which whole numbers and decimals are used to compare.

MATH FUN
Extend Your Thinking

Activity

CREATE A NUMBER

1. You can write 6 three-digit numbers using these 3 digits.

7 8 9

Two of the numbers are 789 and 798. Write the other 4 numbers.

2. You can write 18 three-digit numbers using these 3 digits and a decimal point.

7 8 9

Three of the numbers are 7.89, 78.9, and 789. Write the other 15 numbers.

3. You can write 24 four-digit numbers using these 4 digits.

6 7 8 9

Write the numbers.

4. Write as many four-digit numbers as you can using these 4 digits and a decimal point.

6 7 8 9

Challenge
Number Sense

Look at the underlined digit in each number. Decide which digit has greater value.

1. 7**6**.052　　or　　34.**6**52
2. 3.98**5**　　or　　3.**5**89
3. 45.**7**83　　or　　6**7**.834

Challenge
Calculator

Write a number to tell how many times greater the first number is than the second number.

1. 70 and 0.007
2. 5,000 and 0.05
3. 300 and 0.3

CUMULATIVE REVIEW

CHAPTER 1

Write the letter of the correct answer.

1. Which is the standard form for two hundred seventy-one thousand, sixty-three?

   A. 271,063　　**B.** 271,630
   C. 271,063,000　　**D.** not here

2. Choose the number with the digit 6 in the millions place.

   A. 705,643,218　　**B.** 706,143,852
   C. 715,362,084　　**D.** 715,430,426

3. What is the standard form for 400,000 + 7,000 + 100 + 90 + 2?

   A. 407,129　　**B.** 407,192
   C. 470,192　　**D.** 4,700,192

4. Which is the standard form for one hundred forty-six thousandths?

   A. 0.0146　　**B.** 0.146
   C. 1.46　　**D.** not here

5. Write the value of the underlined digit in the number 631.54$\underline{8}$.

   A. 0.008　　**B.** 0.08
   C. 0.8　　**D.** 8

6. What is 0.23 in word form?

   A. twenty-three thousandths
   B. two and three tenths
   C. twenty-three hundred
   D. not here

7. Which number is greater than 0.75?

   A. 0.079　　**B.** 0.725
   C. 0.749　　**D** 0.76

8. Which is true?

   A. 6,114 = 6,124　　**B.** 6,114 > 6,124
   C. 6,354 < 4,536　　**D.** 6,354 > 4,536

9. Order the numbers from greatest to least.

   A. 61.25; 62.21; 61.52
   B. 61.25; 61.52; 62.21
   C. 61.52; 62.21; 61.25
   D. 62.21; 61.52; 61.25

10. Round 613.89 to the nearest whole number.

    A. 600.00　　**B.** 610.00
    C. 613.00　　**D.** 614.00

11. $10^3 = $ ▨

    A. 10 × 10　　**B.** 100
    C. 1,000　　**D.** not here

12. 5 pennies = ▨

    A. $0.005　　**B.** $0.05
    C. $0.50　　**D.** $5.00

13. Jeff ran a race in 61.32 seconds on Monday, in 61.25 seconds on Tuesday, and in 62.21 seconds on Wednesday. On what day did he run the fastest?

    A. Monday　　**B.** Tuesday
    C. Wednesday　　**D.** Thursday

14. Mr. Jones wants to enclose a square piece of land that is 6 meters on each side. If the fence posts are 3 meters apart, how many posts will there be?

    A. 4 posts　　**B.** 8 posts
    C. 10 posts　　**D.** 12 posts

CHAPTER 2

ADDING AND SUBTRACTING WHOLE NUMBERS AND DECIMALS

Did you know...

... that Barcelona, Spain, hosted over 10,000 athletes at the summer games of the 1992 Olympics?

TALK ABOUT IT

Suppose the seating capacity of an arena for an event is 15,400 seats. On Monday 8,250 tickets were sold, and on Tuesday 5,690 tickets were sold. How can you find the number of tickets that are still available?

CONNECTING ADDITION AND SUBTRACTION

Chris scored 26 points in the first half of the basketball game and 38 points in the whole game. How many points did she score in the second half?

The problem can be solved by finding the missing addend.

points scored in first half		points scored in second half		total points scored
26	+		=	38
26	+	12	=	38

Or, you can use this subtraction sentence.

total points scored		points scored in first half		points scored in second half
38	−	26	=	
38	−	26	=	12

So, Chris scored 12 points in the second half.

Addition and subtraction are **inverse** operations. This means that one operation undoes the other operation.

You can see this in the diagram.

$$38 - 26 = 12 \qquad 12 + 26 = 38$$

The inverse relationship allows you to check an addition computation by using subtraction and to check subtraction by using addition.

Problem	Check	Problem	Check
13	27	754	253
+14	−14	−501	+501
27	13	253	754

- Opening a door is the inverse of closing a door. What other inverse actions can you name?

Check for Understanding

Complete.

1. Write a missing-addend sentence for $38 - 19 = $ ■.

2. Write a subtraction sentence for $52 + $ ■ $ = 83$.

Solve. Use the inverse operation to check each number sentence.

3. $56 - 15 = $ ■

4. $89 = 32 + $ ■

5. $76 + $ ■ $ = 189$

6. $134 - 38 = $ ■

Practice

Write a missing-addend sentence for each.

7. $42 - 12 = \blacksquare$

8. $25 - 16 = \blacksquare$

9. $78 - 14 = \blacksquare$

10. $85 - 56 = \blacksquare$

11. $145 - 97 = \blacksquare$

12. $158 - 95 = \blacksquare$

Write a subtraction sentence for each.

13. $18 + \blacksquare = 74$

14. $32 + \blacksquare = 98$

15. $\blacksquare + 45 = 90$

16. $\blacksquare + 58 = 123$

17. $49 + \blacksquare = 154$

18. $142 + \blacksquare = 174$

Write the inverse operation sentence for each. Solve.

19. $18 + \blacksquare = 78$

20. $\blacksquare + 42 = 98$

21. $146 = 32 + \blacksquare$

Mixed Applications

22. The soccer team plays 14 games each season. They have already played 3 games. How many more games will they play this season? Write a missing-addend sentence and solve.

23. Write at least three number sentences using only the numbers 13, 15, and 28. Are any two of these sentences inverse operation sentences? Explain.

Use the table for Exercises 24–25.

Soccer Team Records			
School	Wins	Losses	Total Games
Westwood Elementary	6	$\blacksquare$	8
Lake Silver Elementary	7	$\blacksquare$	8
Princeton Elementary	$\blacksquare$	5	8

MULTICULTURAL NOTE: Many Costa Ricans enjoy playing soccer, the national sport.

24. Write a missing-addend sentence for each team's record. Solve.

25. **Make Up a Problem** Use the table to write a word problem. Solve.

How would you enter this number sentence in a calculator? $\blacksquare + 49 = 83$

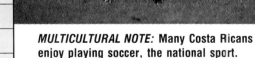

WRAP UP...

ESTIMATING
Whole-Number Sums

Jose collects baseball cards for four teams. He has 42 Astros cards, 86 Cubs cards, 13 Giants cards, and 61 Dodgers cards. About how many baseball cards does Jose have in his collection?

When an exact answer is not needed, you can estimate.

You can use **front-end estimation** to find an estimate.

```
   4 2      Add the lead, or front-end,
   8 6      digits in the group of numbers.
   1 3
 + 6 1
   19▪
```

So, Jose has about 190 baseball cards in his collection.

- When you add only the front-end digits, is your estimate greater or less than the sum?

- How would a rounded estimate differ from your front-end estimate?

Another way to estimate is by using **compatible numbers.** These numbers are easy to compute mentally.

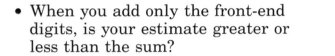

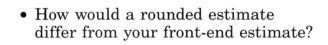

$42 + 61 \approx 100$

$86 + 13 \approx +100$ / 200

$\approx$ is the symbol for "is approximately equal to."

So, $42 + 86 + 13 + 61 \approx 200$.

So, another estimate is about 200 baseball cards.

- Why is the estimate using compatible numbers different from the estimate with front-end digits?

Check for Understanding

Estimate each sum with a method you choose.

1.	2.	3.	4.	5.
89	15	52	116	103
12	34	18	110	268
72	22	77	133	214
+ 26	+ 26	+ 49	+ 142	+ 327

Practice

Estimate each sum. Tell which method you used.

6. 68 +19	**7.** 24 +62	**8.** 403 +113	**9.** 613 +294	**10.** 8,013 + 956

11. 52 89 46 +12	**12.** 18 43 59 +75	**13.** 205 122 540 +616	**14.** 349 728 634 +426	**15.** 114 219 205 +410

16. $431 + 625 \approx$ ▨

17. $3,091 + 515 + 2,125 \approx$ ▨

18. $8,975 + 9,607 + 9,830 \approx$ ▨

Mixed Applications

Use the table for Exercises 19–21.

19. In Weeks 3 and 4, it was estimated that 1,200 tickets were sold. What estimation method was used?

20. About how many tickets were sold in the first two weeks?

Baseball Ticket Sales	Week 1	Week 2	Week 3	Week 4	Week 5
	327	412	629	685	879

21. Number Sense • Estimation How can you use compatible numbers to find the ticket sales for all five weeks?

NUMBER SENSE • ESTIMATION

You can estimate by **finding a range.**

845　845 is between 800 and 900.
+683　683 is between 600 and 700.

Round low.	Round high.
800	900
+ 600	+ 700
1,400	1,600

The range is 1,400 to 1,600.

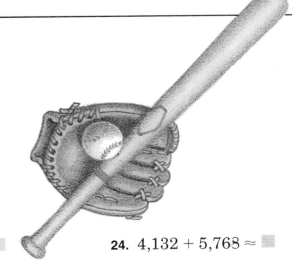

Find a range for each.

22. $635 + 473 \approx$ ▨

23. $987 + 269 \approx$ ▨

24. $4,132 + 5,768 \approx$ ▨

Why is it important to know more than one way to estimate?

WRAP UP...

ADDING
Whole Numbers

In Kenya the most popular sport is soccer. Soccer games between organized teams attract large crowds. Suppose 5,368 spectators attended a soccer game and 3,425 spectators attended another game. What is the total number of people who attended the games?

$$\begin{array}{r} 1 \\ 5,368 \\ +3,425 \\ \hline 8,793 \end{array}$$

Regroup 13 ones as 1 ten 3 ones.

So, 8,793 people attended the games.

More Examples

A. $845 + 796 + 897 =$

$$\begin{array}{r} 21 \\ 845 \\ 796 \\ +897 \\ \hline 2,538 \end{array}$$

B. $46 + 213 + 1,508 =$

$$\begin{array}{r} 1 \\ 46 \\ 213 \\ +1,508 \\ \hline 1,767 \end{array}$$

Line up the addends so that digits of the same place value are in the same column.

Another Method

Use estimation and a calculator to add large numbers. Choose an estimation strategy.

$$\begin{array}{r} 52,738 \rightarrow 50,000 \\ +34,214 \rightarrow +30,000 \\ \hline \text{about }80,000 \end{array}$$

MULTICULTURAL NOTE: Both children and adults play soccer in Kenya.

 You can use a calculator to find the sum.

          = 86952.

Since 86,952 is close to the estimate of 80,000, the sum is reasonable.

Check for Understanding

Estimate the sum. If the estimated sum is greater than 5,000, find the sum.

1. $\begin{array}{r} 916 \\ +584 \\ \hline \end{array}$

2. $\begin{array}{r} 1,439 \\ +2,678 \\ \hline \end{array}$

3. $\begin{array}{r} 11,507 \\ +18,468 \\ \hline \end{array}$

4. $\begin{array}{r} 52,708 \\ +43,695 \\ \hline \end{array}$

Practice

Estimate the sum. If the estimated sum is greater than 10,000, find the sum.

5. 235
+ 742

6. 404
+ 91

7. 7,303
+ 2,143

8. 5,127
+ 795

9. 9,478
+ 2,603

10. 24,305
+ 15,594

11. 37,498
+ 61,537

12. 72,830
+ 4,786

13. 40,340
+ 39,689

14. 92,216
+ 11,595

15. 213
341
+ 724

16. 321
196
+ 254

17. 310
236
+ 134

18. 5,207
3,584
+ 2,671

19. 9,726
5,403
+ 25,312

Complete the table.

Number Sentence	Estimate		Sum	
3,583 + 8,312 = ▧	**20.**	▧	**21.**	▧
4,034 + 968 = ▧	**22.**	▧	**23.**	▧
3,078 + 11,935 = ▧	**24.**	▧	**25.**	▧
11,224 + 30,867 = ▧	**26.**	▧	**27.**	▧

Mixed Applications

28. A soccer team from Kisumu, Kenya, travels to Nakuru, Kenya, by train. The train takes 58 minutes to travel to Londiani. It spends 15 minutes in Londiani and then completes the trip to Nakuru in 38 minutes. How long does the whole trip take?

29. Track and field is the second most popular sport in Kenya. A runner is training for an international event. Her coach wants her to run 55 kilometers this week and then take one day off from running. If she runs 6 kilometers on Sunday, 16 on Monday, 6 on Tuesday, 6 on Wednesday, 13 on Thursday, and 8 on Friday, will she meet this goal? Explain how you know.

When is it easy to use front-end estimation?

WRAP UP...

PROBLEM SOLVING

STRATEGY • Write a Number Sentence

The track coach has 36 students try out for her team, and the swimming coach has 14. The softball coach has 15 more students try out than the swimming coach. If no student is on more than one team, how many students try out in all?

Writing a number sentence may help you solve problems. A number sentence can show how the facts in the problem are related.

▶ **UNDERSTAND**

What are you asked to find?

What facts are given?

▶ **PLAN**

What strategy can you use?

You can write a number sentence, using *n* for the number of students who try out in all.

▶ **SOLVE**

What number sentence can you write?

track tryouts		swimming tryouts		softball tryouts		all tryouts
36	+	14	+	(14 + 15)	=	*n*
↓		↓		↓		↓
36	+	14	+	29	=	79

So, a total of 79 students try out in all.

▶ **LOOK BACK**

Estimate the sum. How can you use your estimate to check the reasonableness of your answer?

How can you check your addition?

WHAT IF... ... the track coach has 52 students try out? What number sentence can you write to find how many more students try out for track than for softball?

44

Apply

Write a number sentence and solve.

1 At swim practice on Monday, Alicia swam 47 laps, Nora swam 62 laps, and Lily swam 10 laps more than Alicia. How many laps did the three girls swim?

2 Brian wants 2 pairs of track shoes that cost $35 a pair. He has a coupon for $10 off the price of one pair. What price will Brian pay for both pairs of shoes?

Mixed Applications → **STRATEGIES** Make a Table • Write a Number Sentence • Make a Drawing

Choose a strategy and solve.

3 There were 98,965 people at the track stadium and 74,930 people at the soccer stadium. How many more people were at the track stadium than at the soccer stadium?

4 Linda swam the freestyle in 52.43 seconds. Wendy's time was 0.05 second slower than Linda's. Patty's time was 0.04 second slower than Wendy's. What was Patty's time for swimming the freestyle?

5 Consuelo spent $14 for shorts, $12 for knee pads, and $27 for track shoes. How much did she spend?

6 A ticket to the soccer game costs $8.75. If Ray has only a $20.00 bill, how much change will he receive?

7 A square bulletin board is 24 inches on each side. If there is a picture of a soccer ball every 8 inches along the edge, including one in each corner, how many soccer balls are on the bulletin board?

8 Eastbrook Community Center has 27 fifth graders and 31 fourth graders on its track team. There are 21 fifth graders and 24 fourth graders on its swim team. How many more fourth graders than fifth graders are on the track and swim teams?

MULTICULTURAL NOTE: Children of the Ukraine enjoy playing in soccer matches.

ESTIMATING
Whole-Number Differences

Scott is on the bowling team. The scores for his first three games were 78, 97, and 126. Estimate the difference between his highest score and his lowest score.

Sometimes, an estimate is all that is needed. You can estimate by **rounding** each number before subtracting.

126 →   130   Round to the nearest ten.
− 78 → − 80   Round to the nearest ten.
            50

So, the estimated difference is 50.

 Find the difference.

| 1 | 2 | 6 | − | 7 | 8 | = | 48. |

• What would happen if you rounded each number to the nearest hundred?

Another Example   Estimate. $3{,}617 - 2{,}392 \approx n$

Round to the nearest thousand.	3,617 → 4,000 −2,392 → −2,000 2,000	Round to the nearest hundred.	3,617 → 3,600 −2,392 → −2,400 1,200

Find the difference.

| 3 | 6 | 1 | 7 | − | 2 | 3 | 9 | 2 | = | 1225. |

Talk About It

Compare the estimates.

▶ Which estimate is closer to the difference? Why?

▶ What reasons can you give for needing a closer estimate?

Check for Understanding

Estimate the difference by rounding each to the nearest thousand and to the nearest hundred.

1. 5,298 − 1,172	**2.** 6,425 − 4,236	**3.** 9,943 − 8,835	**4.** 15,782 − 12,313	**5.** 12,874 − 9,818

Estimate the difference.

| 6. 475
− 284 | 7. 947
− 34 | 8. 982
− 525 | 9. 852
− 34 | 10. 1,962
− 953 |

| 11. 2,685
− 518 | 12. 8,748
− 3,978 | 13. 6,979
− 4,204 | 14. 29,327
− 18,419 | 15. 15,734
− 8,319 |

| 16. 7,832
− 2,643 | 17. 9,840
− 1,298 | 18. 18,479
− 9,521 | 19. 32,205
− 12,084 | 20. 36,231
− 12,059 |

21. $8,918 - 693 \approx n$

22. $13,561 - 3,801 \approx n$

23. $18,793 - 659 \approx n$

24. $8,230 - 4,956 \approx n$

25. $21,857 - 12,104 \approx n$

26. $35,938 - 11,321 \approx n$

27. $16,432 - 3,768 \approx n$

28. $28,697 - 18,430 \approx n$

29. $49,782 - 24,516 \approx n$

Mixed Applications

Use the table for Exercises 30–32.

30. If you round to the nearest ten, is the estimated difference between Randy's first-game score and Rhonda's first-game score greater than or less than 25?

31. **Analyze Data** Round to the nearest ten to estimate the total score of each bowler. Which two bowlers have about a 50-point difference in their total scores?

32. James had about 250 total points for two games. If his first-game score was 130, what are the lowest and highest scores he might have bowled in the second game?

Bowling Scores		
Bowler	**First Game**	**Second Game**
Rhonda	124	118
Randy	94	117
Billy	128	132

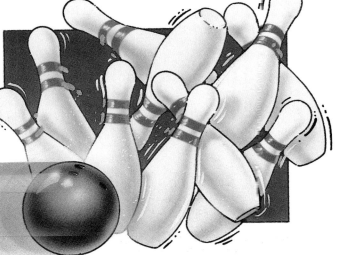

Name situations in which an estimated answer is all you need when you subtract.

WRAP UP...

More Practice, Lesson 2.5, page H39

SUBTRACTING
Whole Numbers

The Olympic Committee received 5,230 requests for tickets in the reserved section for the opening ceremonies. There are 3,592 seats available. How many people will not receive tickets?

Subtract. $5,230 - 3,592 = n$

Step 1	**Step 2**	**Step 3**	**Step 4**
Decide whether to regroup. 2 > 0. So, regroup 3 tens 0 ones as 2 tens 10 ones. Subtract the ones.	9 > 2 So, regroup 2 hundreds 2 tens as 1 hundred 12 tens. Subtract the tens.	5 > 1 So, regroup 5 thousands 1 hundred as 4 thousands 11 hundreds. Subtract the hundreds.	3 < 4 So, subtract the thousands.
2 10 5, 2 3̸ 0̸ − 3, 5 9 2 8	12 1 2̸ 10 5, 2̸ 3̸ 0̸ − 3, 5 9 2 3 8	11 12 4 1̸ 2̸ 10 5̸ 2̸ 3̸ 0̸ − 3, 5 9 2 6 3 8	11 12 4 1̸ 2̸ 10 5̸, 2̸ 3̸ 0̸ − 3, 5 9 2 1, 6 3 8

So, 1,638 people will not receive tickets.

Another Method

A calculator is useful for subtracting large numbers. First, estimate the difference.

$$
\begin{array}{rcl}
87,546 & \rightarrow & 90,000 \\
-48,579 & \rightarrow & -50,000 \\
\hline
 & & 40,000
\end{array}
$$

 Then, use a calculator to find the difference.

8 7 5 4 6 − 4 8 5 7 9 = | 38967.

Since 38,967 is close to the estimate of 40,000, the difference is reasonable.

Check for Understanding

Estimate the difference. If the estimated difference is greater than 1,000, subtract to find the difference.

1. 923 − 367	2. 2,476 − 529	3. 5,208 − 1,759	4. 37,413 − 14,826	5. 58,428 − 39,745

Practice

Estimate each difference. If the estimated difference is greater than 40,000, subtract to find the difference.

6. 7,735
    − 3,634

7. 2,168
    − 1,409

8. 61,213
    − 9,692

9. 57,434
    − 14,765

10. 68,253
     − 19,867

11. 78,531
     − 4,781

12. 42,869
     − 34,739

13. 76,839
     − 17,499

14. 97,467
     − 67,859

15. 89,562
     − 37,619

Complete the table.

Number Sentence	Estimate	Difference
28,476 − 14,825 = n	16.	17.
56,123 − 27,316 = n	18.	19.
89,967 − 30,856 = n	20.	21.
25,406 − 15,399 = n	22.	23.

Mixed Applications

24. In the Heptathlon of the 1992 Olympics, Jackie Joyner-Kersee scored 7,044 points. Her closest competitor scored 6,845 points. How many more points did Jackie Joyner-Kersee score than her competitor?

25. Suppose the combined attendance for the indoor and outdoor events of a track meet was 36,885. If there were 22,103 people at the outdoor events, what was the attendance at the indoor events?

Use the table for Exercises 26–28.

26. How many more points were scored by the Polish team than by the Italian team?

27. What is the difference between the highest and lowest scores?

28. Which two teams' scores were closest to each other?

1992 Modern Pentathlon	
Team	Points
Polish	16,018
Unified	15,924
Italian	15,760
United States	15,649

Why is it important to estimate first when you use a calculator to find a difference?

WRAP
UP...

SUBTRACTING
Across Zeros

William and Harry are competing in the track-and-field events at their school. William ran 3,000 meters. Harry came late and ran only 1,650 meters. How much farther did William run than Harry?

To compare the two numbers, you subtract.

Subtract. $3,000 - 1,650 = n$

Step 1 Subtract the ones.	Step 2 $5 > 0$ So, regroup 3 thousands 0 hundreds as 2 thousands 10 hundreds.	Step 3 Regroup 10 hundreds 0 tens as 9 hundreds 10 tens.	Step 4 Subtract.
$\begin{array}{r} 3,000 \\ -1,650 \\ \hline 0 \end{array}$	$\begin{array}{r} {\scriptstyle 2\ 10} \\ \cancel{3},\cancel{0}00 \\ -1,650 \\ \hline 0 \end{array}$	$\begin{array}{r} {\scriptstyle\ \ \ 9} \\ {\scriptstyle 2\ \cancel{10}\ 10} \\ \cancel{3},\cancel{0}\cancel{0}0 \\ -1,650 \\ \hline 0 \end{array}$	$\begin{array}{r} {\scriptstyle\ \ \ 9} \\ {\scriptstyle 2\ \cancel{10}\ 10} \\ 3,\cancel{0}\cancel{0}0 \\ -1,650 \\ \hline 1,350 \end{array}$

So, William ran 1,350 meters farther than Harry.

More Examples

You can regroup in different ways.

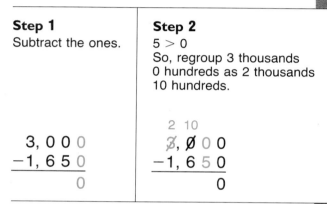

A.
$\begin{array}{r} {\scriptstyle 3\ \ 9\ 9\ 10} \\ 5\cancel{4,00}\cancel{0} \\ -51,863 \\ \hline 2,137 \end{array}$ You can regroup 400 tens as 399 tens 10 ones.

B. $\begin{array}{r} {\scriptstyle 7\ 9\ 10} \\ \cancel{800} \\ -762 \\ \hline 38 \end{array}$

C. $\begin{array}{r} {\scriptstyle 6\ \ 9\ 17\ 13} \\ \cancel{7,083} \\ -5,496 \\ \hline 1,587 \end{array}$

D. $\begin{array}{r} {\scriptstyle 2\ 9\ 9\ 11} \\ \cancel{3,001} \\ -2,567 \\ \hline 434 \end{array}$

E. $\begin{array}{r} {\scriptstyle 6\ 9\ \ 9\ 9\ 10} \\ \cancel{70,000} \\ -59,431 \\ \hline 10,569 \end{array}$

Check for Understanding

Show how you regrouped for each problem. Solve.

1.
$\begin{array}{r} 500 \\ -213 \\ \hline \end{array}$

2.
$\begin{array}{r} 408 \\ -357 \\ \hline \end{array}$

3.
$\begin{array}{r} 7,001 \\ -5,823 \\ \hline \end{array}$

4.
$\begin{array}{r} 4,010 \\ -2,485 \\ \hline \end{array}$

5.
$\begin{array}{r} 90,000 \\ -61,764 \\ \hline \end{array}$

Practice

Show how you regrouped for each problem. Solve.

6.
```
   600
 - 532
```

7.
```
  1,002
 -  983
```

8.
```
  20,005
 -17,416
```

9.
```
  50,004
 -48,756
```

Find the difference.

10.
```
  505
 - 98
```

11.
```
  300
 -137
```

12.
```
  502
 -224
```

13.
```
  830
 -543
```

14.
```
  1,000
 -  168
```

15.
```
  3,002
 -1,765
```

16.
```
  13,004
 -   537
```

17.
```
  7,500
 -  726
```

18.
```
  9,090
 -8,987
```

19.
```
  36,000
 -27,379
```

20.
```
  40,002
 -35,803
```

21.
```
  52,001
 -49,502
```

Mixed Applications

22. Don plays professional basketball. In one year he scored a total of 1,002 points. One teammate scored 150 fewer points. Another teammate scored 234 points fewer than Don. How many points did each of the other players score?

23. **Analyze Data** A leading professional basketball player has made 3,005 free throws in his career. Another leading player has made a total of 1,654. Is 2,351 a reasonable difference between the totals? Explain.

MIXED REVIEW

Compare. Write <, >, or = for each ●.

1. 4.36 ● 4.63

2. 0.20 ● 0.20

3. 1.07 ● 1.70

4. 43.2 ● 42.3

Write each group of numbers in order from least to greatest.

5. 8.9, 7.6, 8.8

6. 1.0, 0.7, 0.5

7. 9.4, 9.1, 8.9

8. 5.3, 2.3, 3.5

9. 3.56, 3.49, 3.4

10. 10.3, 1.03, 1.3

11. 0.01, 1.1, 0.1

12. 0.51, 0.05, 0.5

Look at the regrouping needed in Exercise 11. What is another way to express 300?

WRAP UP...

1. The first tournament hockey game attracted 4,290 fans, the second game had 1,785 fans, and the third game had 6,840 fans. How many fans attended hockey games?

2. Each wall of a square meeting room is 40 feet long. If loudspeakers are placed 20 feet apart around the room, how many loudspeakers are in the room?

I can draw a diagram to solve some problems.

Write in decimal and fraction form.

3. nine tenths

4. four and eighteen thousandths

5. sixty-five hundredths

6. seventeen and twenty-one hundredths

Write the value of the underlined digit as a decimal and a fraction.

7. 6.3<u>8</u>

8. 0.37<u>5</u>

9. 12.0<u>4</u>

10. 3.<u>4</u>09

Order from greatest to least.

11. 8.745, 8.675, 8.750

12. 13.094, 13.940, 13.900, 13.904

Round to the nearest hundredth.

13. 10.609

14. 5.976

15. 13.054

16. 5.546

Write the amount as a decimal form of the whole unit.

17. 30 cents

18. 8 hundredths

19. 4 decimeters

Write the inverse operation sentence for each. Solve.

20. $25 + \blacksquare = 78$

21. $\blacksquare - 85 = 14$

22. $16 + \blacksquare = 98$

23. $\blacksquare - 18 = 56$

24. $\blacksquare + 29 = 63$

25. $\blacksquare - 43 = 69$

Estimate the sum or difference.

26. $489 + 314$

27. $2,968 - 1,296$

28. $27,569 - 12,084$

29. $46,469 + 53,796$

30. $68,312 + 9,839$

Scotland

EUROPE

Visualize the Solution

When you visualize the solution, you take a mental snapshot of how the problem can be solved.

The game of golf originated in Scotland and is a favorite pastime for people around the world. A golfer must visualize in his or her mind how to play each hole.

Suppose you are playing golf with only five clubs: a driver, a 5 iron, a 7 iron, a 9 iron, and a putter. You use the driver for 200-yard shots, the 5 iron for 150-yard shots, the 7 iron for 120-yard shots, and the 9 iron for 90-yard shots. The putter is used on the green.

Study the diagram of each hole. Plan what club to use for each shot from the tee to the green so that the *least* number of shots is used.

1.

Tee — Green

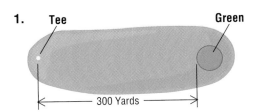

|← 300 Yards →|

2.

Tee — Green

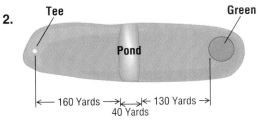

Pond

|← 160 Yards →|←130 Yards →|
40 Yards

3.

Tee — Green

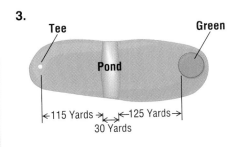

Pond

|←115 Yards →|←125 Yards→|
30 Yards

4.

Green

Woods

Tee

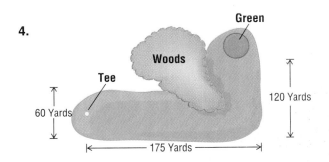

60 Yards

120 Yards

|← 175 Yards →|

ESTIMATING
Decimal Sums and Differences

Sara is saving for a new pair of ice skates. She saved
$42.47 during the summer and $11.49 during the fall.
About how much has she saved?

Front-end estimation can be used to estimate decimal sums.

Step 1	Step 2	Step 3	Step 4
Add the front-end, or lead, digits.	Adjust the estimate.	Think about the value of the other digits.	Adjust the estimate again.
$\begin{array}{r} \$4\,2.4\,7 \\ +\ 1\,1.4\,9 \\ \hline \$5\blacksquare.\blacksquare\blacksquare \end{array}$	$\begin{array}{r} \$4\,2.4\,7 \\ +\ 1\,1.4\,9 \\ \hline \$5\,3.\blacksquare\blacksquare \end{array}$	$\begin{array}{r} \$42.47 \\ +\ 11.49 \\ \hline \end{array}$ 47 cents + 49 cents ≈ $1.00.	$\begin{array}{r} \$53.00 \\ +\ 1.00 \\ \hline \$54.00 \end{array}$

So, Sara has saved about $54.00.

Another Method

Round to the nearest whole number.

$\begin{array}{rcl} 42.47 & \rightarrow & 42 \\ +11.49 & \rightarrow & +11 \\ \hline & & 53 \end{array}$

Round to the nearest ten.

$\begin{array}{rcl} 42.47 & \rightarrow & 40 \\ +11.49 & \rightarrow & +10 \\ \hline & & 50 \end{array}$

- How do the rounded estimates compare to the front-end adjusted estimate?

Rounding can be used to estimate decimal differences.

Round to the nearest whole number and subtract.

$\begin{array}{rcl} 8.3 & \rightarrow & 8 \\ -5.6 & \rightarrow & -6 \\ \hline & & 2 \end{array}$

$\begin{array}{rcl} 5.67 & \rightarrow & 6 \\ -2.42 & \rightarrow & -2 \\ \hline & & 4 \end{array}$

MULTICULTURAL NOTE: The Elfstedentocht is an
ice-skating race held in the Netherlands. The racing
course is over 100 miles long.

Check for Understanding

Estimate the sum or difference. Tell which method you used.

1. $\begin{array}{r} \$8.97 \\ +\ 3.78 \\ \hline \end{array}$
2. $\begin{array}{r} 15.03 \\ -\ 2.90 \\ \hline \end{array}$
3. $\begin{array}{r} \$27.89 \\ +\ 51.68 \\ \hline \end{array}$
4. $\begin{array}{r} 43.86 \\ -\ 21.23 \\ \hline \end{array}$
5. $\begin{array}{r} 56.72 \\ +\ 73.56 \\ \hline \end{array}$

Idea Bank, page 465, Exercise 14

Practice

Estimate the sum or difference. Tell which method you used.

6. $5.84
    + 6.28

7. $7.92
    + 5.03

8. 8.14
    − 4.89

9. 35.24
    − 24.76

10. $26.43
     − 9.58

11. 18.47
     + 62.21

12. $75.24
     − 24.64

13. 524.49
     + 99.52

14. $74.59 + 25.42 \approx n$

15. $375.43 - 190.08 \approx n$

Estimate the sum or difference and compare. Write $<$ or $>$ for each ●.

16. $5.13 + 6.87$ ● $4.82 + 8.09$

17. $9.67 - 6.32$ ● $7.62 - 5.56$

18. $6.48 - 3.36$ ● $6.78 - 2.12$

19. $9 + 14.8 + 6.2$ ● $12.2 + 15.6$

Mixed Applications

20. Juan ran a race in 39.43 seconds. Karen finished in 42.13 seconds. Juan estimates his time was 3 seconds faster than Karen's. Karen estimates a 2-second difference. Whose estimate is closer?

21. Chet skated the first of two laps in 25.87 seconds. He skated his second lap in 24.79 seconds. He estimates his total time to be less than 50 seconds. Is his estimate a good one? Explain.

NUMBER SENSE ● ESTIMATION

Sometimes, sums can be estimated using **clustering.** Clustering is a method to use when addends are close to, or clustered around, a number that is easy to add mentally.

Estimate. $24.8 + 26.42 + 24.3 + 25 = n$ Each addend is close to 25.

$25 + 25 + 25 + 25 = 100$

Estimate each sum. Use clustering.

22. $9.86 + 10.4 + 11.3 \approx n$

23. $50.5 + 49 + 52.1 \approx n$

Is estimating sums with decimals like estimating sums with whole numbers? Why?

ADDING
Tenths and Hundredths

At a concession stand, the small cup of popcorn holds 1.7 ounces. The medium box holds 2.8 ounces. The jumbo tub holds as much as both the small and medium containers. How many ounces does the jumbo tub hold?

You can use base-ten blocks to model decimal place value.

Flat = 1 whole   Long = 0.1   Unit = 0.01

First, estimate. $2.8 + 1.7 \approx n \rightarrow 3 + 2 = 5$
Use base-ten blocks to model $1.7 + 2.8 = n$

Step 1 Model	Step 2 Model

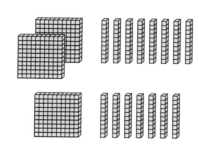

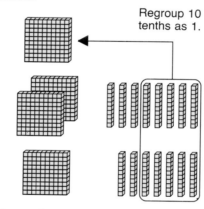

Regroup 10 tenths as 1.

Record

$$\begin{array}{r} 2.8 \\ +1.7 \\ \hline \end{array}$$ Line up the decimal points.

Record

$$\begin{array}{r} 1 \\ 2.8 \\ +1.7 \\ \hline 4.5 \end{array}$$

8 tenths + 7 tenths = 15 tenths or 1 one 5 tenths

↑ Place the decimal point in the sum.

So, the jumbo tub holds 4.5 ounces of popcorn. Since 4.5 ounces is close to the estimate of 5, the answer is reasonable.

More Examples

A.
$$\begin{array}{r} 1 \\ 6.7 \\ +\ 7.5 \\ \hline 14.2 \end{array}$$

B.
$$\begin{array}{r} 1 \\ 0.27 \\ +0.56 \\ \hline 0.83 \end{array}$$

C.
$$\begin{array}{r} 1\ 1 \\ 0.89 \\ +0.35 \\ \hline 1.24 \end{array}$$

D.
$$\begin{array}{r} 1\ 1 \\ \$9.78 \\ +\ \ 5.94 \\ \hline \$15.72 \end{array}$$

Check for Understanding

Use base-ten blocks to model. Write the sum.

1. 1.4
   + 3.5

2. 2.7
   + 0.8

3. 4.91
   + 2.32

4. 1.42
   + 2.76

5. 3.53
   + 1.68

Practice

Estimate the sum to the nearest whole number.

6. 1.6
   + 3.9

7. 4.4
   + 0.6

8. 6.19
   + 8.20

9. 5.05
   + 14.80

10. 19.82
    + 6.03

11. $26.86
    +   0.92

12. 84.7
    + 69.8

13. 29.83
    + 14.29

14. $49.82
    + 27.41

15. $ 4.45
    + 99.89

Find the sum.

16. $9.57
    + 7.90

17. $29.75
    +   8.65

18. $82.68
    + 23.42

19. $140.37
    +   69.90

20. 106.76
    + 18.28

21. 100.22
    + 99.89

22. 234.76
    + 817.09

23. 349.26
    + 67.14

24. 917.61
    + 98.79

25. 987.96
    + 145.34

26. $0.96 + 0.30 + 0.05 = n$

27. $5.3 + 7.8 + 2.1 = n$

28. $6.8 + 3.7 + 9.3 = n$

29. $0.42 + 9.27 + 0.35 = n$

30. $1.65 + 2.86 + 8.73 = n$

31. $9.16 + 72.34 + 29.07 = n$

Mixed Applications

32. At the concession stand, a small drink sells for $0.75, and a large drink sells for $1.15. If Anna purchases two small drinks and two large drinks, what is the total cost?

33. Cora received $1.65 from Elena and $1.45 from Earl. She already had $0.75. Does she have enough money to buy 3 boxes of popcorn if each box costs $1.30?

34. At Bay High, there were 315 fans in the lower seats and 128 fans in the upper seats. The other school had 218 fans in each of the upper and lower seats. Estimate which school had the most fans.

35. **Mental Math** Felicia bought 2 bags of peanuts for $1.05 each. Tommy bought a hot dog for $2.25. How much more did Tommy spend?

How is adding decimals like adding whole numbers?

More Practice, Lesson 2.9, page H40

57

ADDITION PROPERTIES

Addition properties are helpful in finding whole-number sums. You can use the same properties to find decimal sums.

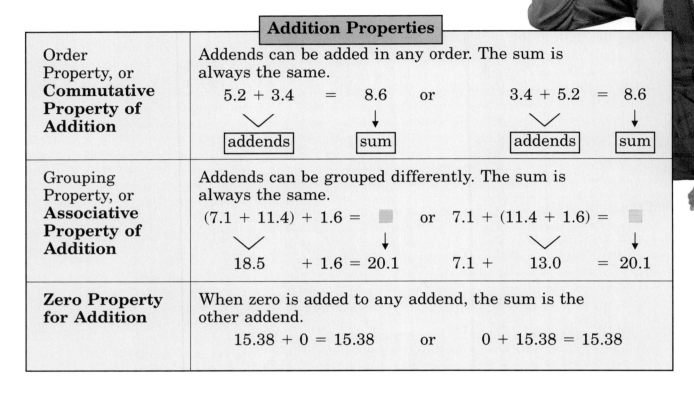

Addition Properties	
Order Property, or **Commutative Property of Addition**	Addends can be added in any order. The sum is always the same. $5.2 + 3.4 = 8.6$ or $3.4 + 5.2 = 8.6$ addends sum addends sum
Grouping Property, or **Associative Property of Addition**	Addends can be grouped differently. The sum is always the same. $(7.1 + 11.4) + 1.6 =$ ▨ or $7.1 + (11.4 + 1.6) =$ ▨ $18.5 + 1.6 = 20.1$ $7.1 + 13.0 = 20.1$
Zero Property for Addition	When zero is added to any addend, the sum is the other addend. $15.38 + 0 = 15.38$ or $0 + 15.38 = 15.38$

Talk About It

▶ How is the Commutative Property different from the Associative Property?

▶ Does the Commutative Property work for subtraction? Explain.

Check for Understanding

Write the name of the addition property used in each number sentence.

1. $12.5 + 5.4 = 5.4 + 12.5$

2. $3.1 + (8.2 + 6.3) = (3.1 + 8.2) + 6.3$

3. $0 + 16.12 = 16.12$

4. $5.78 + 0 = 5.78$

5. $106.7 + 98.2 = 98.2 + 106.7$

6. $(0.5 + 1.5) + 3.9 = 0.5 + (1.5 + 3.9)$

Practice

Complete. Identify the property used.

7. $\blacksquare + 2.5 = 2.5 + 1.4$

8. $4.5 + (\blacksquare + 6) = (4.5 + 1.2) + 6$

9. $1.3 + 7.4 = \blacksquare + 1.3$

10. $(1.3 + 0.7) + 6.8 = 1.3 + (\blacksquare + 6.8)$

11. $14.5 + 0 = \blacksquare$

12. $25.2 + \blacksquare = 4.6 + 25.2$

Use what you know about inverse operations and the Zero Property for Addition to complete each number sentence.

13. $7.25 - 0 = \blacksquare$

14. $4.8 - \blacksquare = 0$

15. $\blacksquare - 2.5 = 0$

16. $1.4 - \blacksquare = 1.4$

Use what you know about the properties to rewrite each number sentence. Use mental math to find the sum.

17. $0.5 + (0.5 + 5.6) = n$

18. $(0.8 + 0.4) + 0.6 = n$

19. $0.2 + (0.8 + 4.5) = n$

20. $(9.50 + 0.25) + 0.75 = n$

21. $(2.7 + 0.1) + 0.9 = n$

22. $0.85 + (0.15 + 0.45) = n$

23. Explain how the Associative Property of Addition can be helpful when you use mental math.

Mixed Applications

Use the properties of addition to write a number sentence. Solve.

24. Carlos ran 0.5 mile on his first day of training, 0.5 mile on the second day, and 1.25 miles on the third. How many total miles did he run?

25. Betty Ann bought socks for $4.25, a shirt for $5.75, and shorts for $7.50. How much did she spend on the three items?

26. Julia bought some watches for her friends. She spent $6.85 for one watch, $5.50 for another, and $4.15 for a third one. How much did she spend on all three watches?

27. The four girls on the 400-meter relay team each ran 100 meters. Their times were 15.6 seconds, 15.1 seconds, 15.4 seconds, and 14.9 seconds. What was their combined time?

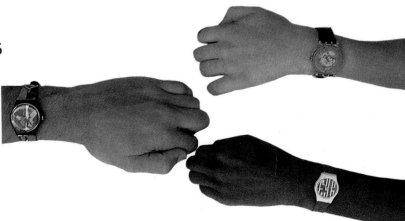

Why is there no Associative Property for subtraction?

SUBTRACTING
Tenths and Hundredths

Jamie is 1.38 meters tall. His hero, Shaquille O'Neal, measures 2.16 meters. How much would Jamie need to grow to be as tall as his hero?

You can subtract decimals the same way you subtract whole numbers. Use base-ten blocks to model $2.16 - 1.38 = n$.

flat = 1 whole   long = 0.1   unit = 0.01

Step 1
Model 2.16 and record.

Flats	Longs	Units
2	1	6

Compute.

Decide whether to regroup.

$$2 . 1\,6$$
$$- 1 . 3\,8$$

Step 2
Regroup.

Flats	Longs	Units
2	0	16

Since 8 > 6, regroup the tenths.

0 16
$$2 . \cancel{1}\,\cancel{6}$$
$$- 1 . 3\,8$$

Step 3
Regroup and remove.

Flats	Longs	Units
1	10	16
− 1	− 3	− 8
0	7	8

Since 3 > 0, regroup the ones. Subtract.

1 10 16
$$\cancel{2} . \cancel{1}\,\cancel{6}$$
$$- 1 . 3\,8$$
$$0 . 7\,8$$

So, Jamie needs to grow 0.78 meter.

Check for Understanding

Draw sets of base-ten blocks to solve.

1. $3.1 - 1.8 = $ ■   **2.** $5.14 - 2.35 = $ ■   **3.** $4.06 - 3.27 = $ ■   **4.** $6.13 - 3.26 = $ ■

Practice

Estimate the difference by rounding to the nearest whole number.

5. 3.4	**6.** 3.0	**7.** 13.5	**8.** 19.53	**9.** 58.00	**10.** 124.68
− 1.8	− 0.9	− 7.8	− 12.29	− 45.24	− 12.49

Find the difference.

11. 12.3	**12.** 28.35	**13.** 84.20	**14.** 320.47	**15.** 675.07	**16.** 840.00
− 9.7	− 14.09	− 43.72	− 213.65	− 434.50	− 759.67

Mixed Applications

17. Ronnie paid $9.45 for a ticket to the basketball game. He had $20.00 before he bought the ticket. How much money does he now have?

18. The tallest player on the basketball team is 1.84 meters tall. The shortest player on the team is 1.57 meters tall. Is the difference in their heights greater than or less than 0.25 meter?

VISUAL THINKING

Tom's hand is 18.4 centimeters from the end of his little finger to the end of his thumb. For Tom to palm a basketball, his hand should be 22.0 centimeters across. How many more centimeters must Tom's hand grow? You can use a number line to see the difference.

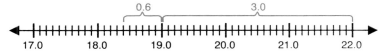

So, Tom's hand needs to grow 3.6 centimeters.

Draw a number line. Solve.

19. Chip's hand is 17.8 centimeters across. How much must his hand grow to be 22.0 centimeters across?

How do base-ten blocks help you understand regrouping?

WRAP UP...

EXPLORING

Equivalent Decimals

You know that numbers have many names.

24 can be expressed in many ways:

$10 + 10 + 4$, $20 + 4$, $12 + 12$,
3×8, 6×4, 24.00, and 24 ones

Equivalent decimals are different names for the same number.

Work Together

Building Understanding

A. Use decimal squares to model each decimal.

1 tenth (0.1) 10 hundredths (0.10) 100 thousandths (0.100)

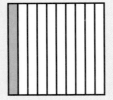 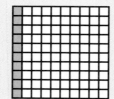 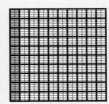

TALK ABOUT IT

- How many tenths are shaded? hundredths? thousandths?

- How are the shaded parts of the decimal squares related?

- Are 0.1, 0.10, and 0.100 equivalent decimals? Why or why not?

B. Use your decimal squares to model the decimals. Then decide whether they are equivalent decimals.

   a. 0.3 and 0.300   **b.** 0.03 and 0.003

- What happens to the size of the parts when additional zeros are at the left of the decimal number, as in Exercise **b**?

- What happens to the value of the digit 3 in Exercise **b**? in Exercise **a**?

Making the Connection

You can make equivalent decimals by annexing zeros. Use them to rewrite addition and subtraction problems.

Find the sum of 0.6 and 1.32.

$$1.3\,2 \rightarrow 1.32$$
$$+\,0.6\; \blacksquare \rightarrow +\,0.60 \leftarrow \text{Annex a zero.}$$
$$1.92$$

You can use a place-value chart to form equivalent decimals.

A. Find $6.9 + 1.452 + 0.68 = n$.

Ones	Tenths	Hundredths	Thousandths
6	9	0	0
1	4	5	2
0	6	8	0

$$
\begin{array}{r}
2\;1\\
6.900\\
1.452\\
+0.680\\
\hline
9.032
\end{array}
$$

B. Find $9.82 - 4.3 = n$.

Ones	Tenths	Hundredths
9	8	2
4	3	0

$$
\begin{array}{r}
9.82\\
-4.30\\
\hline
5.52
\end{array}
$$

TALK ABOUT IT

- Does annexing zeros change the value of the numbers? Explain.

- Why is it helpful to annex zeros to the right of a decimal number when adding or subtracting?

Checking Understanding

Write two equivalent decimals for each.

1. 0.9 **2.** 5.800 **3.** 1.3 **4.** 2.40

Use equivalent decimals to rewrite each problem.

5. $4.8 + 3.64 = n$ **6.** $9.32 - 2.6 = n$ **7.** $7.1 - 4.82 = n$ **8.** $3.68 + 0.9 = n$

Rewrite each problem. Then solve.

9. $0.62 - 0.4 = n$ **10.** $2.7 + 33.85 = n$ **11.** $48.1 + 35 + 17.3 = n$

More Practice, Lesson 2.12, page H41

ADDING AND SUBTRACTING
Thousandths

Measures of distance in many sports events are recorded in meters. What is the difference between 4.163 meters and 1.685 meters?

First, estimate. $4.163 - 1.685 \approx n \rightarrow 4 - 2 = 2$

Subtract.

Step 1	Step 2	Step 3	Step 4
Line up the decimal points.	Since 5 > 3, regroup the hundredths.	Since 8 > 5, regroup the tenths.	Since 6 > 0, regroup the ones. Subtract.
$\begin{array}{r} 4.163 \\ -1.685 \\ \hline \end{array}$	$\begin{array}{r} {}^{5\,13} \\ 4.1\cancel{6}\cancel{3} \\ -1.685 \\ \hline \end{array}$	$\begin{array}{r} {}^{15} \\ 0\,\cancel{5}\cancel{1}3 \\ 4.\cancel{1}\cancel{6}\cancel{3} \\ -1.685 \\ \hline \end{array}$	$\begin{array}{r} {}^{10\ 15} \\ 3\ \ \cancel{0}\,\cancel{5}13 \\ \cancel{4}.\cancel{1}\cancel{6}\cancel{3} \\ -1.685 \\ \hline 2.478 \end{array}$

So, the difference is 2.478 meters. The difference is close to the estimate of 2, so the answer is reasonable.

Another Method

A meterstick or measuring tape is divided into 1,000 equal parts. Each part is 0.001 meter (0.001 m).

Model each addend on the meterstick by *counting on*.

$\longleftarrow \ 0.090 \ \longrightarrow$

0.064   0.026

0mm 10 20 30 40 50 60 70 80 90 100 110 120 130 140 150 160 170

The sum is the total distance you modeled on the stick.

So, the sum is 0.090 meter.

$$\begin{array}{r} {}^{1} \\ 0.064 \\ +0.026 \\ \hline 0.090 \end{array}$$

Check for Understanding

Estimate each sum or difference. If the estimated answer is 7 or greater, find the sum or difference.

| 1. $\begin{array}{r} 0.652 \\ +0.936 \\ \hline \end{array}$ | 2. $\begin{array}{r} 1.503 \\ +6.089 \\ \hline \end{array}$ | 3. $\begin{array}{r} 8.134 \\ -0.867 \\ \hline \end{array}$ | 4. $\begin{array}{r} 3.514 \\ +1.032 \\ \hline \end{array}$ | 5. $\begin{array}{r} 21.346 \\ -\ 9.819 \\ \hline \end{array}$ |

Practice

Estimate the sum or difference to the nearest whole number.

6. $\begin{array}{r} 0.509 \\ + 0.684 \\ \hline \end{array}$ **7.** $\begin{array}{r} 5.982 \\ - 2.175 \\ \hline \end{array}$ **8.** $\begin{array}{r} 9.096 \\ - 7.963 \\ \hline \end{array}$ **9.** $\begin{array}{r} 19.605 \\ + \ 8.796 \\ \hline \end{array}$ **10.** $\begin{array}{r} 24.902 \\ + 12.413 \\ \hline \end{array}$

Find the sum or difference.

11. $\begin{array}{r} 6.574 \\ - 5.634 \\ \hline \end{array}$ **12.** $\begin{array}{r} 3.643 \\ + 24.876 \\ \hline \end{array}$ **13.** $\begin{array}{r} 20.006 \\ - \ 9.346 \\ \hline \end{array}$ **14.** $\begin{array}{r} 35.806 \\ + 40.904 \\ \hline \end{array}$ **15.** $\begin{array}{r} 48.431 \\ - 12.619 \\ \hline \end{array}$

16. $26.398 + 7.438 = n$ **17.** $21.135 - 9.76 = n$

Mixed Applications

Use this table to answer Exercises 18–20.

Indianapolis 500 Race Winners		
Year	Winner	Average Speed (in miles per hour)
1989	E. Fittipaldi	167.581
1990	A. Luyendyk	185.984
1991	R. Mears	176.457
1992	A. Unser, Jr.	134.479

18. How much faster was the average speed for the fastest race than the average speed for the slowest race?

19. How much slower was the winning speed in 1992 than the winning speed in 1991?

20. Analyze Data Between what two years was the difference in the average speed about 20 miles per hour?

MIXED REVIEW

Estimate the sum or difference.

1. $\begin{array}{r} 289 \\ + 423 \\ \hline \end{array}$ **2.** $\begin{array}{r} 875 \\ - 813 \\ \hline \end{array}$ **3.** $\begin{array}{r} 6,154 \\ - \ 968 \\ \hline \end{array}$ **4.** $\begin{array}{r} 5,297 \\ + 4,793 \\ \hline \end{array}$ **5.** $\begin{array}{r} 8,762 \\ - \ 953 \\ \hline \end{array}$

6. $16.5 + 13.2 \approx n$ **7.** $28.9 - 15.1 \approx n$ **8.** $72.5 + 47.3 \approx n$ **9.** $46.2 - 12.4 \approx n$

How is a meterstick like a number line?

PROBLEM SOLVING

Multistep Problems

Robert bought a tennis-racket cover for $2.75, 3 wristbands for $1.05 each, and 2 cans of tennis balls for $1.84 each. How much did he spend?

Sometimes, the information you need to solve a problem is not expressed in the numbers. Some problems have hidden data.

▶ **UNDERSTAND**

What are you asked to find?

What facts are given?

▶ **PLAN**

What plan can you make?

First, find the total cost for each kind of item purchased. Then, add to find the total cost of all items.

What is the hidden data?

It is the total cost of the wristbands and the total cost of the tennis balls.

▶ **SOLVE**

How can you solve the problem?

First, estimate the total cost.

	3	2 cans of		
cover	wristbands	tennis balls		
↓	↓	↓		
$3.00 +	$3.00 +	$4.00	=	$10.00

Then, use these steps to find the exact cost.

Step 1
$1.05
 1.05
+ 1.05 ⎬ 3 wristbands
$3.15

Step 2
$1.84
+ 1.84 ⎬ 2 cans of tennis balls
$3.68

Step 3
$2.75
 3.15
+ 3.68 ⎬ racket cover wristbands tennis balls
$9.58

So, Robert spent $9.58.

▶ **LOOK BACK**

Is your answer reasonable? Explain.

How can you check your computation?

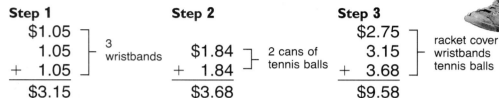

 **WHAT IF...** ... each can of tennis balls costs $2.04? What would the total cost be?

66

Apply

(1) Steve rides his bicycle to the tennis courts to practice 3 days each week. The downhill trip to the courts takes 10 minutes. The uphill trip home takes 20 minutes. How much time does it take Steve to travel each week?

(2) In Tara's first match of the round-robin tournament, she won 6 games. In each of the second and third matches, she won 5 games. In each of Tricia's first and second matches, she won 6 games. In her third match, she won 5 games. Who won more games in the tournament?

> **Mixed Applications** → **STRATEGIES**   **Make a Table • Write a Number Sentence • Make a Drawing**

Choose a strategy and solve.

(3) A total of 2,364 tickets was sold for a two-day tennis tournament. For the first day of the tournament, 1,089 tickets were sold. How many tickets were sold for the second day?

(4) In a tennis tournament, John won 2 matches more than Tiffany. Mary won 1 match more than Tiffany. Mary won a total of 4 matches. Who won the tournament?

(5) Linda, Leslie, Dave, and Diane are sitting together. Leslie is sitting on one end and Linda is sitting between Dave and Diane. If Dave is not sitting next to Leslie, who is sitting next to Leslie?

(6) Steve bought 3 tickets to the tennis tournament and paid $12.50 for each ticket. He also bought a souvenir for $4.75. What is the total cost of the tickets and the souvenir?

WRITER'S CORNER

(7) Use the information in the table. Write a problem with hidden data. Exchange with a partner. Solve.

Number of Students Participating in Sports Programs		
School	Football	Basketball
King School	123	54
McNear School	91	45
St. Mary's School	134	63
Westside School	145	58

CHAPTER REVIEW / TEST

Vocabulary Check

Choose a word from the box to complete each sentence.

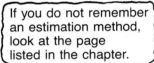

equivalent
Associative
Commutative
compatible
front-end
inverse
rounding
Zero

1. Addition and subtraction are __?__ operations. *(page 38)*

2. Sometimes an exact answer is not needed. You can estimate by __?__ . *(page 46)*

3. Numbers that are easy to add mentally are __?__ numbers. Often their sums are about 100 or about 1,000. *(page 40)*

4. In __?__ estimation the lead digits are used to estimate. *(pages 40, 54)*

5. The number sentences (5 + 15) + 9 = 29 and 5 + (15 + 9) = 29 show the __?__ Property of Addition. *(page 58)*

6. The number sentences 27 + 13 = 40 and 13 + 27 = 40 show the __?__ Property of Addition. *(page 58)*

7. The __?__ Property for Addition is shown by the number sentence 7 + 0 = 7. *(page 58)*

8. You can make __?__ decimals by using different names for the same number. *(page 62)*

If you do not remember an estimation method, look at the page listed in the chapter.

Concept Check

Write the inverse operation sentence for each. Solve. *(page 38)*

9. ▨ + 47 = 64

10. 19 + ▨ = 46

11. 79 = ▨ + 24

Choose the compatible numbers. Estimate the sum. *(page 40)*

12. 43 + 78 + 18 + 59 ≈ ▨

13. 29 + 87 + 70 + 11 ≈ ▨

Estimate the sum. *(pages 40, 54)*

14.   289
    + 724

15.   1,864
    + 4,098

16.   42,153
    + 47,496

17.   1.98
    + 4.23

18.   3.765
    + 8.194

Estimate the difference. *(pages 46, 54)*

19. 627
  − 486

20. 4,845
  − 1,057

21. 72,396
  − 12,546

22. 8.79
  − 1.03

23. 6.127
  − 3.905

Write the name of the addition property used in each number sentence. *(page 58)*

24. $(2.6 + 3.4) + 1.2 = 2.6 + (3.4 + 1.2)$

25. $1.45 + 0 = 1.45$

26. $4.3 + 2.1 = 2.1 + 4.3$

27. $3.5 + (6.5 + 8.9) = (3.5 + 6.5) + 8.9$

Write two equivalent decimals for each. *(page 62)*

28. 0.7   **29.** 1.80   **30.** 4.700   **31.** 2.9   **32.** 0.90

Skill Check

Find the sum. *(pages 42, 56, 64)*

33. 824
  + 347

34. 2,593
  + 3,107

35. 0.7
  + 0.6

36. 0.374
  + 0.782

37. 4.185
  + 8.906

Find the difference. *(pages 48, 50, 60, 64)*

38. 712
  − 256

39. 39,612
  − 1,513

40. 80,000
  − 78,543

41. 0.78
  − 0.49

42. 8.645
  − 6.738

Problem-Solving Check

Solve. *(pages 44, 66)*

43. Susan bought a book for $9.75, an album for $12.50, and a pair of boots for $37.00. How much did she spend in all?

44. The Smithsons bought a new car for $12,489. If they paid a total of $15,459 including $942 for tax and license, $742 for shipping, and payment for accessories, how much were the accessories?

45. Samantha bought 2 loaves of bread for $1.19 each, a tub of margarine for $0.75, and 2 jars of peanut butter for $1.76 each. What was the total cost of the food?

46. Linda jogs 2 hours on Mondays and Fridays. On Tuesdays she rides a bicycle for 1 hour. How much time does she spend exercising each week?

1. Show how to use a subtraction sentence to solve this missing-addend sentence. Solve. 11 + ▇ = 50.

2. Estimate 23.48 + 11.42. Explain your method.

3. Show each step as you find the sum of 834 + 4,281.

4. Show how to use base-ten blocks to model 1.45 + 2.81, and then solve. (Let 1 flat = 1 whole.)

5. Show each step as you find the difference of 7.32 − 2.81.

6. Read Exercise 2 on page 45. Follow the steps on the Problem-Solving Think Along worksheet to show how to solve this problem.

Write About It

7. What do you think is the most important thing to understand about adding and subtracting whole numbers and decimals?

8. Explain why 0.4 and 0.40 are equivalent decimals but 0.20 and 0.02 are not equivalent.

It's easy to use base-ten blocks to model decimal place values.

TEAMWORK Project

POINT AVERAGES FOR BASKETBALL PLAYERS

SCORING AVERAGE (points per game, 400 games minimum)	
Michael Jordan	32.6
Wilt Chamberlain	30.1
Elgin Baylor	27.4
Jerry West	27.0
George Gervin	26.2
Dominique Wilkins	26.1

Basketball players earn 2 or 3 points for each field goal and 1 point for a free throw. This chart shows the scoring averages of professional basketball's scoring leaders. With partners, model these scoring averages.

Michael Jordan

Wilt Chamberlain

Elgin Baylor

SHARE Show your models. Describe how you can compare scoring averages of any two players.

DECIDE

Talk about how you can use graph paper, tape, scissors, and colored paper to show point averages of basketball players.

Work with your teammates. Cut out squares and strips of paper. Divide some of the strips into 10 units. Let 1 square = 1 ten. Let one strip = 1 whole. Let a single unit = 0.1 (1 tenth). Use tape. Combine strips and units to make a model of each average score. Tape each model to a sheet of colored paper. Label your models.

DO

TALK ABOUT IT

Use your models to show the total score of an imaginary basketball game in which five of these players participate.

In your everyday activities, what other whole numbers and decimals have you compared?

MathFun — Extend Your Thinking

Activity

DECIMAL RACE

Gameboard:

START

6.2 3.4 **1**	3.4 1.7 **2**	5.4 3.6 **3**	5.4 0.8 **4**	STOP **5**	8.2 7.3 **6**	8.9 5.6 **7**	9.4 2.7 **8**
5.6 4.0 **9**	STOP **10**	8.3 0.3 **11**	0.8 0.3 **12**	4.8 0.6 **13**	2.9 0.9 **14**	6.4 3.2 **15**	0.9 0.3 **16**
4.6 0.8 **18**	8.3 3.6 **19**	3.2 1.7 **20**	5.0 1.7 **21**	9.6 4.3 **22**	STOP **23**	7.1 5.6 **24**	6.4 4.6 **25**

STOP **17**

FINISH

Decide whether you will play "Addition Race" or "Subtraction Race" on the gameboard. Choose a marker. Take turns rolling the number cube. Move forward the number of spaces you roll. Add or subtract the decimals in the space on which you land. Use the opposite operation to check your answer. If your answer is incorrect, go back to the nearest stop sign. The first player to reach "Finish" wins.

◆ ◆ ◆ ◆ ◆ ◆ ◆ ◆ ◆ ◆ ◆ ◆ ◆ ◆ ◆ ◆ ◆ ◆ ◆ ◆

Challenge — NUMBER PUZZLES

Copy. Fill in each box with one of the three numbers. Then write + or − in the circles to make a true number sentence.

1. 18, 17, 3

■ ● ■ ● ■ = 4

2. 9, 10, 16

■ ● ■ ● ■ = 3

3. 7.6, 0, 16.7

■ ● ■ ● ■ = 24.3

4. 8.4, 3.2, 5.6

■ ● ■ ● ■ = 10.8

Challenge — CALCULATOR

Write decimal points in the correct places to make each difference correct. Use a calculator to check your answer.

 1. 347 − 15 = 3.32
2. 347 − 15 = 1.97
3. 347 − 15 = 19.7
4. 347 − 15 = 33.2
5. 347 − 15 = 346.85

Write the letter of the correct answer.

1. What is the standard form for
$70,000 + 4,000 + 100 + 20 + 5$?

   A. 74,125   **B.** 741,025
   C. 741,205   **D.** 7,040,125

2. Compare. Use $<$, $>$, or $=$ for ⬤.
597,603 ⬤ 597,630

   A. $<$ **B.** $>$
   C. $=$ **D.** not here

3. $1.50 + 4.26 = n$

   A. 4.41   **B.** 5.76
   C. 6.76   **D.** not here

4. What is the best estimate?
$6,182 - 3,941 \approx n$

   A. 200   **B.** 2,000
   C. 4,000   **D.** 9,000

5. What is 54,762 rounded to the
nearest ten thousand?

   A. 50,000   **B.** 54,800
   C. 55,000   **D.** 60,000

6. What is the value of the underlined
digit? 627,541

   A. 7   **B.** 700
   C. 7,000   **D.** 70,000

7. What is the best estimate?
$4,715 + 292 \approx n$

   A. 2,000   **B.** 3,000
   C. 5,000   **D.** 6,000

8. What is the word name for 91,008?

   A. ninety-one, eight
   B. nine thousand, one
   C. ninety thousand, eighty-one
   D. ninety-one thousand, eight

9. $703 - 25 = n$

   A. 678   **B.** 687
   C. 688   **D.** 728

10. $7,639 + 4,836 = n$

   A. 11,465   **B.** 11,475
   C. 12,465   **D.** 12,475

11. $14 + (6 + \blacksquare) = (14 + 6) + 27$

   A. 6   **B.** 14
   C. 27   **D.** not here

12. $4.5 - 2.9 = n$

   A. 1.5   **B.** 2.4
   C. 2.6   **D.** not here

13. A hot-air balloon is flying at a
height of 2,361 feet. An airplane is
flying 28,031 feet higher than the
balloon. How high is the airplane
flying?

   A. 15,670 feet   **B.** 25,670 feet
   C. 30,392 feet   **D.** 31,392 feet

14. Joan practices the piano on
Mondays, Wednesdays, and Fridays
for 30 minutes. She practices for
20 minutes on Tuesdays and
Thursdays. How long does she
practice each week?

   A. 50 minutes   **B.** 90 minutes
   C. 110 minutes   **D.** 130 minutes

MULTIPLYING
WHOLE NUMBERS

Did you know...

... that the heat energy that makes a hot-air balloon rise comes from a propane gas burner?

TALK ABOUT IT

A hot-air balloon can travel at about 11 miles per hour. Jane and Marc have recorded 235 hours in their balloon log this year. Using all or part of this information, write and solve as many problems as you can.

MULTIPLICATION PROPERTIES

Multiplication properties can help you find products.

Multiplication Properties

Commutative Property of Multiplication	You can multiply numbers in any order. The product is always the same. **Example** $4 \times 6 = 24$ $6 \times 4 = 24$ factors product factors product

Associative Property of Multiplication	You can group factors differently. The product is always the same.
	
	Example $(2 \times 5) \times 3 = 2 \times (5 \times 3)$
	    $10 \times 3 = 2 \times 15$
	    $30 = 30$

Property of One	When one of the factors is 1, the product equals the other factor. **Example** $5 \times 1 = 5$ $1 \times 5 = 5$
Zero Property for Multiplication	When one factor is 0, the product is 0. **Example** $7 \times 0 = 0$ $0 \times 7 = 0$

Talk About It

▶ How is the Commutative Property different from the Associative Property?

▶ Explain how the Associative Property of Multiplication can be helpful when you use mental math.

Check for Understanding

Write the name of the multiplication property used in each number sentence.

1. $5 \times (8 \times 3) = (5 \times 8) \times 3$ **2.** $37 \times 6 = 6 \times 37$ **3.** $(7 \times 25) \times 4 = 7 \times (25 \times 4)$

4. $(247 \times 0) \times 8 = 0$ **5.** $5 \times 9 = 9 \times 5$ **6.** $3,857 \times 1 = 3,857$

Practice

Solve. Identify the property used.

7. $68,390 \times \blacksquare = 0$

8. $144 \times 1 = \blacksquare$

9. $6 \times 28 = \blacksquare \times 6$

10. $(25 \times 4) \times \blacksquare = 25 \times (4 \times 5)$

11. $7,468 \times \blacksquare = 7,468$

12. $5 \times (4 \times 7) = (5 \times 4) \times \blacksquare$

Use the Associative Property to find the product. Show your work.

13. $2 \times (50 \times 9) = n$

14. $2 \times (500 \times 7) = n$

15. $(3 \times 5) \times 200 = n$

16. $(8 \times 50) \times 2 = n$

17. $(6 \times 25) \times 4 = n$

18. $50 \times (4 \times 8) = n$

Solve.

19. $5,416 \times 0 = \blacksquare$

20. $35 \times (2 \times 5) = \blacksquare$

21. $(500 \times \blacksquare) \times 6 = 6,000$

22. $(4 \times \blacksquare) \times 8 = 160$

23. $145 \times \blacksquare = 123 \times 145$

24. $6,340 \times \blacksquare = 6,340$

Mixed Applications

25. Lee conserves gasoline by walking to and from school instead of riding in a car. He walks 5 miles a day, 5 days a week. He has done this for 3 weeks. How many miles has he walked?

26. Luis rode his bike 3 miles round-trip to the library one day. He also rode his bike to baseball practice 4 miles round-trip each day for 5 days. How many miles did he ride his bike?

27. Using the factors 3, 6, and 9, give an example of the Associative Property of Multiplication.

28. Using 4 as a factor, give an example of the Commutative Property of Multiplication.

HISTORY CONNECTION

Leonardo Fibonacci (1170–1250) was an Italian mathematician who studied patterns of numbers. These numbers, called the Fibonacci numbers, can be found in nature. The sequence of numbers is: 1, 1, 2, 3, 5, 8, 13 . . . . Look for a pattern in the numbers.

29. Find the next three numbers in the pattern.

Why does the Zero Property for Multiplication give a different answer than the Zero Property for Addition?

WRAP
UP...

USING MENTAL MATH
with Multiples of 10

Electricity is produced using geothermal steam on the North Island of New Zealand. The steam provides energy that generates electricity for the homes and industries on this heavily populated island.

If a refrigerator uses 40 kilowatt-hours of electricity per month, how much does it use in 5 months?

Multiply. $5 \times 40 = n$

So, the refrigerator uses 200 kilowatt-hours of electricity in 5 months.

$$
\begin{array}{r}
4 \text{ tens} \\
\times\ 5 \\
\hline
20 \text{ tens}
\end{array}
\longrightarrow
\begin{array}{r}
40 \\
\times\ 5 \\
\hline
200
\end{array}
$$

Think:
Since $5 \times 4 = 20$,
$5 \times 40 = 200$.

MULTICULTURAL NOTE: The people of New Zealand use their natural resources to produce energy. Geothermal energy has become increasingly important.

You can use a calculator to find patterns with multiples of 10.

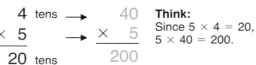

Entry	Display
6 M+ × 7 =	M 42.
MRC × 7 0 =	M 420.
MRC × 7 0 0 =	M 4200.
MRC × 7 0 0 0 =	M 42000.

The M+ key stores one factor in memory.

The MRC key recalls that factor from memory.

More Examples

A.
$8 \times 1 = 8$
$8 \times 10 = 80$
$8 \times 100 = 800$
$8 \times 1,000 = 8,000$

B.
$9 \times (3 \times 1) = 9 \times 3 = 27$
$9 \times (3 \times 10) = 9 \times 30 = 270$
$9 \times (3 \times 100) = 9 \times 300 = 2,700$
$9 \times (3 \times 1,000) = 9 \times 3,000 = 27,000$

Talk About It

▶ How is the pattern in **B** different from the pattern in **A**?

▶ How can you use mental math to find 5×7, 5×70, 5×700, and $5 \times 7,000$?

Check for Understanding

Use mental math to find the product.

1.
$$
\begin{array}{r}
80 \\
\times\ 7 \\
\hline
\end{array}
$$

2.
$$
\begin{array}{r}
500 \\
\times\ 8 \\
\hline
\end{array}
$$

3.
$$
\begin{array}{r}
4,000 \\
\times\ 3 \\
\hline
\end{array}
$$

4.
$$
\begin{array}{r}
9,000 \\
\times\ 5 \\
\hline
\end{array}
$$

5.
$$
\begin{array}{r}
300 \\
\times\ 9 \\
\hline
\end{array}
$$

Practice

Use mental math to find the product.

6.	7.	8.	9.	10.
50 $\times\ 5$	30 $\times\ 7$	800 $\times\ \ \ 2$	900 $\times\ \ \ 4$	500 $\times\ \ \ 6$

11.	12.	13.	14.	15.
400 $\times\ \ \ 8$	900 $\times\ \ \ 3$	4,000 $\times\ \ \ \ \ 6$	2,000 $\times\ \ \ \ \ 7$	7,000 $\times\ \ \ \ \ 9$

Complete each number sentence by using mental math.

16. $700 \times 9 = n$
17. $400 \times 5 = n$
18. $n \times 30 = 240$
19. $50 \times n = 350$

20. $3 \times 200 = n$
21. $500 \times 6 = n$
22. $800 \times n = 4,800$
23. $n \times 200 = 1,200$

24. $2 \times n = 600$
25. $n \times 40 = 320$
26. $6 \times n = 3,000$
27. $800 \times 9 = n$

Multiply each number by 10, 100, and 1,000.

28. 2
29. 4
30. 5

31. 7
32. 9
33. 10

Mixed Applications

Use the table to solve Exercises 34–35.

Cost of Gas and Electricity	
Month	**Amount**
January	$150
April	$ 95
July	$200
October	$ 90

34. How much more was the cost of gas and electricity for January and July than the cost of gas and electricity for April and October?

35. **Find Data** There are 8 houses on the block. If each household paid the same amount for gas and electricity in October, how much did all the households on the block pay?

How does having one or more zeros with a digit change the value of the digit?

WRAP UP...

Modern windmills, called turbines, are used to produce electricity. One type can produce 6 megawatts of electricity in a strong wind. About how many megawatts can 254 of these turbines generate in a strong wind?

Estimate. $6 \times 254 \approx n$

Find the lead, or front-end, digit. Multiply.	Count the places after the lead digit.	Write that number of zeros in the product.
254 $\times$ 6 12	254 $\times$ 6 12	254 $\times$ 6 1,200

So, about 1,200 megawatts can be generated.

- Is the estimate *greater than* or *less than* the actual answer?

_____

Another way to estimate is by rounding.

$254 \rightarrow 300$
$\times 6 \rightarrow \times 6$
about 1,800

Round one of the factors and multiply.

So, another estimate is about 1,800 megawatts.

MULTICULTURAL NOTE: The first windmills probably were built in the A.D. 600's in Iran. They had sails that revolved around a vertical axis. The main purpose of these windmills was to grind grain.

Talk About It

▶ Why is the front-end estimate different from the rounded estimate?

▶ Is the rounded estimate *greater than* or *less than* the exact answer? How do you know?

Check for Understanding

Estimate by using front-end digits.

1. $3 \times 83 \approx n$ 2. $7 \times 543 \approx n$ 3. $9 \times 6,512 \approx n$ 4. $8 \times 9,345 \approx n$

Estimate by rounding.

5. $9 \times 48 \approx n$ 6. $4 \times 679 \approx n$ 7. $8 \times 3,207 \approx n$ 8. $5 \times 9,879 \approx n$

Practice

Estimate each product. Tell which method you used.

9. 35 $\times$ 5	**10.** 78 $\times$ 3	**11.** 212 $\times$ 9	**12.** 499 $\times$ 2
13. 64 $\times$ 8	**14.** 429 $\times$ 2	**15.** 2,648 $\times$ 3	**16.** 15,129 $\times$ 5
17. 2,238 $\times$ 4	**18.** 8,729 $\times$ 5	**19.** 11,132 $\times$ 7	**20.** 19,549 $\times$ 9

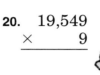

Estimate the product.

21. $678 \times 3 \approx n$

22. $498 \times 5 \approx n$

23. $1,827 \times n \approx 4,000$

24. $10,582 \times n \approx 50,000$

Mixed Applications

Use the table for Exercises 25–28.

Fuel Economy in Cars: Comparing Miles per Gallon			
Size	**City**	**Highway**	**Average Yearly Fuel Cost**
Subcompact	53	58	$287
Compact	37	43	$338
Midsize	23	34	$562
Large	21	30	$657

25. If a midsize car, driven in the city, used 8 gallons of gasoline, about how many miles did it travel?

26. About how many miles can a compact car travel on the highway on 4 gallons of gasoline?

27. Analyze Data If a family owned a large car and a compact car, about how much did they spend on fuel in 2 years?

28. If a subcompact car is driven for 6 years, about how much is spent on fuel?

Why are front-end and rounded estimates both acceptable estimates?

EXPLORING

The Distributive Property

Sometimes, you can break apart numbers to make multiplication with larger numbers easier.

Building Understanding

Use centimeter graph paper.

Outline a rectangle that is 8 units high and 17 units wide.

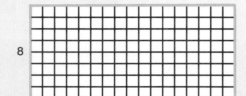

TALK ABOUT IT

- How many units are there inside the rectangle?

- How did you find the number of units inside the rectangle?

- What multiplication number sentence does the rectangle represent?

Move across the top, count off 10 units, and draw a line to break apart the rectangle.

- How many units are in each of the two rectangles?

- What multiplication number sentence can you write for each rectangle?

- What is the sum of the products for the two smaller rectangles?

- Is the product for the large rectangle the same as the sum of the products for the two smaller rectangles?

- How can you use mental math to solve this problem?

Making the Connection

There is an easier way to multiply numbers. You can use the **Distributive Property,** which allows you to break apart numbers to make them easy to multiply.

Compare the two methods.

Multiply. $6 \times 24 = n$

Method 1
Model 6×24 on centimeter graph paper.
Move across the top, count off 20 squares, and draw a line. Write a multiplication sentence for each rectangle. Add the two products.

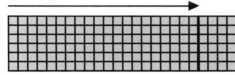

$(6 \times 20) = 120$ $(6 \times 4) = 24$ $120 + 24 = 144$

Method 2
Break apart 24 into 20 + 4.
Rewrite as $6 \times (20 + 4)$.
Multiply. $(6 \times 20) = 120$
$(6 \times 4) = 24$

Add the two products.
$120 + 24 = 144$
$6 \times 24 = 144$

TALK ABOUT IT

• How is Method 2 like Method 1?

• Why does breaking apart the number make the multiplication easier?

• What two operations did you use in both methods?

Checking Understanding

Use centimeter graph paper to find each product.

1. $3 \times 25 = n$

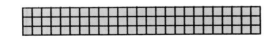

2. $5 \times 37 = n$

Complete. Find each product.

3. Find 3×25.
$3 \times 20 = n$
$3 \times 5 = n$
Add.
$60 + 15 = n$
$3 \times 25 = n$

4. Find 5×37.
$5 \times 30 = n$
$5 \times 7 = n$
Add.
$150 + 35 = n$
$5 \times 37 = n$

More Practice, Lesson 3.4, page H43

MULTIPLYING
by One-Digit Numbers

Solar collectors attached to the roof of a house capture energy from sunlight. If a system for one house uses 6 collectors, how many solar collectors are needed to supply 213 similar homes with solar energy?

First, estimate. $6 \times 200 = 1,200$, so $6 \times 213 \approx 1,200$.

Use four different colors of counters to make a model.

Let ● = 1,000, ● = 100, ● = 10, and = 1.

Step 1

Model the problem.
6 groups of 213

$$213 \times 6$$

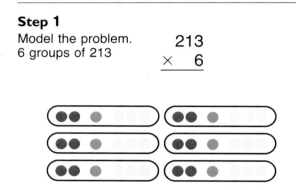

Step 2

Group all counters by color.

Hundreds	Tens	Ones

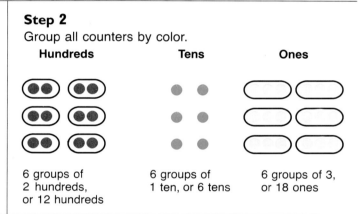

6 groups of 2 hundreds, or 12 hundreds

6 groups of 1 ten, or 6 tens

6 groups of 3, or 18 ones

Step 3

Regroup.

Thousands	Hundreds	Tens	Ones

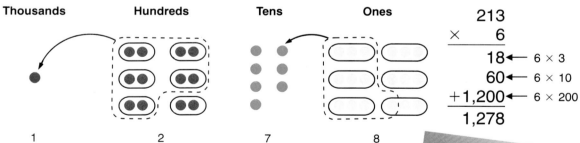

1　　2　　7　　8

$$213 \times 6$$

$18 \leftarrow 6 \times 3$
$60 \leftarrow 6 \times 10$
$+1,200 \leftarrow 6 \times 200$
$1,278$

The standard method of recording this calculation is multiplication.

```
   1
  213
×   6
1,278
```
So, 1,278 solar collectors are needed.

• How is regrouping done in this standard method?

Check for Understanding

Solve. Use counters to model each regrouping.

1. $2 \times 346 = n$ **2.** $3 \times 604 = n$ **3.** $6 \times 365 = n$ **4.** $7 \times 412 = n$

Practice

Estimate each product by rounding. If your estimate is greater than 1,000, find the product.

5. 37 $\times\ 4$	**6.** 63 $\times\ 5$	**7.** 367 $\times\ 7$	**8.** 276 $\times\ 3$	**9.** 1,259 $\times\ 6$	**10.** 3,350 $\times\ 3$

Multiply.

11. 42 $\times\ 3$	**12.** 28 $\times\ 7$	**13.** 64 $\times\ 6$	**14.** 102 $\times\ 5$	**15.** 1,045 $\times\ 5$	**16.** 3,456 $\times\ 8$

Mixed Applications

17. Americans recycle 78 million aluminum cans daily. At this rate, how many aluminum cans do Americans recycle in one week?

18. Is 37,000 a reasonable product for the factors 740 and 5? Explain.

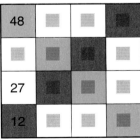

CRITICAL THINKING

Each row, column, and diagonal of a magic square has the same sum. Complete Square A. Multiply each number by 3 to complete Square B.

Square A

16	2	3	13
5		10	8
9	7		12
4	14	15	

Square B

48			
27			
12			

19. What is the sum of each row, column, and diagonal?

20. What is the sum of each row, column, and diagonal?

How is trading counters different from the standard method?

WRAP UP...

PROBLEM SOLVING

Multistep Problems

Mr. Davis wants to use less electricity to heat his home. He bought 3 electric blankets for $32 each, 4 air filters for $2 each, and 2 cords of logs for $95 each. How much money did he have left if he had $350 to start?

Sometimes, you need to use more than one step or operation to solve a problem. There may be hidden data to find first.

▶ **UNDERSTAND**

What are you asked to find?

What facts are given?

▶ **PLAN**

What plan can you make?

First, find the total cost of each kind of item. Then, subtract the total cost of all the items from $350.

▶ **SOLVE**

How can you solve the problem?

First, estimate the cost.

blankets	filters	logs
32	2	95
$\times\ 3$	$\times\ 4$	$\times\ 2$

about 90 + about 10 + about 200 = about 300

Use this number sentence to find the total cost of the purchases, and then subtract to find the amount left from $350.

(3×32) + (4×2) + (2×95) = n

$$
\begin{array}{r}
\$350 \\
-\ 294 \\
\hline
\$\ 56
\end{array}
$$

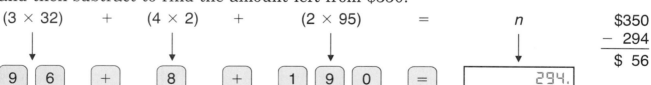

So, Mr. Davis had $56 left.

▶ **LOOK BACK**

How can you check your computation? Is this answer reasonable? How does it compare with the estimate?

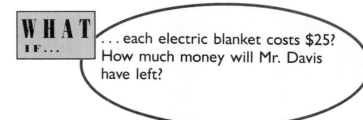

WHAT IF... ... each electric blanket costs $25? How much money will Mr. Davis have left?

Apply

(1) Mr. Gomez wants to conserve energy. He bought 3 ceiling fans for $75 each and 4 window fans for $60 each. He had budgeted $500 for the fans. How much money did he have left after his purchases?

(2) Mr. Gomez hired 2 people to help him install the fans. He paid each of them $10 an hour. One person worked 3 hours, and the other person worked 11 hours. What is the total amount he paid the workers?

> **Mixed Applications** **STRATEGIES** **Make a Drawing • Make a Table • Write a Number Sentence**

Choose a strategy and solve.

(3) A carpenter has one piece of molding 8 feet long, one piece 9 feet long, and one piece 13 feet long. How much more molding does she need to complete a job that requires 45 feet of molding?

(4) Billy rode his bicycle 9 kilometers each day for 5 days. Jim rode his bicycle 8 kilometers each day for 5 days. How many more kilometers did Billy ride than Jim?

(5) A car averages 32 miles to a gallon of gas. Its tank holds 12 gallons of gas. How far can the car be driven on one tank of gas?

(6) Diane counted the fence posts in a fenced-in back yard that was 25 meters long and 15 meters wide. If the posts were 5 meters apart, how many posts were there?

WRITER'S CORNER

(7) List several things you know or can figure out about the information in the table. Then use this information to write and solve as many multistep problems as you can.

Energy-Saving Items

Fluorescent bulbs	$ 4
Window shades	$12
Light-dimmer control	$10

REVIEW AND MAINTENANCE

1. In the first three weeks of selling cookies, Carol sold 319 boxes. If she sold 103 boxes the first week and 98 boxes the second week, how many boxes did she sell the third week?

2. Susan saved $50.00 to buy tennis supplies. She needed 2 cans of tennis balls at $3.45 for each can, a tennis racket for $22.98, and a tennis skirt for $11.95. Did Susan have enough money to buy these items?

Order from least to greatest.

3. 7.23; 8.73; 7.08   4. 1.0; 0.97; 1.07   5. 3.34; 3.034; 3.403

Round to the nearest tenth.

6. 29.07   7. 4.18   8. 6.92   9. 20.455   10. 0.35

> I compare the digits in each place-value position when I put numbers in order.

Find the sum or difference.

| 11. 507
− 283 | 12. 24,792
+ 1,034 | 13. 46,093
+ 78,111 | 14. 37,014
− 12,983 |

| 15. 0.904
+ 0.725 | 16. 9.06
− 5.78 | 17. 40.156
− 13.877 | 18. 79.815
+ 33.245 |

Complete. Identify the multiplication property used.

19. $4,392 \times \blacksquare = 0$

20. $648 \times 1 = \blacksquare$

21. $5 \times 29 = 29 \times \blacksquare$

22. $(15 \times \blacksquare) \times 9 = 15 \times (23 \times 9)$

Estimate.

| 23. 895
× 4 | 24. 4,291
× 4 | 25. 925
× 8 | 26. 18,470
× 5 | 27. 29,562
× 9 |

Multiply.

| 28. 430
× 5 | 29. 6,752
× 7 | 30. 4,978
× 8 | 31. 9,086
× 6 | 32. 8,965
× 4 |

33. $5 \times 923 = n$ 34. $3 \times 3,097 = n$ 35. $2 \times 7,915 = n$ 36. $7 \times 6,893 = n$

Egyptian Multiplication

Egypt

AFRICA

The ancient Egyptians were among the first people to develop a system of mathematics. They invented a form of picture writing called *hieroglyphics*. They used symbols to add, counting the symbols and regrouping when necessary. They also used symbols to double, writing twice as many symbols and counting them as when adding.

Their method of multiplication involved doubling and adding.

first factor   second factor

Example $6 \times 3 = n$

Step 1	**Step 2**
Start with 1 times the second factor. Double until you can find a sum equal to the first factor.	Add the corresponding products. The sum is the final product.

Step 1:
$$1 \times 3 = 3$$
$$6 \begin{cases} 2 \times 3 = 6 \\ 4 \times 3 = 12 \end{cases}$$

Step 2:
$$1 \times 3 = 3$$
$$2 \times 3 = 6 \qquad 6$$
$$4 \times 3 = 12 \quad \underline{+12}$$
$$ 18$$

So, $6 \times 3 = 18$.

Find each product by using the Egyptian method of multiplication.

1. $5 \times 9 = n$ **2.** $10 \times 14 = n$ **3.** $5 \times 17 = n$

4. $3 \times 15 = n$ **5.** $6 \times 24 = n$ **6.** $9 \times 23 = n$

PATTERNS
of Multiples

During one month an employee at the hydroelectric power plant worked 10 hours each day for 20 days. How many hours did the employee work that month?

Multiply. $20 \times 10 = n \longrightarrow$ 2 tens $\times$ 10 = 20 tens

$$20 \times 10 = 200$$

So, the employee worked 200 hours.

Look for the pattern.

20×1	$= 20$	60×7	$= 420$
20×10	$= 200$	60×70	$= 4{,}200$
20×100	$= 2{,}000$	60×700	$= 42{,}000$
$20 \times 1{,}000$	$= 20{,}000$	$60 \times 7{,}000$	$= 420{,}000$

Another Example

Look at the multiplication table. Observe the pattern.

x	40	400	4,000
20	800	8,000	80,000
40	1,600	16,000	160,000
50	2,000	20,000	200,000
60	2,400	24,000	240,000

Talk About It

▶ What pattern do you see?

▶ What do you observe in the pattern of zeros in the products of 50×40, 50×400, and $50 \times 4{,}000$?

▶ Why are there more zeros in the products?

▶ How can you use mental math to multiply $60 \times 40{,}000$?

Check for Understanding

Use mental math to find the product.

1. $10 \times 40 = n$ **2.** $30 \times 700 = n$ **3.** $50 \times 7{,}000 = n$ **4.** $60 \times 50 = n$ **5.** $40 \times 500 = n$

Practice

Use mental math to find the product.

6.	7.	8.	9.	10.
20	40	500	300	600
× 30	× 40	× 70	× 50	× 40

11.	12.	13.	14.	15.
800	900	4,000	2,000	9,000
× 50	× 10	× 30	× 50	× 80

16. $50 \times 30 = n$ **17.** $20 \times 40 = n$ **18.** $90 \times 50 = n$

19. $400 \times 60 = n$ **20.** $3,000 \times 80 = n$ **21.** $800 \times 70 = n$

22. $700 \times 60 = n$ **23.** $5,000 \times 40 = n$ **24.** $60,000 \times 50 = n$

Complete each number sentence.

25. $20 \times 50 = n$ **26.** $40 \times n = 1,200$

27. $n \times 60 = 2,400$ **28.** $600 \times n = 6,000$

29. $4,000 \times n = 200,000$ **30.** $30 \times 6,000 = n$

31. Multiply the number 60 by the numbers 60, 600, and 6,000.

Mixed Applications

32. A science teacher received 20 reports on energy from her class. Each report was 20 pages long. What was the total number of pages in all the reports?

33. At Midway Elementary each of 300 students brought in 20 aluminum cans for recycling. What was the total number of cans brought in?

34. Number Sense • Mental Math How many zeros will be in the product of the numbers 500 and 7,000? What is the product?

35. Number Sense • Mental Math Write a two-digit number and a four-digit number that have a product of 490,000.

Will there be more or fewer zeros in the product when you multiply 30×800 than when you multiply 50×800? Explain.

More Practice, Lesson 3.7, page H44

Carlos burns logs in a fireplace at a lodge. He wants to know how many logs he will need for the 31 days in January. If he burns about 38 logs each day, about how many logs will he need?

Estimate. $31 \times 38 \approx n$

Step 1	**Step 2**
Round each factor to the nearest ten.	Multiply the rounded factors.
$38 \rightarrow 40$ $\times 31 \rightarrow \times 30$	$\begin{array}{r} 40 \\ \times \ \ 30 \\ \hline 1{,}200 \end{array}$ **Think:** $3 \times 40 = 120$, so $30 \times 40 = 1{,}200$

So, Carlos will need about 1,200 logs for January.

Estimate. $38 \times 145 \approx n$

Step 1	**Step 2**
Round each factor to its greatest place-value position.	Multiply the rounded factors.
$145 \rightarrow 100$ $\times \ 38 \rightarrow \times 40$	$\begin{array}{r} 100 \\ \times \ \ 40 \\ \hline 4{,}000 \end{array}$ **Think:** $4 \times 100 = 400$, so $40 \times 100 = 4{,}000$.

Talk About It

▶ How can you use front-end estimation to estimate the product of 38×145?

▶ How can you use rounding to estimate the product?

Check for Understanding

Estimate the product.

| 1. $\begin{array}{r} 57 \\ \times 42 \\ \hline \end{array}$ | 2. $\begin{array}{r} 83 \\ \times 36 \\ \hline \end{array}$ | 3. $\begin{array}{r} 45 \\ \times 31 \\ \hline \end{array}$ | 4. $\begin{array}{r} 203 \\ \times \ 31 \\ \hline \end{array}$ | 5. $\begin{array}{r} 786 \\ \times \ 64 \\ \hline \end{array}$ | 6. $\begin{array}{r} 615 \\ \times \ 89 \\ \hline \end{array}$ |

Practice

Estimate the product.

7. 29
 × 34

8. 24
 × 73

9. 78
 × 16

10. 39
 × 95

11. 47
 × 63

12. 46
 × 54

13. 597
 × 16

14. 635
 × 27

15. 942
 × 93

16. 372
 × 77

17. $89 \times 349 \approx n$

18. $782 \times 41 \approx n$

19. $12 \times 647 \approx n$

20. $24 \times 687 \approx n$

Mixed Applications

21. Wanda's father is going on a business trip. The fuel tank of his car holds 17 gallons, and the car travels 31 miles for each gallon of gasoline. Estimate how far Wanda's father can expect to drive on one tank of gas.

23. Is 10,000 a good estimate for the product of 16 and 483? Explain.

24. A parents' group plans to make new curtains for the 21 classrooms in the school. Each classroom will need 16 curtain panels. Estimate the total number of curtain panels the parents' group needs to make.

22. Number Sense • Estimation If the estimated product of a number and 24 is 800, what could the number be?

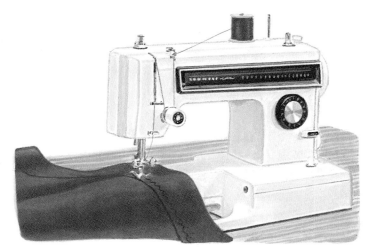

MIXED REVIEW

Find the sum or difference.

1. 6.483
 + 2.418

2. 8.725
 + 3.543

3. 12.403
 − 8.671

4. 21.659
 − 17.804

5. 53.742
 + 25.809

Estimate the product.

6. $8 \times 42 \approx n$

7. $4 \times 258 \approx n$

8. $5 \times 2,697 \approx n$

9. $6 \times 21,018 \approx n$

Tell why rounding, front-end estimation, and mental math are all acceptable methods of estimating.

WRAP
UP...

MULTIPLYING
by Two-Digit Numbers

The fourth and fifth grades plan to visit the new electrical power plant. Each minibus has room for 23 passengers. The teachers have reserved 15 minibuses. How many teachers and students can go on the field trip?

Use graph paper and a ruler to find $15 \times 23 = n$.

Outline an array that is 15 units by 23 units.

Divide the rectangle into smaller parts.

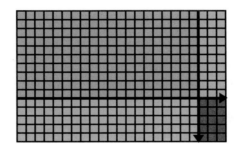

Move across the top, counting off 20 units and 3 units. Then move 10 units and 5 units counting down.

Find the product for each section. Then add the products.

partial products

$$
\begin{array}{r}
23 \\
\times\ 15 \\
\hline
15 \quad \leftarrow\ 5 \times 3 \\
100 \quad \leftarrow\ 5 \times 20 \\
30 \quad \leftarrow\ 10 \times 3 \\
+200 \quad \leftarrow\ 10 \times 20 \\
\hline
345
\end{array}
$$

Use the standard method of recording this calculation.

First, estimate. $20 \times 20 = 400$ So, $15 \times 23 \approx 400$.

Step 1	**Step 2**	**Step 3**
Multiply by the ones.	Multiply by the tens.	Add the partial products.

Step 1
$$
\begin{array}{r}
1 \\
23 \\
\times\ 15 \\
\hline
115 \quad \leftarrow\ 5 \times 23
\end{array}
$$

Step 2
$$
\begin{array}{r}
23 \\
\times\ 15 \\
\hline
115 \\
230 \quad \leftarrow\ 10 \times 23
\end{array}
$$
Use the zero as a placeholder.

Step 3
$$
\begin{array}{r}
23 \\
\times\ 15 \\
\hline
115 \\
+230 \\
\hline
345
\end{array}
$$

So, 345 teachers and students can go on the field trip.

Talk About It

▶ How can you determine whether your answer is reasonable?

▶ Compare the partial products shown on the array with the partial products you added in Step 3. Why are they different?

Check for Understanding

Use graph paper to solve.

1. 16
   × 23

2. 34
   × 12

3. 32
   × 18

4. 25
   × 10

5. 43
   × 13

6. 29
   × 17

Practice

Find the product.

7. 29
   × 28

8. 173
   × 13

9. 382
   × 15

10. 203
    × 14

11. 324
    × 17

12. 150
    × 92

13. $82 \times 12 = n$

14. $23 \times 179 = n$

15. $14 \times 954 = n$

16. $75 \times 875 = n$

Mixed Applications

17. The students toured the power plant in 12 groups of 21 each. Everyone on the tour had to wear a helmet. How many helmets were needed?

18. The plant burns 285 barrels of oil each day to produce electricity. In 4 weeks how many barrels of oil will the power plant use?

19. **Number Sense • Mental Math** What three-digit number can be multiplied by 10 to get a product of 5,500?

20. Is 360,000 a reasonable product for the numbers 450 and 80? Explain.

SCIENCE CONNECTION

Athletes should be aware of their heart rates before, during, and after exercise. To determine your heart rate in beats per minute, count the beats for 6 seconds and multiply by 10, or count the beats for 15 seconds and multiply by 4.

21. If an athlete counts 7 beats in 6 seconds before exercising, what is the heart rate for one minute?

22. If an athlete counts 30 beats in 15 seconds during exercise, what is the heart rate for one minute?

Do you prefer the standard method or the partial-products method of recording multiplication? Why?

WRAP
UP...

MULTIPLYING
by Three-Digit Numbers

Energy is measured in *newtons*. One newton is the amount of work done in moving an object a distance of 1 meter against an opposing force of 1 kilogram.

To find the number of newtons, multiply the number of kilograms by the number of meters. How many newtons are needed to lift a 375-kilogram crate to a height of 125 meters?

Multiply. $125 \times 375 = n$

Estimate. $100 \times 400 = 40,000$ So, $125 \times 375 \approx 40,000$.

```
      375
×     125  ← 100 + 20 + 5
    1,875  ← 5 × 375
    7,500  ← 20 × 375
 + 37,500  ← 100 × 375
   46,875  Since 46,875 is close to the estimate
           of 40,000, the answer is reasonable.
```

So, 46,875 newtons are needed to lift the crate.

Another Example

Multiply. $1,235 \times 304 = n$

Estimate. $1,000 \times 300 = 300,000$ So, $304 \times 1,235 \approx 300,000$.

Paper and Pencil

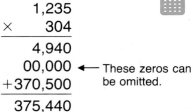

```
     1,235
×      304
     4,940
    00,000  ← These zeros can
  +370,500    be omitted.
   375,440
```

Calculator

3 0 4 $\times$ 1 2 3 5 $=$ ⎸ 375440. ⎹

Check for Understanding

Estimate the product. If your estimate is greater than 200,000, find the product.

1. 216	2. 357	3. 829	4. 2,136	5. 1,846
× 453	× 609	× 750	× 594	× 304

Practice

Estimate the product.

6.	7.	8.	9.	10.
324	372	407	497	7,368
× 212	× 684	× 605	× 195	× 372

 Find the product.

11.	12.	13.	14.	15.
584	635	462	850	936
× 173	× 483	× 648	× 937	× 507

16. $5,849 \times 174 = n$ **17.** $8,340 \times 405 = n$ **18.** $6,930 \times 842 = n$ **19.** $5,600 \times 500 = n$

20. $545 \times 469 = n$ **21.** $949 \times 9,540 = n$ **22.** $498 \times 8,716 = n$ **23.** $609 \times 10,005 = n$

Mixed Applications

24. A factory produces 875 windows each day of the week. It operates Monday through Friday. How many windows are made in 1 year? (HINT: 1 year = 52 weeks)

25. Is 100,000 a reasonable estimate for the product of 615 and 275? Explain.

26. Number Sense • Mental Math What is the product of the smallest three-digit whole number multiplied by the largest four-digit whole number?

27. Number Sense Use a calculator to find the number that when multiplied by itself has a product of 15,625.

MIXED REVIEW

Estimate the difference.

1.	2.	3.	4.
4,592	10,099	25,497	48,375
− 1,348	− 4,599	− 9,632	− 32,896

Write the value of the underlined digit.

5. 0.4<u>5</u>   **6.** 3.2<u>6</u>   **7.** 14.50<u>9</u>   **8.** 9.1<u>2</u>5

How does using partial products help you keep the numbers in proper alignment?

WRAP UP...

PROBLEM SOLVING

STRATEGY • Find a Pattern

Mrs. Owen rents rooms. She is charting the increase in her daily use of kilowatt-hours of electricity as her new renters move in.

Renters	1	2	3	4	5	6	7	8	9	10
Kilowatt-hours	2	5	7	10	12	▨	▨	▨	▨	▨

How many kilowatt-hours can she expect to use when she has 10 renters?

Many problems contain patterns that can be used to determine final results. You should study the information to see whether there are any patterns to be used as clues.

▶ UNDERSTAND

What are you asked to find?

What facts are given?

▶ PLAN

How can you solve this problem?

Look at the kilowatt-hours to see whether there is a pattern.

▶ SOLVE

What pattern do you see in the numbers?

The second number increases by 3. The third number increases by 2. The fourth number increases by 3, and the fifth number increases by 2.

Complete the table by using the pattern.

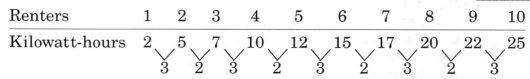

Renters	1	2	3	4	5	6	7	8	9	10
Kilowatt-hours	2	5	7	10	12	15	17	20	22	25

3 2 3 2 3 2 3 2 3

So, Mrs. Owen can expect to use about 25 kilowatt-hours when 10 renters have moved in.

▶ LOOK BACK

How can you check your solution by using subtraction?

WHAT IF... ... Mrs. Owen had 20 renters? What additional numbers would complete the pattern?

 Connection, pages 454–455

Apply

1 One month the power company sent notices to 5,000 of its customers, offering free home-energy inspections. It received 200 replies. A month later the company sent 6,000 notices and received 240 replies. If the pattern continues, how many replies can the company expect to receive if it sends 8,000 notices?

2 It takes 10 minutes for the meter reader to read the 30 meters. She can read 60 meters in 20 minutes and 90 meters in 30 minutes. If the pattern continues, how long would it take to read 150 meters?

Mixed Applications ⟹ **STRATEGIES**

Make a Drawing • Make a Table • Find a Pattern • Write a Number Sentence

Choose a strategy and solve.

3 The power company had 40 new customers in January, in February, and in March. There were no new customers in April, but the company had 35 new customers both in May and in June. Did the company have 200 new customers in the first six months of the year?

4 According to the power company's schedule, the meters at Mrs. Owen's apartment house were read on May 17, June 14, and July 12. If this pattern continues, on what date might the meter reader be scheduled to return? (HINT: Use a calendar.)

5 Many homes in the United States use about 75 kilowatt-hours of electricity each day. If a home used only 70 kilowatt-hours each day, how much electricity could be saved in the month of August?

6 Kristina rode her bicycle to and from her grandparents' house 4 miles away. On the trip she burned 44 calories per mile. If she made this trip 3 times in one week, how many calories did she burn?

CHAPTER REVIEW / TEST

Vocabulary Check

Choose a word or words from the box to complete each sentence.

Associative
Commutative
Distributive
factor
multiples
patterns
Property of One
Zero Property

1. The _?_ Property of Multiplication lets you change the order of factors. *(page 76)*

2. The _?_ Property of Multiplication lets you group factors as you choose. *(page 76)*

3. When you multiply and get a product that is the same as one of the factors, you have used the _?_. *(page 76)*

4. When you multiply and get 0 for the product, you have used the _?_ for Multiplication. *(page 76)*

5. The numbers 10, 100, and 1,000 are _?_ of 10. *(pages 78, 90)*

If you do not understand a problem, look at the page listed in the chapter.

6. When you need to find what comes next in a group of numbers, you should study the information to see whether there are any _?_ to be used as clues. *(page 98)*

7. One way to estimate a product is to round each _?_ to its greatest place value and multiply. *(page 92)*

8. The _?_ Property of Multiplication allows you to break apart numbers and use addition when you multiply. *(page 83)*

Concept Check

Write the name of the multiplication property used in each number sentence. *(pages 76, 82)*

9. $6,584 \times 0 = 0$

10. $78,094 \times 1 = 78,094$

11. $7 \times 50 = 50 \times 7$

12. $(4 \times 50) \times 7 = 4 \times (50 \times 7)$

13. $6 \times (3 + 5) = (6 \times 3) + (6 \times 5)$

14. $8 \times (4 + 2) = (8 \times 4) + (8 \times 2)$

Multiply each by 10, 100, and 1,000. *(pages 78, 90)*

15. 4

16. 23

17. 38

18. 85

19. 43

20. 79

21. 98

22. 17

Skill Check

Use mental math to find the product. *(pages 78, 90)*

23. 70 × 4	24. 500 × 3	25. 6,000 × 7	26. 9,000 × 6	27. 8,000 × 5

28. 30 × 10	29. 600 × 40	30. 4,000 × 30	31. 8,000 × 50	32. 7,000 × 90

Estimate the product. *(pages 80, 92)*

33. 19 × 3	34. 206 × 4	35. 5,128 × 2	36. 42,940 × 7	37. 59,648 × 5

38. 48 × 22	39. 82 × 78	40. 403 × 61	41. 543 × 53	42. 859 × 44

Multiply. *(pages 84, 94, 96)*

43. 56 × 5	44. 342 × 9	45. 3,789 × 6	46. 4,059 × 8	47. 5,167 × 9

48. 50 × 19	49. 262 × 32	50. 295 × 45	51. 340 × 153	52. 905 × 423

Problem-Solving Check *(pages 86, 98)*

53. Corie worked for 16 hours. She earned $5.00 each hour. If she spends $14.95 of her earnings for a sweater, how much money will she have left?

54. Two days a week, Michael works 8 hours each day for $6 per hour. Three days a week, he works 7 hours each day for $5 per hour. How much does he earn each week?

55. The drama club is rehearsing for a play. The first rehearsal lasted 30 minutes, the second rehearsal was 45 minutes long, and the third rehearsal was 1 hour. If the pattern continues, how long will the seventh rehearsal be?

56. On Monday 5 students signed up to run in a race, on Tuesday 15 more students entered the race, and on Wednesday 25 more students signed up. If the pattern continues through Friday, how many students will be signed up to run in the race?

1. Estimate the product of 4 × 357. Show your method.

2. Explain how to use mental math to multiply 30 × 20,000, and give the product.

3. Look at the example on page 84. Using three different colors of counters (red = 100, green = 10, and yellow = 1), model regrouping to find the product of 3 × 142. Draw a picture to show what you did.

4. Show each step as you find the product of 34 × 16.

I know more than one way to multiply.

5. Read Exercise 2 on page 99. Follow the steps on the Problem-Solving Think Along worksheet to show how to solve this problem.

Write About It

6. Which materials that you used with this chapter helped you the most in multiplying whole numbers? Explain.

7. Suppose you estimate the product of two factors as 80,000. When you multiply the factors, the answer you get is 95,424. Would you estimate the product again, multiply the factors again, or consider the answer reasonable? Explain.

Make a Model of Solar Collectors

Solar energy may be captured by solar collector cells, sometimes placed on the roof of a building. It takes 28 panels of 37 cells to produce 1 kilowatt of electricity. With your teammates, model the solar collectors needed to produce 1 kilowatt of electricity.

Do

Work with your teammates. Glue 28 index cards onto a large sheet of colored paper to represent solar collector panels. Use a marker to show 37 "dots" solar collector cells inside each panel.

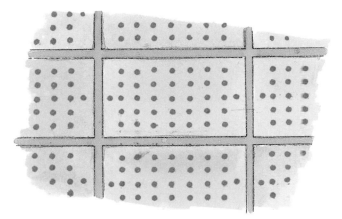

Decide

Talk about how you can use index cards, glue, and markers to model the solar collectors needed to produce 1 kilowatt of electricity.

Share

Show your model. Describe how the number of solar collector cells needed to produce 1 kilowatt of electricity can be calculated.

Talk About It

a. How can you use your model to imagine the number of cells needed to produce 77 kilowatts of electricity?

b. In your everyday activities, what other multiplication situations that involve large products have you noticed?

MathFun
Extend Your Thinking

0	1	2	3	4	5	6	7	8	9
0/0	0/1	0/2	0/3	0/4	0/5	0/6	0/7	0/8	0/9
0/0	0/2	0/4	0/6	0/8	1/0	1/2	1/4	1/6	1/8
0/0	0/3	0/6	0/9	1/2	1/5	1/8	2/1	2/4	2/7
0/0	0/4	0/8	1/2	1/6	2/0	2/4	2/8	3/2	3/6
0/0	0/5	1/0	1/5	2/0	2/5	3/0	3/5	4/0	4/5
0/0	0/6	1/2	1/8	2/4	3/0	3/6	4/2	4/8	5/4
0/0	0/7	1/4	2/1	2/8	3/5	4/2	4/9	5/6	6/3
0/0	0/8	1/6	2/4	3/2	4/0	4/8	5/6	6/4	7/2
0/0	0/9	1/8	2/7	3/6	4/5	5/4	6/3	7/2	8/1

Activity

A Multiplication Machine

Many years ago John Napier, a Scottish mathematician, invented a set of rods, one for each digit 0–9. Each rod shows multiples of a digit. The rods are used to multiply.

2	7
0/2	0/7
0/4	1/4
0/6	2/1
0/8	2/8
1/0	3/5
1/2	4/2
1/4	4/9
1/6	5/6
1/8	6/3

```
    27
  × 86
  ─────
   162  ←
  2160  ←
  ─────
  2,322
```

6 × 27 = 162 ←

8 × 27 = 216 ←

To multiply 86 × 27, place the rods headed 2 and 7 side by side. The partial product of 6 × 27 can be found by looking at the sixth row. The sum of each diagonal from right to left represents each digit in the partial product. Record the results.

To multiply 80 × 27, use the eighth row. Multiply the partial product by 10, and record the result. Then add to find the final product.

Make a set of rods. Try some other multiplication problems, and then check your results with a calculator. Explain to a partner how to use the rods.

Challenge

Number Puzzles

Fill in the missing digits.

1.
```
   1■
 ×  ■
 ────
   45
```

2.
```
   ■8
 ×  3
 ────
  26■
```

3.
```
   47
 ×  ■
 ────
  ■23
```

4.
```
    18
  × ■2
  ────
    36
   3■0
  ────
   396
```

5.
```
    24
  × 1■
  ────
   12■
   240
  ────
   36■
```

6.
```
    70■
  × ■ 4
  ─────
  2,808
  2■060
  ─────
  2■,868
```

Challenge

🖩 Calculator

Find the greatest whole number which, when multiplied by itself, has a product less than or equal to the number given. Use a calculator.

1. 1,290　　　**4.** 14,400

2. 7,564　　　**5.** 49,284

3. 12,400　　　**6.** 279,833

Write the letter of the correct answer.

1. What is the value of the 5 in 354,078?

A. 50
B. 5,000
C. 50,000
D. not here

2. What is the value of the 2 in 16.825?

A. 0.02
B. 0.2
C. 2.0
D. 20.0

3. Round 4,382,568 to the nearest ten thousand.

A. 4,000,000
B. 4,380,000
C. 4,390,000
D. 4,400,000

4. Estimate.
$4,195 + 2,876 \approx n$

A. 5,000
B. 6,500
C. 7,000
D. 70,000

5. $5,000 - 3,875 = n$

A. 2,125
B. 2,235
C. 2,875
D. not here

6. $16.3 - 8.4 = n$

A. 7.9
B. 8.1
C. 8.9
D. 70.9

7. $14.62 + 3.08 = n$

A. 17.60
B. 17.70
C. 18.70
D. not here

8. $25.675 + 37.275 = n$

A. 62.850
B. 62.940
C. 62.950
D. 63.950

9. Estimate. $421 \times 9 \approx n$

A. 360
B. 3,600
C. 36,000
D. 360,000

10. $78 \times 4 = n$

A. 282
B. 302
C. 304
D. 312

11. Estimate. $4,231 \times 21 \approx n$

A. 4,000
B. 8,000
C. 18,000
D. 80,000

12. $48 \times 23 = n$

A. 144
B. 240
C. 1,104
D. not here

13. Erin jogs 2 miles a day every Monday, Wednesday, and Friday. On Tuesday and Thursday, she jogs 4 miles each day. If Erin wants to jog 20 miles a week, how many more miles does she need to jog?

A. 6 miles
B. 10 miles
C. 16 miles
D. 18 miles

14. In the first week of school, 2 students worked on an art project. There were 4 students working on it in the second week, 8 in the third, and 16 in the fourth. If this pattern continues, in which week will there be 128 students?

A. fifth week
B. sixth week
C. seventh week
D. eighth week

CHAPTER 4

GEOMETRY

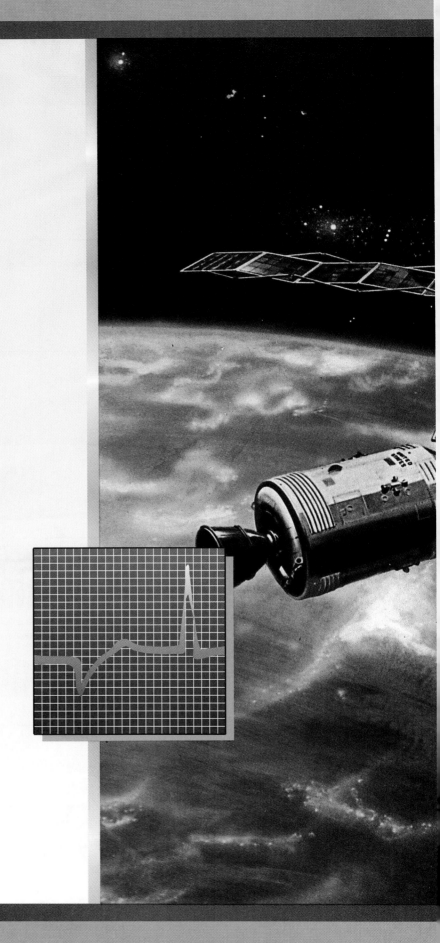

Did you know . . .

. . . that on space flights, astronauts wear monitoring devices that help specialists learn how the human body reacts to conditions in space?

TALK ABOUT IT

Isabel is fascinated with space technology. She describes a space picture over the telephone to her friend. What geometric terms can Isabel use to describe the picture's features?

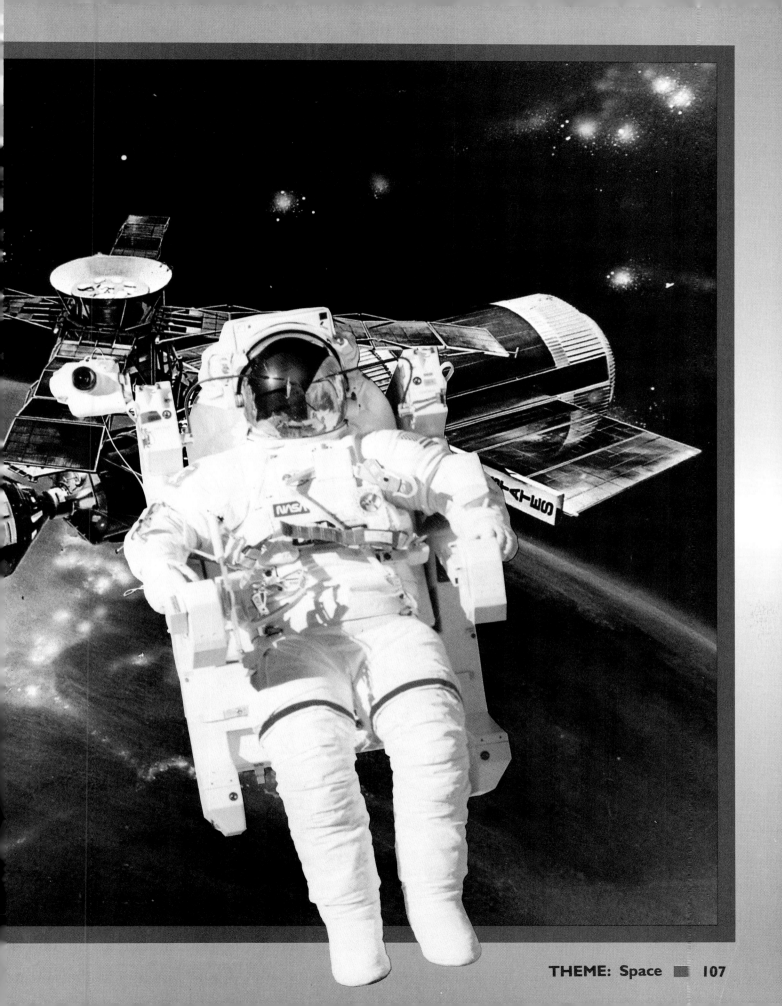

LINE RELATIONSHIPS

The astronauts who explore space discuss the size, shape, and position of things. They use basic ideas from geometry.

A **point** is used to describe an exact location in space.	*P*	Use a capital letter to name a point. *P* • Point *P*, or *P*
A **line** is a straight path made up of points in a plane. A line goes on forever in both directions.	*A* *C*	Use any two points on a line to name a line. Line *AC*, or $\overleftrightarrow{AC}$ Line *CA*, or $\overleftrightarrow{CA}$
A **line segment** is part of a line. It is a straight path with two endpoints.	*E* *F*	Use the endpoints to name a line segment. Line segment *EF*, or $\overline{EF}$ Line segment *FE*, or $\overline{FE}$
All the points that form a flat surface are called a **plane**. A plane extends in all directions.	*E* *F* *A* *B*	Use 3 points to name this plane. Plane *AEF*

• Is line segment *EF* vertical or horizontal?

You can use a sheet of paper to represent a plane and 10 toothpicks to represent line segments.

Drop 10 toothpicks on the paper. Look for different ways the toothpicks can touch or cross. Draw all the different ways you see. Then repeat the process.

Talk About It

▶ How can you describe the positions of the toothpicks?

▶ Name a point where the line segments touch or cross.

Within a plane, lines can be either intersecting or parallel.
Look at the drawings.

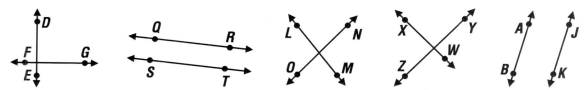

Lines that meet or cross each other at one point are called
intersecting lines.

- Name the intersecting line segments.

Lines that intersect at one point to form square corners are
called **perpendicular** lines.

- Name the perpendicular line segments.

Lines in a plane that will never intersect are the same
distance from each other. They are called **parallel** lines.

- Name the parallel line segments.

Talk About It

▶ When you dropped the toothpicks, did
you draw any line relationships you
do not see in the drawings above?

▶ Do perpendicular lines always
intersect? If so, at how many points
do they intersect?

▶ Are all intersecting line segments
perpendicular? Explain.

▶ How do you know that parallel lines
will never intersect?

Imagine that the toothpicks are lines
that extend in both directions.

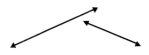

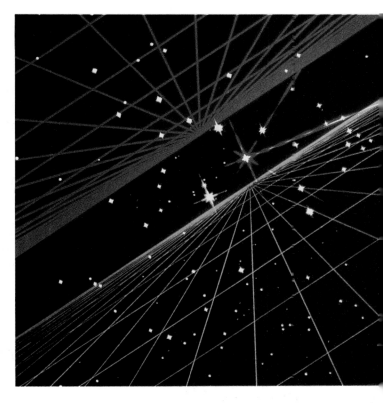

- Are there some lines in the same plane that are neither
intersecting nor parallel? Explain your answer.

Check for Understanding

Complete. Write *always, sometimes,* or *never.*

1. A line segment __?__ forms a straight path.

2. Intersecting lines __?__ cross each other at one point.

3. Intersecting lines are __?__ perpendicular.

4. Parallel lines __?__ intersect.

5. Lines in a plane __?__ intersect if they are not parallel.

Practice

Choose the sentence that describes the relationship of the lines. Write **a, b,** or **c.**

6.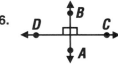

   a. $\overleftrightarrow{AB}$ is not perpendicular to $\overleftrightarrow{DC}$.

   b. $\overline{AB}$ is parallel to $\overline{DC}$.

   c. $\overline{AB}$ is perpendicular to $\overline{DC}$.

7.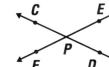

   a. $\overleftrightarrow{CD}$ is parallel to $\overleftrightarrow{EF}$.

   b. $\overleftrightarrow{CD}$ intersects $\overleftrightarrow{EF}$.

   c. $\overleftrightarrow{DC}$ is perpendicular to $\overleftrightarrow{FE}$.

8.

   a. $\overleftrightarrow{GH}$ is perpendicular to $\overleftrightarrow{JK}$.

   b. $\overleftrightarrow{GH}$ intersects $\overleftrightarrow{JK}$.

   c. $\overleftrightarrow{GH}$ is parallel to $\overleftrightarrow{JK}$.

Mixed Applications

Use the map for Exercises 9–12.

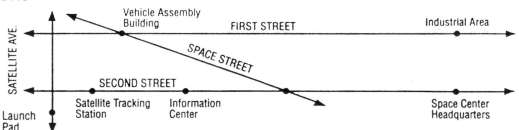

9. Which streets run horizontally? vertically?

10. Explain the relationship between First Street and Space Street.

11. What kind of line relationship do First Street and Second Street represent?

12. **Write a Question** Use the map to write a question about a line segment.

More Practice, Lesson 4.1, page H46

PROBLEM-SOLVING PRACTICE

Oscar's family lives in Spaceville, Earth. Solve each problem to find out about a day in the life of Oscar.

1. Oscar takes the school shuttle to Big Dipper School, located 125.6 space miles away. On the path from his home to school, the shuttle stops to pick up Venus. She lives 27.8 space miles from Oscar. How far does Venus live from Big Dipper School?

2. While at school, Oscar decides to buy some lunch pellets with his starbucks at the spaceteria. He buys a red food pellet for $0.25, a green food pellet for $0.50, 2 blue food pellets for $0.75 each, and an asteroid apple for $0.60. How much change will he receive from $5.00?

3. Henry and Hugo are in Oscar's first class at school. Henry, Hugo, and Venus are in his second class. Hugo and Venus are in Oscar's third class, and Henry, Hugo, and Venus are in his fourth class. Who has the most classes with Oscar?

4. After school Oscar plays spaceball. Oscar imagines that a straight path from first base to second base and one from second base to third base are line segments. At what point would these two line segments intersect?

5. That night Oscar was first to arrive at the intergalactic gig. During the first 5 minutes of the gig, 5 more spacemates arrived. After 10 minutes 12 spacemates were at the gig, and after 15 minutes 24 spacemates were there. If the pattern continued, how long was it before all 96 spacemates were at the gig?

6. Oscar's space pad is located on a path between his friends Henry and Hugo. Venus also lives between Henry and Hugo. If Venus lives next door to Hugo, who lives next door on both sides of Oscar?

NAMING RAYS AND ANGLES

Recently the telescopes of Cerro Tololo Inter-American Observatory in Chile were used to view a supernova. The astronomers used precise angles to aim the telescopes.

You have learned that a line is a never-ending straight path that extends in both directions.

A **ray** is part of a line that has one endpoint and goes on forever in one direction.

A ray is named by its endpoint and any other point on the ray. The endpoint is always named first.

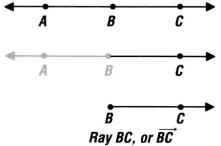

MULTICULTURAL NOTE: The location of Cerro Tololo Observatory, near La Serena, Chile, allows astronomers to observe many stars not visible in the Northern Hemisphere.

Talk About It

▶ Name another ray on line *AC*.

▶ Is a line segment part of a ray? Why or why not?

▶ Name some real things that are examples of rays.

Ray BC, or $\overrightarrow{BC}$

When two rays have the same endpoint, they form an **angle.** The common endpoint is the **vertex** of the angle. The rays are the **sides** of the angle.

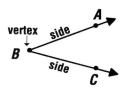

Angle *ABC*, Angle *CBA*, or Angle *B*
∠*ABC*, ∠*CBA*, or ∠*B*

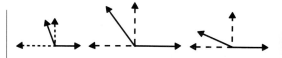

Angles that form square corners are called **right** angles.

Angles that fit inside a right angle are called **acute** angles.

Angles that fit between a right angle and a straight line are called **obtuse** angles.

Talk About It

▶ Can angles be formed by line segments that have the same endpoint? Why or why not?

▶ Name some real things that show examples of angles.

Check for Understanding

Choose a word from the box to complete each sentence.

| acute |
| obtuse |
| ray |
| right |
| vertex |

1. An angle smaller than a right angle is a(n) _?_ angle.

2. An angle larger than a right angle is a(n) _?_ angle.

3. An angle that forms a square corner is a(n) _?_ angle.

4. Part of a line that has one endpoint is a(n) _?_.

5. The common endpoint of an angle is the _?_.

Practice

Identify the angle. Write *right, acute,* or *obtuse.*

6.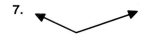

7.

8.

Use the figure for Exercises 9–11.

9. Name two acute angles.

10. Name a right angle.

11. Name an obtuse angle.

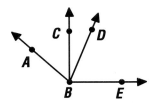

Mixed Applications

12. The stars were viewed at 8:00 P.M. Classify the angle formed by the hands on a clock for this time.

13. The constellation is visible at 9:00 P.M. What angle do the clock hands form for this time?

14. Clara's family drove 5 hours to reach the observatory. If they drove 55 miles each hour, how many miles did they drive?

15. Ralph bought a telescope for $69.99 and 2 calendars for $5.95 each. How much change did he receive from $90.00?

VISUAL THINKING

In this figure, ∠RQT is in a plane. Point S is in the **exterior** of the angle. Point W is in the **interior** of the angle.

16. Draw and name an angle in a plane. Name a point in the interior and exterior of the plane.

Find three angles in your classroom that are right, acute, and obtuse. Describe and draw a picture of each angle.

EXPLORING

Angle Measurement

Just as there are unit names for measuring time or length, there is a unit name for measuring angles. It is called a **degree** (°). A circle is divided into 360 degrees.

A **protractor** is a tool used for measuring the size of the opening of an angle. Its scale is marked from 0° to 180°.

Work Together

Building Understanding

Use a protractor to measure these angles.

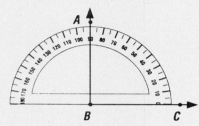

Read the measure of the angle where ray *BA* passes through the scale.

∠ *ABC* is a right angle. Its measure is 90°.

Place the center at the vertex of the angle.

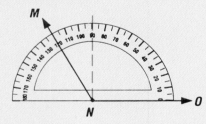

Make sure the rays pass through the marks on the scale.

Obtuse angles measure more than 90° but less than 180°.

Make sure ray *EF* passes through zero (0).

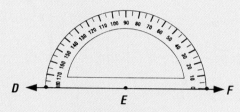

∠ *DEF* is a **straight** angle. Its measure is 180°.

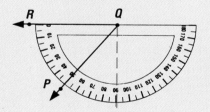

Acute angles measure less than 90°.

TALK ABOUT IT

- What can you conclude about the measure of right angles?

- Suppose you have a ray *PQ*. How can you use a protractor to draw an angle of 45°?

- If the rays are extended, will the angle measure be changed? Why or why not?

Connection, pages 450–451

Making the Connection

Study this diagram. Use what you know about angle measures to explore the angles formed by intersecting lines.

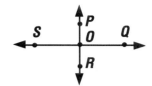

TALK ABOUT IT

- Describe the angles formed by these lines.

- What is the measure of each of the angles formed?

- What relationship do you see between a right angle and a straight angle?

- What is the sum of the degrees of all four angles?

Make a table showing types of angles. Draw two of each type of angle. First, estimate and record the estimated measures. Then, find their actual measures and record.

TALK ABOUT IT

- How did you estimate the measures of the angles you drew in your table?

- How do your estimates compare with the actual measures of the angles?

- How can you measure an angle greater than 180°?

Checking Understanding

Trace each angle. First, estimate the angle measure. Then, use a protractor to measure each angle. You may need to extend the rays.

1.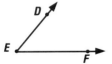

2.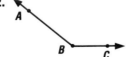

3.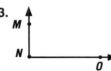

4. Draw an acute angle. Use a protractor to measure the angle. Record the measure.

5. Draw an obtuse angle. Use a protractor to measure the angle. Record the measure.

6. Use a protractor to draw an angle of 60°.

More Practice, Lesson 4.3, pages H46–H47

EXPLORING

Polygons

Work Together

Building Understanding

Since the diagrams below lie on a flat surface, they are called plane figures. They are made up of points that are all in the same plane.

These are **open** figures.   These are **closed** figures.

Use a geoboard or dot paper to make several closed figures.

TALK ABOUT IT

- Describe some of the closed figures you made.

- How many line segments does each of your shapes have? angles?

- What is the relationship between the number of line segments and the number of angles of each shape?

Special closed plane figures are called **polygons.** Polygons are made up of line segments that meet at vertices but do not cross.

A polygon is modeled on each of these geoboards.

• Pentagon •

• Hexagon •

Use a geoboard or dot paper to model six different polygons.

TALK ABOUT IT

Look at your models.

- What relationship can you find between the number of sides and the number of angles of each of your models?

- Name some examples of real objects with polygon shapes.

                    Connection, pages 452–453

Making the Connection

Copy and complete the table, using your polygon models.

Polygons			
Name of Polygon	Number of Sides	Number of Angles	Picture of Your Model
Triangle	3	■	◁
Quadrilateral	■	4	■
Pentagon	5	■	■
Hexagon	■	■	⬡
Octagon	8	■	■

Use the shapes below for clues about regular polygons.

These are polygons.

These are regular polygons.

TALK ABOUT IT
- Look at the two triangles. Describe the angles in both. Describe the sides.

- How are the regular polygons different from the others?

So, some polygons have sides of various lengths and angles of different measures, but **regular** polygons have all sides the same length and all angles the same measure.

Checking Understanding

Name a polygon represented by each object.

1. pennant
2. baseball diamond
3. chalkboard
4. stop sign

Write *true* or *false*.

5. A triangle is an open plane figure.

6. A hexagon has six angles and six sides.

7. A regular pentagon has two sides of unequal length.

8. A polygon has the same number of sides and angles.

More Practice, Lesson 4.4, page H47

CLASSIFYING TRIANGLES

The *Endeavour* is a space shuttle. It moves like a rocket and uses triangular wings to glide to a landing.

A **triangle** has three sides and three angles. Triangles can be classified according to the lengths of their sides.

Use the geoboard, a geoband, and a piece of string to explore triangles. Use your geoband to form a triangle.

Start on the top row of the geoboard. Place the geoband on the center peg. Then loop it around the corner pegs at the bottom.

• How many sides are formed? how many angles?

Use a piece of string to measure the lengths of the sides.

• How many sides are the same length?

A triangle that has at least two sides of equal length is called an **isosceles** triangle.

Form a new triangle by moving the geoband from the center peg to two spaces up from the bottom left corner. Use your string to measure the lengths of the sides.

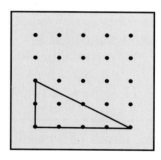

• Is this an isosceles triangle? How do you know?

• What did you find out about the lengths of the three sides?

A triangle in which each side is a different length is called a **scalene** triangle.

Some geoboards have pegs on the back side. These pegs form a circular pattern. Look at the triangle in the example. Measure the lengths of the sides.

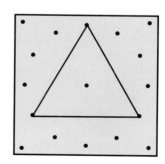

• What did you find out about the length of the three sides?

A triangle with all sides of equal length is called an **equilateral** triangle.

Use a geoboard to model each kind of triangle in three different sizes. Check the lengths of the sides with your string. Record your results, and classify your triangles in a table.

Idea Bank, page 464, Exercise 3

Check for Understanding

Identify the triangle. Write **a**, **b**, or **c**.

1. equilateral
a.
b.
c.

2. scalene
a.
b.
c.

3. isosceles
a.
b.
c.

Practice

Name each triangle. Write *equilateral, scalene,* or *isosceles.*

4.

5.

6.

7.

Mixed Applications

8. Admission to the science center is $3.25 for adults and $2.75 for children. There are 2 adults and 2 children in Kay's family. What will they pay for admission?

9. Models of rockets were on exhibit in 4 different rooms. Tony counted about 39 people in one room. If each room had about the same number of people, about how many people were viewing the exhibit?

CRITICAL THINKING

Complete the activity to discover the sum of the number of degrees of all angles in a triangle.

Use a ruler to draw a picture of a large triangle. Label each vertex with the letters *A, B,* and *C.* Tear the corners as shown. Place the angles together at a point on a straight line.

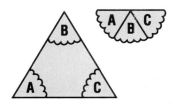

10. What is the total measure of the three angles of the triangle?

11. Draw another triangle and repeat the activity. What are your results?

Name the polygon with the fewest sides and angles.

ANGLES
in a Triangle

The angles of triangles can be used to classify triangles.

Use dot paper and a ruler to explore the angles of triangles.

To draw a triangle on your dot paper, start on a corner dot. Count across three spaces and mark the vertex. Count up three spaces and mark the vertex. Draw line segments between each pair of vertices.

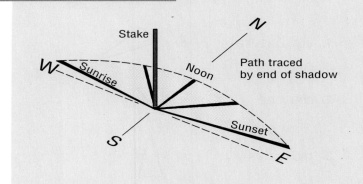

Stake

N

W

Sunrise

Noon

Path traced by end of shadow

S

Sunset

E

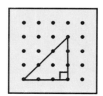

- How many angles are formed inside the triangle?

- How can you estimate the measure of each angle?

- Name each type of angle in the triangle.

A triangle that has a right angle is a **right** triangle.

Draw a triangle that matches this model.

- How do these angles compare with right angles?

- Name each type of angle in the triangle.

MULTICULTURAL NOTE: As the position of the sun changes throughout the day, the angle of the shadow of the triangular rod on a sundial changes to indicate time. The ancient Egyptians were the first people to use this type of sundial.

A triangle that has three acute angles is an **acute** triangle.

Use the dot paper again.
Draw a triangle that matches this model.

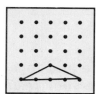

- How do these angles compare with right angles?

- What do you call an angle greater than a right angle?

- Name each type of angle in the triangle.

A triangle that has one obtuse angle is an **obtuse** triangle.

Idea Bank, page 464, Exercise 2

Check for Understanding

Identify the triangle. Write **a**, **b**, or **c**.

1. right   **a.**   **b.**   **c.**

2. acute   **a.**    **b.**   **c.**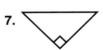

3. obtuse   **a.**   **b.**   **c.**

Practice

Name each triangle. Write *right, acute,* or *obtuse.*

4.   5.   6.   7.

Mixed Applications

8. Suppose you used a sundial to keep track of the time from sunrise to sunset. If sunrise was at 6:50 A.M. and sunset at 5:20 P.M., how many hours passed during the day?

9. **Critical Thinking** Jenny said the wings of a space shuttle were right triangles, and her brother said they were scalene triangles. Could both be correct? Explain.

10. **Critical Thinking** Draw a triangle. By drawing one line, can you divide the triangle into two right triangles? Explain.

11. A spacecraft 200 miles high must travel at a speed of 17,000 miles per hour. At 22,000 miles high, it must travel 6,900 miles per hour. What is the difference in the speeds?

MIXED REVIEW

Complete.

1. Round 16.547 to the nearest tenth, hundredth, and whole number.

Express each as a part of the whole unit.

2. 9 centimeters = ▧ meter   3. 5 decimeters = ▧ meter   4. 8 hundredths = ▧

Name the three words used to classify angles.

EXPLORING

Quadrilaterals

Quadrilaterals are polygons with four sides and four angles. There are several different quadrilaterals. Some of them you already know.

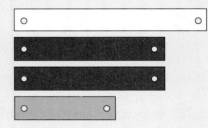

Work Together

Building Understanding

Make larger drawings of these figures. Make cardboard strips from your drawings. Punch holes in the cardboard strips and connect them with fasteners. Record the figures on a sheet of paper.

Make a rectangle.

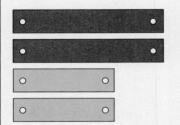

Make a square.

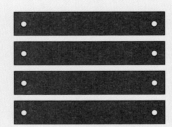

Make a trapezoid.

TALK ABOUT IT

- How many different shapes did you make?

- Which figures have four right angles?

- Which figure has acute and obtuse angles?

- Which figures have two pairs of parallel sides?

- Which figure has only one pair of parallel sides?

Adjust the cardboard strips of the square and the rectangle to form a different kind of quadrilateral for each. Trace these new figures on a sheet of paper.

- Describe the new figures you made.

- Do your new figures have any right angles?

- Do any of your figures have parallel sides? If so, how many?

 Idea Bank, page 464, Exercise 4

Making the Connection

Here are names and examples of some different types of quadrilaterals. Make a table of quadrilaterals. Describe the relationship between the sides and angles.

Quadrilateral	Description	Example
Rectangle	?	▭
Square	?	☐
Rhombus	?	▱
Parallelogram	?	▱
Trapezoid	?	⏢

Checking Understanding

1. parallelogram   trapezoid

   Compare the sides of a parallelogram with the sides of a trapezoid. How are they different?

2. parallelogram   rectangle

   Compare the sides of a parallelogram with the sides of a rectangle. How are they the same?

3. rhombus   trapezoid

   Compare the sides of a rhombus with the sides of a trapezoid. How are they different?

4. rectangle   square

   Compare the angles of a rectangle with the angles of a square. What are their measures?

VISUAL THINKING

5. A tangram is an ancient Chinese puzzle. Copy the seven closed plane figures of a tangram. Cut out the pieces. Rearrange all seven pieces to form different quadrilaterals. How many different quadrilaterals can you make? Name them.

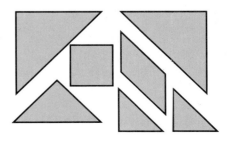

PROBLEM SOLVING

STRATEGY • Guess and Check

The rocket used to launch a space probe has 4 stages. Each stage goes up twice as many miles as the stage before it. The total altitude reached is 75 miles. If the last stage travels 8 times as far as the first stage, how far does each stage travel?

Often problems can be solved by using the strategy *guess and check*. If the first guess is not correct, use the information learned and guess again.

▶ **UNDERSTAND**

What are you asked to find?
What facts are given?

▶ **PLAN**

What plan can you make?

Make a guess for the altitude reached by the first stage.

▶ **SOLVE**

How can you solve the problem?

First, guess 4 miles. Then, check the number by doubling the 4 to get the distance for the second stage. Continue doubling the distance to find the distances for the other stages.

$$4 \; + \; 8 \; + \; 16 \; + \; 32 \; = 60$$
Stage 1   Stage 2   Stage 3   Stage 4

Is the sum 75? No, it is less than 75.
Guess again. Try a larger number. Guess 5.

$$5 \; + \; 10 \; + \; 20 \; + \; 40 \; = 75$$
Stage 1   Stage 2   Stage 3   Stage 4

Is the sum 75? Yes.
So, the 4 rocket stages travel 5, 10, 20, and 40 miles.

▶ **LOOK BACK**

How can you check your answer?

Check by asking these questions:
Does the last stage travel 8 times as far as the first?
Is the total altitude 75 miles?

WHAT IF... ... the rocket only reaches an altitude of 45 miles? How far will each stage travel?

124

Apply

Solve. Use the strategy *guess and check.*

1 A rocket is divided into 4 sections. On the launch pad, the rocket stands 90 feet tall. The second section is twice as long as the first section, the third section is twice as long as the second section, and the fourth section is twice as long as the third section. How long is each section of the rocket?

2 On a space station miles above the earth, a rocket has been assembled with 3 stages. The rocket is designed so that each stage will go 3 times as far as the one before it. If the total altitude to be reached is 6,500 miles, how far will each stage travel?

Mixed Applications > **STRATEGIES**

Guess and Check • Make a Drawing • Find a Pattern • Write a Number Sentence

Choose a strategy and solve.

3 The five planets closest to the sun are Earth, Venus, Mars, Mercury, and Jupiter. Earth is between Venus and Mars. Mercury is between Venus and the sun. Which of these planets is next to Jupiter?

4 Suppose each stage of a rocket could carry it 80,000 miles. The moon is about 240,000 miles away. If you wanted to go to the moon and return, how many stages would your rocket need?

5 A shuttle crew released a satellite into orbit. After 1 minute the satellite was 80 yards from the launch vehicle. After 2 minutes it was 160 yards away. After 3 minutes it was 240 yards away, and after 4 minutes it was 320 yards away. If the pattern continues, how far away will the satellite be after 6 minutes?

6 Mercury is 57,040,000 miles from Earth, and Mars is 48,360,000 miles from Earth. How much farther is Mercury from Earth than Mars is from Earth?

WRITER'S CORNER

7 Find the sum of two numbers. Then write *guess-and-check* problems that ask for the two numbers. The clues should be the sum and either the product or the difference of the numbers. Have a partner solve.

1. A baseball team won 8 more games than it lost. If it played 56 games, how many games did it win?

2. On the first day of practice, Paul did 3 sit-ups. On the second day he did 5, on the third day he did 8, and on the fourth day he did 12. If this pattern continued, how many sit-ups did he do on the sixth day of practice?

> I can look for patterns to help me solve problems.

Write two other forms for each number.

3. 1.35   4. 0.678   5. 14.209   6. 0.003   7. 12.12

Complete.

8. $10^{\blacksquare} = 1,000$ 9. $10 \times 10 \times 10 \times 10 = \blacksquare$ 10. $10^{\blacksquare} = 10,000$

Estimate.

| 11. 495
+ 47 | 12. 780
+115 | 13. 1,423
+ 397 | 14. 28,125
+31,084 | 15. 41,095
+ 6,154 |

Complete. Identify the addition property used.

16. $7,985 + \blacksquare = 7,985$

17. $4.25 + 5.73 = 5.73 + \blacksquare$

18. $275 + 450 = \blacksquare + 275$

19. $(50 + 75) + 125 = \blacksquare + (75 + 125)$

Multiply.

| 20. 60
× 3 | 21. 700
× 5 | 22. 300
× 8 | 23. 8,000
× 4 | 24. 4,000
× 9 |

| 25. 83
× 8 | 26. 254
× 5 | 27. 4,397
× 6 | 28. 6,592
× 4 | 29. 8,543
× 6 |

Identify the angle. Write *acute, obtuse,* or *right.*

30.   31.    32. 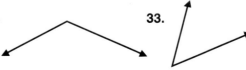   33.

Russia

EUROPE

ASIA

Geometry in Space

A *cosmonaut* is a person from the Commonwealth of Independent States (formerly the Soviet Union) who pilots a spacecraft or works in space. *Cosmonaut* means "sailor of the universe." Cosmonauts have traveled into space in spacecraft called *Soyuz*. They have flown to *Salyut* space stations.

MULTICULTURAL NOTE: In 1987 a Soyuz spacecraft, two other spacecraft, and a Soviet space station docked in space. The length of these four joined vehicles was more than 100 feet.

Study the pictures of a Salyut space station and a Soyuz launching. Work with a partner to answer the questions.

1. What kind of angle does the Soyuz make with the earth at lift-off?

2. How does the lift-off of the Soyuz remind you of a ray?

3. Name the geometric figures you see in the picture of the Salyut space station.

SYMMETRY

A figure has a line of **symmetry** if it can be folded so that the two parts of the figure are identical.

Look at the cutout letters. Each letter is marked with a dotted line of symmetry. Place a mirror along the dotted line to show a **mirror image** of each letter.

- What do you see?

- Which letters have both a vertical and a horizontal line of symmetry?

A figure may have more than one line of symmetry. Use scissors and a regular-hexagon pattern to explore lines of symmetry. Cut out a regular hexagon, and follow these steps:

- Fold the pattern in half so that one side exactly covers the other side.

- Open the pattern and fold in half another way.

- Repeat the process to make as many folds in the pattern as possible.

- Count the number of folds you made.

- How many lines of symmetry does a regular hexagon have?

Cut out a square and an equilateral triangle. Repeat the steps above.

- How many lines of symmetry does a square have? an equilateral triangle?

Record your results. Draw the lines of symmetry.

- Compare the number of sides of the square and the equilateral triangle with the number of lines of symmetry. What do your results tell you about regular polygons and lines of symmetry?

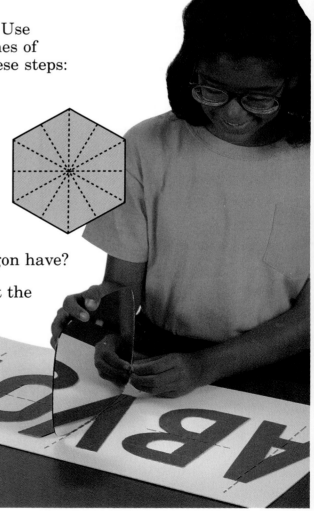

Idea Bank, page 464, Exercise 1

Check for Understanding

Trace each drawing. Draw all the lines of symmetry for each regular polygon.

1.

2.

3.

4.

Practice

Tell whether the picture shows a mirror image. Write *yes* or *no*.

5.

6.

7.

Trace each figure. Draw all the lines of symmetry for each figure.

8.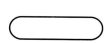

9.

10.

11.

Trace each drawing and complete the design to make a symmetrical figure.

12.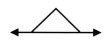

13.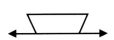

14.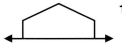

15.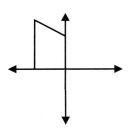

Mixed Applications

Use the list of letters for Exercises 16–19.

N   O   P   Q   R   S   T   U   V   W   X   Y   Z

16. Which of the letters have no lines of symmetry?

17. Which of the letters have only one line of symmetry?

18. Which of the letters have more than one line of symmetry?

19. **Analyze Data** Use only symmetrical letters to write a word.

Name some things found in nature that have line symmetry.

WRAP UP...

EXPLORING

Congruence and Motion

Figures that have the same shape and size are **congruent.**

$\overline{AB}$ is congruent to $\overline{CD}$. $\triangle GHI$ is congruent to $\triangle LMN$.

Figure X is congruent to figure Y.

Work Together

Building Understanding

Use pattern blocks and graph paper to explore different ways to move congruent polygons on a flat surface.

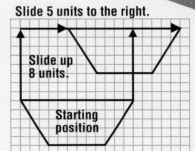

Slide 5 units to the right.

A. Place a trapezoid on graph paper as shown. Trace around it to record a starting position. **Slide,** or move the trapezoid along the lines, going up 8 units and right 5 units.

- Did the trapezoid change its size or shape?

- What changed when you slid the trapezoid?

B. Return the trapezoid to the starting position. **Flip,** or turn over, the trapezoid across a line of symmetry.

- Are the two trapezoids on the graph paper congruent?

- How did the position of the trapezoid change?

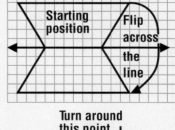

C. Return the trapezoid to the starting position. This time, **turn,** or rotate, the trapezoid around a vertex as shown.

- What changed this time?

- What did not change?

- Turn the trapezoid around another vertex. What happened?

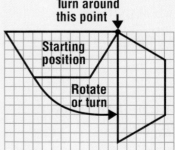

Choose several other polygons. Try sliding, flipping, and turning them.

- What can you say about one figure if you can slide, flip, or turn it to make it look like another figure?

130

Making the Connection

Look at the figures. Decide whether the second figure is a result of a move.

A.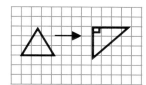

B.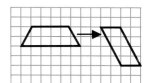

C.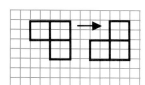

TALK ABOUT IT

• Which of the figures shows motion?

• If any figures do not show motion, explain why.

• Does motion change a figure's shape? Explain.

Checking Understanding

Copy the figures in Exercises 1–3 on graph paper.

1. Flip the squares across the line.

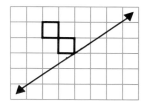

2. Turn the rectangle around this vertex until it sits on another side.

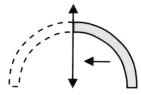

3. Slide the rhombus down 3 units and left 7 units.

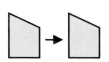

Write *slide, flip,* or *turn* to indicate how each figure was moved.

4.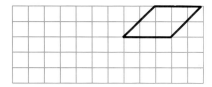

5.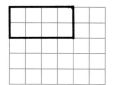

6.

7.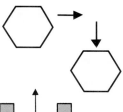

8.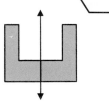

9.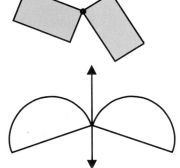

Use Figures *a, b, c,* and *d* for Exercises 10–12.

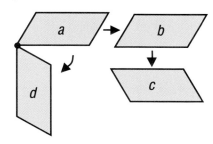

10. Name the motion when *a* is moved to *b*.

11. Name the motions when *a* is moved to *c*.

12. Name the motion when *a* is moved to *d*.

IDENTIFYING SIMILAR FIGURES

Figures that have the same shape are called **similar** figures. They may or may not have the same size.

Use a large sheet of paper, tape, a pencil, and two identical rubber bands to create a similar figure.

Keep your eyes on the knot while the pencil hand does the drawing.

- Knot together two rubber bands.

- Tape a large sheet of paper to the desk.

- Place the figure to be traced on one side of the paper.

- Loop the rubber band around your finger to act as an anchor.

- Stretch the rubber band from the anchor point so that the knot is directly over the figure.

- Place your pencil at the other end of the rubber band, and move the pencil as the knot traces the figure.

Talk About It

▶ Do the two figures have the same shape? the same size?

▶ Is the new figure similar to the first figure?

▶ What will happen if you change the anchor point to another point?

Compare the groups of polygons.

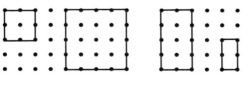
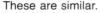
These are similar.

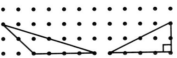
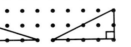

These are not similar.

Talk About It

▶ How can you tell whether two polygons are similar?

▶ Are a pair of regular hexagons always similar? Why or why not?

▶ Are all circles similar? How do you know?

Check for Understanding

Use dot paper to draw a similar figure. Double the length of each side.

1.
2.
3.
4.

Practice

Are the figures similar? Write *yes* or *no*.

5.
6.
7.
8.

9.
10.
11.
12.

On dot paper, draw a larger figure that is similar.

13.
14.
15.

Mixed Applications

16. Explain why triangle *DEF* and triangle *GHI* are not similar.

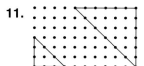

17. Is a baseball similar to a basketball? Explain.

18. If a rocket travels 25,000 miles per hour, how many miles does it travel in 8 hours?

MIXED REVIEW

Multiply.

1. 382	2. 475	3. 693	4. 4,325	5. 6,871
× 2	× 3	× 5	× 4	× 8

Multiply each by 10, 100, and 1,000.

6. 7   7. 18   8. 23   9. 36   10. 49

When the sides of a 2 × 2 square on graph paper are doubled, how many units are in the new figure?

WRAP UP...

EXPLORING

Circles

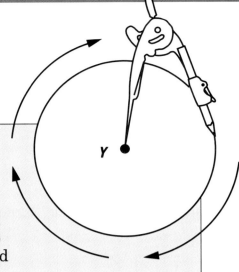

Building Understanding

A **compass** is a tool for constructing circles.

Use a compass or two pencils and a paper clip to draw a circle. Place a point, Y, on a sheet of paper. Place the tip of the compass on the point, and swing the pencil around to form the circle.

The point Y is the center of the circle. A circle is named by its center. The point X is one of many points on the circle.

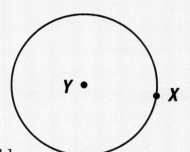

- Using the compass, how can you make larger or smaller circles?

Trace and cut out the circle you have made.

- How many ways can you fold the circle so that the fold passes through the center, Y?

- What do you call these folds?

Using this information about circles, construct a circle on a large sheet of paper. The circle must be larger than one that can be drawn with a compass.

TALK ABOUT IT

- How can you describe the size of your circle?

- How did you make the circle?

Making the Connection

A circle is a closed plane figure formed by all points that are the same distance from a given point in the plane called a **center**.

By connecting points on the circle, or in its center, line segments are formed. These line segments have special names.

A line segment that connects two points on the circle is called a **chord.**

- Name some chords shown in the drawing.

A chord that passes through the center of the circle is called a **diameter**.

- Name the diameter shown in the drawing.

A line segment that connects the center with a point on the circle is called a **radius.**

- Name some radii (plural) shown in the drawing.

Checking Understanding

Write *sometimes*, *always*, or *never* for Exercises 1–4.

1. A chord is _?_ shorter than a diameter.

2. A chord is _?_ longer than a diameter.

3. There are _?_ two radii in a diameter.

4. A radius is _?_ part of a diameter.

Complete.

5. What is the longest chord that can be drawn in a circle?

6. If you know the radius of a circle, how can you determine the diameter?

7. If you know the diameter of a circle, how can you determine the radius?

8. Name some items you could use to draw a circle if you did not have a compass.

9. What line segments in a circle determine the size of the circle?

10. Suppose you draw a circle by tracing around a cylinder. How could you locate the center point? (HINT: Use a cutout circle.)

EXPLORING

Solid Figures

Building Understanding

Use patterns to model solid figures.

Use the pattern on page H91 to model a figure that looks like a shoebox.

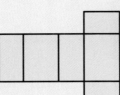

Your model represents a solid figure called a **rectangular prism.**

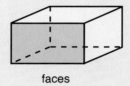

faces

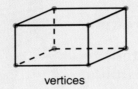

vertices

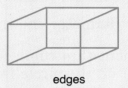

edges

- How many **faces** does the model have?
- What is formed where two faces intersect?
- How many **vertices** does the model have? How many **edges**?

Use the pattern on page H92 to model another prism.

- What do you notice about the lengths of the edges?

- What shape are the faces?
- How is this prism like the rectangular prism above?

- How is it different from the rectangular prism?

This special prism is called a **cube.**
A prism has two congruent faces, called **bases.** Here are other prisms.

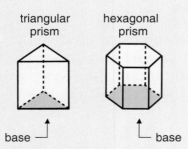

triangular prism

hexagonal prism

base ↑   ↑ base

TALK ABOUT IT

- What shapes are the bases of these prisms?

- What relationship does the name of each prism have with the shape of its base?

Use pipe cleaners to make four congruent equilateral triangles and one square. Use wire ties to hold the polygons together at the vertices to make a **pyramid**. Since the square is the base of the pyramid, this is a square pyramid.

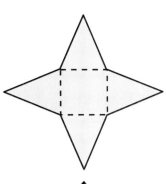

- How many faces does the square pyramid have?

- What shape is each face?

- How many edges does the square pyramid have?

- How do the faces, edges, and vertices of the square pyramid compare with those of the rectangular prism? the cube?

Use pipe cleaners to model triangular and rectangular pyramids.

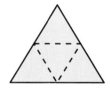

triangular pyramid   rectangular pyramid

- What shapes are the bases of these pyramids?

- How are these pyramids like the square pyramid?

- How are these pyramids different from the square pyramid?

- What relationship does the name of each pyramid have with the shape of its base?

TALK ABOUT IT

Use what you know about pyramids and prisms.

- What do all pyramids have in common?

- What name can you give to a prism with two pentagonal bases?

- What name can you give to a pyramid with a pentagonal base?

- How is a pyramid different from a prism?

- What other pyramids or prisms can you name?

Not all solid figures have flat surfaces. Some 3-dimensional figures have curved surfaces.

Use the pattern to make a cylinder.

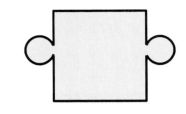

- What shape are the bases of a cylinder?

- How is a cylinder different from a pyramid or a prism?

Use the pattern to make a cone.

- What shape is the base of a cone?

- How are a cone and a cylinder alike?

- How are a cone and a cylinder different?

- How are a cone and a pyramid alike?

Look at this model of a sphere.

- Does a sphere have any flat surfaces?

- How is a sphere different from a cone and a cylinder?

Look at the solid figures from the views given.

Figure A	Figure B	Figure C

Top View   Side View   Side View

TALK ABOUT IT

- Which solid figures could be represented by Figure A?

- Which solid figures could be represented by Figure B?

- In Figure B, what view would you be looking at if this were a triangular prism?

- Which solid figures could be represented by Figure C?

Making the Connection

Think about the solid figure formed by each pattern.

A.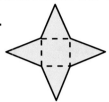

B.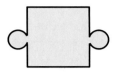

C.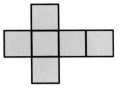

D.

E.

F.

TALK ABOUT IT

- Which figures represent pyramids? prisms?

- Name each pyramid and prism.

- Which figures represent curved surfaces?

- Describe how the figures with curved surfaces differ from those with flat surfaces.

Checking Understanding

Copy and complete the table.

	Solid Figure	Name	Number of Faces	Number of Vertices	Number of Edges
1.		Cube	6	8	■
2.		Square pyramid	■	5	8
3.		■	4	4	6
4.		Triangular prism	5	■	9
5.		Cylinder	2	■	0

6. Name the shapes needed and the number of each shape you would use to build a square pyramid.

7. Name at least two objects that have a shape like a cylinder.

8. Name two solid figures that have at least four triangles.

PROBLEM SOLVING

Choose a Strategy

Understand
Plan
Solve
Look Back

Marlene has a painted cube made up of 64 smaller cubes. Some have 3 faces painted, some have 2 faces painted, some have 1 face painted, and some have 0 faces painted. How many cubes of each type are there?

Sometimes you can solve a difficult problem by using one of several strategies. For this problem you might *solve a simpler problem* or *make a table*.

Strategy: Solve a Simpler Problem

You can build simpler cubes. Break the cubes apart. Decide whether the paint would be on 3 faces, 2 faces, 1 face, or 0 faces of the smaller cubes.

Make a cube of $2 \times 2 \times 2$, or 8, smaller cubes.

Make a cube of $3 \times 3 \times 3$, or 27, smaller cubes.

Count the number of each type of smaller cube.

Strategy: Make a Table

You can organize the data in a table.

Number of Cubes	3 Faces Painted	2 Faces Painted	1 Face Painted	0 Faces Painted
8	8	0	0	0
27	8	12	6	1
64	▪	▪	▪	▪

What cube can you make to complete the table? You can make a cube of $4 \times 4 \times 4$, or 64, smaller cubes. There are 8 cubes with 3 faces painted, 24 cubes with 2 faces painted, 24 cubes with 1 face painted, and 8 cubes with 0 faces painted.

WHAT IF... ... you have a painted cube made up of 125 smaller cubes? How many cubes of each type are there?

Mixed Applications ⟶ STRATEGIES
Make a Table • Guess and Check
• Write a Number Sentence
• Solve a Simpler Problem

Choose a strategy and solve.

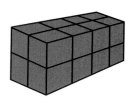

(1) Find the number of cubes with 3 painted faces, 2 painted faces, 1 painted face, and 0 painted faces in this rectangular prism.

(2) Find the number of cubes with 3 painted faces, 2 painted faces, 1 painted face, and 0 painted faces in this rectangular prism.

(3) Ema's family visited the space museum. Her father purchased 2 adult's tickets and 3 child's tickets. Each adult's ticket sold for $1 more than a child's ticket. If her father paid a total of $22 for the tickets, how much was 1 adult's ticket and how much was 1 child's ticket?

(4) Luis began a science club with 2 members. At the end of the first week, he brought in 3 members. At the end of the second week, he brought in 4 more members. If this pattern continued for two more weeks, what was the total membership?

(5) The museum is arranging 15 square tables for seating the students. Each table can seat 1 student on each side. If the tables are pushed together to make one long table, how many students can be seated?

(6) Barry is trying to save $200 so he can attend camp next summer. He has $20 in a savings account. If Barry can deposit $5 a week, how long will it take him to save the $200 he needs for camp?

(7) Each student who plans to attend the field trip needs to pay $8.50. If 125 students are planning to go on the trip and a total of $1,011.50 has been collected, how many students have not yet paid?

(8) While on a field trip, Kitty bought a book for $1.45. She used quarters, dimes, and nickels to pay for the book. If there were 9 coins in all, how many of each type of coin did she use?

CHAPTER REVIEW / TEST

Vocabulary Check

Choose a word from the box to complete each sentence.

chord
diameter
equilateral
intersecting
isosceles
parallel
prism
radius
scalene

1. Lines that never intersect and that are always the same distance from each other are called __?__ lines. *(page 109)*

2. A triangle with all sides of equal length is called an __?__ triangle. *(page 118)*

3. A triangle that has at least two sides of equal length is called an __?__ triangle. *(page 118)*

4. A line segment that has one endpoint on the circle and one endpoint in the center of the circle is called a __?__. *(page 135)*

5. A chord that passes through the center of the circle is called a __?__. *(page 135)*

6. A figure that has two congruent bases is called a __?__. *(page 136)*

7. A triangle in which each side is a different length is called a __?__ triangle. *(page 118)*

8. A line segment inside a circle with endpoints on the circle is called a __?__. *(page 135)*

9. Lines that meet or cross each other at one point are called __?__ lines. *(page 109)*

I can extend the rays of an angle to find the angle measure.

Concept Check

Trace each angle. First, estimate the angle measure. Then, use a protractor to measure each angle. *(page 114)*

10.

11.

12.

13.

Draw all the lines of symmetry for each regular polygon. *(page 128)*

14.   **15.**   **16.**   **17.**

Write *slide, flip,* or *turn* to indicate how each figure was moved. *(page 130)*

18. 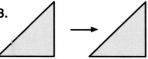 **19.**

Identify the solid figure. *(pages 136–138)*

20.   **21.**   **22.** 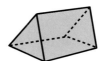 **23.**

Skill Check

Identify the angle. Write *right, acute,* or *obtuse.* *(page 112)*

24.   **25.** 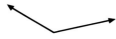 **26.**   **27.**

Are the figures similar? Write *yes* or *no.* *(page 132)*

28.  **29.** 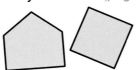 **30.** 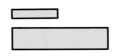 **31.**

Problem-Solving Check

Solve. *(pages 124, 140)*

32. Two numbers have a sum of 19 and a product of 88. What are the two numbers?

33. What is the greatest number of slices of bread you can get by using 12 cuts to slice the bread?

34. A Boy Scout troop had 6 more 13-year-old boys than 12-year-old boys. If there were 24 boys in the troop, how many were 13 years old?

35. A square table can seat one person on each side. How many people can be seated at 10 square tables if the tables are pushed together in a line?

WHAT DID I LEARN?

1. Name objects in the classroom that remind you of a plane surface, perpendicular lines, an acute angle, an obtuse angle, and a quadrilateral. Explain your choices.

2. Draw an obtuse angle. Estimate the measure of the angle. Then measure the angle with a protractor and record the measure.

3. Draw two figures that are similar but not congruent. Explain why the figures are not congruent.

4. Use pattern blocks and graph paper to show how slides, flips, and turns move polygons on a flat surface. Describe each type of move.

5. Use pipe cleaners and wire ties to model a triangular prism and a triangular pyramid. Describe the parts of each model.

6. Read Exercise 2 on page 125. Follow the steps on the Problem-Solving Think Along worksheet to show how to solve this problem.

I can draw figures that are similar but not congruent.

Write About It

7. Describe the lesson or activity in this chapter that was the most interesting to you. What made it interesting?

8. Suppose that the radius of a circle is 4 centimeters long. Is it possible for a chord on that circle to have a length of 8.5 centimeters? Explain.

TEAMWORK Project

MAKE A MODEL

Space-shuttle systems began to operate in the early 1980's. Unlike other space vehicles, a space shuttle can make more than one flight. With your teammates, model a space shuttle.

DECIDE

Talk about how you can use oak tag, tracing paper, and tape to model the solid and plane figures that compose the space shuttle.

DO

Work with your teammates. Trace and cut out the plane figures shown.

Use the traced patterns to cut the same shapes out of oak tag.

Fold along the dotted lines to form cones and cylinders. Tape the edges together.

Tape the solid figures and plane triangles together to form a model of the space shuttle.

SHARE

Show your model. Describe how the shuttle compares with other solid figures you know about.

TALK ABOUT IT

How can you use your model to help you imagine how a space station could be built from a combination of solid figures?

In your everyday activities, what other solid-figure combinations have you noticed?

Activity

CREATE A POLYGON

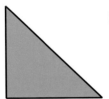 **T**his is an isosceles right triangle.

You can use four congruent isosceles right triangles to make many different polygons.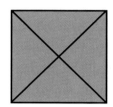

Trace the triangle above. Use your tracing, and cut out four congruent triangles. Use the triangles to make these polygons.

1. a larger triangle

2. a trapezoid

3. a rectangle that is not a square

4. two different parallelograms that are not rectangles

Draw a sketch to show how you made each polygon.
Make as many other polygons with the four triangles as you can.

◆ ◆ ◆ ◆ ◆ ◆ ◆ ◆ ◆ ◆ ◆ ◆ ◆ ◆ ◆ ◆ ◆

Challenge *Visual Thinking*

Use toothpicks to model. Take away four toothpicks to leave four equilateral triangles that are the same size.

Challenge *Visual Thinking*

Use counters to model. Move three circles in triangle *A* so that triangle *A* matches triangle *B*.

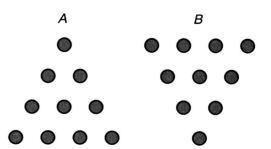

Write the letter of the correct answer.

1. What is 15.463 rounded to the nearest tenth?

- **A.** 15.4
- **B.** 15.46
- **C.** 15.5
- **D.** 20

2. Which decimal represents 7 pennies?

- **A.** $0.007
- **B.** $0.07
- **C.** $0.7
- **D.** $7.00

3. Which is the inverse operation sentence? $\blacksquare + 14 = 30$

- **A.** $14 + 30 = \blacksquare$
- **B.** $30 + 14 = \blacksquare$
- **C.** $30 - 14 = \blacksquare$
- **D.** $\blacksquare = 30 + 14$

4. $(15 + 20) + 6 = 15 + (\blacksquare + 6)$

- **A.** 6
- **B.** 15
- **C.** 20
- **D.** not here

5. $15,679 + 8,341 = n$

- **A.** 7,338
- **B.** 13,910
- **C.** 24,020
- **D.** not here

6. $14.536 - 12.648 = n$

- **A.** 0.888
- **B.** 1.988
- **C.** 1.998
- **D.** not here

7. Which is the estimate? $419 \times 18 \approx n$

- **A.** 800
- **B.** 8,000
- **C.** 80,000
- **D.** 800,000

8. $825 \times 22 = n$

- **A.** 17,150
- **B.** 18,140
- **C.** 18,150
- **D.** not here

9. Which names the polygon?

- **A.** triangle
- **B.** pentagon
- **C.** hexagon
- **D.** octagon

10. Which names the quadrilateral?

- **A.** rhombus
- **B.** parallelogram
- **C.** square
- **D.** trapezoid

11. In a school election, the winner had 5 times as many votes as the loser. If a total of 90 votes were cast, how many votes did the winner get?

- **A.** 70 votes
- **B.** 75 votes
- **C.** 80 votes
- **D.** 85 votes

12. Aretha and 5 other girls went on a picnic. Each girl went on a boat ride with each other girl. If two rode at one time, how many boat rides were taken?

- **A.** 6 rides
- **B.** 10 rides
- **C.** 15 rides
- **D.** 21 rides

DIVIDING WHOLE NUMBERS BY 1-DIGIT NUMBERS

Did you know...

... that Copenhagen, Denmark, is home of the world-famous amusement park called Tivoli Gardens?

TALK ABOUT IT

A carousel at Tivoli Gardens was operated for 8 hours one day. During the 8 hours, it ran 104 times. Suppose it ran the same number of times each hour. How would you explain to a younger student how to find the number of times the carousel ran each hour?

EXPLORING

Divisibility

Building Understanding

Because there is a remainder of zero when you divide 72 by 6, 72 is **divisible** by 6.

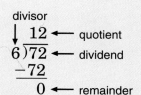

divisor
quotient
dividend
remainder

A. Suppose you want to test the numbers 12, 15, 20, 24, and 30 for divisibility.

- Which are divisible by 2? by 5? by 10?

- Record your data in a table.

- Use the data in your table to look for a relationship between the ones digit and divisibility by 2, 5, and 10. Explain your findings.

B. Now decide whether each of the following numbers is divisible by 2, 5, and 10. How can you check your answers?

218   125   450   360

C. Suppose you want to test the numbers in your table for divisibility by 3. Add 3 to your table, and record your findings.

- Which numbers are divisible by 3?

- Find the sum of the digits of each number that is divisible by 3. What do you notice about each of the sums?

- What rule can you write to show that a number is divisible by 3?

Present your results to the class. Explain how you found which of the numbers are divisible by 2, 3, 5, and 10.

WRITE ABOUT IT

Choose five new numbers. Explain how you know whether the numbers are divisible by 2, 3, 5, and 10.

Making the Connection

There are rules of divisibility that tell whether a number is divisible by 2, 3, 5, or 10.

Even numbers are divisible by 2. These numbers end in 2, 4, 6, 8, or 0. These numbers are divisible by 2.	10, 24, 32, 46, 58
If the sum of the digits is a multiple of 3, then the number is divisible by 3. These numbers are divisible by 3.	12, 15, 33, 42, 54
If there is a 0 or a 5 in the ones place, then the number is divisible by 5. These numbers are divisible by 5.	15, 20, 35, 50, 65
If there is a 0 in the ones place, then the number is divisible by 10. These numbers are divisible by 10.	10, 20, 30, 40, 50, 60

1. Why are all numbers that are divisible by 10 also divisible by 2?

2. Are all numbers that are divisible by 5 also divisible by 2? Explain.

3. Are all numbers that are divisible by 5 also divisible by 3? Explain.

4. Are any numbers that are divisible by 10 also divisible by 3? Explain.

Checking Understanding

Use the rules to decide whether the first number is divisible by the second. Write *yes* or *no*.

5. 8, 2

6. 34, 3

7. 80, 10

8. 95, 5

Use the rules to decide whether each number is divisible by 2, 3, 5, and 10. Complete the table. Write *yes* or *no*.

9.

Divisible by	25	36	38	45	92	100	125
2	?	?	?	?	?	?	?
3	?	?	?	?	?	?	?
5	?	?	?	?	?	?	?
10	?	?	?	?	?	?	?

10. If a number is divisible by 5, is it always divisible by 10?

11. If a number is divisible by 10, is it always divisible by 2 and 5?

ESTIMATING
Quotients

Babs rode in a hot-air balloon 134 times. If she rode the same number of times in each of 7 months, about how many times did she ride in a balloon each month?

Estimate. $134 \div 7 \approx n$

To estimate a quotient, you can use compatible numbers. **Compatible numbers** are numbers close to the actual numbers that can be divided evenly. Compatible numbers for 7 are numbers divisible by 7, such as 14, 21, or 28.

$7\overline{)134}$ **Think:** Since there are not 7 or more hundreds, divide the 13 tens. The first digit will be in the tens place.

$\overset{20}{7\overline{)140}}$ ← estimate **Think:** $7 \times 2 = 14$

So, Babs rode in a balloon about 20 times each month.

More Examples

A. Estimate. $93 \div 4 \approx n$

$4\overline{)93}$ **Think:** $4 \times 2 = 8$ $\quad \overset{20}{4\overline{)80}}$

B. Estimate. $364 \div 5 \approx n$

$5\overline{)364}$ **Think:** $5 \times 7 = 35$ $\quad \overset{70}{5\overline{)350}}$

- Name some other compatible numbers for Examples **A** and **B**.

- What compatible numbers can you use to estimate a quotient for $902 \div 4$? What is the estimated quotient?

- How do compatible numbers help you estimate mentally?

Check for Understanding

Choose the better estimate. Write **a** or **b**.

1. $145 \div 3 \approx n$
   a. 40 b. 50

2. $298 \div 9 \approx n$
   a. 30 b. 40

3. $443 \div 5 \approx n$
   a. 60 b. 90

4. $375 \div 6 \approx n$
   a. 30 b. 60

Estimate each quotient.

5. $64 \div 3 \approx n$

6. $193 \div 6 \approx n$

7. $295 \div 7 \approx n$

8. $337 \div 4 \approx n$

Practice

Choose the better estimate. Write **a** or **b**.

9. $65 \div 8 \approx n$
   a. 7   **b.** 8

10. $138 \div 6 \approx n$
    a. 20   **b.** 30

11. $642 \div 7 \approx n$
    a. 80   **b.** 90

12. $700 \div 9 \approx n$
    a. 30   **b.** 70

Estimate each quotient.

13. $3\overline{)16}$

14. $7\overline{)58}$

15. $5\overline{)32}$

16. $4\overline{)29}$

17. $8\overline{)70}$

18. $2\overline{)13}$

19. $4\overline{)85}$

20. $6\overline{)63}$

21. $3\overline{)95}$

22. $7\overline{)152}$

23. $5\overline{)267}$

24. $9\overline{)908}$

25. $4\overline{)832}$

26. $2\overline{)795}$

27. $6\overline{)850}$

28. $3\overline{)701}$

29. $46 \div 6 \approx n$

30. $29 \div 3 \approx n$

31. $68 \div 5 \approx n$

32. $137 \div 5 \approx n$

33. $396 \div 4 \approx n$

34. $657 \div 8 \approx n$

35. $428 \div 2 \approx n$

36. $615 \div 7 \approx n$

37. $909 \div 9 \approx n$

Mixed Applications

38. A group of 23 students has signed up to learn hang gliding. If there are 4 instructors, about how many students will be with each instructor?

39. Yoko's kite has a tail 325 inches long. If the tail is about 7 times as long as the kite, about how long is the kite?

40. At a public park, 175 people want to take part in a kite festival. Only 8 kites are allowed in each area of the park. Will 16 areas be enough for 175 people to fly kites?

41. **Write a Question** There are 7 hot-air balloons and 18 people waiting to ride them.

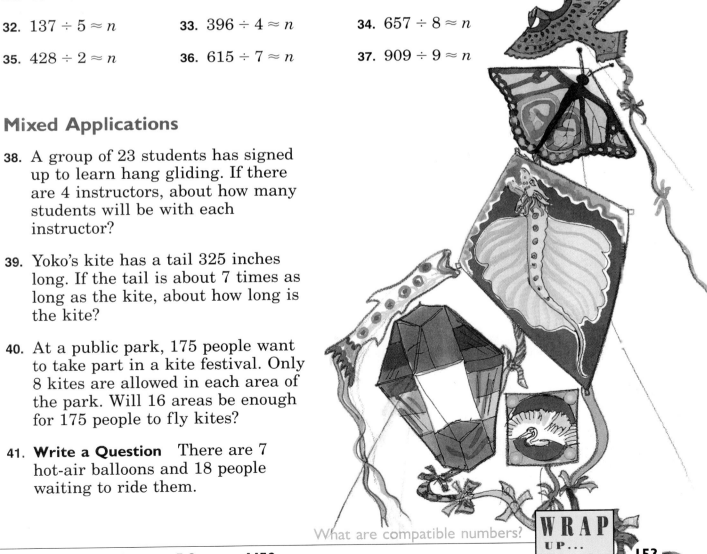

What are compatible numbers?

WRAP UP...

DIVIDING
Two-Digit Numbers

Many people enjoy playing marble games. Patricia, Regina, and Eduardo are dividing a collection of 71 marbles. If each person gets the same number of marbles, how many marbles will each one get?

First, estimate.
 Think:
$3\overline{)71}$ $3 \times 2 = 6$ $\dfrac{20}{3\overline{)60}}$ Since 7 tens can be divided by 3, the first digit of the quotient will be in the tens place.

Divide. $71 \div 3 = n$

Step 1	**Step 2**	**Step 3**
Divide the tens.	Bring down the ones.	Multiply to check.
$3\overline{)7}$	Divide the 11 ones.	
Think: $3 \times n \approx 7$.	Think: $3 \times n \approx 11$.	
	Record the remainder.	

Step 1:
$$\begin{array}{r} 2 \\ 3\overline{)71} \\ -6 \\ \hline 1 \end{array}$$
Multiply.
Subtract.
Compare.
$1 < 3$

Step 2:
$$23 \text{ r2} \leftarrow \text{remainder}$$
$$\begin{array}{r} 3\overline{)71} \\ -6\downarrow \\ \hline 11 \\ -9 \\ \hline 2 \end{array}$$
Multiply.
Subtract.
Compare.
$2 < 3$

Step 3:
$$\begin{array}{r} 23 \leftarrow \text{quotient} \\ \times\ 3 \leftarrow \text{divisor} \\ \hline 69 \\ +\ 2 \leftarrow \text{remainder} \\ \hline 71 \leftarrow \text{dividend} \end{array}$$

MULTICULTURAL NOTE: The game of marbles is an ancient game that was played using such items as pebbles, nuts, and fruit pits.

Since there is a remainder of 2, the marbles cannot be shared equally. So, each person will get 23 marbles, and 2 marbles will be left over.

- Compare the answer to the estimate. Is the answer reasonable?

Talk About It

▶ How can you decide how many digits will be in the quotient?

▶ Why can you use multiplication to check division?

Check for Understanding

Estimate the number of digits in each quotient. Then find the quotient.

1. $39 \div 6 = n$ **2.** $62 \div 7 = n$ **3.** $47 \div 4 = n$ **4.** $87 \div 5 = n$

Practice

Estimate. Write the number of digits in each quotient.

5. $6\overline{)39}$ **6.** $7\overline{)62}$ **7.** $2\overline{)28}$ **8.** $5\overline{)37}$ **9.** $4\overline{)49}$

10. $9\overline{)59}$ **11.** $8\overline{)95}$ **12.** $5\overline{)28}$ **13.** $8\overline{)75}$ **14.** $6\overline{)74}$

Estimate. Then find the quotient.

15. $3\overline{)69}$ **16.** $7\overline{)46}$ **17.** $6\overline{)35}$ **18.** $9\overline{)48}$ **19.** $4\overline{)76}$

20. $3\overline{)33}$ **21.** $8\overline{)78}$ **22.** $7\overline{)67}$ **23.** $4\overline{)48}$ **24.** $5\overline{)92}$

Divide. Then check each quotient.

25. $54 \div 8 = n$ **26.** $58 \div 7 = n$ **27.** $55 \div 5 = n$ **28.** $75 \div 6 = n$

29. $63 \div 3 = n$ **30.** $29 \div 7 = n$ **31.** $74 \div 8 = n$ **32.** $37 \div 3 = n$

Mixed Applications

33. Critical Thinking There are 18 students in Carmen's ballet class. The teacher is planning a dance for the recital and wants the same number of students in each row. What arrangements would have the same number of students in each row?

34. Four friends want to play jacks. They have 38 jacks. If each player gets the same number of jacks, how many jacks will each have? How many extra jacks will there be?

NUMBER SENSE

If the sum of the digits in a number is a multiple of 9, then the number is divisible by 9.

Example   216
$2 + 1 + 6 = 9$ $9 \div 9 = 1$
So, 216 is divisible by 9.

Tell whether the number is divisible by 9. Write *yes* or *no*.

35. 63   **36.** 531   **37.** 138   **38.** 1,260   **39.** 4,312

Explain how estimating first is helpful when you divide.

More Practice, Lesson 5.3, pages H50–H51

DIVIDING
Three-Digit Numbers

Baseball and softball are favorite pastimes of many people. The youth baseball league has 283 games scheduled. The 9 umpires want to share the games equally. At how many games will each umpire work?

First, estimate.
$$9\overline{)283}$$

Think: $9 \times 3 = 27$
$$\overset{30}{9\overline{)270}}$$

Since 28 tens can be divided by 9, the first digit of the quotient is in the tens place.

Divide. $283 \div 9 = n$

Step 1	Step 2	Step 3
Divide the hundreds. $9\overline{)2}$ Since there are not enough hundreds, divide the 28 tens. Think: $9 \times n \approx 28$.	Bring down the ones. Divide the 13 ones. Think: $9 \times n \approx 13$. Record the remainder.	Multiply to check.

Step 1:
$$\overset{3}{9\overline{)283}}$$
$$-27$$
$$\overline{1}$$
Multiply. Subtract. Compare. $1 < 9$

Step 2:
$$\overset{31\ \text{r}4}{9\overline{)283}}$$
$$-27\downarrow$$
$$\overline{13}$$
$$-9$$
$$\overline{4}$$
Multiply. Subtract. Compare. $4 < 9$

Step 3:
$$\begin{array}{r} 31 \\ \times\ \ 9 \\ \hline 279 \\ +\ \ 4 \\ \hline 283 \end{array}$$

So, each umpire will work at least 31 games. The remaining 4 games can be shared by 4 of the umpires.

More Examples

A.
$$\overset{123\ \text{r}3}{5\overline{)618}}$$
$$-5$$
$$\overline{11}$$
$$-10$$
$$\overline{18}$$
$$-15$$
$$\overline{3}$$

Since 6 hundreds can be divided by 5, the first digit of the quotient is in the hundreds place.

B.
$$\overset{74\ \text{r}5}{7\overline{)523}}$$
$$-49$$
$$\overline{33}$$
$$-28$$
$$\overline{5}$$

Since 5 hundreds are not enough, divide the 52 tens. The first digit of the quotient is in the tens place.

Check for Understanding

Estimate each quotient. If the estimate is greater than 50, find the quotient.

1. $159 \div 4 \approx n$ **2.** $247 \div 3 \approx n$ **3.** $589 \div 6 \approx n$

Practice

Estimate each quotient.

4. $8\overline{)546}$ **5.** $7\overline{)589}$ **6.** $5\overline{)495}$ **7.** $3\overline{)129}$ **8.** $4\overline{)358}$ **9.** $6\overline{)713}$

Divide.

10. $7\overline{)291}$ **11.** $8\overline{)746}$ **12.** $9\overline{)909}$ **13.** $7\overline{)590}$ **14.** $6\overline{)555}$ **15.** $4\overline{)854}$

16. $167 \div 7 = n$ **17.** $296 \div 3 = n$

18. $510 \div 8 = n$ **19.** $195 \div 2 = n$

20. $296 \div 2 = n$ **21.** $687 \div 6 = n$

22. $895 \div 9 = n$ **23.** $485 \div 5 = n$

24. Without dividing, tell whether the quotient of $438 \div 3$ has two digits or three digits. Explain.

Mixed Applications

25. A total of 100 people are traveling to a softball tournament. If each car holds 5 people, how many cars will be needed to take everyone to the tournament?

26. Sabrina wants to put her collection of baseball cards in a new album. She has 248 cards, and each page of the album will hold 8 cards. How many pages will she need?

27. There are 18 players on a softball team. At practice, every player is at bat 6 times. If 9 players take turns pitching to each player, how many times will each one get to pitch?

28. **Make Up a Problem** Write a division problem that has a divisor of 6 and a quotient with a remainder of 4.

MIXED REVIEW

Write two other forms for each number.

1. 42,700   **2.** 130,680   **3.** 2,800,050   **4.** 12,009,005

Estimate each sum. Tell which method you used.

5. 61
  $+ 42$

6. 185
  $+ 327$

7. 4,540
  $+ 5,450$

8. 6,342
  $+ 2,105$

Explain how you can tell whether the quotient of $489 \div 6$ will have 2 or 3 digits.

WRAP UP...

SHORT DIVISION

Diane likes to read whenever she has time. She has 4 days to read a 112-page book. How many pages does she need to read each day?

You can use the short form of division to find $112 \div 4$. Multiply and subtract mentally, and write the remainders in the dividend. Write the last remainder as part of the quotient.

First, estimate. $4\overline{)112}$ Think: $4 \times 3 = 12$ $\dfrac{30}{4\overline{)120}}$

Divide. $112 \div 4 = n$

Step 1	Step 2
Divide the 11 tens. Think: $4 \times n \approx 11$.	Divide the 32 ones. Think: $4 \times n = 32$.
$4\overline{)1\,1\,^32}$ $\overset{2}{}$ **Think:** $2 \times 4 = 8$ $11 - 8 = 3$ Place the remainder in the dividend.	$\overset{2\,8}{4\overline{)1\,1\,^32}}$

So, Diane needs to read 28 pages each day.

• How do you know whether your answer is reasonable?

More Examples

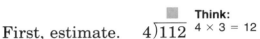

A. $4\overline{)9\,^19\,^37}$ $\overset{2\,4\,9\,r1}{}$

B. $5\overline{)7\,^24\,^43}$ $\overset{1\,4\,8\,r3}{}$

Talk About It

▶ How is short division different from long division?

▶ Why is the estimate of the quotient especially useful in short division?

Check for Understanding

Use short division to find each quotient.

1. $5\overline{)63}$ 2. $7\overline{)125}$ 3. $8\overline{)532}$ 4. $6\overline{)976}$ 5. $4\overline{)395}$

Practice

Use short division to find each quotient.

6. $4\overline{)57}$ 7. $5\overline{)43}$ 8. $3\overline{)85}$ 9. $5\overline{)435}$ 10. $2\overline{)638}$

11. $4\overline{)459}$ 12. $7\overline{)952}$ 13. $7\overline{)837}$ 14. $6\overline{)941}$ 15. $5\overline{)267}$

16. $2\overline{)857}$ 17. $8\overline{)936}$ 18. $5\overline{)828}$ 19. $3\overline{)742}$ 20. $9\overline{)858}$

21. $169 \div 7 = n$ 22. $952 \div 8 = n$ 23. $837 \div 6 = n$

24. $378 \div 4 = n$ 25. $289 \div 9 = n$ 26. $859 \div 7 = n$

27. $981 \div 9 = n$ 28. $857 \div 5 = n$

Mixed Applications

29. Dave likes to help in the school library. He has 435 books to put back on the shelves. He uses 3 carts to carry the books, and each cart can hold 125 books. Will he need another cart? Explain.

30. Megan is making a quilt out of 4 different fabrics. She has cut out a total of 664 pieces. She cut the same number of pieces from each fabric. How many pieces did she cut from each fabric?

EVERYDAY MATH CONNECTION

Some things are commonly separated into parts, while other things are never divided. A remainder in division must be handled according to the situation.

Examples

A. There are 71 apples to make 2 batches of applesauce. The apples are to be shared equally by 2 classes. The extra apple can be cut in half. How many apples are in each batch?

B. There are 71 paper cups to be shared equally by 2 classes. The extra cup would not be cut in half. How many cups does each class get? How many cups are left over?

Divide the items equally among 6 people. Then write how many each person gets.

31. 140 pencils   32. 105 cookies   33. 81 books

What steps are not written when you use short division?

PROBLEM SOLVING

Choose the Operation

Some students from Princeton Elementary School are performing in a play. All the tickets for 4 performances have been sold. If 1,080 tickets were sold and an equal number were sold for each performance, how many were sold for each performance?

Many times you can look for the relationships in a problem. These relationships can help you decide whether you should add, subtract, multiply, or divide.

▶ **UNDERSTAND**

What are you asked to find?

What facts are given?

▶ **PLAN**

What plan can you make?

First, study the problem. What relationships can help you decide which operation to use?
You are asked to find how many tickets were sold for each performance. You know an equal number were sold for each performance. So, you divide.

▶ **SOLVE**

How can you solve the problem?

Find 1,080 ÷ 4.

Operation	Relationships
Add	• Joining of groups
Subtract	• Taking away some of a group • Comparing one group with another
Multiply	• Joining equal-sized groups
Divide	• Separating into equal-sized groups • Finding how many groups

Number of tickets				Number of performances		Number of tickets for each performance
1	0	8	0	÷	4	= 270.

So, 270 tickets were sold for each performance.

▶ **LOOK BACK**

How can you check your answer?

WHAT IF... . . . each ticket cost $2? How much money was earned for each performance?

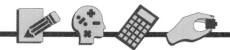

Apply

Choose the correct operation and solve.

(1) A group of 5 buses will take 130 fifth graders to see a play. If each bus takes the same number of students, how many students will be on each bus?

(2) Jessie is organizing his stamp collection. He has 1,367 U.S. stamps and 2,094 foreign stamps. How many stamps does he have?

Mixed Applications ⟩ STRATEGIES

Make a Drawing
• **Make a Table** • **Find a Pattern**
• **Write a Number Sentence**

Choose a strategy and solve.

(3) Some fifth graders are making beaded jewelry. They have a kit with a total of 1,200 beads in 8 different colors. How many beads of each color are there if there is the same number of each color?

(4) In a volleyball tournament, the 6 best teams played 8 games each. Another 6 teams were eliminated after playing 4 games each. What was the total number of games played in the tournament?

(5) The first week Frances played her new video game, her highest score was 450 points. The second week it was 700 points, the third week 1,000 points, and the fourth week 1,350 points. If this pattern continues, what will be her highest score in the seventh week?

(6) Pat and Terry are playing video games. In the first game, Terry scored 30 more points than Pat, and Pat scored 650 points. In the second game, Pat scored 70 more points than Terry, and Pat scored 748 points. In which game did Terry score more points?

WRITER'S CORNER

(7) Write two different problems about your favorite school activity. Use two different operations and the numbers 5 and 50. Explain how you would solve your problems.

More Practice, Lesson 5.6, page H52

1. The cans in a display were stacked to form a square pyramid. At the very top was 1 can. Beneath it were 4 cans, 9 cans, then 16 cans. How many cans were in the stack if there were 6 layers?

> Use the inverse operation to check your answer.

2. A painter uses 3 cans of paint for each room he paints. How many rooms can he paint if he has 123 cans?

Write two other forms for each number.

3. 87,953 4. 450,708 5. 2,800,075 6. 12,006,003

Estimate.

7.	8.	9.	10.
6.231	19.75	19.5	78.23
$+\,5.897$	$+\,32.68$	$-\,10.4$	$-\,17.75$

Find the sum or difference.

11.	12.	13.	14.	15.
$3,085$	$8,207$	$43,087$	$956,000$	$52,820$
$+\,2,974$	$-\,4,683$	$+\,36,953$	$-\,368,009$	$-\,16,045$

Estimate the product.

16.	17.	18.	19.	20.
186	$4,738$	82	$5,390$	634
$\times\quad 4$	$\times\quad 9$	$\times\,48$	$\times\quad 47$	$\times\quad 29$

Use the figure for Exercises 21–24.

21. Name two lines.

22. Name two intersecting lines.

23. Name three rays.

24. Name three line segments.

Divide.

25. $4\overline{)75}$ 26. $3\overline{)50}$ 27. $6\overline{)69}$ 28. $2\overline{)77}$

29. $3\overline{)287}$ 30. $5\overline{)460}$ 31. $7\overline{)652}$ 32. $8\overline{)848}$

ASIA

China

Interpret Remainders

Dragon dances are a long-standing tradition at festivals in China. The heads of the dragons are made of bamboo covered with silk and can weigh as much as 26 pounds.

Zhu is a craftsperson from China who makes dragon and lion heads that are used for festivals. A lion head takes Zhu 2 weeks to make.

To find out how many lion heads he can make in 15 weeks, Zhu divides 15 by 2.
$15 \div 2 = 7 \text{ r}1$

MULTICULTURAL NOTE: Some Chinese dragons can be as long as 300 feet.

So, there are 7 2-week periods, which will allow Zhu to complete 7 heads. The remaining week can be dropped, because Zhu cannot finish a head in 1 week.

When you solve a division problem that has a remainder, the way you interpret the remainder depends on the situation. You may round the quotient to the next greater number. You may drop the remainder. You may use only the remainder for your answer.

Answer each question. Tell which way you interpreted the remainder. Be prepared to discuss how the remainder affects the answer.

1. How many lion heads can Zhu finish in 25 weeks?

2. Zhu needs 8 weeks to make a dragon head. How many dragon heads can he make in 25 weeks?

3. Suppose Zhu has 27 weeks to make dragon heads for the Chinese New Year celebration. He wants to make as many as possible in that time. Will he have any time left to make lion heads? If so, how many?

4. Zhu also makes Chinese lanterns. He puts the lanterns in boxes. Each box holds 9 lanterns. How many boxes does he need for 40 lanterns?

ZEROS IN THE QUOTIENT

Iliti lives in Fiji. She collects seashells and designs shell necklaces. If she has 327 seashells, how many shells can she use for each of 3 necklaces?

First, estimate.

Think:
$3 \times 100 = 300$

$$3\overline{)327}$$

$$\overset{100}{3\overline{)300}}$$

Since 3 hundreds can be divided by 3, the first digit in the quotient will be in the hundreds place.

Divide. $327 \div 3 = n$

Step 1	**Step 2**	**Step 3**
Divide the 3 hundreds. Think: $3 \times n = 3$.	Bring down the tens. Divide the 2 tens. Think: Since $3 > 2$, write 0 in the quotient.	Bring down the ones. Divide the 27 ones. Think: $3 \times n = 27$.

Step 1:
$$\begin{array}{r} 1 \\ 3\overline{)327} \\ -3 \\ \hline 0 \end{array}$$
Multiply. Subtract. Compare. $0 < 3$

Step 2:
$$\begin{array}{r} 10 \\ 3\overline{)327} \\ -3\downarrow \\ \hline 02 \\ -\ 0 \\ \hline 2 \end{array}$$

Step 3:
$$\begin{array}{r} 109 \\ 3\overline{)327} \\ -3\downarrow\downarrow \\ \hline 02\ \\ -\ 0\downarrow \\ \hline 27 \\ -\ 27 \\ \hline 0 \end{array}$$
Multiply. Subtract. Compare. $0 < 3$

Since 109 is close to the estimate of 100, the answer is reasonable.

So, Iliti can use 109 seashells for each necklace.

MULTICULTURAL NOTE: Many beautiful shells are found on Fiji and other islands of the South Pacific.

- What happens to your answer if you forget to write the zero in the quotient?

- How can you tell whether your answer is reasonable?

More Examples

A.
$$\begin{array}{r} 106 \\ 5\overline{)530} \\ -5 \\ \hline 03 \\ -\ 0 \\ \hline 30 \\ -30 \\ \hline 0 \end{array}$$
Since $5 > 3$, write 0 in the quotient.

B.
$$\begin{array}{r} 204\ \text{r1} \\ 4\overline{)817} \\ -8 \\ \hline 01 \\ -0 \\ \hline 17 \\ -16 \\ \hline 1 \end{array}$$
Since $4 > 1$, write 0 in the quotient.

C.
$$\begin{array}{r} 330 \\ 3\overline{)990} \\ -9 \\ \hline 09 \\ -9 \\ \hline 00 \end{array}$$
Since there are zero ones, write 0 in the quotient.

Check for Understanding

Estimate each quotient. If the estimate is greater than 100, find the quotient.

1. $5\overline{)250}$ **2.** $7\overline{)734}$ **3.** $4\overline{)824}$ **4.** $6\overline{)365}$ **5.** $3\overline{)9,273}$

Practice

Divide.

6. $4\overline{)80}$ **7.** $2\overline{)61}$ **8.** $4\overline{)816}$ **9.** $3\overline{)918}$ **10.** $6\overline{)612}$

11. $5\overline{)525}$ **12.** $6\overline{)624}$ **13.** $7\overline{)745}$ **14.** $9\overline{)980}$ **15.** $2\overline{)121}$

16. $5\overline{)544}$ **17.** $2\overline{)801}$ **18.** $3\overline{)961}$ **19.** $8\overline{)887}$ **20.** $5\overline{)454}$

21. $7\overline{)754}$ **22.** $3\overline{)6,129}$ **23.** $4\overline{)8,036}$ **24.** $2\overline{)2,101}$ **25.** $5\overline{)5,154}$

26. $417 \div 2 = n$ **27.** $836 \div 4 = n$ **28.** $965 \div 6 = n$ **29.** $623 \div 3 = n$

30. $122 \div 4 = n$ **31.** $5,045 \div 5 = n$ **32.** $8,247 \div 8 = n$ **33.** $2,122 \div 7 = n$

Mixed Applications

34. On Saturday and Sunday a total of 414 people visited a local beach. If the same number of people came each day, how many visited the beach on Saturday?

35. Mental Math Is 14 a reasonable quotient for $312 \div 3$? Explain.

36. A surfing competition will last 5 days and have 325 competitors. If the same number of people compete each day, how many will compete in one day?

37. Coconuts are one of the leading agricultural products of Fiji. Suppose 20 coconuts are harvested from each of 36 trees and all of these coconuts are boxed for shipping. If each box holds 8 coconuts, how many boxes are needed?

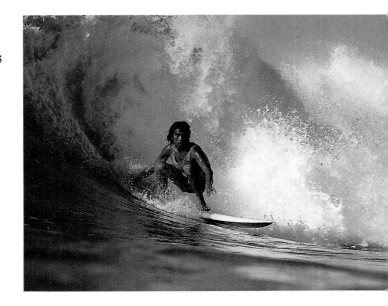

When must a zero be placed in a quotient?

DIVIDING
Larger Numbers

Melanie collects stamps. She has 9 albums and a total of 11,250 stamps. If she has the same number of stamps in each album, how many does she have in each album?

First, estimate. $9\overline{)11{,}250}$

Think: $9 \times 1{,}000$

$$9\overline{)9{,}000}$$ $1{,}000$

Since 11 thousands can be divided by 9, the first digit of the quotient is in the thousands place.

Divide. $11{,}250 \div 9 = n$

Step 1	**Step 2**	**Step 3**
Divide the 11 thousands. Think: $9 \times n \approx 11$.	Bring down the hundreds. Divide the 22 hundreds. Think: $9 \times n \approx 22$.	Bring down the tens. Divide the 45 tens. Think: $9 \times n = 45$.

Step 1:
$$\begin{array}{r} 1 \\ 9\overline{)11{,}250} \\ -\ 9 \\ \hline 2 \end{array}$$
Multiply. Subtract. Compare. $2 < 9$

Step 2:
$$\begin{array}{r} 1\,2 \\ 9\overline{)11{,}250} \\ -\ 9\downarrow \\ \hline 2\,2 \\ -\ 1\,8 \\ \hline 4 \end{array}$$
Multiply. Subtract. Compare. $4 < 9$

Step 3:
$$\begin{array}{r} 1{,}250 \\ 9\overline{)11{,}250} \\ -\ 9\downarrow \\ \hline 2\,2 \\ -\ 1\,8\downarrow \\ \hline 45 \\ -\ 45\downarrow \\ \hline 00 \end{array}$$
Since there are zero ones, write a zero in the quotient.

Multiply. Subtract. Compare. $0 < 9$

So, Melanie has 1,250 stamps in each album.

Another Method

A calculator can help you divide larger numbers.

$56{,}387 \div 4 = n$

          [5] [6] [3] [8] [7] [÷] [4] [=] $\boxed{14096.75}$

So, $56{,}387 \div 4 = 14{,}096.75$.

- What do you think .75 represents?
- How can you find the whole-number remainder?

Check for Understanding

Find each quotient.

1. $5\overline{)72{,}855}$
2. $3\overline{)6{,}858}$
3. $6\overline{)43{,}878}$
4. $8\overline{)37{,}624}$
5. $3\overline{)79{,}245}$

Practice

Estimate each quotient. If the estimate is greater than 1,000, find the quotient.

6. $8)\overline{4,936}$

7. $7)\overline{4,728}$

8. $5)\overline{5,159}$

9. $4)\overline{3,748}$

10. $6)\overline{20,442}$

11. $3)\overline{6,357}$

12. $7)\overline{6,987}$

13. $3)\overline{4,578}$

14. $2)\overline{16,443}$

15. $4)\overline{9,785}$

16. $6)\overline{11,478}$

17. $8)\overline{24,688}$

18. $9)\overline{28,897}$

19. $4)\overline{84,483}$

20. $5)\overline{37,650}$

Estimate. Then find the quotient.

21. $3,480 \div 8 = n$

22. $8,073 \div 9 = n$

23. $12,456 \div 6 = n$

24. $41,494 \div 2 = n$

25. $36,276 \div 3 = n$

26. $23,900 \div 5 = n$

27. $45,000 \div 8 = n$

28. $89,991 \div 9 = n$

29. $83,616 \div 4 = n$

Mixed Applications

30. Collectors often pay large amounts of money for rare stamps. A group of collectors purchased 4 British stamps for $13,000. How much did each stamp cost if each stamp cost the same?

31. Angela keeps her stamp collection in 4 boxes. In 3 of the boxes, she has the same number of stamps, and in the fourth box she has 1,500 stamps. If she has a total of 5,250 stamps, how many stamps are in each of the 3 boxes?

32. Leon will put 6,254 stamps in 3 albums. Can he put the same number of stamps in each album? Explain.

33. **Make Up a Problem** Randy has 1,396 stamps and 6 albums for stamps.

Tell how estimating before you divide 27,535 by 5 helps you decide whether your actual answer is reasonable.

WRAP
UP...

FINDING THE AVERAGE
Using Statistics

You can explain or summarize a group of numbers with one number, the **average.** Another name for the average is the **mean.**

Roger, the manager of Video Village, kept a record of the number of movie videotapes he rented during a 5-day period. He rented 35 tapes on Monday, 41 on Tuesday, 38 on Wednesday, 43 on Thursday, and 48 on Friday. How can Roger find the average number of tapes he rented each day?

Step 1 Add to find the total number of rentals.	**Step 2** Divide the sum by the number of addends.
35 41 38 43 + 48 ----- 205 ← sum of rentals	number of days → $\begin{array}{r} 41 \leftarrow \text{average} \\ 5\overline{)205} \leftarrow \text{sum of} \\ -20\downarrow \quad \text{rentals} \\ \hline 05 \\ -\ 5 \\ \hline 0 \end{array}$

So, Roger rented an average of 41 tapes each day.

• How can you estimate the average?

Another Example

Find the average of 125, 115, and 108.

• Is your average reasonable? Explain.

$$\begin{array}{r} 125 \\ 115 \\ +108 \\ \hline 348 \end{array} \qquad \begin{array}{r} 116 \leftarrow \text{average} \\ 3\overline{)348} \\ -3 \\ \hline 04 \\ -\ 3 \\ \hline 18 \\ -18 \\ \hline 0 \end{array}$$

Check for Understanding

Find the average.

1. 93; 89; 97   **2.** 27; 28; 37; 52   **3.** 325; 215   **4.** 125; 136; 201

Practice

Find the average.

5. 24; 36; 42

6. 45; 48; 52; 47

7. 125; 145; 165

8. 228; 247; 269; 272

9. 657; 890; 1,240

10. 2,350; 2,070; 2,000

11. 1,647; 2,537; 4,392; 3,364

12. 295; 647; 598; 312; 458

Mixed Applications

Use the table for Exercises 13–16.

October Movie Rentals				
Week	**Children's**	**Adventure**	**Science Fiction**	**Mystery**
1	17	37	26	12
2	22	26	34	18
3	13	25	28	18
4	16	32	36	24

13. What was the average number of mystery movies rented each week?

14. Which type of movie averaged more rentals each week, children's movies or mysteries?

15. Which week averaged the greatest number of movie rentals?

16. Analyze Data Which type of movie had the greatest average number of rentals each week?

MIXED REVIEW

Find the difference.

1. 800
      − 652

2. 2,004
      − 1,495

3. 8,000
      − 5,697

4. 20,050
      − 14,609

5. 98,009
      − 19,991

Complete. Identify the multiplication property used.

6. $659 \times \blacksquare = 659$

7. $475 \times 3 = \blacksquare \times 475$

8. $932 \times \blacksquare = 0$

9. $4 \times (5 \times 3) = (\blacksquare \times 5) \times 3$ **10.** $847 \times 0 = \blacksquare$

11. $419 \times 1 = \blacksquare$

Name some situations in which averages are used.

WRAP UP...

PROBLEM SOLVING

STRATEGY • Work Backward

Shirley and her family are planning a trip to the beach. She has $12.50 left after buying a beach towel for $5.00, an audiocassette for $10.00, and a bottle of sunscreen for $4.50. She received a $2.00 refund on the sunscreen by using a coupon. How much money did Shirley have before her purchases?

Sometimes a problem can be worked by starting with a given number and then using inverse operations to find the answer. This strategy is called *work backward*.

► **UNDERSTAND**

What are you asked to find?

What facts are given?

► **PLAN**

What plan can you make?

One plan is to make a flowchart of the given data. Then write the inverse operations in another flowchart and work backward to solve the problem.

► **SOLVE**

What flowchart can you make?

Step 1 Show the steps of the problem.

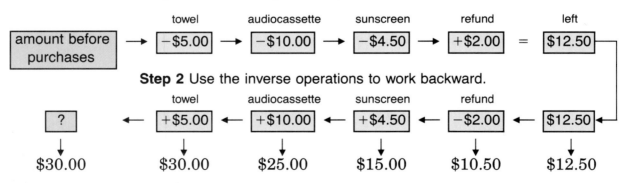

Step 2 Use the inverse operations to work backward.

So, Shirley had $30.00 before her purchases.

► **LOOK BACK**

How can you check your answer?

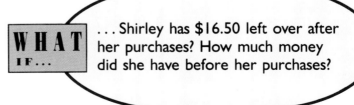

WHAT IF... ... Shirley has $16.50 left over after her purchases? How much money did she have before her purchases?

 Connection, pages 456–457

Apply

Work backward and solve.

1 At a concession stand, Luisa bought 2 drinks for $0.75 each, a plain hot dog for $1.25, and 3 bags of peanuts for $0.30 each. She was given $1.35 in change. How much money did she give the cashier at the concession stand?

2 Glenn's family made a trip to the beach. When they got home, the odometer on the car read 32,458 miles. If the beach is 65 miles from their home and they drove an additional 12 miles each of the three days of their trip, what did the odometer read before the trip?

Mixed Applications ⟩ **STRATEGIES**

Make a Drawing • Find a Pattern • Write a Number Sentence • Work Backward

Choose a strategy and solve.

3 The drama club will present a play to 1,482 students in 6 different assemblies. If each assembly has the same number of students, how many students will be at each performance?

4 At the school swim meet, Sandra was in the first lane, and Gwen and Paula were next to each other. If 4 lanes were used for the race and Paula was between Ruth and Sandra, in which lane was Ruth?

5 The school swim team practices 2 hours each Monday and 1 hour each Wednesday and Friday. For how many hours will the team practice in 4 weeks?

6 Eric joined the running club. At the first practice, he ran for only 5 minutes. On the second day of practice, he ran for 10 minutes. On the third day of practice, he ran for 15 minutes. If this pattern continued, on which day of practice did Eric run for 30 minutes?

More Practice, Lesson 5.10, page H53

CHAPTER REVIEW / TEST

Vocabulary Check

Choose a word or words from the box to complete each sentence.

average
compatible
dividend
divisible
divisor
inverse
mean
quotient
short division

1. A number is ___?___ by another number when it can be divided evenly with a remainder of zero. *(page 150)*

2. A number that is a summary of a group of numbers is the ___?___ . *(page 168)*

3. The number that is divided is the ___?___ . *(page 150)*

4. When using ___?___ , write in the dividend each remainder except the last one. *(page 158)*

5. Another name for the average is the ___?___ . *(page 168)*

6. To estimate a quotient, you can use ___?___ numbers. *(page 152)*

7. Multiplication is the ___?___ of division. *(page 154)*

8. The number that divides the dividend is the ___?___ . *(page 150)*

9. The result of a division is a ___?___ . *(page 150)*

Concept Check

Use the rules for divisibility to decide whether the first number is divisible by the second. Write *yes* or *no*. *(page 150)*

> Look for numbers that divide into equal groups with a remainder of zero.

10. 248; 2
11. 323; 3
12. 815; 5
13. 240; 10

14. 510; 5
15. 480; 3
16. 2,005; 10
17. 865; 2

Estimate each quotient. *(page 152)*

18. $3\overline{)58}$
19. $4\overline{)39}$
20. $6\overline{)350}$
21. $8\overline{)319}$

22. $5\overline{)4,670}$
23. $2\overline{)5,807}$
24. $7\overline{)7,218}$
25. $9\overline{)3,550}$

Find the average. *(page 168)*

26. 125; 472; 231
27. 32; 50; 62; 48
28. 1.7; 6.8; 6.5; 5.0

Skill Check

Estimate each quotient. *(page 152)*

29. $65 \div 9 \approx n$ **30.** $80 \div 9 \approx n$ **31.** $126 \div 4 \approx n$

32. $523 \div 5 \approx n$ **33.** $1{,}578 \div 8 \approx n$ **34.** $2{,}795 \div 7 \approx n$

Divide. *(pages 154, 156, 164, 166)*

35. $4\overline{)57}$ **36.** $5\overline{)82}$ **37.** $9\overline{)203}$ **38.** $7\overline{)814}$

39. $8\overline{)96}$ **40.** $5\overline{)48}$ **41.** $6\overline{)56}$ **42.** $5\overline{)129}$

43. $9\overline{)658}$ **44.** $3\overline{)253}$ **45.** $9\overline{)1{,}496}$ **46.** $6\overline{)2{,}349}$

47. $2\overline{)416}$ **48.** $8\overline{)874}$ **49.** $6\overline{)425}$ **50.** $8\overline{)3{,}746}$

51. $4\overline{)5{,}767}$ **52.** $6\overline{)5{,}653}$ **53.** $8\overline{)3{,}466}$ **54.** $6\overline{)47{,}087}$

Use short division to find each quotient. *(page 158)*

55. $6\overline{)1{,}503}$ **56.** $4\overline{)3{,}078}$ **57.** $6\overline{)4{,}113}$ **58.** $5\overline{)3{,}046}$

Find the average. *(page 168)*

59. 428; 463; 492   **60.** 214; 219; 247; 268

61. 1,250; 1,463; 1,783; 2,000   **62.** 10,950; 14,764; 17,210

Problem-Solving Check *(pages 160, 170)*

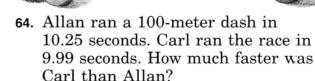

63. Leo has an 8-page folder that can hold 192 stamps. How many stamps can he put on each page?

64. Allan ran a 100-meter dash in 10.25 seconds. Carl ran the race in 9.99 seconds. How much faster was Carl than Allan?

65. One day Clara went shopping. She bought a book for $15. She received $11 for a pen set that she returned. She spent $5 on lunch and found that she had $8 left. How much money did she have before she went shopping?

66. Rhonda bought a bag of marbles. She gave half of them to her brother. Then she lost half plus 6 more of the remaining marbles in a match. She had 24 marbles left after the match. How many marbles did Rhonda buy?

WHAT DID I LEARN?

1. Explain how to determine whether 45 is divisible by 2, 3, 5, and 10. Then determine the divisibility.

2. Use compatible numbers to estimate $158 \div 8$. Show your work.

3. Show each step as you find the quotient of $812 \div 4$.

4. Show each step as you find the average of 35, 43, 36.

5. Read Exercise 2 on page 171. Follow the steps on the Problem-Solving Think Along worksheet to show how to solve this problem.

I can use the rules for divisibility to tell whether a number is divisible by 2, 3, 5, or 10.

Write About It

6. Explain how estimation is helpful to you when finding quotients.

7. How is understanding place value important in division? Use an example in your explanation.

TEAMWORK
Project

MAKE A MODEL

Amusement park rides are built to hold many people at one time. With your teammates, model a roller coaster.

 **DECIDE** Talk about how you can use oak tag, scissors, index cards, glue, and stickers to model a roller coaster ride.

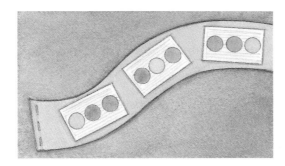

 **DO** Work with your teammates. Use 57 small stickers to represent 3 riders per car. Let each index card represent a roller coaster passenger car.

Tape index cards to a strip of oak tag.

Staple the strip to a piece of colored paper.

SHARE Show your model. Describe how the number of cars on the roller coaster can be calculated.

TALK ABOUT IT

1 How can you use your model to determine the number of cars needed for 57 passengers if 3 people ride in each car?

2 In your everyday activities, what other uses for division have you noticed?

Activity

PERFECT NUMBERS

In ancient Greece a group of men studied relationships among numbers. The leader was Pythagoras, and group members were known as Pythagoreans. They investigated *perfect numbers*.

A perfect number is one that equals the sum of all its different factors. The number itself is not included. Look at the table at the right.

Example

Factors of 496: 1, 2, 4, 8, 16, 31, 62, 124, 248, 496

Sum of the factors (not including the number itself):

$1 + 2 + 4 + 8 + 16 + 31 + 62 + 124 + 248 = 496$

So, 496 is a perfect number.

NUMBER	FACTORS EXCEPT THE NUMBER ITSELF						SUM OF FACTORS
1							
4	1	2					3
9	1	3					4
18	1	2	3	6	9		21

Make a table like the one above. Include all the numbers from 1 to 28. Use the table to answer the following questions.

1. What are the perfect numbers between 1 and 28?

2. Why is the number itself not included?

3. Why can you not consider 1 as a perfect number?

Challenge

Number Puzzles

Use the clues to find the number.

1. I am greater than 70, less than 77, and divisible by 6.

2. If you divide me by 6, you will have 6 r4.

3. If you divide me by 5, you will have 5 r1.

Critical Thinking

Beth is 7 years older than Nora.
Nora is 1 year older than Kathy.
Kathy is one half as old as Beth.
Beth is 1 year older than Jana.
Nora, who is 9 years old, was born 6 years after Jana.
List the girls and their ages from oldest to youngest.

Write the letter of the correct answer.

1. What is the value of the 5 in 15,234,678?

A. 500
B. 5,000
C. 500,000
D. 5,000,000

2. Which decimals are in order from least to greatest?

A. 5.12; 5.71; 5.60
B. 5.71; 5.60; 5.12
C. 5.12; 5.60; 5.71
D. not here

3.
$$865,437$$
$$+429,543$$

A. 1,284,970   B. 1,295,970
C. 1,295,980   D. not here

4.
$$603,455$$
$$-215,378$$

A. 388,077   B. 408,177
C. 412,077   D. 423,177

5.
$$5.72$$
$$-1.46$$

A. 3.26   B. 4.26
C. 4.34   D. 4.36

6. Which name describes this figure?

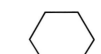

A. pentagon
B. hexagon
C. octagon
D. not here

7. Which figures are similar?

A.   B.

C.   D.

8. Which figure shows a line of symmetry?

A.   B.

C. 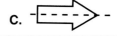   D.

9. $500 \times 40 = n$

A. 2,000   B. 20,000
C. 200,000   D. 2,000,000

10. $7,864 \div 6 = n$

A. 1,210 r4   B. 1,310
C. 1,310 r4   D. 1,410 r6

11. Jared unpacked pencils for the school secretary. Jared unpacked 5 boxes that held 125 pencils each. How many pencils did he unpack?

A. 125 pencils   B. 130 pencils
C. 525 pencils   D. 625 pencils

12. Beatrice put some money in her wallet. She spent $3.75 and found $1.00. When she counted the money in her wallet, she had $6.50. How much money did she put in her wallet at first?

A. $1.75   B. $3.75
C. $9.25   D. $11.25

DIVIDING WHOLE NUMBERS BY 2-DIGIT NUMBERS

Did you know ...

... that the St. Bernard is a dog famous for rescuing lost travelers? It was trained in the Alps of Switzerland to rescue people who were lost.

TALK ABOUT IT

Suppose a St. Bernard eats 1,800 pounds of dog food in a 12-month period. Based on this information, list everything you can figure out about the food a St. Bernard eats. Explain how you arrived at your answers.

DIVISION PATTERNS

Ginny wanted to set a record by growing the largest watermelon. After trying for several years, Ginny grew a watermelon that weighed 160 pounds. If she cut the watermelon into 40 equal pieces, how much did each piece weigh?

Divide.

Think:

weight of the watermelon	number of equal pieces	weight of each piece
160	÷ 40	= n

You know that multiplication and division are inverse, or opposite, operations. So, you can use a multiplication sentence to help find a quotient.

Since $4 \times 40 = 160$, you know that $160 \div 40 = 4$. So, each piece of Ginny's watermelon weighed 4 pounds.

Look at these division patterns.

A.
$60 \div 30 = 2$
$600 \div 30 = 20$
$6,000 \div 30 = 200$

B.
$420 \div 70 = 6$
$4,200 \div 70 = 60$
$42,000 \div 70 = 600$

C.
$600 \div 20 = 30$
$6,000 \div 20 = 300$
$60,000 \div 20 = 3,000$

Talk About It

▶ What pattern do you see?

▶ How can the pattern help you determine the number of zeros in the quotient?

▶ How many zeros will be in the quotient of $40,000 \div 50$? How does this differ from the pattern?

Check for Understanding

Complete the pattern.

1.
$80 \div 40 = 2$
$800 \div 40 = n$
$8,000 \div 40 = 200$

2.
$90 \div 30 = 3$
$900 \div 30 = 30$
$9,000 \div 30 = n$

3.
$250 \div 50 = n$
$2,500 \div 50 = 50$
$25,000 \div 50 = 500$

4.
$180 \div 60 = 3$
$1,800 \div 60 = n$
$18,000 \div 60 = 300$

Write the number of zeros in the quotient.

5. $60\overline{)1,200}$ **6.** $70\overline{)14,000}$ **7.** $60\overline{)30,000}$ **8.** $80\overline{)160,000}$ **9.** $50\overline{)50,000}$

Practice

Find the quotient.

10. $60 \div 20 = n$ **11.** $80 \div 40 = n$ **12.** $540 \div 60 = n$ **13.** $640 \div 80 = n$

14. $560 \div 80 = n$ **15.** $2,400 \div 30 = n$ **16.** $3,600 \div 40 = n$ **17.** $36,000 \div 30 = n$

18. $20\overline{)80}$ **19.** $30\overline{)90}$ **20.** $10\overline{)90}$ **21.** $50\overline{)50}$ **22.** $70\overline{)210}$

23. $40\overline{)800}$ **24.** $80\overline{)160}$ **25.** $90\overline{)270}$ **26.** $60\overline{)360}$ **27.** $20\overline{)1,000}$

28. $70\overline{)4,900}$ **29.** $20\overline{)6,000}$ **30.** $30\overline{)1,800}$ **31.** $80\overline{)80,000}$ **32.** $50\overline{)150,000}$

Mixed Applications

33. The fifth-grade classes had a contest to find out which classroom had the tallest students. The winning class had 30 students measuring a total of 1,800 inches. What was the average height of the students?

34. Mrs. Ramsey's class set a school record by collecting the most newspapers for recycling. If each of her 30 students collected 60 newspapers, how many newspapers did they collect in all?

35. Mrs. Brooks has 20 students in her class who want to set a school record for domino toppling. If there are 800 dominoes and each student sets up the same number, how many dominoes will each student set up?

36. Mental Math Is 60 a reasonable quotient for $480 \div 80$? Explain.

MIXED REVIEW

Find the difference.

1. 6.8
    $- 4.9$

2. 8.35
    $- 5.46$

3. 12.48
    $- 9.39$

4. 123.75
    $- 106.57$

Find the product.

5. 28
    $\times \ 3$

6. 248
    $\times \ 4$

7. 197
    $\times \ 7$

8. $6,503$
    $\times \ 2$

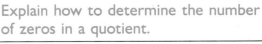

Explain how to determine the number of zeros in a quotient.

WRAP UP...

ESTIMATING
Whole-Number Quotients

Karen Stevenson holds the record for eating the most baked beans in the least amount of time. Using a toothpick, she ate 2,780 beans in 30 minutes. About how many baked beans did she eat each minute?

Since an exact number is not needed, estimate the quotient. Choose compatible numbers that are close to the original numbers that divide easily.

Estimate. $2{,}780 \div 30 \approx n$

Think: $30 \times n = 2{,}700$
$30 \times 90 = 2{,}700$ $\overset{90 \;\leftarrow \text{estimate}}{30\overline{)2{,}700}}$

So, Karen ate about 90 baked beans each minute.

• Is 90 greater than or less than the actual quotient? How can you tell?

Another Method

Sometimes you can use more than one pair of compatible numbers to estimate a quotient. Finding more than one estimate will give you two possible quotients.

Estimate. $43\overline{)2{,}752}$

Talk About It

▶ Does $2{,}400 \div 40$ give a good estimate? Why or why not?

▶ Does $2{,}800 \div 40$ give a good estimate? Why or why not?

▶ What are the two possible estimates?

▶ Name two pairs of compatible numbers for $1{,}572 \div 35$.

Check for Understanding

Name two pairs of compatible numbers.

1. $158 \div 34 \approx n$
2. $620 \div 87 \approx n$
3. $1{,}425 \div 27 \approx n$

Estimate the quotient.

4. $18\overline{)178}$
5. $23\overline{)138}$
6. $28\overline{)627}$
7. $32\overline{)7{,}120}$
8. $68\overline{)6{,}216}$

Practice

Write two pairs of compatible numbers for each. Give two possible estimates.

9. $153 \div 34 \approx n$ **10.** $640 \div 87 \approx n$ **11.** $153 \div 18 \approx n$

12. $275 \div 32 \approx n$ **13.** $1{,}425 \div 27 \approx n$ **14.** $3{,}050 \div 56 \approx n$

Estimate the quotient.

15. $17\overline{)163}$ **16.** $33\overline{)315}$ **17.** $57\overline{)305}$ **18.** $28\overline{)281}$ **19.** $46\overline{)379}$

20. $37\overline{)162}$ **21.** $59\overline{)382}$ **22.** $75\overline{)540}$ **23.** $92\overline{)790}$ **24.** $72\overline{)581}$

25. $26\overline{)809}$ **26.** $48\overline{)470}$ **27.** $12\overline{)789}$ **28.** $24\overline{)812}$ **29.** $43\overline{)736}$

30. $53\overline{)2{,}470}$ **31.** $13\overline{)4{,}900}$ **32.** $74\overline{)5{,}780}$ **33.** $31\overline{)2{,}650}$ **34.** $64\overline{)1{,}738}$

35. $530 \div 72 \approx n$ **36.** $625 \div 27 \approx n$ **37.** $4{,}680 \div 47 \approx n$ **38.** $5{,}716 \div 81 \approx n$

39. $3{,}469 \div 43 \approx n$ **40.** $6{,}250 \div 87 \approx n$ **41.** $6{,}321 \div 34 \approx n$ **42.** $9{,}800 \div 97 \approx n$

Mixed Applications

43. Cucumbers have 73 calories per pound. The largest cucumber on record weighed about 18 pounds. If it had been divided into 15 equal slices, about how many calories would have been in each slice?

44. Number Sense   The largest pecan pie ever baked weighed 40,266 pounds. If 4 pounds of pecan pie can feed about 10 people, about how many people could the record-setting pie have fed?

45. Write a Question   The longest continuous loaf of bread ever baked in the United States was about 2,350 feet long. Aluminum foil comes in rolls of 75 feet.

46. The largest gingerbread house ever made was 52 feet high. If 1,650 pounds of icing were used, about how many pounds of icing were used for each foot?

How does using compatible numbers help you estimate quotients?   **WRAP UP...**

DIVIDING
Two-Digit Numbers

Cross-country skiing is very popular in Sweden. A ski run called the Vasa Race is about 90 kilometers long. Sigrid is responsible for checkpoints to be placed about every 15 kilometers along the race course. For how many checkpoints is Sigrid responsible?

First, estimate. $90 \div 15 \approx n$

Think: $20 \times n = 100$, so $n = 5$.

Then, divide. $15\overline{)90}$

Step 1	Step 2
Since the estimate is a one-digit number, divide the 90 ones.	Since the remainder is equal to the divisor, increase the quotient.
$\begin{array}{r} 5 \\ 15\overline{)90} \\ -75 \\ \hline 15 \end{array}$ Multiply. Subtract. Compare. $15 = 15$	$\begin{array}{r} 6 \\ 15\overline{)90} \\ -90 \\ \hline 0 \end{array}$ Multiply. Subtract. Compare. $0 < 15$

So, Sigrid is responsible for 6 checkpoints.

MULTICULTURAL NOTE: Each year thousands of Swedes participate in the Vasa Race. Skiing is a popular sport because snow covers the ground from two to six months a year.

More Examples

A. Estimate. $18\overline{)84}$

Think: $20 \times n = 80$ or
$15 \times n = 75$, so $n = 4$ or 5.

$\begin{array}{r} 4 \text{ r}12 \\ 18\overline{)84} \\ -72 \\ \hline 12 \end{array}$ Write the remainder next to the quotient.

Check
$\begin{array}{r} 18 \\ \times\ 4 \\ \hline 72 \\ +12 \\ \hline 84 \end{array}$ ← divisor
← quotient

← remainder
← dividend

B. Estimate. $26\overline{)67}$

Think: $30 \times n = 60$ or
$25 \times n = 75$, so $n = 2$ or 3.

$\begin{array}{r} 2 \text{ r}15 \\ 26\overline{)67} \\ -52 \\ \hline 15 \end{array}$

Check
$\begin{array}{r} 26 \\ \times\ 2 \\ \hline 52 \\ +15 \\ \hline 67 \end{array}$ ← divisor
← quotient

← remainder
← dividend

Talk About It

▶ How can you determine the place value of the first digit in the quotient?

▶ How is your estimate part of the division process?

Check for Understanding

Estimate. Then find the quotient.

1. $12\overline{)62}$ **2.** $18\overline{)41}$ **3.** $37\overline{)84}$ **4.** $48\overline{)95}$ **5.** $53\overline{)167}$

Practice

Estimate.

6. $52 \div 12 \approx n$ **7.** $82 \div 38 \approx n$ **8.** $90 \div 25 \approx n$ **9.** $45 \div 13 \approx n$

10. $65 \div 32 \approx n$ **11.** $73 \div 40 \approx n$ **12.** $49 \div 17 \approx n$ **13.** $89 \div 26 \approx n$

Divide. Check with multiplication.

14. $22\overline{)88}$ **15.** $34\overline{)94}$ **16.** $16\overline{)80}$ **17.** $21\overline{)62}$ **18.** $12\overline{)79}$

19. $51\overline{)58}$ **20.** $32\overline{)96}$ **21.** $27\overline{)81}$ **22.** $42\overline{)88}$ **23.** $34\overline{)86}$

24. $12\overline{)70}$ **25.** $48\overline{)98}$ **26.** $65\overline{)72}$ **27.** $13\overline{)99}$ **28.** $13\overline{)97}$

29. $85 \div 32 = n$ **30.** $74 \div 12 = n$

31. $57 \div 22 = n$ **32.** $49 \div 19 = n$

33. $90 \div 18 = n$ **34.** $98 \div 47 = n$

Mixed Applications

35. Critical Thinking When a two-digit number is divided by a two-digit number, is the quotient ever a two-digit number? Explain.

36. Robert's van can hold 11 people plus the driver. If Robert plans to transport 40 friends to see a race, how many trips will he need to make?

37. The Swedish unit of money is the krona. A vendor at the race sells sandwiches for 20 kronor each. He can make 25 sandwiches for 215 kronor. How much profit does he make on the sale of 25 sandwiches?

38. When Helga does cross-country skiing, she stops to rest every 12 kilometers. If she tries the Vasa Race, how many times will she stop to rest? How far will she have to ski after her last rest stop to finish the race?

Explain why you sometimes get a remainder when you divide.

WRAP UP...

CORRECTING QUOTIENTS

A group of students at a high school set a record for the longest volleyball game. The game lasted a little more than 118 hours. How many continuous days did the students play volleyball?

Since there are 24 hours in a day, divide 118 hours by 24 hours.

Estimate. $118 \div 24 \approx n$ **Think:** $20 \times n = 100$ or
 $30 \times n = 120$,
 so $n = 5$ or 4.

Divide. $24\overline{)118}$

Try 5.

$\begin{array}{r} 5 \\ 24\overline{)118} \\ -120 \end{array}$ Since 120 > 118, this estimate is too large.

Try 4.

$\begin{array}{r} 4 r22 \\ 24\overline{)118} \\ -96 \\ \hline 22 \end{array}$

So, the students played for 4 days and 22 hours.

Another Example

Estimate. $269 \div 38 \approx n$
Think: $40 \times n = 240$ or
 $40 \times n = 280$, so $n = 6$ or 7.

Divide. $38\overline{)269}$

Try 6.

$\begin{array}{r} 6 \\ 38\overline{)269} \\ -228 \\ \hline 41 \end{array}$ Since 41 > 38, the estimate is too small.

Try 7.

$\begin{array}{r} 7 r3 \\ 38\overline{)269} \\ -266 \\ \hline 3 \end{array}$

Talk About It

▶ How do you know when an estimated quotient is too large?

▶ How do you know when an estimated quotient is too small?

▶ What can you do to correct an estimate that is too large? too small?

▶ How do you know when an estimated quotient is correct?

Check for Understanding

Look at each estimated quotient. Write whether the estimated quotient is *too large, too small,* or *just right.*

1. $15\overline{)76}$ with quotient 6

2. $86\overline{)351}$ with quotient 4

3. $53\overline{)349}$ with quotient 7

4. $65\overline{)336}$ with quotient 4

5. $78\overline{)496}$ with quotient 6

Practice

Choose the correct estimate to use in the quotient. Write **a** or **b**.

6. $22\overline{)185}$ **a.** 8   **b.** 9

7. $54\overline{)194}$ **a.** 3   **b.** 4

8. $42\overline{)352}$ **a.** 8   **b.** 9

9. $37\overline{)268}$ **a.** 6   **b.** 7

10. $16\overline{)150}$ **a.** 9   **b.** 10

Divide.

11. $19\overline{)74}$ 12. $25\overline{)85}$ 13. $33\overline{)80}$

14. $14\overline{)94}$ 15. $27\overline{)134}$ 16. $44\overline{)175}$

17. $54\overline{)235}$ 18. $65\overline{)342}$ 19. $46\overline{)456}$

20. $38\overline{)270}$ 21. $22\overline{)119}$ 22. $49\overline{)489}$

23. $29\overline{)234}$ 24. $36\overline{)191}$ 25. $52\overline{)335}$

Mixed Applications

26. A total of 84 students signed up for a volleyball tournament. The principal asked 6 teachers to coach one team each. If there are 12 students on each team, is another coach needed?

27. The volleyball team practices each Monday, Wednesday, and Friday after school. If each practice is 2 hours long, how many hours does the team practice in 8 weeks?

28. The captain of the volleyball team has collected $140 to buy new balls for the tournament. If the balls cost $32 each, how many can he buy?

29. **Analyze Data** The uniforms for the 12 team members cost $42 each. If the players have earned $360 at a car wash to be used toward the purchase of the uniforms, how much additional money will each player have to pay for a uniform?

How do you know whether your first estimate in the quotient is too large or too small?

DIVIDING
Three-Digit Numbers

Collecting postcards is a popular hobby. One of the largest collections in the world has 1,000,265 postcards.

Ted's grandmother has a collection of 579 postcards. She wants to divide them equally among her 17 grandchildren. How many postcards can she give to each of her grandchildren?

Estimate.　　$579 \div 17 \approx n$ **Think:** $20 \times n = 600$ or
$15 \times n = 600$, so $n = 30$ or 40.

Divide.　$17\overline{)579}$

Step 1	Step 2	Step 3
Since the estimate is a two-digit number, divide the 57 tens.	Bring down the ones. Divide the 69 ones.	Since the remainder is greater than the divisor, correct the quotient.

Step 1

$$\begin{array}{r} 3 \\ 17\overline{)579} \\ -51 \\ \hline 6 \end{array}$$
Multiply.
Subtract.
Compare.
$6 < 17$

Step 2

$$\begin{array}{r} 33 \\ 17\overline{)579} \\ -51\downarrow \\ \hline 69 \\ -51 \\ \hline 18 \end{array}$$
Multiply.
Subtract.
Compare.
$18 > 17$

Step 3

$$\begin{array}{r} 34 \text{ r1} \\ 17\overline{)579} \\ -51\downarrow \\ \hline 69 \\ -68 \\ \hline 1 \end{array}$$
Multiply.
Subtract.
Compare.
$1 < 17$

So, Ted's grandmother can give 34 postcards to each of her grandchildren. She will have 1 postcard left.

More Examples

A. Estimate.　$35\overline{)843}$

Think: $40 \times n = 800$ or
$30 \times n = 900$, so $n = 20$ or 30.

$$\begin{array}{r} 24 \text{ r3} \\ 35\overline{)843} \\ -70 \\ \hline 143 \\ -140 \\ \hline 3 \end{array}$$

B. Estimate.　$28\overline{)720}$

Think: $30 \times n = 600$ or
$25 \times n = 750$,
so $n = 20$ or 30.

$$\begin{array}{r} 25 \text{ r20} \\ 28\overline{)720} \\ -56 \\ \hline 160 \\ -140 \\ \hline 20 \end{array}$$

- How can you tell whether your answer is reasonable?

Check for Understanding

Estimate. Then find the quotient.

1. $31\overline{)975}$
2. $41\overline{)820}$
3. $28\overline{)564}$
4. $87\overline{)931}$

Practice

Find the quotient.

5. $21\overline{)875}$
6. $35\overline{)842}$
7. $16\overline{)850}$
8. $24\overline{)521}$

9. $12\overline{)706}$
10. $30\overline{)275}$
11. $42\overline{)168}$
12. $54\overline{)302}$

13. $53\overline{)968}$
14. $63\overline{)567}$
15. $31\overline{)618}$
16. $47\overline{)987}$

17. $23\overline{)385}$
18. $34\overline{)400}$
19. $23\overline{)414}$
20. $13\overline{)415}$

21. $819 \div 39 = n$
22. $500 \div 14 = n$
23. $605 \div 52 = n$

Mixed Applications

24. Alex started his rock collection with 4 rocks. He collected 6 more rocks the first week, 8 rocks the next week, and 10 rocks the third week. If this pattern continues, how many rocks will he have after 6 weeks?

25. Flora collects dolls from different countries. She has 132 dolls in her collection. If she can place 15 dolls on a shelf, how many shelves will she need to display all her dolls?

26. Lloyd has the largest baseball-card collection in his class. He collected 15 cards each week for 18 weeks. If he divided these cards evenly into the 30 pages of his album, how many cards were on each page?

27. **Mental Math** Edith has 200 shells in her collection. She wants to make 6 wind chimes and use 50 shells for each. How many more shells does she need to collect?

CRITICAL THINKING

28. Using the digits 1, 3, 5, 7, and 9, write a division problem that has a two-digit divisor, a three-digit dividend, and the greatest possible quotient. Make sure that you use each digit at least once.

Why is it helpful to have more than one estimate?

PROBLEM SOLVING

STRATEGY • Use Estimation

The Grand Canyon is one of the largest land gorges in the world. Tim and his family have saved $1,235 to spend on a visit to Grand Canyon National Park. If their expenses will average $185 per day, will they have enough money for a 6-day visit?

Sometimes an exact answer is not needed to solve a problem. In such a situation, you can decide whether to overestimate or to underestimate.

▶ **UNDERSTAND**

What are you asked to find?

What facts are given?

▶ **PLAN**

Do you need an exact answer to solve the problem?

No, an estimate is reasonable.

Do you need to overestimate or to underestimate to find the solution?

You need to overestimate the cost per day and underestimate the amount saved to be sure that Tim and his family will have enough money.

▶ **SOLVE**

How will you carry out the plan?

To estimate the quotient, increase the divisor and decrease the dividend. Choose compatible numbers to divide.

$1,235 ÷ $185 = n   The exact quotient will be more
   ↓   ↓   ↓   than the estimated quotient.
$1,200 ÷ $200 = 6

So, Tim and his family will have enough money to stay about 6 days.

▶ **LOOK BACK**

What would happen if you estimated by using $1,200 ÷ $100?

... Tim and his family have saved $1,020 and expect expenses to average $175 per day? Will they have enough money for a 5-day visit?

Apply

Tell whether an exact answer is needed. Solve.

1 Some tourists plan to spend 5 days traveling about 400 miles in Grand Canyon National Park. They will travel about 185 miles in a minibus for 1 day. They will bicycle for 4 days. About how many miles will they travel each day on bicycles?

2 Jack and his family will spend 10 days touring the Grand Canyon. They purchased 8 rolls of film with 36 exposures on each roll. About how many pictures can they take on each of the 10 days if they take about the same number every day?

> **Mixed Applications** ▷ STRATEGIES

Write a Number Sentence
• **Guess and Check**
• **Find a Pattern** • **Work Backward**

Choose a strategy and solve.

3 Lake Superior is in both the United States and Canada. Its surface area of about 31,800 square miles is the greatest of any freshwater lake. About how many square miles are in Canada if about 20,700 square miles are in the United States?

4 Rudy was the first to board a tour bus at the stop. It stopped at the next corner, and 3 passengers got on. At the third stop, 5 passengers got on. If the pattern continues, how many people will be on the bus after 5 stops?

5 The Carsons used traveler's checks on their vacation. By the end of the fourth day, they had spent $185.74 for lodging, $212.48 for food, and $56.91 for gas. They had $340.00 in traveler's checks and about $5.00 in change left. How many dollars worth of traveler's checks did they begin with?

6 There are 350 burros in the park. The park rangers want to move them to another area. They plan to move 30 burros the first month. If they move 20 more burros each month than the month before, how many months will it take to move all the burros?

More Practice, Lesson 6.6, page H55

REVIEW AND MAINTENANCE

1. When Janice deposited her birthday money in her savings account, her total savings increased from $484.96 to $522.56. Janice received $15.00 from her aunt and the rest from her parents. How much did her parents give her?

2. Luis went grocery shopping and bought 2 chickens for $2.12 each, milk for $1.05, potatoes for $1.69, and eggs for $0.89. About how much change did he receive from $20.00?

Watch for hidden data in problems.

Find the sum or difference.

3. 12.45
    $+ 17.57$

4. 45.78
    $- 28.95$

5. 236.705
    $+ 874.365$

6. 485.932
    $- 269.064$

Multiply.

7. 498
    $\times\ 14$

8. $6,725$
    $\times\ \ \ 6$

9. $16,430$
    $\times\ \ \ \ 25$

10. $45,893$
    $\times\ \ \ \ \ 3$

Name each triangle. Write *equilateral, isosceles,* or *scalene.*

11.

12.

13.

14.

Estimate each quotient.

15. $6\overline{)55}$

16. $8\overline{)333}$

17. $4\overline{)1,789}$

18. $5\overline{)4,345}$

19. $17\overline{)380}$

20. $29\overline{)875}$

21. $42\overline{)3,300}$

22. $62\overline{)4,605}$

Divide.

23. $7\overline{)64}$

24. $9\overline{)238}$

25. $3\overline{)976}$

26. $8\overline{)1,875}$

27. $16\overline{)83}$

28. $35\overline{)79}$

29. $24\overline{)194}$

30. $32\overline{)580}$

Find the average.

31. $45, 57, 68, 74, 76$

32. $139, 275, 398, 420$

33. $1,275; 1,485; 1,803$

34. $2,575; 3,012; 4,985$

35. $3,576; 1,475; 1,288$

36. $7,648; 4,875; 5,327$

Whole-Number Operations

NORTH AMERICA

El Salvador

El Salvador is a small but heavily populated country in Central America. Many of the people live in the middle of the country, where agriculture and industry are concentrated.

Most Latin American countries, such as El Salvador, use similar methods for adding, subtracting, multiplying, and dividing. The methods involve showing symbols and digits at the right of the problem.

Examples

Addition	Subtraction
Read:	**Read:**
$45 +$ 45 plus 23 equals 68.	$45 -$ 45 minus 23 equals 22.
$23 =$	$23 =$
68	22

Multiplication

Step 1

Read:

$\overset{1}{2}4 \times 3$

2

3 times 24

Step 2

$\overset{1}{2}4 \times 3$

72

Division

Step 1

Read:

192 | 6
18   3
1

192 divided by 6

Step 2

192 | 6
18   32
12
12
0

Work Together

Try the methods above for operating with whole numbers.

1. $62 +$
   $35 =$

2. $59 -$
   $43 =$

3. $125 -$
   $34 =$

4. 36×4

5. $280 | 5$

6. $496 | 8$

DIVIDING
Larger Numbers

Karting is a sports event in which people try to set records. In one such event, the most mileage recorded in 24 hours on a closed, twisting circuit was 1,018 one-mile laps. On the average, how many laps were completed in an hour?

Estimate. $1,018 \div 24 \approx n$

Think: $25 \times n = 1,000$ or $20 \times 50 = 1,000$, so $n = 40$ or 50.

Divide. $24\overline{)1,018}$

Step 1	**Step 2**
Since the estimate has two digits, divide the 101 tens.	Bring down the 8 ones. Divide the 58 ones.
	Think: $25 \times n = 50$.

Step 1

$$\begin{array}{r} 4 \\ 24\overline{)1,018} \\ -96 \\ \hline 5 \end{array}$$

Multiply.
Subtract.
Compare. $5 < 24$

Step 2

$$\begin{array}{r} 42 \ \text{r}10 \\ 24\overline{)1,018} \\ -96\downarrow \\ \hline 58 \\ -48 \\ \hline 10 \end{array}$$

Multiply.
Subtract.
Compare. $10 < 24$

So, on the average, 42 laps were completed each hour. The remainder of 10 represents only parts of laps.

Another Method

A calculator can help you divide large numbers.

Estimate. $14,304 \div 48 \approx n$

Think: $50 \times n = 15,000$
        $50 \times 300 = 15,000$

             298.

So, $14,304 \div 48 = 298$.

Talk About It

▶ Compare your estimate with the quotient. Is your answer reasonable? Explain.

▶ Is your estimate an overestimate or an underestimate? Why?

Idea Bank, page 464, Exercise 5

Check for Understanding

Choose the correct answer. Write **a, b,** or **c.**

1. $16\overline{)3,568}$
   a. 22
   b. 222
   c. 223

2. $27\overline{)1,382}$
   a. 51
   b. 51 r5
   c. 515

3. $42\overline{)8,904}$
   a. 21
   b. 221
   c. 212

4. $53\overline{)2,385}$
   a. 45
   b. 450
   c. 455 r5

Practice

Estimate. Then find the quotient.

5. $5,751 \div 81 = n$

6. $6,050 \div 93 = n$

7. $3,620 \div 27 = n$

8. $8,589 \div 11 = n$

9. $2,398 \div 46 = n$

10. $4,580 \div 32 = n$

Divide.

11. $37\overline{)1,036}$

12. $23\overline{)2,185}$

13. $54\overline{)5,508}$

14. $68\overline{)4,624}$

15. $24\overline{)68,976}$

16. $12\overline{)45,984}$

17. $17\overline{)55,403}$

18. $32\overline{)33,024}$

Mixed Applications

19. The original Ferris wheel was erected in 1893 at the World's Columbian Exposition in Chicago. The wheel carried 36 cars, each seating 60 people. What was the total number of passengers that could be seated?

20. **Number Sense** What is the smallest four-digit number that can be divided by 20 and leave a remainder of 15?

21. **Number Sense** If a motorcycle traveled 1,502 miles in 24 hours, was its average speed more than 50 miles per hour?

NUMBER SENSE

Compare. Use < or > for ●.

22. $6,539 \div 13 ● 6,539 \div 19$

23. $8,250 \div 12 ● 6,250 \div 12$

24. $1,034 \div 24 ● 3,098 \div 24$

25. $4,195 \div 27 ● 4,195 \div 17$

Why is an estimate needed when you use a calculator to find quotients?

WRAP UP...

ZEROS IN THE QUOTIENT

The largest barbecue ever recorded, at the May Festival in Memphis, Tennessee, was attended by 80,000 people. Rosa and her friends are planning a smaller barbecue to be held on Saturday. Over a period of 12 hours, a team of cooks will prepare 1,248 pounds of beef. What is the average number of pounds of beef they will prepare each hour?

Estimate. $1,248 \div 12 \approx n$ **Think:** $12 \times n = 1,200$ or
$10 \times n = 1,200$, so $n = 100$ or 120.

Divide. $12\overline{)1,248}$

Step 1	**Step 2**	**Step 3**
Since the estimate is three digits, divide the 12 hundreds. $12 \times n = 12$	Bring down the tens. Divide the 4 tens. **Think:** Since $12 > 4$, write 0 tens in the quotient.	Bring down the ones. Divide the 48 ones.
$\begin{array}{r} 1 \\ 12\overline{)1,248} \\ -12 \\ \hline 0 \end{array}$	$\begin{array}{r} 10 \\ 12\overline{)1,248} \\ -12\downarrow \\ \hline 04 \\ -0 \\ \hline 4 \end{array}$	$\begin{array}{r} 104 \\ 12\overline{)1,248} \\ -12 \\ \hline 04 \\ -0\downarrow \\ \hline 48 \\ -48 \\ \hline 0 \end{array}$

So, on the average, the cooks will prepare 104 pounds of beef each hour.

• What would happen if you did not write a zero in the tens place?

Check for Understanding

Choose the correct answer. Write **a, b,** or **c.**

1. $26\overline{)5,382}$ **a.** 27   **b.** 207   **c.** 270

2. $34\overline{)3,604}$ **a.** 16   **b.** 160   **c.** 106

3. $53\overline{)6,364}$ **a.** 120 r4   **b.** 12 r4   **c.** 102 r4

4. $47\overline{)4,841}$ **a.** 13   **b.** 103   **c.** 130

Practice

Divide.

5. $25\overline{)500}$

6. $12\overline{)360}$

7. $13\overline{)390}$

8. $29\overline{)585}$

9. $58\overline{)2,900}$

10. $56\overline{)5,040}$

11. $38\overline{)4,066}$

12. $11\overline{)7,812}$

13. $93\overline{)9,594}$

14. $41\overline{)4,141}$

15. $35\overline{)14,070}$

16. $41\overline{)16,769}$

17. $240 \div 12 = n$

18. $155 \div 15 = n$

19. $3,570 \div 34 = n$

20. $4,769 \div 23 = n$

21. $9,421 \div 31 = n$

22. $31,310 \div 62 = n$

23. $17,650 \div 44 = n$

24. $16,082 \div 52 = n$

Mixed Applications

25. A county set a record in its state for having the largest barbecue. Lonnie sold a total of 1,350 tickets in two weeks. If he sold 100 more tickets the second week than he sold the first week, how many tickets did he sell each week?

26. There were 3,000 people who attended the barbecue. There were supposed to be enough tables to seat half that number at one time. If 70 tables were ordered and each table seated 20 people, how many more tables should have been ordered?

27. **Making Decisions** Tickets to the barbecue were $10 for use anytime or 20 for $160 at a special group price for a one-day event. Which type of ticket would you have bought? Explain your answer.

28. **Number Sense** Explain why a quotient of 15 is incorrect for $3,150 \div 30$.

MIXED REVIEW

Write in standard form.

1. six tenths

2. twelve hundredths

3. five hundredths

Find the sum.

4. 398
   $+ 876$

5. 2,187
   $+ 7,950$

6. 89.50
   $+ 64.98$

7. 264.20
   $+ 857.95$

Explain why the zero in a quotient is important.

WRAP UP...

EXPLORING

Division with a Calculator

A calculator is a useful tool. Use a calculator to explore division.

Work Together

Building Understanding

Estimate. $45,236 \div 16 \approx n$

Divide. $16\overline{)45,236}$

Think: $20 \times n = 50,000$
$15 \times n = 45,000$;
so $n = 2,500$ or $3,000$.

TALK ABOUT IT

• How do you read $16\overline{)45,236}$?

• When you enter division on a calculator, does the divisor or the dividend come first?

$\boxed{4}$ $\boxed{5}$ $\boxed{2}$ $\boxed{3}$ $\boxed{6}$ $\boxed{\div}$ $\boxed{1}$ $\boxed{6}$ $\boxed{=}$

• When you press the $\boxed{=}$ key, what shows on the display?

• Name the whole-number part of the display.

• How does your quotient compare with your estimate?

• What does the decimal part of the display represent? How do you know?

• How can you find 0.25 of 16?

• If you do this division by paper and pencil, what is the remainder?

Making the Connection

When you use a calculator for division and there is a remainder, the display shows a decimal. Suppose you need to know the whole number this decimal represents.

Do this division on a calculator.

 [3] [0] [4] [2] [0] [÷] [4] [7] [=] | 647.23404 |

The whole-number part of the display is the quotient. Use this number to find the remainder. Multiply this number by the divisor, 47. Then subtract the product from the dividend, 30,420.

You can use the **memory keys** on your calculator to do this.

Step 1 [6] [4] [7] [×] [4] [7] [=] | 30409. | [M+] M | 30409. |

Step 2 [3] [0] [4] [2] [0] [−] [MRC] [=] M | 11. |

So, the remainder is 11.

↳ recalls the product from memory

Some calculators use [MR] for memory recall.

TALK ABOUT IT

- How can you check that this remainder is correct?

- What happened when you pressed the [M+] key?

- What does the *M* on the display represent?

- What happened when you pressed the [MRC] key?

- What happens when you press [MRC] [MRC] [ON/C] ?

Checking Understanding

Use a calculator to divide. Then find the remainder.

1. $16\overline{)26{,}136}$
2. $25\overline{)48{,}920}$
3. $63\overline{)56{,}850}$
4. $58\overline{)28{,}720}$

PROBLEM SOLVING

Choose a Strategy

The most extensive cave system in the world is under Mammoth Cave National Park in Kentucky. Many visitors tour the caves. Rod and his father are purchasing tickets for one of the tours. The cost is $7.50 for one child and one adult. The adult's ticket costs $3.00 more than the child's ticket. What is the cost of each ticket?

Understand
Plan
Solve
Look Back

You have learned many problem-solving strategies. It is important to remember that some problems can be solved by using more than one strategy.

One strategy you can use is *guess and check*.

Guess. $2.00 for the child's ticket

child's ticket	+	child's ticket plus $3	= n
$2	+	($2 + $3)	= n
$2	+	$5	= $7

Is this sum $7.50? No, it is less than $7.50. Guess again. Try a larger number.

Guess. $2.25 for the child's ticket

$2.25 + ($2.25 + $3.00) = n
$2.25 + $5.25   = $7.50

Another strategy you can use is *work backward*.

child's ticket ?	→	× 2 tickets	→	+ $3.00 for adult	→	$7.50
?	←	÷ 2	←	− $3.00	←	$7.50
$2.25		$2.25		$4.50		$7.50

So, the child's ticket costs $2.25, and the adult's ticket costs $5.25.

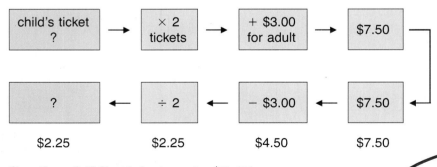

WHAT IF... ...the total cost of admission is $10.00? What is the cost of each ticket?

200

Mixed Applications ➤ **STRATEGIES** Make a Table • Find a Pattern
• Guess and Check • Write a Number
Sentence • Work Backward

Choose a strategy and solve.

1 The largest cake ever baked was made from 31,026 boxes of cake mix. If each box required 2 eggs, how many dozen eggs were used in the cake?

2 You are to find two 2-digit numbers. The sum of the two numbers is 50, and the difference is 22. What are the two numbers?

3 Otis is practicing to set a new record with his yo-yo. The first day he practiced, he made 70 loops. The second day he made 100 loops, and the third day he made 140 loops. If he continues at this rate, how many days of practice will it take before he makes 400 loops?

4 Sue Ann now has 15,000 postcards in her collection. On her twelfth birthday, she received half of this total from her brother, 500 cards from her aunt, and 125 cards from friends. How many cards did she have before her twelfth birthday?

5 The heaviest cat on record weighed about 47 pounds, and the lightest adult cat weighed about 2 pounds. The heaviest dog on record weighed about 338 pounds, and the lightest adult dog weighed about 1 pound. What is the difference in weight between the heaviest cat and dog? between the lightest cat and dog?

6 Jack and Lucinda played a number game. Jack told Lucinda to choose a number. Then he told her to multiply it by 4, add 6, divide by 2, and subtract 5. When Lucinda said that her answer was 6, Jack told her what number she began with. What was Lucinda's starting number?

WRITER'S CORNER

7 Write a brief news article about an imaginary record-breaking event at school. Include several number facts. Then make up a problem based on those number facts. Exchange your article and problem with a partner. Solve.

CHAPTER REVIEW / TEST

Vocabulary Check

Choose a word from the box to complete each sentence.

| memory |
| pattern |
| reasonable |
| remainder |
| strategy |

1. When 40, 400, and 4,000 are divided by 50, you can see a ___?___ in the quotients. *(page 180)*

2. The ⎡M+⎤ key on the calculator is a ___?___ key. *(page 199)*

3. Some problems can be solved by using more than one problem-solving ___?___ . *(page 200)*

4. If you multiply the whole-number quotient in the display of a calculator by the divisor and subtract this product from the dividend, you can find the ___?___ . *(page 199)*

5. An important part of the problem-solving process is to check whether your solution is ___?___ . *(page 188)*

Concept Check

> Compatible numbers are close to the original numbers, and they divide easily.

Complete the pattern. *(page 180)*

6. $60 \div 20 = 3$
   $600 \div 20 = 30$
   $6,000 \div 20 = n$

7. $120 \div 60 = n$
   $1,200 \div 60 = 20$
   $12,000 \div 60 = 200$

8. $240 \div 30 = 8$
   $2,400 \div 30 = n$
   $24,000 \div 30 = 800$

Name a pair of compatible numbers for each. *(page 182)*

9. $260 \div 77 \approx n$

10. $475 \div 58 \approx n$

11. $1,697 \div 26 \approx n$

12. $146 \div 43 \approx n$

13. $317 \div 26 \approx n$

14. $1,587 \div 68 \approx n$

Estimate the quotient. *(page 182)*

15. $18\overline{)83}$

16. $13\overline{)47}$

17. $29\overline{)85}$

18. $43\overline{)78}$

19. $47\overline{)287}$

20. $32\overline{)936}$

21. $24\overline{)389}$

22. $53\overline{)997}$

23. $36\overline{)3,750}$

24. $27\overline{)2,792}$

25. $42\overline{)8,106}$

26. $61\overline{)5,500}$

Look at each estimated quotient. Write whether the estimated quotient is *too large*, *too small*, or *just right*. *(page 186)*

27. $21\overline{)86}$ with estimate 5

28. $73\overline{)149}$ with estimate 2

29. $45\overline{)287}$ with estimate 5

30. $86\overline{)317}$ with estimate 4

Skill Check

Find the quotient. (page 180)

31. $20\overline{)60}$

32. $30\overline{)90}$

33. $10\overline{)800}$

34. $40\overline{)160}$

35. $50\overline{)250}$

36. $60\overline{)480}$

37. $70\overline{)6,300}$

38. $40\overline{)2,800}$

Estimate the quotient. (page 182)

39. $41\overline{)825}$

40. $12\overline{)710}$

41. $25\overline{)595}$

42. $71\overline{)139}$

43. $60\overline{)4,328}$

44. $54\overline{)3,050}$

45. $82\overline{)2,500}$

46. $93\overline{)8,000}$

Find the quotient. (pages 184, 186, 188, 194, 196)

47. $15\overline{)67}$

48. $25\overline{)85}$

49. $24\overline{)72}$

50. $36\overline{)547}$

51. $56\overline{)896}$

52. $35\overline{)770}$

53. $45\overline{)1,043}$

54. $19\overline{)986}$

55. $1,470 \div 42 = n$

56. $2,890 \div 65 = n$

57. $5,602 \div 12 = n$

58. $640 \div 32 = n$

59. $9,246 \div 23 = n$

60. $10,285 \div 17 = n$

Problem-Solving Check (pages 190, 200)

61. Heather needs to make 150 hearts for the crafts fair. She has made 48. If she completes 10 each day, about how many days will it take her to finish making the hearts?

62. Larry worked a total of 18 hours on Monday and Tuesday. If he worked 4 more hours on Tuesday than he did on Monday, how many hours did he work each day?

63. At a crafts fair, Alma sold 7 baskets for $15 each, 3 wreaths for $12 each, and a rug for $24. The cost of entering the fair was $15. After deducting the cost of her materials, Alma made $95. How much did her materials cost?

64. Ryan and his family will travel a total of 1,870 miles in 6 days. The first day they will drive 430 miles. To divide the travel evenly, about how many miles will they have to travel each of the remaining days?

WHAT DID I LEARN?

1. Estimate 421 ÷ 58. Explain your method.

2. Explain how to use mental math to find the quotient of 6,000 ÷ 20, and give the quotient.

3. Show each step as you find the quotient of 175 ÷ 42.

4. Read Exercise 3 on page 201. Follow the steps on the Problem-Solving Think Along worksheet to show how to solve this problem.

I can use a multiplication sentence to find a quotient.

Write About It

5. Describe a recent time when you or someone else in your family needed to divide a number by a two-digit number, other than at school.

6. Without actually dividing, decide whether the quotient of 459 ÷ 45 is greater than or less than 10. Explain how you determined this.

TEAMWORK Project

ORGANIZE A SPORTS ACTIVITY

There are many record-setting events in the sports world. One such event was the longest roller-skating marathon. The winner skated continuously for more than 344 hours.

Alvarez Takes First In Skate Race

On June 25, Seminole County sponsored the first ever roller-skate race. There were 48 skaters participating in the 2-mile race down Sand Lake Road. The street was closed to traffic, and fans lined the road to cheer on the competitors.

Find out about some other record-setting events. With your teammates, organize a sports activity for your team.

SHARE

Prepare a booklet describing the event. Explain how the activity was set up, what the rules were, and how the record-keeping was done. You can relate stories about the participants' experiences and give a statistic of a team member's record-setting performance.

Discuss interesting information about each team's event. Compare record-keeping methods. Combine the team booklets into one book of class records.

DECIDE

Create a sports activity in which all of your teammates can participate. Discuss the materials you will need and the way you will conduct the competition.

DO

Gather the necessary materials. Schedule times when individuals will perform the activity. Design record-keeping sheets. Carry out the planned event.

TALK ABOUT IT

☐ What interesting facts did you learn?

☐ If the class chooses to sponsor a school-wide sports activity, which event would work best for the school?

☐ Based on the performances of the participants, could an average time for an event be calculated?

☐ How was multiplication or division used in this project?

Activity

High-Low Division

Play the game with 1, 2, or 3 players. You will need a spinner and a calculator. Each player will also need a worksheet of blank grids like the ones above.

The first player calls "high" or "low" to tell the other players whether to try to form a problem with the greatest or the least quotient. The first player then spins the spinner. Each player writes the number shown on the spinner until all the boxes in the first grid are full.

Each player solves his or her problem and then checks the answer with the

calculator. The player with the greatest (or least) correct quotient wins the round and receives a score of 1 point.

The second player then spins numbers for the next round. The game continues until the grids are filled.

The winner is the player with the most points at the end of the game.

Challenge

Critical Thinking

What is the smallest number that gives a remainder of 1 when it is divided by each of the following? What is the pattern in the answers?

1. 2 and 3   **6.** 7 and 3
2. 2 and 5   **7.** 2 and 7
3. 3 and 5   **8.** 4 and 5
4. 5 and 7   **9.** 2, 3, and 7
5. 2, 3, and 5   **10.** 3, 4, and 5

Calculator

Radio Station WMON is giving away $1,000,000 at the rate of $50 an hour.

1. Will it take more than two years to give away the money?
2. Will it take more than three years to give away the money?

Use a calculator to find about how long it will take to give away the money. Explain your answer.

Write the letter of the correct answer.

1. Which is in order from least to greatest?

A. 12,497; 12,507; 12,521
B. 12,497; 12,521; 12,507
C. 12,507; 12,497; 12,521
D. 12,521; 12,507; 12,497

2. What is the value of the digit 5 in 12.157?

A. 0.05   B. 0.5
C. 5   D. 50

3. What is 25.39 rounded to the nearest whole number?

A. 24   B. 25
C. 26   D. 30

4.
$$3,376$$
$$+2,941$$

A. 5,317   B. 6,217
C. 6,317   D. not here

5. $23.7 - 4.9 = n$

A. 19.2   B. 19.8
C. 21.8   D. not here

6. $468 \times 3 = n$

A. 1,384   B. 1,404
C. 4,112   D. not here

7. $300 \times 40 = n$

A. 120   B. 1,200
C. 12,000   D. 120,000

8. $52 \times 17 = n$

A. 416   B. 874
C. 884   D. not here

9. Which triangle is an equilateral triangle?

A.   B.

C.   D.

10. Which figure shows a slide?

A.   B.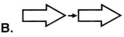

C.   D.

11. Jack is reading a 312-page book. He has already read 62 pages. If Jack needs to finish the book in 6 days, about how many pages should he read each day?

A. about 30 pages B. about 40 pages
C. about 50 pages D. about 60 pages

12. A fifth-grade class has 4 more girls than boys. If there are 28 students in the class, how many of them are girls?

A. 12 girls   B. 14 girls
C. 16 girls   D. 18 girls

CHAPTER 7

STATISTICS AND GRAPHING

Did you know...

...that the earliest restaurant was opened in 1725 in Madrid, Spain?

TALK ABOUT IT

A Mexican-restaurant owner keeps a record of his income each month. He wants to determine his busiest months. How can he organize the data to show the pattern of income for the year?

EXPLORING

Sample Groups

Work Together

Building Understanding

Brian's favorite sport is soccer. He thinks most fifth graders' favorite sport is soccer. He predicted 15 students in his class would name soccer as their favorite sport. He surveyed his class and organized the data in a frequency table.

Brian's Prediction					
Choice	Archery	Baseball	Basketball	Football	Soccer
Votes	1	5	4	5	15

Brian's Survey					
Choice	Archery	Baseball	Basketball	Football	Soccer
Votes	8	7	3	10	2

← **Frequency tables** show how often events occur.

TALK ABOUT IT

- Why do you think his prediction was so different from the survey?

- What do you think would happen if Brian surveyed a different fifth-grade class?

One way to find the sport that most fifth graders like best is to ask a small group, or **sample group,** of fifth graders. The larger your sample group is, and the more it is like most fifth graders, the better it is.

One way to choose a sample group is to choose names at **random.** When names are selected at random, all students have the same chance of being chosen. One way to select a random group is by drawing names from a bag.

Suggestions for sample groups were given by these students:

Susan	Bill	Andre
10 Art Club members 10 chorus members 10 girls	10 eleven-year-olds 10 boys 10 Math Club members	50 fifth graders chosen at random

- Which sample group is best? Why?

Making the Connection

A fifth-grade class won $50 in a safety contest. Predict how most of the class would spend the money. Then survey a sample group from your class.

- With a partner, select a sample group.

- Decide what choices to include in your survey.

- Decide how you will record the data.

- Conduct your survey.

- Organize the data.

TALK ABOUT IT

- How large is your sample group, and how did you select it?

- What was the most frequent choice of your sample group?

- How do the results of your sample group differ from those of other sample groups?

- How do you think the results would have differed if you had surveyed only students who participate in sports?

Checking Understanding

1. Tell which sample group would better predict the choice of fifth graders. Defend your answer.

   30 Math Club members or 50 fifth-grade students chosen at random

Choose a word or words from the box to complete each sentence.

| predict |
| random |
| sample group |
| survey |

2. When you choose a group at __?__, all students have the same chance of being chosen.

3. A __?__ can be conducted to find the most frequent choice of a group.

4. Data collected from a __?__ can help you __?__ the most frequent choice of a larger group.

RANGE, MODE, MEDIAN, AND MEAN

Carla surveyed fifth-grade students to find out how many hours a week they watch television. The frequency table shows the results of Carla's survey.

Weekly Hours of TV Watched					
Student	Kyle	Leandra	Tanya	Jody	Steven
Hours	8	10	5	2	5

Use connecting cubes to model the number of hours each student watches television. Find the difference between the number of cubes in the tallest and the shortest stacks. This is called the **range.**
$10 - 2 = 8$ So, the range is 8.

Look for stacks that have the same number of cubes. The number that appears most often is 5. So, 5 is the **mode**.

Place the stacks of cubes in order from greatest to least. The number in the middle stack contains 5 cubes. So, 5 is the **median**.

Put the cubes in one stack. Separate the stack into five equal stacks. Count the cubes in each new stack. This number, called the **mean,** is the average number of cubes in the original stacks. You can compute the mean.

Find the total number of cubes.	Divide by the number of stacks.
$8 + 10 + 5 + 2 + 5 = 30$	$30 \div 5 = 6$

Talk About It

▶ In what ways are the median and the mode different?

▶ In what ways do the median and the mode differ from the mean? the range?

Check for Understanding

Find the range, mode, median, and mean for each set of data.

1. 7, 3, 2, 3, 5

2. 19, 9, 7, 5, 5

3. 6, 10, 18, 6, 25

Connection, pages 460–461

Practice

Find the range, mode, median, and mean.

4. $27, 31, 34, 31, 32$

5. $55, 59, 60, 59, 57$

6. $15, 20, 25, 15, 30$

7. $30, 45, 50, 45, 65$

8. $24, 37, 42, 15, 42$

9. $\$28, \$42, \$59, \$42, \$64$

10. $\$271, \$298, \$271$

11. $575, 630, 720, 575, 525$

12. $13, 22, 13, 15, 12$

Mixed Applications

13. A football team has scored 14 points, 7 points, 10 points, and 17 points in its last four games. Find the mean of the points scored in the four games.

14. **Critical Thinking** Sheila scored 95, 82, 90, and 83 on four tests. After the fifth test, the mode of her scores was 83. What did she score on the fifth test?

15. Buses will be used to take students to a football game. How many buses will be needed if 225 tickets are sold and each bus holds 48 people?

16. A math quiz has 25 problems. If each problem has a value of 4 points, how many problems did Pedro miss if he scored 84?

CALCULATOR

You can use a calculator to find the mean of a set of data.

Example Sharon scored 86, 92, 95, 100, and 92 on five tests. What is her average score?

Press $\boxed{86}$ $\boxed{+}$ $\boxed{92}$ $\boxed{+}$ $\boxed{95}$ $\boxed{+}$ $\boxed{100}$ $\boxed{+}$ $\boxed{92}$ $\boxed{=}$

$\boxed{465.}$ $\boxed{\div}$ $\boxed{5}$ $\boxed{=}$ $\boxed{93.}$

Find the mean of each set of data.

17. 59, 63, 53, 75, 65

18. 135, 375, 450

19. 13, 19, 28, 13, 17

How can a set of data have more than one mode?

W R A P
U P...

PICTOGRAPHS

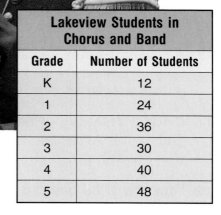

Loren surveyed students at Lakeview School to find out how many participate in chorus and band. She recorded the results in a frequency table. She made a pictograph to compare the numbers.

A pictograph uses a **key** to tell how many students are shown by each symbol in the graph.

Talk About It

▶ How many students are represented by one symbol in Loren's key?

▶ How many students does half a symbol represent?

▶ What problems will Loren have if she uses one symbol to represent each student?

▶ How can Loren show 30 if she chooses one symbol to represent 12 students?

▶ What is the greatest number that Loren can use as her key if she wants to have all whole symbols?

Check for Understanding

Use the data that shows each grade's Computer Club membership. Plan a pictograph.

1. What title would you use?

2. Tell what you would label each column.

3. Where would you write the grade levels?

4. What symbol would you use to represent students?

5. How many students would each symbol represent?

6. What are two questions that could be answered by using your graph?

Lakeview Students in Chorus and Band	
Grade	Number of Students
K	12
1	24
2	36
3	30
4	40
5	48

Lakeview Students in Chorus and Band	
Grade	Number of Students
K	●●●
1	●●●●●●
2	●●●●●●●●●
3	●●●●●●●◖
4	●●●●●●●●●●
5	●●●●●●●●●●●●

Key ● = 4 students

Computer Club Data	
Grade	Number of Club Members
K	4
1	7
2	10
3	10
4	12
5	8
6	3

Practice

Use the pictograph for Exercises 7–9.

7. Which type of book was checked out most often in one week?

8. How many joke books were checked out?

9. How many fiction and science fiction books were checked out in one week?

10. Use the data from the table to make a pictograph. Title and label your graph and choose a key.

Types of Books Checked Out from Library in One Week	
Type of Book	**Number of Books**
Biography	📖📖📖📖📖📖📖
Fiction	📖📖📖📖📖📖📖📖📖📖
Science fiction	📖📖📖📖
Puzzles	📖📖📖📖
Joke book	📖📖📖
History	📖📖📖📖

Key 📖 = 2 books

Students Playing Musical Instruments							
Type of Instrument	Guitar	Piano	Accordion	Recorder	Flute	Organ	Violin
Number of Students	8	48	6	14	16	4	12

Mixed Applications

11. Write a Question Make up a question that can be answered by using the pictograph you made in Exercise 10.

12. If the key in a pictograph has a symbol that represents 6 students, how many symbols will be used to show 75 students?

13. A flute sells for $450. If the rental fee, $25 a month, can be used toward the purchase of the flute, how many months will it take to pay for the flute?

14. There were 65 students in the band at the end of the year. If twelve students joined and seven left the band, how many students were in the band at the start?

VISUAL THINKING

The symbols used in some pictographs indicate the subject of the graphs.

For each symbol shown, describe the kind of information that might be on the graph.

15.

16.

17.

18.

BAR GRAPHS

The table shows the data Miss Whittier's class collected from fifth graders about their family homes.

Miss Whittier's students tallied and then counted their data. They wanted to display the data so that it could be read quickly and easily. They decided to make a bar graph. A bar graph has these parts.

- A bar graph has a **title.**

- Each part of the graph has a **label.**

- A **scale** is used on the graph to tell what each unit length represents.

- Bars can be drawn either vertically or horizontally.

Bar graphs make it easy to compare data that can be counted. The title, labels, and scale help you understand the information on the bar graph.

Family Homes of Fifth Graders		
Type of Home	**Number of Students**	
Apartment	⁄⁄⁄⁄ ⁄⁄⁄⁄ ⁄⁄⁄⁄ ⁄⁄⁄⁄ ⁄⁄⁄⁄	25
Condominium	////	4
Duplex	⁄⁄⁄⁄ ⁄⁄⁄⁄	10
House	⁄⁄⁄⁄ ⁄⁄⁄⁄ ⁄⁄⁄⁄ ⁄⁄⁄⁄ ⁄⁄⁄⁄ /	26
Mobile home	⁄⁄⁄⁄ ///	8

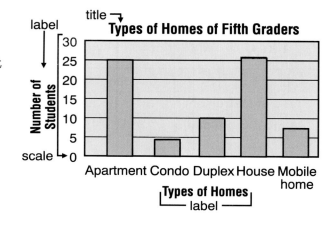

Talk About It

▶ Is a bar graph a reasonable way to show the data? Explain.

▶ How does a bar graph make the data easy to read?

▶ How many students does each unit length represent?

▶ How do you read a bar that ends between unit lengths?

Check for Understanding

Use the bar graph for Exercises 1–3.

1. About how many more students live in houses than in apartments?

2. About how many more students live in apartments than in mobile homes?

3. About how many students do not live in a house?

Practice

Use the bar graph about Longwood Elementary School for Exercises 4–7.

4. What is each unit length shown on the scale?

5. Are there more students in first grade or fourth grade?

6. Which grades have fewer than 120 students?

7. How many students are in kindergarten?

8. A class survey showed the type of fast food preferred by each student. Use the data from the table to make a bar graph. Choose a scale, title and label your graph, and then color in the bars.

Students at Longwood Elementary

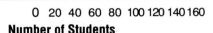

Grades	
Kindergarten	
First	
Second	
Third	
Fourth	
Fifth	

0 20 40 60 80 100 120 140 160
Number of Students

Favorite Fast Food	
Food	Number of Students
Chicken	1
Hamburgers	8
Pizza	12
Tacos	4
Other	3

Mixed Applications

Use the bar graph about school fund-raising projects for Exercises 9–11.

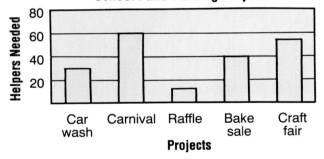

School Fund-Raising Projects

Helpers Needed

80
60
40
20

Car wash   Carnival   Raffle   Bake sale   Craft fair

Projects

9. Which project needs the most helpers?

10. **Analyze Data** How many more helpers are needed at the carnival than at the bake sale?

11. Which project represents the median for all helpers needed?

Solve.

12. At the bake sale, 120 cookies were sold. Half of the cookies were oatmeal. The rest were raisin or carob-chip. If there were 10 more carob-chip cookies than raisin, how many cookies were carob-chip?

13. At the car wash, 5 cars were washed the first hour, 10 cars the second hour, and 15 cars the third hour. If the pattern continues, how many cars will be washed the sixth hour?

Would you rather read a pictograph or a bar graph? Explain.

WRAP UP...

CHOOSING THE APPROPRIATE SCALE

There are 179 fifth graders in Jay's school. Jay surveyed them to find how they travel to and from school. The frequency table shows his results. He wants to choose a scale so he can display his data on a graph.

My data includes numbers from 4 to 63. If I start my scale at zero and number each line to 63, I'll run out of room on my paper.

Transportation					
Type	Car	Bicycle	School bus	Walk	Van
Number of Students	43	30	63	39	4

The scale is made up of **intervals**, or units that are equal in number.

Jay drew three different scales:

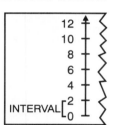

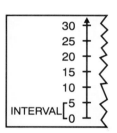

Jay's First Attempt
Each interval stands for 1 person.

Jay's Second Attempt
Each interval stands for 2 persons.

Jay's Third Attempt
Each interval stands for 5 persons.

Talk About It

▶ With what number should you start each scale?

▶ How are Jay's attempts different? How are they similar?

▶ What is a reasonable scale for Jay's set of data? Explain.

Check for Understanding

Choose the most reasonable scale for the set of data. Write **a**, **b**, or **c.** Explain your choice.

1.

Favorite Kinds of Books				
Books	Poetry	Biography	Fiction	Science Fiction
Number of Students	15	19	25	10

a.
100
80
60
40
20
0

b.
25
20
15
10
5
0

c.
20
14
12
8
2
0

Practice

Choose the most reasonable scale for each set of data. Write **a**, **b**, or **c**.

2.

Fifth-Grade Girls					
Bicycle Color	Green	Pink	Purple	White	Other
Number of Students	10	20	25	5	18

a. 10, 8, 6, 4, 2, 0
b. 25, 20, 15, 10, 5, 0
c. 15, 12, 9, 6, 3, 0

3.

Favorite Types of Television Shows					
Shows	Cartoon	Comedy	Drama	News	Sports
Number of Students	5	8	4	2	3

a. 100, 80, 60, 40, 20, 0
b. 75, 60, 45, 30, 15, 0
c. 10, 8, 6, 4, 2, 0

4.

After-School Activities					
Activity	Band	Chorus	Computer	Newspaper	Track
Number of Students	75	36	12	21	53

a. 25, 20, 15, 10, 5, 0
b. 100, 80, 60, 40, 20, 0
c. 30, 24, 18, 12, 6, 0

Mixed Applications

5. Tyrone is taking a survey of 125 fifth-grade students. If there are 15 more boys than girls, how many students are boys and how many are girls?

6. **Critical Thinking** Would it be reasonable to mark a scale off in ones if the graph is going to show the numbers of different kinds of books in a library? Explain.

7. **Making Decisions** If a graph is to show the number of pets owned by students in a class of 30, do you think the scale should be marked off in ones, tens, or fifties? Explain.

8. Pauline wants to know how many copies of her survey she should make. Each student will receive one copy. If there are 29 students in each of 3 classes and 32 students in each of 2 classes, how many copies should she make?

What is true of the intervals of all scales?

WRAP UP...

PROBLEM SOLVING

Choose a Strategy

Understand
Plan
Solve
Look Back

As a gift to a class in Panama, Mr. Snyder's students made a friendship quilt. First, the students made 36 small quilt squares. Then, they began sewing 4 small squares together to make 1 larger square. If it took 18 minutes to make 1 larger square, how long did it take to sew all the small squares into larger squares?

Sometimes you can use one of several strategies to solve a problem.

What strategies can you use for this problem? You can draw a diagram or make a table.

Strategy: Draw a Diagram

You can *draw a diagram* to help you solve the problem.

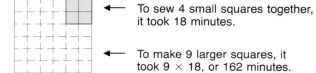

← To sew 4 small squares together, it took 18 minutes.

← To make 9 larger squares, it took 9 × 18, or 162 minutes.

Strategy: Make a Table

You can *make a table* to help you find the answer.

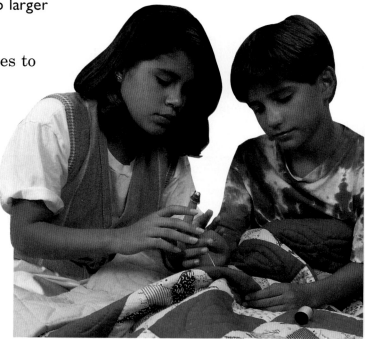

MULTICULTURAL NOTE: Quilting involves sewing together two layers of cloth with insulating material between. During colonial times in the United States, people made quilts at parties called quilting bees.

	× 2	× 3	× 4	× 5	× 6	× 7	× 8	× 9
Squares Used	4	8	12	16	20	24	28	32	36
Time in Minutes	18	36	54	72	90	108	126	144	162
	× 2	× 3	× 4	× 5	× 6	× 7	× 8	× 9

So, the table shows it took 162 minutes to make the larger squares.

 WHAT IF... ... the class made 64 small squares? How long would it take the class to sew them into larger squares?

220

Mixed Applications ➡ **STRATEGIES**

Work Backward • Draw a Diagram
• Make a Table • Guess and Check
• Write a Number Sentence

Choose a strategy and solve.

1 At the opening of a school carnival, a booth has 108 prizes to give away. If every 15 minutes 9 prizes are given away, how long will it take to give away all the prizes?

2 Sonia is making a pot holder with 42 loops. If her pattern uses 4 red loops for every 6 loops in the design, how many red loops will be used for the pot holder?

3 A pottery booth sold a total of 32 pieces of pottery. If 8 more pieces were sold in the afternoon than in the morning, how many pieces were sold in the afternoon?

4 An industrial arts class can complete 5 projects every 9 weeks. How many projects can 5 classes complete in the 36 weeks of the school year?

5 Construction paper is sold in packages of 24 sheets. An art teacher has 3 classes with 28 students in each class and 2 classes with 30 students in each class. How many packages of paper should she buy if each student needs one sheet?

6 When Neil arrived home after purchasing art supplies, he had $4.35. He bought paper for $3.89, paint for $5.19, and brushes for $4.12. He received a $2.00 discount on his total bill. How much money did he have to start?

7 Two buses will transport people to an art festival. Each bus holds 52 people. A total of 1,248 people will be transported. If each bus makes the same number of trips, how many trips will each bus make?

8 At an outdoor art show, there were five different booths on a block. Photography was on the corner, and pottery was between photography and woodworking. Jewelry was between woodworking and pottery. If the oil paintings were next to jewelry and pottery, in what order were the five booths on the block?

More Practice, Lesson 7.6, page H59

Choose a strategy and solve.

1. Jason took some baseball cards to Matt's house. Matt gave Jason 12 cards. Jason gave Matt 5 cards. Jason then had 23 cards. How many cards did Jason have when he went to Matt's house?

2. It takes Meredith about 25 minutes to type 2 pages of her report. If she has a total of 10 pages to type, about how long will it take her to type the report?

Some problems can be solved using more than one strategy.

Write the value of the underlined digit.

3. 4.5̲27

4. 12.40̲6

5. 15.28̲5

6. 25.7̲50

Complete each number sentence.

7. 6.55 + ■ = 6.55

8. 9.8 + 6.3 = ■ + 9.8

9. 7.25 + (3.75 + 2.50) = (7.25 + ■) + 2.50

Multiply.

10. 485
   × 4

11. 7,081
   × 8

12. 5,902
   × 8

13. 6,875
   × 16

14. 809
   × 25

Identify each angle. Write *right, acute,* or *obtuse.*

15.

16.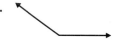

17.

18.

Use the rules for divisibility to decide whether the first number is divisible by the second. Write *yes* or *no.*

19. 794; 2

20. 534; 3

21. 507; 5

22. 6,480; 10

23. 642; 3

Estimate.

24. 8)555

25. 3)259

26. 6)3,780

27. 9)8,000

28. 7)6,498

Divide.

29. 12)348

30. 36)2,358

31. 25)2,515

32. 43)5,762

33. 28)2,688

ASIA

Bangladesh

Making Inferences

**Average Rainfall for
Chittagong, Bangladesh**

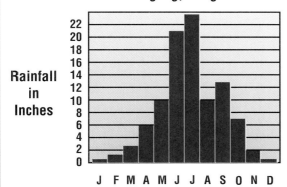

Rainfall
in
Inches

J F M A M J J A S O N D
Months of the Year

You can use a graph to help you compare data. You can also use a graph to answer questions whose answers are not directly shown by the data. When you do this kind of thinking, you are **making an inference.** Study the graph.

Bangladesh is a small country in Asia on the Indian Ocean. Because of the country's location, its weather changes often during the year. It alternates from very dry weather to periods of very heavy rains. These rains are helpful for growing rice, the largest crop of Bangladesh. The rainy season is called the *monsoon* season. During that time people often use waterways instead of roads as transportation.

Use the graph to answer the questions.

1. Which month has the most rainfall?

2. Which months have the least rainfall?

3. What season of the year do you think is the monsoon season?

4. Why do you think rice is the leading crop in Bangladesh?

5. Name a plant that you would *not* expect to find in Bangladesh.

6. Why do you think waterways are more important transportation routes than paved highways in Bangladesh?

7. Estimate the yearly rainfall in Chittagong, Bangladesh.

8. How does the yearly rainfall in Chittagong compare with the rainfall in your town?

LINE GRAPHS

Cher went on a bicycle trip. She made a table to record her average miles per hour for each hour of her trip.

Average Miles Per Hour for Each Hour of Cher's Trip					
Hours	1	2	3	4	5
Average Miles Per Hour	15	10	0	15	5

She recorded the data in a line graph. **Line graphs** are used to make comparisons and show changes over time. Bar graphs and pictographs are used to compare data that is counted. A bar graph has one scale, and a pictograph has a scale and a key. A line graph has a scale on the vertical and the horizontal axis.

AVERAGE MILES PER HOUR
For Each Hour of Cher's Trip

label → | Average Miles Per Hour (vertical axis) — 25, 20, 15, 10, 5, 0 — Hours (label) 1, 2, 3, 4, 5 → horizontal axis

Talk About It

▶ Why is a line graph a good choice to compare the average miles per hour Cher rode for each hour of her trip?

▶ What does each mark on the **vertical axis,** or left side of the line graph, represent?

▶ What does each mark on the **horizontal axis,** or bottom line, represent?

▶ How do you think Cher chose the scale on the vertical axis?

▶ What does each point on the graph represent?

▶ Which part of the graph shows whether there is an increase, a decrease, or no change in the miles?

Check for Understanding

Use the line graph for Exercises 1–2.

1. What is represented by the scale on the vertical axis?

2. What does the line show?

AVERAGE MILES PER HOUR
For Each Hour of Cassandra's Trip

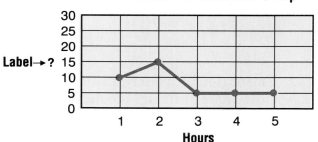

Practice

Use the line graph for Exercises 3–8.

3. In which month did the most new members join?

4. In which two months did the same number of new members join?

5. How many new members were there in May?

6. Between which two months was there the greatest increase in new members?

7. How many new members were there for the first two months of the year?

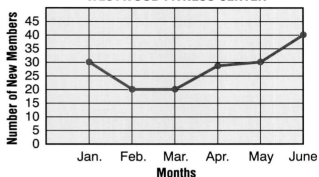

NEW MEMBERS AT WESTWOOD FITNESS CENTER

8. **Analyze Data** In which month was there a decrease in membership growth and in which months was there an increase in membership growth?

Mixed Applications

9. One day each week, 48 students participate in an aerobics class. If 3 different students lead the class each week, how many weeks will it take for all the students to lead the class?

10. Mario joined a running club that meets 3 days a week. He runs for 15 minutes each day the club meets. Mario also runs on weekends for 20 minutes each day. For how many minutes does he run each week?

CRITICAL THINKING

A Venn diagram uses geometric shapes to show relationships.

Use this Venn diagram of student participation in school sports for Exercises 11–13.

11. How many students participate only in basketball?

12. How many students participate in both soccer and baseball, but not in basketball?

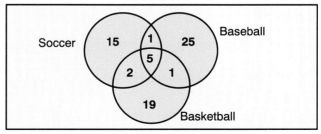

STUDENTS PARTICIPATING IN SPORTS

13. What is the total number of students participating in these three sports?

Why does the distance between the lines on a line graph need to be the same?

WRAP UP...

MAKING A LINE GRAPH

Paula's family bought a rowing machine. Paula could easily row 200 times in the first 5 minutes. She made a table showing her rate of rowing in 5-minute intervals for 30 minutes. You can make a line graph using the data from the table to show the changes in her rowing rate over time.

Rowing rate per 5 minutes	200	200	150	150	0	200
Time in minutes	5	10	15	20	25	30

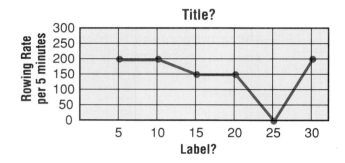

Talk About It

▶ What should the title of the graph be?

▶ What does each unit on the horizontal axis represent? on the vertical axis?

▶ How should you label the horizontal axis?

▶ What do you think happened after 25 minutes?

Check for Understanding

Use the data on the line graph for Exercises 1–3.

1. What are some other possible titles for the graph?

2. In what way are the labels helpful?

3. What are the intervals of the horizontal axis and the vertical axis?

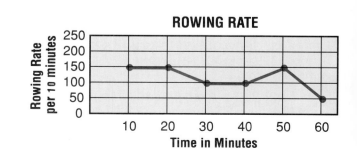

Practice

4. Use the data in the table to make a line graph.

Average Yearly Muffin Sales					
Year	1989	1990	1991	1992	1993
Average Sales	$18,000	$25,000	$43,000	$35,000	$60,000

Use the line graph for Exercises 5–7.

5. What should the label be on the vertical axis? on the horizontal axis?

6. What happened to the total sales between January and February?

7. Would it be reasonable to use intervals of $1,000? Explain.

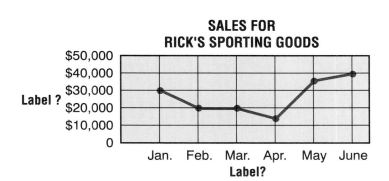

SALES FOR
RICK'S SPORTING GOODS

Mixed Applications

Solve.

8. Mai's mother is going to buy Mai and her sister each a pair of skates. If the total price for each pair of skates is $23.45, how much change will Mai's mother receive from $50.00?

9. **Mental Math** Estimate to determine whether $30.00 will be enough for Angelo to buy a tennis racket for $18.95, tennis balls for $0.99, and a shirt for $10.99.

Use the data in the table for Exercises 10–12.

10. If you make a line graph of the data, what will the intervals be in the scale on the vertical axis?

11. Why is a line graph a good way to display this data?

12. **Analyze Data** In which hours did the amount of rain that fell measure more than 0.10 cm?

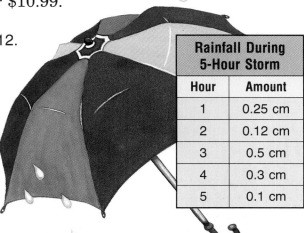

Rainfall During 5-Hour Storm	
Hour	Amount
1	0.25 cm
2	0.12 cm
3	0.5 cm
4	0.3 cm
5	0.1 cm

When do you think it is appropriate to use a line graph to show data?

W R A P
U P . . .

EXPLORING

Circle Graphs

Building Understanding

Miss Colletti's class has 36 students. She gave them a choice of vegetables for lunch. Of the students, $\frac{1}{2}$ chose green beans, $\frac{1}{4}$ preferred corn, and $\frac{1}{4}$ selected beets.

The data from Miss Colletti's class can be shown on a **circle graph.** Fraction-circle pieces can be put together to show a whole circle. Use circle pieces to help you understand and make a circle graph.

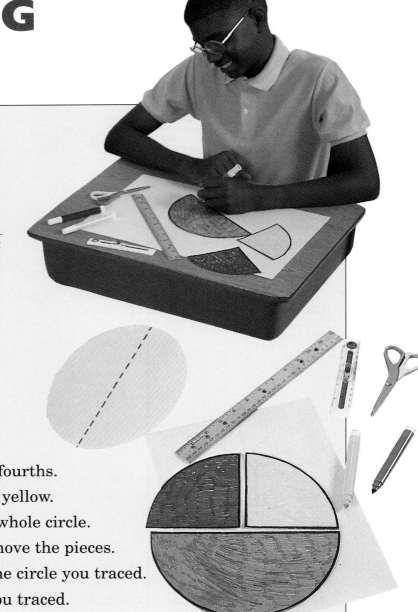

- Mark and cut out a circle.

- Cut the circle in half.

- Color one half of the circle green. Cut the other half in half to make fourths.

- Color one fourth red and the other yellow.

- Put the pieces together to make a whole circle.

- Trace around the whole circle. Remove the pieces.

- Put the red and yellow pieces on the circle you traced.

- Put the green piece on the circle you traced.

TALK ABOUT IT

- How is the whole class represented?

- What section of the circle shows the part of the class that chose green beans?

- What do you think the red and the yellow sections of the circle represent?

228

Making the Connection

A circle graph shows how parts are related to the whole. It also shows how the parts are related to each other.

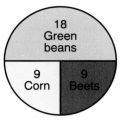

Vegetable Choices of 36 Students

18 Green beans
9 Corn
9 Beets

TALK ABOUT IT

- What is the title of this graph?

- How is each part of the circle graph labeled?

- How does the part of the class that prefers corn compare with the part of the class that prefers beets?

- How does the part of the class that prefers green beans compare with the part of the class that prefers beets?

- How would you change the graph if the same number of students liked green beans, corn, and beets?

- How would the graph change if there were 6 vegetable choices and some students chose each?

Checking Understanding

Use circle pieces to draw graphs that show the number of people represented by each part of the circle.

1. Miss Colletti brought juice for the 36 students at the class picnic. Of the students, $\frac{3}{4}$ wanted apple juice and $\frac{1}{4}$ wanted grape juice. Show this in a circle graph.

2. During the picnic, $\frac{1}{4}$ of the students entered sack races, $\frac{1}{4}$ played horseshoes, $\frac{1}{4}$ played softball, and $\frac{1}{4}$ ran in the three-legged race. Show this in a circle graph.

3. The picnic was attended by 24 parents who helped Miss Colletti. Of the parents, $\frac{1}{2}$ helped serve food, $\frac{1}{4}$ helped with games, and $\frac{1}{4}$ read stories to the students. Show this in a circle graph.

More Practice, Lesson 7.9, page H60

COMPARING GRAPHS

You can use graphs to present facts in different ways. Graphs are often easier to understand than written descriptions because they show a large amount of information in picture form. While graphs have some things in common, each type has advantages and disadvantages.

Bar Graphs

Advantages
- used with countable data
- used to compare facts about groups
- show patterns in data

Disadvantages
- bars nearly the same length are difficult to compare
- scale can be used to make small differences look large

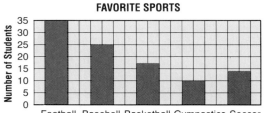

FAVORITE SPORTS

Pictographs

Advantages
- used with countable data
- used to compare facts about groups

Disadvantages
- parts of pictures may be needed to show exact amounts
- calculations may be needed for exact amounts

FAVORITE SPORTS

Football	●●●●●●●●●●●●●●●●
Baseball	●●●●●●●●●●●
Basketball	●●●●●●●●
Gymnastics	●●●●●
Soccer	●●●●●●●
	● = 2 students

Line Graphs

Advantages
- used for comparisons
- show changes over time

Disadvantage
- not the best to use when counting objects

AMOUNT OF PRACTICE TIME

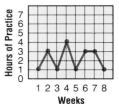

Circle Graphs

Advantage
- good when comparing part of a group to whole group

Disadvantage
- difficult to use when the parts of the number cannot be shown by simple fractions

STUDENTS' FAVORITE CLUBS

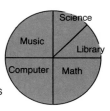

Check for Understanding

1. Which type of graph would you use to show how you usually spend all 24 hours of a weekday?

2. Which type of graph would you use to show the number of pages read each month during a year?

Practice

Choose a type of graph for Exercises 3–6. Explain your choice.

3. yearly incomes for several different jobs

4. height development for boys

5. types of books preferred by a fifth-grade class

6. how a student spends $10

Mixed Applications

Use the data in the table for Exercises 7–9.

7. Would you use a line graph to display this data? Explain.

8. **Analyze Data** What type of graph would you use to display this data? Explain.

9. What is the total number of students surveyed?

10. Maureen's test scores in math are 95, 92, 83, and 78. What is the mean of her test scores?

11. There are 53 students in the chorus. If there are 15 more girls than boys, how many boys and how many girls are in the chorus?

Favorite Subject	
Subject	Number of Students
English	6
Math	8
Social studies	7
Science	5
Music	4

MIXED REVIEW

Estimate.

1. $12\overline{)230}$ **2.** $18\overline{)395}$ **3.** $38\overline{)150}$ **4.** $41\overline{)280}$ **5.** $28\overline{)3,217}$

Find the sum or difference.

6. $\begin{array}{r} 2.345 \\ +\,9.745 \end{array}$ **7.** $\begin{array}{r} 8.975 \\ -\,5.896 \end{array}$ **8.** $\begin{array}{r} 12.427 \\ +\,89.582 \end{array}$ **9.** $\begin{array}{r} 14.312 \\ +\,38.721 \end{array}$ **10.** $\begin{array}{r} 25.602 \\ -\,7.093 \end{array}$

Could a circle graph be used for the data in the Favorite Subject table? Explain.

WRAP UP...

PROBLEM SOLVING

Use Logical Reasoning

Leah, Dennis, Dena, and Eli own one vehicle each. Altogether, they own a moped, a station wagon, a jeep, and a van. Eli does not own a van or a jeep. Leah went to a restaurant with the owner of the van. Dena owns a moped. Which vehicle does Dennis own?

▶ **UNDERSTAND**

What are you asked to find?

What facts are given?

▶ **PLAN**

How can you solve the problem?

You can make a table to organize the data.

▶ **SOLVE**

How can you carry out your plan?

Use logical reasoning to show all the possibilities. Since each person owns one vehicle, there can be only one *yes* in each row and column.

A.	Van	Jeep	Station Wagon	Moped
Leah				No
Dennis				No
Dena	No	No	No	Yes
Eli				No

B.	Van	Jeep	Station Wagon	Moped
Leah			No	No
Dennis			No	No
Dena	No	No	No	Yes
Eli	No	No	Yes	No

C.	Van	Jeep	Station Wagon	Moped
Leah	No	Yes	No	No
Dennis	Yes	No	No	No
Dena	No	No	No	Yes
Eli	No	No	Yes	No

A. Dena owns a moped.

B. Since Eli does not own the van, jeep, or moped, he must own the station wagon.

C. Since Leah does not own the van, she must own the jeep.

So, Dennis must own the van.

▶ **LOOK BACK**

How can you make sure your answers make sense?

 WHAT IF... . . . the problem did not state that Dena owns a moped? Could you solve the problem? Explain.

232

Apply

Organize the information in a table. Use logical reasoning to solve.

(1) Diego, Becky, Leon, and Lonnie won the first four prizes in an art contest. Diego won second prize. Lonnie did not win third prize. Leon won fourth prize. What prize did Becky win?

(2) Andy, Pete, and Bea each bring a different type of sandwich for lunch. One brings peanut butter, one brings cheese, and one brings meat. Andy does not like meat, and Pete does not like meat or cheese. Who brings each sandwich?

| Mixed Applications | ⟹ | STRATEGIES | Write a Number Sentence • Find a Pattern • Use Estimation • Work Backward |

Choose a strategy and solve.

(3) Molly wants to buy a sweater that costs $38. If she saves $7 each week from her baby-sitting job, how many weeks will it take her to earn enough money?

(4) Brian earns $2.75 an hour for baby-sitting. If he baby-sits from 7:00 P.M. to 12:45 A.M., about how much will he earn?

(5) Tomas mows lawns for 2 hours the first week, 4 hours the second week, and 6 hours the third week. If he follows this pattern, for how many hours will he mow lawns in the eighth week?

(6) Leslie wants to earn $1,000 mowing lawns this summer. If she works for 10 weeks and mows 5 lawns each week, how much should she charge for each lawn?

WRITER'S CORNER

(7) Write a problem in which logical reasoning is used to arrive at the table given below. Exchange with a partner. Solve.

Monday	Tuesday	Wednesday	Thursday
98°	85°	75°	82°

GRAPHING
Ordered Pairs

Kelly's class planned to visit the museums at Central State University. To help the students find the museums, their teacher put a grid over a map of the campus.

You can locate points on a grid by using an **ordered pair** of numbers. The two numbers in an ordered pair are called **coordinates.** The first number tells how far to move to the right. The second number tells how far up to move.

To locate point *A*, follow these steps:

- Start at coordinates (0,0).

- Move 7 spaces to the right.

- Move up 4 spaces to the parking lot represented by point *A*.

  So, the location of the parking lot has the coordinates (7,4).

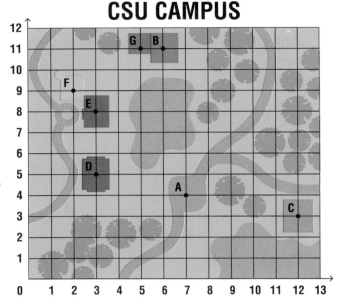

CSU CAMPUS

Legend

A — Parking lot
B — Space Museum
C — Natural History Museum
D — Art Museum
E — Marine Sciences Museum
F — Planetarium
G — Snack Shack

Talk About it

▶ Why can't you locate the parking lot using the coordinates (4,7)?

▶ What are the coordinates of the Space Museum?

▶ Can you use the coordinates (11,6) to find the Space Museum? Explain.

Check for Understanding

Name the building at each of the following coordinates.

1. (2,9)   **2.** (3,8)   **3.** (6,11)   **4.** (5,11)

Name the coordinates of each location.

5. Snack Shack   **6.** Art Museum   **7.** Natural History Museum

Practice

Use the grid and legend for Exercises 8–15. Name the coordinates of each location.

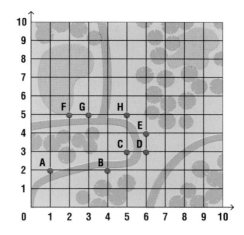

Legend
A — Grocery store
B — School
C — Post Office
D — Neighbor's house
E — Park
F — Lake
G — Library
H — Friend's house

8. School

9. Lake

10. Library

11. Park

Name the building at each of the following coordinates.

12. (5,3)   **13.** (5,5)   **14.** (1,2)   **15.** (6,3)

Mixed Applications

16. Make a grid like the one above. Mark points at coordinates (1,1), (2,2), (3,3), (4,4), and (5,5). Connect the points. What figure did you make?

17. Use the grid from Exercise 16. Draw a rectangle on the grid. Write the coordinates for the four corners of the rectangle.

18. Julio walked from his house to the lake each day for 5 days. On 3 of those days he went directly home, but on the other days, he continued walking to the library. The lake is 1 mile from Julio's house and 1 mile from the library. The library is 2 miles from Julio's house. How many miles did Julio walk in all?

19. One day Nori paid $3.79 to mail a package. Then she bought groceries for $7.89 and received $5.00 a friend owed her. When Nori got home, she had $9.12. How much money did she have at the beginning of the day?

MIXED REVIEW

Find the range, mode, median, and mean.

1. 76, 58, 58   **2.** 76, 85, 92, 76, 81   **3.** 275, 350, 350

Multiply.

4. 52
     × 26

5. 78
     × 39

6. 136
     × 18

7. 842
     × 45

8. 237
     × 34

What do you notice about ordered pairs that have the same first coordinate?

WRAP UP...

CHAPTER REVIEW / TEST

Vocabulary Check

Choose a word or words from the box to complete each sentence.

coordinates
horizontal axis
key
mean
median
mode
ordered pair
range
sample group
scale
vertical axis

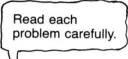

1. The left side of a line graph is called the __?__ . *(page 224)*

2. The bottom of a line graph is called the __?__ . *(page 224)*

3. The difference between the greatest and least numbers is the __?__ . *(page 212)*

4. You can locate points on a map or grid by using an __?__ . *(page 234)*

5. The two numbers in an ordered pair are the __?__ . *(page 234)*

6. The number that appears most often in a set of numbers is the __?__ . *(page 212)*

7. The middle number in an ordered set of numbers is the __?__ . *(page 212)*

8. The average of the numbers is the __?__ . *(page 212)*

9. You can collect data from a __?__ to help you make predictions. *(page 210)*

10. The unit length on a line compared with the number it stands for is the __?__ . *(page 218)*

11. A __?__ tells how many are represented by each picture in a pictograph. *(page 214)*

> Read each problem carefully.

Concept Check

Use the data to find the range, mode, median, and mean. *(page 212)*

12. 12, 1, 4, 9, 4   13. 10, 20, 15, 20, 30

Tell which sample group would better predict the choice of fifth graders. Write **a** or **b**. *(page 210)*

14. favorite after-school activity
    a. members of a fifth-grade class
    b. members of a football team

Choose a type of graph for Exercises 15–18. Explain your choice. *(page 230)*

15. careers chosen by your classmates

16. how a fifth grader spent $20

17. changes in enrollment at your school during the past five years

18. favorite movies seen this year by your classmates

Skill Check

Use the data in the table for Exercises 19–20.
(pages 214, 218)

Bicycle Colors	
Colors	Number of Students
White	3
Red	12
Blue	24
Pink	15

19. Decide on a scale and labels for the vertical and horizontal axes, and make a bar graph.

20. Make a pictograph using the data in the table.

Use the grid to find the coordinates for each point. *(page 234)*

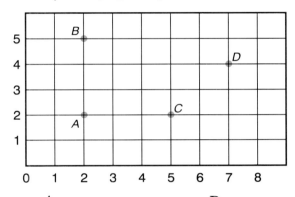

21. *A*
22. *B*
23. *C*
24. *D*

Use the line graph for Exercises 25–26. *(page 224)*

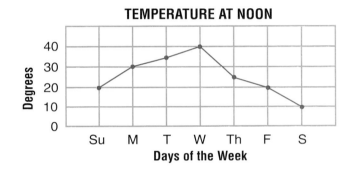

25. For which two days was the temperature at noon the same?

26. How much warmer was it on Thursday than on Saturday?

Problem-Solving Check *(pages 220, 232)*

27. Mr. Suarez plans to walk 35 city blocks. He decides to rest for 3 minutes after every 7 blocks he walks. For how many minutes will he rest on the 35-block walk?

28. Each of 20 large squares was made by gluing 9 small squares together. It took 4 minutes to make 1 large square. How long did it take to make all 20 large squares?

29. Chris, Wes, and Alicia each caught a fish. The fish they caught are a grouper, snapper, and a grunt. Chris did not catch the grunt or the snapper. Alicia did not catch the snapper or the grouper. Who caught each fish?

30. Phil, Kenesha, and Darryl finished first, second, and third in a gymnastics tournament. Phil did not finish first or third. Kenesha finished third. In what place did Darryl finish?

WHAT DID I LEARN?

1. Use connecting cubes to find the range, mode, median, and mean for this set of data: 3, 8, 4, 5, 5. Explain how you found each.

2. Identify the type of graph you would use to display the outside temperature at noon each day for one week. Explain your choice.

3. Locate the coordinates (3,5) on a grid. Explain your method.

4. Read Exercise 2 on page 233. Follow the steps on the Problem-Solving Think Along worksheet to show how to solve this problem.

To find the coordinates, I move right and then up.

Write About It

5. What lesson or activity did you enjoy the most in this chapter on statistics and graphing? What did you like about it?

6. Would a circle graph be a good way to represent data showing how the price of something has increased over the last ten years? Explain your answer.

TEAMWORK Project

Make a Survey

"More people like Brand A than Brand B." How do people find out who likes one thing more than another? They can use a survey. A survey is a set of questions that a group of people are asked.

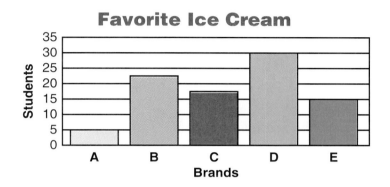

Favorite Ice Cream

Decide
Work with your team. Talk about making a survey of the class. Decide how you can learn about other students' likes and dislikes. Decide what kind of information will be learned from the survey. Determine what questions will be asked on the survey and who will ask them.

Choose at random the people your team will question, and decide how you will record their answers.

Do
Conduct your survey, and record the results. Choose the type of graph you think would best show your data. Determine the title, labels, and scale, and then make your graph.

Share
Let the other teams examine your graph, and ask them to tell you what conclusions they can draw from your data. Ask them to make predictions by using the data from your graph.

TALK ABOUT IT

a. How many questions were in your survey?

b. How many people were in your sample group?

c. Do you think the number of people in your sample group affected your data? Explain.

d. What type of graph did you use, and why did you choose it?

e. How could a business use the data from your survey?

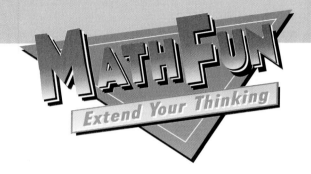

Extend Your Thinking

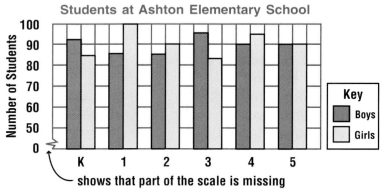

Students at Ashton Elementary School

Number of Students

100
90
80
70
60
50
0

K   1   2   3   4   5

shows that part of the scale is missing

Key
Boys
Girls

Activity

Double-Bar Graphs

Double-bar graphs are used to compare similar kinds of data. This bar graph shows the number of boys and girls in each grade at Ashton Elementary School. The key explains how to read the bars in the graph.

Use the graph for Exercises 1–3.

1. Which grades have more than 90 girls?
2. In which grade are there 15 more girls than boys?
3. Can you use the data from the graph to predict the number of boys and girls in the fifth grade at your school? Explain.

Find out how many boys and how many girls are in each grade level at your school.

4. Use your data to make a frequency table and a double-bar graph.
5. Compare your graph with the graphs made by your classmates. List two ways the graphs are alike and two ways the graphs are different.

Math Connection

Challenge

Critical Thinking

1. On a sheet of graph paper, mark and connect these points on a coordinate grid.

   (1,1) (6,1) (5,3) (5,5) (4,5)
   (4,7) (3,7) (3,5) (2,5) (2,3)

2. Multiply by 2 the first number in each ordered pair in Exercise 1. Graph the new set of points.

3. Multiply by 2 the second number in each ordered pair in Exercise 1. Graph the new set of points.

Jason forgot his locker number at school. He remembered that the sum of the digits of the number is 11 and that the digits are odd numbers. He also knows that the lockers are numbered from 1 to 120.

What is Jason's locker number?

CUMULATIVE REVIEW
CHAPTERS 1–7

Write the letter of the correct answer.

1. What is 813,567 rounded to the nearest thousand?

    A. 810,000   **B.** 813,000
    C. 813,600   **D.** 814,000

2. Which is sixty-two hundredths in standard form?

    A. 0.062   **B.** 0.62
    C. 6.20   **D.** 62.00

3.
$$8.05$$
$$-0.46$$

    A. 7.59   **B.** 7.69
    C. 8.51   **D.** not here

4.
$$46.18$$
$$+ 3.86$$

    A. 49.04   **B.** 50.04
    C. 50.94   **D.** not here

5. Which figure shows perpendicular lines?

    A.   **B.**
    C.   **D.**

6. What is the number of faces?

    A. 1   **B.** 4
    C. 5   **D.** 6

7. Which is the best estimate?
$6,159 \times 5 \approx n$

    A. 3,000   **B.** 30,000
    C. 300,000   **D.** 3,000,000

8. $775 \times 8 = n$

    A. 5,600   **B.** 5,660
    C. 6,200   **D.** not here

9. Which is the best estimate.
$489 \times 68 \approx n$

    A. 2,400   **B.** 3,500
    C. 35,000   **D.** 350,000

10. $26 \times 43 = n$

    A. 182   **B.** 918
    C. 2,018   **D.** not here

11. $8\overline{)76,864}$

    A. 968   **B.** 9,108
    C. 9,180   **D.** 9,608

12. $17\overline{)3,954}$

    A. 23 r10   **B.** 232
    C. 232 r10   **D.** 2,321

13. Meredith took 15 minutes to unpack 4 boxes of books. If she unpacked a total of 28 boxes, how long did it take her to unpack all the boxes?

    A. 30 min   **B.** 60 min
    C. 75 min   **D.** 105 min

14. Sam, Diane, Carla, and Cliff each participate in a sport. Sam does not play soccer, basketball, or softball. Diane does not play volleyball, soccer, or softball. Carla plays soccer. What sport does Cliff play?

    A. soccer   **B.** basketball
    C. volleyball   **D.** softball

CHAPTER 8

MULTIPLYING AND DIVIDING
DECIMALS

Did you know...

... that in many places cash registers are terminals that are connected to a computer? The system is called a *point-of-sale*, or *POS*, system.

TALK ABOUT IT

Crystal bought 3 pairs of socks at $1.79 each while shopping at the mall. She also purchased a belt for $5.99. How can she determine the amount of change she should have from $20.00?

USING MENTAL MATH
to Multiply Decimals

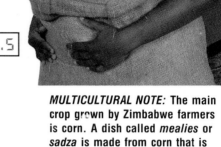

Bevil lives in Zimbabwe. He helps his father, a farmer, by selling some of their crops. If he sells a bag of corn for 15.25 Zimbabwe dollars (Z.$), how much should he receive for 10 bags of corn?

 You can use a calculator to multiply.
$10 \times 15.25 = n$

| 1 | 0 | × | 1 | 5 | . | 2 | 5 | = | 152.5 |

So, Bevil should receive Z.$152.5, or Z.$152.50, for 10 bags of corn.

MULTICULTURAL NOTE: The main crop grown by Zimbabwe farmers is corn. A dish called *mealies* or *sadza* is made from corn that is pounded into a flour.

More Examples

A. $100 \times 15.25 = n$

| 1 | 0 | 0 | × | 1 | 5 | . | 2 | 5 | = | 1525. |

B. $1,000 \times 15.25 = n$

| 1 | 0 | 0 | 0 | × | 1 | 5 | . | 2 | 5 | = | 15250. |

- What happens to the position of the decimal point when you multiply by 10? by 100? by 1,000?

Mental math can be as fast as a calculator when you multiply by 10, 100, or 1,000.

$1 \times 0.06 = 0.06$	$1 \times 0.35 = 0.35$	$1 \times 8.23 = 8.23$
$10 \times 0.06 = 0.6$	$10 \times 0.35 = 3.5$	$10 \times 8.23 = 82.3$
$100 \times 0.06 = 6.0$	$100 \times 0.35 = 35.0$	$100 \times 8.23 = 823.0$
$1,000 \times 0.06 = 60.0$	$1,000 \times 0.35 = 350.0$	$1,000 \times 8.23 = 8,230.0$

Talk About It

▶ What pattern do you see in the placement of the decimal point?

▶ Why is multiplying by 10, 100, and 1,000 easy to compute mentally?

Check for Understanding

Copy each exercise. Place the decimal point in each product.

1. $10 \times 0.67 = 67$ **2.** $100 \times 0.007 = 07$ **3.** $1,000 \times 0.024 = 240$

Practice

Use mental math to complete the pattern.

4. $1 \times 0.28 = 0.28$
$10 \times 0.28 = 2.8$
$100 \times 0.28 = n$
$1,000 \times 0.28 = 280.0$

5. $1 \times 1.37 = 1.37$
$10 \times 1.37 = 13.7$
$100 \times 1.37 = 137.0$
$1,000 \times 1.37 = n$

6. $1 \times 10.7 = 10.7$
$10 \times 10.7 = n$
$100 \times 10.7 = 1,070.0$
$1,000 \times 10.7 = 10,700.0$

Multiply each number by 10, 100, and 1,000.

7. 0.9   **8.** 2.3   **9.** 1.45   **10.** 0.83   **11.** 23.8

12. 34.73   **13.** 0.642   **14.** 3.596   **15.** 0.057   **16.** 56.079

Find each product.

17. $10 \times 0.4 = n$

18. $10 \times 1.5 = n$

19. $100 \times 0.6 = n$

20. $100 \times 4.7 = n$

21. $100 \times 25.34 = n$

22. $10 \times 78.65 = n$

23. $1,000 \times 0.85 = n$

24. $100 \times 6.932 = n$

25. $1,000 \times 42.054 = n$

Mixed Applications

26. Bevil's family sells a pound of cotton for Z.$14.00. How much will they receive for 10 pounds of cotton?

27. If 2 bushels of wheat cost Z.$32.00, what do 20 bushels of wheat cost?

28. Bevil's family is trying to save Z.$240 to buy a cow. If they save Z.$22 a month, in how many months will they have enough money for the cow?

29. Mental Math A quarter is 0.25 of a dollar. What is the value of 100 quarters? of 1,000 quarters?

MULTICULTURAL NOTE: Cattle raising is important in Zimbabwe's economy.

How will the position of the decimal point change if you multiply $10,000 \times 2.1$? $100,000 \times 2.1$?

WRAP UP...

ESTIMATING
Decimal Products

You can estimate decimal products the same way you estimate whole-number products.

Claudia earns $2.25 an hour at baby-sitting jobs. About how much can she earn in 18 hours?

Estimate.

$$2.25 \times 18 \approx n$$

Round each factor and multiply.

$$2 \times 20 = 40$$

So, Claudia earns about $40 in 18 hours.

More Examples

A. $6.32 \times 65 \approx n$

$$6 \times 70 = 420$$

B. $3.78 \times 23 \approx n$

$$4 \times 20 = 80$$

C.
$$\begin{array}{r} 29 \\ \times 4.9 \end{array} \rightarrow \begin{array}{r} 30 \\ \times 5 \\ \hline 150 \end{array}$$

Sometimes, you can use factors close to 10, 100, or 1,000 to multiply mentally. If a factor is close to 10, 100, or 1,000, you can use mental math to find or estimate the product.

D. $56.9 \times 94 \approx n$

$$56.9 \times 100 = 5,690$$

E. $98 \times 3.76 \approx n$

$$100 \times 3.76 = 376$$

F. $972 \times 0.123 \approx n$

$$1,000 \times 0.123 = 123$$

Talk About It

▶ In Example **D,** would 60×90 give a reasonable estimate? Explain.

▶ In Example **E,** how can you tell whether 376 is an overestimate or an underestimate?

Check for Understanding

Choose the best estimate. Write **a, b,** or **c.**

1. $21 \times 5.63 \approx n$	**a.** 120	**b.** 200	**c.** 240
2. $48 \times 3.21 \approx n$	**a.** 100	**b.** 150	**c.** 250
3. $4.65 \times 92 \approx n$	**a.** 320	**b.** 360	**c.** 450
4. $2.42 \times 96 \approx n$	**a.** 242	**b.** 342	**c.** 400

Practice

Estimate each product.

5. 5.8 $\times$ 11	6. 8.2 $\times$ 47	7. 9.7 $\times$ 35	8. 5.2 $\times$ 52	9. 1.6 $\times$ 99

10. 2.16 $\times$ 28	11. 6.07 $\times$ 17	12. 9.89 $\times$ 55	13. 8.68 $\times$ 19	14. 1.74 $\times$ 43

15. $3.8 \times 42 \approx n$

16. $6.7 \times 68 \approx n$

17. $9.5 \times 73 \approx n$

18. $2.68 \times 57 \approx n$

19. $2.75 \times 92 \approx n$

20. $6.16 \times 31 \approx n$

21. $58 \times 2.97 \approx n$

22. $4.21 \times 86 \approx n$

23. $93 \times 5.98 \approx n$

24. $33.1 \times 97 \approx n$

25. $98.7 \times 23 \approx n$

26. $19.8 \times 22 \approx n$

Because of mistakes in pressing the keys, the answer in a calculator display may not be reasonable. Estimate each product. Write **R** for each display that is reasonable. If the display is unreasonable, write the number and place the decimal correctly.

27. 8×2.27

   | 181.6 |

28. 9×1.23

   | 1.107 |

29. 7.94×61

   | 484.34 |

30. 4.68×12

   | 561.6 |

31. 11.4×48

   | 547.2 |

32. 20.3×92

   | 186.76 |

Mixed Applications

33. Isabel wants to buy 3 tapes that cost $4.29 each. If she earns $2.25 an hour baby-sitting, about how many hours will she have to baby-sit to earn enough for the tapes?

34. Melvin wants a tape player that costs $95. If he earns $4 an hour, how many hours will he have to work to earn enough to buy the tape player?

35. Felix earns $23.50 a week delivering papers. About how much money does he earn in 12 weeks?

36. **Mental Math**   Teresa earns $18.75 each day at her job. How much does she earn in 10 days?

Is 15,000 a reasonable estimate for 15.12 $\times$ 1,000? How do you know?

EXPLORING

Decimal Multiplication

Work Together

Building Understanding

You can use graph paper to show decimal products.

A. Work with a partner. Use a 10-by-10 section of graph paper and three different-colored markers. Remember that the model represents 100 squares. Each square is $\frac{1}{100}$, or 0.01.

Multiply. $3 \times 0.16 = n$

Show 3 of the 16 hundredths. Shade 0.16 of the section three times. Use a different color each time.

TALK ABOUT IT

- What is the product? How do you know?

- Is the product greater than or less than one whole?

- How is multiplying 3×0.16 similar to multiplying 3×16?

B. Work with a partner. Use another 10-by-10 section of graph paper. Remember that 1 column or 1 row is 0.1 of the square.

Multiply. $0.4 \times 0.3 = n$

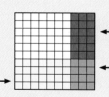

Shade 0.4 of the rows another color. →

← Shade 0.3 of the columns one color.

← 0.12 of the squares are shaded by both colors.

TALK ABOUT IT

- How does the shading help you find the product?

- Are the sections of each color more than or less than one whole?

- How is multiplying 0.3×0.4 different from multiplying 3×4?

C. Use a graph-paper model to find each product.

a. $0.4 \times 0.2 = n$ **b.** $0.8 \times 0.6 = n$ **c.** $0.7 \times 0.5 = n$ **d.** $0.9 \times 0.8 = n$

Making the Connection

The graph-paper squares show some decimal products. You can also multiply to find decimal products.

Find the product. $0.3 \times 0.5 = n$

Use the graph-paper model.

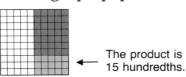

The product is 15 hundredths.

Multiply.

$$\begin{array}{r} 0.5 \\ \times\ 0.3 \\ \hline 0.15 \end{array}$$

Use the model to place the decimal point.

- Is 0.5 greater than or less than one whole?

- Is 0.3 greater than or less than one whole?

- Is the product of 0.3×0.5 greater than or less than either factor?

Multiply. Use the model to help you place the decimal point.

1.

$0.2 \times 0.8 = n$

2.

$0.9 \times 0.5 = n$

3.

$0.6 \times 0.3 = n$

TALK ABOUT IT

- In Exercise 2, what part of the whole does 0.5 cover? What part of the 0.9 does the 0.5 cover?

- When you multiply tenths times tenths, is the product greater than or less than either factor? Explain.

Checking Understanding

Use 10-by-10 sections of graph paper to show each product.

4. $0.4 \times 0.6 = n$

5. $0.8 \times 0.3 = n$

6. $0.4 \times 0.7 = n$

Use multiplication to find each product.

7. $0.9 \times 0.2 = n$

8. $0.7 \times 0.8 = n$

9. $0.1 \times 0.6 = n$

MULTIPLYING A DECIMAL
by a Whole Number

Americans throw away an average of 3.5 pounds of trash per person per day. On the average, how many pounds of trash does a family of 5 throw away per day?

First, estimate. Then, multiply to find the solution. Use your estimate to place the decimal point in the product.

Step 1 Estimate the product.	**Step 2** Multiply as with whole numbers.	**Step 3** Use the estimate to place the decimal point in the product.
$5 \times 3.5 \approx n$ ↓ ↓ ↓ $5 \times 4 = 20$	$\begin{array}{r} 2 \\ 3.5 \\ \times\ \ 5 \\ \hline 175 \end{array}$	$\begin{array}{r} 2 \\ 3.5 \\ \times\ \ 5 \\ \hline 17.5 \end{array}$ Since the estimate is 20, it is reasonable that the decimal point follows 17.

So, a family of 5 throws away an average of 17.5 pounds of trash per day.

Another Example

Multiply. $19 \times 12.35 = n$ Estimate. $20 \times 12 = 240$

$$
\begin{array}{r}
12.35 \\
\times\ \ \ \ \ 19 \\
\hline
111\ 15 \\
+\ 123\ 50 \\
\hline
234.65
\end{array}
$$

← 2 decimal places (for 12.35)
← 2 decimal places (for 234.65)

Since the estimate is 240, place the decimal point after the digit 4.

Talk About It

▶ Why is it important to estimate?

▶ How do you use your estimate to help you place the decimal point?

▶ What is another way to estimate $19 \times 12.35 = n$?

Check for Understanding

Estimate. Then find the product.

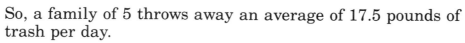

1. $6 \times 5.4 = n$ **2.** $8 \times 21.34 = n$ **3.** $12 \times 6.89 = n$ **4.** $18 \times 39.07 = n$

Practice

Copy each exercise. Place the decimal point in the product.

5.   4.2
   $\times$ 3
   ───────
     126

6. $1.36
   $\times$ 9
   ───────
    $1224

7. $2.95
   $\times$ 14
   ───────
    $4130

8.   3.48
   $\times$ 26
   ───────
     9048

9.   23.4
   $\times$ 42
   ───────
     9828

Estimate. Then find the product.

10.   1.4
    $\times$ 4
    ───────

11.   3.7
    $\times$ 8
    ───────

12.   1.3
    $\times$ 9
    ───────

13.   2.37
    $\times$ 42
    ───────

14. $61.46
    $\times$ 6
    ───────

15. $82.19
    $\times$ 12
    ───────

16.   0.962
    $\times$ 25
    ───────

17.   5.68
    $\times$ 39
    ───────

18.   9.423
    $\times$ 73
    ───────

19. $511.05
    $\times$ 43
    ───────

20. $3 \times 2.9 = n$

21. $8 \times 13.7 = n$

22. $20 \times 5.25 = n$

23. $27 \times 19.16 = n$

24. $32 \times 80.6 = n$

25. $20 \times 75.25 = n$

26. $68 \times 908.4 = n$

27. $89 \times 792.41 = n$

Mixed Applications

28. The Willis family pays $32.40 for 3 months of trash pickup. How much do they pay each year for this service?

29. If 0.35 pound of trash is recycled per person per day, how many pounds of trash are recycled in one week for a family of 3?

30. Robert's family uses 2 garbage bags each day. If the bags come in boxes of 15, how long will 4 boxes last?

31. **Write a Question** Flora's family pays $11.40 each month for trash pickup.

MIXED REVIEW

Write *slide, flip,* or *turn* to indicate how each figure was moved.

1.

2.

3.

Estimate the quotient.

4. $4\overline{)319}$

5. $8\overline{)6,197}$

6. $5\overline{)4,900}$

7. $9\overline{)8,029}$

If an estimated product is 18, explain where to place the decimal in 1809.

MULTIPLYING DECIMALS

Emily collected 5.8 pounds of aluminum cans to recycle. If she earned $0.40 for each pound, how much money did she earn in all?

Multiply. $5.8 \times 0.40 = n$ Estimate. $6 \times 0.40 = 2.40$

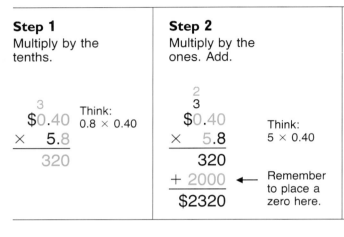

Step 1
Multiply by the tenths.

$$\begin{array}{r} 3 \\ \$0.40 \\ \times\ \ 5.8 \\ \hline 320 \end{array}$$

Think:
0.8×0.40

Step 2
Multiply by the ones. Add.

$$\begin{array}{r} 2 \\ 3 \\ \$0.40 \\ \times\ \ 5.8 \\ \hline 320 \\ +\ 2000 \\ \hline \$2320 \end{array}$$

Think:
5×0.40

← Remember to place a zero here.

Step 3
Use your estimate to place the decimal point in the product.

$$\begin{array}{r} 2 \\ 3 \\ \$0.40 \\ \times\ \ 5.8 \\ \hline 320 \\ +\ 2000 \\ \hline \$2.32\emptyset \end{array}$$

Round money to the nearest cent.

MULTICULTURAL NOTE: In 1888 an Austrian chemist named Karl Joseph Bayer developed a technique for producing aluminum.

So, Emily earned $2.32 in all.

How does the answer compare to the estimate?

You can use a calculator to multiply.

$\boxed{.}\ \boxed{4}\ \boxed{0}\ \boxed{\times}\ \boxed{5}\ \boxed{.}\ \boxed{8}\ \boxed{=}\ \boxed{2.32}$

Why does the calculator display only two decimal places?

Talk About It

▶ What relationship do you see between the number of decimal places in the product and the total number of decimal places in the factors?

▶ How many decimal places are in the product of 1.86×0.43?

▶ What can you write about this relationship?

Check for Understanding

Estimate. Then find the product.

1. $\begin{array}{r} 0.8 \\ \times 0.7 \\ \hline \end{array}$

2. $\begin{array}{r} 2.41 \\ \times\ \ 0.8 \\ \hline \end{array}$

3. $\begin{array}{r} \$12.36 \\ \times\ \ \ \ 1.5 \\ \hline \end{array}$

4. $\begin{array}{r} 0.7 \\ \times 0.6 \\ \hline \end{array}$

5. $\begin{array}{r} 32.8 \\ \times 0.95 \\ \hline \end{array}$

Idea Bank, page 464, Exercise 5

Practice

Estimate. Then find the product.

6. 0.9
    × 0.8

7. 0.6
    × 0.7

8. 6.2
    × 3.1

9. 5.43
    × 3.8

10. 9.26
    × 4.9

11. 7.89
    × 4.2

12. 32.5
    × 0.95

13. $45.60
    ×   5.5

14. 856.4
    × 0.84

15. 602.74
    ×   2.8

16. $0.7 \times 0.9 = n$

17. $8.5 \times 2.7 = n$

18. $5.9 \times 6.3 = n$

19. $4.95 \times 1.6 = n$

20. $8.25 \times 1.3 = n$

21. $713.2 \times 8.9 = n$

Compare. Write $<$, $>$, or $=$ for ⬤.

22. 2.5×3.1 ⬤ 0.25×31

23. 0.8×4.5 ⬤ 1.4×4.4

24. 2.4×0.8 ⬤ 2.5×0.6

Mixed Applications

25. The recycling center pays $0.28 a pound for aluminum. Owen has collected 75.5 pounds of aluminum. How much will he earn?

26. Every recycled ton of paper saves 17 trees. If 850 trees are saved, how many tons of paper were recycled?

27. A recycled ton of glass saves 37 liters of oil. If people recycle 4,575 tons of glass each day, how many liters of oil are saved?

28. **Number Sense** Both factors are the same number. The product is 420.25. Use a calculator to find the number.

PATTERNS AND RELATIONSHIPS

Tell whether each number is multiplied by a *decimal* or by a *whole number*, and complete the pattern.

29. $2.1, 4.2, 8.4,$ ▨, ▨

30. $1.5, 7.5, 37.5,$ ▨, ▨

31. $50, 25, 12.5,$ ▨, ▨

32. $12, 18, 27,$ ▨, ▨

33. $3.4, 10.2, 30.6,$ ▨, ▨

34. $10, 25, 62.5,$ ▨, ▨

How do you know where to place the decimal point in the product of two decimals?

WRAP
UP...

ZEROS IN THE PRODUCT

Deeanne wants to purchase a greeting card for $0.75.
She must pay a state sales tax of $0.06 on each dollar.
How much tax will Deeanne have to pay?

To find the amount of the sales tax, multiply the cost of
the greeting card times 0.06.

Multiply. $0.75 \times 0.06 = n$ Estimate. $1 \times 0.06 = 0.06$

Step 1 Multiply as with whole numbers.	Step 2 Count the number of decimal places in both factors.	Step 3 Write a zero in the product to place the decimal point.
3 $0.75 $\times$ 0.06 ——— 450	3 $0.75 ← 2 decimal places $\times$ 0.06 ← 2 decimal places ——— 450	3 $0.75 $\times$ .06 ——— $0.0450 ← 4 decimal places

Round $0.0450 to the nearest cent. ⟶ $0.05
So, Deeanne has to pay $0.05 sales tax on the greeting card.

- Does 0.80×0.06 also give a reasonable estimate? Explain.

More Examples

A.
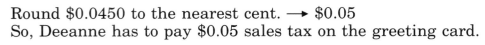
```
        0.04  ← 2 decimal places
    ×    0.2  ← 1 decimal place
       0.008  ← 3 decimal places
         ↑↑ Write zeros for these places.
```

B.
```
          16
     ×0.005  ← 3 decimal places
      0.080  ← 3 decimal places
        ↑ Write a zero for this place.
```

- How do you know when to add a zero to the final product?

Check for Understanding

Copy each exercise. Place the decimal point in each product.

1. $0.09 \times 7 = 063$

2. $0.04 \times 12 = 048$

3. $0.07 \times 0.8 = 0056$

Find each product.

4. 0.054 $\times$ 16	**5.** 3.09 $\times$ 2.1	**6.** 0.45 $\times$ 0.08	**7.** 0.93 $\times$ 1.8	**8.** 0.005 $\times$ 0.6

Practice

Copy each exercise. Place the decimal point in each product.
Write zeros if they are needed.

9. $\begin{array}{r} 0.09 \\ \times\ 0.9 \\ \hline 81 \end{array}$

10. $\begin{array}{r} 0.06 \\ \times\ 0.7 \\ \hline 42 \end{array}$

11. $\begin{array}{r} 0.047 \\ \times\ \ \ \ 3 \\ \hline 141 \end{array}$

12. $\begin{array}{r} 0.105 \\ \times\ \ \ 15 \\ \hline 1575 \end{array}$

Find the product.

13. $\begin{array}{r} 0.07 \\ \times\ 0.3 \\ \hline \end{array}$

14. $\begin{array}{r} 0.04 \\ \times\ 0.8 \\ \hline \end{array}$

15. $\begin{array}{r} 0.15 \\ \times\ 0.6 \\ \hline \end{array}$

16. $\begin{array}{r} 0.25 \\ \times\ 0.4 \\ \hline \end{array}$

17. $\begin{array}{r} 0.62 \\ \times\ 0.5 \\ \hline \end{array}$

18. $\begin{array}{r} 0.705 \\ \times\ \ 1.4 \\ \hline \end{array}$

19. $\begin{array}{r} 1.008 \\ \times\ \ 5.5 \\ \hline \end{array}$

20. $\begin{array}{r} 3.006 \\ \times\ \ \ 43 \\ \hline \end{array}$

21. $0.08 \times 0.2 = n$

22. $0.003 \times 5 = n$

23. $5.006 \times 0.5 = n$

24. $4.005 \times 0.6 = n$

Mixed Applications

25. Paula bought a record cleaner for $0.69. If she paid a sales tax of $0.06 on each dollar, what did she spend on the record cleaner?

26. Is 2 a reasonable product for the numbers 0.04 and 0.05? Explain.

Use the table for Exercises 27–30.

27. What is the difference in the price of tapes at Record City and at Discount Music?

28. How much are 3 tapes at The Music Store?

29. What will be the cost of 2 CDs bought at Music Town, including a sales tax of $0.06 on each dollar?

30. **Making Decisions**   If you buy both tapes and CDs, at which store should you shop? Explain.

Music Store Prices		
Store	Tape	Compact Disc (CD)
The Music Store	$ 8.99	$14.99
Music Town	$ 8.49	$11.99
Discount Music	$ 7.89	$12.98
Record City	$10.49	$15.99

How do you know whether to write zeros in a product before placing the decimal point?

WRAP UP...

PROBLEM SOLVING

Choose the Method of Computation

In one month Gordon collected $540.45 from his paper route. Of this amount, he paid $433.50 to the newspaper company. He saved $20.85 toward a new bicycle and put $30.50 in his savings account. The rest was his to spend. How much spending money did he have that month?

Decide which method of computation you should use to solve the problem.

▶ **UNDERSTAND**

What are you asked to find?

What facts are given?

▶ **PLAN**

How can you decide which method of computation to use?

Think about the methods you have used in problem solving.

- If an exact answer is not needed, try estimation.
- If mental math is too difficult, choose paper and pencil or a calculator.

▶ **SOLVE**

How will you carry out the plan?

Subtract to find the amount Gordon kept for himself.

[5] [4] [0] [.] [4] [5] [−] [4] [3] [3] [.] [5] [0] [M+] M `106.95`

Add to find the amount he set aside for the bicycle and his savings account.

[2] [0] [.] [8] [5] [+] [3] [0] [.] [5] [0] [M−] M `51.35` ← The [M−] key subtracts the sum from the value already in memory.

Press the memory recall key to find the difference.

[MRC] M `55.6` ← Remember to place a zero here.

So, Gordon had $55.60 for spending money that month.

▶ **LOOK BACK**

How can you check your solution?

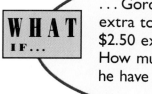

WHAT IF... ... Gordon decided to save $5 extra toward the bicycle and put $2.50 extra into his savings account? How much spending money would he have left?

256

Apply

Choose a method of computation and solve.

1 The Lopez family spent $48.50 each night for 3 nights on its vacation. The family spent $27.89, $48.25, $32.95, and $41.30 on meals and $52.50 for admissions to parks. About how much did the family spend on its vacation?

2 The Jacksons spent $17.98 for gasoline the first day of their vacation. Their meals cost $13.67 and $25.76. Their motel room cost $55.00. If they brought $500.00 for their vacation, how much money is left?

| Mixed Applications | STRATEGIES |

Make a Table • Find a Pattern
• Write a Number Sentence
• Work Backward • Guess and Check
• Use Estimation

Choose a strategy and solve.

3 The Nelsons traveled 242 miles the first day of their trip and 285 miles the second day. If they drove about 60 miles per hour, about how many hours did they spend driving?

4 Pearl has saved $90. She received half of this money on her birthday. She earned the rest from her paper route. If she has worked 3 weeks, how much did she earn each week?

5 Sammy has 140 papers to deliver. If he can deliver 10 papers in 5 minutes, how long will it take him to deliver all the papers?

6 Laura needs $130 to buy a coat. She has $45. If she saves $5 each week, how many weeks will it take her to save enough money?

7 One week Ruben earned money doing chores around the house. For vacuuming and washing windows, he earned $1.00 per job. He earned $2.50 for cleaning the garage and $1.75 for washing the kitchen floor. How much did he earn?

8 Paco figured how much he spent for meals during his vacation. On Friday he spent $1.89, $2.49, and $6.75. On Saturday he spent $2.29, $2.10, and $6.50. On Sunday he spent $2.45, $3.05, and $5.80. On which day did he spend the most for meals?

MULTICULTURAL NOTE: The Mesa Verde National Park in southwestern Colorado is known as the home of the ancient Anasazi people. These cliff dwellers built their homes along canyon walls and under rock overhangs.

1. Barbara bought a radio-controlled car for $38.95. She bought a battery for $5.98 and used it for the transmitter. She needed 8 more batteries for the car. The batteries were sold in packages of 4 for $5.29. What was the total cost of the car and batteries?

2. Tikaya compared her sales of radio-controlled cars during a four-month period. The totals sold in each of the four months were 35, 28, 45, and 42. She sold the fewest cars in April and the most in July. If she sold more than 40 cars in May, how many did she sell in June?

3. Richard compared speeds of radio-controlled cars Big Bandit, Cyclone, White Lion, and Prancer. The speeds of the cars were 4, 7, 8, and 12 miles per hour. White Lion did not go less than 10 miles per hour, and Prancer did not go more than 5 miles per hour. If Cyclone had a speed of 7 miles per hour, what was the speed of Big Bandit?

4. Brian went to the store and bought 2 packages of batteries for $4.98 each and a radio-controlled truck for $27.95. He had about $15.00 when he returned home. About how much did he have when he started?

> I can make a table to solve a problem.

Order from least to greatest.

5. 1,789; 179; 1,798; 178

6. 25,465; 24,456; 24,465

7. 45.02; 4.50; 45.20; 4.52

8. 6.578; 60.508; 6.057; 6.508

Use mental math to find the product.

9. $\begin{array}{r} 40 \\ \times\ 6 \\ \hline \end{array}$

10. $\begin{array}{r} 500 \\ \times\ 5 \\ \hline \end{array}$

11. $\begin{array}{r} 800 \\ \times\ 3 \\ \hline \end{array}$

12. $\begin{array}{r} 3,000 \\ \times\ 9 \\ \hline \end{array}$

13. $\begin{array}{r} 8,000 \\ \times\ 5 \\ \hline \end{array}$

Are the figures similar? Write *yes* or *no*.

14.

15.

16.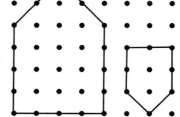

Find the quotient.

17. $3\overline{)471}$

18. $6\overline{)549}$

19. $8\overline{)969}$

20. $36\overline{)728}$

21. $42\overline{)4,209}$

22. $13\overline{)2,613}$

Find the range, mode, median, and mean.

23. 87, 93, 90, 93, 82

24. 325, 250, 175, 275, 175

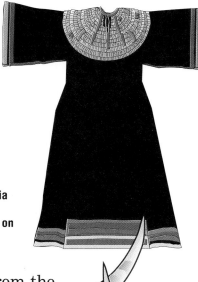

Vancouver Island

NORTH AMERICA

Another Form of Money

Trading was once an important activity for most Native American people. Some Native Americans used an early form of money called *dentalia,* which means "teeth." Dentalia are curved, toothlike shells that were used as money throughout the western part of North America.

A researcher of Native Americans has investigated the source of dentalia near Canada's Vancouver Island. He built special equipment to gather the shells from underwater shell beds 50 to 60 feet deep.

MULTICULTURAL NOTE: Dentalia shells were used not only as money but also as decorations on clothes and jewelry.

Talk About It

- How do you think the dentalia were retrieved from the shell beds?

- Why do you think dentalia were the only shells that became true currency?

Solve. Be prepared to explain how you solved each problem.

1. One dentalia bed lies 15.43 m below the water's surface. A rope that brings up the shells is 3 times that long. How long is the rope?

2. Dentalia were strung lengthwise like beads to hang around the neck. If each dentalium took up 4.5 cm on a string, how long was a string of 16 shells?

3. Suppose rows of dentalia are used to decorate a dress. The first row consists of 90 shells side by side, the second row has 120 shells, and the third has 150 shells. If this pattern continues, how many shells will be in the tenth row?

USING MENTAL MATH
to Divide Decimals

Ramona has saved her money for several months. Her goal is to save $375.50. This amount is 10 times more than she has saved already. How much money has Ramona saved?

 You can use a calculator to divide. $375.50 ÷ 10 = n

 | 3 | 7 | 5 | . | 5 | 0 | ÷ | 1 | 0 | = | ┌─────────┐ 37.55 └─────────┘

So, Ramona has saved $37.55 toward her goal.

Divide. 132 ÷ 100 = n

132 | ÷ | 100 | = | ┌─────────┐ 1.32 └─────────┘

Divide. 2,416 ÷ 1,000 = n

2,416 | ÷ | 1,000 | = | ┌─────────┐ 2.416 └─────────┘

- What happens to the position of the decimal point when you divide by 10? by 100? by 1,000?

Mental math can be as fast as a calculator when you divide by 10, 100, or 1,000.

372 ÷ 10 = 37.2	2,418 ÷ 10 = 241.8	40 ÷ 10 = 4.0
372 ÷ 100 = 3.72	2,418 ÷ 100 = 24.18	40 ÷ 100 = 0.4
372 ÷ 1,000 = 0.372	2,418 ÷ 1,000 = 2.418	40 ÷ 1,000 = 0.04

Talk About It

▶ What pattern do you see in the placement of the decimal point?

▶ Why do you need to write zeros in the quotient?

▶ Why is dividing by 10, 100, and 1,000 easy to compute mentally?

Check for Understanding

Use mental math to complete the pattern.

1. 14 ÷ 10 = 1.4
   14 ÷ 100 = n
   14 ÷ 1,000 = 0.014

2. 250 ÷ 10 = 25
   250 ÷ 100 = 2.5
   250 ÷ 1,000 = n

3. 1,354 ÷ 10 = n
   1,354 ÷ 100 = 13.54
   1,354 ÷ 1,000 = 1.354

Practice

Use mental math to complete each pattern.

4. $24 \div 10 = n$
$24 \div 100 = 0.24$

5. $2.5 \div 10 = n$
$2.5 \div 100 = 0.025$

6. $654 \div 10 = 65.4$
$654 \div 100 = n$

7. $34.5 \div 10 = 3.45$
$34.5 \div 100 = n$

8. $61.9 \div 10 = 6.19$
$61.9 \div 100 = n$

9. $128 \div 100 = n$
$128 \div 1,000 = 0.128$

Divide each number by 10, 100, and 1,000.

10. 45 **11.** 106 **12.** 295 **13.** 3,872 **14.** 13,912

Divide.

15. $6.8 \div 10 = n$ **16.** $49 \div 10 = n$ **17.** $148 \div 100 = n$

18. $19.7 \div 100 = n$ **19.** $895 \div 100 = n$ **20.** $425 \div 1,000 = n$

Mixed Applications

21. Davie has deposited $555.00 in his savings account. If he made 10 equal deposits, how much was each deposit?

22. Juana bought a sweater for $18.95 and a pair of jeans for $16.99. If she paid a sales tax of $0.06 for each dollar of her purchase, how much did she pay in sales tax?

23. Each week Nina saves $9.75 from her pay. In 12 weeks, how much money will she have saved?

24. Albert has collected 1,372 pennies. How much money does he have in dollars and cents?

MIXED REVIEW

Find the sum or difference.

1. 4.567
$+ 5.443$

2. 12.906
$- 9.879$

3. 8.952
$+ 5.139$

4. 25.475
$- 18.685$

5. 39.654
$+ 14.048$

Divide.

6. $12\overline{)99}$ **7.** $14\overline{)784}$ **8.** $25\overline{)955}$ **9.** $32\overline{)992}$ **10.** $48\overline{)866}$

How will the position of the decimal point change if you divide by 10,000? by 100,000?

WRAP UP...

EXPLORING

Decimal Division

Building Understanding

You can use base-ten blocks to explore dividing with decimals.

Divide. $5.36 \div 4 = n$

Work with a partner. Model 5.36 using base-ten blocks. If you let the flat represent 1, you can make the following chart.

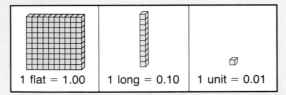		
1 flat = 1.00	1 long = 0.10	1 unit = 0.01

- What blocks can you use to model 5.36?

- How many flats can be sorted evenly into 4 groups?

- Are there any flats left over?

- What regrouping can be made?

Regroup.

- How many longs are there now?

- How many longs can be sorted evenly into each of the 4 groups?

- Are there any longs left over?

- What regrouping can be made to use the other long?

Regroup.

- How many units are there now?

- How many units can be sorted evenly into each of the 4 groups?

- Did you use all of the blocks?

- What blocks are in each of the 4 groups?

TALK ABOUT IT

- What decimal number represents the amount in each of the 4 equal groups?

- How can you compare division to this sorting process?

262

Making the Connection

The base-ten blocks can help you divide a decimal into groups to find the amount in each group. The steps are the same as when you divide with whole numbers. Remember, the values of the base-ten blocks are different for decimals.

Divide. $9.51 \div 3 = n$

Base-Ten Blocks

Recording

Base-Ten Blocks	Recording
Show 9.51 as 9 flats, 5 longs, 1 unit. 	$3\overline{)9.51}$
Divide the flats into 3 equal groups. How many flats can be placed in each group? 	$\begin{array}{r} 3 \\ 3\overline{)9.51} \\ -9 \\ \hline 0 \end{array}$ ← 3 ones in each group ← 9 ones shared in all ← 0 ones left over
How many longs can be placed in each group? 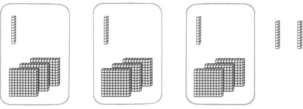	Remember to place the decimal in the quotient. $\begin{array}{r} 3.1 \\ 3\overline{)9.51} \\ -9 \downarrow \\ \hline 0\,5 \\ -\ 3 \\ \hline 2 \end{array}$ ← 1 tenth in each group ← 3 tenths shared in all ← 2 tenths left over
Regroup the 2 longs left over as 20 units. How many units can be placed in each group? 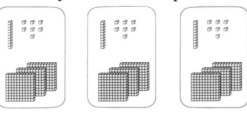	$\begin{array}{r} 3.17 \\ 3\overline{)9.51} \\ -9 \\ \hline 0\,5 \\ -\ 3 \\ \hline 21 \\ -21 \\ \hline 0 \end{array}$ ← 7 hundredths in each group ← 21 hundredths shared in all ← 0 left over

Checking Understanding

Divide. Use base-ten blocks to model each problem. Then record.

1. $3.74 \div 2 = n$ **2.** $5.16 \div 3 = n$ **3.** $2.10 \div 6 = n$ **4.** $6.24 \div 4 = n$

More Practice, Lesson 8.9, page H64

DIVIDING DECIMALS
by Whole Numbers

Joan and 3 classmates bought some food to share. The total bill was $25.40. If they share the bill equally, how much will each owe?

First estimate. $4\overline{)25.40}$

Think: $4 \times n = 24$
$4 \times 6 = 24$

$4\overline{)24.00}$ with 6.00 on top

Divide. $25.40 \div 4 = n$

Step 1	Step 2	Step 3
Divide as with whole numbers. Since the estimate is 6 dollars, put the decimal point after the 6.	Continue to divide.	Check.

Step 1

$$4\overline{)\$25.40}$$ with $6.$ on top
$$-24$$
$$\overline{1}$$

Step 2

$$4\overline{)\$25.40}$$ with $\$6.35$ on top
$$-24\downarrow$$
$$1\ 4$$
$$-1\ 2\downarrow$$
$$20$$
$$-20$$
$$\overline{0}$$

Step 3

$$\$6.35$$
$$\times4$$
$$\overline{\$25.40}$$

So, each one will owe $6.35 for a share of the food.

More Examples

A.
$$7\overline{)423.5}$$ with 60.5 on top
$$-42$$
$$\overline{03}$$
$$-0$$
$$\overline{35}$$
$$-35$$
$$\overline{0}$$

There are 0 ones, so place a zero in the ones place.

B.
$$21\overline{)1.47}$$ with 0.07 on top
$$-0$$
$$\overline{1\ 4}$$
$$-0$$
$$\overline{1\ 47}$$
$$-1\ 47$$
$$\overline{0}$$

There are 0 ones and 0 tenths, so place a zero in the ones and tenths places.

- Why do you write zero in the quotient in Example **A**? in Example **B**?

Check for Understanding

Divide.

1. $5\overline{)19.75}$ 2. $6\overline{)276.48}$ 3. $23\overline{)25.07}$ 4. $37\overline{)51.06}$ 5. $42\overline{)3.612}$

Practice

Estimate the cost for one item.

6. 5 bars of soap for $1.47 **7.** 6 apples for $1.25 **8.** 6 boxes of raisins for $_.79

9. 3 bags of popcorn for $1.00 **10.** 4 onions for $0.25 **11.** 4 oranges for $0.99

Find the quotient.

12. $3\overline{)1.8}$ **13.** $4\overline{)2.0}$ **14.** $6\overline{)0.24}$ **15.** $5\overline{)3.5}$ **16.** $8\overline{)8.72}$

17. $7\overline{)1.47}$ **18.** $3\overline{)3.69}$ **19.** $9\overline{)83.7}$ **20.** $4\overline{)44.8}$ **21.** $6\overline{)49.26}$

22. $8\overline{)56.8}$ **23.** $6\overline{)54.48}$ **24.** $2\overline{)19.62}$ **25.** $8\overline{)496.16}$ **26.** $41\overline{)438.7}$

27. $15\overline{)52.5}$ **28.** $24\overline{)115.2}$ **29.** $36\overline{)442.8}$ **30.** $12\overline{)902.4}$ **31.** $19\overline{)1.026}$

Mixed Applications

Use the price list for Exercises 32–35.

32. Estimate the cost of 1 pound of potatoes.

33. Evan bought a dozen eggs and 2 loaves of bread. How much did he spend?

34. **Making Decisions** If you need one gallon of milk, would 2 half-gallon containers or 1 one-gallon container be less expensive?

35. **Write a Question** Use the price list to write a question.

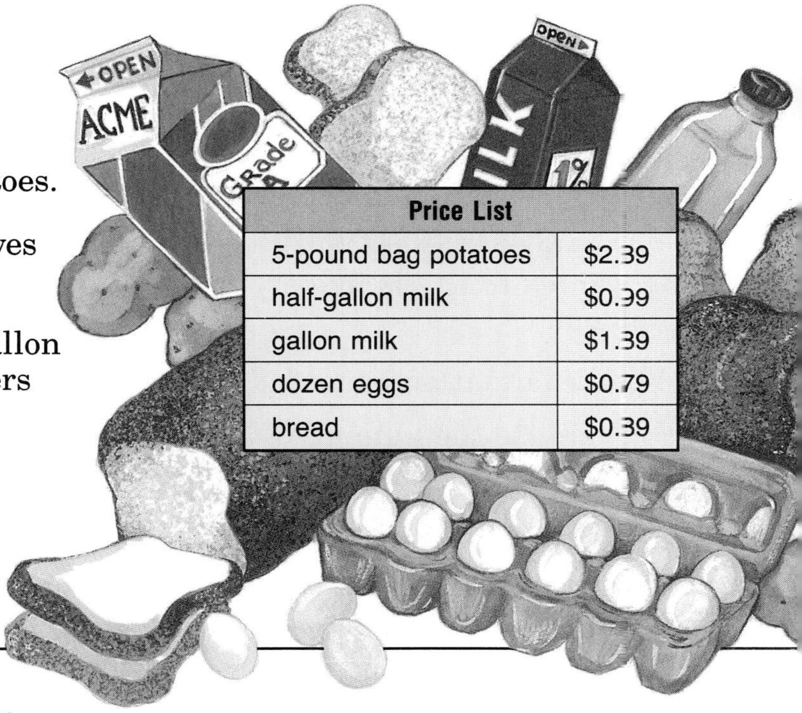

Price List	
5-pound bag potatoes	$2.39
half-gallon milk	$0.39
gallon milk	$1.39
dozen eggs	$0.79
bread	$0.39

CALCULATOR

Use your calculator to complete each pattern.

36. $8.5 \div 0.1 = n$
$8.5 \div 0.01 = n$
$8.5 \div 0.001 = n$

37. $12.4 \div 0.2 = n$
$12.4 \div 0.02 = n$
$12.4 \div 0.002 = n$

38. $12.5 \div 0.5 = n$
$1.25 \div 0.5 = n$
$0.125 \div 0.5 = n$

39. $21.6 \div 0.3 = n$
$2.16 \div 0.3 = n$
$0.216 \div 0.3 = n$

How is division with decimals like division with whole numbers? How is it different?

WRAP
UP...

PROBLEM SOLVING

Relevant/Irrelevant Information

Chuck spent $10.11 for 3 audiocassettes. The price was $1.00 more than he wanted to pay. Carolee spent $5.12 for 2 audiocassettes. Did Chuck or Carolee pay less money for a single audiocassette?

Sometimes, a problem may contain more information than you need to answer a question. **Relevant** means that something is important in the situation. **Irrelevant** means that something is not important in the situation.

▶ **UNDERSTAND**

What are you asked to find?

What facts are given?

▶ **PLAN**

What information is irrelevant to the question?

The statement that Chuck paid $1.00 more than he wanted to pay is irrelevant in solving the problem.

What information is needed to solve the problem?

You can use the number of audiocassettes and the amount spent for both purchases.

▶ **SOLVE**

How will you carry out the plan?

Use the relevant information to find the solution.

Divide.

	Amount of Purchase		Number of Audiocassettes Purchased		Amount Paid for Each Audiocassette
Chuck	$10.11	÷	3	=	$3.37
Carolee	$ 5.12	÷	2	=	$2.56

So, Carolee paid less money for a single audiocassette.

▶ **LOOK BACK**

How can you check your solution?

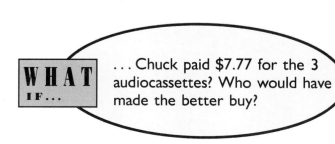

WHAT IF... ...Chuck paid $7.77 for the 3 audiocassettes? Who would have made the better buy?

Apply

List the relevant information and solve.

(1) Sara Ann wants to buy 2 new video games. At a store 4.5 miles from her house, she can buy 2 games for $39.98. At a store 2 miles from her house, the games are $21.95 each. What is the difference in cost for a video game?

(2) Cesar receives an allowance of $3.75 a week. He says that most of his friends receive between $2.00 and $5.00. His friend Alfred receives $3.25. If Cesar saves all his allowance, how much will he have in 4 weeks?

Mixed Applications ⟹ **STRATEGIES**

Make a Table • Use Estimation • Write a Number Sentence • Guess and Check

Choose a strategy and solve.

(3) Daphne bought oranges and grapefruits at the grocery store. She bought a total of 12 pieces of fruit for $3.36. If oranges cost $0.24 each and grapefruits cost $0.36 each, how many of each type of fruit did Daphne buy?

(4) Nancy made a phone call that cost $2.00 for the first minute and $0.45 for each additional minute. If she was on the phone for 5 minutes, what was the cost of the phone call?

(5) Jared and his brother have been saving baseball cards for 4 years. Jared has 1,123 cards, and his brother has 792 cards. If they continue to save at the same rate over the next 4 years, about how many cards will they have?

(6) Ralph buys a package of meat that weighs 1.20 pounds and costs $2.25 per pound. How much change will he receive from $5.00?

WRITER'S CORNER

(7) Write a question about a purchase you made recently. The question should contain more information than needed to solve the problem.

CHAPTER REVIEW/TEST

Vocabulary Check

Choose a word or words from the box to complete each sentence.

> decimal point
> irrelevant
> relevant
> zero

1. Sometimes you need to write a __?__ in the product to place the decimal point. *(page 254)*

2. Information given in a problem that is not important for solving the problem is __?__ information. *(page 266)*

3. Information that is needed to solve a problem is __?__ information. *(page 266)*

4. When you divide by 10, the __?__ moves one place to the left. *(page 260)*

> An estimate helps me place the decimal point in the product.

Concept Check

Copy each exercise. Place the decimal point in the product. *(pages 244, 250)*

5.	6.	7.	8.
0.32	0.045	0.68	0.279
× 10	× 100	× 100	× 1,000
0320	004500	06800	0279000

9.	10.	11.	12.
0.02	0.07	0.005	0.404
× 5	× 4	× 6	× 5
010	028	0030	2020

Choose the best estimate. Write **a, b,** or **c.** *(page 246)*

13. 18×4.9 **a.** 100   **b.** 800   **c.** 1,000

14. 31×6.3 **a.** 18   **b.** 180   **c.** 210

15. 48×3.8 **a.** 120   **b.** 200   **c.** 2,000

Use mental math to complete the pattern. *(pages 244, 260)*

16. $10 \times 0.07 = 0.7$
$100 \times 0.07 = 7$
$1,000 \times 0.07 = n$

17. $10 \times 0.24 = 2.4$
$100 \times 0.24 = n$
$1,000 \times 0.24 = 240$

18. $10 \times 1.4 = 14$
$100 \times 1.4 = 140$
$1,000 \times 1.4 = n$

19. $12 \div 10 = 1.2$
$12 \div 100 = n$
$12 \div 1,000 = 0.012$

20. $145 \div 10 = n$
$145 \div 100 = 1.45$
$145 \div 1,000 = 0.145$

21. $1,756 \div 10 = 175.6$
$1,756 \div 100 = n$
$1,756 \div 1,000 = 1.756$

Skill Check

Find each product. *(page 244)*

22. $10 \times 0.5 = n$

23. $10 \times 2.8 = n$

24. $100 \times 0.7 = n$

25. $100 \times 5.6 = n$

26. $1{,}000 \times 0.75 = n$

27. $1{,}000 \times 0.123 = n$

Estimate each product. *(page 246)*

28.
$$\begin{array}{r} 4.7 \\ \times\ 12 \\ \hline \end{array}$$

29.
$$\begin{array}{r} 6.9 \\ \times\ 23 \\ \hline \end{array}$$

30.
$$\begin{array}{r} 18.5 \\ \times\ \ 32 \\ \hline \end{array}$$

31.
$$\begin{array}{r} 1.72 \\ \times\ \ 58 \\ \hline \end{array}$$

32.
$$\begin{array}{r} 3.9 \\ \times\ 83 \\ \hline \end{array}$$

Find the product. *(pages 248, 250, 252, 254)*

33.
$$\begin{array}{r} 1.8 \\ \times\ \ 6 \\ \hline \end{array}$$

34.
$$\begin{array}{r} \$12.48 \\ \times\ \ \ \ \ 15 \\ \hline \end{array}$$

35.
$$\begin{array}{r} 0.985 \\ \times\ \ \ \ 27 \\ \hline \end{array}$$

36.
$$\begin{array}{r} 0.8 \\ \times\ 0.4 \\ \hline \end{array}$$

37.
$$\begin{array}{r} 1.9 \\ \times\ 0.6 \\ \hline \end{array}$$

38.
$$\begin{array}{r} 2.5 \\ \times\ 3.8 \\ \hline \end{array}$$

39.
$$\begin{array}{r} 4.52 \\ \times\ \ 3.2 \\ \hline \end{array}$$

40.
$$\begin{array}{r} 0.08 \\ \times\ 0.05 \\ \hline \end{array}$$

41.
$$\begin{array}{r} 0.52 \\ \times\ \ 0.6 \\ \hline \end{array}$$

42.
$$\begin{array}{r} 0.455 \\ \times\ \ \ \ 0.4 \\ \hline \end{array}$$

Find the quotient. *(pages 260, 262, 264)*

43. $4.9 \div 10 = n$

44. $75 \div 10 = n$

45. $14.8 \div 100 = n$

46. $72.5 \div 100 = n$

47. $632 \div 100 = n$

48. $3{,}180 \div 1{,}000 = n$

49. $6\overline{)28.8}$

50. $13\overline{)282.1}$

51. $21\overline{)787.50}$

52. $32\overline{)540.8}$

53. $23\overline{)646.99}$

Problem-Solving Check *(pages 256, 266)*

54. A merchant bought 6 pairs of skis for $45.50 a pair, 3 pairs of poles for $8.50 a pair, 8 pairs of boots for $38.00 a pair, and 5 parkas for $29.00 each. How much did he pay for the skis?

55. Amy is comparing breakfast cereals. A box of Brand A has 10 grams of sugar, weighs 13 ounces, and sells for $2.08. A box of Brand B has 12 grams of sugar, weighs 14 ounces, and sells for $2.10. Which cereal costs less per ounce?

56. Janell bought 2 shirts for $11.98 each, a sweater for $18.95, and 3 pairs of socks for $2.05 a pair. About how much did all of these items cost?

57. Each week for 6 weeks Harry deposited his check of $74.28 into his bank. He also deposited $25.00 he received as a gift. How much did Harry deposit during the 6 weeks?

WHAT DID I LEARN?

1. Estimate the product of 3.21×78. Explain your method.

2. Use 10-by-10 sections of graph paper and colored markers to show the product of 0.4×0.6. Explain what part of the grid shows the product.

3. Find the product of 2.4×0.61. Show your work.

4. Use base-ten blocks to model $5.24 \div 2$. (Let the flat represent 1.) Solve. Draw a picture to show what you did.

5. Find the quotient of $32.8 \div 8$. Show your work.

6. Read Exercise 2 on page 257. Follow the steps on the Problem-Solving Think Along worksheet to show how to solve this problem.

Dividing decimals is like dividing whole numbers.

Write About It

7. What part of this chapter on multiplying and dividing decimals was the most challenging for you? Explain.

8. How is multiplying decimals like multiplying whole numbers? How are these operations different?

TEAMWORK Project

Make a Graph

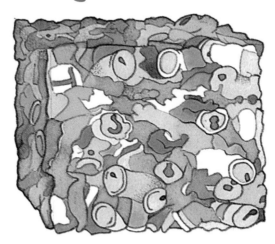

Suppose your class wants to keep track of money earned from a recycling project. The goal is to earn $250 by collecting aluminum cans for recycling. The recycling center pays $0.28 a pound for aluminum cans. With your teammates, decide on the number of weeks for the project, and make a frequency table to show the amount earned each week.

Decide

Work with your team. Talk about what kind of graph you can use to display the data on your frequency table.

Do Decide on a title, labels, and a scale, and make your graph. Each week, compute the amount of money earned. To do this, multiply the number of pounds collected by the amount paid by the recycling center for each pound. Add this amount each week to the previous week's total, and continue marking your graph until the goal is reached.

Share **Let other teams study your graph. Discuss whether your graph clearly shows the progress made each week.**

TALK ABOUT IT

- What type of graph did you use?
- How could you use your graph to find the amount of money earned each week?
- How is the graph helpful in keeping track of the progress in reaching the goal?
- In your everyday activities, what other situations require multiplication and division with decimals?

Activity

A Game from Ghana

The Ashanti live in the country of Ghana in western Africa. Ashanti children like to play a game similar to tic-tac-toe. They draw a figure like the one at the right in the dirt.

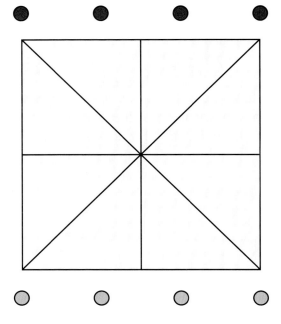

- Each of two players has four colored stones. Players take turns placing one of their stones on one of the empty intersections.

- Once all of the stones are in place, the players take turns moving one stone along a line to the next empty intersection.

- The first player to get three stones in a row wins.

Draw the figure for this game. Play the game with a partner. Use counters as stones.

Challenge

Estimation

Estimate the products. List the number sentences in order from least to greatest according to the estimated product.

$47.3 \times 0.9 = n$
$19.31 \times 22 = n$
$107.89 \times 4.9 = n$
$43.9 \times 0.8 = n$
$92.63 \times 2.6 = n$

Calculator

Find the number that, when multiplied by itself, has a product close to the number given. Use a calculator to help you find the numbers.

1. 240.25
2. 404.01
3. 1,317.69
4. 10,100.25

Write the letter of the correct answer.

1. Which is in order from least to greatest?

   A. 7.350, 7.503, 7.530
   B. 7.350, 7.530, 7.503
   C. 7.503, 7.350, 7.530
   D. 7.530, 7.350, 7.503

2. Which is the best estimate?
$7{,}269 - 5{,}188 \approx n$

   A. 1,000   **B.** 2,000
   C. 3,000   **D.** 12,000

3. $34.62 + 3.50 = n$

   A. 34.97   **B.** 37.12
   C. 71.62   **D.** not here

4. $2{,}940 \times 5 = n$

   A. 14,200   **B.** 14,500
   C. 14,700   **D.** not here

5. Which names the type of angle?

   A. acute   **B.** obtuse
   C. right   **D.** not here

6. How many faces are on a triangular prism?

   A. 3 faces   **B.** 4 faces
   C. 5 faces   **D.** 6 faces

7. $239 \div 7 = n$

   A. 34   **B.** 34 r1
   C. 35   **D.** 341

8. $20\overline{)200}$

   A. 10   **B.** 20
   C. 100   **D.** not here

Use the graph for Exercises 9–10.

9. In which month did Jim earn the most money?

   A. January   **B.** February
   C. March   **D.** April

10. How much more did Jim earn in April than in February?

   A. $10   **B.** $20
   C. $30   **D.** $40

11. Phil spent $12.45 for a gift for his mother, $14.84 for a gift for his father, and $8.16 for a gift for his sister. How much money does he have left from $75.00?

   A. $35.45   **B.** $39.55
   C. $40.45   **D.** $40.55

12. Maria bowled 2 games at $2.45 a game, rented shoes for $1.30, and bought a drink for $0.75. What was the cost of bowling 2 games?

   A. $4.80   **B.** $4.90
   C. $5.20   **D.** $6.95

NUMBER THEORY AND FRACTIONS

Did you know...

... that Dutch growers produce nearly 2,000 varieties of tulips? Tulips grow from bulbs, and the leaves, stems, and flowers grow directly out of the bulb.

TALK ABOUT IT

Janie Chang plants tulips of different colors in her garden. Of the tulips in her garden, $\frac{1}{16}$ are red, $\frac{5}{16}$ are orange, $\frac{1}{4}$ are yellow, and $\frac{3}{8}$ are pink. How can Janie compare the parts of her garden that are different colors?

FRACTIONS

Mr. Notowidigdo owns a small farm in Malaysia. He grows a variety of crops on 8 sections of land. What fraction represents the sections of his farm planted with rice?

🥜 Rice	🥜 Rice	🍍 Pineapples	🍍 Pineapples
🥜 Rice	🫑 Peppers	🫑 Peppers	🫘 Cacao

You can use a fraction to describe the parts of a whole.

numerator $\longrightarrow$ $\dfrac{3}{8}$ $\longleftarrow$ number of parts planted with rice
denominator $\longrightarrow$ 8 $\longleftarrow$ total number of equal parts

Read: three eighths $\longrightarrow$ **Write:** $\frac{3}{8}$

So, $\frac{3}{8}$ of Mr. Notowidigdo's farm is planted with rice.

MULTICULTURAL NOTE: Rice is an important part of the diet of the people of Malaysia.

You can also use a fraction to describe part of a group. What part of the bouquet of flowers is red?

The Whole Group

6 flowers

numerator $\longrightarrow$ $\dfrac{3}{6}$ $\longleftarrow$ number of red flowers
denominator $\longrightarrow$ 6 $\longleftarrow$ total number of flowers

Read: three sixths $\longrightarrow$ **Write:** $\frac{3}{6}$

So, $\frac{3}{6}$ of the flowers are red.

Each flower is $\frac{1}{6}$.
Six flowers are $\frac{6}{6}$, or the whole.

Check for Understanding

Write the fraction for the part that is shaded. Tell whether the fraction represents *part of a whole* or *part of a group*.

1.

2.

3.

4.

Draw a shape. Divide it into the correct number of equal parts. Shade some of the parts to represent the fraction.

5. $\dfrac{1}{4}$

6. $\dfrac{2}{3}$

7. $\dfrac{2}{8}$

8. $\dfrac{3}{5}$

Practice

Write the fraction for the part that is shaded.

9.

10.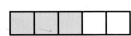

11.

12.

Draw two pictures for each fraction. Show part of a whole with one picture and part of a group with the other picture.

13. $\dfrac{7}{8}$

14. $\dfrac{5}{9}$

15. $\dfrac{2}{5}$

16. $\dfrac{6}{8}$

Complete each sentence by using a fraction.

17. April and May are ▓ of a year.

18. The letters *A, B, C,* and *D* are ▓ of the letters in the alphabet.

Mixed Applications

19. A garden has 4 rows of pineapple plants with 8 plants in each row. If each plant produces a total of 3 pineapples, how many pineapples in all will the plants produce?

20. Abdul sells pineapples. He has 96. If he sells 14, what fraction of the pineapples will he sell?

21. Suki plants 2 pepper shrubs a day. If she plants a total of 14 pepper shrubs in a week, what fraction of the shrubs does she plant each day?

22. **Write a Question** There are 3 red flowers, 4 yellow flowers, and 5 white flowers in a bouquet. Write a question using fractions.

VISUAL THINKING

Look at this list of fractions:
$\dfrac{1}{1}, \dfrac{1}{2}, \dfrac{1}{3}, \dfrac{1}{4}.$

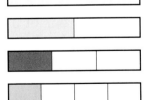

Look at this list of fractions:
$\dfrac{1}{8}, \dfrac{2}{8}, \dfrac{3}{8}, \dfrac{4}{8}.$

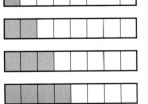

23. If the denominator increases and the numerator stays the same, what happens to the sizes of the fractions?

24. If the denominator stays the same and the numerator increases, what happens to the sizes of the fractions?

If $\frac{4}{5}$ of 5 flowers are yellow, how many are yellow?

W R A P
UP...

EXPLORING

Equivalent Fractions

A fraction such as $\frac{1}{2}$ can be renamed as different fractions with the same value. How many fractions can you find that name the same amount as $\frac{1}{2}$?

Work Together

Building Understanding

Use the fraction bars or fraction circles on pages H98–H100. Start with a whole for each model.

- Model other fractions that show the same amount as $\frac{1}{2}$.

- Draw a picture of each of your models, and record the fractions. Make sure all the models of $\frac{1}{2}$ have the same overall size.

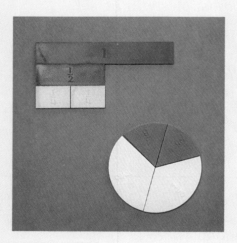

Model $\frac{1}{3}$.

- Use the same steps as you used above.

Present pictures of your models to the class. Explain how you know each picture represents the same amount as $\frac{1}{2}$ or $\frac{1}{3}$.

WRITE ABOUT IT

Fractions that name the same number or amount are called **equivalent fractions.** Choose an equivalent fraction for $\frac{1}{2}$ and another for $\frac{1}{3}$. Write a conclusion that explains why the fractions in each pair are equivalent fractions.

Making the Connection

You can fold and shade a piece of paper to rename a fraction.

Fold and shade a strip of paper to make equal parts as shown in Figure A.

A.

Fold the model in half as shown in Figure B.

B.

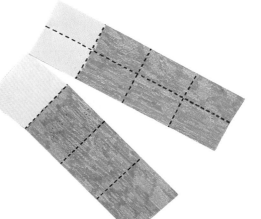

TALK ABOUT IT

- Describe the size of the whole after both folds.

- What happens to the total number of parts when you fold the model in half?

- What happens to the number of shaded parts when you fold the model in half?

- How can you use paper folding to rename $\frac{3}{4}$ using eighths?

Checking Understanding

Write the equivalent fractions for each pair of pictures.

1.
2.
3.
4.
5.

Draw two pictures to find an equivalent fraction.

6. $\frac{4}{20}$ 7. $\frac{2}{3}$ 8. $\frac{12}{16}$ 9. $\frac{3}{8}$ 10. $\frac{4}{24}$

MORE EQUIVALENT FRACTIONS

Lana folded a sheet of paper into thirds. She colored $\frac{2}{3}$ red. Then she folded her paper in half. The result was 6 parts instead of 3. Then how much was colored red?

$\frac{2}{3}$  →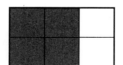

You can find equivalent fractions by multiplying or dividing the numerator and the denominator by the same number.

$\frac{2 \times 2}{3 \times 2} = \frac{4}{6}$ When the paper is folded in half, the number of parts is doubled, so both the numerator and denominator are multiplied by 2.

So, $\frac{4}{6}$ of Lana's paper was colored red.

When fractions are equivalent, you can find a missing numerator or denominator. You can multiply or divide to find the missing number.

Examples

A. Multiply.

$\frac{3}{5} = \frac{\blacksquare}{15}$ Think: By what was 5 multiplied to get 15?

$\frac{3 \times \blacksquare}{5 \times 3} = \frac{\blacksquare}{15}$

$\frac{3}{5} = \frac{9}{15}$

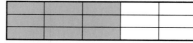

B. Divide.

$\frac{9}{15} = \frac{\blacksquare}{5}$ Think: By what was 15 divided to get 5?

$\frac{9 \div \blacksquare}{15 \div 3} = \frac{\blacksquare}{5}$

$\frac{9}{15} = \frac{3}{5}$

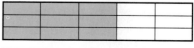
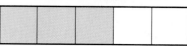

Check for Understanding

Tell by what number you multiply or divide to find the missing number. Write the missing number.

1. $\frac{1}{2} = \frac{\blacksquare}{8}$

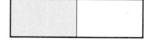
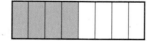

2. $\frac{1}{8} = \frac{\blacksquare}{32}$

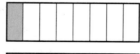
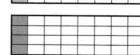

3. $\frac{2}{3} = \frac{\blacksquare}{18}$

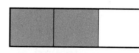
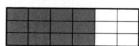

Practice

Find the missing numerator or denominator.

4. $\frac{1}{3} = \frac{\blacksquare}{6}$

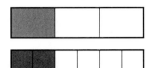

5. $\frac{2}{5} = \frac{\blacksquare}{10}$

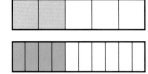

6. $\frac{1}{4} = \frac{2}{\blacksquare}$

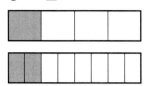

7. $\frac{4}{16} = \frac{\blacksquare}{4}$

8. $\frac{2}{3} = \frac{14}{\blacksquare}$

9. $\frac{9}{21} = \frac{\blacksquare}{7}$

Which fraction is *not* equivalent to the given fraction? Write **a, b,** or **c.**

10. $\frac{1}{2}$ **a.** $\frac{5}{10}$ **b.** $\frac{6}{14}$ **c.** $\frac{8}{16}$

11. $\frac{2}{3}$ **a.** $\frac{4}{6}$ **b.** $\frac{8}{12}$ **c.** $\frac{5}{9}$

12. $\frac{3}{4}$ **a.** $\frac{6}{12}$ **b.** $\frac{12}{16}$ **c.** $\frac{15}{20}$

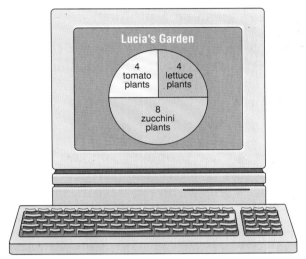

Mixed Applications

Use the graph for Exercises 13–15.

13. Write a fraction to show what part of Lucia's garden is planted with tomato plants.

14. Write two equivalent fractions to show what part of Lucia's garden is planted with zucchini plants.

15. **Analyze Data**   If Lucia had 3 times as many tomato plants, 4 times as many lettuce plants, and 2 times as many zucchini plants, how many plants would she have?

MIXED REVIEW

Divide.

1. $6\overline{)58}$ **2.** $5\overline{)83}$ **3.** $4\overline{)68}$ **4.** $7\overline{)504}$ **5.** $3\overline{)705}$

Identify the triangle. Write *equilateral, scalene,* or *isosceles.*

6. 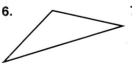   **7.** 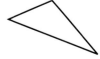   **8.**   **9.** 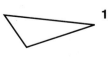   **10.**

How do you compute to find equivalent fractions?   **WRAP UP...**

PROBLEM SOLVING

Choose a Strategy

Understand
Plan
Solve
Look Back

Bernard's azalea garden was planted in a circle. He liked to water the bushes in a pattern. One day he watered every third bush starting with the first bush. If he stayed on the path shown, did he water each of the 8 bushes before coming back to the first?

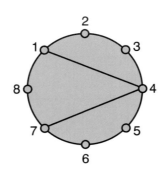

Sometimes you can use more than one strategy to solve a problem.

What strategy can you use for this problem? You can *act it out* or *draw a diagram* to solve the problem.

Strategy: Act It Out

To *act out* the problem, you can set up 8 chairs in the pattern described. Keep a record of the watering results for the 8 bushes.

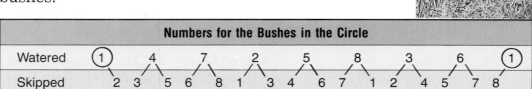

Numbers for the Bushes in the Circle															
Watered	①		4		7		2		5		8		3		6	①
Skipped		2 3		5 6		8 1		3 4		6 7		1 2		4 5		7 8

Strategy: Draw a Diagram

Or you can *draw a diagram* of the 8 bushes in a circle. Beginning with number one, show the whole path for the watering pattern.

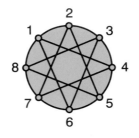

So, Bernard did water each bush before coming back to the first.

WHAT
IF...
... Bernard chose a different pattern? Which patterns would take him to all the bushes?

Mixed Applications ⟩ **STRATEGIES** Act It Out • Make a Table • Solve a Simpler Problem • Write a Number Sentence • Draw a Diagram

Choose a strategy and solve.

(1) Samuel's garden has 10 bushes planted in a circle. If he weeds every third bush, will he weed each of the 10 bushes before coming back to the first?

(2) Margaret dug 11 holes to plant trees in a circle. If she skips 2 holes after each tree she plants, will she plant each of the 11 trees before coming back to the first?

(3) One row of carrots produces 2.5 kg of carrots. One row of beets produces 2.3 kg of beets. How many more kilograms of carrots than beets would come from 5 rows of carrots and 4 rows of beets?

(4) There are 8 vegetables being planted in a garden. There will be 2 different vegetables in each row. If every vegetable is planted with each of the other vegetables, how many rows will be in the garden?

(5) Emilia can plant 8 flowers in 5 minutes. How long will it take her to plant 120 flowers?

(6) There are 4 tomatoes in a circular display. If a customer examines every third tomato, will all the tomatoes be examined before the customer examines the first tomato again?

(7) Jamie and Erika operate the family produce stand during the summer. On the first day, Jamie took in $150 between 9:00 A.M. and noon. Erika took in $270 between noon and 5:00 P.M. How much more did Erika take in each hour?

WRITER'S CORNER

(8) Write a problem that can be solved by *acting it out* or *drawing a diagram*. Solve your problem to make sure it works. Exchange your problem with a classmate.

1. Pang purchased 6 azaleas for $8.99 each and 3 oleanders for $5.99 each. How much did Pang pay for the azalea plants?

2. There are 10 plants in a circle. If Billy weeds every other plant, will he weed each of the 10 plants before coming back to the first? Why or why not?

3. There are 7 flowers planted in a circle. If Aki waters every third flower, how many times will she go around the circle before each flower is watered?

4. Flo makes arrangements. She sold 4 large arrangements for $40 each and 3 small arrangements for $25 each. How much did she receive for her large arrangements?

Round to the nearest whole number.

5. 3.68
6. 0.84
7. 45.094
8. 32.846

> Sometimes a problem has more information than I need to answer the question.

Find the sum or difference.

9. 23,845
   + 60,275

10. 4.78
    + 6.32

11. 36,842
    − 19,689

12. 8.78
    − 4.23

Match each polygon with its name. Write **a, b, c,** or **d.**

| **a.** triangle | **b.** pentagon | **c.** hexagon | **d.** octagon |

13.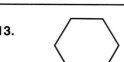

14.

15.

16.

Divide.

17. $17\overline{)136}$
18. $14\overline{)295}$
19. $21\overline{)5,570}$
20. $32\overline{)96,640}$
21. $15\overline{)32,805}$

Multiply.

22. 451
    × 3.5

23. 6.52
    × 22

24. 0.07
    × 8

25. 45.38
    × 24

26. 35.04
    × 1.9

Find the missing numerator or denominator.

27. $\frac{1}{3} = \frac{\blacksquare}{18}$

28. $\frac{3}{7} = \frac{\blacksquare}{49}$

29. $\frac{2}{3} = \frac{\blacksquare}{9}$

30. $\frac{8}{12} = \frac{\blacksquare}{3}$

MULTICULTURAL CONNECTION

AFRICA

South Africa —

Using Equivalent Fractions

Many of South Africa's flowers, such as geraniums, have become popular in Europe and the United States. Two popular flowers grown in South Africa are the chincherinchee (chin chuh rin CHEE) and the bird-of-paradise.

Abasi makes floral arrangements. One of his arrangements is $\frac{1}{3}$ bird-of-paradise flowers. If he makes this arrangement using 12 flowers, how many bird-of-paradise flowers will he need?

Step 1

$$\frac{1}{3} = \frac{\blacksquare}{12}$$

Step 2

$$\frac{1 \times 4}{3 \times 4} = \frac{4}{12}$$

MULTICULTURAL NOTE: South Africa exports bird-of-paradise flowers to florists around the world.

Since $\frac{1}{3} = \frac{4}{12}$, he will need 4 bird-of-paradise flowers.

Suppose each arrangement below is $\frac{1}{3}$ bird-of-paradise flowers. Use an equivalent fraction to find each solution.

1. If there are 15 flowers, how many are bird-of-paradise flowers?

2. If there are 30 flowers, how many are not bird-of-paradise?

3. If 8 of the flowers are bird-of-paradise, how many flowers are in the arrangement?

Suppose each arrangement below is $\frac{2}{5}$ chincherinchees. Use an equivalent fraction to find each solution.

4. If there are 15 flowers, how many are chincherinchees?

5. If 10 of the flowers are chincherinchees, how many flowers are in the arrangement?

6. If there are 20 flowers, how many flowers are not chincherinchees?

EXPLORING

Prime and Composite Numbers

People in cities may not have as much room to plant gardens as people with large yards or farms, but they can grow flowers or vegetables in boxes on porches or in window boxes.

This "box garden" shows one way 8 boxes can be arranged in the shape of a rectangle.

Work Together

Building Understanding

With connecting cubes you can show all the ways that 8 boxes can be arranged to represent a rectangular box garden.

There are four ways that 8 boxes can be arranged as rectangles. Use connecting cubes to show the rectangles. Rectangles can be described by naming their length times their width. The length and width are factors.

2 × 4 ⬜⬜⬜⬜
⬜⬜⬜⬜

1 × 8   4 × 2 ⬜⬜   8 × 1 ⬜
⬜⬜   ⬜
⬜⬜   ⬜
⬜⬜   ⬜
⬜⬜⬜⬜⬜⬜⬜⬜   ⬜
                ⬜
                ⬜
                ⬜

- Show all the possible ways 4 boxes can be arranged to represent a rectangular box garden.

- Show all the possible ways 12 boxes can be arranged to represent a rectangular box garden.

TALK ABOUT IT
- What factors were used in the rectangles for 8 boxes?

- What factors were used in the rectangles you made with 4 boxes? 12 boxes?

Making the Connection

Copy and complete the table. Use cubes to make the rectangles.

Number of Boxes	Arrangement of Rectangles	The Different Factors	Number of Different Factors
2	1 × 2; 2 × 1	1, 2	2
3	1 × 3; 3 × 1	1, 3	■
4	1 × 4; 4 × 1; 2 × 2	1, 2, 4	3
5	1 × 5; 5 × 1	■	■
6	■ × ■; ■ × ■; ■ × ■; ■ × ■	■	■
7	■ × ■; ■ × ■	■	■
8	1 × 8; 8 × 1; 2 × 4; 4 × 2	■	■
9	■ × ■; ■ × ■; ■ × ■	■	■
10	■ × ■; ■ × ■; ■ × ■; ■ × ■	■	■

- List the numbers of boxes that make only two different arrangements.

  Each of these numbers has two different factors: 1 and the number itself. They are called **prime numbers.**

1 is neither prime nor composite.

- List the numbers in the table that make more than two different arrangements.

  Each of these numbers has more than two factors. They are called **composite numbers.**

Checking Understanding

Use the Sieve of Eratosthenes to find prime numbers. Copy the table onto graph paper.

1. Cross out 1. It is neither prime nor composite.

2. Circle 2, 3, 5, and 7. They are all prime. How do you know?

3. Cross out all the multiples of 2, 3, 5, and 7. What kind of numbers are they?

4. Circle the remaining numbers. How many factors does each have? What kind of numbers are they?

5. Continue the table to 100. List all the prime numbers.

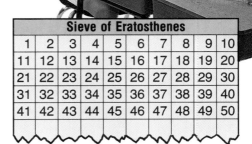

Sieve of Eratosthenes									
1	2	3	4	5	6	7	8	9	10
11	12	13	14	15	16	17	18	19	20
21	22	23	24	25	26	27	28	29	30
31	32	33	34	35	36	37	38	39	40
41	42	43	44	45	46	47	48	49	50

EXPLORING

Common Factors

Max has 12 marigold and 18 pepper plants. He wants to put them in containers that hold the same number and same kind of plants. What is the greatest number of marigold or pepper plants that each container should hold?

Work Together

Building Understanding

Use 12 yellow connecting cubes to represent the marigold plants and 18 green connecting cubes to represent the pepper plants.

- With a partner, find and draw as many different arrangements as you can using the 12 yellow cubes.

Examples

2 × 6   1 × 12

- List the multiplication facts that describe these arrangements.

- Find and draw as many different arrangements as you can using the 18 green cubes.

- List the multiplication facts that describe these arrangements.

- List the factors of 12.

- List the factors of 18.

TALK ABOUT IT

- What factors in both lists are the same?

- Of the factors that are the same, which is the greatest?

- What is the greatest number of marigold or pepper plants each container should hold?

288

Making the Connection

Max solved his problem by finding the **greatest common factor** of 12 and 18. The greatest common factor is the greatest factor a pair of numbers have in common.

If Max wanted to package 18 garlic plants and 27 tomato plants equally without mixing the plants and with none left over, what would be the greatest number of plants he could put in each package?

You can find this number of plants by finding the greatest common factor of 18 and 27.

- Begin by listing all the factors of 18 and 27.

Factors of 18: 1, ▦, ▦, ▦, ▦, 18

Factors of 27: 1, ▦, ▦, 27

TALK ABOUT IT

- Why is it useful to list factors in order?

- What are the common factors of 18 and 27?

- What is the greatest common factor of 18 and 27?

- What is the greatest number of plants Max can put in each package?

Checking Understanding

List the factors of each number.

1. 16　　　　2. 28　　　　3. 36　　　　4. 48　　　　5. 64

List the factors of each number. Write the greatest common factor for each pair of numbers.

6. 6, 12　　　7. 3, 4　　　8. 4, 5　　　9. 6, 8　　　10. 4, 8

FRACTIONS
in Simplest Form

Sherry experimented to see if all of her seeds would grow into seedlings. She found that 8 of the 12 seeds she planted grew into seedlings. How can she express her results as a fraction in simplest form?

A fraction is in **simplest form** when the greatest common factor, or GCF, of the numerator and denominator is 1.

The fraction $\frac{8}{12}$ is not in simplest form. To write $\frac{8}{12}$ in simplest form, follow these steps.

Step 1	**Step 2**
Find the greatest common factor of 8 and 12.	Divide the numerator and denominator by the GCF.
Factors of 8: 1, 2, 4	
Factors of 12: 1, 2, 3, 4, 6, 12	
	$\dfrac{8 \div 4}{12 \div 4} = \dfrac{2}{3}$ ← The GCF of 2 and 3 is 1.
The GCF is 4.	

So, $\frac{8}{12}$ in simplest form is $\frac{2}{3}$.

Another Method

You can write a fraction in simplest form by dividing the numerator and denominator by any common factor. Divide until the greatest common factor of the numerator and denominator is 1.

$$\frac{18 \div 3}{24 \div 3} = \frac{6}{8} \longrightarrow \frac{6 \div 2}{8 \div 2} = \frac{3}{4} \longrightarrow \frac{18}{24} = \frac{3}{4} \longleftarrow \text{simplest form}$$

Talk About It

▶ How are the two methods for writing fractions in simplest form different?

▶ When is it easier to use the second method for writing a fraction in simplest form?

Check for Understanding

Write in simplest form.

1. $\dfrac{4}{8}$

2. $\dfrac{9}{12}$

3. $\dfrac{4}{12}$

4. $\dfrac{8}{24}$

5. $\dfrac{10}{20}$

Practice

Tell whether the fraction is in simplest form. Write *yes* or *no*.

6. $\dfrac{3}{6}$ **7.** $\dfrac{2}{5}$ **8.** $\dfrac{3}{4}$ **9.** $\dfrac{4}{12}$ **10.** $\dfrac{7}{9}$

Write in simplest form.

11. $\dfrac{12}{15}$ **12.** $\dfrac{9}{12}$ **13.** $\dfrac{10}{12}$ **14.** $\dfrac{15}{18}$ **15.** $\dfrac{10}{25}$

16. $\dfrac{6}{15}$ **17.** $\dfrac{12}{14}$ **18.** $\dfrac{16}{32}$ **19.** $\dfrac{30}{40}$ **20.** $\dfrac{18}{45}$

Mixed Applications

21. Yori brought 8 plants to school for a science project. A total of 24 plants were brought to school. Write in simplest form the fraction of all the plants brought in that were Yori's.

22. Critical Thinking If a fraction is in simplest form, can the greatest common factor of the numerator and denominator be 2? Explain.

23. One store sells 3 packages of seeds for $5.25. Another store sells each package for $1.49. What is the difference in the price per package between the stores?

24. Kathleen scored 87, 91, 95, 92, and 85 on 5 science tests. What is her average score?

VISUAL THINKING

25. Use the picture to find the greatest common factor.

factors of 18   factors of 24

9 18   1 2 3 6   4 8 12 24

common factors

EXPLORING

Least Common Multiples

Mr. Hamilton wants to plant one row with tulip bulbs and another row with an equal number of crocus bulbs. Tulip bulbs come 3 to a box. Crocus bulbs come 4 to a box. If all the bulbs from all the boxes are used, what is the least number of bulbs he can put in each row?

Knowing about **multiples** can help you find the answer.

A **multiple** is the product of two or more numbers. → Multiples of 2: 2, 4, 6, 8, . . .
Multiples of 3: 3, 6, 9, 12, . . .

Work Together

Building Understanding

Use geometric shapes and what you know about multiples to help determine the least number Mr. Hamilton can plant in each row.

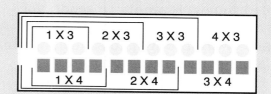

- Line up a row of 3 circle shapes to represent one box of tulip bulbs.
- Line up a row of 4 square shapes to represent one box of crocus bulbs.
- Compare the rows. Are they equal?

- Place groups of 3 circles in the circle row and groups of 4 squares in the square row until both rows have the same number of shapes.

TALK ABOUT IT

- If Mr. Hamilton wants the least number of bulbs in each row, how many bulbs should he plant in each row?

- Name some multiples of 3 greater than 0.

- Name some multiples of 4 greater than 0.

- Which multiples of 3 are also multiples of 4?

Multiples of one number that are also multiples of another number are called **common multiples.** The smallest number that is a common multiple is called the **least common multiple** (LCM).

- What is the least common multiple of 3 and 4? How does this compare to the number of bulbs Mr. Hamilton should plant in each row?

Making the Connection

Some multiples of 2 and of 8 that are
greater than 0 are shown on the
number line.

Some common multiples are 8 and 16.
The smallest number that is a common
multiple is 8. So, 8 is the least common
multiple of 2 and 8.

TALK ABOUT IT

- How are using the number line
  and lining up shapes alike?

- How can you find the least common
  multiple of two numbers without using
  a number line or lining up shapes?

Checking Understanding

Use geometric shapes, draw a number line, or list multiples to solve.

1. What is the least common multiple of 6 and 9?

2. What is the least common multiple of 8 and 3?

3. Paving stones come in boxes. Mr. Hamilton will use
   triangular and rectangular patio stones for a sidewalk,
   and he will use all the stones he buys. If he uses the
   same number of each shape, how many stones will be
   in the shortest sidewalk he makes?

4. If Mr. Hamilton uses the same number of circular and
   triangular stones, how many stones will be in the
   sidewalk he makes?

5. If Mr. Hamilton uses the same number of circular,
   triangular, and rectangular stones, how many stones
   will be in the sidewalk he makes?

shape of stone	number in a box
○	6
◺	3
▭	5

More Practice, Lesson 9.8, page H68

COMPARING FRACTIONS

Mr. Sigman planted flower seeds in $\frac{2}{3}$ of the garden. Mrs. Sigman planted $\frac{3}{9}$ of the garden with herbs. Is more of the garden planted with flowers or herbs?

You can compare numerators or use fraction bars to compare fractions with like denominators. Which is greater, $\frac{2}{5}$ or $\frac{4}{5}$?

| $\frac{1}{5}$ | $\frac{1}{5}$ | $\frac{1}{5}$ | $\frac{1}{5}$ | $\frac{1}{5}$ |

| $\frac{1}{5}$ | $\frac{1}{5}$ | $\frac{1}{5}$ | $\frac{1}{5}$ | $\frac{1}{5}$ |

The fraction bar shows that $\frac{4}{5}$ is longer. Also, $4 > 2$. So, $\frac{4}{5} > \frac{2}{5}$.

You can use fraction bars to compare fractions with unlike denominators.

| $\frac{1}{3}$ | $\frac{1}{3}$ | $\frac{1}{3}$ |

| $\frac{1}{9}$ | $\frac{1}{9}$ | $\frac{1}{9}$ | $\frac{1}{9}$ | $\frac{1}{9}$ | $\frac{1}{9}$ | $\frac{1}{9}$ | $\frac{1}{9}$ | $\frac{1}{9}$ |

The fraction bars show that $\frac{2}{3}$ is longer. So, $\frac{2}{3} > \frac{3}{9}$. More of the garden is planted with flowers.

Another Method

Compare $\frac{2}{3}$ and $\frac{3}{9}$ by renaming them as fractions with like denominators.

Step 1 Find the least common multiple (LCM) of 3 and 9.	**Step 2** Write an equivalent fraction. Use the LCM as the denominator.	**Step 3** Compare the numerators.
3: 3, 6, 9 9: 9	$\dfrac{2 \times 3}{3 \times 3} = \dfrac{\blacksquare}{9}$ $\quad \dfrac{2}{3} = \dfrac{6}{9}$	$\dfrac{6}{9} > \dfrac{3}{9}$ $\quad$ So, $\dfrac{2}{3} > \dfrac{3}{9}$.

• Why do you change fractions to have like denominators?

Check for Understanding

Compare. Write the greater fraction in each pair.

1. $\frac{5}{7}, \frac{6}{7}$
2. $\frac{3}{4}, \frac{5}{8}$
3. $\frac{5}{6}, \frac{2}{4}$
4. $\frac{1}{2}, \frac{3}{8}$
5. $\frac{3}{12}, \frac{7}{24}$
6. $\frac{5}{15}, \frac{3}{5}$

Practice

Compare. Write <, >, or = for .

7. $\frac{2}{4}$ ● $\frac{3}{4}$ 8. $\frac{1}{4}$ ● $\frac{1}{8}$ 9. $\frac{2}{3}$ ● $\frac{5}{6}$ 10. $\frac{7}{8}$ ● $\frac{5}{6}$

11. $\frac{5}{6}$ ● $\frac{3}{4}$ 12. $\frac{1}{2}$ ● $\frac{3}{6}$ 13. $\frac{5}{8}$ ● $\frac{2}{3}$ 14. $\frac{6}{8}$ ● $\frac{3}{4}$

15. $\frac{3}{4}$ ● $\frac{5}{8}$ 16. $\frac{1}{8}$ ● $\frac{1}{6}$ 17. $\frac{1}{2}$ ● $\frac{3}{8}$ 18. $\frac{2}{3}$ ● $\frac{4}{6}$

Mixed Applications

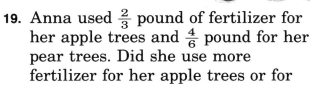
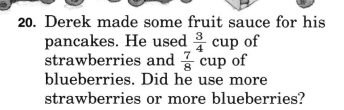

19. Anna used $\frac{2}{3}$ pound of fertilizer for her apple trees and $\frac{4}{6}$ pound for her pear trees. Did she use more fertilizer for her apple trees or for her pear trees?

20. Derek made some fruit sauce for his pancakes. He used $\frac{3}{4}$ cup of strawberries and $\frac{7}{8}$ cup of blueberries. Did he use more strawberries or more blueberries?

21. The members of the garden club are purchasing seeds. One catalog advertises $\frac{5}{6}$ pound of pumpkin seeds for $1, and another catalog offers $\frac{7}{8}$ pound of pumpkin seeds for $1. Which is the better buy?

22. Brent planted $\frac{1}{3}$ of his garden with tomato plants, and Jill planted $\frac{2}{5}$ of her garden with tomato plants. Who has more tomato plants if both the gardens have the same number of plants?

23. Rhonda bought a total of 12 packages of seeds, 4 packages of which were flower seeds. Write in simplest form the fraction that were flower seeds.

24. **Write a Question** Using the fractions $\frac{1}{2}$ and $\frac{3}{5}$, write a question in which the fractions are compared.

MIXED REVIEW

Find the range, mode, median, and mean.

1. $75, 80, 80, 100, 90$ 2. $14.40; $15.75; $15.75   3. $425, 505, 375, 425, 350$

Find the product.

4. 6.7×5 5. 12.8×9 6. 6.32×1.4 7. 12.93×12 8. 10.95×21

Describe how to compare fractions with unlike denominators.

WRAP UP...

ORDERING FRACTIONS

Lynette plants $\frac{1}{6}$ of the garden with vegetables. Larry plants $\frac{1}{2}$ of the garden with flowers, and Jeff plants $\frac{1}{3}$ of the garden with strawberries. How can they find who plants the greatest and the least amounts of space in the garden?

You can compare the amounts of garden space by using fraction bars to order from least to greatest.

| $\frac{1}{6}$ | $\frac{1}{6}$ | $\frac{1}{6}$ | $\frac{1}{6}$ | $\frac{1}{6}$ | $\frac{1}{6}$ |

| $\frac{1}{3}$ | $\frac{1}{3}$ | $\frac{1}{3}$ |

| $\frac{1}{2}$ | $\frac{1}{2}$ |

The fraction bars show that $\frac{1}{6} < \frac{1}{3} < \frac{1}{2}$. So, Larry plants the greatest amount of garden space, and Lynette plants the least amount of garden space.

Another Method

Another way to compare is to use the least common multiple to rename the fractions so they have like denominators.

$\frac{1}{2} \longrightarrow$ 2: 2, 4, 6
$\frac{1}{3} \longrightarrow$ 3: 3, 6, 9
$\frac{1}{6} \longrightarrow$ 6: 6

The least common multiple of 2, 3, and 6 is 6.

Step 1
Write equivalent fractions with like denominators.

$\frac{1}{6} = \frac{1}{6}$ $\frac{1}{3} = \frac{\blacksquare}{6}$ $\frac{1}{2} = \frac{\blacksquare}{6}$

$\frac{1}{3} = \frac{2}{6}$ $\frac{1}{2} = \frac{3}{6}$

Step 2
Compare the numerators.

$\frac{1}{6} \bullet \frac{2}{6} \bullet \frac{3}{6}$

So, $\frac{1}{6} < \frac{1}{3} < \frac{1}{2}$.

Check for Understanding

Use like denominators to rename the fractions. Order the fractions from least to greatest. You may use a number line if you want.

1. $\frac{2}{4}, \frac{1}{3}, \frac{3}{8}$

2. $\frac{2}{10}, \frac{8}{12}, \frac{2}{5}$

3. $\frac{2}{3}, \frac{3}{9}, \frac{3}{27}$

Practice

Write in order from least to greatest.

4. $\dfrac{3}{4}, \dfrac{2}{8}, \dfrac{1}{2}$

5. $\dfrac{1}{3}, \dfrac{2}{3}, \dfrac{1}{6}$

6. $\dfrac{6}{8}, \dfrac{1}{8}, \dfrac{2}{4}$

Write in order from greatest to least.

7. $\dfrac{3}{8}, \dfrac{2}{4}, \dfrac{5}{16}$

8. $\dfrac{2}{3}, \dfrac{3}{15}, \dfrac{4}{5}$

9. $\dfrac{1}{2}, \dfrac{3}{4}, \dfrac{7}{12}$

Mixed Applications

10. Alfonso made punch for a party. The recipe called for $\frac{1}{2}$ gallon of orange juice, $\frac{3}{4}$ gallon of pineapple juice, and $\frac{4}{5}$ gallon of grape juice. List the ingredients in order from greatest to least.

11. Cara used a recipe calling for $\frac{3}{4}$ cup of cherries, $\frac{5}{8}$ cup of water, and $\frac{1}{2}$ cup of honey. List the ingredients in order from the least amount used to the greatest amount used.

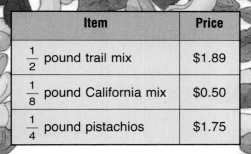

Use the price list for Exercises 12–14.

12. Esther bought each of the items listed. Write the fractions in order from least to greatest.

Item	Price
$\frac{1}{2}$ pound trail mix	$1.89
$\frac{1}{8}$ pound California mix	$0.50
$\frac{1}{4}$ pound pistachios	$1.75

13. Critical Thinking Is a pound of trail mix or a pound of pistachios more expensive?

14. Analyze Data If Esther bought each of the items listed, did she have enough left over from $6.00 to buy another $\frac{1}{2}$ pound of trail mix?

VISUAL THINKING

15. Copy the number line. At the correct place, write each fraction.

$$\dfrac{1}{4}, \dfrac{5}{12}, \dfrac{2}{3}, \dfrac{1}{3}, \dfrac{3}{4}, \dfrac{1}{6}$$

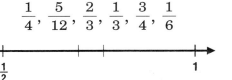

16. Which is greater, $\frac{5}{12}$ or $\frac{1}{2}$?

17. Which is less, $\frac{1}{4}$ or $\frac{1}{6}$?

What skill for comparing numbers is needed to order unlike fractions? **WRAP UP...**

EXPLORING

Mixed Numbers

Mr. Fedler planted two gardens. He divided each garden into four parts and planted some of them with corn. How many parts of both gardens were planted with corn?

A   B

Work Together

Building Understanding

Use fraction bars to represent Mr. Fedler's two gardens.

Remember: $1 = \frac{2}{2}, \frac{3}{3}, \frac{4}{4}, \frac{5}{5}, \ldots$

TALK ABOUT IT

- In garden A, how many fourths were planted with corn?

- In garden B, how many fourths were planted with corn?

- In both gardens, how many fourths were planted with corn?

- Which is greater, $\frac{5}{4}$ or 1?

Andy Fedler had two pumpkin patches. Each patch was divided into fourths, and all were planted with pumpkins.

Use fraction bars to show Andy's pumpkin patches.

TALK ABOUT IT

- In patch C, how many fourths were planted with pumpkins?

- What fraction describes the number of fourths planted in patches C and D?

- What whole number describes the patches that were planted with pumpkins?

C

D

298

Making the Connection

Some fractions greater than 1 are renamed as whole numbers.

Here is one way to rename $\frac{16}{8}$.

$\frac{8}{8} = 1$ $\frac{8}{8} = 1$

| $\frac{8}{8}$ | $+$ | $\frac{8}{8}$ | $=$ | $\frac{16}{8}$ |
| 1 | $+$ | 1 | $=$ | 2 |

You can also divide to rename a fraction greater than 1 as a whole number.

$$\frac{16}{8} \longrightarrow \begin{array}{r} 2 \\ 8\overline{)16} \\ -16 \\ \hline 0 \end{array}$$

So, another name for $\frac{16}{8}$ is 2.

In the fraction $\frac{9}{8}$, the numerator, 9, is greater than the denominator, 8.

You can rename $\frac{9}{8}$ as a mixed number.

A **mixed number** is a whole number with a fraction.
Here is one way to rename $\frac{9}{8}$.

$\frac{8}{8} = 1$ $\frac{1}{8}$

| 1 | $+$ | $\frac{1}{8}$ | $=$ | $1\frac{1}{8}$ |

You can also divide to rename a fraction greater than 1 as a mixed number.

$$\frac{9}{8} \longrightarrow \begin{array}{r} 1 \\ 8\overline{)9} \\ -8 \\ \hline 1 \end{array}$$ Write the remainder as the fraction $\frac{1}{8}$.

So, another name for $\frac{9}{8}$ is $1\frac{1}{8}$.

Sometimes you need to rename a mixed number as a fraction greater than 1.

$2\frac{1}{3} \longrightarrow$ $1 = \frac{3}{3}$ $1 = \frac{3}{3}$ $\frac{1}{3}$

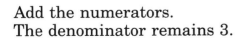

Add the numerators.
The denominator remains 3.

$$\frac{3}{3} + \frac{3}{3} + \frac{1}{3} = \frac{3 + 3 + 1}{3} = \frac{7}{3}$$

So, $2\frac{1}{3} = \frac{3}{3} + \frac{3}{3} + \frac{1}{3} = \frac{7}{3}$.

You can also use multiplication and addition to change a mixed number to a fraction greater than 1.

$$2\frac{1}{3} = \frac{(3 \times 2) + 1}{3} = \frac{6 + 1}{3} = \frac{7}{3}$$

So, another name for $2\frac{1}{3}$ is $\frac{7}{3}$.

A. How can you order $2\frac{3}{16}$, $2\frac{3}{8}$, and $2\frac{1}{4}$?

To put mixed numbers in order, first compare the whole numbers. You can see that the whole numbers are equal.

$$2\frac{3}{16} \quad 2\frac{3}{8} \quad 2\frac{1}{4}$$

Next, rename the fractions so they have a common denominator.

$$2\frac{3}{16} = 2\frac{3}{16}; \qquad 2\frac{3}{8} = 2\frac{6}{16}; \qquad 2\frac{1}{4} = 2\frac{4}{16}$$

Arrange the mixed numbers in order from least to greatest. So, $2\frac{3}{16} < 2\frac{1}{4} < 2\frac{3}{8}$.

B. When the whole numbers are not the same, put them in order first.

$$3\frac{2}{4}; \ 4\frac{1}{12}; \ 3\frac{4}{6}; \ 4\frac{1}{3}$$

$$3\frac{2}{4}; \ 3\frac{4}{6}; \ 4\frac{1}{12}; \ 4\frac{1}{3}$$

Next, rename the fractions. Use a common denominator.

$$3\frac{2}{4} = 3\frac{6}{12}; 3\frac{4}{6} = 3\frac{8}{12}; 4\frac{1}{12} = 4\frac{1}{12}; 4\frac{1}{3} = 4\frac{4}{12}$$

Order the mixed numbers from least to greatest. So, $3\frac{2}{4} < 3\frac{4}{6} < 4\frac{1}{12} < 4\frac{1}{3}$.

Checking Understanding

Write a whole number or a mixed number for each picture.

1.

2.

3.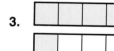

Rename each as a mixed number or a whole number.

4. $\dfrac{8}{5}$

5. $\dfrac{9}{5}$

6. $\dfrac{7}{4}$

7. $\dfrac{12}{3}$

Rename each as a fraction.

8. $7\dfrac{3}{4}$

9. $2\dfrac{1}{2}$

10. $5\dfrac{1}{3}$

11. $3\dfrac{6}{8}$

Arrange in order from least to greatest.

12. $5\dfrac{8}{12}; 5\dfrac{3}{6}; 5\dfrac{1}{3}$

13. $2\dfrac{3}{6}; 4\dfrac{4}{12}; 3\dfrac{2}{3}$

PROBLEM-SOLVING PRACTICE

Sammy the earthworm has set a goal of traveling through Mr. Fedler's garden in less than one month.

1. Sammy is $\frac{1}{4}$ inch wide. His sister is $\frac{7}{16}$ inch wide, and his brother is $\frac{3}{8}$ inch wide. Write in order from least to greatest the sizes of Sammy and his brother and sister.

2. Sammy measures $\frac{11}{8}$ inches long. His sister is $\frac{13}{8}$ inches long, and his brother is $\frac{3}{2}$ inches long. Rename each of these fractions as a mixed number.

3. Sammy wants to estimate the number of vegetables in Mr. Fedler's garden. Based on the garden he was in last month, he thinks there will be 12 rows, with 14 plants in each row. About how many plants does Sammy estimate are in the garden?

4. Mr. Fedler planted 5 different vegetables in his garden. Each row has 2 different kinds of vegetables. In different rows, each vegetable is planted with each other vegetable once. How many rows are in Mr. Fedler's garden?

5. In 4 hours, Sammy travels 12 inches. At this rate, how many inches does Sammy travel in 24 hours?

6. If there are 10 plants in each row, how many plants are in the garden? (HINT: Use the answer from Exercise 4.)

7. If each plant in the garden takes up about 18 inches, how many plants does Sammy travel by in 24 hours? (HINT: Use the answer from Exercise 5.)

8. Sammy can travel from one row in the garden to the next row in 4 hours. How many days did it take Sammy to travel through Mr. Fedler's garden? Did he reach his goal?

PROBLEM SOLVING

STRATEGY • Draw a Picture

Mrs. Poe and Mrs. Beasley had gardens that were the same size. Each woman grew three crops: tomatoes, corn, and strawberries. The table shows the part of each garden planted with each crop. How much land is left in each garden?

Vegetable Gardens		
Crop	Mrs. Poe's Garden	Mrs. Beasley's Garden
Tomatoes	$\frac{2}{5}$	$\frac{1}{6}$
Corn	$\frac{1}{10}$	$\frac{1}{3}$
Strawberries	$\frac{1}{5}$	$\frac{4}{12}$

▶ **UNDERSTAND**

What are you asked to find?

What facts are given?

▶ **PLAN**

What strategy can you use?

You can *draw a picture* to find the amount of land that is not used in each garden.

▶ **SOLVE**

How can you solve the problem?

Since the sum of the fractional parts of a whole is 1, you can draw 2 whole fraction bars to represent each garden.

Draw and color each fractional part of the crops in each garden. The missing part of the whole in each drawing represents the amount of land that is left in each garden.

So, Mrs. Poe has $\frac{3}{10}$ of her land left and Mrs. Beasley has $\frac{2}{12}$ of her land left.

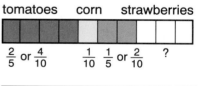

Mrs. Poe's Garden

tomatoes   corn   strawberries

$\frac{2}{5}$ or $\frac{4}{10}$ $\frac{1}{10}$ $\frac{1}{5}$ or $\frac{2}{10}$?

Mrs. Beasley's Garden

$\frac{1}{6}$ or $\frac{2}{12}$ $\frac{1}{3}$ or $\frac{4}{12}$ $\frac{4}{12}$?

▶ **LOOK BACK**

What other strategy can you use to solve the problem?

WHAT IF...

...Mrs. Beasley did not plant tomatoes and she doubled the amount of land used to grow strawberries?

CHOOSE

Apply

Draw a picture and solve.

1 The 36 students in Mrs. Day's class and the 36 students in Mr. Lee's class were asked to name their favorite vegetable. Which class has more students who like corn?

Favorite Vegetable		
Vegetable	Mrs. Day's Class	Mr. Lee's Class
Broccoli	$\frac{1}{3}$	$\frac{1}{9}$
Peas	$\frac{2}{9}$	$\frac{1}{18}$
Corn	■	$\frac{5}{6}$

2 Alfonso and Arlene estimated the amount of time they each have spent on their garden. The table shows their estimates. Who spends the most time weeding?

Gardening		
Activity	Alfonso	Arlene
Planting	$\frac{1}{8}$	$\frac{3}{8}$
Weeding	$\frac{3}{4}$	■
Watering	$\frac{1}{16}$	$\frac{1}{16}$
Picking	$\frac{1}{16}$	$\frac{1}{8}$

Mixed Applications **STRATEGIES** Work Backward • Guess and Check • Find a Pattern

Choose a strategy and solve.

3 Bonnie has $5.40 when she returns from the nursery. She knows she spent $4.95 on potting soil, $3.50 on planting tools, and $5.15 on seeds. How much did she have when she left for the nursery?

4 Mariana spent 20 minutes in her garden on Monday, 30 minutes on Tuesday, 45 minutes on Wednesday, and 65 minutes on Thursday. If the pattern continues, for how many minutes will she work in her garden on Friday? on Saturday?

5 Roscoe's vegetable stand sold tomatoes for $0.50 each and onions for $0.40 each. The same number of vegetables were brought to the stand in the morning. At noon Roscoe had $19.50 and twice as many tomatoes as onions left to sell. How many of each did he sell?

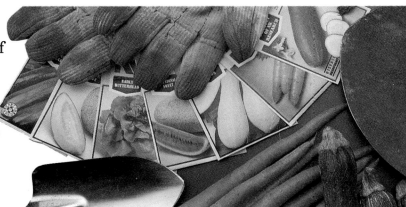

More Practice, Lesson 9.12, page H69

303

CHAPTER REVIEW/TEST

Vocabulary Check

Choose a word or words from the box to complete each sentence.

composite numbers
equivalent fractions
greatest common factor
least common multiple
mixed number
prime numbers
simplest form

1. Numbers with only two different factors are called __?__ . *(page 287)*

2. Fractions that name the same number or amount are called __?__ . *(page 279)*

3. Numbers with more than two different factors are called __?__ . *(page 287)*

4. The __?__ is the greatest factor a pair of numbers have in common. *(page 289)*

5. When a fraction is in __?__ , the greatest common factor of the numerator and denominator is 1. *(page 290)*

6. The smallest number that is a common multiple of each of two or more numbers is called the __?__ . *(page 292)*

7. A(n) __?__ has a whole number and a fractional part. *(page 299)*

Concept Check

Write two equivalent fractions for each picture. *(page 278)*

8.   9.   10.   11.

List the factors of each number. Write the greatest common factor for each pair of numbers. *(page 288)*

12. $3, 6$ 13. $4, 7$ 14. $5, 10$ 15. $6, 15$

Write the least common multiple for each pair of numbers. *(page 292)*

16. $3, 4$ 17. $2, 5$ 18. $4, 6$ 19. $5, 8$

Rename as a mixed number or a whole number. *(page 298)*

20. $\dfrac{15}{4}$ 21. $\dfrac{13}{3}$ 22. $\dfrac{17}{5}$ 23. $\dfrac{11}{2}$

> A multiple is the product of two or more numbers.

Skill Check

Write the fraction for the part that is shaded. *(page 276)*

24.   **25.** 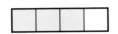 **26.**  **27.**

Find the missing numerator or denominator. *(page 280)*

28. $\dfrac{1}{2} = \dfrac{\blacksquare}{8}$

29. $\dfrac{2}{3} = \dfrac{\blacksquare}{6}$

30. $\dfrac{2}{5} = \dfrac{\blacksquare}{15}$

31. $\dfrac{\blacksquare}{4} = \dfrac{6}{8}$

32. $\dfrac{2}{5} = \dfrac{4}{\blacksquare}$

33. $\dfrac{4}{7} = \dfrac{12}{\blacksquare}$

34. $\dfrac{5}{8} = \dfrac{\blacksquare}{24}$

35. $\dfrac{2}{3} = \dfrac{\blacksquare}{21}$

Write in simplest form. *(page 290)*

36. $\dfrac{9}{27}$

37. $\dfrac{10}{50}$

38. $\dfrac{12}{15}$

39. $\dfrac{16}{28}$

40. $\dfrac{15}{18}$

Compare. Write $<$, $>$, or $=$ for ●.
(page 294)

41. $\dfrac{3}{5}$ ● $\dfrac{4}{5}$

42. $\dfrac{2}{3}$ ● $\dfrac{6}{9}$

43. $\dfrac{3}{4}$ ● $\dfrac{1}{8}$

Write in order from least to greatest.
(page 296)

44. $\dfrac{1}{2}, \dfrac{1}{4}, \dfrac{6}{8}$

45. $\dfrac{2}{3}, \dfrac{10}{12}, \dfrac{1}{6}$

Problem-Solving Check *(pages 282, 302)*

46. If there are 11 rosebushes in a circle, could Chico pick roses from every third bush and complete picking from all 11 bushes before returning to the first bush?

47. If there are 11 shrubs in a circle, could Bena water every fourth shrub and complete watering all 11 shrubs before returning to the first shrub?

48. Jerry and Felicia estimated how much of an hour they each spend on homework. The table shows their estimates. Who spends more time doing math homework?

49. Mr. Cruz and Ms. Harris each have 27 students. The table shows which parts of their classes did projects on different subjects. Which class had more students doing projects on astronomy?

Homework		
Subject	Jerry	Felicia
Science	$\dfrac{1}{8}$	$\dfrac{1}{4}$
Math	■	$\dfrac{3}{8}$
English	$\dfrac{1}{8}$	$\dfrac{3}{8}$

Projects		
Subject	Mr. Cruz's Class	Ms. Harris's Class
Astronomy	■	$\dfrac{1}{3}$
Biology	$\dfrac{1}{3}$	$\dfrac{4}{9}$
Ecology	$\dfrac{2}{9}$	$\dfrac{2}{9}$

WHAT DID I LEARN?

1. Fold and shade a piece of paper to show the fraction $\frac{1}{4}$ and a fraction equivalent to $\frac{1}{4}$.

2. Use connecting cubes to determine whether 9 is a prime number or a composite number. Explain your method.

3. Use geometric shapes or a number line to find the least common multiple of 4 and 6. Explain what you did.

4. Rename $2\frac{1}{4}$ as a fraction greater than 1. Show your method.

5. Order these fractions from least to greatest: $\frac{1}{2}$, $\frac{3}{4}$, $\frac{2}{3}$. Explain your method.

6. Read Exercise 2 on page 283. Follow the steps on the Problem-Solving Think Along worksheet to show how to solve this problem.

You can multiply or divide to find an equivalent fraction.

Write About It

7. What is something you now understand more clearly about fractions than you did before studying this chapter? Explain.

8. Explain the difference between greatest common factor and least common multiple.

TEAMWORK *Project*

Make a Garden Model

Landscapers plan and create beautiful gardens that surround buildings and homes. With your teammates, create a model of a landscaped garden.

DECIDE ■ ■ ■ ■ ■ ■ ■

Talk about how you can use a ruler, markers, and an encyclopedia to model a landscaped garden.

DO ■ ■ ■ ■ ■ ■ ■ ■ ■

Work with your teammates. Draw a garden plot on a large sheet of manila paper. Divide the plot into 12 equal sections. Find types of trees, shrubs, and flowers in an encyclopedia. Plan and draw a garden that is $\frac{1}{4}$ trees, $\frac{1}{3}$ shrubs, $\frac{1}{6}$ perennial flowers, and $\frac{3}{12}$ very colorful annual flowers.

Show your model. Tell

SHARE

about the plants you chose and the layout.

TALK ABOUT IT

○ How could you use a model to plan the landscaping around a building?

○ In your everyday activities, what other fractional parts have you noticed?

Extend Your Thinking

Activity

ART CONNECTION

A **tessellation** is an arrangement of geometric figures that cover a flat surface without leaving gaps and without overlapping. Some polygons, such as equilateral triangles and hexagons, can form tessellations. Others, such as pentagons, cannot.

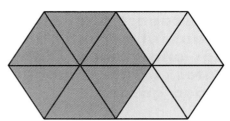

Figure A

1. Look at Figure A. How many equilateral triangles make up the figure? What fraction of the triangles are red? What fraction are blue?

2. Look at Figure B. What fraction names the equilateral triangles that are not red? that are not green?

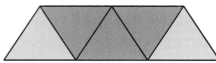

Figure B

3. Trace this figure, and use it to make a tessellation pattern. Color the part of the pattern that is equivalent to $\frac{1}{3}$.

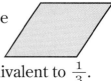

Challenge

Calculator

Use your calculator to find equivalent fractions.

Example $\frac{5}{9} = \frac{\blacksquare}{126}$

$\boxed{1}\boxed{2}\boxed{6}\boxed{\div}\boxed{9}\boxed{=}$ $\boxed{14.}$

$\boxed{\times}\boxed{5}\boxed{=}$ $\boxed{70.}$

1. $\frac{3}{8} = \frac{\blacksquare}{96}$

2. $\frac{7}{12} = \frac{\blacksquare}{132}$

Critical Thinking

Compare these fractions. Put them in order from least to greatest.

1. $\frac{9}{2}, \frac{9}{4}, \frac{14}{3}$

2. $\frac{17}{8}, \frac{13}{4}, \frac{5}{2}$

3. $\frac{16}{7}, \frac{45}{21}, \frac{8}{3}$

CUMULATIVE REVIEW
CHAPTERS 1–9

Write the letter of the correct answer.

1. $10^3 =$

   A. 10   B. 100
   C. 1,000   D. not here

2. $12,905 - 5,234 = n$

   A. 7,671   B. 7,731
   C. 7,771   D. not here

3. $600 \times 8 = n$

   A. 480   B. 4,800
   C. 48,000   D. 480,000

4. Which is the best estimate?
   $268 \div 3 \approx n$

   A. 9   B. 50
   C. 90   D. 900

5. Which word names the figure?

   A. pentagon   B. rectangle
   C. octagon   D. hexagon

6. Which figure is similar to △?

   A.   B.
   C.   D.

7. Which is the best estimate?
   $626 \div 83 \approx n$

   A. 8   B. 50   C. 80   D. 800

8. Which is the mean? 87, 85, 98

   A. 85   B. 87   C. 90   D. 98

9. $3.27 \times 4 = n$

   A. 1.208   B. 12.08
   C. 13.8   D. not here

10. $65.43 \div 3 = n$

    A. 2.181   B. 21.81
    C. 21.83   D. not here

11. If Jay delivers a paper to every third house, how many times will he circle the block before each of 14 houses has a paper?

    A. 1 time   B. 2 times
    C. 3 times   D. 4 times

12. Nicole's and Justin's flower gardens are the same size. Use the table to decide what part of Nicole's garden is violets.

    A. $\frac{1}{8}$ B. $\frac{1}{4}$ C. $\frac{3}{8}$ D. $\frac{3}{4}$

13. Each of 5 rows is planted with a different vegetable. Lettuce and onions are on the ends and carrots and beans are next to each other. If the beans are next to the onions, what two vegetables are next to the spinach?

    A. onions/carrots   B. carrots/lettuce
    C. lettuce/onions   D. beans/lettuce

Flower Gardens		
Flower	Nicole's Garden	Justin's Garden
Marigolds	$\frac{1}{2}$	$\frac{1}{8}$
Daisies	$\frac{1}{4}$	$\frac{1}{2}$
Violets		$\frac{3}{8}$

USING FRACTIONS

Did you know . . .

. . . that kabuki is a type of Japanese drama that dates back to the seventeenth century?

TALK ABOUT IT

Masato is painting scenery for a Kabuki play. He needs $3\frac{1}{2}$ liters of paint. He already has $1\frac{3}{4}$ liters of paint. What must Masato consider to find out how much more paint he needs to buy?

ESTIMATING FRACTIONS

Fraction circles are helpful when you are estimating the value of fractions. It is easy to think about fractions as being close to 0, $\frac{1}{2}$, or 1.

$\frac{1}{12}$ is about 0. $\frac{3}{8}$ is about $\frac{1}{2}$. $\frac{5}{6}$ is about 1.

You can compare the numerator with the denominator to estimate sums and differences of fractions.

A. Estimate. $\dfrac{3}{8} + \dfrac{1}{5} \approx n$

$\dfrac{3}{8}$ The numerator is about one half the denominator. $\dfrac{3}{8}$ is close to $\dfrac{1}{2}$. ⟶ $\dfrac{1}{2}$

$\dfrac{1}{5}$ The numerator is much less than the denominator. $\dfrac{1}{5}$ is close to 0. ⟶ 0

So, $\dfrac{3}{8} + \dfrac{1}{5}$ is close to $\dfrac{1}{2}$.

B. Estimate. $\dfrac{11}{12} - \dfrac{7}{8} \approx n$

$\dfrac{11}{12}$ The numerator is about the same as the denominator. $\dfrac{11}{12}$ is close to 1. ⟶ 1

$\dfrac{7}{8}$ The numerator is about the same as the denominator. $\dfrac{7}{8}$ is close to 1. ⟶ 1

So, $\dfrac{11}{12} - \dfrac{7}{8}$ is close to 0.

Talk About It

▶ Without fraction circles, how do you know when a fraction is close to $\frac{1}{2}$?

▶ How do you know when a fraction is close to 0?

▶ What can you say about the numerator and denominator when a fraction is close to 1?

▶ Does $\frac{1}{4}$ round to 0 or $\frac{1}{2}$? Explain.

Check for Understanding

Estimate whether each fraction is closer to 0, $\frac{1}{2}$, or 1.

1. $\frac{1}{10}$
2. $\frac{3}{7}$
3. $\frac{5}{8}$
4. $\frac{8}{9}$
5. $\frac{7}{15}$
6. $\frac{2}{11}$

Practice

Estimate the sum or difference.

7. $\frac{9}{10}$ $+\frac{3}{5}$

8. $\frac{8}{9}$ $-\frac{7}{8}$

9. $\frac{5}{11}$ $+\frac{6}{13}$

10. $\frac{1}{12}$ $+\frac{2}{15}$

11. $\frac{7}{15}$ $-\frac{1}{14}$

12. $\frac{8}{14}$ $+\frac{1}{11}$

13. $\frac{8}{9} + \frac{2}{13} \approx n$

14. $\frac{9}{10} - \frac{6}{7} \approx n$

15. $\frac{4}{9} + \frac{10}{12} \approx n$

Mixed Applications

16. There are 11 members in a band. If 3 members play guitar and 2 other members play keyboard, what fraction of the band plays guitar and keyboard?

17. **Mental Math** Ann practiced for about $\frac{9}{10}$ hour on Monday, about $\frac{4}{5}$ hour on Tuesday, and about $\frac{5}{6}$ hour on Wednesday. For about how long did she practice altogether?

18. The first band class completed about $\frac{7}{8}$ of the book, and the second band class completed about $\frac{3}{5}$ of the book. Estimate the difference in the amounts completed by the first and second band classes.

19. Callie has practiced about $\frac{3}{4}$ of a new song. Bryan has practiced about $\frac{1}{2}$ of it. If Lorrie has practiced more than Bryan but less than Callie, write a fraction that shows about how much of the song Lorrie has practiced.

CRITICAL THINKING

Use any four of the digits 1 through 5. Write a fraction for each.

20. a sum close to 1

21. a difference close to 0

How can you determine that a fraction is close to 1?

WRAP UP...

Adding and Subtracting Fractions

In a jazz band, $\frac{3}{8}$ of the musicians play trumpets, and $\frac{2}{8}$ play trombones. Trumpets and trombones are brass instruments. What fraction of the musicians in the band play these brass instruments?

Add. $\frac{3}{8} + \frac{2}{8} = n$

Step 1	**Step 2**	**Step 3**
Compare the denominators. They are the same.	Add the numerators mentally.	Write the sum over the denominator.
$\begin{array}{r} \frac{3}{8} \\ +\frac{2}{8} \\ \hline \end{array}$	$\begin{array}{r} \frac{3}{8} \leftarrow \text{3 eighths} \\ +\frac{2}{8} \leftarrow \text{+ 2 eighths} \\ \hline \end{array}$ **Think:**	$\begin{array}{r} \frac{3}{8} \\ +\frac{2}{8} \\ \hline \frac{5}{8} \leftarrow \text{5 eighths} \end{array}$

So, $\frac{5}{8}$ of the musicians in the band play these brass instruments.

MULTICULTURAL NOTE: Jazz music comes from a variety of sources, including West African rhythms, European classical music, gospel songs and spirituals, and American folk music.

Subtract. $\frac{7}{8} - \frac{5}{8} = n$

Step 1	**Step 2**	**Step 3**
Compare the denominators. They are the same.	Subtract the numerators mentally.	Write the difference over the denominator.
$\begin{array}{r} \frac{7}{8} \\ -\frac{5}{8} \\ \hline \end{array}$	$\begin{array}{r} \frac{7}{8} \leftarrow \text{7 eighths} \\ -\frac{5}{8} \leftarrow \text{- 5 eighths} \\ \hline \end{array}$ **Think:**	$\begin{array}{r} \frac{7}{8} \\ -\frac{5}{8} \\ \hline \frac{2}{8} \end{array}$ Remember to write the answer in simplest form. **Think:** $\frac{2}{8} = \frac{2 \div 2}{8 \div 2} = \frac{1}{4}$

Check for Understanding

Find the sum or difference. Write the answer in simplest form.

1. $\begin{array}{r} \frac{5}{6} \\ -\frac{4}{6} \\ \hline \end{array}$

2. $\begin{array}{r} \frac{2}{9} \\ +\frac{1}{9} \\ \hline \end{array}$

3. $\begin{array}{r} \frac{7}{8} \\ -\frac{2}{8} \\ \hline \end{array}$

4. $\begin{array}{r} \frac{3}{10} \\ +\frac{4}{10} \\ \hline \end{array}$

5. $\begin{array}{r} \frac{8}{12} \\ -\frac{4}{12} \\ \hline \end{array}$

Practice

Write an addition or a subtraction sentence for each drawing.

6.

7.

8.

Use mental math to find the sum or difference. Write the answer in simplest form.

9. $\dfrac{1}{8}$
$+\dfrac{5}{8}$
___

10. $\dfrac{6}{10}$
$-\dfrac{1}{10}$
___

11. $\dfrac{5}{9}$
$-\dfrac{2}{9}$
___

12. $\dfrac{1}{6}$
$+\dfrac{2}{6}$
___

13. $\dfrac{3}{5}$
$-\dfrac{1}{5}$
___

14. $\dfrac{3}{7}$
$-\dfrac{2}{7}$
___

15. $\dfrac{5}{12} + \dfrac{3}{12} = n$

16. $\dfrac{1}{8} + \dfrac{4}{8} + \dfrac{2}{8} = n$

17. $\dfrac{2}{9} + \dfrac{4}{9} + \dfrac{3}{9} = n$

18. $\dfrac{5}{12} + \dfrac{4}{12} = n$

19. $\dfrac{9}{15} - \dfrac{4}{15} = n$

20. $\dfrac{9}{16} + \dfrac{7}{16} = n$

Mixed Applications

21. A jazz band is made up of $\frac{1}{3}$ trumpets, $\frac{1}{9}$ trombones, and $\frac{2}{9}$ clarinets. List the instruments in order from the greatest number to the least number.

22. Make Up a Problem A jazz band has 1 piano, 1 string bass, 1 drum, 3 trumpets, 2 trombones, and 4 saxophones. Use fractions to write an addition problem.

MIXED REVIEW

Identify the angle. Write *right, acute,* or *obtuse.*

1.

2.

3.

4.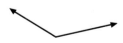

Divide.

5. $18\overline{)365}$

6. $25\overline{)5,075}$

7. $31\overline{)9,308}$

8. $46\overline{)31,510}$

When you add like fractions, what parts of the fractions are computed? **WRAP**

More Practice, Lesson 10.2, page H70

EXPLORING

Unlike Fractions

Fractions such as $\frac{1}{4}$ and $\frac{3}{8}$ are unlike
fractions. How can you use fraction
bars to find their sum?

Building Understanding

A. Begin with a whole bar.
Use fraction bars to model
$\frac{1}{4} + \frac{3}{8} = n$.

- Decide how you will change the
model to show both addends
with like pieces.

- Record a number sentence to
show how you found the sum.

B. Begin with a whole bar. Use fraction
bars to model $\frac{7}{10} - \frac{1}{5} = n$.

- Discuss how using fraction bars to find the
difference is different from using them to
find the sum.

- Solve the problem by using the same
steps as you used above.

Use what you have learned about
adding and subtracting unlike fractions
to present a new problem to the class.
Show pictures of models for your problem.
Record the number sentence and solution
for the problem.

WRITE ABOUT IT

Write a conclusion that explains why unlike fractions
should be changed to like fractions before you find the
sum or difference.

Making the Connection

To find the sum or difference of fractions with *unlike* denominators, you first need to change the fractions to *like* fractions that have a common denominator.

When you add fourths and halves, the sum is expressed in fourths.

$$\frac{1}{4} + \frac{1}{2} = \frac{1}{4} + \frac{2}{4} = \frac{3}{4}$$

When you subtract thirds from sixths, the difference is expressed in sixths.

$$\frac{5}{6} - \frac{2}{3} = \frac{5}{6} - \frac{4}{6} = \frac{1}{6}$$

One unlike denominator may be a multiple of the other.

$\frac{1}{4}$ and $\frac{1}{8}$ $\longrightarrow$ 8 is a multiple of 4.

$\frac{1}{5}$ and $\frac{1}{10}$ $\longrightarrow$ 10 is a multiple of 5.

$\frac{1}{4}$ and $\frac{1}{9}$ $\longrightarrow$ 9 is not a multiple of 4.

$\frac{1}{6}$ and $\frac{1}{7}$ $\longrightarrow$ 7 is not a multiple of 6.

TALK ABOUT IT

- Are sixths multiples of thirds? Explain.

- Name another multiple of 3.

Checking Understanding

Tell whether one number is a multiple of the other. Write *yes* or *no*.

1. $5, 15$ **2.** $3, 9$ **3.** $4, 16$ **4.** $7, 15$ **5.** $2, 20$

Tell whether one denominator is a multiple of the other. Write *yes* or *no*.

6. $\frac{1}{5}, \frac{2}{10}$ **7.** $\frac{1}{4}, \frac{3}{8}$ **8.** $\frac{2}{3}, \frac{3}{5}$ **9.** $\frac{5}{6}, \frac{3}{12}$

Use fraction bars to find the sum or difference.

10. $\frac{2}{5} + \frac{3}{10} = n$ **11.** $\frac{3}{4} - \frac{1}{8} = n$ **12.** $\frac{1}{6} + \frac{2}{3} = n$ **13.** $\frac{2}{3} - \frac{4}{9} = n$

EXPLORING

Unlike Fractions

Alida and Gwen made a drapery skirt to put across the stage for the school orchestra. The first piece covered $\frac{1}{2}$ of the stage. The second piece covered $\frac{2}{5}$ of the stage.

Work Together

Building Understanding

A. Use fraction bars to show $\frac{1}{2} + \frac{2}{5} = n$.

1 whole		
$\frac{1}{2}$	$\frac{1}{5}$	$\frac{1}{5}$

TALK ABOUT IT

- Are fifths multiples of halves? Explain.

- Which like fraction bars will fit exactly over the $\frac{1}{2}$ and the $\frac{2}{5}$ lengths?

- Use the fraction bars to find the sum. What number sentence do the bars represent?

- How much of the stage did the two pieces cover?

B. Use fraction bars to show $\frac{1}{2} - \frac{1}{3} = n$.

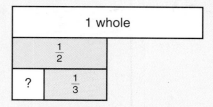

1 whole	
$\frac{1}{2}$	
?	$\frac{1}{3}$

TALK ABOUT IT

- Which like fraction bars can be used to cover exactly both $\frac{1}{2}$ and $\frac{1}{3}$?

- How many of these pieces fill the space that shows $\frac{1}{2} - \frac{1}{3}$?

- Use the fraction pieces to find the difference. What number sentence do the bars represent?

Making the Connection

These fraction bars show that $\frac{1}{6}$ and $\frac{3}{4}$ match 11 of the twelfths pieces.

1 whole

$\frac{1}{6}$	$\frac{1}{4}$	$\frac{1}{4}$	$\frac{1}{4}$

$\frac{1}{12}$	$\frac{1}{12}$	$\frac{1}{12}$	$\frac{1}{12}$	$\frac{1}{12}$	$\frac{1}{12}$	$\frac{1}{12}$	$\frac{1}{12}$	$\frac{1}{12}$	$\frac{1}{12}$	$\frac{1}{12}$

$$\frac{1}{6} = \frac{2}{12} \qquad \frac{3}{4} = \frac{9}{12}$$

You can find the sum or difference of fractions with unlike denominators in another way. First you need to find a common denominator and then use it to rewrite the fractions.

To add $\frac{1}{6}$ and $\frac{3}{4}$, first find the common multiples. Since 6 is not a multiple of 4, search for common multiples of 4 and 6.

Multiples of 6:   6, 12, 18, 24, 30, 36, . . .
Multiples of 4:   4, 8, 12, 16, 20, 24, 28, 32, 36, . . .

Three common multiples of 6 and 4 are 12, 24, and 36. The least common multiple of 6 and 4 is 12. Use the least common multiple as the **least common denominator,** or **LCD.**

TALK ABOUT IT

• What is the least common multiple of 5 and 3? 5 and 4?

• How does knowing the least common multiple help you find the least common denominator?

Checking Understanding

Use fraction bars to find the sum or difference.

1. $\frac{2}{3} + \frac{2}{9} = n$ 2. $\frac{7}{8} - \frac{3}{4} = n$ 3. $\frac{1}{2} + \frac{2}{10} = n$ 4. $\frac{7}{10} - \frac{1}{2} = n$

Find the least common multiple.

5. $5, 7$ 6. $4, 10$ 7. $9, 6$ 8. $2, 5$

Find the least common denominator.

9. $\frac{1}{5}, \frac{2}{3}$ 10. $\frac{3}{4}, \frac{4}{10}$ 11. $\frac{2}{9}, \frac{5}{6}$ 12. $\frac{1}{2}, \frac{4}{5}$

More Practice, Lesson 10.4, page H70

ADDING AND SUBTRACTING UNLIKE FRACTIONS

Joan made a program for the school play. The names of the cast filled $\frac{2}{4}$ page. The names of the stage crew filled $\frac{1}{6}$ page. How much of a page was used to list the names of the students involved in the play?

Add. $\frac{2}{4} + \frac{1}{6} = n$

Step 1	**Step 2**	**Step 3**
To add unlike fractions, first look at the denominators.	Change the fractions to like fractions. Find the least common denominator, or LCD.	Add the fractions. Write the answer in simplest form.
$\begin{array}{r}\frac{2}{4}\\[4pt]+\frac{1}{6}\end{array}$	$\frac{2}{4} = \frac{2 \times 3}{4 \times 3} = \frac{6}{12}$ $+\frac{1}{6} = \frac{1 \times 2}{6 \times 2} = \frac{2}{12}$	$\begin{array}{r}\frac{6}{12}\\[4pt]+\frac{2}{12}\\ \hline \frac{8}{12} = \frac{2}{3}\end{array}$
	The LCM of 4 and 6 is 12, so the LCD is twelfths.	

So, $\frac{2}{3}$ page was used to list the names of the students in the play.

Subtract. $\frac{3}{5} - \frac{1}{3} = n$

Step 1	**Step 2**	**Step 3**
To subtract unlike fractions, first look at the denominators.	Change the fractions to like fractions. Find the least common denominator, or LCD.	Subtract the fractions.
$\begin{array}{r}\frac{3}{5}\\[4pt]-\frac{1}{3}\end{array}$	$\frac{3}{5} = \frac{3 \times 3}{5 \times 3} = \frac{9}{15}$ $-\frac{1}{3} = \frac{1 \times 5}{3 \times 5} = \frac{5}{15}$	$\begin{array}{r}\frac{9}{15}\\[4pt]-\frac{5}{15}\\ \hline \frac{4}{15}\end{array}$
	The LCM of 5 and 3 is 15, so the LCD is fifteenths.	

- How can you find the LCM of two numbers?

- What other method can be used to find the LCM of numbers such as 5 and 3?

Check for Understanding

Find the least common denominator. Then find the sum or difference.

1. $\dfrac{1}{3}$
    $+\dfrac{2}{5}$

2. $\dfrac{7}{8}$
    $-\dfrac{1}{3}$

3. $\dfrac{2}{5}$
    $+\dfrac{3}{10}$

4. $\dfrac{9}{10}$
    $-\dfrac{3}{5}$

5. $\dfrac{5}{12}$
    $+\dfrac{1}{6}$

6. $\dfrac{2}{3}$
    $-\dfrac{3}{6}$

Practice

Add or subtract. Write the answer in simplest form.

7. $\dfrac{1}{8}$
    $+\dfrac{3}{4}$

8. $\dfrac{5}{9}$
    $-\dfrac{1}{6}$

9. $\dfrac{1}{4}$
    $+\dfrac{3}{5}$

10. $\dfrac{3}{8}$
     $-\dfrac{1}{16}$

11. $\dfrac{2}{9}$
     $+\dfrac{2}{3}$

12. $\dfrac{1}{2}$
     $-\dfrac{2}{20}$

13. $\dfrac{4}{5} - \dfrac{3}{10} = n$

14. $\dfrac{5}{6} - \dfrac{2}{3} = n$

15. $\dfrac{7}{9} + \dfrac{1}{18} = n$

16. $\dfrac{1}{12} + \dfrac{3}{4} = n$

17. $\dfrac{1}{4} - \dfrac{1}{5} = n$

18. $\dfrac{2}{12} + \dfrac{1}{3} = n$

19. $\dfrac{3}{7} - \dfrac{2}{14} = n$

20. $\dfrac{1}{7} + \dfrac{1}{5} = n$

Mixed Applications

21. Flo has $\frac{3}{8}$ yard of ribbon. The costume she is making requires $\frac{3}{4}$ yard. How much more ribbon does she need?

22. In the program for a school play, a $\frac{1}{8}$-page ad cost $5.25 and a $\frac{1}{4}$-page ad cost $9.75. How much did three $\frac{1}{8}$-page ads and four $\frac{1}{4}$-page ads cost?

SOCIAL STUDIES CONNECTION

In early times Egyptians wrote all fractions as sums of unit fractions. Fractions such as $\frac{1}{2}$, $\frac{1}{3}$, $\frac{1}{4}$, $\frac{1}{5}$, and $\frac{1}{6}$ are called unit fractions because the numerator in each fraction is a 1, or a unit. For example, $\frac{3}{4} = \frac{1}{2} + \frac{1}{4}$.

Write each fraction as the sum of unit fractions. Use fraction bars.

23. $\dfrac{3}{8}$

24. $\dfrac{7}{12}$

25. $\dfrac{5}{6}$

26. $\dfrac{7}{10}$

27. $\dfrac{4}{9}$

If you use twelfths as a common denominator when you add $\frac{1}{2} + \frac{1}{3}$, what must you do to the sum?

WRAP UP...

EXPLORING

Adding Mixed Numbers

Dimitri was in a play. The first week he learned $2\frac{3}{4}$ pages of his part. The second week he learned $2\frac{1}{2}$ pages. How many pages did he learn in the two weeks?

Work Together

Building Understanding

The numbers $2\frac{3}{4}$ and $2\frac{1}{2}$ are called mixed numbers. Each is a number written as a whole number and a fraction.

Add. $2\frac{3}{4} + 2\frac{1}{2} = n$

Estimate. $2\frac{3}{4}$ is close to 3. $\longrightarrow$ $3 + 2\frac{1}{2} = 5\frac{1}{2}$

You can use fraction squares to help you add mixed numbers.

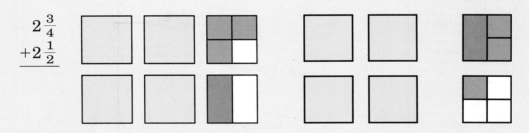

$2\frac{3}{4}$
$+2\frac{1}{2}$

- What happens when you join the partial squares?

- What fraction names the amount that is more than the whole?

- How many whole fraction squares are there now?

So, Dimitri learned $5\frac{1}{4}$ pages in the two weeks.

TALK ABOUT IT • What happened when $\frac{3}{4}$ and $\frac{1}{2}$ were joined?

- How did the sum of $\frac{3}{4}$ and $\frac{1}{2}$ affect the sum of the whole numbers?

- How does the sum compare with the estimate? Is the sum reasonable?

Making the Connection

Sometimes you need to rename mixed numbers before you can add. Compare this with regrouping in the addition of whole numbers.

A. Add. $15 + 78 = n$

Step 1 Add the ones. Regroup 1 ten.	**Step 2** Add the tens.
$\begin{array}{r} 1 \\ 78 \\ +15 \\ \hline 3 \end{array}$ 13 = 1 ten 3 ones	$\begin{array}{r} 1 \\ 78 \\ +15 \\ \hline 93 \end{array}$

B. Add. $5\frac{3}{4} + 2\frac{3}{4} = n$

Step 1 Add the fractions. Rename $\frac{6}{4}$.	**Step 2** Regroup 1 whole. Add the ones. Write in simplest form.
$\begin{array}{r} 5\frac{3}{4} \\ +2\frac{3}{4} \\ \hline \frac{6}{4} = 1\frac{2}{4} \end{array}$	$\begin{array}{r} \overset{1}{5}\frac{3}{4} \\ +2\frac{3}{4} \\ \hline 8\frac{2}{4} = 8\frac{1}{2} \end{array}$

TALK ABOUT IT

- In Exercise A, why do you need to regroup?

- In Exercise B, why do you need to rename?

- What happens when the sum of two fractions is greater than one?

- How can you rename $1\frac{6}{5} + \frac{6}{5}$?

Checking Understanding

Use fraction squares to find the sum.

1. $\begin{array}{r} 3\frac{2}{3} \\ +2\frac{2}{3} \\ \hline \end{array}$

2. $\begin{array}{r} 4\frac{2}{5} \\ +3\frac{3}{5} \\ \hline \end{array}$

3. $\begin{array}{r} 2\frac{3}{4} \\ +1\frac{3}{8} \\ \hline \end{array}$

4. $\begin{array}{r} 1\frac{5}{6} \\ +5\frac{2}{3} \\ \hline \end{array}$

Tell whether or not you need to rename the sum. Write *yes* or *no.*

5. $\begin{array}{r} 4\frac{3}{5} \\ +3\frac{1}{5} \\ \hline \end{array}$

6. $\begin{array}{r} 5\frac{2}{7} \\ +1\frac{6}{7} \\ \hline \end{array}$

7. $\begin{array}{r} 3\frac{5}{8} \\ +5\frac{3}{4} \\ \hline \end{array}$

8. $\begin{array}{r} 8\frac{1}{6} \\ +\ \frac{2}{3} \\ \hline \end{array}$

EXPLORING

Subtracting Mixed Numbers

Paige played the piano for the school play. She played for $5\frac{1}{4}$ minutes during the first half of the play. During the second half, she played for $2\frac{3}{4}$ minutes. For how much longer did she play in the first half?

Work Together

Building Understanding

Estimate.　　$5\frac{1}{4}$　is close to 5. ➡　5

　　　　　　$-2\frac{3}{4}$　is close to 3. ➡　-3

　　　　　　　　　　　　　　　　　　2

A. Use fraction circles to help you subtract $2\frac{3}{4}$ from $5\frac{1}{4}$.

This is one way to model $5\frac{1}{4}$.

This is another way to model $5\frac{1}{4}$.

TALK ABOUT IT

- What fraction is shaded in the first picture? in the second picture?

- How is the second picture different from the first picture?

- Which model of the larger fraction can be used so that $2\frac{3}{4}$ can be removed?

- What is left when you subtract $2\frac{3}{4}$?

- For how much longer did Paige play in the first half?

- How does the difference compare with the estimate?

B. Use fraction circles to subtract $1\frac{1}{3}$ from 4.

- How can you model the whole number, 4, so that $1\frac{1}{3}$ can be removed?

- How can you subtract a mixed number from a whole number?

324

Making the Connection

Sometimes you need to rename mixed numbers before you can subtract. Compare this with regrouping in the subtraction of whole numbers.

A. Subtract. $46 - 19 = n$

Step 1	**Step 2**
Since $9 > 6$, regroup 4 tens 6 ones as 3 tens 16 ones.	Subtract.
$\begin{array}{r} \scriptstyle 3\;\;16 \\ \cancel{4}\,\cancel{6} \\ -1\;9 \\ \hline \end{array}$	$\begin{array}{r} \scriptstyle 3\;\;16 \\ \cancel{4}\,\cancel{6} \\ -1\;9 \\ \hline 2\;7 \end{array}$

B. Subtract. $3\frac{2}{8} - 1\frac{5}{8} = n$

Step 1	**Step 2**
Since $\frac{5}{8} > \frac{2}{8}$, rename 3 ones $\frac{2}{8}$ as 2 ones $\frac{10}{8}$.	Subtract.
$3\frac{2}{8}$ Think: $2 + \frac{8}{8} + \frac{2}{8} =$ $2\frac{10}{8}$ $-1\frac{5}{8}$	$2\frac{10}{8}$ $-1\frac{5}{8}$ $\overline{1\frac{5}{8}}$

TALK ABOUT IT

- In Example A, why do you need to regroup?

- In Example B, why do you need to rename the mixed number?

- How can you rename the larger fraction to find $5\frac{1}{5} - 3\frac{4}{5}$?

- Do you need to rename $4\frac{5}{6} - 3\frac{1}{6}$? Explain.

Checking Understanding

Use fraction circles to find the difference. Write the answer in simplest form.

1. $4\frac{1}{4}$ $-2\frac{3}{4}$

2. $3\frac{3}{8}$ $-\frac{3}{4}$

3. 5 $-1\frac{7}{8}$

4. $2\frac{2}{3}$ $-1\frac{5}{6}$

5. $2\frac{1}{2}$ $-\frac{5}{6}$

Tell whether you need to rename. Write *yes* or *no*.

6. $3 - 2\frac{1}{3} = n$

7. $2\frac{3}{8} - 1\frac{1}{8} = n$

8. $8\frac{2}{5} - 5\frac{3}{5} = n$

9. $10\frac{1}{2} - 7\frac{1}{2} = n$

RENAMING MIXED NUMBERS

Mrs. Hsing is adding a step to the platform for the chorus performance. She needs to nail together two boards to go across the front tier. One board measures $7\frac{5}{16}$ feet, and another measures $8\frac{3}{4}$ feet. How long will the two boards together measure?

Add. $7\frac{5}{16} + 8\frac{3}{4} = n$ Estimate. $7\frac{1}{2} + 9 = 16\frac{1}{2}$

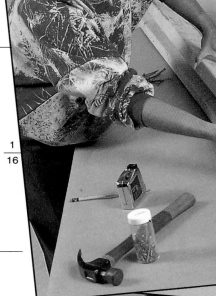

Step 1	**Step 2**	**Step 3**
The fractions are unlike. Find the least common denominator (LCD).	Rename each fraction. Use the LCD. Add.	Rename the sum.
16: **16**, 32 4: 4, 8, 12, **16** The LCM of 16 and 4 is 16, so the LCD is sixteenths.	$7\frac{5}{16} = 7\frac{5}{16}$ $+8\frac{3}{4} = +8\frac{12}{16}$ $\overline{ 15\frac{17}{16}}$	$15\frac{17}{16}$ Think: $= 15 + \frac{16}{16} + \frac{1}{16}$ $16\frac{1}{16}$

So, the two boards together will measure $16\frac{1}{16}$ feet.

Subtract. $16\frac{1}{6} - 4\frac{3}{8} = n$ Estimate. $16 - 4\frac{1}{2} = 11\frac{1}{2}$

Step 1	**Step 2**	**Step 3**
Rename the fractions. Use the LCD.	Decide if you can subtract. $\frac{6}{16} > \frac{1}{16}$ Rename to subtract.	Subtract.
$16\frac{1}{16} = 16\frac{1}{16}$ $-4\frac{3}{8} = -4\frac{6}{16}$ The LCD is sixteenths.	$16\frac{1}{16}$ Think: $15\frac{16}{16} + \frac{1}{16} = 15\frac{17}{16}$ $-4\frac{6}{16}$	$15\frac{17}{16}$ $-4\frac{6}{16}$ $\overline{11\frac{11}{16}}$

- How do the solutions compare with the estimates?

Check for Understanding

Find the sum or difference. Write the answer in simplest form.

1. $10\frac{1}{3} - 6\frac{2}{5} = n$ **2.** $12\frac{5}{6} + 9\frac{3}{4} = n$ **3.** $15\frac{1}{8} - 6\frac{3}{8} = n$

Practice

Estimate the sum or difference.

4. $6\frac{1}{2} + 1\frac{3}{4} \approx n$

5. $5\frac{6}{7} + 1\frac{1}{14} \approx n$

6. $3\frac{7}{8} + 2\frac{1}{3} \approx n$

7. $12\frac{1}{14} - 1\frac{2}{7} \approx n$

8. $11\frac{4}{5} - 3\frac{2}{15} \approx n$

9. $25\frac{2}{9} - 16\frac{3}{5} \approx n$

Add or subtract. Write the answer in simplest form.

10. $5\frac{3}{8}$
$+4\frac{3}{4}$

11. $6\frac{2}{3}$
$+4\frac{3}{4}$

12. $4\frac{7}{20}$
$+2\frac{4}{5}$

13. $4\frac{1}{2}$
$+1\frac{3}{5}$

14. $6\frac{3}{4}$
$-1\frac{7}{8}$

15. $4\frac{2}{3}$
$-1\frac{5}{6}$

16. $10\frac{1}{5}$
$-3\frac{3}{10}$

17. $5\frac{1}{8}$
$-2\frac{3}{4}$

18. $4\frac{5}{6}$
$+4\frac{2}{3}$

19. $3\frac{11}{12}$
$+2\frac{1}{4}$

20. $8\frac{3}{15}$
$+2\frac{4}{5}$

21. $9\frac{1}{10}$
$-6\frac{2}{15}$

Mixed Applications

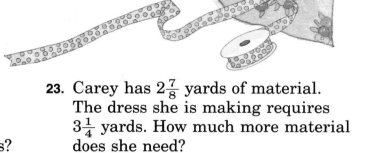

22. The chorus practiced for $2\frac{3}{4}$ hours on Saturday and $3\frac{2}{3}$ hours on Sunday. Was the total time practiced more or less than 6 hours? How do you know?

23. Carey has $2\frac{7}{8}$ yards of material. The dress she is making requires $3\frac{1}{4}$ yards. How much more material does she need?

Use the table for Exercises 24–26.

24. Charlene bought fabric for costumes. How many total yards of cotton, felt, and metallic fabric did she buy?

Fabrics Purchased			
Amount	$3\frac{2}{3}$ yards	$1\frac{1}{2}$ yards	$\frac{3}{4}$ yard
Type	Cotton	Felt	Metallic

25. **Write a Question** Use the information in the table to write a question with fractions.

26. How much more cotton than felt did Charlene buy?

How do you rename $8\frac{11}{6}$?

PROBLEM SOLVING

STRATEGY • Make a Table

At a gathering of Native Americans, several groups participate in native dances. The size and location of each group are shown in this diagram.

Pueblo Laguna (4)	Sioux Santee (2)		Iroquois Mohawk (5)	
Iroquois Onondaga (2)	Pueblo Taos (3)		Sioux Yankton (3)	
Iroquois Cayuga (3)	Sioux Oglala (3)		Pueblo Zuni (3)	
Pueblo Hopi (3)	Sioux Teton (3)	Iroquois Seneca (4)	Pueblo Zia (2)	

Red Cloud is a Sioux. Do the Sioux dancers make up more than or less than $\frac{1}{4}$ of the total number of dancers?

MULTICULTURAL NOTE: A Sioux in elaborate dress demonstrates a native dance. The Sioux have many festivals in celebration of their heritage.

▶ **UNDERSTAND**

What are you asked to find?

What facts are given?

▶ **PLAN**

What strategy can you use?

You can *make a table* that shows the number of each group participating.

▶ **SOLVE**

How will you carry out the plan?

Make a table of the information from the diagram.

Native American Dancers (40)		
Iroquois	**Pueblo**	**Sioux**
Mohawk (5)	Zuni (3)	Yankton (3)
Seneca (4)	Hopi (3)	Santee (2)
Onondaga (2)	Laguna (4)	Teton (3)
Cayuga (3)	Zia (2)	Oglala (3)
	Taos (3)	

The Sioux are $\frac{11}{40}$ of the dancers, so they make up more than $\frac{1}{4}$ of the total number of dancers.

▶ **LOOK BACK**

Does your answer seem reasonable?

WHAT IF... ...there were 10 more Iroquois dancers? Would the Sioux dancers make up more than or less than $\frac{1}{4}$ of the total number of dancers?

Apply

Use the table of Native American dancers on page 328 for Exercises 1–4.

1 What fraction of the Iroquois are from the Seneca group?

2 What fraction of the Pueblo Native Americans are not from the Zia or Taos groups?

3 Do the Iroquois, the Pueblo, or the Sioux make up the greatest fraction of the dancers?

4 What fraction of the dancers are Iroquois?

| Mixed Applications | STRATEGIES | Make a Model • Guess and Check • Write a Number Sentence |

Choose a strategy and solve.

5 Some Native Americans at the gathering demonstrate basket weaving, pottery making, weaving, and carving. Others tell folktales. The table shows the fractions of the people participating in the crafts and story telling. What fraction of the storytellers are Sioux? If the same number of people participate in the crafts as in the story telling, which activity has more Sioux?

Group Activities		
	Crafts	**Story Telling**
Iroquois	$\frac{2}{5}$	$\frac{1}{6}$
Pueblo	$\frac{1}{3}$	$\frac{1}{2}$
Sioux	$\frac{4}{15}$	▩

6 Claudio bought tickets to see the Native American dancers. If children's tickets were $1.50 less than adults' tickets and Claudio paid $11.00 for 2 adults' tickets and 2 children's tickets, how much did each type of ticket cost?

7 Dee bought 9 yards of material to make costumes for two of her Native American friends. If she needs $4\frac{1}{2}$ yards for one costume and $4\frac{1}{3}$ yards for the other, how much material will be left over?

MULTICULTURAL NOTE: This Pueblo girl is wearing traditional dress at a festival. The Pueblos have strong ties to their traditions and homeland.

WRITER'S CORNER

8 Use the diagram of the Native American dancers to make up problems with fractions. Write at least one addition problem and one subtraction problem.

More Practice, Lesson 10.9, page H72

329

REVIEW AND MAINTENANCE

1. Two high schools each have a chorus with the same number of singers. The table shows the part of each chorus singing soprano, tenor, bass, and alto. What fraction of the West High chorus sings alto? Which chorus has more students singing alto?

Chorus		
Singer	**East High**	**West High**
Soprano	$\frac{2}{5}$	$\frac{3}{8}$
Tenor	$\frac{1}{5}$	$\frac{1}{4}$
Bass	$\frac{1}{10}$	$\frac{1}{8}$
Alto	$\frac{3}{10}$	

2. There are 75 people in a chorus. There are 35 singing soprano, 20 singing tenor, 15 singing alto, and 5 singing bass. What fraction of the chorus is tenors?

3. Greta went to see an orchestra that had 81 instruments. There were 36 in the string section, 7 in percussion, 18 in brass, and 20 in woodwind. What fraction of the orchestra was brass?

I can draw a picture to solve a problem.

Find the sum or difference.

4. $\begin{array}{r} 456.85 \\ + 837.45 \\ \hline \end{array}$

5. $\begin{array}{r} 9.057 \\ + 9.943 \\ \hline \end{array}$

6. $\begin{array}{r} 18.73 \\ - 14.84 \\ \hline \end{array}$

7. $\begin{array}{r} 8.095 \\ - 6.986 \\ \hline \end{array}$

Estimate.

8. $\begin{array}{r} 395 \\ \times \quad 5 \\ \hline \end{array}$

9. $\begin{array}{r} 880 \\ \times \quad 9 \\ \hline \end{array}$

10. $\begin{array}{r} 1,032 \\ \times \quad 7 \\ \hline \end{array}$

11. $\begin{array}{r} 9,845 \\ \times \quad 8 \\ \hline \end{array}$

Write the number of faces for each solid figure.

12. rectangular prism

13. hexagonal pyramid

14. cube

Find the range, mode, median, and mean.

15. 75; 80; 100; 95; 80

16. 200; 150; 220; 180; 220

Divide.

17. $8\overline{)49.6}$

18. $5\overline{)139.05}$

19. $12\overline{)57.6}$

20. $21\overline{)115.5}$

Write each fraction as a whole or mixed number.

21. $\frac{18}{9}$

22. $\frac{9}{6}$

23. $\frac{12}{7}$

24. $\frac{24}{3}$

Using Mixed Numbers

A group of Irish descendants is planning an Irish festival as part of a St. Patrick's Day celebration. For entertainment, it plans to sponsor a *hurling* game, which is a very fast ball-and-stick game popular in Ireland. It is also planning to sing Irish songs and to demonstrate Irish folk dances.

Ireland → EUROPE

For these demonstrations, 3 groups of dancers will each demonstrate 2 Irish jigs. Use this information to answer the questions.

MULTICULTURAL NOTE: Irish dances tend to be lively and exciting. Two popular Irish folk dances are reels and jigs.

1. The first dance group will perform a $3\frac{1}{4}$-minute dance and a $1\frac{3}{4}$-minute dance sequence. What is the total amount of time the group will perform?

2. The second dance group will perform for a total of $5\frac{1}{4}$ minutes. If the first dance takes $2\frac{1}{2}$ minutes, what will be the length of the second dance?

3. The third dance group will perform two $2\frac{3}{4}$-minute dances. What is the total amount of time it will perform?

4. Which group will dance the longest dance?

5. Which group will dance the longest amount of time? the shortest amount of time?

6. Make up a problem using mixed numbers. Exchange with a partner and solve.

MULTIPLYING FRACTIONS
and Whole Numbers

Mrs. Bruner has 12 fancy costume hats. Alice asked to use $\frac{1}{3}$ of the hats for a play. How many hats does Alice need?

You can draw a picture to show $\frac{1}{3}$ of 12.

A. Use circles to show the total number of hats.

B. Separate the hats into 3 equal-sized groups.

C. Shade 1 of the 3 groups, or $\frac{1}{3}$ of the total.

So, Alice needs 4 hats.

• How can you use the picture to show $\frac{2}{3}$ of 12?

Here is another way you can draw the picture.

• How do you know whether this picture shows 3 equal-sized groups?

A.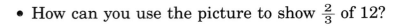

B.

C.

$\frac{1}{3}$ of 12 = 4

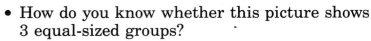

You can use multiplication of fractions instead of pictures.

Multiply. $\frac{1}{3} \times 12 = n$

Step 1	**Step 2**	**Step 3**
Write the whole number as a fraction.	Multiply numerators. Multiply denominators.	Write the answer in simplest form.
$\frac{1}{3} \times \frac{12}{1}$ **Think:** $12 = \frac{12}{1}$	$\frac{1}{3} \times \frac{12}{1} = \frac{12}{3}$	$\frac{12 \div 3}{3 \div 3} = \frac{4}{1} = 4$

Check for Understanding

Write a number sentence for each picture.

1.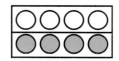

2.

3.

4.

Multiply. Write the product as a whole or mixed number.

5. $\frac{1}{4} \times 16 = n$ **6.** $\frac{1}{5} \times 10 = n$ **7.** $9 \times \frac{3}{4} = n$ **8.** $\frac{3}{5} \times 25 = n$

Idea Bank, page 464, Exercise 5

Practice

Multiply. Write the product as a whole or mixed number.

9. $12 \times \frac{1}{3} = n$

10. $15 \times \frac{2}{3} = n$

11. $4 \times \frac{2}{3} = n$

12. $18 \times \frac{2}{9} = n$

13. $8 \times \frac{3}{4} = n$

14. $6 \times \frac{2}{3} = n$

15. $5 \times \frac{7}{8} = n$

16. $6 \times \frac{4}{9} = n$

17. $\frac{3}{5} \times 5 = n$

18. $\frac{2}{5} \times 6 = n$

19. $\frac{6}{7} \times 5 = n$

20. $\frac{3}{4} \times 6 = n$

21. $\frac{3}{5} \times 15 = n$

22. $\frac{6}{7} \times 21 = n$

23. $\frac{7}{12} \times 7 = n$

24. $\frac{5}{8} \times 15 = n$

Mixed Applications

25. J.D. walked a total of $\frac{3}{4}$ mile to and from school each day. How far did he walk to and from school in 5 days?

26. There were 360 people who saw the school play. If $\frac{4}{9}$ were adults, how many adults saw the play?

27. There were 32 students in the play. How many were girls if $\frac{3}{8}$ of the students in the play were boys?

28. Dolores used $\frac{1}{4}$ yard of silk to make a scarf, $\frac{5}{8}$ yard for a cape, and $\frac{1}{2}$ yard for a headpiece. How much silk did she use?

29. The students in the play want to earn money for new costumes. Their goal is to raise $500. If they have sold 130 plants for $3.75 each, how many more plants do they need to sell to reach their goal?

30. **Analyze Data** On Monday night the play was held in the multipurpose room. The audience occupied $\frac{4}{5}$ of the 200 seats. On Tuesday night the play was held in the media center. The audience occupied $\frac{5}{6}$ of the 180 seats. On which night did more people see the play?

MIXED REVIEW

Multiply.

1.   0.4
  $\times 0.7$

2.   3.21
  $\times 0.3$

3.   64.5
  $\times 0.2$

4.   8.5
  $\times 6.2$

5.   9.54
  $\times 0.25$

Divide.

6. $4\overline{)6.52}$

7. $5\overline{)110.65}$

8. $16\overline{)32.48}$

9. $21\overline{)30.45}$

10. $25\overline{)458.75}$

When you multiply a number by $\frac{1}{4}$, what are you doing?

MULTIPLYING FRACTIONS

Some members of a stage crew were covering frames for a backdrop for their play. They covered $\frac{2}{3}$ of one of the frames with paper. Then they painted $\frac{1}{5}$ of the paper. What part of the whole frame did they paint?

You can use pictures of fraction squares to multiply fractions.

Multiply. $\frac{1}{5} \times \frac{2}{3} = n$ **Think:** $\frac{1}{5}$ of $\frac{2}{3} = n$

Step 1	**Step 2**	**Step 3**
Show thirds of the square. Shade $\frac{2}{3}$ yellow.	Show fifths of the square. Shade $\frac{1}{5}$ blue.	2 of 15 parts are both yellow and blue.

- Into how many sections did you divide the square?

- How much of the square is shaded by both colors?

- What number sentence can you write?

- How does shading help you find the product?

So, the stage crew painted $\frac{2}{15}$ of the whole frame.

Talk About It

▶ Is the product of $\frac{1}{5} \times \frac{2}{3}$ greater than or less than 1?

▶ How is the numerator of the product found?

▶ How is the denominator of the product found?

▶ What happens if you multiply the denominators before the numerators?

Check for Understanding

Draw fraction squares to help you multiply these fractions.

1. $\frac{1}{4}$ of $\frac{1}{3} = n$
2. $\frac{3}{4} \times \frac{1}{2} = n$
3. $\frac{2}{3} \times \frac{3}{4} = n$
4. $\frac{1}{3} \times \frac{2}{3} = n$

Practice

Write a number sentence for each drawing.

5.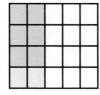
6.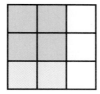
7.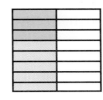
8.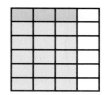

Multiply. Write the answer in simplest form.

9. $\frac{1}{4} \times \frac{1}{2} = n$

10. $\frac{4}{5} \times \frac{1}{5} = n$

11. $\frac{2}{5} \times \frac{3}{7} = n$

12. $\frac{3}{8} \times \frac{2}{3} = n$

13. $\frac{1}{8} \times \frac{2}{3} = n$

14. $\frac{1}{5} \times \frac{5}{12} = n$

15. $\frac{3}{4} \times \frac{3}{8} = n$

16. $\frac{3}{10} \times \frac{1}{6} = n$

17. $\frac{2}{9} \times \frac{3}{9} = n$

18. $\frac{2}{3} \times \frac{5}{6} = n$

19. $\frac{2}{15} \times \frac{3}{4} = n$

20. $\frac{3}{7} \times \frac{2}{9} = n$

21. $\frac{4}{7} \times \frac{2}{3} = n$

22. $\frac{3}{8} \times \frac{2}{7} = n$

23. $\frac{5}{12} \times \frac{3}{10} = n$

24. $\frac{5}{8} \times \frac{1}{2} = n$

Mixed Applications

25. Critical Thinking When you multiply a fraction by a fraction, will the product change if the order of the fractions changes?

26. Taro spent $\frac{2}{3}$ hour painting a prop. She spent $\frac{1}{4}$ of that time sanding the prop. What part of an hour did she spend sanding the prop?

27. Johnny has $\frac{1}{2}$ gallon of paint. He needs 5 times as much to paint the props. How much paint does he need?

28. Freda mixed $\frac{1}{4}$ gallon of white paint, $\frac{3}{8}$ gallon of blue paint, and $\frac{1}{2}$ gallon of green paint. How much paint did she have?

29. Carlotta painted scenery for the play. She painted $\frac{1}{2}$ of a wall yellow. Then she painted a design on $\frac{1}{3}$ of the yellow part. What part of the wall had a design on it?

30. Number Sense Will the product of two fractions ever be greater than 1 if each fraction is less than 1? Explain.

When you multiply two whole numbers greater than 1, the product is greater than either factor. What happens to the product when you multiply two fractions?

More Practice, Lesson 10.11, page H72

335

MULTIPLYING FRACTIONS
and Mixed Numbers

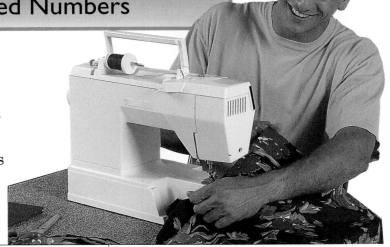

Diego made props for the school play. He used $2\frac{1}{3}$ yards of cloth to make a tablecloth. He used $\frac{1}{4}$ as much cloth to make a set of napkins. How much cloth did he use to make the napkins?

You can use pictures of fraction squares to multiply fractions and mixed numbers.

Multiply. $\frac{1}{4} \times 2\frac{1}{3} = n$

Step 1	**Step 2**	**Step 3**
Show 3 whole squares. Show each square in thirds. Shade $2\frac{1}{3}$ squares yellow.	Show fourths of the squares. Shade $\frac{1}{4}$ blue.	Each whole has 12 parts. 7 of 12 parts are both yellow and blue, making green.
	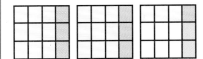	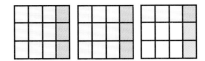

- How does shading help you find the product?

- How many equal parts are in each square?

- How many of these parts are shaded by both colors?

- What is the product of $\frac{1}{4} \times 2\frac{1}{3}$?

So, Diego used $\frac{7}{12}$ yard of cloth to make the napkins.

Check for Understanding

Write a number sentence for each picture.

1.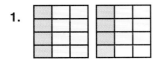

2.

3.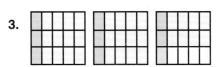

Draw fraction squares to help you find each product.

4. $\frac{3}{4} \times 1\frac{1}{6} = n$

5. $\frac{2}{5} \times 3\frac{2}{3} = n$

6. $\frac{2}{3} \times 2\frac{1}{5} = n$

Practice

Write a number sentence for each picture.

7.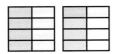

8.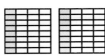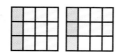

9.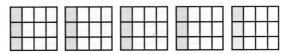

10. **11.** **12.**

Draw fraction squares to help you find each product.

13. $\frac{1}{4} \times 2\frac{1}{2} = n$

14. $\frac{1}{4} \times 3\frac{1}{2} = n$

15. $\frac{2}{3} \times 1\frac{1}{3} = n$

16. $\frac{2}{3} \times 3\frac{1}{4} = n$

17. $\frac{1}{2} \times 4\frac{1}{3} = n$

18. $\frac{3}{4} \times 2\frac{3}{4} = n$

Mixed Applications

19. Sidney had $3\frac{1}{2}$ pages of the play to learn. He learned $\frac{1}{3}$ of the pages on Friday afternoon. How many pages did he learn on Friday afternoon?

20. Velma had $2\frac{1}{2}$ dozen roses. She used $\frac{1}{2}$ of them in a bouquet for the party. How many dozen roses did she use in the bouquet?

21. After the play $\frac{2}{3}$ of the cast stayed for a party. If 24 people were in the play, how many people stayed for the party?

22. The recipe for the punch served at the party called for $2\frac{1}{2}$ cups of orange juice and $1\frac{1}{3}$ cups of pineapple juice. If Leroy made 6 times this amount, how many cups of punch did he make?

Is the product of $\frac{3}{4} \times 1\frac{1}{2}$ the same as $1\frac{1}{2} \times \frac{3}{4}$? How do you know?

WRAP UP...

EXPLORING

Dividing Fractions

Randy cut a large sub sandwich into 10 pieces to serve at the cast party. He put out $\frac{9}{10}$ of the sub. If each person eats exactly $\frac{3}{10}$ of the sandwich, how many people can be served?

Work Together

Building Understanding

A. You can use fraction bars to divide fractions.

$\frac{9}{10}$  $\frac{3}{10}$

- How many $\frac{3}{10}$ pieces fit on the $\frac{9}{10}$ piece?
- How many people can each be served $\frac{3}{10}$ of the sandwich? Write a number sentence.

B. Sometimes you can use counters to divide fractions.

A muffin pan can hold 12 muffins. Randy's pan is $\frac{2}{3}$ full. How many servings that are $\frac{1}{3}$ of the pan can be made from the muffins Randy has?

$\frac{2}{3}$ $\frac{1}{3}$

- How many sets of counters that show $\frac{1}{3}$ can be made from $\frac{2}{3}$ of a set of counters? How many servings of muffins can be made?

C. You can also use fraction circles to divide fractions.

There are three large pizzas at the party. The pizzas were cut into 4 pieces each. If each person has $\frac{1}{4}$ of a pizza, how many people can have pizza?

$\frac{4}{4}$ + $\frac{4}{4}$ + $\frac{4}{4}$ = $\frac{12}{4}$

- How many people can eat $\frac{1}{4}$ piece from $\frac{12}{4}$ pieces?

Making the Connection

Think about what you learned using the fraction bars, counters, and fraction circles to divide fractions.

1. How many sets of 2 are in 8?
   $8 \div 2 = n$?

2. How many sets of $\frac{2}{10}$ are in $\frac{8}{10}$?
   $\frac{8}{10} \div \frac{2}{10} = n$?

3. How many sets of $\frac{2}{8}$ are in $\frac{8}{8}$?
   $\frac{8}{8} \div \frac{2}{8} = n$?

4. How many sets of $\frac{2}{12}$ are in $\frac{8}{12}$?
   $\frac{8}{12} \div \frac{2}{12} = n$?

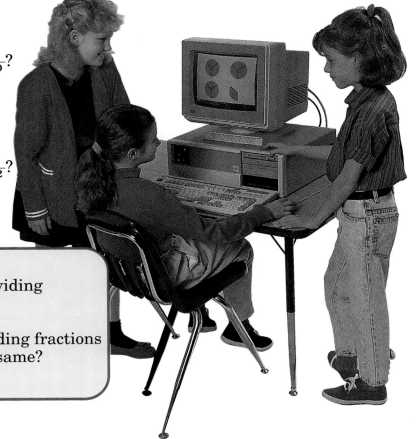

TALK ABOUT IT

- How is dividing fractions like dividing whole numbers?

- What rule can you write for dividing fractions when the denominators are the same?

Checking Understanding

Complete.

5. How many fours are in sixteen?

6. How many threes are in twenty-four?

Write a division number sentence for each picture.

7.

8.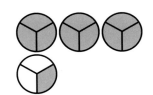

9.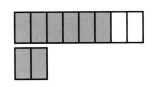

Use your rule for dividing fractions with like denominators.

10. $\frac{8}{10} \div \frac{4}{10} = n$

11. $\frac{12}{3} \div \frac{2}{3} = n$

12. $\frac{3}{4} \div \frac{1}{4} = n$

PROBLEM SOLVING

STRATEGY • Make a Diagram

Mrs. Yentz's students are enrolled in three different kinds of activities. She has $\frac{1}{3}$ of her students in music, $\frac{1}{2}$ in athletics, and $\frac{1}{6}$ in acting. If 5 of the students are actors, how many students are in her class?

In solving problems, it helps to make a diagram of the information given in the problem.

▶ **UNDERSTAND**

What are you asked to find?

What facts are given?

▶ **PLAN**

What strategy will you use?

Making a diagram is a good strategy.

▶ **SOLVE**

How can you solve the problem?

Make a diagram of the information by using fraction bars to model the problem.

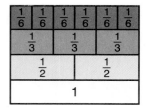 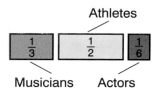

Musicians   Actors

Use the fraction bars to draw a diagram of $\frac{1}{3}$ and $\frac{1}{2}$. Then, make a cutout of the fraction bar that shows the number of actors.

Use the cutout to mark how many of these bars it takes to cover $\frac{1}{2}$ and $\frac{1}{3}$ on your diagram.

It takes three bars to cover $\frac{1}{2}$ and two bars to cover $\frac{1}{3}$.

$\frac{1}{6}$ bar = 5 student actors

$\frac{3}{6}$ bars = 15 student athletes

$\frac{2}{6}$ bars = 10 student musicians

$5 + 10 + 15 = 30$

So, there are 30 students in Mrs. Yentz's class.

▶ **LOOK BACK**

In what other way can you solve the problem?

… $\frac{1}{4}$ of the students are musicians, $\frac{1}{2}$ are athletes, and $\frac{1}{4}$ are actors? If 5 of the students are actors, how many students are in the class?

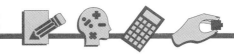
Apply

Make a diagram and solve.

(1) There will be three ballets in a dance program. Each dancer will be in only one ballet. Of the dancers, $\frac{2}{5}$ will be in the classical ballet, $\frac{1}{2}$ will be in the modern ballet, and $\frac{1}{10}$ will be in the pas de deux. There are 2 dancers in a pas de deux. How many dancers will be in the modern ballet?

(2) Mrs. Hicks asked the students in her drama class to tell whether they would prefer acting in movies, television, or theater. Of the students, $\frac{1}{4}$ chose television, $\frac{5}{8}$ chose movies, and $\frac{1}{8}$ chose theater. If 4 of the students chose theater, how many students are in the drama class?

Mixed Applications	STRATEGIES

Write a Number Sentence • Guess and Check • Solve a Simpler Problem • Work Backward • Find a Pattern

Choose a strategy and solve.

(3) The fifth graders are going to see a play. If one bus can hold 40 students, how many buses will be needed if there are 138 students going to the play?

(4) There are 6 dancers in a program. Each dancer will perform a short dance with each of the other dancers before the program is over. How many dances will there be?

(5) There will be two performances of *Jack and the Beanstalk*. If a total of 230 tickets were sold and 18 more tickets were sold for the second performance than for the first, how many tickets were sold for each performance?

(6) One day Rebecca withdrew $100.00 from her account to purchase 2 tickets to a concert. That day she also bought shoes for $32.50 and a purse for $12.90. She had $12.60 left from the $100.00. How much was 1 ticket to the concert?

(7) Corey is studying the script for a play. He learned $\frac{1}{4}$ page the first day, $\frac{1}{2}$ page the second day, and $\frac{3}{4}$ page the third day. If the pattern continues, how many pages will Corey learn on the eighth day?

(8) As of today $\frac{2}{5}$ of the costumes for an opera are completed. If there are 50 costumes being made, how many costumes are completed?

CHAPTER REVIEW / TEST

Vocabulary Check

Choose a word or words from the box to complete each sentence.

> least common
> denominator
> like fractions
> multiples
> unlike fractions

1. When you find a common denominator for fractions, you change the fractions to __?__. *(page 317)*

2. Fractions that have different denominators are called __?__. *(page 317)*

3. Denominators such as eighths are __?__ of fourths. *(page 317)*

4. You can use the least common multiple of two denominators to write fractions with the __?__. *(page 319)*

Concept Check

Tell whether one number is a multiple of the other. Write *yes* or *no.* *(page 316)*

5. $2, 21$ 6. $3, 12$ 7. $5, 25$ 8. $8, 28$ 9. $10, 70$

Tell whether one denominator is a multiple of the other. Write *yes* or *no.* *(page 316)*

10. $\dfrac{1}{2}, \dfrac{5}{8}$ 11. $\dfrac{3}{5}, \dfrac{4}{20}$ 12. $\dfrac{2}{3}, \dfrac{5}{9}$ 13. $\dfrac{3}{4}, \dfrac{3}{14}$ 14. $\dfrac{4}{5}, \dfrac{4}{9}$

> When the denominators are the same, I can divide the numerators as if they are whole numbers.

Find the least common multiple. *(page 318)*

15. $2, 3$ 16. $4, 6$ 17. $5, 4$ 18. $6, 8$ 19. $3, 7$

Find the least common denominator. *(page 318)*

20. $\dfrac{1}{2}, \dfrac{2}{3}$ 21. $\dfrac{3}{4}, \dfrac{4}{5}$ 22. $\dfrac{4}{9}, \dfrac{5}{6}$ 23. $\dfrac{2}{5}, \dfrac{5}{6}$

Estimate the sum or difference. *(page 312)*

24. $3\dfrac{2}{5} + 2\dfrac{4}{5} \approx n$ 25. $4\dfrac{3}{8} - 2\dfrac{5}{8} \approx n$ 26. $2\dfrac{1}{3} + 5\dfrac{5}{6} \approx n$

Draw fraction squares to help you find each product. *(page 336)*

27. $\dfrac{1}{2} \times 1\dfrac{1}{3} = n$ 28. $\dfrac{2}{3} \times 2\dfrac{1}{2} = n$ 29. $\dfrac{1}{4} \times 1\dfrac{1}{2} = n$

Divide. *(page 338)*

30. $\dfrac{2}{5} \div \dfrac{1}{5} = n$ 31. $\dfrac{9}{12} \div \dfrac{3}{12} = n$ 32. $\dfrac{12}{4} \div \dfrac{3}{4} = n$

Skill Check

Add or subtract. Write the answer in simplest form. *(pages 314–327)*

33. $\dfrac{3}{4}$ $-\dfrac{1}{4}$

34. $\dfrac{5}{7}$ $+\dfrac{2}{7}$

35. $8\dfrac{2}{3}$ $-4\dfrac{1}{6}$

36. $2\dfrac{3}{5}$ $-1\dfrac{1}{4}$

37. $9\dfrac{3}{4}$ $+3\dfrac{1}{6}$

38. $2\dfrac{1}{4}$ $+4\dfrac{7}{8}$

39. $6\dfrac{7}{8}$ $+5\dfrac{4}{12}$

40. $4\dfrac{1}{10}$ $-2\dfrac{3}{5}$

41. $5\dfrac{3}{8}$ $-1\dfrac{5}{12}$

42. $8\dfrac{2}{3}$ $-3\dfrac{9}{10}$

Multiply. Write each product as a whole or mixed number. *(page 332)*

43. $5 \times \dfrac{2}{7} = n$

44. $6 \times \dfrac{2}{3} = n$

45. $\dfrac{3}{4} \times 8 = n$

46. $\dfrac{5}{8} \times 7 = n$

Multiply. Write the answer in simplest form. *(page 334)*

47. $\dfrac{2}{3} \times \dfrac{3}{5} = n$

48. $\dfrac{3}{4} \times \dfrac{5}{6} = n$

49. $\dfrac{4}{7} \times \dfrac{5}{6} = n$

50. $\dfrac{1}{4} \times \dfrac{1}{5} = n$

Problem-Solving Check *(pages 328, 340)*

51. Randy counted 50 instruments in the orchestra. The table shows the number of instruments in each section. What fraction of the orchestra is percussion?

52. The cast in a local play was $\frac{1}{5}$ adults, $\frac{1}{2}$ girls under 16 years old, and $\frac{3}{10}$ boys under 16 years old. If there were 4 adults in the play, how many boys under 16 years old were in the play?

53. The dance recital was $\frac{3}{4}$ ballet dances, $\frac{1}{6}$ tap dances, and $\frac{1}{12}$ jazz dances. If there were 3 jazz dances, how many tap dances were in the recital?

Symphony Orchestra	
Section	**Number**
Woodwinds	12
Percussion	5
Strings	25
Brass	8

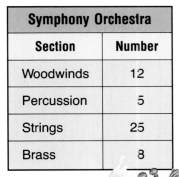

1. Estimate $\frac{1}{8} + \frac{5}{9}$. Explain your method.

2. Use fraction bars to find the sum of $\frac{2}{3} + \frac{1}{6}$. Draw a picture to show what you did.

3. Show each step as you find the difference of $4\frac{3}{8} - 1\frac{5}{8}$.

4. Draw a fraction square to help you find $\frac{3}{4} \times \frac{1}{2}$.

5. Use fraction bars, counters, or fraction circles to find the quotient of $\frac{6}{8} \div \frac{2}{8}$. Draw a picture to show what you did.

6. Read Exercise 2 on page 341. Follow the steps on the Problem-Solving Think Along worksheet to show how to solve this problem.

It's easy to think about fractions as being close to 0, $\frac{1}{2}$, or 1.

Write About It

7. Which concept in this chapter on using fractions was the easiest for you? Which was the hardest? Explain.

8. Write a word problem to go with the following number sentence, and give the solution. $\frac{1}{2} \times \frac{2}{3} = n$

TEAMWORK Project

Compose Music

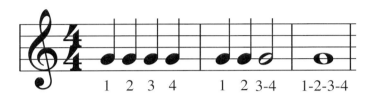

1 2 3 4   1 2 3-4   1-2-3-4

Composers write music, using time
signatures and musical notes.
**With your teammates, compose and
perform your own music.**

MUSICAL NOTE CHART	
Musical Note	**Number of Beats**
o Whole note	4
♩ Half note	2
♪ Quarter note	1
♪ Eighth note	$\frac{1}{2}$

Decide

**Talk about how you can use tracing paper
and pencils to create and perform a
musical composition.**

Share

Show your composition.
Describe how the length of an
eighth note compares with the
lengths of quarter, half, and
whole notes.

Do

■ Trace the staff and
meter signature shown. Use
a ruler to make each
line on the staff 8 inches
long.

■ Use the table to
develop 4-beat measures.
Separate measures with
vertical lines.

■ Write the beats below
the notes, counting from
1 to 4 for each measure.

■ Perform your composition by tapping out the
beats with a pencil.

Talk About It

a. How can you use your
composition to
imagine the number of
eighth notes in a
quarter note? a half
note? a whole note?
an entire measure?

b. In your everyday
activities, what other
fractional parts do you
measure?

MATH FUN
Extend Your Thinking

Activity

MAGIC SQUARES

4	9	2
3	5	7
8	1	6

An ancient Chinese book tells the story of a turtle with a magic square on its back, like the one at the right.

In a magic square, the sum of each column, row, and diagonal is the same number. The sum of each column, row, and diagonal of this special magic square is 15.

Magic squares can also be made up of mixed numbers. Copy and complete the following magic squares.

1.

$1\frac{3}{4}$	■	$2\frac{3}{4}$
■	$2\frac{1}{2}$	■
■	■	$3\frac{1}{4}$

2.

■	$\frac{7}{8}$	■
■	■	■
$1\frac{1}{4}$	$1\frac{3}{8}$	$\frac{3}{4}$

Challenge

Number Puzzles

Write + or − in each ● to make true sentences.

1. $\frac{8}{10} ● \frac{4}{10} ● \frac{7}{10} = \frac{1}{2}$

2. $\frac{6}{9} ● \frac{5}{9} ● \frac{2}{9} = \frac{1}{3}$

3. $\frac{3}{10} ● \frac{1}{5} ● \frac{2}{3} = 1\frac{1}{6}$

4. $5\frac{5}{7} ● 2\frac{5}{14} ● 2\frac{6}{7} = 6\frac{3}{14}$

Critical Thinking

Ms. Jackson kept a record of the number of hours students worked in the library during a week. Sue worked $\frac{1}{4}$ hour. Pete worked 2 times as long as Sue. Jose worked $\frac{1}{2}$ as long as Pete. Anne worked $4\frac{2}{3}$ times as long as Jose. Max worked $\frac{3}{7}$ as long as Anne worked. How many hours did each student work?

Write the letter of the correct answer.

1.
$$8.905$$
$$-4.896$$

A. 4.009   **B.** 4.109
C. 4.119   **D.** not here

2. Which is the best estimate?
$6,152 \times 5 \approx n$

A. 3,000   **B.** 30,000
C. 300,000   **D.** not here

3. Which figure shows parallel lines?

A.
B.
C.   **D.**

4. Which is the average of 85, 90, 100, 83, and 87?

A. 85   **B.** 87
C. 89   **D.** 90

5. $4\overline{)1,216}$

A. 34   **B.** 304
C. 340   **D.** not here

6. $26\overline{)31,028}$

A. 1,093   **B.** 1,193
C. 1,293   **D.** not here

Use the grid for Exercises 7–8.

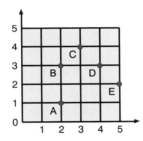

7. Which are the coordinates of Point E?

A. (2,5)   **B.** (5,2)
C. (2,2)   **D.** (5,5)

8. Which is the point at (3,4)?

A. Point A **B.** Point B
C. Point C **D.** Point D

9. Which is the best estimate?
$31 \times 6.84 \approx n$

A. 18   **B.** 21
C. 210   **D.** 2,100

10. Which fraction is equivalent to $\frac{2}{3}$?

A. $\frac{4}{12}$ **B.** $\frac{4}{9}$
C. $\frac{4}{8}$ **D.** $\frac{4}{6}$

11. There are 60 students in the chorus. For the concert 16 students stood in the first row, 20 stood in the second row, and 24 stood in the third row. What fraction of the chorus stood in the third row?

A. $\frac{4}{15}$ of the chorus   **B.** $\frac{1}{3}$ of the chorus

C. $\frac{2}{5}$ of the chorus   **D.** $\frac{1}{2}$ of the chorus

12. Tickets for a concert sold for $15, $12, and $9. Of the total number of tickets, $\frac{3}{4}$ sold for $15, $\frac{1}{8}$ sold for $12, and $\frac{1}{8}$ sold for $9. If 200 tickets sold for $9, how many tickets sold for $15?

A. 200 tickets   **B.** 400 tickets
C. 1,200 tickets   **D.** 1,600 tickets

CHAPTER 11

MEASUREMENT

Did you know . . .

. . . that Scouting began in 1907? Today there are over 15 million young people and Scout leaders belonging to Scouting units in nearly 120 countries.

TALK ABOUT IT

A Boy Scout troop is constructing rafts to be used at the next jamboree. Each board for the rafts measures 6 in. wide, and the rafts will be 5 ft. wide. What are some things the Scout leader should consider to find out how much wood is needed for 3 rafts?

Kimiko and Nat must choose a unit to measure their model ship.

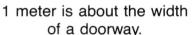

Units of Length
1,000 millimeters (mm) = 1 meter (m)
100 centimeters (cm) = 1 meter
10 decimeters (dm) = 1 meter
1 kilometer (km) = 1,000 meters

1 meter is about the width of a doorway.

1 centimeter is about the width of a large paper clip.

1 millimeter is about the thickness of a dime.

The model ship is smaller than a meter. Centimeters can be used to measure objects smaller than a meter.

So, it is reasonable to measure the model ship in centimeters.

Talk About It

▶ Which units are smaller than a meter? larger than a meter?

▶ Which unit would you use to measure the height of your desk? Explain why you think your choice is reasonable.

▶ What objects in your classroom would you measure in meters? Explain why you think your choices are reasonable.

Check for Understanding

Choose the most reasonable unit of measure. Write *mm, cm, m,* or *km.*

1. thickness of paper   2. distance to the next town

Write **a, b,** or **c** to tell which measurement is the most reasonable.

3.    **a.** 6 dm   **b.** 6 cm   **c.** 60 m

4.   **a.** 15 m   **b.** 15 cm   **c.** 15 mm

Practice

Choose the most reasonable unit of measure. Write *mm, cm, m,* or *km.*

5. length of a spelling book

6. distance from the earth to the moon

7. height of a chalkboard

8. distance around a baseball field

9. thickness of a dime

10. length of a piece of chalk

11. length of a bus

12. distance from your home to school

Write **a, b,** or **c** to tell which measurement is the most reasonable.

13. width of a window   **a.** 10 cm   **b.** 10 dm   **c.** 10 km

14. diameter of a ring   **a.** 15 mm   **b.** 15 cm   **c.** 15 km

15.  length of a crayon   **a.** 8 mm   **b.** 8 cm   **c.** 8 dm

16.  length of a car   **a.** 4 dm   **b.** 4 m   **c.** 4 km

Mixed Applications

17. **Write a Question** Chin measured his plant's growth on each of seven days. By the seventh day his plant had grown 21 mm.

18. Franklin and Candy cut 12 pieces of wire that were each 20.5 cm long. How many centimeters of wire did they cut?

19. Mildred kept track of rainfall during four weeks for her science project. She measured 1.4 cm the first week, 2.1 cm the second week, 1.8 cm the third week, and 2.9 cm the fourth week. How many centimeters of rain fell during four weeks?

20. Greta and Mario measured the length of the chalkboard. Greta said it measured 3 dm long, and Mario said it measured 3 m long. Whose measurement was more reasonable?

How can you compare the length of a centimeter with the length of a meter?

EXPLORING

with Metric Units

Building Understanding

To measure length, you can use a meterstick or a metric ruler. Both may be marked to show millimeters and centimeters. A decimeter is equal to 10 centimeters. A meterstick is marked to show decimeters.

Find the marks that represent each unit on your ruler.

1mm ⊦ 1cm ⊢——⊣ 1dm ⊢————————————————————⊣

Use a metric ruler. Measure the length of an index card in cm.

TALK ABOUT IT

- How can you find the length of the index card in mm? in dm?

Measure the length of your desk with a metric ruler. When you reach the end of the ruler, use chalk to mark the spot on your desk.

Slide the ruler to the right. Line it up with your chalk mark.

Draw a mark at 30cm.

| | | | | | | | | | |
21 22 23 24 25 26 27 28 29 30

Slide the ruler to the chalk mark.

Line up the end of the ruler with the chalk mark.

| | | | | | | |
1 2 3 4 5 6 7 8
Centimeters

Measure and mark the rest of the length of your desk. Add the measurements to find the length of your desk.

- What metric measuring instrument would have made measuring your desk as easy as measuring the index card?

- How many mm long is your metric ruler? How many cm? How many dm?

- How many mm long is your meterstick? How many cm? How many dm?

Making the Connection

The reason you have for measuring an object will determine the unit of measure you use. The smaller the unit you use, the more precise your measurement will be. When you measure an object, you measure to the nearest unit.

Measuring to the nearest unit is like rounding numbers.

Measure

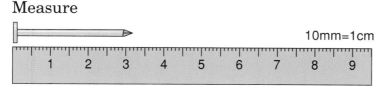

10mm=1cm

Round 473

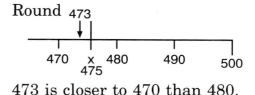

473 is closer to 470 than 480.

The length of the nail is closer to 3 cm than 4 cm.

It is about 3 cm.

Measure the nail in mm to find a more precise measure.

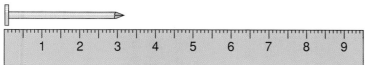

The length of the nail is 32 mm.

Measure each side of the rectangle to the nearest cm. Add the measurements. This is the perimeter of the rectangle.

Checking Understanding

Write the measure to the nearest cm and then write a more precise measure.

1.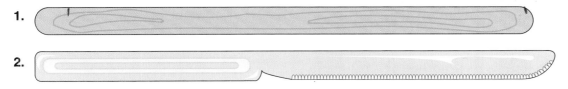

2.

Measure each side of the rectangle to the nearest cm. Add the measurements to find the perimeter.

3.

4.

Use a metric ruler. Draw a line to show each length.

5. 25 cm

6. 58 mm

7. 2 dm

8. 153 mm

METRIC
Units of Capacity

Ed makes paste by mixing powder with 1 liter of water. How can he find a container that will hold the mixture, or that has a **capacity** of about 1 liter?

The total capacity of 3 soda cans is about 1 L.

So, Ed can choose a container that holds about 3 soda cans of liquid.

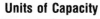

Because containers come in different sizes and shapes, estimating capacity can be challenging. Use empty containers and water to practice estimating capacity.

- Choose five empty containers of different sizes and shapes.
- Label each container as shown.
- Estimate how much liquid each container holds. Order the containers from least to greatest. Copy the table and record the order.
- Use a metric measuring cup. Measure the capacity of each container in mL. Record the measurements. Write *yes* or *no* to tell whether the container holds more than a liter.

Container	A	B	C	D	E
mL	■	■	■	■	■
More than a liter	?	?	?	?	?

- Why does the shape of a container make it difficult to estimate its capacity?

Check for Understanding

Choose the more reasonable unit of measure. Write *L* or *mL*.

1. a fishbowl

2. a kitchen sink

3. a juice glass

Practice

Choose the more reasonable unit of measure. Write *mL* or *L*.

4. an eyedropper

5. an aquarium

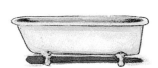

6. a soup can

7. a birdbath

8. a bathtub

9. a yogurt cup

Choose the more reasonable estimate of capacity. Write **a** or **b**.

10. gasoline tank	**a.** 40 mL	**b.** 40 L
11. water given a houseplant	**a.** 300 mL	**b.** 300 L
12. juice for a class party	**a.** 2 mL	**b.** 2 L
13. glass of water	**a.** 250 mL	**b.** 250 L

Mixed Applications

14. Mavis is having a hard time reading a recipe. Would a recipe for 12–14 pancakes call for 300 mL of milk or 30 L of milk?

15. Mario wants to know the length of a piece of wood that is $\frac{4}{5}$ the length of his arm. If his arm is 65 cm long, how long is the piece of wood?

16. Jaime measured the width of his paper and said it was 212 cm wide. Is this a reasonable measurement? Explain.

17. Julian filled a bowl with 5 glasses of water. If each glass had a capacity of 300 mL, how many milliliters of water did the bowl hold?

MIXED REVIEW

Multiply.

1. $15 \times 100 = n$ **2.** $370 \times 10 = n$ **3.** $68 \times 1,000 = n$ **4.** $1,000 \times 100 = n$

Divide.

5. $63 \div 1,000 = n$ **6.** $82 \div 100 = n$ **7.** $7 \div 10 = n$ **8.** $41 \div 100 = n$

How do milliliters compare to liters?

METRIC
Units of Mass

Linda wants to know the mass of a nickel and a pair of men's shoes. She remembered that the mass of a paper clip is about 1 gram. She can estimate the mass of each object by comparing it to the mass of a paper clip.

Units of Mass
1,000 milligrams (mg) = 1 gram (g)
1,000 grams = 1 kilogram (kg)

What is the mass of the nickel?

It takes 5 paper clips to balance a nickel. So, 1 nickel has a mass of about 5 g.

It takes 1,000 paper clips to balance a pair of men's shoes. So, a pair of men's shoes has a mass of 1,000 grams, or about 1 kg.

- Choose five objects of different sizes and weights.
- Label each object as shown.
- Estimate the mass of each object. Put the objects in order from least mass to greatest mass. Copy the table and record the order.
- Use a metric scale. Find the mass of each object in grams. Write *yes* or *no* to tell whether the mass is more than a kilogram.

Object	A	B	C	D	E
Mass in grams	▪	▪	▪	▪	▪
More or less than a kilogram	?	?	?	?	?

Talk About It

▶ Which objects were the most difficult to estimate? Why?

▶ Which objects in your classroom would you measure in kilograms? in grams?

Check for Understanding

Choose the most reasonable unit. Write *kg, g,* or *mg.*

1. a full box of cereal

2. a grain of rice

3. a loaf of bread

4. an iron

Practice

Choose the most reasonable unit. Write *kg, g,* or *mg.*

5. a full suitcase   **6.** a cat   **7.** a pencil   **8.** a grain of salt

9. a cookie   **10.** a snowflake   **11.** a book   **12.** a bag of oranges

Choose the more reasonable estimate of mass. Write **a** or **b**.

13.
a. 30 mg
b. 30 g

14.
a. 10 g
b. 10 kg

15.
a. 1 mg
b. 1 kg

16.
a. 15 g
b. 15 kg

17.
a. 4 mg
b. 4 g

18.
a. 200 g
b. 200 kg

19.
a. 500 mg
b. 500 kg

20.
a. 10 g
b. 10 kg

Mixed Applications

For Exercises 21–24, write how many servings can be made from each item.

21. 25-g bags of peanuts

22. 50-g servings of granola

23. 20-g servings of popcorn

24. 60-g bags of peanuts

25. For a cooking project, Hoshie bought 3 bags of nuts for $1.29 each, 1 bag of flour for $1.69, and 2 bags of coconut for $0.95 each. How much did he spend for all the items?

26. Peggy is using a recipe that makes 12 cookies. Would the mass of the cookies be greater or less than a kilogram?

Name some items that are usually measured in grams and kilograms.

THE METRIC SYSTEM

Bárbara is from Colombia, South America. She is working on a project, using only units from the **metric system.** There are metric units of length, capacity, and mass. The same prefixes are used with different base units to name all the other units in the system. These prefixes relate to place value.

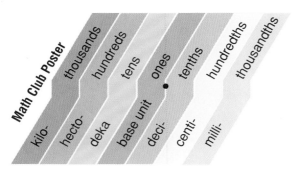

Math Club Poster

| thousands | hundreds | tens | ones | tenths | hundredths | thousandths |
| kilo- | hecto- | deka | base unit | deci- | centi- | milli- |

MULTICULTURAL NOTE: Metric units are used in many countries throughout the world. A group of French scientists created the metric system in the 1790's.

Metric units use a <u>prefix</u> and a base unit.

<u>centi</u> *meter*   <u>milli</u> *liter*   <u>kilo</u> *gram*

You can change each measurement to the base unit.

Prefix	Base Unit	Measurement
kilo-	gram	1,000 grams
centi-	meter	0.01 meter
milli-	liter	0.001 liter

A. 7 kilograms = ■ grams
Think: 1 kilogram = 1,000 grams
7 × 1,000 = 7,000
7 kilograms = 7,000 grams

B. 4 centimeters = ■ meter
Think: 1 centimeter = 0.01 meter
4 × 0.01 = 0.04
4 centimeters = 0.04 meter

C. 3 milliliters = ■ liter
Think: 1 milliliter = 0.001 liter
3 × 0.001 = 0.003
3 milliliters = 0.003 liter

Talk About It

▶ Which prefixes indicate units smaller than the base units?

▶ Which prefix indicates a unit 1,000 times greater than the base unit?

Check for Understanding

Write each measurement as a decimal, using the base unit.

1. 4 cm   **2.** 5 mg   **3.** 7 L   **4.** 6 mm   **5.** 8 cm

Practice

Choose the smaller unit of measure. Write **a** or **b**.

6. a. milliliter   **7. a.** gram   **8. a.** kilometer
   b. liter   **b.** milligram   **b.** meter

Choose the larger unit of measure. Write **a** or **b**.

9. a. gram   **10. a.** milliliter   **11. a.** decimeter
   b. kilogram   **b.** liter   **b.** centimeter

Give the decimal meaning for each prefix.
Write **a, b, c,** or **d** for Exercises 12–15.

12. milli-   **a.** tenth
13. deci-   **b.** thousand
14. kilo-   **c.** hundredth
15. centi-   **d.** thousandth

Use the place-value chart on page 358. Change each
measurement to the base unit.

16. 5 dm   **17.** 3 mL   **18.** 8 g   **19.** 2 mm   **20.** 9 mg

21. 2 mL   **22.** 13 mL   **23.** 6 cm   **24.** 12 mg   **25.** 25 mg

Mixed Applications

26. Ricardo is painting his display board. He already has 0.25 L of paint. If the board requires 1.5 L of paint, how much more paint does he need?

27. Kristen and Sara need string for their projects. Kristen needs 2.5 m of string, and Sara needs 3.4 m of string. How much string do both girls need?

28. For her science project, Lois needs a board that is 1 m long. Alex needs a board that is 1 dm long. Who needs a longer board?

29. Cornelius is using an object that weighs 1 kg. Mark is using an object that weighs 1 mg. Who is using the lighter object?

How can you tell that a decimeter is longer than a centimeter?

CHANGING METRIC UNITS

The directions say Suki's model will be 2.4 meters long. Her ruler has only centimeter units. How can she find the number of centimeters in 2.4 meters?

Changing units in the metric system is like moving from one place-value position to another.

	×10	×10	×10	×10	×10	×10	
kilo- thousands	hecto- hundreds	deka- tens	base- ones	deci- tenths	centi- hundredths	milli- thousandths	
	÷10	÷10	÷10	÷10	÷10	÷10	

To change larger units to smaller units, multiply by 10 for each place you move to the right.

km thousands	hm hundreds	dam tens	m ones	dm tenths	cm hundredths	mm thousandths

2.4 m = ■ cm

2.4 × 100 = 240

To change meters to centimeters, move two places to the right, so multiply by 100.

Suki can multiply by 100 to change 2.4 m to 240 cm.

To change smaller units to larger units, divide by 10 for each place you move to the left.

km thousands	hm hundreds	dam tens	m ones	dm tenths	cm hundredths	mm thousandths

200 cm = ■ m

Divide. 200 ÷ 100 = 2

200 cm = 2 m

To change centimeters to meters, move 2 places to the left, so divide by 100.

Talk About It

▶ If you change 7 meters to centimeters, does the number become greater or lesser?

▶ Why do you multiply to change 7 kilograms to grams?

▶ Why do you divide to change meters to kilometers?

▶ How can you determine how many times you must multiply or divide by 10 to change units in the metric system?

Check for Understanding

1. Is a gram larger or smaller than a kilogram?

2. How many grams are equal to 9 kg?

3. Do you multiply or divide to change 9.5 kg to g?

Practice

Complete.

4. 3 kg = 3,000 _?_

5. 50 km = 50,000 _?_

6. 4.309 L = 4,309 _?_

7. 9.813 kg = 9,813 _?_

8. 6,200 g = 6.2 _?_

9. 760 mL = 0.760 _?_

10. 5.8 m = 580 _?_

11. 50 m = 5,000 _?_

12. 5,850 mm = 5.85 _?_

 Write *multiply* or *divide* for each exercise. Then solve.

13. 5.2 cm = ■ mm

14. 80 mm = ■ cm

15. 4.5 m = ■ cm

16. 15 L = ■ mL

17. 25,000 mL = ■ L

18. 120 L = ■ mL

19. 4,000 mg = ■ g

20. 6.52 g = ■ mg

21. 23,000 mg = ■ g

22. 3.75 m = ■ cm

23. 50 mm = ■ dm

24. 8.754 g = ■ mg

Mixed Applications

25. Thelma poured 0.5 L of water into a beaker. During an experiment, she added 200 mL of water. How much water was in the beaker at the end of the experiment?

26. While doing a science project, Roberto learned that weather balloons burst at an altitude of 27 km. What is this altitude in meters?

27. Marvin had a piece of wire that was 2.7 m long. He cut the wire into 3 equal pieces. Was each piece of wire greater than or less than 1 m?

28. **Analyze Data** Darlene and Jason collected rocks for science class. Darlene's rock weighed 0.3 kg, and Jason's rock weighed 350 g. Whose rock weighed more?

Why do you multiply to change kilometers to meters?

COMPUTING TEMPERATURE CHANGES

Mandy used a Fahrenheit thermometer to find the difference between the high and low temperatures on Monday.

In the customary system, temperature is measured in degrees **Fahrenheit (°F)**. This is a Fahrenheit thermometer. It shows room temperature at 68°F.

The low temperature on Monday was 10 degrees below zero, or ⁻10°F. The high temperature was 29°F.

You can find the difference in temperature by comparing the starting temperature with the number of degrees it rises or falls.

Starting Temperature	Change in Temperature
⁻10°F	from ⁻10° to 0° ⟶ 10° from 0° to 29° ⟶ +29° ———— 39°

The temperature rose 39°F.

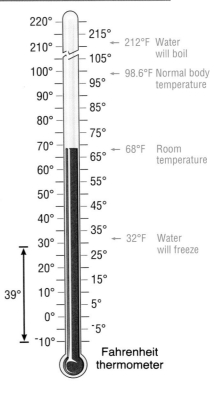

In the metric system, temperature is recorded in degrees **Celsius (°C)**. This is a Celsius thermometer. It shows room temperature at 20°C.

On Tuesday the high temperature was 15°C. The low temperature was ⁻5°C.

Starting Temperature	Change in Temperature
15°C	from 15° to 0° ⟶ 15° from 0° to ⁻5° ⟶ + 5° ———— 20°

The temperature fell 20°C.

Check for Understanding

Use the thermometers. Find the difference in temperature.

1. high 25°F, low ⁻7°F

2. high 20°C, low ⁻5°C

3. high 33°C, low 20°C

4. high 68°F, low 32°F

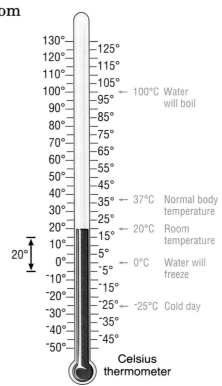

Practice

Use the starting temperature on each thermometer to find the new temperature.

5. 12° colder   **6.** 56° warmer   **7.** 8° colder   **8.** 15° warmer

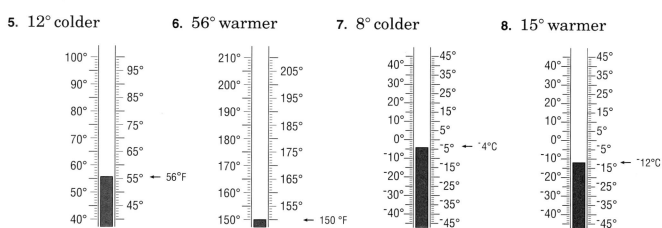

Copy and complete the table. Use the thermometers on page 362.

Starting Temperature	62°F	**10.**	10°C	45°C
Change in Temperature	rose 10°	rose 15°	fell 12°	**12.**
Final Temperature	**9.**	52°F	**11.**	32°C

Mixed Applications

13. The highest temperature ever recorded in the United States was 134°F in Death Valley in 1913. The lowest temperature was ⁻80°F in Prospect Creek, Alaska, in 1971. What is the difference between the highest and the lowest temperatures?

14. Rosalinda recorded the afternoon temperature in her backyard for 5 days. On Monday the temperature was 16°C. On Tuesday and Wednesday the temperature was 18°C. On Thursday it was 17°C, and on Friday it was 16°C. What was the average temperature for these 5 days?

Use the graph for Exercises 15–17.

15. What was the coldest time of the day?

16. How many degrees did the temperature rise between 8:30 A.M. and noon?

17. What was the difference between the temperature at 10:00 A.M. and the temperature at 3:30 P.M.?

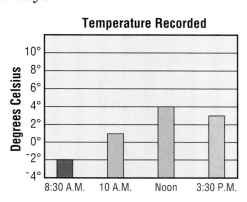

What are the units on a customary and a metric thermometer?

PROBLEM SOLVING

Evaluate Answers for Reasonableness

Tom measured the 24 bookshelves in his classroom. Each shelf was 105 cm long. When his teacher asked how many meters of bookshelves there were, Tom said 5 meters. Did Tom give a reasonable answer?

▶ **UNDERSTAND**

What are you asked to find?

What facts are given?

▶ **PLAN**

What strategy can you use?

You can estimate the total number of meters in 24 bookshelves. Then compare.

▶ **SOLVE**

How can you solve the problem?

Round 105 to 100. ◀————— cm length of 1 shelf
Multiply:
   $100 \times 24 = 2,400$ ◀— cm length of 24 shelves

Compare your estimate of 2,400 cm with 5 m.

5 m = 500 cm
500 cm is much less than 2,400 cm.

Another Method

2,400 cm = 24 m
24 m is much more than 5 m.

So, Tom did not give a reasonable answer.

▶ **LOOK BACK**

What is another way to solve the problem?

WHAT IF... ... there were 35 bookshelves 90 cm long and Tom told his teacher there were 3.5 m of bookshelves? Did Tom give a reasonable answer?

Apply

1 Geraldo walks a total of 3 km to and from school each day. At the end of the 180-day school year, Geraldo said, "I have walked 540 m to and from school this year." Is this reasonable? Explain.

2 The mass of 1 granola bar is 100 grams. When Francine's friend asked her what the mass of 12 granola bars was, Francine answered it was more than 1 kg. Was her answer reasonable? Explain.

3 If it rained 2 cm on Monday, 1 cm on Tuesday, 2.5 cm on Wednesday, 3.5 cm on Thursday, and 2 cm on Friday, is it reasonable to say that more than a decimeter of rain fell in 5 days? Explain.

4 Ming Chin poured 4 cups of water into a container. Each cup held 250 mL of water. Is it reasonable to say that the container held 10 L of water? Explain.

Mixed Applications	STRATEGIES	Find a Pattern • Work Backward • Make a Table • Make a Diagram

Choose a strategy and solve.

5 Ken, Michael, Marcia, and Larry each did a science project on a different topic. The topics were electricity, sea life, space, and weather. Ken did his project on space. Michael did not do his project on sea life. Larry did his project on electricity. What project did each person do?

6 Students in the industrial arts class had a choice of making a planter, bookends, or a shelf. Of the students, $\frac{1}{2}$ chose to make a planter, $\frac{1}{3}$ chose to make bookends, and $\frac{1}{6}$ chose to make a shelf. If 5 of the students chose to make a shelf, how many students are in the class?

7 A student listed a temperature of 85°F at 1:00 P.M., 82°F at 3:00 P.M., 78°F at 5:00 P.M., and 73°F at 7:00 P.M. If this pattern continued, what was the temperature at 11:00 P.M.?

8 Cristina spent half of her project money for a display board. Then she spent half of what was left for paint. After that she had $2.50 left. How much did she have at the start?

More Practice, Lesson 11.8, page H76

1. Of the rooms in Zachary's house, $\frac{1}{2}$ are white, $\frac{1}{3}$ are yellow, and $\frac{1}{6}$ are blue. If there is one blue room in Zachary's house, how many yellow rooms are in his house?

2. Linda's garden is $\frac{2}{5}$ tomato plants, $\frac{1}{2}$ green vegetable plants, and $\frac{1}{10}$ strawberry plants. If she has 4 strawberry plants, how many tomato plants does she have?

3. The window in Yosi's room is 1.5 m wide. Yosi tells the salesclerk he needs a window shade 15 cm wide. Is this reasonable? Explain.

4. Emily's cat weighs about 3 kg. She told her friend that her cat weighs 300 g. Is this reasonable? Explain.

Think about the meaning of the prefix to decide if a metric measure is reasonable.

Write the amount as a decimal form of the whole unit.

5. 6 dimes   6. 7 dm   7. 4 tenths   8. 5 pennies

Solve.

9. $8{,}230 \times 0 =$

10. $(3 \times$ $) \times 5 = 75$

11. $20 \times (3 \times 2) =$

12. $2{,}380 \times$ $= 2{,}380$

Trace each figure. Draw all the lines of symmetry for each shape.

13.
14.
15.
16.

Estimate the quotient.

17. $4\overline{)79}$

18. $8\overline{)231}$

19. $18\overline{)395}$

20. $28\overline{)1{,}470}$

Use the graph for Exercises 21–23.

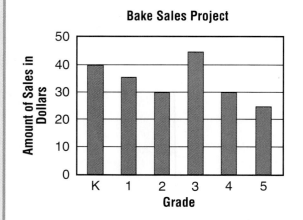

Bake Sales Project

Amount of Sales in Dollars vs. Grade

21. How much did the kindergarten earn in bake sales?

22. How much more did the first grade earn than the fifth grade?

23. How much did all the grades earn in bake sales?

NORTH AMERICA

Reading a Time-Zone Map

Neighboring countries such as Canada, Mexico, and the United States share some of the same time zones. There are six time zones in the United States. The map shows the difference in time between zones.

Hawaii	Alaska	Pacific	Mountain	Central	Eastern
1:00 P.M.	2:00 P.M.	3:00 P.M.	4:00 P.M.	5:00 P.M.	6:00 P.M.

Talk About It

- Why do you think there are time zones in the United States?

- Why do you think that time gets earlier as you move from east to west?

- If you live in Florida, in the Eastern time zone, would you call someone at a school in California at 8:00 A.M.? Why or why not?

Use the time-zone map for Exercises 1–4.

1. Maria lives in the Central time zone. She wants to call her grandmother in California at 8:00 A.M. Pacific time to wish her a happy birthday. At what time should she place the call?

2. If David places a call to central Texas from Hawaii at 2:00 P.M. Hawaiian time, what time is it in central Texas?

3. Robert lives in Alaska. He received a call from a friend in Denver at 11:00 P.M. At what time did his friend place the call from the Mountain time zone?

4. If business hours at a California business are 9:30 A.M. to 5:30 P.M., at what times could a person in the Central time zone call and reach someone at the business?

USING A CUSTOMARY RULER

Lisa did an experiment on plant growth. She measured and recorded the height of a plant in five different ways.

Customary Units of Length

12 inches (in.)	=	1 foot (ft)
3 ft	=	1 yard (yd)
5,280 ft or 1,760 yd	=	1 mile (mi)

Plant Height

Measurement	Week 1	Week 4
Nearest inch	4 in.	4 in.
Nearest $\frac{1}{2}$ inch	4 in.	4 in.
Nearest $\frac{1}{4}$ inch	$3\frac{3}{4}$ in.	$4\frac{1}{4}$ in.
Nearest $\frac{1}{8}$ inch	$3\frac{7}{8}$ in.	$4\frac{2}{8}$ in.
Nearest $\frac{1}{16}$ inch	$3\frac{13}{16}$ in.	$4\frac{3}{16}$ in.

1 inch

$\frac{1}{2}$ inch

$\frac{1}{4}$ inch

$\frac{1}{8}$ inch

$\frac{1}{16}$ inch

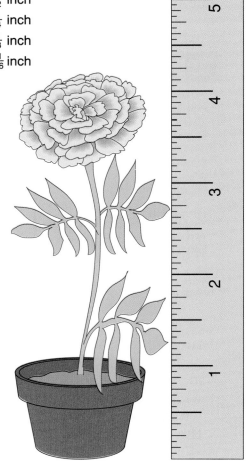

- If Lisa measures only to the nearest inch or the nearest $\frac{1}{2}$ inch, what would her report show?

- Why are some measurements the same from Week 1 to Week 4?

- Using the most precise measurements, what was the height of the plant in Week 1? Week 4?

- How much did the plant grow in 4 weeks?

Measure the width of your mathematics book to the nearest inch and to the nearest $\frac{1}{2}$ in., $\frac{1}{4}$ in., $\frac{1}{8}$ in., and $\frac{1}{16}$ in. Record your measurements.

Talk About It

▶ Which measurement is the most precise?

▶ When are less precise measurements just as good? When are more precise measurements necessary?

Check for Understanding

Draw a line to the given length.

1. $5\frac{1}{4}$ in. **2.** $2\frac{3}{8}$ in. **3.** $6\frac{1}{2}$ in. **4.** $7\frac{5}{16}$ in. **5.** $\frac{3}{4}$ in.

Practice

Using an inch ruler, measure each line segment as precisely as you can.

6. ————————————————————————————

7. ——————————————————————

8. ————————————————

9. ————————

Draw a line to the given length.

10. $4\frac{3}{4}$ in.   **11.** $1\frac{3}{8}$ in.   **12.** $\frac{5}{16}$ in.   **13.** $7\frac{1}{2}$ in.   **14.** $4\frac{5}{8}$ in.

Complete each riddle.

15. I measure long distances. There are 5,280 feet in me. My name is ? , and my abbreviation is ? .

16. I measure small things. There are 12 of me in 1 foot. My name is ? , and my abbreviation is ? .

17. I measure large things. There are 3 feet in me. My name is ? , and my abbreviation is ? .

Mixed Applications

18. Lauren's plant has grown to a height of $5\frac{1}{4}$ in. Lynn's plant has grown to a height of $5\frac{3}{8}$ in. Whose plant is taller?

19. Caroline measured a butterfly's wingspan at $2\frac{3}{8}$ in. What is the measurement to the nearest $\frac{1}{2}$ in.?

20. Mills watered his plant twice a week. If he gave the plant 250 mL of water each time he watered, how much water did he give the plant in 4 weeks?

21. Dillan measured the height of 5 flowers in his mother's garden. They measured 7 in., 5 in., $8\frac{3}{4}$ in., $7\frac{1}{4}$ in., and 7 in. What is the average height of the flowers?

Measure the length of your desk in customary units. What is the length to the nearest inch?

WRAP UP...

CUSTOMARY UNITS
Changing and Computing

Lloyd marked the standing long jump for Field Day. He tested his setup and jumped 60 in. How many feet did he jump?

Customary Units of Length	
12 inches (in.)	= 1 foot (ft)
36 in. or 3 ft	= 1 yard (yd)
5,280 ft. or 1,760 yd	= 1 mile (mi)

You can multiply or divide to change units of length.

To change smaller units to larger units, divide.

60 in. = ■ ft **Think:** 12 in. = 1 ft
60 ÷ 12 = 5
60 in. = 5 ft
So, Lloyd jumped 5 ft.

To change larger units to smaller units, multiply.

5 ft = ■ in. **Think:** 1 ft = 12 in.
5 × 12 = 60
5 ft = 60 in.

You may need to change units to add or subtract measurements.

Examples

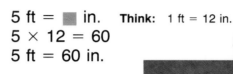

$$\begin{array}{r} 2\ \text{ft} \quad 8\ \text{in.} \\ +\ 3\ \text{ft} \quad 9\ \text{in.} \\ \hline 5\ \text{ft} \quad 17\ \text{in.} \end{array}$$

5 ft 17 in. = 5 ft + Rename 17 in. $\overbrace{12\ \text{in.} + 5\ \text{in.}}$ =
5 ft + 1 ft + 5 in. = **6 ft 5 in.**

Another Example

Rename 7 ft.

$$\begin{array}{r} 7\ \text{ft} \quad 9\ \text{in.} \\ -\ 4\ \text{ft} \quad 11\ \text{in.} \end{array} \quad \overbrace{6\ \text{ft} + 1\ \text{ft}} + 9\ \text{in.} =$$
6 ft + 12 in. + 9 in. =

$$\begin{array}{r} 6\ \text{ft}\ 21\ \text{in.} \\ \cancel{7}\ \text{ft}\quad \cancel{9}\ \text{in.} \\ -\ 4\ \text{ft}\ 11\ \text{in.} \\ \hline 2\ \text{ft}\ 10\ \text{in.} \end{array}$$

Check for Understanding

Write *multiply* or *divide*. Complete.

1. 3 ft = ■ in.
2. 5 mi = ■ ft
3. 120 ft = ■ yd
4. 3 yd = ■ ft
5. 252 in. = ■ yd
6. 228 in. = ■ ft

Add or subtract.

7. $\begin{array}{r} 4\ \text{ft}\ 7\ \text{in.} \\ +3\ \text{ft}\ 6\ \text{in.} \end{array}$

8. $\begin{array}{r} 9\ \text{yd}\ 2\ \text{ft} \\ -5\ \text{yd}\ 5\ \text{ft} \end{array}$

9. $\begin{array}{r} 14\ \text{ft}\ 3\ \text{in.} \\ -\ 9\ \text{ft}\ 6\ \text{in.} \end{array}$

Practice

Complete.

10. 36 in. = ■ ft

11. 5,280 ft = ■ yd

12. 6 ft = ■ yd

13. 2 ft = ■ in.

14. 144 in. = ■ yd

15. 2 mi = ■ yd

16. 10,560 ft = ■ mi

17. 21,120 ft = ■ mi

18. 7,040 yd = ■ mi

Add or subtract.

19.
```
  8 ft  11 in.
+ 6 ft   9 in.
```

20.
```
  4 yd  1 ft
- 2 yd  2 ft
```

21.
```
  6 ft   8 in.
+ 7 ft  10 in.
```

22.
```
  11 ft  7 in.
- 10 ft  9 in.
```

Mixed Applications

23. Janet made a dollhouse. Each of the 8 windows needed 1 ft of trim. Trim came in pieces that were 1 ft 2 in. long. How many pieces of trim did Janet need?

24. **Analyze Data** Josie needed 16 ft of wood to line a sidewalk. She had 3 pieces that were 5 ft 4 in., 4 ft 6 in., and 6 ft 10 in. Did she have enough wood to line the sidewalk?

25. Alan needs 38 ft of red paper for the border of a mural. The paper comes in pieces that are 4 ft 10 in. long. About how many pieces of paper will Alan need?

26. Carla is trimming a bed cover with lace. She has put on 16 ft 8 in. of lace. If the bed cover is 22 ft 9 in. around, how much more does she need to put on?

LANGUAGE CONNECTION

Words we use to name customary units of measurement are based upon the human body. One *foot* describes the length of a human foot. One *hand* describes the width of a hand (4 inches). The word *inch* comes from the Latin word *uncia*, which describes the width of the thumb. One *inch* can be thought of as the width of one thumb.

27. How wide is your desk in feet and thumbs?

28. How wide is your desk in hands and thumbs?

How do you change feet into inches?

WRAP UP...

CHANGING CUSTOMARY UNITS
of Capacity and Weight

Kenesha needs to mix 5 quarts of water with powder for a papier-mâché project. She is using a pint jar to measure the water. How many times will she have to fill the jar to get 5 quarts of water?

Customary Units of Capacity
8 fluid ounces (fl oz) = 1 cup (c)
2 c = 1 pint (pt)
2 pt = 1 quart (qt)
4 qt = 1 gallon (gal)

To change larger units to smaller units, multiply.

5 qt = ■ pt   **Think:** 1 qt = 2 pt
5 × 2 = 10
5 qt = 10 pt

To change smaller units to larger units, divide.

10 pt = ■ qt   **Think:** 1 qt = 2 pt
10 ÷ 2 = 5
10 pt = 5 qt

So, Kenesha will have to fill the pint jar 10 times to get 5 quarts of water.

• Why do you divide to change pints to quarts?

• Why do you multiply to change quarts to pints?

Customary units of weight can also be changed by multiplying or dividing.

Customary Units of Weight
16 ounces (oz) = 1 pound (lb)
2,000 lb = 1 ton (T)

To change larger units to smaller units, multiply.

3 T = ■ lb   **Think:** 1 T = 2,000 lb
3 × 2,000 = 6,000
3 T = 6,000 lb

To change smaller units to larger units, divide.

36 oz = ■ lb   **Think:** 16 oz = 1 lb
36 ÷ 16 = 2 r4
36 oz = 2 lb 4 oz

Talk About It

▶ Why do you multiply to change tons to pounds?

▶ Why do you divide to change ounces to pounds?

Check for Understanding

Write *multiply* or *divide*. Complete.

1. 1 gal = ■ qt
2. 4 c = ■ pt
3. 5 lb = ■ oz
4. 32 oz = ■ lb

5. 6,000 lb = ■ T
6. 96 oz = ■ lb
7. 4 T = ■ lb
8. 4 gal = ■ qt

Practice

Write *multiply* or *divide*.

9. to change cups to pints

10. to change gallons to quarts

11. to change cups to ounces

12. to change pints to quarts

13. to change ounces to pounds

14. to change tons to pounds

Complete.

15. $3 \text{ gal} = \blacksquare \text{ qt}$

16. $2 \text{ gal} = \blacksquare \text{ pt}$

17. $16 \text{ qt} = \blacksquare \text{ pt}$

18. $20 \text{ qt} = \blacksquare \text{ gal}$

19. $17 \text{ qt} = \blacksquare \text{ c}$

20. $5 \text{ pt} = \blacksquare \text{ c}$

21. $16 \text{ c} = \blacksquare \text{ fl oz}$

22. $12 \text{ pt} = \blacksquare \text{ qt}$

23. $5\frac{1}{2} \text{ gal} = \blacksquare \text{ qt}$

24. $12 \text{ lb} = \blacksquare \text{ oz}$

25. $4,000 \text{ lb} = \blacksquare \text{ T}$

26. $3 \text{ T} = \blacksquare \text{ lb}$

27. $208 \text{ oz} = \blacksquare \text{ lb}$

28. $5 \text{ T} = \blacksquare \text{ lb}$

29. $80 \text{ oz} = \blacksquare \text{ lb}$

30. $5\frac{1}{2} \text{ T} = \blacksquare \text{ lb}$

31. $9\frac{1}{2} \text{ lb} = \blacksquare \text{ oz}$

32. $9,000 \text{ lb} = \blacksquare \text{ T}$

Mixed Applications

33. **Making Decisions** Lucas needs to buy 1 gal of paint. The store sells 1 qt of paint for $4.95 or 1 gal of paint for $18.49. Which is the less expensive way for him to buy 1 gal of paint?

34. An art teacher has 3 classes of 28 students each and 2 classes of 32 students each. If each student needs 3 qt of papier-mâché paste, how many gallons of paste does the art teacher need to buy?

35. George needs 2 gal of water. How many times will he need to fill an 8-oz cup to get the water he needs?

36. **Number Sense** If Ashley mixes $\frac{1}{4}$ c of liquid with $\frac{1}{2}$ c of liquid, how many ounces will she have?

How can you find the number of cups in a gallon?

WRAP UP...

UNITS OF TIME

The fifth graders spent 190 minutes in one week working on class projects. The teacher had set aside 4 hours a week for work on their projects. Did he allow enough time?

Find the number of hours in 190 minutes. Change 190 minutes to hours.

190 min = ■ hr   **Think:** 60 min = 1 hr

190 ÷ 60 = 3 r10

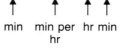

min   min per   hr min
        hr

190 min = 3 hr 10 min

Since 3 hr 10 min is less than 4 hr, the teacher allowed enough time to work on projects.

You can multiply to change units of time.

3 hr 10 min = ■ min   **Think:** 1 hr = 60 min

3 × 60 = 180

3 hr 10 min = 190 min

Units of Time
60 seconds (sec) = 1 minute (min)
60 minutes = 1 hour (hr)
24 hours = 1 day
7 days = 1 week (wk)
52 weeks = 1 year (yr)
12 months (mo) = 1 year
365 days = 1 year
366 days = 1 leap year

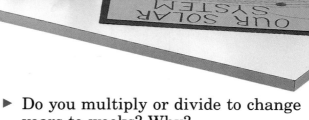

Talk About It

▶ Do you multiply or divide to change seconds to minutes? Why?

▶ Do you multiply or divide to change years to weeks? Why?

Check for Understanding

Write *multiply* or *divide*.

1. change days to years

2. change weeks to days

3. change days to hours

Complete.

4. 4 wk = ■ days

5. 49 hr = ■ days ■ hr

6. 48 mo = ■ yr

7. 3 yr = ■ wk

8. 1,460 days = ■ yr

9. 180 sec = ■ min

Idea Bank, page 464, Exercise 8

Practice

Complete.

10. 20 min = ☒ sec

11. 6 wk = ☒ days

12. 5 yr = ☒ mo

13. 96 hr = ☒ days

14. 5 days = ☒ hr

15. 3 yr = ☒ days

16. 4 yr = ☒ wk

17. 9 min = ☒ sec

18. 104 wk = ☒ yr

19. 4 hr = ☒ min

20. 84 days = ☒ wk

21. 36 mo = ☒ yr

22. 4 hr 15 min = ☒ min

23. 150 hr = ☒ days ☒ hr

24. 327 sec = ☒ min ☒ sec

25. 55 mo = ☒ yr ☒ mo

Mixed Applications

26. Number Sense How many seconds are in 2 hr?

27. Number Sense How many hours are in 2 non-leap years?

28. Ellen has worked on her sewing project 45 min each night for 5 nights. She plans to spend 4 hr on her project during one week. How much more time does she need to spend on her project?

29. Steven wants to know how many hours he has spent in school this year. If he has been in school 145 days, and each day he has spent 7 hr at school, how many hours has he been in school this year?

SCIENCE CONNECTION

Our system of telling time is many centuries old. It was developed by people who observed the earth's rotation and its revolution about the sun. Days, months, and years are based on these movements.

The earth rotates, or turns, on its axis once every 24 hr, or 1 day. The earth revolves around the sun once every $365\frac{1}{4}$ day, or 1 yr. (We have a leap year every 4 yr to account for the $\frac{1}{4}$ day.) The moon revolves around the earth one time in about 28 days, or 1 mo.

30. About how many times does the moon go around the earth in 215 days?

31. How many times does the earth rotate in 288 hr?

Explain how to find the number of seconds in a day.

WRAP UP...

Kevin worked on his project from 9:00 A.M. to 12:15 P.M. How much time did he spend working?

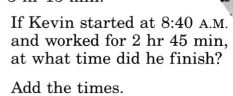

A.M. is 12 midnight to 12 noon.
P.M. is 12 noon to 12 midnight.

Count forward from the starting time to find the elapsed time.

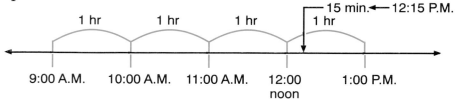

— 15 min. ← 12:15 P.M.

1 hr · 1 hr · 1 hr · 1 hr

9:00 A.M. 10:00 A.M. 11:00 A.M. 12:00 noon 1:00 P.M.

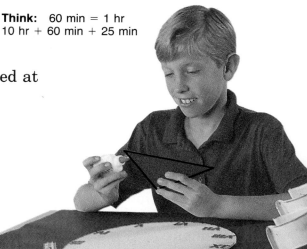

So, Kevin worked on his project for 3 hr 15 min.

For how long would Kevin have worked if he had taken a 30-min break?

Subtract the times.

```
  2 hr 75 min
  3 hr 15 min
 −      30 min
  _____
  2 hr 45 min
```

Think: 60 min = 1 hr
2 hr + 60 min + 15 min

So, Kevin would have worked 2 hr 45 min.

If Kevin started at 8:40 A.M. and worked for 2 hr 45 min, at what time did he finish?

Add the times.

```
    8 hr 40 min
 +  2 hr 45 min
  _____
   10 hr 85 min
   11 hr 25 min
```

Think: 60 min = 1 hr
10 hr + 60 min + 25 min

So, Kevin finished at 11:25 A.M.

Talk About It

▶ What is the elapsed time from 8:25 A.M. to 8:30 P.M.?

▶ What time is it 30 minutes after 11:45 A.M.?

Check for Understanding

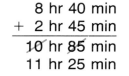

Count forward to find the elapsed time.

1. 5:25 A.M. to 7:10 A.M.   **2.** 8:03 A.M. to 2:27 P.M.   **3.** 10:15 A.M. to 10:30 P.M.

Add or subtract.

4.
```
  3 min  27 sec
 +        58 sec
```

5.
```
  4 hr  15 min
 −2 hr  37 min
```

6.
```
  2 hr  20 min
 +4 hr  25 min
```

7.
```
  6 hr  45 min
 +1 hr  32 min
```

Practice

Compute the time when each event began or ended.

8. Dinner is served at 6:15 P.M. It takes 30 min to eat.

9. Dinner is served at 5:35 P.M. It takes 27 min to prepare.

10. A plane arrived at 8:02 P.M. It took 2 hr and 17 min for the flight.

11. A spacecraft was launched at 7:45 A.M. on Monday. It was in flight for 5 days 3 hr 18 min.

Add or subtract.

12.
$$\begin{array}{rr} 2\,\text{hr} & 43\,\text{min} \\ +5\,\text{hr} & 50\,\text{min} \\ \hline \end{array}$$

13.
$$\begin{array}{rr} 6\,\text{min} & 55\,\text{sec} \\ -4\,\text{min} & 14\,\text{sec} \\ \hline \end{array}$$

14.
$$\begin{array}{rr} 5\,\text{min} & 10\,\text{sec} \\ -3\,\text{min} & 22\,\text{sec} \\ \hline \end{array}$$

15.
$$\begin{array}{rr} 6\,\text{hr} & 18\,\text{min} \\ -3\,\text{hr} & 25\,\text{min} \\ \hline \end{array}$$

16.
$$\begin{array}{rr} 4\,\text{hr} & 35\,\text{min} \\ +4\,\text{hr} & 35\,\text{min} \\ \hline \end{array}$$

17.
$$\begin{array}{rr} 8\,\text{min} & 50\,\text{sec} \\ +48\,\text{min} & 30\,\text{sec} \\ \hline \end{array}$$

Mixed Applications

18. Each of the two scenes in a school play lasted 45 min. The intermission was 10 min long, and the play began at 7:10 P.M. At what time was the play over?

19. Roland began working on his science project at 6:45 P.M. He took a 15-min break at 8:00 P.M. He finished working at 9:50 P.M. For how long did he work on his science project?

20. The 36 students in a social studies class each made a covered wagon. The project was completed on the first day by $\frac{3}{4}$ of the class. How many students did not complete the project on the first day?

21. Make Up a Problem Phoebe spent 3 hr 15 min working on a math project.

MIXED REVIEW

Divide.

1. $5.4 \div 10 = n$ **2.** $24 \div 100 = n$ **3.** $679 \div 1,000 = n$ **4.** $42.6 \div 10 = n$ **5.** $6.7 \div 100 = n$

Compare. Write $<$, $>$, or $=$ for ●.

6. $\frac{5}{8}$ ● $\frac{4}{8}$

7. $\frac{1}{3}$ ● $\frac{5}{6}$

8. $\frac{3}{4}$ ● $\frac{9}{12}$

9. $\frac{2}{5}$ ● $\frac{1}{4}$

10. $\frac{5}{10}$ ● $\frac{1}{2}$

Explain how adding and subtracting time is different from adding and subtracting whole numbers.

WRAP UP...

PROBLEM SOLVING

Use a Schedule

Irma read this schedule. It shows presentation times for Career Day. Each presentation will last 1 hr 15 min. Irma wants to see the potter, the musician, or the filmmaker. It takes 5 min for Irma to walk back to class. She must be back in class by 10:50 A.M. Which presentation can she see?

Schedule of Career Day Speakers		
Speaker	**Location**	**Start**
Filmmaker	Rm 104	9:30 A.M.
Musician	Rm 107	9:45 A.M.
Architect	Rm 102	10:00 A.M.
Potter	Rm 203	10:20 A.M.
Waiter	Rm 103	10:30 A.M.

▶ **UNDERSTAND**

What are you asked to find?

What facts are given?

▶ **PLAN**

What strategy can you use to solve the problem?

Use the schedule to find the starting time of each presentation. Compute to find the ending time of each.

▶ **SOLVE**

How can you solve the problem?

Use the information from the schedule.

Speaker	Starting Time	Duration of Presentation	Ending Time
Potter	10:20	1 hr 15 min	11:35 (too late)
Musician	9:45	1 hr 15 min	11:00 (still too late)
Filmmaker	9:30	1 hr 15 min	10:45

If Irma sees the potter or the musician she will not be back to class on time.

So, Irma can see the filmmaker and have 5 min to walk back to class.

▶ **LOOK BACK**

How can you check your answer?

... Irma had to be back in class by 11:20 A.M.? Which two speakers could she choose between?

378

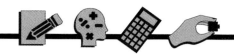

Apply

Use the schedule for Exercises 1–4.

(1) How long is the flight that takes the most time?

(2) How long is the flight that takes the least time?

(3) If it takes 35 min to check in for a flight, when should you arrive at the airport for a flight to Buffalo?

(4) Which flights to New York will arrive before noon?

Schedule of Departures from Middleburg		
Leave	Destination	Arrive
6:05 A.M.	New York	8:23 A.M.
6:18 A.M.	Atlanta	7:21 A.M.
6:25 A.M.	Miami	7:14 A.M.
7:42 A.M.	New York	10:02 A.M.
8:07 A.M.	Buffalo	10:52 A.M.
10:56 A.M.	New York	1:15 P.M.
11:05 A.M.	Miami	11:59 A.M.
11:17 A.M.	Atlanta	12:25 P.M.

Mixed Applications ⇒ **STRATEGIES** Make a Diagram • Guess and Check • Solve a Simpler Problem • Work Backward

Choose a strategy and solve.

(5) If 2 projects can be displayed on each side of a square table, how many projects can be displayed on 12 square tables that are pushed together end to end to form a rectangle?

(6) On Saturday morning, 46 students showed up to plant a garden. If 12 more girls than boys showed up, how many boys and how many girls showed up to plant a garden?

(7) A school carnival needed the help of volunteers. Of the volunteers needed, $\frac{1}{2}$ worked in booths, $\frac{2}{5}$ worked at food stands, and $\frac{1}{10}$ worked at the bake sale. If 5 volunteers worked at the bake sale, how many worked at food stands?

(8) Some fifth graders sold cupcakes at a carnival and collected a total of $50.00. They sold some for $0.25 each and some at 3 for $0.50. They collected $30.00 from the sale of single cupcakes. How many cupcakes did they sell?

WRITER'S CORNER

(9) Use the schedule above to write a question. Answer your question. Then exchange with a partner and answer the partner's question.

More Practice, Lesson 11.14, page H77

Vocabulary Check

Choose a word or words from the box to complete each sentence.

capacity
Celsius
customary system
Fahrenheit
gram
liter
mass
meter
metric system

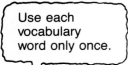

Use each vocabulary word only once.

1. The base unit of mass in the metric system is the __?__ . *(page 358)*

2. One hundred centimeters is the same as one __?__ . *(page 350)*

3. In the metric system, temperature is measured in degrees __?__ . *(page 362)*

4. The same prefixes are used with different base units to name all other units in the __?__ . *(page 358)*

5. The amount of liquid a container can hold is its __?__ . *(page 354)*

6. In the customary system, temperature is measured in degrees __?__ . *(page 362)*

7. One thousand milliliters is the same as one __?__ . *(page 354)*

8. The weight of objects on earth is measured in metric units of __?__ . *(page 356)*

9. The inch, foot, yard, and mile are standard units of length in the __?__ of measurement. *(page 368)*

Concept Check

Choose the more reasonable unit. Write **a** or **b**. *(pages 350, 354, 356)*

10. length of a thumbtack	a. mm	b. cm
11. liquid in a fishbowl	a. mL	b. L
12. mass of a tube of toothpaste	a. g	b. kg

Find the difference in temperature. *(page 362)*

13. high 58°F, low 39°F   14. high 7°C, low ⁻9°C   15. high 32°C, low 16°C

Complete.

16. $30\,cm = \blacksquare\,m$ 17. $6.5\,m = \blacksquare\,cm$ 18. $18\,L = \blacksquare\,mL$ 19. $5{,}000\,mg = \blacksquare\,g$

Use a customary ruler. Draw a line to represent each length.
(page 368)

20. $1\frac{3}{4}$ in.   **21.** $2\frac{1}{2}$ in.   **22.** $3\frac{5}{8}$ in.   **23.** $4\frac{1}{4}$ in.   **24.** $5\frac{1}{16}$ in.

Skill Check

Use a metric ruler. Write the measure to the nearest centimeter, and then write a more precise measurement. (page 352)

25. _____   **26.** _____

Choose the larger unit. (page 358)

27. meter or kilometer   **28.** milliliter or liter   **29.** milligram or gram

Complete. (page 360)

30. $6 \text{ km} = 6,000 \underline{\ ?\ }$ **31.** $25 \text{ g} = 25,000 \underline{\ ?\ }$ **32.** $3,000 \text{ mL} = 3 \underline{\ ?\ }$

Add or subtract. (page 370)

33.   4 ft   6 in.
        +5 ft   8 in.

34.   5 yd   1 ft
        −3 yd   2 ft

35.   2 ft   4 in.
        −1 ft   8 in.

Complete. (pages 372, 374)

36. $8 \text{ lb} = \blacksquare \text{ oz}$ **37.** $3 \text{ qt} = \blacksquare \text{ c}$ **38.** $4 \text{ gal} = \blacksquare \text{ pt}$

39. $6 \text{ wk} = \blacksquare \text{ day}$ **40.** $3 \text{ yr} = \blacksquare \text{ wk}$ **41.** $7 \text{ min} = \blacksquare \text{ sec}$

Problem-Solving Check (pages 364, 378)

42. Cora has 2 L of grape juice. She says she has enough for one cup for each of the 120 fifth graders. Is this reasonable? Explain.

9:10	Tardy bell and opening
9:25	First class begins
10:15	First class ends
10:20	Second class begins
11:10	Second class ends
11:15	Third class begins
12:05	Third class ends—Lunch
12:35	Lunch ends

43. A plane arrived at 10:02 A.M. The flight took 3 hr 17 min. Is it reasonable to say the flight began at 1:19 A.M.? Explain.

Use the morning bell schedule for Exercises 44–45.

44. How long is each class?

45. How much time is there between the tardy bell and the end of lunch?

WHAT DID I LEARN?

1. Explain how you would decide which metric units to use for measuring the length of an ant, the capacity of a kitchen sink, and the mass of a dog. Name your choices.

2. Show each step as you find the difference of 6 ft 2 in. − 3 ft 10 in.

3. Determine the elapsed time from 10:30 A.M. to 2:45 P.M. Explain your method.

4. Measure the length of the cover of your math book to the nearest millimeter and to the nearest $\frac{1}{16}$ of an inch. Record the measurements.

5. Read Exercise 2 on page 379. Follow the steps on the Problem-Solving Think Along worksheet to show how to solve this problem.

To measure length, you can use a meterstick or a metric ruler.

Write About It

6. Describe a situation in which you have used, or plan to use, something you learned in this chapter on measurement.

7. Explain how meters, liters, and grams differ. Give an example of something that is measured with each of these units.

TEAMWORK Project

Compare Temperatures in Different Cities

Temperatures in the United States may vary greatly, particularly during winter months. With your teammates, draw a weather map for the east coast of the United States.

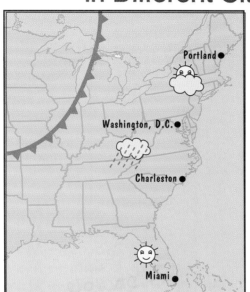

Portland

Washington, D.C.

Charleston

Miami

Do Work with your teammates. Trace the map of the east coast. Find and mark these cities on your map: Portland, ME; Washington, DC; Charleston, SC; Miami, FL. Draw a line connecting the cities. Use a United States mileage chart, an almanac, or an encyclopedia. Make a table showing the distance between the cities and the normal temperature for each city during the month of January.

Decide Talk about how you can compare the temperatures of certain cities along the east coast of the United States. Discuss how you can find the distance in mileage between these cities.

Share Show your map. Describe how the temperature is related to the location of a city.

TALK ABOUT IT

- What do you notice about the temperature of each city as you move farther north?

- About how many miles apart are the cities?

- How can you use your information to estimate the temperature in January of a city about 500–600 miles north of Portland?

- How do you think the temperature of each city during the month of June will compare with the temperature of each city during the month of January? Explain your answer.

Activity

The Game of Patolli

The Aztecs played a game called *patolli* on a board like the one shown.

Two to four people can play. Draw the board on a large piece of paper or cardboard. Use a marking pen to place a single dot on one side of each of five dried lima beans. Each player needs six game pieces to move around the board.

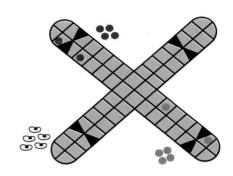

- The players start at opposite ends of the board.

- Each player tosses the beans.

- The number of dots facing up determines the number of spaces the player moves.

1 dot — Move 1 space.
2 dots — Move 2 spaces.
3 dots — Move 3 spaces.
4 dots — Move 4 spaces.
5 dots — Move 10 spaces.

- A player may not land on a space occupied by an opponent but may move another of his or her pieces instead.

- The player who gets all six pieces around the board first is the winner.

◆ ◆ ◆ ◆ ◆ ◆ ◆ ◆ **Challenge** ◆ ◆ ◆ ◆ ◆ ◆ ◆ ◆

Visual Thinking

Without using a ruler, draw a vertical line segment and a horizontal line segment that are the measures given below. Then use a ruler to check your drawings. Tell how your drawings compare with the given measures.

1. 3 in.
2. 4 in.
3. 5 in.
4. 7 in.

Critical Thinking

You have two pails. One holds exactly 3 L, and the other holds exactly 5 L. Without using any other container, and assuming you have an unlimited supply of water, how could you put exactly 4 L of water into the 5-L pail?

Write the letter of the correct answer.

1. Which is the standard form for seven and three hundred eighty-seven thousandths?

   A. 7.387
   B. 70.387
   C. 7,387
   D. not here

2. Which is the best estimate?
   $$\begin{array}{r} \$5.79 \\ +\ 3.83 \\ \hline \end{array}$$

   A. $8.00
   B. $10.00
   C. $12.00
   D. $14.00

3. $27 \times 43 = n$

   A. 1,091
   B. 1,161
   C. 1,211
   D. not here

4. $16.75 \div 5 = n$

   A. 3.65
   B. 33.5
   C. 36.5
   D. not here

5. $33\overline{)9{,}943}$

   A. 298 r8
   B. 301 r10
   C. 310
   D. 310 r10

6. $0.09 \times 5 = n$

   A. 0.045
   B. 0.45
   C. 4.5
   D. not here

7. Which names the diameter?

   A. $\overline{AO}$
   B. $\overline{OB}$
   C. $\overline{AC}$
   D. $\overline{AB}$

8. $5 \times \dfrac{2}{3} = n$

   A. $\dfrac{2}{15}$
   B. $2\dfrac{1}{3}$
   C. $3\dfrac{1}{3}$
   D. $5\dfrac{2}{3}$

9. What is another name for $\dfrac{11}{3}$?

   A. $\dfrac{3}{11}$
   B. 3
   C. $3\dfrac{1}{3}$
   D. $3\dfrac{2}{3}$

10. Which metric unit would you use to measure the length of a pencil point?

    A. millimeter
    B. centimeter
    C. meter
    D. kilometer

11. What is the change in temperature? high 82°F, low 65°F

    A. 7°
    B. 17°
    C. 27°
    D. 150°

12. 126 day = ▩ wk

    A. 12
    B. 18
    C. 126
    D. 882

13. Which program is the longest?

ASSEMBLY SCHEDULE	
TIME	PROGRAMS
12:10 – 12:35	CHORUS
12:45 – 1:00	BAND
1:10 – 1:30	DRAMA
1:40 – 2:15	AWARDS

    A. Chorus
    B. Band
    C. Drama
    D. Awards

14. Alana needs $2\dfrac{1}{2}$ ft of material for each of the 10 costumes she is making. What is a reasonable estimate of the number of yards she will need?

    A. 2 yd
    B. 8 yd
    C. 20 yd
    D. 250 yd

CHAPTER 12

PERIMETER, AREA, AND VOLUME

Did you know . . .

. . . that the building with the largest area of land under one roof is in the Netherlands? The building measures 2,546 ft by 1,794 ft.

TALK ABOUT IT

Matt and his sister are planning to build a doghouse for their dog, Rex. They want the floor of the doghouse to measure 5 ft long by $3\frac{3}{4}$ ft wide. What can you determine about the floor of the doghouse from the measurements given? What other dimensions will Matt and his sister need to know to build the doghouse?

EXPLORING

Perimeter

The distance around a figure is its **perimeter.**

Work Together

Building Understanding

You can use a geoboard and a geoband to explore perimeter.

The distance between two pegs on a geoboard is one unit length.

A. On the geoboard, make the smallest square possible. Count the unit lengths.

one unit length

- How many unit lengths is the perimeter of the square?

On the geoboard, make the largest square possible.

- How many unit lengths is the perimeter of the square?

B. Make a square with a perimeter of 12 units.

- How many unit lengths is each side of the square?

C. Make the smallest and the largest rectangles that are not squares.

- How many unit lengths is the perimeter of the smallest rectangle?

- How many unit lengths is the perimeter of the largest rectangle?

D. Make as many different shapes as you can that have a perimeter of 16 unit lengths. Record each shape on dot paper.

- How many of the shapes you made have sides with the same number of unit lengths?

TALK ABOUT IT

- How many sides of a square have the same lengths?

- How many sides of a rectangle have the same lengths?

388

Making the Connection

Another way you can find the perimeter
of a rectangle is to add the measures of
the sides.

Figure A

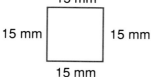

15 mm + 15 mm + 15 mm + 15 mm = 60 mm

Figure B

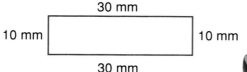

$$\underbrace{10 \text{ mm} + 10 \text{ mm}}_{20 \text{ mm}} + \underbrace{30 \text{ mm} + 30 \text{ mm}}_{60 \text{ mm}} = n$$
$$= 80 \text{ mm}$$

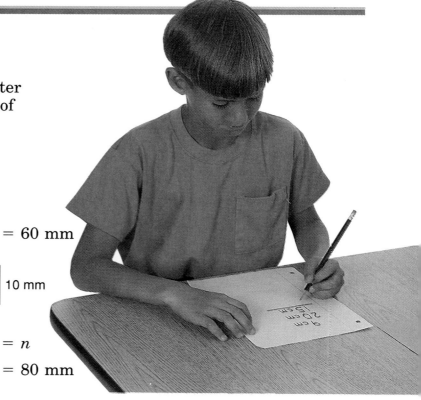

TALK ABOUT IT

- How can you find the perimeter of a square if you know the
  length of one side is 6 mm?

- How can you find the perimeter of a rectangle if you know that
  the length of one side is 3 mm and the width of one side is 5 mm?

- Is there an easier way to find the perimeter of squares and
  rectangles than adding? Explain your answer.

You can add the measures of the sides to find the perimeter
of other polygons.

- How can you find
  the perimeter
  of this figure?

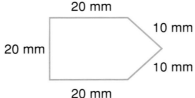

Checking Understanding

Measure the sides and find the perimeter of each figure in mm.

1.

2.

3.

More Practice, Lesson 12.1, page H78   **389**

FINDING PERIMETER

Mr. Verteks wants to install new baseboards in a recreation room. How much baseboard will he need to go around the room and the platform?

Finding the perimeter of the recreation room and the platform will give the amount of baseboard needed.

The recreation room is in the shape of a rectangle. You can use this formula to find the perimeter of the rectangle.

$$
\begin{aligned}
\text{Perimeter} &= (2 \times \text{length}) + (2 \times \text{width}) \\
P &= (2 \times l) + (2 \times w) \\
P &= (2 \times 45) + (2 \times 25) \\
P &= 90 + 50 = 140
\end{aligned}
$$

The perimeter of the room is 140 ft.

The platform is in the shape of a square. Each of the four sides measures the same length, 3 ft. You can use this formula to find the perimeter of the square.

$$
\begin{aligned}
\text{Perimeter} &= 4 \times \text{side} \\
P &= 4 \times s \\
P &= 4 \times 3 = 12
\end{aligned}
$$

The perimeter of the platform is 12 ft.

So, Mr. Verteks needs 140 ft + 12 ft, or 152 ft, of baseboard.

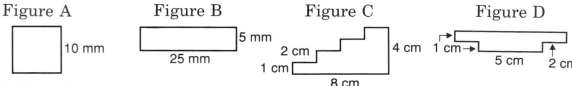

Figure A — 10 mm

Figure B — 5 mm, 25 mm

Figure C — 2 cm, 1 cm, 4 cm, 8 cm

Figure D — 1 cm, 5 cm, 2 cm

Talk About It

▶ Which formula can you use to find the perimeter of Figure A? Figure B?

▶ On what does the choice of a formula depend?

▶ How can you find the perimeter of Figures C and D? What are the perimeters?

▶ Describe some real-life situations for using perimeter measures.

Idea Bank, page 465, Exercises 12–13

Check for Understanding

Find the perimeter.

1.

5 m

2.
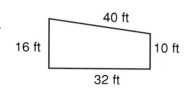
40 ft
16 ft   10 ft
32 ft

3.
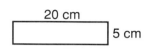
20 cm
5 cm

Practice

Find the perimeter of each figure.

4.

4 ft

5.
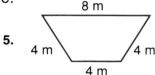
8 m
4 m   4 m
4 m

6.

16 cm
8 cm

Find the missing length in each figure.

7.
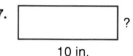
?
10 in.
perimeter = 30 in.

8.
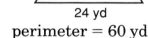
?
12 yd   12 yd
24 yd
perimeter = 60 yd

9.
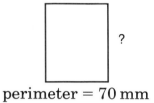
15 mm
?
perimeter = 70 mm

Mixed Applications

10. Lynn is gathering ingredients for a recipe. For 15 muffins, does she need 500 mL or 500 L of milk?

11. If Richard mixes $\frac{1}{4}$ c of paint with $\frac{1}{2}$ c of paint, how much paint will he have?

12. Four different-sized gardens measure 5 m by 4 m, 6 m by 5 m, 4 m by 6 m, and 7 m by 3 m. How much fencing is around the gardens?

13. Aretha wants to put paper trim around 5 square tables. If the side of each table is 0.5 m, how many meters of paper trim will she need?

CRITICAL THINKING

To write a mathematical rule, you must use critical thinking based on examples you have examined.

Write a perimeter rule for each figure.

14.
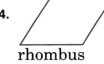
rhombus

15.

equilateral triangle

16.

parallelogram

How do you decide whether you can use a formula to find the perimeter of a figure?

WRAP UP...

EXPLORING

Circumference

The distance around a shape is the perimeter. The perimeter of a circle is called the **circumference.**

Work Together

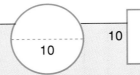

Building Understanding

A. You can use string to find the circumference of a large circular object such as a wastebasket.

- Wrap the string around the largest part of the wastebasket.
- Cut the string to fit around the wastebasket.

Now, cut the string that fit around the wastebasket so that it is the same length as the diameter of the wastebasket. Cut as many diameter lengths as you can.

- About how many diameter lengths of string did you cut?

B. You can use string, a ruler, and three different-sized lids to explore the circumference of smaller circular objects.

- Wrap string around each lid to fit exactly, and then cut the string.

- Measure each string to the nearest centimeter. Record the length of each circumference in a table.

- Measure the diameter of each lid to the nearest centimeter. Record the length of each diameter in the table.

Lid	Circumference (in cm)	Diameter (in cm)
Number 1		
Number 2		
Number 3		

TALK ABOUT IT

- What relationship do you see between the circumference and the diameter of each lid?

- Is the relationship between the circumference and diameter of the large wastebasket the same as between the circumference and diameter of the small lid? Explain.

Making the Connection

The circumference and diameter of all circles are related in the same way. The relationship of the circumference divided by the diameter is always a little more than 3. This number is given the name *pi*, and its symbol is π.

Use a calculator. Divide the circumference of each object by its diameter. Complete the table by rounding to the nearest hundredth.

Object	Circumference	Diameter	$\frac{C}{d}$
Bowl	61 cm	19.5 cm	
Glass	31.5 cm	10 cm	
Lampshade	68 cm	21.5 cm	
Vase	24.5 cm	7.8 cm	

- How can you describe the result of $\frac{C}{d}$?

When more precise measurements are used, π is equal to approximately 3.14.

You can use this formula to find the circumference of a circle.

Circumference = π × diameter
$$C = \pi \times d$$

Example $C = \pi \times d$
$C \approx 3.14 \times 27.5$
$C \approx 86.35$

27.5 mm

The circumference of the circle is about 86.35 mm.

TALK ABOUT IT

- If you know the diameter of a circle, how can you find the circumference?

- If you know the circumference of a circle, how can you find the diameter?

Checking Understanding

Find the circumference. Round to the nearest tenth.

1. 18.8 mm

2. 9.4 mm

3. 6.5 mm

Find the diameter. Round to the nearest tenth.

4. $C = 59.7$ cm

5. $C = 37.5$ in.

6. $C = 163.3$ cm

FINDING AREA
of Rectangles

Mefuhva is a game played in Malawi, Africa. It is played with beans on a wooden board with shallow cups carved in it. Mosi is making a mefuhva board with 4 rows of 12 shallow cups. What is the area of the wood he needs to make the board?

Area is the number of square units, or units², needed to cover the surface. Assume the space needed for each cup is a square that is 1 in. by 1 in.

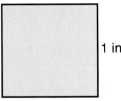

1 square inch, or 1 in.²

1 in.

1 in.

Talk About It

▶ How many 1-in. squares can you count along the length of one side of the rectangle?

▶ How many rows of 1-in. squares fill the rectangle?

▶ How many 1-in. squares fill the rectangle?

▶ How much area will be used for cups?

So, the area of the wood he needs must be more than 48 in.²

You can use this formula to find the area of any rectangle.

Area = length × width
$A = l \times w$

Example

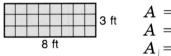

3 ft

8 ft

$A = l \times w$
$A = 8 \text{ ft} \times 3 \text{ ft}$
$A = 24 \text{ ft}^2$

Talk About It

▶ How is finding an area like using an array?

MULTICULTURAL NOTE: Mefuhva is a form of the mancala, or wari, game. There are many versions of this popular game throughout Africa.

Check for Understanding

Find each area. Each square equals 1 cm².

1.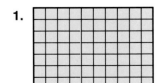

2.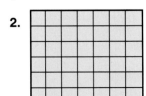

3.

Connection, pages 458–459

Practice

Find each area. Each square equals 1 cm².

4.

5.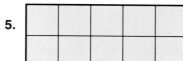

6.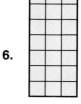

Use the formula to find the area of each rectangle.

7. 6 in. / 11 in.

8. 1.5 m / 8 m

9. 1 ft / 5 ft

Measure each side to the nearest millimeter. Then find the area.

10.

11.

12.

Mixed Applications

13. Munyoro is making a mefuhva board with 4 rows and 24 cups in each row. Each cup is 1 in. by 1 in. How much area is used for cups?

14. Naftali is painting an area 10 ft high and 36 ft long. If 1 gallon of paint covers 180 ft², how many gallons does he need?

15. A rectangular farm in Malawi is 230 meters by 110 meters. What is the area of the farm?

16. The board used to play the game Kiuthi is 8 in. long and 2 in. wide. What is the perimeter of the board?

MIXED REVIEW

Estimate each product.

1. 9.1×42

2. 8.3×59

3. 4.7×21

4. 6.18×63

5. 2.75×38

Add or subtract. Write the answer in simplest form.

6. $3\frac{3}{8} + 4\frac{1}{8}$

7. $8\frac{4}{5} - 2\frac{1}{10}$

8. $6\frac{1}{3} + 2\frac{1}{6}$

9. $7\frac{1}{2} - 5\frac{1}{5}$

10. $9\frac{3}{5} + 6\frac{1}{3}$

How are the units used to measure the perimeter of a figure different from the units used to measure the area of a figure?

WRAP UP...

FINDING AREA
of Parallelograms and Triangles

You can use what you know about finding the area of a rectangle to help you find the area of other polygons.

Use centimeter graph paper, a pencil, and scissors to find the area of a parallelogram.

- Draw the parallelogram *ABCD* on your graph paper.

- Measure and record its base (*b*) and height (*h*).

- Cut out the parallelogram.

- Then cut along the dotted line. Start where the right angle is formed.

- Move the triangular piece to form a four-sided polygon.

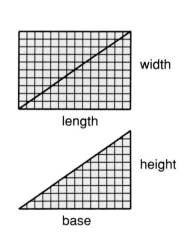

Talk About It

▶ What new figure did you form?

▶ How can you find the area of the rectangle?

▶ How is the area of the parallelogram related to the area of the rectangle?

▶ How do the base and the height of the parallelogram relate to the length and the width of the rectangle?

Now, try this. On graph paper, draw a rectangle that measures 10 by 14 units.

- What is the area of the rectangle?

Cut across the rectangle to make two triangles.

- What fractional part of the rectangle is one triangle?

- What is the area of half the rectangle, or one triangle?

Talk About It

▶ How do the base and the height of one triangle relate to the length and the width of the corresponding rectangle?

▶ What formula could you use to find the area of a right triangle?

Check for Understanding

Find the base and the height of each figure. Let the side of
1 square equal 1 unit.

1.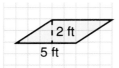

2.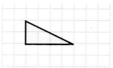

3.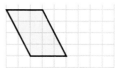

Find the area of each figure.

4.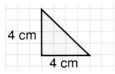
4 cm
4 cm

5.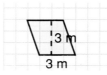
3 m
3 m

6.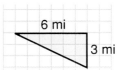
6 mi
3 mi

Practice

Find the area of each figure.

7.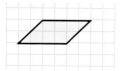
2 ft
5 ft

8.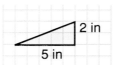
2 in
5 in

9.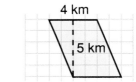
4 km
5 km

10. triangle
$b = 5$ yd
$h = 2$ yd

11. triangle
$b = 6$ m
$h = 2.5$ m

12. parallelogram
$b = 12$ mi
$h = 6\frac{1}{2}$ mi

Mixed Applications

13. A house is being built on a rectangular lot measuring 80 ft by 125 ft. What is the area of the lot?

14. Greg has a piece of plywood $2\frac{3}{4}$ ft long. He cuts a piece $1\frac{1}{2}$ ft long from that piece for his project. How much plywood does he have left?

15. Dawn has a rectangular piece of lumber 60 cm long and 40 cm wide. She cuts it in half diagonally to make two triangular pieces. What is the area of each triangular piece of lumber?

16. Critical Thinking Which has the greater area, a triangle with a base of 4 cm and a height of 4 cm or a parallelogram with a base of 4 cm and a height of 4 cm? Explain.

What two measurements are needed for finding the
areas of parallelograms and triangles?

WRAP
UP...

PROBLEM SOLVING

Choose a Strategy

Jason and Melissa have 48 ft of fencing. They want to make a rectangular pen for their dog. They want to build a pen with the greatest possible area. What dimensions should the pen have?

Sometimes you can use different strategies to solve the same problem.

What strategies can you use for this problem?

You can *make a model* or *make a table*.

**Understand
Plan
Solve
Look Back**

Strategy: Make a Model

To find the dimensions the pen should have, you can *make a model*. Cut a piece of string 48 in. long to represent the 48 ft of fencing. Use the string to model rectangles with different whole-number dimensions. Draw the rectangles on graph paper.

HINT: If the perimeter of the rectangle is 48 in., the sum of the length and the width must be 24 in.

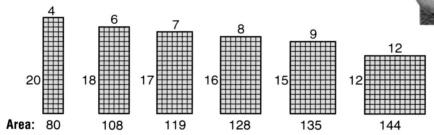

Area: 80   108   119   128   135   144

Strategy: Make a Table

You can *make a table* to record the data as you investigate each length and width for the pen.

So, a rectangle that is a square will have the greatest area. The dimensions of the dog pen should be 12 ft by 12 ft.

Length	Width	Perimeter	Area
20	4	48	80
18	6	48	108
17	7	48	119
16	8	48	128
15	9	48	135
12	12	48	144

WHAT IF... . . . Melissa and Jason have 96 ft of fencing? What dimensions would a pen with the greatest area have?

398

Mixed Applications ⟩ **STRATEGIES** **Use a Formula • Make a Table • Make a Model • Guess and Check**

Choose a strategy and solve.

1 J.W. has 24 ft of wood to use as a border for his flower bed. He wants to build a rectangular border with the greatest possible area. What dimensions should the border have?

2 Ted and Kate want to fence in a rectangular part of their yard. They have 60 m of fence to use. What dimensions should the fence be to give the greatest possible area?

3 Marlene uses 3 nails in every 10 in. of wood. How many nails will she use in 5 ft of wood?

4 A bulletin board is 4 ft by 3 ft. How much paper is needed to make a border around the bulletin board?

5 Judd made a bookcase on Monday. He finished at 5:30 P.M. He worked a total of 8 hr on the bookcase. If he took off 45 min for lunch and 30 min for an afternoon break, what time did he start the bookcase?

6 A carpenter worked a total of 14 hr 30 min on a project. If the project took two days to complete and the carpenter worked 1 hr 50 min more the second day than the first day, how much time did the carpenter work the second day?

7 Tracy has a 2-ft board, a $2\frac{1}{2}$-ft board, and a 3-ft board. One board goes on the front of a doghouse, one goes on the back, and one goes on the roof. If the shortest board does not go on the front or the back, and the longest board does not go on the front, which board goes on the back?

8 Ginny built a mailbox. She spent $\frac{1}{6}$ of the time sanding the wood, $\frac{3}{6}$ of the time putting the wood together, and $\frac{2}{6}$ of the time painting the mailbox. If she spent 1 hr sanding the wood, how long did she spend painting the mailbox?

More Practice, Lesson 12.6, page H80

Use the schedule for Exercises 1–2.

Theme Park Schedule		
Show	**Times**	**Duration**
Ice Skating	10:00 2:00	1 hr 15 min
Musical	10:30 2:45	1 hr 10 min
Magic	10:50 1:30	45 min
Animal	11:30 3:00	1 hr

1. If Dick sees the first ice-skating show, how long will he have to wait for the magic show?

2. If Marla wants to see all four shows in one day, in what order will she have to see the shows?

3. Wyatt and Vernon have 44 yd of fencing to fence in a rectangular play area. What dimensions should the play area be to give the greatest possible area?

4. A rectangular part of the playground at Carver School is being roped off for a contest. If there is 36 m of rope and the greatest possible area is needed, what should be the dimensions of the roped-off area?

Write the place-value position of each underlined digit.

5. 6.5$\underline{2}$

6. 3.8$\underline{9}$5

7. 0.01$\underline{5}$

8. $\underline{4}$.297

9. 1.9$\underline{6}$3

Estimate the sum or difference.

10. $\begin{array}{r} \$2.98 \\ +\ 7.20 \\ \hline \end{array}$

11. $\begin{array}{r} 46.251 \\ -23.916 \\ \hline \end{array}$

12. $\begin{array}{r} 84.576 \\ +12.410 \\ \hline \end{array}$

13. $\begin{array}{r} \$19.75 \\ -\ 4.95 \\ \hline \end{array}$

14. $\begin{array}{r} 52.734 \\ +46.802 \\ \hline \end{array}$

Use the rules for divisibility to decide whether the first number is divisible by the second. Write *yes* or *no*.

15. 684; 2

16. 342; 3

17. 508; 5

18. 605; 10

> Numbers that end in 2, 4, 6, 8, or 0 are even numbers. They are divisible by 2.

Multiply.

19. $\begin{array}{r} 2.4 \\ \times\ 6 \\ \hline \end{array}$

20. $\begin{array}{r} 0.315 \\ \times\ \ \ \ 5 \\ \hline \end{array}$

21. $\begin{array}{r} 0.5 \\ \times 0.5 \\ \hline \end{array}$

22. $\begin{array}{r} 3.63 \\ \times\ 0.6 \\ \hline \end{array}$

Compare. Write $<$, $>$, or $=$ for ●.

23. $\dfrac{2}{3}$ ● $\dfrac{1}{3}$

24. $\dfrac{3}{10}$ ● $\dfrac{2}{5}$

25. $\dfrac{3}{4}$ ● $\dfrac{6}{8}$

Multiply. Write the answer in simplest form.

26. $\dfrac{1}{2} \times \dfrac{2}{3} = n$

27. $\dfrac{3}{8} \times \dfrac{5}{6} = n$

28. $\dfrac{1}{4} \times \dfrac{2}{5} = n$

Visualize the Situation

To **visualize** means to make a mental picture of something. Making mental pictures can help you understand and solve problems.

Volunteers from Douala, Cameroon, in western Africa, are building a clinic in the village. The clinic is on the same side of a road as the school and the market.

The clinic is 80 m from the market and 35 m from the school. How far apart are the market and the school?

MULTICULTURAL NOTE: This small village is typical of villages in Cameroon. More than half the people of Cameroon live in rural areas.

Visualize a road with the three buildings on it. It may help to sketch a picture of what you see in your mind to answer the questions.

Talk About It

- Describe the order of the three buildings on the road you visualized. What is the distance between the market and the school?

- Is it possible to solve the problem by ordering the buildings in another way? Explain your answer.

Visualize the results as you read each problem. Draw a sketch of what you see in your mind. Solve.

1. Ama rode her bicycle north for 3 miles. Then she rode 4 miles west, 2 miles south, and 5 miles east. How far had she traveled when she crossed her route?

2. A craft store and a hotel are on the same road as the theater. The craft store is 2 blocks from the theater, and the hotel is 4 blocks from the theater. How far apart are the craft store and the hotel?

3. Tengo is visiting Yaoundé, the capital of Cameroon. She walked 2 blocks north, 3 blocks west, 2 blocks south, and 6 blocks east. How far is she from where she started her walk?

FINDING AREA
Complex and Curved Figures

A carpenter can count the square units to find the area of this figure. The area is $4 + 15 = 19$ units^2. How can he find the area of a complex figure if it is not drawn on graph paper?

Look at this figure. Mentally divide the figure into a square and a rectangle.

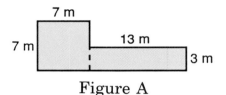

Figure A

The area of the square is $7 \times 7 = 49$ m^2.
The area of the rectangle is $13 \times 3 = 39$ m^2.

Add the areas of the two rectangles to find the area of the original figure.

$49 + 39 = 88 \longrightarrow$ The area of the original figure is 88 m^2.

So, the carpenter can mentally divide the figure into two simpler figures. Then he can compute and add the two areas to find the area of the complex figure.

Estimate the area of the curved figure.

$\square = 1$ cm^2

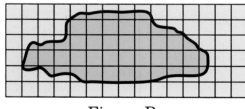

Figure B

- What was your estimate?

You can use averaging to estimate the area of a curved figure.

- Count only the whole units in the figure. Record the number.

- Then count all the partial units in the figure. Divide by 2 to find the estimated average. Record the number.

- Add the two numbers you recorded to find the estimated area of the curved figure.

- How did your first estimate compare with your averaged estimate?

Check for Understanding

Find the area of each complex figure.

1.

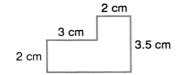

25 cm

20 cm

10 cm

5 cm

2. 10 mm

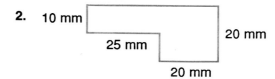

20 mm

25 mm

20 mm

Use averaging to estimate the area of each curved figure.
Each unit equals 1 cm².

3.

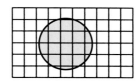

4.

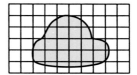

Practice

Find the area of each complex figure.

5.

2 cm

3 cm

3.5 cm

2 cm

6. 15 mm

15 mm

30 mm

10 mm

7.

5 mm

15 mm

5 mm

15 mm

Estimate the area of each curved figure. Each unit equals 1 cm².

8.

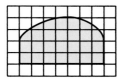

9.

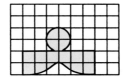

10.

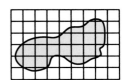

Mixed Applications

11. Brett worked on his report for 35 min on each of 6 nights. He needs to spend at least 5 hr on his report. How much more time does he need to spend on his report?

12. Lori traced around her shoe on centimeter graph paper. Her shoe covered 151 squares and 48 partial squares. Estimate the area of Lori's shoe.

13. The low temperature on Monday was ⁻15°F, and the high temperature was 47°F. What was the difference between the high and low temperatures on Monday?

14. The dimensions of Dee's room are 14 ft by 12 ft. What is the shape and the area of her room?

Explain what you can do to find the area of your foot in square inches.

WRAP UP...

EXPLORING

Three-Dimensional Figures

Building Understanding

Sandra thinks she can build each of the figures below with 20 cubes.

 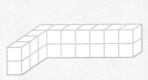

Figure A   Figure B   Figure C

Use connecting cubes to build each figure.

- Which figure can be made using exactly 20 cubes?

- How does the number of cubes you used to build each figure compare with the number of cubes visible in the drawings?

The top, bottom, front, and back views of a figure can be seen in the following drawings.

   top   bottom   front   back

Use connecting cubes to build the figure from each view.

TALK ABOUT IT

- Which views show how high the figure is? Tell how high it is.

- If you did not have a front or back view, what figure would you have made? How many cubes would you have used?

- How many cubes did your completed figure take?

- Which views show the open spaces in the figure?

Making the Connection

Some of the cubes needed to build a three-dimensional figure may not be visible in a drawing. Use paper, a pencil, and connecting cubes to compare different views of a figure.

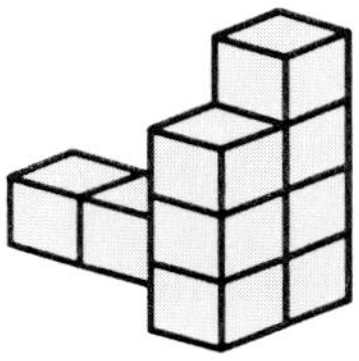
View A

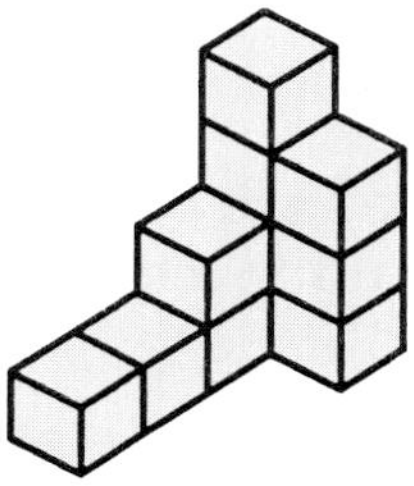
View B

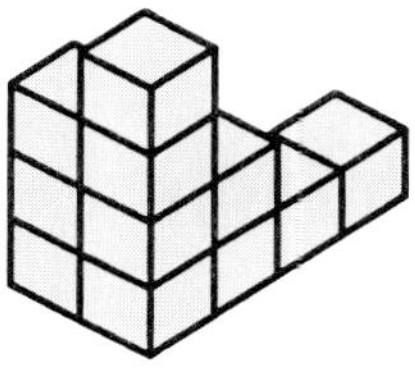
View C

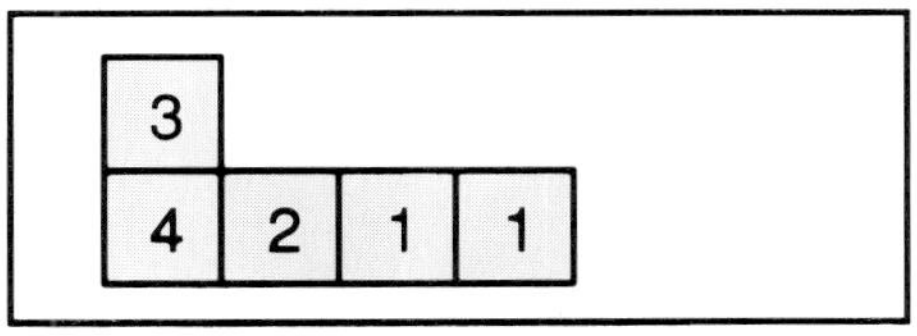

Build the figure on the paper to match the number in each box.

Turn the paper until each view shown above is visible.

Draw the top, bottom, front, and back views as shown on page 404.

TALK ABOUT IT

- How many cubes do you see when you view the figure as in **A**? in **B**? in **C**?
- How many cubes are not visible in **A, B,** and **C**?
- Why are some of the cubes in the figure not visible in the drawings?
- In which view are the most cubes visible?
- Do your drawings differ from the views shown above? Explain.

Checking Understanding

Use what you know about hidden cubes to find the number of cubes used to build each figure.

1. 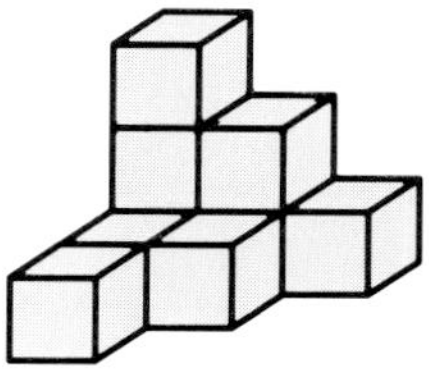

2. 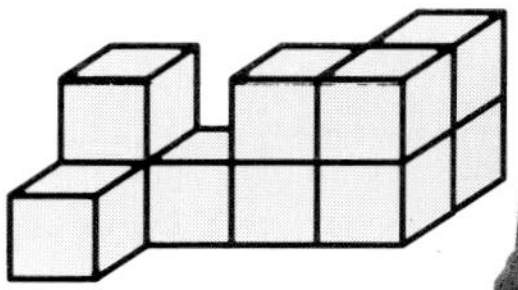

3. 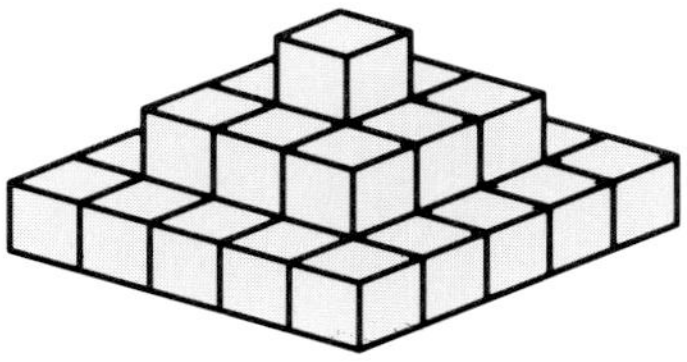

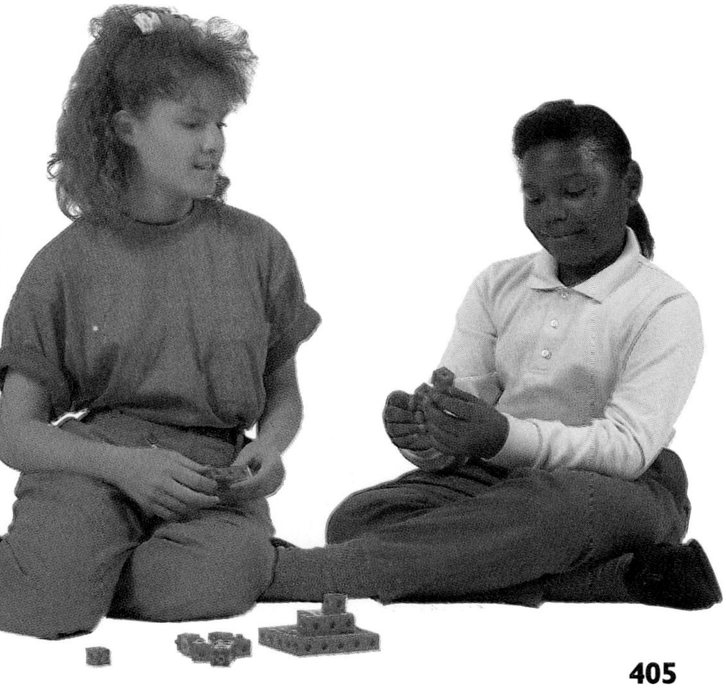

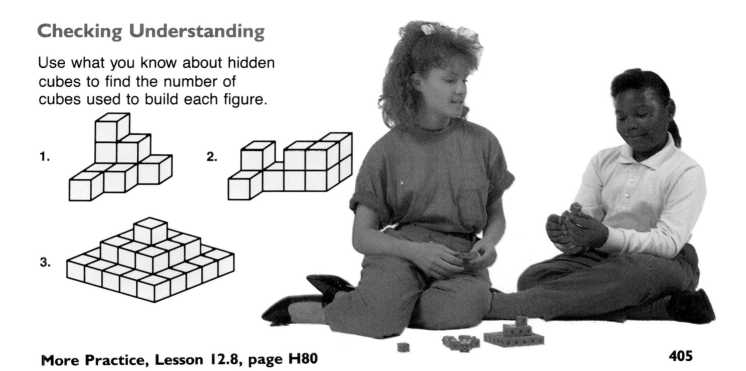

EXPLORING

Volume

Volume is the measure of the space inside a solid figure. Volume can be found by counting cubic units.

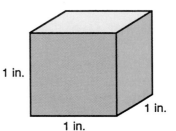

1 in.

1 in.

1 in.

1 cubic inch

Work Together

Building Understanding

Use connecting cubes to explore volume. Let 1 connecting cube represent 1 cubic inch (1 in. × 1 in. × 1 in.)

Build a rectangular prism like this one.

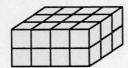

- What is the area of the bottom layer?

- How many layers of cubes are there?

- How many cubes did it take to build the prism?

Now, use the cubes to build all the different rectangular prisms possible with 24 cubes.

Use a table to record what you find.

Example

Length	Width	Height	Volume
24	1	1	24

TALK ABOUT IT

- How many dimensions are used in measuring volume? What are they?

- Which dimension used in measuring volume is not used in measuring area?

Making the Connection

Each picture represents a rectangular prism.

Figure A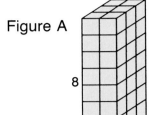

8
3
2

Figure B

3
7
2

- Which do you think has the greater volume? Why?

Use connecting cubes to build each figure.

TALK ABOUT IT

- Which figure has a greater volume? Why?

- Suppose you made a $2 \times 2 \times 9$ rectangular prism and a $3 \times 3 \times 5$ rectangular prism. Does the taller prism have a greater volume than the shorter prism? Why?

- If you change the taller rectangular prism to measure $3 \times 3 \times 9$, which has the greater volume? Why?

Checking Understanding

Use cubes to find the number of all the possible rectangular prisms.

1. 8 cubes

2. 12 cubes

3. 18 cubes

Guess which rectangular prism has the greater volume. Use connecting cubes to find the volume of each prism in cubic centimeters.

4.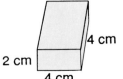

4 cm
2 cm
4 cm

5.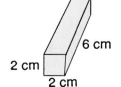

6 cm
2 cm
2 cm

6.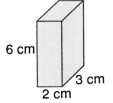

6 cm
3 cm
2 cm

7. Write a formula that you can use to find the volume of a rectangular prism instead of using the cubes.

FINDING VOLUME

A carpenter wants to buy the portable toolbox with the greatest volume. Which toolbox should she choose?

Toolbox A

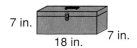

7 in.
18 in. 7 in.

Toolbox B

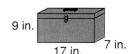

9 in.
17 in. 7 in.

Toolbox C

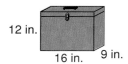

12 in.
16 in. 9 in.

The volume of a solid figure can be described by the number and size of cubic units that will fit inside it. Common units of volume are the cubic inch (in.^{3}) and the cubic foot (ft^3).

You can use this formula to find the volume of a rectangular prism.

Volume = length × width × height
$V = l \times w \times h$

Toolbox A	Toolbox B	Toolbox C
$V = l \times w \times h$	$V = l \times w \times h$	$V = l \times w \times h$
$V = 18 \times 7 \times 7$	$V = 17 \times 7 \times 9$	$V = 16 \times 9 \times 12$
$V = 126 \times 7$	$V = 119 \times 9$	$V = 144 \times 12$
$V = 882$ in.^{3}	$V = 1{,}071$ in.^{3}	$V = 1{,}728$ in.^{3}

Toolbox C has the greatest volume of the three toolboxes. So, the carpenter should choose Toolbox C.

Talk About It

▶ Some dimensions of Toolbox A and Toolbox C are close in size. Why do you think the volume of Toolbox C is so much greater?

Check for Understanding

Write the volume of each in cubic inches or in cubic feet.

1.
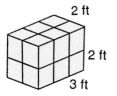

2 ft
2 ft
3 ft

2.
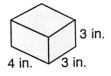

3 in.
4 in. 3 in.

3.
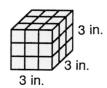

3 in.
3 in.
3 in.

4. a rectangular prism that measures 4 in. × 5 in. × 2 in.

Practice

Find the volume of each.

5.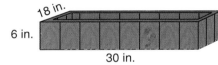
18 in. / 6 in. / 30 in.

6. 24 ft / 24 ft / 24 ft
ACE OCEAN TRANSPORT COMPANY

7. 44 cm / 35 cm / 60 cm

8. $42\,\text{mm} \times 34\,\text{mm} \times 28\,\text{mm} = \blacksquare\,\text{mm}^3$

9. $4\,\text{yd} \times 5\,\text{yd} \times 3\,\text{yd} = \blacksquare\,\text{yd}^3$

10. $7\,\text{cm} \times 14\,\text{cm} \times 12\,\text{cm} = \blacksquare\,\text{cm}^3$

11. $12\,\text{ft} \times 4\,\text{ft} \times 3\,\text{ft} = \blacksquare\,\text{ft}^3$

12. $l = 5\,\text{in.}$
$w = 3\,\text{in.}$
$h = 7\,\text{in.}$
$V = \blacksquare\,\text{in.}^3$

13. $l = 10\,\text{cm}$
$w = 8\,\text{cm}$
$h = 9\,\text{cm}$
$V = \blacksquare\,\text{cm}^3$

14. $l = 51\,\text{m}$
$w = 14\,\text{m}$
$h = 5\,\text{m}$
$V = \blacksquare\,\text{m}^3$

15. $l = 2.8\,\text{m}$
$w = 1.6\,\text{m}$
$h = 0.9\,\text{m}$
$V = \blacksquare\,\text{m}^3$

Mixed Applications

16. Sophie has three pieces of wood that are 3 ft 2 in., 4 ft 6 in., and 4 ft 11 in. long. If she needs 13 ft of wood, does she have enough?

17. Brett wants to know the length of a piece of wood that is $\frac{2}{5}$ the length of his leg. If his leg is 100 cm long, how long is the piece of wood?

18. The Woods' swimming pool is 38 ft long, 22 ft wide, and 6 ft deep. What is the volume of the pool?

19. The Gonzalez family is building a patio. The patio will be 9 ft long by 12 ft wide. If the concrete is poured $\frac{1}{2}$ ft deep, what will be the volume of the patio?

MIXED REVIEW

Find the product.

1. $10 \times 0.5 = n$

2. $100 \times 6.3 = n$

3. $1{,}000 \times 8.905 = n$

Add or subtract. Write the answer in simplest form.

4. $2\frac{2}{3}$
$+ 1\frac{5}{6}$

5. $4\frac{4}{5}$
$- 2\frac{9}{10}$

6. $1\frac{7}{9}$
$+ 2\frac{2}{3}$

7. $10\frac{1}{2}$
$- 5\frac{3}{4}$

8. $6\frac{3}{4}$
$+ 5\frac{2}{5}$

How are the units used to measure the area of a figure different from the units used to measure the volume of a figure?

WRAP UP...

ESTIMATING
Volume

Sam and Barbara want to build a box large enough to hold an apple. Sam wants to build the box with a volume of 1 cubic centimeter (cm³). Barbara wants to build the box with a volume of 1 cubic decimeter (dm³). Which size is more reasonable for an apple?

 1 cubic centimeter   1 cubic decimeter

- Use centimeter graph paper, a pencil, tape, and scissors to build a box with a volume of 1 dm³.

- Place a decimeter cube on your graph paper.

- Trace around the cube, or draw each face as a square with 10 cm on each side to form this pattern.

- Cut out the pattern.

- Tape the pattern to form a box with a volume of 1 dm³.

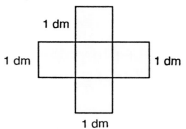

Talk About It

▶ Is this a reasonable size to hold an apple? What else would fit?

▶ What would fit in a box with a volume of 1 cm³?

Work in a small group. Use butcher paper, a marker, scissors, and a meterstick to model a box with a volume of 1 m³.

- Each of five groups should make one square face for the box.

- Join the faces by taping the squares to model a box with a volume of 1 m³.

Talk About It

▶ Did your class make enough 1-dm³ boxes to fill the 1-m³ box?

▶ How many would you need?

Check for Understanding

Choose the most reasonable measure. Write **a, b,** or **c.**

1. box for 30 math books   **a.** 100 cm³   **b.** 100 dm³   **c.** 100 m³
2. crayon box   **a.** 500 cm³   **b.** 500 dm³   **c.** 500 m³

Practice

Choose the most reasonable measure. Write **a, b,** or **c.**

3. tissue box	**a.** 90 in.^{3}	**b.** 90 ft^3	**c.** 90 yd^3
4. lunch box	**a.** 4,500 mm^3	**b.** 4,500 cm^3	**c.** 4,500 m^3
5. shoebox	**a.** 400 in.^{3}	**b.** 400 ft^3	**c.** 400 yd^3
6. ice-cream carton	**a.** 120 yd^3	**b.** 120 ft^3	**c.** 120 in.^{3}
7. refrigerator	**a.** 32 yd^3	**b.** 32 ft^3	**c.** 32 in.^{3}

Mixed Applications

8. At a construction site, some workers are digging a pit. The pit will be 3 ft deep, 2 ft wide, and 5 ft long. How many cubic feet of dirt must be removed?

9. There are 2 crates at the construction site. Each crate is 3 ft long, 9 ft wide, and 6 ft high. What is the combined volume of the crates?

10. The carpenters worked for 3 hr 15 min. Then they took a 45-min lunch break. They worked for 4 hr 15 min after lunch. If they began work at 8:30 A.M., at what time did they finish work?

11. A group of volunteers built a shelter. Of all the volunteers, $\frac{1}{2}$ measured and sawed boards, $\frac{1}{4}$ nailed boards, and $\frac{2}{8}$ sanded boards. If 8 volunteers nailed boards, how many sanded boards?

VISUAL THINKING

12. Find the volume of each box shown.

13. How many 1 ft^3 are there in a box with a volume of 1 yd^3?

14. How can you find the number of 1 in.^{3} there are in a box with a volume of 1 ft^3?

15. Compare the volume of the boxes shown. Are they the same or different?

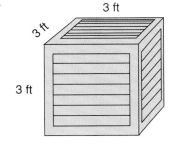
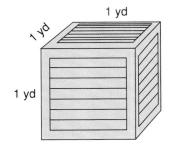

3 ft

3 ft

3 ft

1 yd

1 yd

1 yd

How many cm^3 equal 1 dm^3? How many dm^3 equal 1 m^3?

WRAP UP...

PROBLEM SOLVING

STRATEGY • Use a Formula

Debbie wants to mount a poster on a piece of plywood. Then she will use molding to make a frame for the poster. The poster is 2 ft by 3 ft. How many square feet of plywood will Debbie need? How many feet of molding will she need?

Sometimes you can solve problems by *using formulas* you know.

▶ **UNDERSTAND**

What are you asked to find?

What facts are given?

▶ **PLAN**

What strategy can you use?

You can use formulas to solve this problem.

Use the formula for area of a rectangle to find the number of square feet of plywood needed.

Use the formula for perimeter of a rectangle to find the number of feet of molding needed.

Formulas	
Perimeter of rectangle	$P = (2 \times l) + (2 \times w)$
Circumference	$C = \pi \times d$
Area of rectangle	$A = l \times w$
Volume of prism	$V = l \times w \times h$

▶ **SOLVE**

How will you solve the problem?

	Plywood	Molding
Write the formula.	$A = l \times w$	$P = (2 \times l) + (2 \times w)$
Replace the l and w.	$A = 2 \times 3$	$P = (2 \times 2) + (2 \times 3)$
Solve.	$A = 6 \text{ ft}^2$	$P = \quad 4 \quad + \quad 6$
		$P = 10 \text{ ft}$

So, Debbie needs 6 ft² of plywood and 10 ft of molding for her poster.

▶ **LOOK BACK**

How can you check your answer?

WHAT IF... ... Debbie's poster is 3 ft by 4 ft? How many square feet of plywood and how many feet of molding will she need?

412

Apply

Use a formula and solve.

(1) The length of a school playground is 95 m, and the width is 64 m. If the school board wants to build a fence around the playground, how much fencing will be needed?

(2) Terri and Greg are building a circular border around a flagpole. They stand where the border will be on opposite sides of the flagpole. The distance between them is 7.5 m. Using 3.14 as a value of *pi*, find the circumference of the circular border rounded to the nearest tenth of a meter.

Mixed Applications ⟹ **STRATEGIES** **Make a Table • Solve a Simpler Problem • Write a Number Sentence**

Choose a strategy and solve.

(3) A carpenter can build 2 shelves in 25 min. How long will it take the carpenter to build 6 shelves?

(4) Annie put paper trim around 12 tables. How much trim did she use if each table was 4 ft by 6 ft?

(5) Brian uses two different-sized nails. The larger nails are $2\frac{1}{8}$ in. long. The smaller nails are $\frac{1}{4}$ in. shorter. How long are the smaller nails?

(6) How many cuts need to be made in a rectangular board if 10 equal pieces of wood are needed?

(7) Billy, Sara, Zach, and Joe are building a doghouse. They need wood, a hammer, nails, and paint. Each person will get one item. Billy will not get paint, and Sara will not get a hammer or paint. Zach will get the wood. What item will each person get?

(8) A carpenter is building a corner bookcase with four shelves. Each shelf is $1\frac{3}{4}$ in. wider than the shelf above it. The top shelf is $14\frac{1}{2}$ in. wide. How wide is the bottom shelf?

WRITER'S CORNER

(9) Design a rectangular clubhouse with a fence around it. Decide on the dimensions of the clubhouse and the fence. Use this information to write as many problems as you can. Be sure each problem can be solved by using a formula. Exchange with a partner and solve.

Vocabulary Check

Choose a word or words from the box to complete each sentence.

area
circumference
cubic centimeter
perimeter
square foot
volume

1. The measure of the space inside a solid figure is the ___?___ .
   (page 406)

2. A(n) ___?___ is a unit of volume. *(page 407)*

3. The distance around a figure is its ___?___ . *(page 388)*

4. The number of square units needed to cover a surface is the ___?___ . *(page 394)*

5. The distance around a circle is called the ___?___ .
   (page 392)

6. A(n) ___?___ is a unit of area. *(page 394)*

Concept Check

Measure the sides and find the perimeter of each figure in mm. *(pages 388, 390)*

7.

8.

9.

Find the circumference. Round to the nearest tenth. *(page 392)*

10.
    62 mm

11.
    17 mm

12. 44 mm

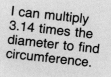

I can multiply 3.14 times the diameter to find circumference.

Use what you know about hidden cubes to find the number of cubes used to build each figure. *(page 404)*

13.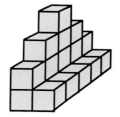

14.

15.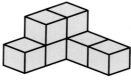

Use cubes to find the number of all the possible rectangular prisms. *(page 406)*

16. 16 cubes

17. 10 cubes

18. 20 cubes

Skill Check

Measure the sides and find the perimeter of each figure in mm.
(pages 388, 390)

19.

20.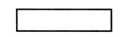

21.

Use the formula to find the area of each rectangle. *(page 394)*

22.
9 cm
14 cm

23.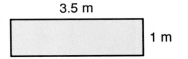
3.5 m
1 m

24.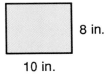
8 in.
10 in.

Find the area of each figure.

25.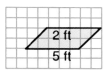
2 ft
5 ft

26.
2 cm
3 cm

27.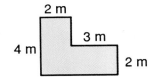
2 m
4 m
3 m
2 m

Find the volume of each. *(page 408)*

28. $l = 6$ in.
$w = 4$ in.
$h = 5$ in.
$V = \blacksquare$ in.^{3}

29. $l = 2.5$ m
$w = 1.5$ m
$h = 3.2$ m
$V = \blacksquare$ m^3

30. $l = 12$ yd
$w = 30$ yd
$h = 12$ yd
$V = \blacksquare$ yd^3

31. $l = 5$ cm
$w = 18$ cm
$h = 6$ cm
$V = \blacksquare$ cm^3

Problem-Solving Check *(pages 398, 412)*

32. Aaron wants to plant a rectangular flower garden with an area of 24 ft^2. He has 20 ft of edging that he will put around the outside of the garden. What dimensions should his garden have?

33. Morgan is building a rectangular pen for her dog. She has 40 ft of fencing to use for the pen. What dimensions should she make the pen so that it has the greatest possible area?

34. One side of a square frame measures 12 in. What is the perimeter of the frame?

35. A builder is ordering carpeting for a room that is 10 ft by 12 ft. How many square feet of carpeting should he order?

1. Find the perimeter of the cover of a book. Explain your method.

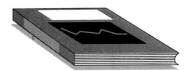

2. Use a piece of string to find the circumference and the diameter of a circular lid. Give each measure, and describe the relationship between circumference and diameter.

3. Look at the polygons on page 396. Use these polygons to help you explain how the areas of a parallelogram and a triangle are related to the area of a rectangle.

4. Look at the rectangular prism below. Explain how to find the volume of a solid figure. Then find the volume of this prism.

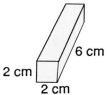

6 cm

2 cm

2 cm

5. Read Exercise 2 on page 399. Follow the steps on the Problem-Solving Think Along worksheet to show how to solve this problem.

I can use the formula $l \times w \times h$ to find volume.

Write About It

6. What is something you learned about perimeter; area, or volume that you did not know before studying this chapter? Explain.

7. Explain how you would find the volume of a rectangular box in your classroom.

TEAMWORK *Project*

MODEL A HOUSE AND ITS FENCE

Homeowners often surround their property with a fence. With your teammates, model a house and a surrounding fence.

DECIDE

Talk about how you can use graph paper, markers, scissors, glue, string, and craft sticks to make your model.

SHARE

Show your model. Describe how the area of the house compares with the area of the property.

DO

Work with your teammates. Use graph paper. Draw and color a rectangular house 11 units long and 15 units wide. Cut a 3-unit frame surrounding the house to show the property line. Glue craft-stick fence posts around the property line. Use string to connect the fence posts.

TALK ABOUT IT

☐ Suppose you had a 1-unit frame around the house. How would the model be different?

☐ Why might you need to know the area between a fence and a house?

☐ What happens to the area between a fence and a house if a room is added to the house?

Activity

Surface Area

Alaskan Eskimos call themselves *Inupiat,* or "people." During winter, some Inupiat hunt for food. As they move from one hunting spot to another, they build temporary houses of ice or hard-packed snow. These houses are called *igloos.* An igloo can be built in less than two hours.

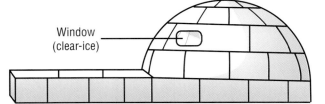

Window (clear-ice)

Suppose an igloo builder begins by cutting blocks of hard-packed snow 3 feet long by 2 feet wide by 2 feet thick. What is the surface area of one block of snow?

The surface area of a figure is the sum of the areas of all its faces. To find the surface area of a figure, it sometimes helps to visualize what the figure would look like if it were "unfolded." Find the surface area of the block of snow.

The surface area of the block of snow is 32 ft².

FACE	AREA OF FACE (ft.²)
A	2 x 3 = 6
B	2 x 3 = 6
C	2 x 3 = 6
D	2 x 3 = 6
E	2 x 2 = 4
F	2 x 2 = 4
TOTAL	**32**

Draw a picture to show each block of ice unfolded. Then find the surface area of each.

1. a clear-ice window 2 ft × 1.5 ft × 1 ft

2. a platform inside the igloo 5 ft × 1 ft × 1 ft

Challenge

CRITICAL THINKING

Each face should be only one color. Any two faces that touch should be different colors. What is the smallest number of colors you would need for painting the whole cube?

VISUAL THINKING

8 ft

10 ft

Draw five other polygons that have the same perimeter as the rectangle. One of your polygons may be a rectangle, but it must not be congruent to the one shown.

Write the letter of the correct answer.

1. Which is 104.536 rounded to the nearest tenth?

   A. 100   B. 104.5
   C. 104.54   D. 105

2. $5.8 + 3.5 = \blacksquare + 5.8$

   A. 0   B. 3.5
   C. 9.3   D. not here

3. $2 \times (50 \times 6) = n$

   A. 106   B. 112
   C. 302   D. 600

4. Which identifies the triangle?

   A. isosceles
   B. equilateral
   C. scalene
   D. right

5. Which number is divisible by 3?

   A. 103   B. 313
   C. 350   D. 471

6. Which is the best estimate?
   $5.26 \times 38 \approx n$

   A. 20   B. 200
   C. 1,500   D. 2,000

7. Which is the mean of 84, 86, 92, 95, and 98?

   A. 14   B. 91
   C. 92   D. 95

8. Which is the greatest common factor of 18 and 24?

   A. 3   B. 6
   C. 8   D. 9

9. Which is true?

   A. $\frac{3}{8} < \frac{1}{3}$ B. $\frac{3}{8} = \frac{1}{3}$
   C. $\frac{3}{8} > \frac{1}{3}$ D. not here

10. $4\frac{2}{3} - 1\frac{1}{4} = n$

    A. $2\frac{5}{12}$ B. $3\frac{1}{12}$
    C. $3\frac{5}{8}$ D. not here

11. Corliss is building a rectangular pen for her dog. She has 56 ft of fencing. What should be the dimensions of the pen if she wants to have the greatest area possible?

    A. 14 ft × 14 ft
    B. 16 ft × 12 ft
    C. 18 ft × 10 ft
    D. 20 ft × 8 ft

12. The Lings' yard is 22 m long and 10 m wide. If they want to build a fence around their yard, how much fencing will they need?

    A. 32 m of fencing
    B. 54 m of fencing
    C. 64 m of fencing
    D. 220 m of fencing

RATIO, PERCENT, AND PROBABILITY

Did you know . . .

. . . that there are over 44,000 miles of highway in the United States interstate system?

TALK ABOUT IT

Jan draws a map to record the places she visits on her summer vacation. The scale on Jan's map shows that 1 inch stands for 25 miles. So far, Jan has recorded 5 inches of travel on her map. Using this information, make a table. Then use the information in the table to write and solve as many problems as you can.

EXPLORING

Ratio

In Mrs. Appleton's class, 3 of the 5 students who ride bicycles to school ride red bicycles. In Mr. Brown's class, 4 of the 6 students who ride bicycles to school ride red ones. In Ms. Chester's class, 2 students ride bicycles to school. They both ride red bicycles.

Work Together

Building Understanding

You can compare the number of students who ride red bicycles to the total number of students who ride bicycles to school.

Mrs. Appleton
3 to 5

You can use counters to show comparisons and explore ratio. Work with a partner for this activity.

A. Use counters to represent all five students in Mrs. Appleton's class who ride bicycles to school. Each counter represents one student.

Turn the red side of the counters up to represent the number of students with red bicycles.

B. Use counters to show the comparison of the number of students who ride red bicycles with all students who ride bicycles in Mr. Brown's class.

C. Use counters to show the comparison of the number of students who ride red bicycles with all students who ride bicycles in Ms. Chester's class.

TALK ABOUT IT

- How many of Mrs. Appleton's students who ride bicycles do *not* ride red bicycles?

- For all classes combined, compare the number of students who ride red bicycles to the number of students who ride bicycles that are not red.

Making the Connection

You can use a **ratio** to compare two numbers. A ratio can be written in any one of three ways. The ratio of students in Mrs. Appleton's class who ride red bicycles to all students who ride bicycles can be written in these three ways.

3 to 5   3:5 $\frac{3}{5}$

Read each ratio "three to five."

You can use ratios to make other comparisons about the students who ride bicycles in Mrs. Appleton's class.

The counters that represent Mrs. Appleton's class show three relationships.

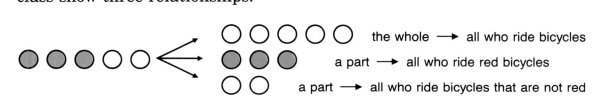

the whole ⟶ all who ride bicycles

a part ⟶ all who ride red bicycles

a part ⟶ all who ride bicycles that are not red

Here are other ratios for Mrs. Appleton's class.	part:whole not red:all 2:5	whole:part all:red 5:3	part:part red:not red 3:2

TALK ABOUT IT

- For Mrs. Appleton's class, what does the ratio $\frac{5}{2}$ describe?

- Is the ratio $\frac{5}{2}$ the same as $\frac{2}{5}$? Explain.

Checking Understanding

In Exercises 1–3, write each ratio in three ways.

1. stars to circles

2. circles to all shapes

3. all shapes to stars

For Exercises 4–6, write *part to whole, whole to part,* or *part to part* for each description in Exercises 1–3.

4. _?_   5. _?_   6. _?_

EQUIVALENT RATIOS

Lake Tanganyika, near Tanzania in eastern Africa, is the longest freshwater lake in the world. Hadiya counts canoes and rowboats on the lake. On Thursday he counted 2 canoes and 3 rowboats. On Friday he counted 4 canoes and 6 rowboats. On Saturday he counted 6 canoes and 9 rowboats.

You can draw pictures to show the relationship of canoes to rowboats counted.

Let ⬭ represent a canoe and ▱ represent a rowboat.

$\frac{2}{3}$ → canoes → rowboats	Thursday's count
$\frac{4}{6}$ → canoes → rowboats	Friday's count
$\frac{6}{9}$ → canoes → rowboats	Saturday's count

You can make a ratio table.

Canoes	2	4	6
Rowboats	3	6	9

You can multiply or divide both terms of a ratio by the same number.

$$\frac{2}{3} \overset{\times 2}{\underset{\times 2}{=}} \frac{4}{6} \qquad \frac{2}{3} \overset{\times 3}{\underset{\times 3}{=}} \frac{6}{9}$$

So, the ratios of canoes to rowboats counted were **equivalent,** or had the same relationship, each day.

Talk About It

▶ How can you use multiplication to find a ratio equivalent to $\frac{1}{4}$?

▶ How can you use division to find a ratio equivalent to $\frac{10}{15}$?

▶ Name two other ratios equivalent to $\frac{2}{3}$.

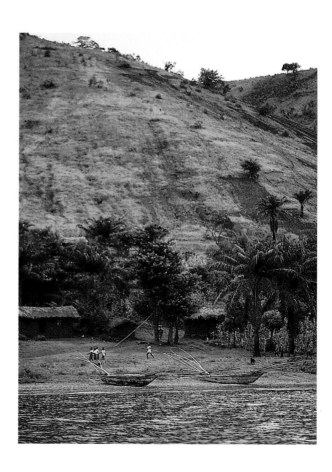

Check for Understanding

Draw pictures to show whether these ratios are equivalent. Write *yes* or *no*.

1. $\dfrac{1}{3}, \dfrac{2}{6}, \dfrac{3}{9}$

2. $\dfrac{1}{4}, \dfrac{2}{8}, \dfrac{3}{9}$

3. $\dfrac{1}{8}, \dfrac{2}{16}, \dfrac{3}{24}$

4. $\dfrac{1}{6}, \dfrac{2}{12}, \dfrac{3}{18}$

Write three ratios that are equivalent to the given ratio.

5. $\dfrac{3}{4}$

6. $\dfrac{1}{2}$

7. $\dfrac{1}{5}$

8. $\dfrac{2}{3}$

Practice

Tell whether the ratios are equivalent. Write *yes* or *no*.

9. $\dfrac{2}{3}$ and $\dfrac{3}{4}$

10. 1:4 and 3:12

11. 3 to 5 and 6 to 10

12. Use multiplication to write two ratios that are equivalent to $\frac{2}{5}$.

13. Use division to write two ratios that are equivalent to $\frac{6}{12}$.

Write two ratios that are equivalent to the given ratio.

14. 1:6

15. 4:5

16. 4:6

17. 3:5

18. $\dfrac{8}{12}$

Mixed Applications

19. **Critical Thinking** Find two numbers between 20 and 25 that have a ratio equivalent to 7:8.

20. John worked for 2 hours and earned $7. For how many hours must he work to earn $35?

21. There are 4 children and 2 adults in the car. There are 6 children and 4 adults in the van. Are the ratios of children to adults the same in both vehicles?

22. On Sunday Hadiya counted 2 more rowboats than canoes. He counted 14 boats in all. How many canoes did he count?

MIXED REVIEW

Multiply. Write the answer in simplest form.

1. $\dfrac{2}{5} \times \dfrac{1}{2} = n$

2. $\dfrac{1}{3} \times \dfrac{3}{4} = n$

3. $\dfrac{5}{6} \times \dfrac{2}{3} = n$

4. $\dfrac{1}{6} \times \dfrac{3}{8} = n$

Complete.

5. $2.54\,\text{m} = \blacksquare\,\text{cm}$

6. $55\,\text{g} = \blacksquare\,\text{mg}$

7. $3{,}000\,\text{mL} = \blacksquare\,\text{L}$

8. $17{,}000\,\text{mm} = \blacksquare\,\text{m}$

Explain how you can multiply to find the missing number. $\frac{3}{4} = \frac{n}{20}$ **WRAP UP...**

EXPLORING

Scale Drawings

On their vacation trip to the Florida Keys, Jared and his family drove on the Overseas Highway from Key Largo to Key West. They discussed how many kilometers it is from Plantation to Long Key.

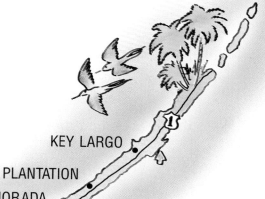

KEY LARGO

PLANTATION

ISLAMORADA

LONG KEY

KEY WEST

MARATHON

cm	0	1	2	3	4	5	6
km	0	10	20	30	40	50	60

LEGEND
⬆ STATE PARKS
🏛 STATE MONUMENTS

Work Together

Building Understanding

You can use a map and a ruler to explore scale drawings and to estimate distances.

Copy and complete the table. On the map, measure to the nearest centimeter the number of centimeters between the cities.

Cities	Distance on Map (in cm)
Key Largo and Islamorada	▪
Key Largo and Long Key	▪
Key Largo and Marathon	▪
Key Largo and Key West	▪

TALK ABOUT IT

- What is an estimate of the distance between Plantation and Long Key?

- Is the distance greater between Marathon and Key West or between Key Largo and Marathon? How do you know?

426

Making the Connection

A ratio that compares the distance on the map with the actual distance is a **scale.**

The scale of the map on page 426 is 1 cm : 10 km.

The scale tells you that 1 centimeter on the map represents an actual distance of 10 kilometers.

You can use equivalent ratios to find the actual distance between the cities listed in the table on page 426.

distance on map in cm ⟶ $\dfrac{1}{10} \overset{\times 3}{=} \dfrac{3}{30}$ cm
actual distance in km ⟶ $\phantom{\dfrac{1}{10}}$ km
$\times 3$

So, the actual distance from Plantation to Long Key is about 30 kilometers.

Checking Understanding

1. Add a third column to the table you made on page 426.

2. Use "Actual Distance (in km)" as the heading at the top of the column.

Cities	Distance on Map (in cm)	Actual Distance (in km)
Key Largo and Islamorada		
Key Largo and Long Key		
Key Largo and Marathon		
Key Largo and Key West		

3. Use equivalent ratios to find the actual distances between the cities in the table.

SOCIAL STUDIES CONNECTION

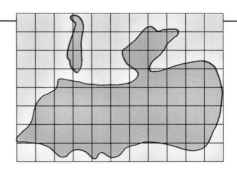

In scale drawings, dimensions are sometimes enlarged and sometimes reduced.

This map of Key West has been drawn on graph paper. Each square on the graph paper is 0.5 cm by 0.5 cm.

4. Enlarge the map of Key West by drawing it on graph paper on which each square is 1 cm by 1 cm.

5. What size graph paper can be used to reduce the map of Key West?

EXPLORING

Percent

You can use colored markers or crayons and graph paper with 10-by-10 grids to explore percent. Work with a partner for these activities.

Work Together

Building Understanding

Activity 1 On a 10-by-10 grid, color some squares blue. Then color all the other squares on the grid red.

TALK ABOUT IT

- How many squares are on the grid?

- How many squares are blue? How many are red?

- What is the ratio of blue squares to all the squares on the grid? of red squares to all the squares on the grid?

- How can you shade a grid to show a ratio of blue squares to all squares of 75 to 100? 23:100? $\frac{50}{100}$?

Activity 2
On a 10-by-10 grid, color all the squares blue. On another 10-by-10 grid, do not color any squares.

TALK ABOUT IT

- Look at the first grid. How many squares are blue?

- What is the ratio of blue squares to all squares?

- Look at the other grid. How many squares are blue?

- What is the ratio of blue squares to all squares?

- How can you shade a grid to show a ratio of red squares to all squares of 100:100?

Making the Connection

Percent is a ratio of some number to 100. Percent means "per hundred." The symbol for percent is %.

Look at this 10-by-10 grid.

The ratio of blue squares to all squares is 35 to 100.

Thirty-five percent of the grid is blue.

- What percent of the grid is red?

- What percent of the grid is not colored?

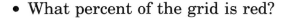

Percent is often used with money.

Think of $1.00 as 100 pennies with each penny, or counter, in a square of a 10-by-10 grid.

35% of $1.00 is $0.35.

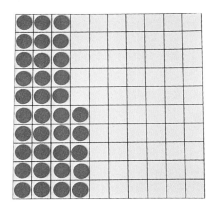

TALK ABOUT IT

- What is 50% of $1.00? 10% of $1.00? 36% of $1.00?

- What part of a dollar do you have if you have 0% of it? 100% of it?

- What does 200% of a number mean?

Checking Understanding

1. Color a 10-by-10 grid so that it is 25% blue, 50% red, and 25% yellow. How much of the grid is colored? What is the sum of the three percents?

2. Suppose you have $1.00 in your wallet. What percent of your money is $1.00? is $0.75? is $0.50? is $0.25? is $0.00?

PERCENT

Mr. Richards observed the number of people who rode the train on his Monday and Wednesday routes. He counted 100 people on Monday. On Wednesday, 75% of this group rode the train. Write the fraction and decimal that represents 75%.

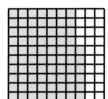

Think: 75% is $\frac{75}{100}$.

$$75\% = \frac{75 \div 25}{100 \div 25} = \frac{3}{4} \longleftarrow \text{simplest form}$$

$$75\% = 75 \text{ hundredths, or } 0.75$$

So, the fraction that represents 75% is $\frac{3}{4}$ and the decimal is 0.75.

More Examples

A. Write the fraction for 40%.

Think: 40% is 40 hundredths.

$$40\% = \frac{40 \div 20}{100 \div 20} = \frac{2}{5}$$

B. Write the decimal for 8%.

Think: 8% is 8 hundredths.

$$8\% = 0.08$$

Talk About It

▶ How do you express 42% as a decimal and as a fraction in simplest form?

▶ How do you express $\frac{5}{10}$ as a percent? Explain why $\frac{5}{10}$ is not 5%.

Check for Understanding

Write each as a percent, a decimal, and a fraction in simplest form.

1.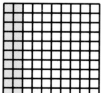

2.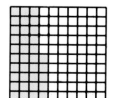

3.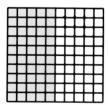

4. 3 percent

5. fifteen per hundred

6. thirty-seven hundredths

Practice

Write each as a percent, a decimal, and a fraction in simplest form.

7.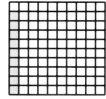

8.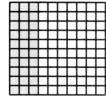

9.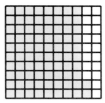

10. seven hundredths

11. sixteen percent

12. 32 per hundred

13. ninety percent

14. 78 per hundred

15. twenty-one hundredths

Mixed Applications

16. If one car is needed for every 4 students going on a field trip, how many cars are needed if 30 students are going on the trip?

17. Brett and his family took a trip by interstate highway. He counted 46 white cars out of 100 cars. What percent of the cars were white?

18. Mr. Wolf is a salesman. He spends 60% of his time driving in his car. What is this percent expressed as a fraction?

19. Babs received $1.00 to spend on snacks. If she spent 80% of her money, how much money does she have left?

CRITICAL THINKING

Mrs. Raibourn drives to work and back each day through a toll booth. She stops 3 times each way to deposit the tolls. Each toll is either $0.50 or $0.75. The ratio of $0.50 tolls to $0.75 tolls is 1:2 each way.

20. Do you have enough information to know how much Mrs. Raibourn spends each day on tolls? If so, how much does she spend?

Explain how a student can score 80% on a test of 10 questions.

PROBLEM SOLVING

Choose a Strategy

Understand
Plan
Solve
Look Back

Ahmed is planning to travel from England to France. He can leave on Monday or on Wednesday. He can go to France by airplane, or he can cross the English Channel by Hovercraft or by auto ferry. What are Ahmed's travel choices?

Sometimes you can use different strategies to solve the same problem.

What strategies can you use for this problem?

You can *make an organized list* or *write a number sentence.*

Strategy: Make an Organized List

You can make a **tree diagram,** a type of organized list, to show all the choices Ahmed has for traveling to France. The tree diagram shows both days and each type of transportation given in the problem.

Days	Transportation	Possibilities
Monday	Airplane	Monday/Airplane
	Hovercraft	Monday/Hovercraft
	Auto ferry	Monday/Auto ferry
Wednesday	Airplane	Wednesday/Airplane
	Hovercraft	Wednesday/Hovercraft
	Auto ferry	Wednesday/Auto ferry

Strategy: Write a Number Sentence

If you want to find just the number of travel choices, you can write a multiplication number sentence.

$$2 \times 3 = 6$$

days	types of transportation	possible choices

So, Ahmed's travel choices are: Monday/airplane, Monday/ Hovercraft, Monday/auto ferry, Wednesday/airplane, Wednesday/Hovercraft, Wednesday/auto ferry.

WHAT IF... ...a tunnel to France is open for train travel on Monday and Wednesday? How many choices does Ahmed have for traveling to France? What are the choices?

Idea Bank, page 465, Exercises 10–11

Mixed Applications ➔ STRATEGIES

Make a Table • Work Backward • Make an Organized List • Write a Number Sentence • Use a Formula

Choose a strategy and solve.

1 Pepita left her hotel at 8:00 A.M. She spent 1 hr 20 min eating breakfast, 30 min traveling to a museum, and 3 hr 45 min at the museum. If it took Pepita 35 min to get back to the hotel, at what time did she arrive back at the hotel?

2 For lunch Winsie may order a sandwich with chicken, tuna fish, or peanut butter. She can have the sandwich on white bread, wheat bread, rye bread, or a roll. How many choices does she have?

3 Elston is staying in a hotel that is 14 blocks from the Empire State Building. If Elston can walk 2 blocks in 5 min, how long will it take him to walk from his hotel to the Empire State Building?

4 Norman packed green pants, black pants, and blue pants. He packed a white shirt, a yellow shirt, and a red shirt. Describe each outfit he can make.

5 Percy rode his bicycle once around the perimeter of Central Park. The park is $2\frac{1}{2}$ mi long and $\frac{1}{2}$ mi wide. How far did Percy ride his bicycle?

6 On Tuesday, Wednesday, and Thursday, Caroline visited a different museum in Paris each day. The museums were the Louvre, the Orsay Museum, and the Museum of Man. She did not visit the Louvre on Tuesday, and she did visit the Museum of Man on Wednesday. On which day did she visit each museum?

MULTICULTURAL NOTE: The Louvre was originally built as a royal fort in the 1200's. It has about 8 mi of galleries and is one of the world's largest art museums.

WRITER'S CORNER

7 Imagine that you can ask 1 person to take a trip to 1 place with you. Choose 3 people with whom you might travel and 3 places you might visit. Using this information, write and solve as many problems as you can.

1. Maria can use either Red Avenue, Main Street, or Elm Street to get to school. She can ride her bicycle, walk, or ride in the car. In how many different ways can she go to school?

2. Both the school and the city bus systems drop off students at the main entrance, the cafeteria, and the parking lot. In how many different ways can a student arrive at school by bus?

3. Julia walked around a square city block. If each side of the block is 500 ft long, how far did Julia walk?

4. Paul went camping at a state park that was about $1\frac{1}{2}$ mi long and $\frac{3}{4}$ mi wide. About how many square miles is the area of the state park?

Multiply.

5. $\begin{array}{r} 542 \\ \times\ \ 8 \\ \hline \end{array}$

6. $\begin{array}{r} 1{,}793 \\ \times\ \ \ \ 6 \\ \hline \end{array}$

7. $\begin{array}{r} 68 \\ \times 17 \\ \hline \end{array}$

8. $\begin{array}{r} 405 \\ \times 24 \\ \hline \end{array}$

I can use a formula to solve a problem.

Write *slide, flip,* or *turn* to indicate how each figure was moved.

9.
10.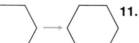
11.

Find the quotient.

12. $3\overline{)2{,}981}$
13. $4\overline{)9{,}860}$
14. $13\overline{)957}$
15. $24\overline{)1{,}370}$

Use the graph for Exercises 16–17.

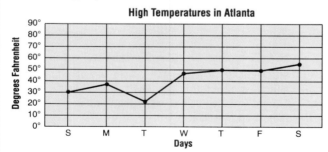

High Temperatures in Atlanta

16. Between which two days was the increase in temperature greatest?

17. What was the difference in the high temperature on Sunday and the high temperature on Saturday?

Write the greatest common factor for each pair of numbers.

18. 6, 9
19. 10, 35
20. 4, 14

21. 8, 24
22. 12, 20
23. 8, 12

Add or subtract. Write the answer in simplest form.

24. $\begin{array}{r} 2\frac{1}{3} \\ +1\frac{1}{6} \\ \hline \end{array}$

25. $\begin{array}{r} 4\frac{5}{8} \\ -2\frac{1}{4} \\ \hline \end{array}$

26. $\begin{array}{r} 10\frac{4}{5} \\ -\ 3\frac{2}{3} \\ \hline \end{array}$

Make a Scale Drawing

A scale drawing is like a photograph. It can be enlarged or reduced to change the size of the pictured object.

Travelers flying above the desert mesas of southern Peru can see huge figures scratched in the earth. These figures, called the Nazca lines, may date back a thousand years. One of these figures is a monkey. How could you enlarge or reduce this picture of the monkey?

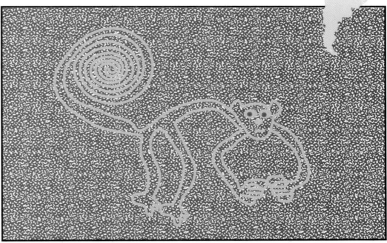

MULTICULTURAL NOTE: The left hand of the monkey is about 40 feet across. The monkey is so large it can be recognized only from the air.

You can make a sketch and use graph paper to make a scale drawing.

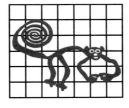 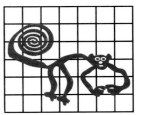

Work Together

- Use tracing paper to make a simple sketch.

- Draw a square grid over the sketch.

- Enlarge and reduce the sketch by copying the lines in the squares onto grids of smaller and larger squares.

Use graph paper to reduce or enlarge the animal figures.

1.

2.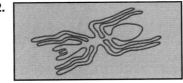

3. Explain how you are able to draw an object in a larger or smaller form.

EXPLORING

Probability

You can do a coin-tossing experiment to explore probability and to learn how to make good predictions.

When you toss a coin, the coin can land in two possible ways. It can land heads up or tails up. These are the **possible outcomes** of tossing one coin.

For this experiment you will
• predict the results of tossing two coins at one time.
• compare your results with your predictions.

Work Together

Building Understanding

Step 1 Copy the table. The possible outcome HH means that the first coin landed heads up and the second coin landed heads up.

Coin-Tossing Experiment				
Possible Outcomes	Prediction for 5 Tosses	Result for 5 Tosses	Prediction for 50 Tosses	Result for 50 Tosses
HH				
HT				
TH				
TT				

• What does the outcome TH mean?

Step 2 Predict the number of times you think each outcome will occur for 5 tosses and then for 50 tosses.

Step 3 Toss the 2 coins 5 times. Use tally marks to record your results in the table.

Step 4 Now toss the two coins 50 times. Record your results.

TALK ABOUT IT

• Describe how you made your predictions.

• How did your results for the 5 tosses and for the 50 tosses compare with your predictions?

• How many times do you think each outcome would occur if you tossed the coins 100 times? 1,000 times?

• Combine your results with those of all others in your class. How does this total compare to your results?

436

Making the Connection

The chance of something happening is called **probability**.

Probability is a ratio.

When you toss a coin, there are two possible outcomes: heads and tails. There is 1 chance in 2 of tossing heads.

The probability can be written as a fraction.

$$\text{Probability} = \frac{\text{number of favorable outcomes (heads)}}{\text{number of possible outcomes (heads, tails)}} = \frac{1}{2}$$

TALK ABOUT IT

- When you toss two coins at one time, how many possible outcomes are there? List the possible outcomes.

- What is the probability of the result being HH? HT? TH? TT?

- For how many possible outcomes is there at least 1 heads? What is the probability of tossing heads?

- For how many possible outcomes is there 1 heads and 1 tails? What is the probability of tossing 1 heads and 1 tails?

Checking Understanding

Suppose this spinner is used in the experiment.

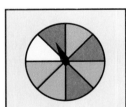

1. How many equivalent sections does the spinner have?

2. What are the possible outcomes of spinning the spinner?

3. What is the probability of the spinner landing on yellow? on blue? on red?

4. If you spin the spinner eight times, how many times do you think it will land on yellow? on blue? on red?

5. On what color will the spinner probably land most often? Why?

More Practice, Lesson 13.7, page H84

PROBABILITY

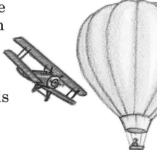

For a report Melinda wants to choose one type of early transportation from this table. She writes each type on slips of paper that are all the same, puts the slips into a bag, and, without looking, chooses one. What is the probability that she will pick *Biplane*?

Early Air Transportation	
Type	**Country**
Linen balloon	France
Glider (no passengers)	Britain
Manned glider	Germany
Steam-powered model airplane	U.S.A.
Biplane	U.S.A.
Four-engine plane	Russia
Single-engine transport	U.S.A.

It is **equally likely** that any 1 of the 7 types of transportation will be chosen.

$$\text{Probability} = \frac{\text{number of favorable outcomes (Biplane)}}{\text{number of possible outcomes (all types)}} = \frac{1}{7}$$

So, the probability that Melinda will pick *Biplane* is $\frac{1}{7}$.

The probability of an event occurring can always be expressed as 0, 1, or a number between 0 and 1.

impossible ← less likely   more likely → certain

0        $\frac{1}{2}$ 1

- Is it equally likely that Melinda will choose a type of air transportation from Britain as one from the United States?

From Britain:

$$\frac{\text{favorable outcomes}}{\text{possible outcomes}} = \frac{1}{7}$$

From the United States:

$$\frac{\text{favorable outcomes}}{\text{possible outcomes}} = \frac{3}{7}$$

Since $\frac{1}{7}$ is not equal to $\frac{3}{7}$, the two events are not equally likely.

Since $\frac{3}{7} > \frac{1}{7}$, it is more likely that she will choose one from the United States.

Find the probability of choosing a type of transportation from Canada.

$$\frac{\text{favorable outcomes}}{\text{possible outcomes}} = \frac{0}{7}, \text{ or } 0$$

Melinda's choosing a type of transportation from Canada is **impossible**.

Find the probability of choosing one of the types of transportation in the table.

$$\frac{\text{favorable outcomes}}{\text{possible outcomes}} = \frac{7}{7}, \text{ or } 1$$

Melinda's choosing one of the types of transportation in the table is **certain**.

Check for Understanding

Write a fraction for the probability of picking each marble from the bag.

1. a red marble
2. a green marble
3. a blue marble
4. a yellow marble

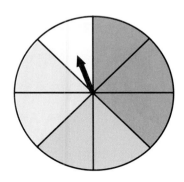

Practice

Use the spinner for Exercises 5–10.

5. What are the possible outcomes of spinning the spinner?

6. On what color is the spinner most likely to land? least likely to land? Explain.

Suppose you spin the spinner once. Write a fraction for the probability that the spinner will land on each.

7. yellow
8. green
9. red
10. black

Mixed Applications

11. If you put the names of all your classmates in a hat, what is the probability you will draw your name? a girl's name?

12. Copy and label this spinner to show outcomes that are equally likely and not equally likely.

13. A bag has red and blue marbles. After each draw you replace the marble. After 50 draws you have drawn a red marble 35 times. Do you think there are more red or blue marbles?

MIXED REVIEW

Add or subtract.

1. 6 hr 35 min
   + 4 hr 37 min

2. 8 min 14 sec
   − 3 min 45 sec

3. 5 hr 13 min
   + 7 hr 53 min

Find the perimeter.

4. 6 mm
   25 mm

5. 12 cm

6. 3 m
   9 m

Explain why the probability of an event cannot be greater than 1.

WRAP UP...

PROBLEM SOLVING

Conduct a Simulation

Mrs. Wooldridge must choose a student for a part in a play. Four students are equally qualified. How can a choice be made so that each student has an equal chance of being selected?

Student 1 ⟶ Brett
Student 2 ⟶ Linda
Student 3 ⟶ Renee
Student 4 ⟶ David

▶ UNDERSTAND

What are you asked to find?

What facts are given?

▶ PLAN

What process can you use?

You can choose the student by drawing numbers from a bag.
- On each of four slips of paper, write a student's number. Put the slips in a bag.
- Without looking, select one slip of paper. Make a tally mark next to the student's number in a table. Return the slip to the bag.
- Repeat this activity 50 times. The number selected most often will determine Mrs. Wooldridge's choice.

▶ SOLVE

How can you conduct a simulation?

You can use a computer program to simulate the experiment.

This BASIC program will generate the digits 1–4 at random 50 times.

```
10 REM THIS PROGRAM PRINTS
20 REM 50 RANDOM NUMBERS
30 REM BETWEEN 1 AND 4
40 PRINT "THE 50 RANDOM NUMBERS ARE:"
50 FOR I = 1 TO 49
60 X = INT ( RND (1) * 4) + 1
70 PRINT X; ",";
80 NEXT I
90 PRINT INT ( RND (1) * 4) + 1
100 END
```

On one computer run, these numbers were generated.

2,4,4,2,4,2,2,3,1,3,3,3,4,4,
2,4,3,2,4,2,3,3,4,1,4,3,1,4,
3,2,4,1,2,1,1,2,4,4,2,1,1,3,
4,2,1,2,3,3,1,1

Summary: 1 = 11
2 = 13
3 = 12
4 = 14

So, student number 4, David, was the choice.

▶ LOOK BACK

If you repeat the activity, will you get the same results?

 WHAT IF... ... there are five students who are equally qualified? How will the computer program have to be changed?

Apply

1 A program generates the digits 1–5 at random 100 times. Write a problem that this program could simulate.

2 If a program generates the digits 1–4 at random 100 times, about how many times would you expect each digit to occur?

Mixed Applications	>	**STRATEGIES**	**Make a Diagram • Work Backward** **• Use a Table • Guess and Check** **• Solve a Simpler Problem**

Choose a strategy and solve.

3 When Saki got back to her hotel after a day of sightseeing, she had $32.45. She had spent $9.50 on food, $14.80 on souvenirs, $13.75 on admission tickets, and $4.50 on transportation. How much money did she have at the beginning of the day?

4 Mrs. Berry assigned 38 students to do a report on England, France, Spain, Germany, or Italy. One half of the class chose to do a report on Spain, Germany, or Italy. France was chosen 5 more times than England. How many students did a report on France?

5 Look at the table below. In which month does Paris have the greatest difference between its average high and low temperatures?

6 Mr. Aviles asked his students if they would rather take a trip to Egypt, Mexico, or Thailand. Of the students, $\frac{1}{2}$ chose Mexico, $\frac{2}{5}$ chose Egypt, and $\frac{1}{10}$ chose Thailand. If 3 students chose Thailand, how many students chose Mexico?

Average Temperatures in Paris		
Month	**High**	**Low**
January	42°F	32°F
April	60°F	41°F
July	76°F	55°F
October	59°F	44°F

MULTICULTURAL NOTE: The people of Thailand enjoy the traditional stories called wannakhadi. These stories are acted out by classical dancers wearing decorative costumes.

CHAPTER REVIEW/TEST

Vocabulary Check

Choose a word or words from the box to complete each sentence.

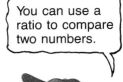

equivalent
  ratios
scale
percent
probability
ratio
scale drawing
tree diagram

1. You can use a __?__ to compare two numbers. *(page 423)*

2. If you want to show enlarged or reduced parts of an object, you can make a __?__ . *(page 427)*

3. A ratio of some number to 100 is a __?__ . *(page 429)*

4. A ratio that compares the distance on a map with the actual distance is a __?__ . *(page 427)*

5. A ratio that gives the chance that something will happen is a __?__ . *(page 437)*

6. A diagram that is an organized list is a __?__ . *(page 432)*

7. Ratios that show the same relationships are __?__ . *(page 424)*

You can use a ratio to compare two numbers.

Concept Check

Write the ratio for each comparison. *(page 422)*

8. triangles to circles

9. squares to all shapes

10. all shapes to triangles

Write the ratio in three ways. *(page 422)*

11. the ratio of red hats to all hats

12. the ratio of red hats to green hats

Use the map for Exercises 13–14. *(page 426)*

13. What is the distance on the map between points *A* and *B*?

14. Use the map scale to find the actual distance between points *A* and *B*.

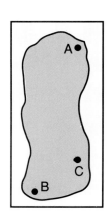

Scale 1 cm: 100 km

442 • **Chapter 13**

Use the grid for Exercises 15–16. *(page 428)*

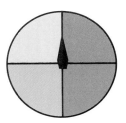

15. What percent of the grid is blue?

16. What percent of the grid is not colored?

Write the amount of money for each. *(page 428)*

17. 25% of $1.00 **18.** 100% of $1.00 **19.** 200% of $1.00

Write each as a percent, a decimal, and a fraction in simplest form. *(page 430)*

20. 4 percent
21. thirteen per hundred
22. 26 hundredths

Skill Check

Write a ratio equivalent to the given ratio. *(page 424)*

23. 1:3
24. 2 to 5
25. $\dfrac{3}{2}$
26. 10:12
27. $\dfrac{15}{10}$

Use the spinner for Exercises 28–30. *(pages 436, 438)*

28. What are the possible outcomes of spinning the spinner?

29. What is the probability of the spinner landing on red?

30. What is the probability of the spinner landing on green?

Problem-Solving Check *(pages 432, 440)*

31. A program generates the digits 1–3 at random 25 times. Write a problem that this program could simulate.

32. If a computer program generates the digits 1–3 at random 100 times, about how many times would you expect each digit to occur?

33. Jon can travel from Rutland to Simon by car, bus, or train. He can travel from Simon to Titan by boat or jet. In how many different ways can he travel from Rutland to Simon to Titan?

34. Becky can paint the walls in her room yellow, pink, or blue. She can paint the trim white, tan, or green. In how many different ways can Becky paint her room?

WHAT DID I LEARN?

1. Determine the ratio of students wearing sneakers to all students in your class. Explain your method.

2. Color a 10-by-10 grid so that it is 25% blue and 50% red. Explain the meaning of *percent*.

3. There are 3 red marbles, 2 blue marbles, and 1 yellow marble in a bag. Explain what probability is. Then determine the probability of picking
   a. a red marble.
   b. a red, blue, or yellow marble.
   c. a green marble.

4. Read Exercise 2 on page 433. Follow the steps on the Problem-Solving Think Along worksheet to show how to solve this problem.

Percent is a ratio that means "per hundred."

Write About It

5. How do you think the concepts you studied in this chapter on ratio, percent, and probability will be useful to you, other than in school?

6. Write what you know about the meaning of the ratio 2:3. Draw a picture to show the meaning.

TEAMWORK
Project

Conduct a Survey

Vacationers have many types of transportation from which to choose. With your teammates, conduct and analyze a survey about transportation.

Decide — Talk about how you can use a table and graph paper to show and analyze the results of a survey.

MODES OF TRANSPORTATION	
CAR	
BUS	
TRAIN	
PLANE	

Do — Work with your teammates. Survey a total of 100 students. Ask them what type of transportation they used the last time they took a trip. Use tally marks to record responses in a table, as shown.

Combine results for the team. Find ratios and percentages for each type of transportation. Color the grids on the graph paper to show the percentages.

Share — Show your tables and graph paper. Find the ratio of car use to each of the other types of transportation.

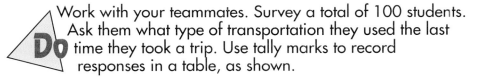

Modes of Transportation

TALK ABOUT IT

How can you use your results to predict the results of a survey of 1,000 people?

In your everyday activities, what other ratios and percentages have you noticed?

Extend Your Thinking

Activity

Probability of Independent Events

The probability of the coin landing heads up is $\frac{1}{2}$.

The probability of the spinner landing on red is $\frac{1}{3}$.

What is the probability of the coin landing heads up and the spinner landing on red?

You can make a tree diagram to show the possible outcomes.

Coin	Spinner	Outcomes
heads	red	heads, red
	green	heads, green
	blue	heads, blue
tails	red	tails, red
	green	tails, green
	blue	tails, blue

There are 6 different outcomes. The probability of the coin landing heads up and the spinner landing on red is $\frac{1}{6}$.

The result of the coin toss does not affect the spin of the spinner. The two events are independent. To find the probability that two independent events will occur, you can multiply the probability of each event occurring.

$$\frac{1}{2} \times \frac{1}{3} = \frac{1}{6}$$

Suppose you have a number cube with the numbers 1–6 on the faces. You also have a coin.

What is the probability of

1. the cube landing on 2 and the coin landing on heads?

2. the cube landing on an odd number and the coin landing on heads?

3. the cube landing on a number greater than 2 and the coin landing on tails?

Challenge

EVERYDAY MATH

Make a scale drawing of your classroom.

Use graph paper and a ruler.

Be sure to include the scale you used.

NUMBER PUZZLE

In a parking lot, the ratio of four-door cars to two-door cars is 2:3. If there were 6 fewer four-door cars, the ratio would be 1:2.

How many two-door cars are in the parking lot?

CUMULATIVE REVIEW

CHAPTERS 1–13

Write the letter of the correct answer.

1. Which numbers are in order from greatest to least?

A. 3.609; 3.690; 3.069
B. 3.690; 3.069; 3.609
C. 3.690; 3.609; 3.069
D. 3.069; 3.609; 3.690

2. Which figure shows a line of symmetry?

A. ← ⬡ →   B. ← △ →

C. ⬜ ← - - - →   D. ○

3. $400 \times 50 = n$

A. 2,000   B. 20,000
C. 200,000   D. not here

4. Which is the best estimate? $3\overline{)281}$

A. 9   B. 80
C. 90   D. 900

5. Which is the median of 50, 15, 45, 50, and 25?

A. 35   B. 37
C. 45   D. 50

6.
$$\begin{array}{r} 0.05 \\ \times\ 0.3 \\ \hline \end{array}$$

A. 0.015   B. 0.15
C. 1.5   D. not here

7. Which is the least common multiple of 4 and 10?

A. 10   B. 20
C. 30   D. 40

8. Which fraction is in simplest form?

A. $\frac{3}{15}$ B. $\frac{5}{20}$
C. $\frac{4}{12}$ D. $\frac{4}{9}$

9. $\frac{2}{3} + \frac{5}{6} = n$

A. $\frac{3}{4}$ B. $\frac{7}{9}$
C. $1\frac{1}{6}$ D. not here

10. 400 oz = ▮ lb

A. 25   B. 30
C. 40   D. not here

11.
$$\begin{array}{r} 6\ \text{min}\quad 34\ \text{sec} \\ +\ 5\ \text{min}\quad 47\ \text{sec} \\ \hline \end{array}$$

A. 47 sec   B. 11 min 21 sec
C. 12 min   D. 12 min 21 sec

12. Which is the perimeter of the rectangle?

3 m
9 m

A. 3 m   B. 9 m
C. 24 m   D. 27 m

13. Alan can take a vacation in June, July, or August. He can go to the mountains, go to the beach, or visit Washington, D.C. How many choices does he have?

A. 3 choices   B. 6 choices
C. 9 choices   D. 12 choices

14. A computer program generates the digits 1–3 at random 50 times. About how many times would you expect each digit to occur?

A. about 1 time   B. about 3 times
C. about 17 times   D. about 50 times

COMPUTER
Connection

Computers can do many kinds of work, They help writers, business people, artists, doctors, and lawyers. They can also do work for you in mathematics.

In this section you will explore LOGO, use a word processor, make a spreadsheet, and build a data base. You will be using the kinds of computer programs that many people use at their jobs and at home.

Table of Contents

▶ ▶ ▶ ▶ ▶ ▶ ▶ ▶

LOGO Graphics
Introducing Variables

You can use different numbers and turtle commands to draw interesting pictures. The computer will remember and do a series of these commands if you put them in a **procedure**.

LOGO COMMANDS	
FD 30	The turtle moves FORWARD 30 steps.
BK 50	The turtle moves BACKWARD 50 steps.
LT 90	The turtle turns to the LEFT 90°.
RT 135	The turtle turns to the RIGHT 135°.
PU	(PENUP) The turtle moves without leaving a trail.
PD	(PENDOWN) The turtle moves and leaves a trail.
DRAW	The screen clears and the turtle returns HOME.
HOME	The turtle returns to the center of the screen.

a. The procedure STAR tells the turtle to draw a star every time the procedure is called.

```
TO STAR
   REPEAT 5 [FD 30 RT 144]
END
```

b. Suppose you want to change the size of the star. To make the star bigger, you can change the FORWARD command to FD 50. To make the star smaller, you can change the FORWARD command to FD 20. A **variable** lets you change the numbers in a procedure. This procedure with the variable :SIZE draws a star of any size.

```
TO STAR :SIZE
   REPEAT 5 [FD :SIZE RT 144]
END
```

c. This example shows how the value 60 replaced the variable :SIZE in the procedure STAR to draw this figure.

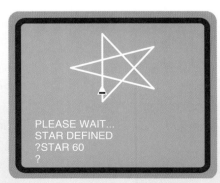

PLEASE WAIT...
STAR DEFINED
?STAR 60
?

At the Computer

1. Experiment with different turtle commands. Then write a procedure to draw these five angles.
   a. obtuse **b.** acute **c.** right **d.** straight **e.** 72°

2. Write a procedure that will make angles of any size. Name the procedure ANGLE, and use a variable called X.

3. Look at the computer screens below. Type the procedure TIME. Input different times from 1 to 12. Name the kind of angle the hands of the clock make. For example, the procedure TIME with a variable value of 3 makes a right angle. The variable value 8 makes an obtuse angle.

```
TO TIME :HOUR
    REPEAT 36 [FD 10 RT 10]
    PU RT 90 FD 55 PD LT 90 FD 40
    LT 135 FD 8 BK 8 RT 270
    FD 8 BK 8 LT 135 BK 40
    RT: HOUR * 30 FD 25
    LT 135 FD 8 BK 8 RT 270 FD 8
END

EDIT: CTRL-C TO DEFINE, CTRL-G
TO ABORT
```

```
PLEASE  WAIT...
TIME  DEFINED
?TIME 3
?HT
```

```
PLEASE  WAIT...
TIME  DEFINED
?TIME 8
?HT
```

Talk About It

▶ In the procedure TIME, what commands draw the circle?

▶ How can you identify a variable in a procedure?

▶ What times on the clock make right angles?

▶ If the hands on the clock were extended, what would happen to the size of the angle?

▶ Why is it useful to use a variable in the procedure TIME to draw 12 clock faces?

LOGO Graphics

Procedures, Variables, and Geometry

You can teach the turtle to repeat a procedure or a group of commands. The REPEAT command was used to make these polygons.

OCTAGON

REPEAT 8 [FD 30 LT 45]

PENTAGON

REPEAT 5 [FD 30 LT 72]

The number after REPEAT tells the turtle how many times to do the commands in the brackets [ ] that follow. Can you find a relationship between the distance of the LEFT turn and the number of times the steps are repeated? What is the product of those two numbers?

At the Computer

Write procedures to make these polygons.

1. hexagon (six sides)

2. decagon (ten sides)

3. square (four sides)

4. triangle (three sides)

Talk About It

▶ What happens when you change the FORWARD command?

▶ How can you use multiplication or division to draw polygons?

▶ What two numbers in the procedures, whose product is 360, close the figure?

▶ What are the only things that change in the procedures?

Variables can help you make polygons of many different sizes and shapes with the same procedure. For example, this procedure can draw pentagons of many different sizes.

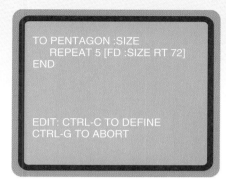

```
TO PENTAGON :SIZE
    REPEAT 5 [FD :SIZE RT 72]
END



EDIT: CTRL-C TO DEFINE
CTRL-G TO ABORT
```

```
PLEASE WAIT...
PENTAGON DEFINED
?PENTAGON 70
?
```

At the Computer

1. Test the procedure PENTAGON with different numbers. Then change your other polygon procedures so that they use variables for the FORWARD steps.

2. Type the procedure below, and test different numbers to see what polygons you and your partner can make. For example, typing POLYGON 3 50 after the procedure POLYGON is defined will make a triangle. Each side is 50 turtle steps.

```
TO POLYGON :NUMSIDES :SIZE
    REPEAT :NUMSIDES [FD :SIZE RT 360/ :NUMSIDES]
END
```

3. Why does the command RT 360/ :NUMSIDES give the proper angle turn for each polygon?

4. What numbers will complete these commands to make the figure below?

REPEAT ▨ [RT 60 REPEAT 120 [FD 2 RT ▨]]

Recursion is a way of doing something over and over. To understand what it means, look at this math application.

Jamie and four classmates are sitting in a circle, playing the math recursion game. Jamie thinks of the number 7 and uses the rule to add 3 to her number. Her new number is 10. She tells Ken, the person to her right, to do the same thing. Ken adds 3 to the number 10 and gets 13. He tells Maria to do the same thing. This can continue forever since they are sitting in a circle. The only way to stop it is to interrupt the game.

At the Computer

Look at the computer screen. You can draw the design on the right by using computer recursion. Like Jamie and her friends, the computer starts with a number and follows the computer commands until it is interrupted. Some computers have different ways of being interrupted.

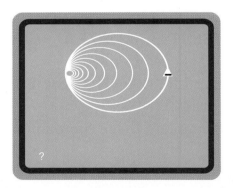

The following recursive procedure tells the computer to move 2 more steps forward every time it reads the REPEAT command to make an oval. The process is repeated until interrupted. Find how your LOGO program can be interrupted.

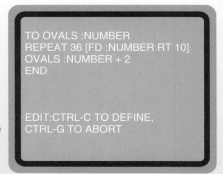

```
TO OVALS :NUMBER
REPEAT 36 [FD :NUMBER RT 10]
OVALS :NUMBER + 2
END



EDIT:CTRL-C TO DEFINE,
CTRL-G TO ABORT
```

At the Computer

1. How can you finish the following procedure so that it uses recursion to make a spiral of triangles?

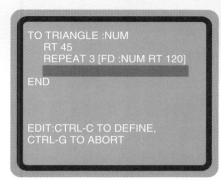 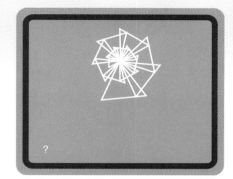

2. Use the REPEAT command, variables, and recursion to make pictures similar to the following ones. Both pictures were made by the same procedure!

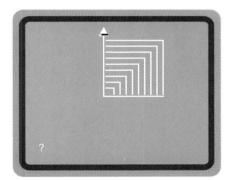 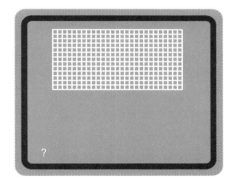

Talk About It

► How can you interrupt a recursive procedure on *your* computer?

► Why does the drawing continue to "grow" if you do not interrupt the procedure?

► What happens when the turtle goes off the screen?

► What command in procedure TRIANGLE, Exercise 1, turns the triangle?

► How can you tell if a LOGO procedure is recursive?

► What step in procedure TRIANGLE, Exercise 1, makes the procedure recursive?

A **word processing** program can help you plan complicated LOGO, spreadsheet, and data base problems. The programming steps that follow will help you plan a LOGO drawing.

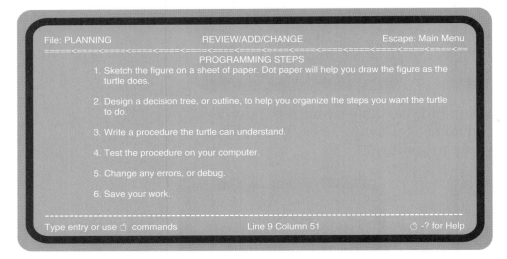

```
File: PLANNING              REVIEW/ADD/CHANGE              Escape: Main Menu
=====<====<====<====<====<====<====<====<====<====<====<====<====<====<==
                        PROGRAMMING STEPS
        1. Sketch the figure on a sheet of paper. Dot paper will help you draw the figure as the
           turtle does.

        2. Design a decision tree, or outline, to help you organize the steps you want the turtle
           to do.

        3. Write a procedure the turtle can understand.

        4. Test the procedure on your computer.

        5. Change any errors, or debug.

        6. Save your work.

----------------------------------------------------------------------
Type entry or use ⌂ commands            Line 9 Column 51            ⌂ -? for Help
```

At the Computer

1. After you learn about *your* word processor, type the programming steps. You will need to use these word processing operations.

   a. Start a new document.
   b. Correct typing mistakes by deleting or inserting characters.
   c. Save your document on a formatted disk.
   d. Print your document.

2. Using the programming steps, plan a LOGO drawing. Use your word processor to write a plan for the drawing.

Talk About It

▶ Why is planning important?

▶ What steps in the planning process are easy to do on a word processer? What steps are hard to do?

▶ What are some advantages and disadvantages of planning on a word processor rather than on a sheet of paper?

Investigate at the Computer

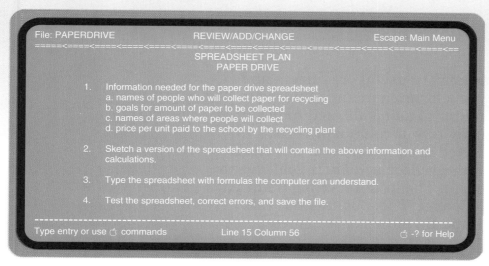

File: PAPERDRIVE   REVIEW/ADD/CHANGE   Escape: Main Menu

SPREADSHEET PLAN
PAPER DRIVE

1. Information needed for the paper drive spreadsheet
   a. names of people who will collect paper for recycling
   b. goals for amount of paper to be collected
   c. names of areas where people will collect
   d. price per unit paid to the school by the recycling plant

2. Sketch a version of the spreadsheet that will contain the above information and calculations.

3. Type the spreadsheet with formulas the computer can understand.

4. Test the spreadsheet, correct errors, and save the file.

Type entry or use ⌂ commands   Line 15 Column 56   ⌂ -? for Help

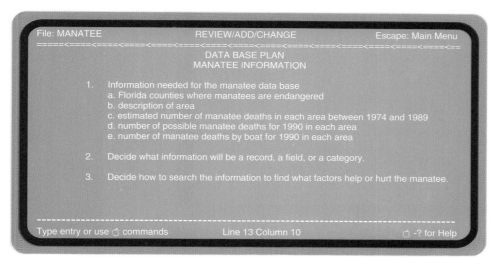

File: MANATEE   REVIEW/ADD/CHANGE   Escape: Main Menu

DATA BASE PLAN
MANATEE INFORMATION

1. Information needed for the manatee data base
   a. Florida counties where manatees are endangered
   b. description of area
   c. estimated number of manatee deaths in each area between 1974 and 1989
   d. number of possible manatee deaths for 1990 in each area
   e. number of manatee deaths by boat for 1990 in each area

2. Decide what information will be a record, a field, or a category.

3. Decide how to search the information to find what factors help or hurt the manatee.

Type entry or use ⌂ commands   Line 13 Column 10   ⌂ -? for Help

At the Computer

3. Look at the computer screens. Practice using your word processor by typing the spreadsheet plan. Name the document PAPERDRIVE.

4. Learn to copy the spreadsheet plan into another document. Then revise the document to make your own plan to collect aluminum cans for recycling. Name the new document CANDRIVE.

5. Use your word processor to type the data base plan. Name the document MANATEE. Copy the data base plan into another document. Type your own plan for a data base that will contain information about an animal species you care about. Give the document an appropriate file name.

Spreadsheet Math

Working with Formulas

Spreadsheet programs are useful organizers and calculators. You can type a formula in any of the cells. The formula can tell a computer to add, subtract, multiply, or divide the numbers in any row or column of **cells.**

Seven students collected used paper from two cities to raise money for their fifth-grade class. Their goal was to collect 100 pounds of paper. The local recycling plant pays $0.50 for every pound of paper. The students put this information in cells B1 and B2 of this spreadsheet.

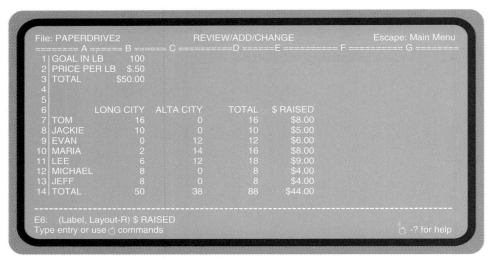

```
File: PAPERDRIVE2              REVIEW/ADD/CHANGE              Escape: Main Menu
======== A ====== B ====== C ==========D ======E =========== F =========== G ========
  1 | GOAL IN LB      100
  2 | PRICE PER LB   $.50
  3 | TOTAL         $50.00
  4 |
  5 |
  6 |           LONG CITY   ALTA CITY    TOTAL    $ RAISED
  7 | TOM          16          0          16       $8.00
  8 | JACKIE       10          0          10       $5.00
  9 | EVAN          0         12          12       $6.00
 10 | MARIA         2         14          16       $8.00
 11 | LEE           6         12          18       $9.00
 12 | MICHAEL       8          0           8       $4.00
 13 | JEFF          8          0           8       $4.00
 14 | TOTAL        50         38          88      $44.00

------------------------------------------------------------------------
E6:    (Label, Layout-R) $ RAISED
Type entry or use ☐ commands                              ☐ -? for help
```

The students typed the formula (B1*B2) in cell B3 to determine how much they could earn. The computer uses the * symbol as a multiplication sign. The formula tells the computer to see what numbers live in cells B1 and B2. Then it tells the computer to multiply the two numbers and to put the answer in cell B3 where the formula lives. Both the formula and the answer can live in the same cell.

Talk About It

▶ How can the computer calculate Maria's contribution?

▶ What does the number in cell D14 represent?

▶ Describe what the numbers in column E represent?

▶ What information do you need to calculate how much money each student earned for the class?

At the Computer

1. Learn how to format *your* spreadsheet by practicing the following operations.

   a. Widen columns.

   b. Add or delete rows and columns.

   c. Add $, %, or ¢ signs to special numbers.

   d. Write numbers as characters, not values, Example: Type 16/100 as a label, not as the formula 16/100.

   e. Copy a formula using an **absolute** cell reference. This will not change the cell addresses in the formula.

   f. Copy a formula using a **relative** cell reference. This will change the cell addresses in the formula in the direction you are copying.

   g. Lay out words or titles in the cells (right, left, or center).

   h. Erase a cell.

2. Format the following spreadsheet on your computer. These are some of the formulas.

   a. Cell B14 contains the formula @SUM(B7..B13).

   b. Cell D7 contains the formula (B7+C7).

   c. Cell E11 contains "18/100.

   d. Cell F12 contains the formula (D12/B1).

   e. Cell G8 contains the formula (D8*B2).

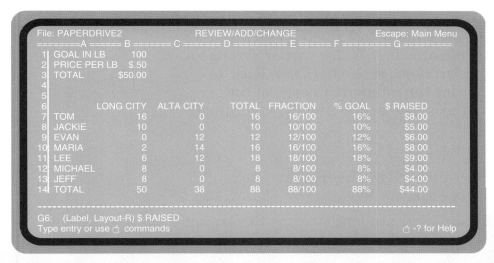

File: PAPERDRIVE2			REVIEW/ADD/CHANGE			Escape: Main Menu	
A	B	C	D	E	F	G	
1 GOAL IN LB	100						
2 PRICE PER LB	$.50						
3 TOTAL	$50.00						
4							
5							
6	LONG CITY	ALTA CITY		TOTAL	FRACTION	% GOAL	$ RAISED
7 TOM	16	0		16	16/100	16%	$8.00
8 JACKIE	10	0		10	10/100	10%	$5.00
9 EVAN	0	12		12	12/100	12%	$6.00
10 MARIA	2	14		16	16/100	16%	$8.00
11 LEE	6	12		18	18/100	18%	$9.00
12 MICHAEL	8	0		8	8/100	8%	$4.00
13 JEFF	8	0		8	8/100	8%	$4.00
14 TOTAL	50	38		88	88/100	88%	$44.00

G6:   (Label, Layout-R) $ RAISED
Type entry or use ⌂ commands   ⌂ -? for Help

Talk About It

▶ What do the numbers in column F represent?

▶ What is the relationship between the numbers in columns E and F?

▶ What do the formulas in column G calculate?

Spreadsheet
Sorting

Some fifth graders at Lake Teague Elementary School collected aluminum cans for recycling. They organized their information on this spreadsheet. They will use the data to find the mean, median, mode, and range for the number of cans collected each day of the week.

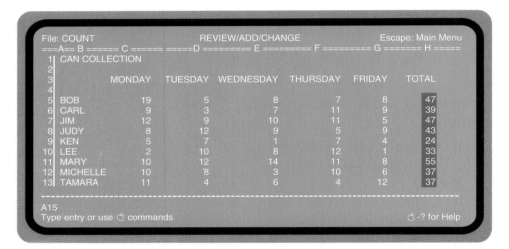

```
File: COUNT                    REVIEW/ADD/CHANGE              Escape: Main Menu
===A== B ===== C ===== =====D ========= E ========= F ========= G ======= H =====
  1| CAN COLLECTION
  2|
  3|            MONDAY   TUESDAY  WEDNESDAY  THURSDAY   FRIDAY    TOTAL
  4|
  5| BOB          19        5         8         7         8        47
  6| CARL          9        3         7        11         9        39
  7| JIM          12        9        10        11         5        47
  8| JUDY          8       12         9         5         9        43
  9| KEN           5        7         1         7         4        24
 10| LEE           2       10         8        12         1        33
 11| MARY         10       12        14        11         8        55
 12| MICHELLE     10        8         3        10         6        37
 13| TAMARA       11        4         6         4        12        37

A15
Type entry or use ⌘ commands                              ⌘ -? for Help
```

The spreadsheet program has a tool that can sort a column of words alphabetically. It will also sort or arrange a column of numbers from greatest to least or from least to greatest. The tool can order the numbers in each of the columns so that you can pick the median, mode, and range.

At the Computer

1. Group project: Choose a recyclable item and make a spreadsheet like the one above.

2. Work with three or four other students to type the example spreadsheet (or your own) so that the names of the people are not in alphabetical order. Then use the **arrange** or **sorting** tool on *your* computer to alphabetize the list.

3. Copy a formula like (C5+D5+E5+F5+G5) in the cells of column H to add all the items collected during the week by each person.

4. Learn to use the sorting command on your computer. Practice by arranging the numbers in the Monday column from greatest to least.

At the Computer

5. Sort the numbers in each of the days of the week to help you find the median, mode, and range for each day. Keep track of your discoveries on a separate sheet of paper or on another section of the same spreadsheet.

6. Finally, copy a formula that will calculate the mean number of items collected each day. For example, the formula ((F5+F6+F7+F8+F9+F10+F11+F12+F13)/9) in cell F18 calculates the mean for Thursday.

This is part of the spreadsheet for the Lake Teague Elementary School can collection.

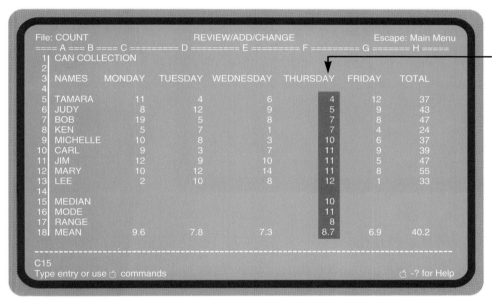

```
File: COUNT                    REVIEW/ADD/CHANGE                  Escape: Main Menu
==== A === B ==== C ========= D ========= E ========= F ========= G ======= H =====
 1| CAN COLLECTION
 2|
 3| NAMES    MONDAY    TUESDAY  WEDNESDAY   THURSDAY  FRIDAY    TOTAL
 4|
 5| TAMARA     11         4          6          4       12        37
 6| JUDY        8        12          9          5        9        43
 7| BOB        19         5          8          7        8        47
 8| KEN         5         7          1          7        4        24
 9| MICHELLE   10         8          3         10        6        37
10| CARL        9         3          7         11        9        39
11| JIM        12         9         10         11        5        47
12| MARY       10        12         14         11        8        55
13| LEE         2        10          8         12        1        33
14|
15| MEDIAN                                     10
16| MODE                                       11
17| RANGE                                       8
18| MEAN       9.6        7.8        7.3        8.7      6.9       40.2


C15
Type entry or use ⌂ commands                                   ⌂ -? for Help
```

The median will be in the middle of the list. The modes will be listed together. The greatest and least numbers will be at the top and bottom of the list to calculate the range.

Talk About It

▶ How can you be sure a formula is working correctly in a spreadsheet?

▶ When you arrange a column, what happens to the information in the other columns?

▶ How does ordering the numbers help you to find the median, mode, and range?

▶ What happens to the formulas when you sort a column?

▶ How is finding the median, mode, and range different from finding the mean?

Data Base

Searching for Information

The following data base contains information about the West Indian manatee, a large, gentle mammal. The manatee is an endangered species that lives along the Florida coast. The data base lists five counties where many manatee deaths have occurred in the past 16 years. The purpose of the data base is to organize information and to search a list for clues about manatee deaths.

FIGURE 1

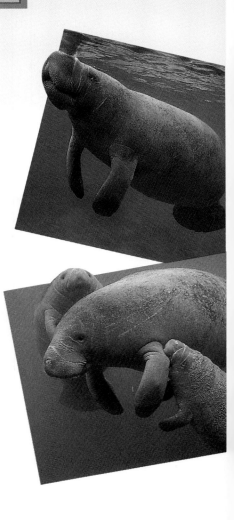

File:SAVEMANATEE		REVIEW/ADD/CHANGE		Escape: Main Menu
Selection: All records				
COUNTY	DESCRIPTION	1974-1989 DEATHS	1990 DEATHS	1990 BOAT DEATHS
BREVARD	RIVER & COASTLINE	285	62	7
DADE	EVERGLADES SWAMP	95	4	1
COLLIER	MARCO ISLAND	127	13	7
LEE	RIVER AREA	222	27	5
DUVAL	RIVER & COASTLINE	142	13	1

Type entry or use ♢ commands · 32K Avail.

Answer the questions about the data base.

1. How many **categories** does the manatee data base have? One category is 1990 DEATHS.

2. How many **records** does the manatee data base have? This is an example of a record.

   BREVARD   RIVER & COASTLINE   285   62   7

3. The BOAT DEATHS category indicates how many manatees were killed by boats in 1990 in each county. Compare the numbers in the 1990 BOAT DEATHS category to the 1990 DEATHS category. How can this comparison be used to help the manatee?

Talk About It

▶ What other categories can you add to the manatee data base? Why?

▶ If you get more information about the manatee from other counties, how can you add it to the data base?

At the Computer

4. Type the manatee data base on your computer.

5. Save the information on a disk.

6. Tell the computer to organize the counties from greatest to least number of manatee deaths.

7. Tell the computer to list the record that contains the words MARCO ISLAND.

8. Tell the computer to print a list of the records.

The following computer screen shows that the computer selected records containing the word RIVER, showing more than 130 manatee deaths in 1974–1989, and more than 4 boat deaths in 1990. The computer listed all the records that followed the search rules entered.

FIGURE 2

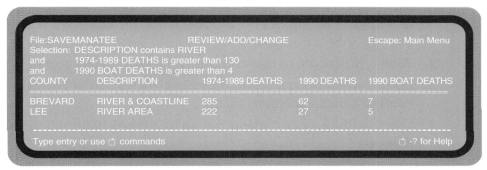

Look at Figure 1 on page 462 to answer the following questions.

9. List the records that contain the word RIVER.

10. List the records that contain numbers greater than 130 in the 1974–1989 DEATHS category.

11. List the records that contain numbers greater than 4 in the BOAT DEATHS category.

12. Now, list the records that contain the information in numbers 1, 2, and 3. Does your list look like the computer list in Figure 1?

Talk About It

▶ When is it better to let the computer search a list for information?

▶ What is the purpose of setting up rules for a computer search?

IDEA BANK

LOGO IDEAS

1. Use this procedure to draw a spiral.
   TO SP :ANGLE :SIDE
      RT :ANGLE
      FD :SIDE
      SP :ANGLE :SIDE +4
   END

Use different numbers for the angle and the side. Save and print your best designs.

2. Write a procedure to draw obtuse, acute, and straight angles.

3. Make several polygons with sides and angles that are equal. What are these polygons called?

4. Use the REPEAT command, variables, and recursion to make a design.

WORD PROCESSING IDEAS

5. Write a story about a time when you had to multiply or divide numbers outside of school.

6. Write a plan for a spreadsheet to gather information about a fund raiser. Make a list of the data and calculations that will make the spreadsheet useful.

7. Explain to a visitor from another planet how to draw a design by using LOGO and recursion.

8. Write a plan to design a data base that will contain information about your classmates. Make a list of things that you want to remember, such as each person's birthday, phone number, address, and favorite color.

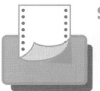

SPREADSHEET AND DATA BASE IDEAS

9. Make a spreadsheet to organize fund raising information discussed in Exercise 6. Consider organizing the names of people who participated, the number of items collected, and total dollars raised.

10. Make a data base to organize the information you collected about your classmates in Exercise 8. Direct the computer to sort and find data that is important to you.

11. Make a spreadsheet that contains the same information in Exercise 10. Use the sorting command to arrange the data. Which program, data base, or spreadsheet is the better organizer? Why?

12. Make a spreadsheet that calculates the perimeter of your bedroom, bed, desk, and math book. All your data should be in inches. What spreadsheet formula will convert inches into feet for large measurements?

13. With four or five classmates, gather the information in Exercise 12, and put all the results in a group data base. Tell the computer to print a list of the larger objects.

14. Ask a group of classmates these questions.

a. What is your full name?

b. How much money do you spend on dessert per week?

c. How much money do you spend on drinks per week?

d. How much money do you spend in the cafeteria per week?

Put the information in a data base program. Tell the computer to sort through the list to find the people who spend more than $5.00 on food and drinks per week.

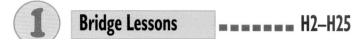

Student **H**andbook

Bridge Lessons

CHAPTER I

Numbers to Thousands

In this lesson you will explore how ones, tens, hundreds, and thousands are related.

WORK TOGETHER

Building Understanding

Use graph paper to make place-value models.

Color 1 square, and label it *one*.

Color 10 squares in a row, and label them *ten*.

Color 100 squares in 10 rows of 10, and label them *one hundred.*

Since □ = 1, then ▯ = 10, and ▦ = 100.

one   ten   one hundred

Use graph paper to make models for 40, 90, 200, and 600.

Talk About It

▶ How many hundreds are in each number?

▶ How many tens are in each number? How many ones?

Since ▦ = 100, then 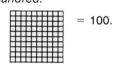 = 1,000.

one hundred   one thousand

▶ How many hundreds are in 1,000? How many tens? How many ones?

———————————

Numbers can be expressed in different ways.

Standard Form: 600
Expanded Form: $(6 \times 100) + (0 \times 10) + (0 \times 1)$
Word Form: six hundred

• How can you express 657 in two other forms?

Practice

Here are some statements about 1,000. Write *true* or *false*.

1. There are more than 1,000 books in the classroom.

2. A line of one thousand squares (■) would reach from the classroom door to the principal's office.

3. One thousand equals 10 hundreds.

Use place-value models to show each number. Then write how many thousands, hundreds, tens, or ones you used.

4. 846 = ■ hundreds, ■ tens, ■ ones

5. 406 = ■ hundreds, ■ tens, ■ ones

6. 8,374 = ■ thousands, ■ hundreds, ■ tens, ■ ones

7. 30 = ■ tens, ■ ones

8. 866 = ■ hundreds, ■ tens, ■ ones

9. 5,559 = ■ thousands, ■ hundreds, ■ tens, ■ ones

What kind of container would hold 1,000 pencils?

What item could you buy with 1,000 pennies?

From the front door of the school, where would you be if you took 1,000 steps?

Write two other forms for each number.

10. $(4 \times 100) + (8 \times 10) + (5 \times 1)$

11. twenty-nine

12. $(9 \times 10) + (3 \times 1)$

13. eight hundred three

14. three hundred fifty-three

15. 675

16. $(2 \times 100) + (0 \times 10) + (4 \times 1)$

17. 700

18. five thousand, forty-seven

19. 6,110

20. $(6 \times 1,000) + (0 \times 100) + (0 \times 10) + (3 \times 1)$

Write the value of the underlined digit.

21. 3<u>4</u>5

22. <u>1</u>6

23. 1,0<u>7</u>5

24. <u>5</u>89

25. <u>7</u>,900

26. 2,43<u>9</u>

27. 90<u>0</u>

28. 6,0<u>9</u>8

29. 4<u>3</u>5

30. 8,4<u>5</u>2

Solve.

31. I am a number greater than 99 but less than 101. What am I?

32. I am a number less than 1,050 but greater than 1,048. What am I?

Patterns in Addition and Subtraction

Counting On

$5 + 3 = 8$

Think: 5 . . . 6, 7, 8

$$\begin{array}{r} 5 \\ +3 \\ \hline 8 \end{array}$$ ← addend ← addend ← sum

Zero

$8 + 0 = 8$

$$\begin{array}{r} 8 \\ +0 \\ \hline 8 \end{array}$$

Doubles

$4 + 4 = 8$

$$\begin{array}{r} 4 \\ +4 \\ \hline 8 \end{array}$$

Doubles Plus One

$6 + 5 = 11$

Think: 1 more than 5 + 5

$$\begin{array}{r} 6 \\ + 5 \\ \hline 11 \end{array}$$

When one of the addends is 1, 2, or 3, *count on* to find the sum.

When you add *zero* to a number, the sum is that number.

If both addends are the same, you are adding *doubles*.

When one addend is one more than the other, you can use *doubles plus one* to find the sum.

You can use the addition methods to find patterns in the table.

- Use the *zero* method to find sums on the addition table. What pattern do you notice?

- Use the *doubles* method to find sums on the addition table. What pattern do you notice?

- Use the *doubles plus one* method to find sums on the addition table. What pattern do you notice?

+	0	1	2	3	4	5	6	7	8	9
0	0	1	2	3	4	5	6	7	8	9
1	1	2	3	4	5	6	7	8	9	10
2	2	3	4	5	6	7	8	9	10	11
3	3	4	5	6	7	8	9	10	11	12
4	4	5	6	7	8	9	10	11	12	13
5	5	6	7	8	9	10	11	12	13	14
6	6	7	8	9	10	11	12	13	14	15
7	7	8	9	10	11	12	13	14	15	16
8	8	9	10	11	12	13	14	15	16	17
9	9	10	11	12	13	14	15	16	17	18

Since addition and subtraction are opposite operations, you can use the addition table to subtract.

Example: $10 - 6 = 4$

Begin at 6 in the first row.

Move down the column to 10.

From 10, move left to the first column to find the difference.

+	0	1	2	3	4	5	6	7	8	9
0	0	1	2	3	4	5	6	7	8	9
1	1	2	3	4	5	6	7	8	9	10
2	2	3	4	5	6	7	8	9	10	11
3	3	4	5	6	7	8	9	10	11	12
4	4	5	6	7	8	9	10	11	12	13
5	5	6	7	8	9	10	11	12	13	14
6	6	7	8	9	10	11	12	13	14	15
7	7	8	9	10	11	12	13	14	15	16
8	8	9	10	11	12	13	14	15	16	17
9	9	10	11	12	13	14	15	16	17	18

Practice

Find the sum. Name the addition method.

1. $4 + 5 = $ ▨
2. $6 + 0 = $ ▨
3. $7 + 2 = $ ▨

4. $7 + 8 = $ ▨
5. $8 + 8 = $ ▨
6. $3 + 4 = $ ▨

7. $12 + 0 = $ ▨
8. $9 + 3 = $ ▨
9. $1 + 9 = $ ▨

10. $4 + 0 = $ ▨
11. $2 + 3 = $ ▨
12. $3 + 7 = $ ▨

13. $6 + 2 = $ ▨
14. $4 + 4 = $ ▨
15. $1 + 4 = $ ▨

16. $7 + 7 = $ ▨
17. $6 + 6 = $ ▨
18. $5 + 3 = $ ▨

19. $8 + 0 = $ ▨
20. $5 + 6 = $ ▨
21. $9 + 1 = $ ▨

22. $\begin{array}{r} 7 \\ +6 \\ \hline \end{array}$
23. $\begin{array}{r} 3 \\ +5 \\ \hline \end{array}$
24. $\begin{array}{r} 2 \\ +9 \\ \hline \end{array}$
25. $\begin{array}{r} 6 \\ +0 \\ \hline \end{array}$
26. $\begin{array}{r} 8 \\ +9 \\ \hline \end{array}$

27. $\begin{array}{r} 3 \\ +6 \\ \hline \end{array}$
28. $\begin{array}{r} 1 \\ +8 \\ \hline \end{array}$
29. $\begin{array}{r} 2 \\ +6 \\ \hline \end{array}$
30. $\begin{array}{r} 5 \\ +5 \\ \hline \end{array}$
31. $\begin{array}{r} 0 \\ +4 \\ \hline \end{array}$

Find the missing addend. Write a subtraction sentence.

32. $6 + $ ▨ $= 13$
33. $3 + $ ▨ $= 8$
34. $9 + $ ▨ $= 13$

35. $8 + $ ▨ $= 14$
36. $5 + $ ▨ $= 10$
37. $6 + $ ▨ $= 12$

38. $9 + $ ▨ $= 16$
39. $3 + $ ▨ $= 5$
40. $3 + $ ▨ $= 10$

Add or subtract.

41. $\begin{array}{r} 15 \\ -\ 7 \\ \hline \end{array}$
42. $\begin{array}{r} 7 \\ +7 \\ \hline \end{array}$
43. $\begin{array}{r} 9 \\ +3 \\ \hline \end{array}$
44. $\begin{array}{r} 14 \\ -\ 4 \\ \hline \end{array}$
45. $\begin{array}{r} 13 \\ -\ 5 \\ \hline \end{array}$

Solve.

46. Claire waited 6 minutes for Mark at the baseball game. Then she waited 5 minutes for Cherie. How long did Claire wait for Mark and Cherie?

47. Robbie won 4 stuffed bears and 5 stuffed rabbits. How many stuffed animals did Robbie win?

Adding 2- and 3-Digit Numbers

A basketball team scored 27 points in the first half of a game and 35 points in the second half. How many points did the team score in all?

You can add to find how many points the team scored in all.

Add: 27 + 35 = ▨

Step 1 Add the ones.	**Step 2** Regroup 12 ones as 1 ten 2 ones.	**Step 3** Add the tens.
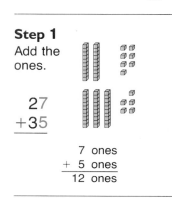 27 +35 7 ones + 5 ones 12 ones	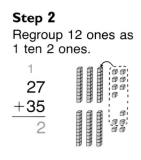 1 27 +35 2	1 27 +35 62

So, the team scored 62 points in all.

More Examples

A.	47 +32 79	**B.**	1 35 +59 94	**C.**	83 +65 148	**D.**	1 58 +74 132

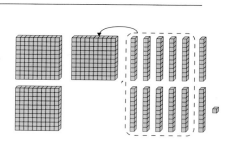

- What columns were regrouped in Examples B, C, and D?

  _____

You can use what you know about adding two-digit numbers to help you add three-digit numbers.

Add: 154 + 167 = ▨

Step 1 Add the ones. Regroup 11 ones as 1 ten 1 one.	**Step 2** Add the tens. Regroup 12 tens as 1 hundred 2 tens. Add the hundreds.
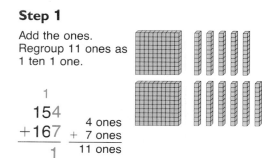 1 154 +167 1 4 ones + 7 ones 11 ones	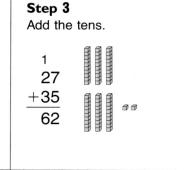 11 154 +167 321 1 ten 5 tens + 6 tens 12 tens

Practice

Find the sum. In Exercises 1–15, circle the columns in which you regrouped.

1. $\begin{array}{r} 52 \\ +\ 9 \\ \hline \end{array}$	**2.** $\begin{array}{r} 15 \\ +\ 6 \\ \hline \end{array}$	**3.** $\begin{array}{r} 14 \\ +\ 9 \\ \hline \end{array}$	**4.** $\begin{array}{r} 63 \\ +12 \\ \hline \end{array}$	**5.** $\begin{array}{r} 21 \\ +19 \\ \hline \end{array}$
6. $\begin{array}{r} 13 \\ +47 \\ \hline \end{array}$	**7.** $\begin{array}{r} 18 \\ +17 \\ \hline \end{array}$	**8.** $\begin{array}{r} 65 \\ +39 \\ \hline \end{array}$	**9.** $\begin{array}{r} 24 \\ +16 \\ \hline \end{array}$	**10.** $\begin{array}{r} 44 \\ +28 \\ \hline \end{array}$
11. $\begin{array}{r} 38 \\ +69 \\ \hline \end{array}$	**12.** $\begin{array}{r} 69 \\ +36 \\ \hline \end{array}$	**13.** $\begin{array}{r} 27 \\ +46 \\ \hline \end{array}$	**14.** $\begin{array}{r} 33 \\ +39 \\ \hline \end{array}$	**15.** $\begin{array}{r} 54 \\ +18 \\ \hline \end{array}$

Find the sum.

16. $72 + 19 = $ ▨ **17.** $29 + 32 = $ ▨ **18.** $66 + 28 = $ ▨ **19.** $33 + 64 = $ ▨

20. $48 + 65 = $ ▨ **21.** $69 + 37 = $ ▨ **22.** $98 + 89 = $ ▨ **23.** $13 + 79 = $ ▨

24. $45 + 39 = $ ▨ **25.** $58 + 77 = $ ▨ **26.** $34 + 79 = $ ▨ **27.** $17 + 56 = $ ▨

Find the sum. In Exercises 28–37, circle the columns in which you regrouped.

28. $\begin{array}{r} 169 \\ +\ 26 \\ \hline \end{array}$	**29.** $\begin{array}{r} 213 \\ +\ 94 \\ \hline \end{array}$	**30.** $\begin{array}{r} 462 \\ +318 \\ \hline \end{array}$	**31.** $\begin{array}{r} 610 \\ +297 \\ \hline \end{array}$	**32.** $\begin{array}{r} 337 \\ +145 \\ \hline \end{array}$
33. $\begin{array}{r} 318 \\ +198 \\ \hline \end{array}$	**34.** $\begin{array}{r} 422 \\ +278 \\ \hline \end{array}$	**35.** $\begin{array}{r} 197 \\ +413 \\ \hline \end{array}$	**36.** $\begin{array}{r} 276 \\ +935 \\ \hline \end{array}$	**37.** $\begin{array}{r} 479 \\ +460 \\ \hline \end{array}$

Find the sum.

38. $399 + 211 = $ ▨ **39.** $255 + 546 = $ ▨ **40.** $483 + 118 = $ ▨

41. $855 + 295 = $ ▨ **42.** $469 + 545 = $ ▨ **43.** $633 + 749 = $ ▨

44. $909 + 321 = $ ▨ **45.** $594 + 398 = $ ▨ **46.** $212 + 727 = $ ▨

Solve.

47. The Oak Street School band traveled 38 miles to the game. On the return trip, they went a different way and traveled 29 miles. How many miles did they travel?

48. On Thursday 293 tickets were sold for the game. On Friday 428 tickets were sold for the game. How many tickets were sold in all?

CHAPTER 2

Subtracting 2- and 3-Digit Numbers

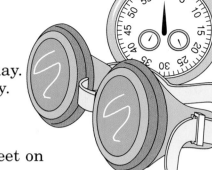

There were 43 students at the swim meet on Wednesday. There were 19 students at the swim meet on Thursday. How many more students were at the swim meet on Wednesday than on Thursday?

To find how many more students were at the swim meet on Wednesday than on Thursday, subtract.

Subtract: $43 - 19 = n$

Step 1	Step 2	Step 3
Decide whether to regroup. Since $9 > 3$, regroup 4 tens 3 ones as 3 tens 13 ones.	Subtract the ones.	Subtract the tens.
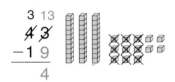		

So, 24 more students were at the swim meet.

You can use what you know about subtracting two-digit numbers to help you subtract three-digit numbers.

Subtract: $243 - 197 = n$

Step 1	Step 2	Step 3
Decide whether to regroup. Since $7 > 3$, regroup 4 tens 3 ones as 3 tens 13 ones. Subtract the ones.	Since $9 > 3$, regroup 2 hundreds 3 tens as 1 hundred 13 tens. Subtract the tens.	Subtract the hundreds.

- How would you have estimated the difference?
- How can you check your subtraction?

Practice

Find the difference. In Exercises 1–15, circle the columns in which you regrouped.

1. 99
   − 23

2. 36
   − 12

3. 43
   − 34

4. 67
   − 27

5. 80
   − 49

6. 78
   − 19

7. 56
   − 27

8. 22
   − 13

9. 75
   − 57

10. 41
    − 29

11. 56
    − 28

12. 31
    − 18

13. 47
    − 18

14. 95
    − 76

15. 80
    − 35

Find the difference.

16. $33 - 26 = n$ 17. $98 - 47 = n$ 18. $60 - 39 = n$

19. $56 - 27 = n$ 20. $87 - 49 = n$ 21. $39 - 25 = n$

Find the difference. In Exercises 22–36, circle the columns in which you regrouped.

22. 465
    − 124

23. 688
    − 317

24. 975
    − 461

25. 738
    − 527

26. 437
    − 218

27. 971
    − 337

28. 396
    − 218

29. 882
    − 713

30. 452
    − 126

31. 532
    − 346

32. 213
    − 98

33. 435
    − 146

34. 582
    − 394

35. 732
    − 545

36. 848
    − 459

Find the difference.

37. $313 - 234 = n$ 38. $463 - 372 = n$ 39. $898 - 789 = n$

40. $244 - 198 = n$ 41. $749 - 568 = n$ 42. $900 - 699 = n$

Solve.

43. Last year the team won 17 basketball games. This year they won 24 basketball games. How many more basketball games did they win this year than last year?

44. On Thursday morning there were 182 tickets to be sold. At the end of the day, 114 tickets had not been sold. How many tickets were sold during the day?

CHAPTER 3

Multiplying 2-Digit Numbers

Meg McNeil likes to make sun catchers. She uses 16 pieces of colored plastic for each flower. How many pieces of plastic does she need to make 4 flowers?

Estimate.   Front-end: $4 \times 10 = 40$

Rounding: $4 \times 20 = 80$

Use place-value blocks to model 4×16.
Then compare your model with this method.

Step 1	**Step 2**	**Step 3**
Multiply the ones. 4 × 6 ones = 24 ones	Regroup 24 ones as 2 tens 4 ones. Record the 2 tens above the 1 ten.	Multiply the tens. Then add the regrouped tens. 4 tens + 2 tens = 6 tens
16 × 4	2 16 × 4 ——— 4	2 16 × 4 ——— 64

So, Meg needs 64 pieces of plastic. Since 64 is close to 80, the answer is reasonable.

Talk About It

▶ Compare the method shown at the right with the shorter method shown above. Explain how the methods differ.

▶ Explain why the 40 is not shown in the problem above.

▶ How does your estimate help you determine whether your answer is reasonable?

T	**O**
1	6
×	4
2	4
4	0
6	4

Practice

Estimate the product.

1. $2 \times 32 = n$

2. $3 \times 26 = n$

3. $2 \times 37 = n$

4. $3 \times 12 = n$

5. $6 \times 23 = n$

6. $3 \times 28 = n$

Find the product.

7. $\begin{array}{r} 18 \\ \times\ 4 \\ \hline \end{array}$

8. $\begin{array}{r} 23 \\ \times\ 3 \\ \hline \end{array}$

9. $\begin{array}{r} 34 \\ \times\ 6 \\ \hline \end{array}$

10. $\begin{array}{r} 43 \\ \times\ 7 \\ \hline \end{array}$

11. $\begin{array}{r} 52 \\ \times\ 8 \\ \hline \end{array}$

12. $\begin{array}{r} 79 \\ \times\ 4 \\ \hline \end{array}$

13. $\begin{array}{r} 45 \\ \times\ 2 \\ \hline \end{array}$

14. $\begin{array}{r} 54 \\ \times\ 4 \\ \hline \end{array}$

15. $\begin{array}{r} 28 \\ \times\ 3 \\ \hline \end{array}$

16. $\begin{array}{r} 29 \\ \times\ 5 \\ \hline \end{array}$

17. $\begin{array}{r} 28 \\ \times\ 5 \\ \hline \end{array}$

18. $\begin{array}{r} 62 \\ \times\ 7 \\ \hline \end{array}$

19. $\begin{array}{r} 37 \\ \times\ 4 \\ \hline \end{array}$

20. $\begin{array}{r} 52 \\ \times\ 6 \\ \hline \end{array}$

21. $\begin{array}{r} 43 \\ \times\ 8 \\ \hline \end{array}$

22. $\begin{array}{r} 35 \\ \times\ 2 \\ \hline \end{array}$

23. $\begin{array}{r} 78 \\ \times\ 8 \\ \hline \end{array}$

24. $\begin{array}{r} 19 \\ \times\ 8 \\ \hline \end{array}$

25. $\begin{array}{r} 24 \\ \times\ 5 \\ \hline \end{array}$

26. $\begin{array}{r} 67 \\ \times\ 9 \\ \hline \end{array}$

27. $\begin{array}{r} 43 \\ \times\ 5 \\ \hline \end{array}$

28. $\begin{array}{r} 32 \\ \times\ 3 \\ \hline \end{array}$

29. $\begin{array}{r} 97 \\ \times\ 4 \\ \hline \end{array}$

30. $\begin{array}{r} 62 \\ \times\ 3 \\ \hline \end{array}$

31. $\begin{array}{r} 40 \\ \times\ 7 \\ \hline \end{array}$

32. $\begin{array}{r} 77 \\ \times\ 3 \\ \hline \end{array}$

33. $\begin{array}{r} 21 \\ \times\ 5 \\ \hline \end{array}$

34. $\begin{array}{r} 36 \\ \times\ 6 \\ \hline \end{array}$

35. $\begin{array}{r} 87 \\ \times\ 8 \\ \hline \end{array}$

36. $\begin{array}{r} 14 \\ \times\ 9 \\ \hline \end{array}$

37. $\begin{array}{r} 45 \\ \times\ 4 \\ \hline \end{array}$

38. $\begin{array}{r} 31 \\ \times\ 7 \\ \hline \end{array}$

39. $\begin{array}{r} 67 \\ \times\ 5 \\ \hline \end{array}$

40. $\begin{array}{r} 54 \\ \times\ 6 \\ \hline \end{array}$

41. $\begin{array}{r} 13 \\ \times\ 8 \\ \hline \end{array}$

42. $7 \times 64 = n$

43. $5 \times 48 = n$

44. $3 \times 86 = n$

45. $6 \times 17 = n$

46. $9 \times 56 = n$

47. $8 \times 43 = n$

48. $3 \times 39 = n$

49. $4 \times 42 = n$

50. $5 \times 27 = n$

51. $3 \times 72 = n$

52. $6 \times 35 = n$

53. $4 \times 59 = n$

Solve.

54. Leon sold 27 sun catchers. Pete sold twice as many as Leon. How many sun catchers did Pete sell?

55. Maria sold 4 sun catchers for $12 each. How much money did she receive for the sun catchers?

CHAPTER 4

Exploring Plane Figures and Polygons

Some plane figures are polygons.

| triangle | square | rectangle | | curve | angle | circle | figure with crossed lines |

These are polygons.   These are *not* polygons.

Polygons are made up of line segments that do not cross.

WORK TOGETHER

Use string to model plane figures.

Cut a piece of string about 6 feet long. Lay the string on a flat table or a desk top. Make sure that the ends do not touch. This is an **open figure.**

Talk About It

▶ How do you know that the string forms a plane figure?

▶ How can you make a closed figure with the string?

Tie the ends of the string. Now, have three people in the group each hold a point on the string. Each point shows where two line segments meet and is called a **vertex.**

▶ What is the figure that you made? Is it a closed figure?

▶ Is the figure a plane figure? How do you know?

▶ If one person lifts up a point, will the figure be in a different plane?

▶ Is the figure a polygon? What is this polygon called?

▶ What makes a polygon different from other plane figures?

▶ Why are curves, angles, and circles not polygons?

Practice

Use string to make a model of each of these polygons. Then make two different examples of each type of polygon, and draw them.

triangle

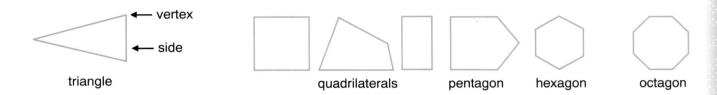

quadrilaterals   pentagon   hexagon   octagon

Write *true* or *false.*

1. A quadrilateral can be a rectangle, a square, or a figure with four sides that are not parallel.

2. The point where the sides meet is called the vertex.

3. A circle is a polygon.

4. All plane figures are polygons.

Write *yes* or *no* to tell whether the figure is a polygon. Give a reason for your answer.

5.

6.

7.

8.

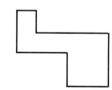

9.

10.

11.

12.

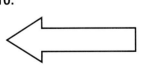

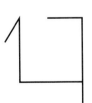

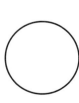

Name each figure.

13.

14.

15.

16.

17. a polygon with four sides

18. a quadrilateral with four equal sides

CHAPTER 5

Exploring Division

WHBJ-TV produces 52 children's programs per season on their 3 soundstages. Each soundstage can handle about the same number of programs. How many programs are produced on each soundstage?

Divide: $52 \div 3 = n$ $\qquad 3\overline{)52}^{\,n}$

Building Understanding

Use place-value blocks to model the problem. Record the numbers as you complete each step.

Step 1 Draw 3 circles. Show 52 as 5 tens 2 ones. 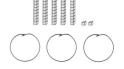 Record: $3\overline{)52}$	**Step 2** Place an equal number of tens into each circle. 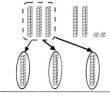 Record: $\begin{array}{r} 1 \\ 3\overline{)52} \\ -3 \\ \hline 2 \end{array}$ ← 1 ten in each group ← 3 tens used ← 2 tens left
Step 3 Regroup the 2 tens left over into ones. 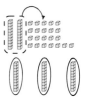 Record: $\begin{array}{r} 1 \\ 3\overline{)52} \\ -3\downarrow \\ \hline 22 \end{array}$ ← bring down ones	**Step 4** Place an equal number of ones into each circle. Record the remainder. 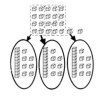 Record: $\begin{array}{r} 17 \ \text{r1} \\ 3\overline{)52} \\ -3\downarrow \\ \hline 22 \\ -21 \\ \hline 1 \end{array}$

So, 17 programs are produced on each of 2 soundstages and 18 programs are produced on 1 soundstage.

Talk About It

▶ In Step 2, why did you put only 1 ten in each circle?

▶ Why did you have to regroup the 2 leftover tens?

▶ Why must you bring down the ones before you can divide again?

▶ After Step 4, how many blocks are in each circle?

Practice

Use place-value blocks to model each problem. Then find the quotient.

1. $2\overline{)46}$
2. $3\overline{)48}$
3. $2\overline{)38}$
4. $3\overline{)42}$
5. $4\overline{)34}$

6. $4\overline{)57}$
7. $6\overline{)89}$
8. $8\overline{)29}$
9. $3\overline{)74}$
10. $5\overline{)73}$

Find the quotient.

11. $5\overline{)75}$
12. $2\overline{)52}$
13. $3\overline{)57}$
14. $4\overline{)72}$
15. $6\overline{)78}$

16. $2\overline{)59}$
17. $4\overline{)79}$
18. $7\overline{)66}$
19. $5\overline{)47}$
20. $3\overline{)32}$

21. $8\overline{)96}$
22. $3\overline{)87}$
23. $6\overline{)78}$
24. $4\overline{)39}$
25. $9\overline{)24}$

26. $7\overline{)96}$
27. $7\overline{)51}$
28. $2\overline{)93}$
29. $3\overline{)77}$
30. $6\overline{)43}$

31. $90 \div 7 = n$
32. $88 \div 5 = n$
33. $81 \div 4 = n$

34. $36 \div 7 = n$
35. $82 \div 3 = n$
36. $33 \div 8 = n$

37. $41 \div 5 = n$
38. $42 \div 4 = n$
39. $65 \div 3 = n$

40. $67 \div 2 = n$
41. $56 \div 5 = n$
42. $75 \div 8 = n$

43. $35 \div 2 = n$
44. $85 \div 7 = n$
45. $39 \div 8 = n$

Solve.

46. A science program showed a total of 21 experiments in 5 days. If on each day except one the program showed the same number of experiments, how many experiments were shown each day?

47. Gary videotaped 3 programs on a 90-minute tape. If each program was the same length, how long was each program?

48. In one episode of the television show, *Dandy Lions,* Dandy and his 2 friends are building a clubhouse. The materials will cost $54. If they share the cost equally, how much will each person pay?

49. In another episode, Dandy has to pack 68 books into boxes. Each box will hold 8 books. How many boxes will Dandy need to pack all the books?

CHAPTER 7

Collecting Data

Angela and Eric took a survey for a social studies project. They asked students to name their favorite restaurant at the Maple Mall. They used tally marks (/) to record the data and then made a frequency table. How can they find the total number of people who participated in the survey?

Tally Table

Restaurant	Tallies
Burger World	ЖЖ IIII
Taco-Ria	ЖЖ ЖЖ III
Hot Dog Haven	ЖЖ
Julie's Pizza	ЖЖ ЖЖ ЖЖ
Sizzling Subs	ЖЖ
Pasta Factory	III

Frequency Table

Restaurant Choice	Number of Votes Frequency
Burger World	9
Taco-Ria	13
Hot Dog Haven	5
Julie's Pizza	15
Sizzling Subs	5
Pasta Factory	3

A **frequency table** is a table that shows how often an item occurs.

You can add to find the total number of people surveyed.

9 + 1 3 + 5 + 1 5 + 5 + 3 =   50.

So, 50 people were surveyed in all.

Talk About It

▶ What do you need to think about when you plan a survey?

▶ How many votes does each tally mark (/) represent?

▶ How was the data displayed for this project?

▶ How do you know what numbers to put in the frequency table?

Practice

Use the tally table for Exercises 1–5.

Favorite Fruit Juices

Juice	Tally
Orange	卌 卌 I
Grape	III
Apple	卌 卌 卌
Pineapple	卌 II

1. Which juice is most popular?

2. Which juice is least popular?

3. How many people like apple or orange juice?

4. Change the tally table into a frequency table.

5. How many people participated in this survey?

Use the frequency table for Exercises 6–8.

Stan's Juice Stand	
Day	**Bottles Sold**
Monday	120
Tuesday	194
Wednesday	239
Thursday	248
Friday	219

6. On which day did Stan sell the most bottles of juice?

7. How many more bottles of juice did he sell on Thursday than on Wednesday?

8. How many bottles of juice did Stan sell in all?

Use the frequency table for Exercises 9–11.

9. On which days did Mona sell the same number of salads?

10. How many more salads did Mona sell on Friday than on Tuesday?

11. How many salads did Mona sell in all?

Mona's Health Salads	
Day	**Salads Sold**
Monday	56
Tuesday	38
Wednesday	70
Thursday	38
Friday	63

CHAPTER 9

Fractions in Simplest Form

$\frac{8}{24}$

8 out of 24

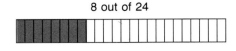

Chandra has 24 plants in her garden. Of these plants, 8 are tomato plants. What is the simplest form of a fraction that tells the part of Chandra's garden that is planted in tomato plants?

$\frac{4}{12}$

4 out of 12

Look at the fraction bars. Find the fraction bar with the largest piece that is the same size as $\frac{8}{24}$. This shows the **simplest form** of the fraction.

$\frac{2}{6}$

2 out of 6

The $\frac{1}{3}$ piece of the fraction bar is the same size as $\frac{8}{24}$. So, $\frac{1}{3}$ is the simplest form of $\frac{8}{24}$.

$\frac{1}{3}$

1 out of 3

To **simplify** a fraction, divide the numerator and the denominator by the same number. This number is a **common factor.**

More Examples

A.

$$\frac{3}{12} = \frac{1}{4}$$

A common factor of 3 and 12 is 3.

B.

$$\frac{6}{12} = \frac{3}{6} = \frac{1}{2}$$

Both 2 and 3 are common factors of 6 and 12.

C.

$$\frac{1}{13}$$

The only common factor of 1 and 13 is 1. So, $\frac{1}{13}$ is in simplest form.

Talk About It

▶ How can you test whether a fraction is in its simplest form?

▶ Why does dividing both the numerator and the denominator by the same number not change the value of the fraction?

▶ What is the largest number you can use to divide the numerator and the denominator of $\frac{6}{12}$?

Practice

Complete.

1.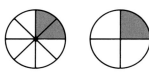

$$\frac{2}{8} = \frac{\blacksquare}{4}$$

2.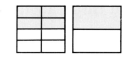

$$\frac{4}{8} = \frac{\blacksquare}{2}$$

3.

$$\frac{6}{8} = \frac{\blacksquare}{4}$$

4.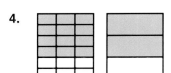

$$\frac{12}{\blacksquare} = \frac{\blacksquare}{3}$$

5.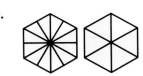

$$\frac{4}{16} = \frac{\blacksquare}{\blacksquare}$$

6.

$$\frac{\blacksquare}{\blacksquare} = \frac{\blacksquare}{\blacksquare}$$

7.

$$\frac{6}{16} = \frac{\blacksquare}{\blacksquare}$$

8.

$$\frac{10}{\blacksquare} = \frac{\blacksquare}{6}$$

9.

$$\frac{\blacksquare}{\blacksquare} = \frac{\blacksquare}{\blacksquare}$$

10. $\dfrac{6}{9} = \dfrac{6 \div 3}{9 \div 3} = \dfrac{\blacksquare}{\blacksquare}$

11. $\dfrac{12}{14} = \dfrac{12 \div 2}{14 \div 2} = \dfrac{\blacksquare}{\blacksquare}$

12. $\dfrac{4}{12} = \dfrac{4 \div 4}{12 \div 4} = \dfrac{\blacksquare}{\blacksquare}$

13. $\dfrac{9}{12} = \dfrac{9 \div 3}{12 \div 3} = \dfrac{\blacksquare}{\blacksquare}$

14. $\dfrac{6}{10} = \dfrac{6 \div 2}{10 \div 2} = \dfrac{\blacksquare}{\blacksquare}$

15. $\dfrac{15}{30} = \dfrac{15 \div 15}{30 \div 15} = \dfrac{\blacksquare}{\blacksquare}$

Write in simplest form.

16. $\dfrac{2}{4}$ **17.** $\dfrac{3}{9}$ **18.** $\dfrac{4}{12}$ **19.** $\dfrac{4}{16}$ **20.** $\dfrac{6}{12}$

21. $\dfrac{3}{15}$ **22.** $\dfrac{5}{10}$ **23.** $\dfrac{4}{6}$ **24.** $\dfrac{2}{6}$ **25.** $\dfrac{2}{16}$

26. $\dfrac{8}{18}$ **27.** $\dfrac{12}{36}$ **28.** $\dfrac{10}{24}$ **29.** $\dfrac{14}{16}$ **30.** $\dfrac{30}{60}$

Solve.

31. Helene works in her garden 2 hours every day. What is the simplest form of a fraction that tells the part of a day Helene works in her garden?

32. Robert is in school 6 hours each day. What is the simplest form of a fraction that tells the part of a day Robert is in school?

Metric Units

These pictures of animals will help you think about **metric** units for measuring length.

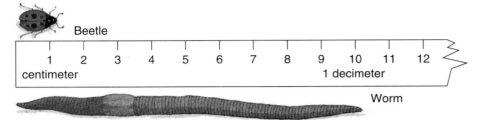

Beetle

centimeter

1 decimeter

Worm

- The beetle is about 1 centimeter long and the worm is about 1 decimeter long. What other living creatures are about 1 centimeter long? 1 decimeter long?

Here is a table of metric units.

A **centimeter** is about the width of your index finger.

| 1 cm |

Metric Units	
10 centimeters (cm)	= 1 decimeter (dm)
10 decimeters (dm)	= 1 meter (m)
100 centimeters (cm)	= 1 meter (m)
1,000 meters (m)	= 1 kilometer (km)

A **decimeter** is about the width of an adult's hand.

| 1 dm |

- Which unit is equal to 10 cm? 100 cm?

A meter is about the distance from one hand to the other when your arms are stretched out.

A kilometer is about how far you can walk in 15 minutes.

Talk About It

▶ If you and a partner stand side by side and measure your outstretched arms, about how far do your arms reach?

▶ If you walk around Palm Lake for 30 minutes, about how many kilometers will you walk?

Practice

Write the unit that is longer.

1. 1 cm or 1 dm
2. 1 km or 1 m
3. 1 dm or 1 m

4. 4 dm or 4 cm
5. 5 m or 5 cm
6. 700 dm or 700 km

7. 2 km or 2 m
8. 30 cm or 2 dm
9. 10 dm or 2 m

Use your index finger to measure each. Label in centimeters.

10. |———————————|
11. |———————————|

12. |———————————————————|
13. |———————————————————|

Name the longer unit.

14. 4 dm or 4 cm
15. 5 m or 5 cm
16. 700 dm or 700 km
17. 2 km or 2 m

Choose the appropriate unit for each. Write *cm*, *dm*, *m*, or *km*.

18. length of a ladybug
19. distance a car travels in 1 hour

20. width of a garage door
21. length of the classroom

22. distance you can walk in 40 minutes
23. height of a classroom wall

24. width of a table
25. height of a garbage can

26. length of a window
27. width of a sheet of paper

28. width of a book
29. length of a pencil

30. length of your index finger
31. length of a playground

Draw a line of each length.

32. 5 cm
33. 1 dm
34. 12 cm
35. 2 dm

Solve.

36. Corky says she has a bookmark that is 9 dm long. Is this reasonable? Explain.

37. Holly wants to tie a ribbon in her hair. Would she need 25 cm or 25 dm?

38. Patti walked 1 km on a hike. Then she walked 500 m farther to a new trail. Pam walked 2 km on a hike. Who walked farther? How many meters farther?

39. Mr. Cruz drove 57 km to Elk City and 72 km to St. Cloud. Estimate the total distance that he drove.

CHAPTER 11

Length in Customary Units

These pictures of things Ryan found in his desk will help you think about customary units for measuring length.

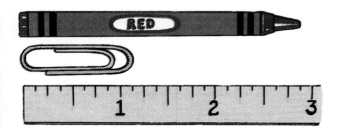

Talk About It

▶ About how long is the paper clip?

▶ About how long is the crayon?

Here is a table of customary units.

Customary Units	
12 inches (in.)	= 1 foot (ft.)
3 feet	= 1 yard (yd)
36 inches	= 1 yard
5,280 feet	= 1 mile (mi)
1,760 yards	= 1 mile

An **inch** is about the length of your thumb from the first knuckle to the tip.

1 in.

A **yard** is about the length of a baseball bat.

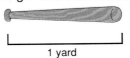

1 yard

A **foot** is about the length of a man's shoe.

1 foot

A **mile** is about the distance you can walk in 20 minutes.

1 mile

Talk About It

▶ Which unit is most appropriate to measure the length of a football field? the length of a pencil?

▶ Which part of your hand can you use to help you estimate 10 in.?

▶ How many baseball bats laid end to end measure about 12 yds?

Practice

Write the unit that is longer.

1. 2 yd or 2 ft
2. 72 in. or 72 ft
3. 1 yd or 1 mi
4. 5,000 mi or 5,000 ft
5. 10 yd or 10 ft
6. 33 ft or 33 in.

Choose the appropriate unit. Write *in.*, *ft*, *yd*, or *mi*.

7. The distance from the floor to the chalkboard is about 3 _?_.

8. Mrs. McBee bought 4 _?_ of fabric to make a dress.

9. The length of a fishing pole is about 5 _?_.

10. A football player rushed for 10 _?_ in the last game.

11. The height of a skyscraper is about 1,000 _?_.

12. The distance from home to the supermarket is about 3 _?_.

13. The length of a table is about 8 _?_.

14. The height of a dog is about 24 _?_.

15. The length of a bus is about 20 _?_.

16. The width of a piece of notebook paper is about 9 _?_.

17. The width of a toy boat is 5 _?_.

18. The height of a desk is 25 _?_.

Draw a line of each length.

19. 4 in.
20. 7 in.
21. 10 in.

Solve.

22. Nathan rides his bike 5,000 ft to school. Teri rides 1 mi to school. Who rides the greater distance?

23. Bonnie's room is 4 yd long. Carol's room is 11 ft long. Whose room is longer?

24. Nan's desk measures 38 in. long. Jennifer's desk measures 3 ft in length. Who has the longer desk?

25. John walks 1 mi to school every day. Gary walks 2,000 yards. Who has the longer walk to school?

CHAPTER 12

Connecting Geometry and Measurement

Geometric figures can be one-dimensional, two-dimensional, or three-dimensional. Sort the figures in the picture by drawing them on a table.

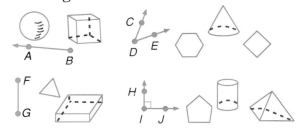

One-Dimensional	Two-Dimensional	Three-Dimensional
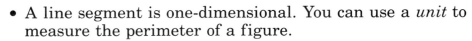		

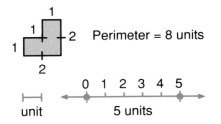

Perimeter = 8 units

- A line segment is one-dimensional. You can use a *unit* to measure the perimeter of a figure.

- A polygon is two-dimensional. You can use a *square unit* to measure the area of a polygon.

- A solid figure is three-dimensional. You can use a *cubic unit* to measure the volume of a three-dimensional figure.

unit

5 units

square unit

8 square units

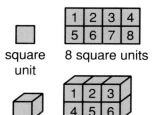

cubic unit

6 cubic units

What three dimensions do you use to find the volume of a rectangular prism?

_____

Use 18 connecting cubes. Make as many different-shaped prisms as you can. In a table, record the results.

Measuring Volume			
Length	Width	Height	Volume
9	2	1	18 cubic units

Talk About It

► What is the volume of each model you made?

► If the length of one model is 18 units, what are the other two measurements?

► How can you use multiplication to find the volume of a prism?

► If a prism is 2 units in length, 6 units in width, and 4 units in height, what is the volume?

Practice

Find the volume. Use connecting cubes to help you.

1.

2.

3.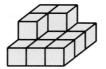

4.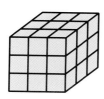

5.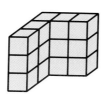

6.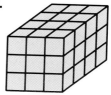

Write a multiplication sentence to find the volume of each.

7.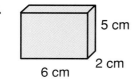
5 cm
2 cm
6 cm

8.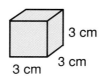
3 cm
3 cm
3 cm

9.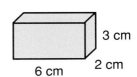
3 cm
2 cm
6 cm

10.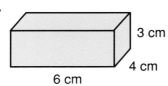
3 cm
4 cm
6 cm

11.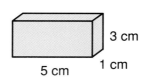
3 cm
1 cm
5 cm

12.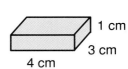
1 cm
3 cm
4 cm

Complete this table for rectangular prisms.

	Length	Width	Height	Volume
13.	2 cm	3 cm	1 cm	▨
14.	5 cm	3 cm	2 cm	▨
15.	3 cm	2 cm	▨	18 cubic cm
16.	4 cm	▨	1 cm	8 cubic cm
17.	▨	4 cm	3 cm	60 cubic cm

School-Home Connection

CHAPTER 1

Place Value: Whole Numbers and Decimals

Project: Plan a Meal

Use a grocery store receipt with a total of at least $15.00. Circle at least three items that total about $5.00. Record your choices. Use a calculator. Compare your estimate to the actual cost of the items.

Now Try This

Create a breakfast, lunch, or dinner menu from items on your grocery store receipt. Plan a meal with foods that cost about $5.00 by estimating the cost of each item.

Example

eggs	$0.89
milk	$1.79
cheese	$1.89
bread	$0.99
juice	$0.89
napkins	$2.19
meat	$2.49

Breakfast

eggs ⟶ $1.00
bread ⟶ $1.00
juice ⟶ $1.00
meat ⟶ $2.00

CHAPTER 2

Adding and Subtracting Whole Numbers and Decimals

Application: Comparing Field Dimensions

Modern field hockey is played on a field that is 100 yards long by 55 yards wide.

A football field is 120 yards long by 53.3 yards wide.

How much longer is a football field than a hockey field?

$120 - 100 = 20$
It is 20 yards longer.

How much wider is a football field than a hockey field?

$55 - 53.3 = 1.7$
It is 1.7 yards wider.

Now Try This

Find the length and width of a soccer field. Compare these dimensions to those of football and hockey fields.

School-Home Connection

CHAPTER 3

Multiplying Whole Numbers

Application: Using a Lattice to Multiply

You can use a lattice to multiply two numbers.
Follow these steps to multiply 531 × 274.

1. Write 531 along the top of the lattice, and 274 down the right side.

2. For each small box, multiply the number at the top of its column by the number at the right of its row. Write one digit of the product in each half of the box.

3. Add along the diagonals. Start in the lower right corner. Regroup to the next diagonal. Write the sums along the edges of the lattice.

4. Read the product, moving down the left side and across the bottom.

Now Try This

Use lattice multiplication to find these products.

  1. 421 × 265   **2.** 205 × 156   **3.** 951 × 607   **4.** 123 × 456

CHAPTER 4

Geometry

Project: Design a Moon House

Architecture is the art of designing buildings. An architect uses geometric ideas and shapes to design and create structures.

Now Try This

Design a house you might build on the moon. Use a combination of solid shapes and the geometric ideas of congruence and symmetry. Make a model of your moon house.

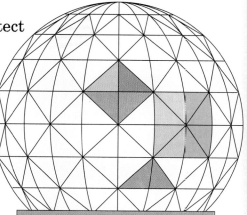

CHAPTER 5

Dividing Whole Numbers by 1-Digit Numbers

Application: Determining Speed

You can find the speed at which something travels by dividing the distance traveled by the time taken to travel the distance.

If you travel 150 miles in 3 hours, then divide 150 by 3 to determine the average speed of the trip.

$150 \div 3 = 50$

The average speed is 50 miles per hour.

Now Try This

The next time you take an automobile trip, record the number of hours and the number of miles you travel. (Round the number of hours to the nearest whole number.) Use the data to record the average number of miles you traveled per hour.

. . . .

CHAPTER 6

Dividing Whole Numbers by 2-Digit Numbers

Application: Determining Leap Years

A calendar year has 365 days except in a leap year, when it has 366 days. A leap year occurs every 4 years. Leap years make the calendar year nearly the same as the solar year.

Every 400 years there is an error of 3 days in the calendar. To correct this error, a year ending in 00 that cannot be divided evenly by 40 is NOT a leap year. It has 365 days. A year ending in 00 that can be divided evenly by 40 is a leap year. The year 1500 was not a leap year; the year 1600 was.

Now Try This

Tell whether each year is or is not a leap year.

1. 1900   **2.** 1800   **3.** 2300   **4.** 2400

CHAPTER 7

Statistics and Graphing

Project: Displaying Temperature Data

Temperature is important to many people. People decide what clothes to wear or what activities to pursue by the temperature. Record the daily high and low temperatures for a week. You can use your own thermometer or listen to weather reports on radio or television.

Now Try This

Make a pair of line graphs that show the daily high and low temperatures for one week. One graph should show the daily high temperatures and the other should show the daily low temperatures. Look at the line on each graph to see the pattern of the high and low temperatures for the week.

CHAPTER 8

Multiplying and Dividing Decimals

Application: Determining the Best Buy

Items you buy in a grocery store are often sold in different-sized packages or containers. To determine which is the best buy, you find the cost per ounce by dividing the cost of the item by the weight of the package.

For example, the same kind of peanut butter might be sold in three different-sized jars.

Size of Jar	Cost	Cost per Ounce	Round to the Nearest Cent
12 oz	$1.67	$1.67 \div 12 = 0.139$	$0.14
18 oz	$2.08	$2.08 \div 18 = 0.116$	$0.12
40 oz	$5.25	$5.25 \div 40 = 0.131$	$0.13

So, the 18-oz jar is the best buy.

Now Try This

Next time you go to a grocery store, choose an item that is sold in at least three different-sized containers. Use a calculator to determine the best buy.

CHAPTER 9

Number Theory and Fractions

Project: Sketch a Garden Plan

Gardening is a popular hobby. You can gather information about gardening from books, seed catalogs, plant dealers, or your county agricultural extension agent. Some gardeners sketch a plan before they select or plant seeds. This sketch shows that $\frac{3}{8}$ of the garden will be planted with leaf lettuce, $\frac{1}{8}$ with tomatoes, $\frac{1}{8}$ with spinach, $\frac{2}{8}$, or $\frac{1}{4}$, with carrots, and $\frac{1}{8}$ with snap beans.

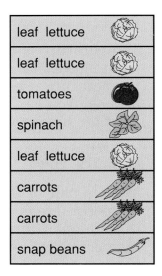

leaf lettuce	
leaf lettuce	
tomatoes	
spinach	
leaf lettuce	
carrots	
carrots	
snap beans	

Now Try This

Sketch a garden plan. Determine what fraction of your garden you want to plant with each type of seed you select. You may wish to plant the garden.

CHAPTER 10

Using Fractions

Project: Design a Costume

Madame Barbara Karinska designed and made the costumes for a New York City Ballet production of *The Nutcracker*. *The Nutcracker* is the story of a nutcracker that comes to life during the winter holiday season. This is one costume design for the character of the Nutcracker.

Now Try This

Sketch your own costume design for the Nutcracker. Suppose your design requires $2\frac{1}{2}$ yards of fabric. Find the number of yards of fabric you would need to make 4 identical costumes.

CHAPTER 11

Measurement

Project: Make a Weighing Device

One nickel weighs about 5 grams. You can use nickels, cardboard, paper clips, a paper fastener, a paper punch, glue, scissors, a marker, and a heavy object like a washer or a rock to make a weighing device.

Large versions of these three pieces can be found in *Learning Resources*, page H101. Use carbon paper to trace them onto cardboard. Cut out the pieces and punch out the holes as shown. Cut out a 2-cm by 2-cm square of cardboard. Glue the square between B and C. Attach B and C on either side of A with a paper fastener. Put the fastener through the holes marked X.

Use a paper clip to fasten a heavy object to A at the hole marked Y. Use a paper clip at the hole marked Z to hold things you want to weigh. You may want to attach a plastic cup to the paper clip.

To mark your device, first mark the position when nothing is hanging from the paper clip. Then hang from 1–10 nickels and mark where the arrow points for 5 to 50 grams. You can use a set of standard weights to mark your device if it is available.

Now Try This

Estimate the weight of an object. Then weigh it on your weighing device.

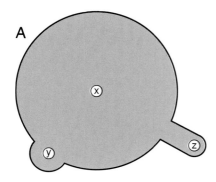
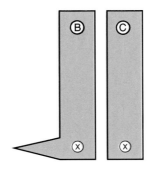

CHAPTER 12

Perimeter, Area, and Volume

Project: Tiling the Kitchen Floor

If you want to tile a floor, you must first determine the area so you will know how much tile you need.

Now Try This

Measure the length and width of your kitchen. Find the area in square feet.

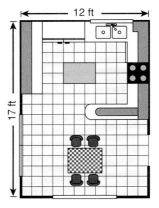

Compute the total area of the places that would not be tiled, such as under the cabinets. Subtract this measurement from the total that you found above.

What is the total area that needs to be tiled?

Suppose you buy 1-ft-square tiles that come 24 to a box. How many boxes would you need? How many squares of tile would be left?

CHAPTER 13

Ratio, Percent, and Probability

Project: Draw a Map

A life-size drawing of a large area would be very difficult to use. Therefore, maps have scales to show small but accurate representations of many areas.

School

Now Try This

Make a map of your usual route to school. Use an odometer to measure the actual distance you travel. Assign a scale to show the relationship between the actual distance and the distance on your map. Can you find a shorter route to school? Make a map of the new route if you find one.

CREDITS

Harcourt Brace & Company Photographs

KEY: (t) top, (b) bottom, (l) left, (r) right, (c) center

viii, Maria Paraskevas; xi(b), Charlie Burton; xii(b), Maria Paraskevas; xiii(r) & xiv(l), Terry Sinclair; xvi, Jerry White; xvii(t) & (b), Earl Kogler; xviii & xxii, Richard Haynes; xxiii, Jerry White; xvi–xvii, Terry Sinclair; 2, Rob Downey; 3, Maria Paraskevas; 5(t), 8 & 12(inset), Jerry White; 16(t), Maria Paraskevas; 16(b) & 17, Jerry White; 18(t) & (b), Maria Paraskevas; 23, Carroll Morgan; 24, Annette Stahl; 25–29, Jerry White; 42, Maria Paraskevas; 46 & 56(t), Earl Kogler; 56(b), Jerry White; 58 & 59, Annette Stahl; 61, Jerry White; 62, Maria Paraskevas; 63, Rob Downey; 64(b) & 69, Jerry White; 70, Maria Paraskevas; 76, Richard Haynes; 82, Maria Paraskevas; 86, Earl Kogler; 90(inset), Annette Stahl; 92, Richard Haynes; 94, Earl Kogler; 97, Victoria Bowen; 98, Jerry White; 99, Annette Stahl; 102, Maria Paraskevas; 108 & 110, Jerry White; 114, Beverly Brosius; 115, Jerry White; 116–117, Rodney Jones; 118, Jerry White; 122–123, Rob Downey; 128, Jerry White; 130, Rob Downey; 132(t) & (b), Jerry White; 134(l) & (r), Maria Paraskevas; 135, Greg Leary; 136, Maria Paraskevas; 137, 138, 139 & 140, Jerry White; 144, Maria Paraskevas; 148(inset), Jerry White; 149(inset) & 150, Maria Paraskevas; 151, Beverly Brosius; 154(t), Richard Haynes; 154(b), Beverly Brosius; 158 & 161, Jerry White; 166, Annette Stahl; 170 & 171, Greg Leary; 174, Maria Paraskevas; 179(inset), Greg Leary; 186, Maria Paraskevas; 188(t) & (b), Annette Stahl; 191(r), Jerry White; 196(t), Chris Lowery; 198(t), Victoria Bowen; 198(b), Beverly Brosius; 199(t) & (b), Rob Downey; 200(inset), Greg Leary; 201, Jerry White; 204, Maria Paraskevas; 208–209(background) & 208(inset), Greg Leary; 210 & 211, Richard Haynes; 212 & 213, Jerry White; 216 & 218, Julie Fletcher; 228(t) & (b), Rob Downey; 229 & 230, Jerry White; 232 & 233, Annette Stahl; 234(inset), Greg Leary; 238, Maria Paraskevas; 242–243(background), Charlie Burton/courtesy of "Kidding Around"; 243(inset), Jerry White; 242(inset), Charlie Burton; 244, Maria Paraskevas; 248, Victoria Bowen; 249, Rob Downey; 250, Annette Stahl; 252, Rodney Jones; 256, Charlie Burton; 260(t) & (b), Jerry White; 262, Rob Downey; 263, Maria Paraskevas; 266, Charlie Burton; 270, Maria Paraskevas; 274(inset) & 275(inset), Richard Haynes; 278(l) & (r), Maria Paraskevas; 279(t) & (b), Victoria Bowen; 280 & 282(t), Charlie Burton; 286, Victoria Bowen; 287, Maria Paraskevas; 288, Rob Downey; 289, Richard Haynes; 290, Greg Leary; 292, Victoria Bowen; 293, Annette Stahl; 298, Victoria Bowen; 299, Maria Paraskevas; 300, Rob Downey; 306, Maria Paraskevas; 312, Jerry White; 316(l) & (r), Maria Paraskevas; 317, Richard Haynes; 318 & 319, Rob Downey; 320(t) & (b), Annette Stahl; 322, Maria Paraskevas; 323, Richard Haynes; 324, Rob Downey; 325, Richard Haynes; 326(t) & (b), Annette Stahl; 332, Charlie Burton; 334, Jerry White; 336, Charlie Burton; 338 & 339, Rob Downey; 334, Maria Paraskevas; 348(inset) & 349(inset), Greg Leary; 350, Charlie Burton; 352, Maria Paraskevas; 353, Victoria Bowen; 354, Jerry White; 356(l), Terry Sinclair; (r), Jerry White; 358 & 359, Maria Paraskevas; 360, Richard Haynes; 364, 365 & 370, Charlie Burton; 372 & 374, Jerry White; 376(t) & (b) & 378, Charlie Burton; 382, Debi Harbin; 386(inset) & 387(inset), Richard Haynes; 388, Victoria Bowen; 389, Beverly Brosius; 390, Annette Stahl; 392, Jerry White; 393, Beverly Brosius; 396, Richard Haynes; 398 & 399, Charlie Burton; 402, Jerry White; 404, Maria Paraskevas; 405, Rob Downey; 406, Maria Paraskevas; 407, Rob Downey; 408, Charlie Burton; 410, 412(t) & (b), Jerry White; 413, Richard Haynes; 416, Terry Sinclair; 420–421(background), Greg Leary; 420(inset), Charlie Burton; 421(inset), Richard Haynes; 422, 423, 426 & 427, Maria Paraskevas; 428(t) & (b), Rob Downey; 429, Maria Paraskevas; 432, Richard Haynes; 436, Rob Downey; 437, Victoria Bowen; 440, Richard Haynes; 444(t) & (b), Terry Sinclair; 445, Jerry White; 448, Greg Leary; H0–H22(all), Jerry White.

All Other Photographs

iv, Mike Yamashita/Woodfin Camp & Assoc.; v, Mitchell Layton/duomo; vi, Farrell Grehan/Photo Researchers; vii, Clifford Hausner/Leo deWys, Inc.; ix, Michal Heron/Woodfin Camp & Assoc.; x(t), Walter Chandoha; x(b), Dwight Kuhn; xi(t), Jerry Sinkovec/Artwerks; xii(l), Steve Vidler/Superstock; xiii(tl), Robert Frerck/Odyssey Productions; xiii(bl), Milton & Joan Mann/Cameramann International; xiv(r), Kennan Ward; 0–1(background), Culver Pictures; 0(inset), Lee Bolton Photo, courtesy of Bawne & Co., South Street Seaport Museum; 4, Lawrence Migdale/Photo Researchers; 5(b), H. Armstrong Roberts; 6, Mike Yamashita/Woodfin Camp & Assoc.; 9, George Rose/Gamma-Liaison; 10, Troy Maben/David R. Frazier Photolibrary; 12(background), Wally Hampton Photography; 15, Charlyn Zlotnik/Woodfin Camp & Assoc.; 20, Steve Vidler/Nawrocki Stock Photo; 22, Photo Library International/Stock Imagery; 31, L. Willinger/Superstock; 36–37(background), Paul J. Sutton/duomo; 36(inset), William H. Sallaz/duomo; 37(inset), Paul J. Sutton/duomo; 38, Bob Daemmrich/TSW; 39, David J. Sams/Texas Imprint; 40, Richard Hutchings/Photo Researchers; 43, Paul J. Sutton/duomo; 44, Grant LeDuc/Monkmeyer Press; 45, Bruno Barbey/Magnum Photos; 48, Al Tielemans/duomo; 49, Wide World Photos; 50, Paul Slaughter/The Image Bank; 51, Brian Drake/Sportschrome East/West; 54, E. N. Van Loo/TSW; 60, Mitchell Layton/duomo; 64–65, Richard Dole/duomo; 66, Alvin Upitis/The Image Bank; 67, Bob Abraham, Pacific Rim Productions/The Stock Market; 74–75(background), James Blank/Stock Imagery; 74(inset), LaTrobe Barnitz/The Picture Cube; 75(inset), Stock Imagery; 78, G. R. Roberts; 79, Ray Pfortner/Peter Arnold, Inc.; 80, Robert V. Eckert, Jr./The Picture Cube; 84(t), Greig Cranna/Stock, Boston; 84(b), Dennis Junor/Superstock; 87, Frank P. Rossotto/The Stock Market; 89, Ferrill Grehan/Photo Researchers; 90(background), David Pollack/The Stock Market; 95, David Madison/duomo; 96, Arnold J. Kaplan/Berg & Assoc.; 106–107(background), NASA; 106(inset), Harry J. Przekop/MediChrome-The Stock Shop; 107(inset), NASA; 109, Comstock; 112, Roger Ressmeyer; 125, Helmut Wimmer; 127(t), SPL/Photo Researchers; 127(b), TASS from Sovfoto; 145, NASA; 148–149(background), R. Kord/H. Armstrong Roberts; 152, Bob Daemmrich; 156, Clifford Hausner/Leo deWys, Inc.; 160, Bob Daemmrich; 163, John Roberts/The Stock Market; 164(t), Bill Schildge/Pacific Stock; 164(b), James H. Carmichael/Bruce Coleman, Inc. New York; 165, Ddarodents/Pacific Stock; 168, David R. Frazier Photolibrary; 175, David Lissy/The Picture Cube; 178–179(background), Ric Ergenbright Photography; 178(inset), A. Devaney/Devaney Stock Photos; 180, Royce Bair/The Stock Solution; 182, Jerome F. Shaw/Take Stock; 184, Lori Adamski Peek/Tony Stone Worldwide/Chicago; 190, Tom Bean/The Stock Market; 191(l), Tony Freeman/PhotoEdit; 193, Cardoni/Bruce Coleman, Inc. New York; 194(t), B.J. Adams/Devaney Stock Photos; 194(b), John Pineda/Miami Herald; 196(b) & 197, Gale Beery/Stock Imagery; 200(background), Mark E. and Audrey Gibson/The Stock Market; 214 & 219, Tom Myers; 220, Bob Daemmrich; 223, Bill Gillette/Stock, Boston; 224, Richard Hutchings/InfoEdit; 226, David Young-Wolff/PhotoEdit; 234(background), Superstock; 245, David Reed/Panos Pictures; 246, Dick Wade/Berg & Assoc.; 253, Stock Imagery; 254, David R. Frazier Photolibrary; 257, Michal Heron/Woodfin Camp & Assoc.; 264, Chris Jones/The Stock Market; 267, John M. Touscany/Third Coast Stock Source; 274–275(background), Larry Lefever/Grant Heilman Photography; 276, R. Ian Lloyd/Stock Market; 282(b), Walter Chandoha; 283, John Lei/Stock, Boston; 285, E. R. Degginger/Bruce Coleman, Inc. New York; 294, Walter Chandoha; 296, Dwight Kuhn; 302, Larry Lefever/Grant Heilman Photography; 303, Christopher Rogers/The Stock Market; 310–311(background), Jacques Jangoux/Peter Arnold, Inc.; 310(inset), Jaime Martorano/Superstock; 311(inset), Luca Gavagna/Photo Researchers; 314, Bob Daemmrich/The Image Works; 321, Steve Drexler/Stockphotos-The Image Bank; 328 & 329, Jerry Sinkovac Artwerks; 331(l), Carol Simowitz; 331(r), Steve Vidler/Superstock; 340, Tony Freeman/PhotoEdit; 341, Lawrence Migdale; 348–349(background), Richard Steedman/The Stock Market; 394, Christiana Dittmann/Rainbow; 401, Les Everett; 424, Kennan Ward; 433, Milton & Joan Mann/Cameramann International; 438, Chris Sorensen/The Stock Market; 441, Robert Frerck/Odyssey Productions; 448–449, Jay Freis/The Image Bank; 449, Mug Shots/The Stock Market; 462(t) & (b), Douglas Faulkner/Photo Researchers.

Illustrations

Michael Adams 175, M8; **Tim Bowers** xiv, 14, 30, 32, 52, 68, 70, 88, 100, 102, 126, 142, 144, 172, 174, 202, 204, 236, 238, 268, 270, 304, 306, 342, 344, 380, 382, 414, 416, 442, 444, M1, M16; **Congraf** 15, 53, 89, 127, 163, 193, 223, 259, 285, 331, 367, 401, 435; **Suzanne Clee** 369, 371, 373, 375, 377, 379, 381, 417, 445; **Eldon Doty** 50, 111, 174, 301; **Don Dyen** xi, 103, 153, 157, 159, 167, 173, 337, 355, 357, 361, H82, H85; **Electronic Publishing Center** 53, 120, 215, 231, 234, 235, 251, 359; **Barbara Erickson** ix, 259, H31, H48, H74; **Roger Hart** 247; **Kathy Hendrickson** 180, 183, 185, 187, 189, 195, 203, 217, 221, 227, 250, 255, 261, 265, 269; **J.A.K. Graphics** 34, 72, 145, 276, 281, 286, 291, 350, 352, 353, 358, 359, 362, 363, 367, 368, 383, 408, 409, 424, 439, 442, H8, H27, H30, H31, H32; **Bryce Lee** 387; **Polly K. Lewis** x, 33, 287, 295, 297, 313, 321, 327, 333, 335; **Laurie Marks** 307; **Tom Powers** 47; **Eileen Rosen** 240, 446; **Ed Sauk** viii, 77, 85, 91, 93, 99, 155, 165, 169, 181, 205, 343, 351, 354; **Nancy Schill** 271; **Den Shofield** 431, 443; **Brad Strode** 385, 411, 425, 438; **George Ulrich** 197, 430; **Jan Verbraeken** 89; **Nina Winters** 7, 21, 27, 418

CHAPTER I

Lesson 1.1 *(pages 2–3)*

Complete.

1. $10 \times 10 = \blacksquare$ **2.** $10\blacksquare = 1{,}000$ **3.** $10^5 = \blacksquare$

	Number Name	Number	Multiplication	Power of Ten
4.	$\blacksquare$	10	10×1	10^1
5.	hundred	100	$\blacksquare$	10^2
6.	thousand	1,000	$10 \times 10 \times 10$	$\blacksquare$
7.	ten thousand	$\blacksquare$	$10 \times 10 \times 10 \times 10$	10^4
8.	$\blacksquare$	100,000	$\blacksquare$	10^5

Lesson 1.2 *(pages 4–5)*

Write two other forms for each number.

1. $800{,}000 + 3{,}000 + 60 + 5$ **2.** six thousand, thirty   **3.** 50,312

Write the value of each underlined digit.

4. $\underline{3}1{,}254$ **5.** $2\underline{1}9{,}005$ **6.** $67{,}\underline{4}91$ **7.** $429{,}2\underline{9}3$

Lesson 1.3 *(pages 6–7)*

Write the value of each underlined digit.

1. $\underline{2}{,}756{,}489$ **2.** $7{,}0\underline{6}3{,}495$ **3.** $1\underline{8}{,}487{,}003$ **4.** $\underline{3}96{,}652{,}105$

Lesson 1.4 *(pages 8–9)*

Write $<$, $>$, or $=$ for $\bullet$.

1. $2{,}967 \bullet 2{,}769$ **2.** $84{,}817 \bullet 84{,}987$ **3.** $4{,}298{,}178 \bullet 4{,}298{,}178$

4. $14{,}670 \bullet 13{,}760$ **5.** $423{,}470 \bullet 424{,}370$ **6.** $7{,}425{,}367 \bullet 7{,}425{,}367$

Order from least to greatest.

7. 4,298; 4,098; 3,980   **8.** 29,600; 27,860; 29,060   **9.** 630,030; 603,300; 630,300

Lesson 1.5 *(pages 10–11)*

Round to the nearest ten.

1. 643   2. 789   3. 399   4. 884   5. 2,121

Round to the nearest hundred.

6. 574   7. 316   8. 974   9. 6,498   10. 1,951

Round to the nearest thousand.

11. 4,289   12. 7,030   13. 9,800   14. 8,154   15. 18,550

Round to the nearest ten thousand.

16. 47,260   17. 69,982   18. 364,531   19. 745,715

Round to the nearest hundred thousand.

20. 582,263   21. 787,060   22. 549,200   23. 675,800

24. 463,975   25. 723,842   26. 976,590   27. 14,672,400

Round to the nearest million.

28. 8,781,200   29. 10,821,700   30. 92,989,432

31. 82,398,114   32. 15,786,456   33. 672,899,243

Lesson 1.6 *(pages 12–13)*

Make a table and answer the questions.

In a recycling contest, Mrs. Reed's class collected 99 cans the
first week, 80 cans the second week, and 118 cans the third
week. Mr. Mason's class collected 207 cans the first week,
170 cans the second week, and 244 cans the third week.
Mrs. Jenner's class collected 197 cans the first week, 95 cans
the second week, and 102 cans the third week.

1. Which class collected the most cans the first week? the
   second week?

2. How many more cans did Mr. Mason's class collect than
   Mrs. Reed's class?

3. How many more cans did Mr. Mason's class collect than
   Mrs. Jenner's class?

4. How many cans were collected in all?

Lesson 1.7 *(pages 16–17)*

Write the amount as a decimal form of the whole unit.

1. 6 dimes 2. 2 decimeters 3. 8 tenths 4. 1 dime

5. 5 pennies 6. 4 centimeters 7. 3 hundredths 8. 15 centimeters

Complete.

9. ▓ dimes = 1 dollar

10. 1 meter = ▓ centimeters

11. ▓ cents = $0.10

12. 1 decimeter = ▓ meter

Lesson 1.8 *(pages 18–19)*

Write the value of each underlined digit as a decimal and a fraction.

1. 0.<u>1</u> 2. <u>1</u>4.36 3. 0.9<u>6</u> 4. 3<u>2</u>.09 5. <u>3</u>00.08

Write the word form for each decimal.

6. 0.8 7. 0.25 8. 0.04

9. 35.79 10. 0.10 11. 7.02

Lesson 1.9 *(pages 20–21)*

Write in standard form.

1. twenty-one thousandths

2. six and fourteen thousandths

3. one hundred seventy-two thousandths

Write the place-value position of each underlined digit.

4. 7.1<u>3</u>1 5. 0.80<u>4</u> 6. <u>9</u>.25 7. 5.<u>2</u>13 8. 0.00<u>6</u>

Lesson 1.10 *(pages 22–23)*

Write in standard form.

1. two thousand, four hundred sixty and fifty-one hundredths

2. thirty-seven and five hundred twenty-nine thousandths

3. eight thousand and two hundredths

Write the value of the digit 5 in each number.

4. 715.01 5. 298.05 6. 5,006.12 7. 39.5

Lesson 1.11 (pages 24–25)

Write <, >, or = for ●.

1. 42.13 ● 42.15   2. 2.900 ● 2.90   3. 819.65 ● 819.56

4. 0.710 ● 0.700   5. 0.040 ● 0.004   6. 0.210 ● 0.201

7. 0.105 ● 0.150   8. 0.003 ● 0.300   9. 0.110 ● 0.101

Order from least to greatest.

10. 1.7; 1.9; 1.8; 1.6   11. 34.33; 39.43; 34.03; 32.94   12. 0.2; 2.0; 2.3; 0.3

13. 4.72; 3.02; 5.23; 2.76   14. 453.2; 258.3; 233.9; 347.2   15. 0.45; 0.27; 1.58; 5.33

In which number of each pair does the digit 5 have the greater value?

16. 15.7 or 51.7   17. 307.5 or 318.15   18. 6.05 or 6.56   19. 2.125 or 0.05

Lesson 1.12 (pages 26–27)

Round to the nearest tenth.

1. 65.06   2. 129.81   3. 0.97   4. 3.425   5. 2,190.049

Round to the nearest hundredth.

6. 0.894   7. 7.639   8. 219.017   9. 67.259   10. 0.996

Round to the nearest dollar.

11. $6.02   12. $4.93   13. $13.86   14. $299.48   15. $49.85

Round to the nearest whole number.

16. 4.75   17. 300.53   18. 17.6   19. 34.26   20. 81.97

Lesson 1.13 (pages 28–29)

Choose a strategy and solve.

1. Five students lined up to receive their school lunch tickets. Tasha was first in line. If Karen was between Don and Sergio, and Don was behind Tasha, where was Sandra in line?

2. The school lunch tickets cost $1.15 each. Mrs. Rosen collected 10 quarters, 9 dimes, and 1 nickel from Sergio. How many tickets did he buy?

CHAPTER 2

Lesson 2.1 *(pages 38–39)*

Write a missing-addend sentence for each.

1. $63 - 15 = $ ▨

2. $31 - 19 = $ ▨

3. $72 - 59 = $ ▨

4. $123 - 48 = $ ▨

Write the inverse operation sentence for each. Solve.

5. $16 + $ ▨ $= 93$

6. $112 + $ ▨ $= 139$

7. ▨ $+ 13 = 27$

8. $109 = 45 + $ ▨

Lesson 2.2 *(pages 40–41)*

Estimate each sum. Tell which method you used.

1.   58
   +17
	2. 32
	   +41
		3. 510
		   +293
			4. 326
			   +569
				5. 7,019
				   + 895

6.   43
   78
   61
   +34
	7. 75
	   12
	   93
	   +34
		8. 207
		   629
		   341
		   +537
			9. 362
			   517
			   721
			   +542
				10. 1,293
				   6,742
				   2,140
				   +3,291

Lesson 2.3 *(pages 42–43)*

Estimate the sum. If the estimated sum is greater than 10,000, find the sum.

1.   634
   +329
	2. 207
	   + 84
		3. 6,407
		   +2,317
			4. 34,413
			   +14,793

5.   34,507
   +16,894
	6. 47,598
	   +61,423
		7. 82,730
		   + 5,896
			8. 60,320
			   +29,798

Complete the table.

Number Sentence	Estimate		Sum	
$6,212 + 5,324 = $ ▨	**9.**	▨	**10.**	▨
$3,104 + 828 = $ ▨	**11.**	▨	**12.**	▨
$1,212 + 10,462 = $ ▨	**13.**	▨	**14.**	▨
$16,412 + 3,892 = $ ▨	**15.**	▨	**16.**	▨
$12,142 + 30,912 = $ ▨	**17.**	▨	**18.**	▨

Lesson 2.4 *(pages 44–45)*

Write a number sentence and solve.

1. At basketball practice Manuel made 21 baskets, Nathan made 19 baskets, and Lucas made 8 more than Nathan. How many baskets did the three boys make?

2. Kaitlin bought 2 pairs of soccer shoes that cost $42 a pair. The store ran a special, $21 off the price of a second pair of shoes. How much did Kaitlin pay for both pairs of shoes?

Lesson 2.5 *(pages 46–47)*

Estimate the difference.

1. 525
   −214

2. 829
   −416

3. 920
   −186

4. 791
   − 57

5. 3,512
   − 219

6. 4,692
   −1,921

7. 38,192
   −17,893

8. 16,412
   − 9,843

Lesson 2.6 *(pages 48–49)*

Complete the table.

Number Sentence		Estimate		Difference
36,129 − 13,208 = *n*	1.	▦	2.	▦
82,929 − 40,127 = *n*	3.	▦	4.	▦
47,291 − 19,260 = *n*	5.	▦	6.	▦
76,928 − 23,619 = *n*	7.	▦	8.	▦

Lesson 2.7 *(pages 50–51)*

Find the difference.

1. 700
   −264

2. 1,007
   − 698

3. 30,000
   −18,534

4. 60,009
   −53,874

5. 4,500
   − 692

6. 3,007
   −1,689

7. 400
   −265

8. 940
   −679

9. 8,400
   − 625

10. 12,001
    − 436

11. 60,002
    −25,913

12. 73,004
    −39,425

Lesson 2.8 *(pages 54–55)*

Estimate the sum or difference. Tell which method you used.

1. $7.94
    + 3.62

2. $4.83
    + 7.09

3. 9.14
    −2.69

4. 83.92
    −44.23

5. $21.27
    − 11.23

6. 219.54
    + 99.52

7. $75.62
    − 14.89

8. 51.69
    −29.86

Estimate the sum or difference and compare. Write $<$ or $>$ for ●.

9. $6.13 + 2.97$ ● $7.14 + 1.23$

10. $4.69 - 1.03$ ● $3.97 - 2.01$

11. $5.47 - 2.39$ ● $5.78 - 1.12$

12. $7 + 12.8 + 4.3$ ● $8.2 + 13.7$

Lesson 2.9 *(pages 56–57)*

Estimate the sum to the nearest whole number.

1. 2.6
    +5.8

2. 4.8
    +0.7

3. $7.29
    + 6.43

4. 9.03
    +13.71

5. $21.97
    + 0.83

6. 67.89
    + 9.76

7. 37.26
    +46.17

8. 41.23
    +69.84

Find the sum.

9. 0.25
    +0.67

10. 0.27
    +0.98

11. 6.34
    +9.86

12. $9.27
    + 3.31

13. $87.64
    + 26.79

14. 142.98
    + 69.23

15. 842.78
    +291.60

16. 421.63
    +743.39

Lesson 2.10 *(pages 58–59)*

Complete. Identify the property used.

1. ■ $+ 3.7 = 3.7 + 2.4$

2. $1.8 + (9.3 + 5) = (1.8 + ■) + 5$

3. $7.1 + ■ = 1.6 + 7.1$

4. $(6.4 + 0.9) + 11.2 = 6.4 + (■ + 11.2)$

5. $18.9 + ■ = 18.9$

6. $31.5 + 8.3 = ■ + 31.5$

Lesson 2.11 *(pages 60–61)*

Estimate the difference by rounding to the nearest whole number.

1. $\begin{array}{r} 3.6 \\ -1.2 \\ \hline \end{array}$
2. $\begin{array}{r} 7.4 \\ -6.8 \\ \hline \end{array}$
3. $\begin{array}{r} 32.4 \\ -11.5 \\ \hline \end{array}$
4. $\begin{array}{r} 59.23 \\ -\ 6.45 \\ \hline \end{array}$

Find the difference.

5. $84.73 - 75.68 = n$
6. $9.73 - 4.39 = n$
7. $478.09 - 219.63 = n$

Lesson 2.12 *(pages 62–63)*

Write two equivalent decimals for each.

1. 0.7
2. 2.30
3. 6.5
4. 8.100

Rewrite each problem. Then solve.

5. $0.95 - 0.7 = n$
6. $0.4 + 1.29 = n$
7. $7.1 + 41.23 = n$

Lesson 2.13 *(pages 64–65)*

Estimate the sum or difference to the nearest whole number.

1. $\begin{array}{r} 0.813 \\ +0.594 \\ \hline \end{array}$
2. $\begin{array}{r} 6.815 \\ -3.136 \\ \hline \end{array}$
3. $\begin{array}{r} 8.739 \\ -7.243 \\ \hline \end{array}$
4. $\begin{array}{r} 18.702 \\ +\ 6.914 \\ \hline \end{array}$

Find the sum or difference.

5. $\begin{array}{r} 7.621 \\ +3.147 \\ \hline \end{array}$
6. $\begin{array}{r} 23.194 \\ -16.217 \\ \hline \end{array}$
7. $\begin{array}{r} 83.129 \\ +\ 7.604 \\ \hline \end{array}$
8. $\begin{array}{r} 25.709 \\ +30.827 \\ \hline \end{array}$

9. $3.98 + 0.876 = n$
10. $34.928 - 16.537 = n$
11. $62.401 + 0.983 = n$

12. $31.204 - 14.315 = n$
13. $74.005 + 3.897 = n$
14. $51.001 - 23.174 = n$

Lesson 2.14 *(pages 66–67)*

Solve.

1. Small slides cost $110.75 each. Large slides cost $216.90 each. Susan orders 2 of each. How much will they cost?

2. Marty walks to school 4 days each week. The walk to school takes 15 minutes. The walk home takes 20 minutes. How much time does it take Marty to walk to school and home each week?

More Practice

CHAPTER 3

Chapter 3.1 *(pages 76–77)*

Solve. Identify the property used.

1. $4{,}298 \times \blacksquare = 0$ **2.** $123 \times 1 = \blacksquare$ **3.** $7 \times 42 = \blacksquare \times 7$

4. $(3 \times \blacksquare) \times 40 = 3 \times (6 \times 40)$ **5.** $9 \times 16 = \blacksquare \times 9$ **6.** $(12 \times 2) \times \blacksquare = 12 \times (2 \times 30)$

Solve.

7. $3{,}924 \times 0 = \blacksquare$ **8.** $1{,}118 \times \blacksquare = 3 \times 1{,}118$ **9.** $1{,}294 \times \blacksquare = 1{,}294$

10. $(3 \times 4) \times 10 = 3 \times (\blacksquare \times 10)$ **11.** $74 \times 23 = \blacksquare \times 74$ **12.** $495 \times \blacksquare = 0$

Lesson 3.2 *(pages 78–79)*

Use mental math to find the product.

1. $\begin{array}{r} 30 \\ \times\ 4 \\ \hline \end{array}$	**2.** $\begin{array}{r} 500 \\ \times\ 8 \\ \hline \end{array}$	**3.** $\begin{array}{r} 600 \\ \times\ 2 \\ \hline \end{array}$	**4.** $\begin{array}{r} 2{,}000 \\ \times\ 9 \\ \hline \end{array}$	**5.** $\begin{array}{r} 8{,}000 \\ \times\ 3 \\ \hline \end{array}$
6. $\begin{array}{r} 7{,}000 \\ \times\ 7 \\ \hline \end{array}$	**7.** $\begin{array}{r} 9{,}000 \\ \times\ 6 \\ \hline \end{array}$	**8.** $\begin{array}{r} 600 \\ \times\ 5 \\ \hline \end{array}$	**9.** $\begin{array}{r} 1{,}000 \\ \times\ 8 \\ \hline \end{array}$	**10.** $\begin{array}{r} 10{,}000 \\ \times\ 9 \\ \hline \end{array}$

Complete each number sentence by using mental math.

11. $500 \times 4 = n$ **12.** $300 \times 7 = n$ **13.** $n \times 60 = 360$

14. $3 \times n = 2{,}700$ **15.** $8 \times n = 5{,}600$ **16.** $900 \times n = 8{,}100$

Multiply each number by 10, 100, and 1,000.

17. 3 **18.** 6 **19.** 8 **20.** 10

Lesson 3.3 *(pages 80–81)*

Estimate each product. Tell which method you used.

1. $\begin{array}{r} 46 \\ \times\ 5 \\ \hline \end{array}$	**2.** $\begin{array}{r} 82 \\ \times\ 4 \\ \hline \end{array}$	**3.** $\begin{array}{r} 192 \\ \times\ 6 \\ \hline \end{array}$	**4.** $\begin{array}{r} 599 \\ \times\ 2 \\ \hline \end{array}$
5. $\begin{array}{r} 2{,}921 \\ \times\ 3 \\ \hline \end{array}$	**6.** $\begin{array}{r} 1{,}134 \\ \times\ 6 \\ \hline \end{array}$	**7.** $\begin{array}{r} 12{,}921 \\ \times\ 3 \\ \hline \end{array}$	**8.** $\begin{array}{r} 17{,}547 \\ \times\ 9 \\ \hline \end{array}$

Lesson 3.4 *(pages 82–83)*

Complete. Find each product.

1. Find 6×34.
$6 \times 30 = n$
$6 \times 4 = n$
Add.
$180 + 24 = n$
$6 \times 34 = n$

2. Find 4×62.
$4 \times 60 = n$
$4 \times 2 = n$
Add.
$240 + 8 = n$
$4 \times 62 = n$

3. Find 8×29.
$8 \times 20 = n$
$8 \times 9 = n$
Add.
$160 + 72 = n$
$8 \times 29 = n$

Lesson 3.5 *(pages 84–85)*

Solve. Use counters to model each regrouping.

1. $5 \times 23 = n$

2. $9 \times 37 = n$

3. $3 \times 56 = n$

4. $4 \times 83 = n$

5. $7 \times 29 = n$

6. $5 \times 43 = n$

7. $6 \times 48 = n$

8. $8 \times 92 = n$

9. $7 \times 68 = n$

Estimate each product by rounding. If the estimate is greater than 1,000, find the product.

10. $\begin{array}{r} 42 \\ \times\ 5 \\ \hline \end{array}$

11. $\begin{array}{r} 87 \\ \times\ 3 \\ \hline \end{array}$

12. $\begin{array}{r} 294 \\ \times\ \ 6 \\ \hline \end{array}$

13. $\begin{array}{r} 819 \\ \times\ \ 2 \\ \hline \end{array}$

14. $\begin{array}{r} 119 \\ \times\ \ 4 \\ \hline \end{array}$

15. $\begin{array}{r} 1{,}123 \\ \times\ \ \ \ 7 \\ \hline \end{array}$

16. $\begin{array}{r} 3{,}175 \\ \times\ \ \ \ 3 \\ \hline \end{array}$

17. $\begin{array}{r} 6{,}543 \\ \times\ \ \ \ 5 \\ \hline \end{array}$

18. $\begin{array}{r} 593 \\ \times\ \ 2 \\ \hline \end{array}$

19. $\begin{array}{r} 2{,}403 \\ \times\ \ \ \ 6 \\ \hline \end{array}$

Lesson 3.6 *(pages 86–87)*

Solve.

1. Mrs. Lee ordered 15 copies of *Introduction to the Microscope* at $8 each. She bought 23 pamphlets about starfish at $4 each. How much money did she spend on books and pamphlets?

2. Felipe bought 2 sets of microscope slides at $22 per set and a lab manual for $8. He paid for his purchases with two $50 bills. How much change did he receive?

3. Elliot bought 4 toy trucks at $2 each and 3 action figures at $3 each. How much money did he have left if he started with $25?

4. Danielle had $45. She bought 2 compact discs at $14 each and a calculator at $12. How much money did she have left after her purchases?

Lesson 3.7 (pages 90–91)

Use mental math to find the product.

| 1. 40 $\times 20$ | 2. 30 $\times 30$ | 3. 200 $\times 60$ | 4. 600 $\times 30$ | 5. 500 $\times 10$ |

| 6. 700 $\times 50$ | 7. 1,000 $\times 20$ | 8. 900 $\times 10$ | 9. 4,000 $\times 40$ | 10. 8,000 $\times 90$ |

11. $5,000 \times 60 = n$ 12. $80 \times 70 = n$ 13. $700 \times 30 = n$

14. $7,000 \times 40 = n$ 15. $3,000 \times 60 = n$ 16. $50,000 \times 60 = n$

Lesson 3.8 (pages 92–93)

Estimate the product.

| 1. 59 $\times 24$ | 2. 32 $\times 61$ | 3. 68 $\times 17$ | 4. 47 $\times 86$ | 5. 55 $\times 62$ |

| 6. 76 $\times 34$ | 7. 493 $\times 17$ | 8. 738 $\times 25$ | 9. 949 $\times 94$ | 10. 563 $\times 81$ |

11. $79 \times 293 \approx n$ 12. $32 \times 687 \approx n$ 13. $16 \times 827 \approx n$

14. $56 \times 473 \approx n$ 15. $23 \times 842 \approx n$ 16. $14 \times 921 \approx n$

Lesson 3.9 (pages 94–95)

Find the product.

| 1. 18 $\times 33$ | 2. 48 $\times 17$ | 3. 29 $\times 43$ | 4. 192 $\times 14$ | 5. 438 $\times 16$ |

| 6. 509 $\times 15$ | 7. 224 $\times 17$ | 8. 250 $\times 54$ | 9. 619 $\times 92$ | 10. 423 $\times 75$ |

11. $64 \times 17 = n$ 12. $43 \times 291 = n$ 13. $13 \times 964 = n$

14. $32 \times 456 = n$ 15. $67 \times 949 = n$ 16. $43 \times 608 = n$

17. $83 \times 127 = n$ 18. $45 \times 350 = n$ 19. $95 \times 435 = n$

Lesson 3.10 *(pages 96–97)*

Estimate the product.

1. 421 ×192	**2.** 294 ×623	**3.** 609 ×302	**4.** 521 ×347	**5.** 732 ×121
6. 1,293 × 550	**7.** 6,529 × 143	**8.** 927 ×314	**9.** 4,293 × 617	**10.** 2,654 × 692

Find the product.

11. 320 ×403	**12.** 780 ×680	**13.** 348 ×627	**14.** 647 ×432	**15.** 427 ×806
16. 5,423 × 143	**17.** 8,234 × 203	**18.** 9,615 × 981	**19.** 4,530 × 705	**20.** 2,746 × 825
21. 8,743 × 403	**22.** 5,090 × 672	**23.** 4,302 × 430	**24.** 3,487 × 226	**25.** 6,821 × 376

Lesson 3.11 *(pages 98–99)*

Solve.

1. A custodian at the zoo cleaned the bird cages on August 4, 7, and 10. He cleaned the monkey cages on August 11, 15, and 19. If the custodian continues the same cleaning pattern, what is the next date he will clean the bird cages? What is the next date he will clean the monkey cages?

2. An animal trainer was teaching a monkey to catch a ball. When he stood 3 feet from the monkey, the monkey caught 6 of 8 balls. When he stood 4 feet from the monkey, the monkey caught 5 of 8 balls. At 5 feet the monkey caught every other ball. If the pattern continues, how many balls will the monkey catch at a distance of 8 feet?

3. The snakes were fed on July 1, 9, and 17. The tigers were fed on July 7, 9, and 11. If the same pattern of feeding continues, what is the next date the snakes will be fed? What is the next date the tigers will be fed?

4. The zoo closes early every third day so the trainers can exercise the animals. If it closes early on Monday, on what other day of the week will it close early?

CHAPTER 4

Lesson 4.1 *(pages 108–110)*

Choose the sentence or sentences that describe the
relationship of the lines. Write **a, b,** or **c.**

1.

a. $\overleftrightarrow{FG}$ is parallel to $\overleftrightarrow{HI}$.

b. $\overleftrightarrow{FG}$ is perpendicular
to $\overleftrightarrow{HI}$.

c. $\overleftrightarrow{FG}$ intersects $\overleftrightarrow{HI}$.

2.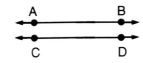

a. $\overleftrightarrow{AB}$ is not parallel to
$\overleftrightarrow{CD}$.

b. $\overline{AB}$ intersects $\overline{CD}$.

c. $\overleftrightarrow{AB}$ is parallel to
$\overleftrightarrow{CD}$.

3.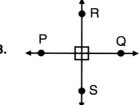

a. $\overleftrightarrow{PQ}$ is parallel to $\overleftrightarrow{RS}$.

b. $\overleftrightarrow{PQ}$ is perpendicular
to $\overleftrightarrow{RS}$.

c. $\overleftrightarrow{PQ}$ intersects $\overleftrightarrow{RS}$.

Lesson 4.2 *(pages 112–113)*

Identify the angle. Write *right*, *acute*, or *obtuse*.

1.

2.

3.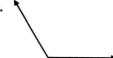

Use the figure for Exercises 4–6.

4. Name two acute angles.

5. Name an obtuse angle.

6. Name a right angle.

Lesson 4.3 *(pages 114–115)*

Trace each angle. First, estimate the angle measure. Then, use
a protractor to measure each angle. You may need to extend
the rays.

1.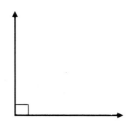

2.

3.

Use a protractor to solve.

4. Use a protractor to draw an angle of 70°.

5. Draw an acute angle and an obtuse angle. Use a protractor to measure each angle. Record the measures.

Lesson 4.4 *(pages 116–117)*

Copy and complete the table.

Polygons		
Name of Polygon	**Number of Sides**	**Number of Angles**
Rectangle	1. ▢	2. ▢
Quadrilateral	3. ▢	4. ▢
Pentagon	5. ▢	6. ▢
Octagon	7. ▢	8. ▢

Write *true* or *false*.

9. A sixagon has six angles and six sides.

10. A pentagon has five angles and five sides.

11. All polygons are quadrilaterals.

12. All quadrilaterals are polygons.

Lesson 4.5 *(pages 118–119)*

Identify the triangle. Write *equilateral*, *isosceles*, or *scalene*.

1. 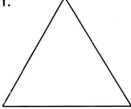 **2.**  **3.** 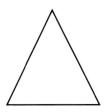 **4.**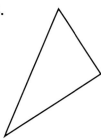

Lesson 4.6 *(pages 120–121)*

Name each triangle. Write *right*, *acute*, or *obtuse*.

1. 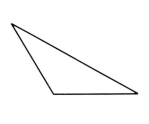 **2.**  **3.** **4.**

Lesson 4.7 *(pages 122–123)*

Name the quadrilaterals.

1.
2.
3.
4.

Lesson 4.8 *(pages 124–125)*

Solve. Use the strategy guess and check.

1. A survey of 60 students was taken to find whether they preferred soccer or baseball. There were 22 fewer students who preferred soccer. How many students preferred soccer?

2. Jamal bought a new camera and lens. The total cost for both items was $450. The camera cost $150 more than the lens. What was the cost of the camera?

3. The sum of two numbers is 14. The difference of the numbers is 2. What are the numbers?

4. The sum of two numbers is 15. The difference of the numbers is 3. What are the numbers?

Lesson 4.9 *(pages 128–129)*

Tell whether the picture shows a mirror image. Write *yes* or *no*.

1.
2.
3.

Trace each figure. Draw all the lines of symmetry for each figure.

4.
5.
6.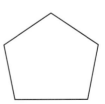

Lesson 4.10 *(pages 130–131)*

Write *slide*, *flip*, or *turn* to indicate how each figure was moved.

1.
2.
3.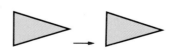

Lesson 4.11 *(pages 132–133)*

Are the figures similar? Write *yes* or *no.*

1.    **2.** 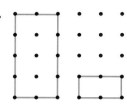   **3.** 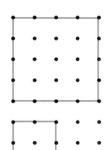   **4.**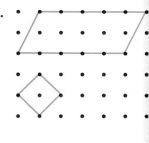

Lesson 4.12 *(pages 134–135)*

Use the diagram to answer Exercises 1–5.

1. What is the name of the circle?

2. Name the chords.

3. Name a radius.

4. What line segment would you multiply by 2 to find the diameter?

5. What line segment is both a chord and diameter?

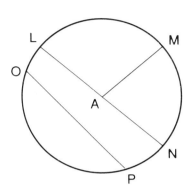

Write *sometimes*, *always*, or *never* for Exercises 6–7.

6. A diameter __?__ passes through the center of a circle.

7. A chord is __?__ shorter than a diameter.

Lesson 4.13 *(pages 136–139)*

Name the solid figures.

1.   **2.**   **3.**   **4.**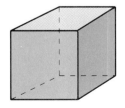

Lesson 4.14 *(pages 140–141)*

Choose a strategy and solve.

1. Jerome is arranging 8 square tables to seat his friends at a party. Each table can seat 1 friend on each side. If the tables are pushed together to make one long table, how many friends can be seated?

2. Mrs. Revell and 4 friends are planning to visit the museum. If every person goes once with each of the other persons, how many visits will be made to the museum?

CHAPTER 5

Lesson 5.1 *(pages 150–151)*

Use the rules to decide whether the first number is divisible by the second number. Write *yes* or *no*.

1. $64, 9$	**2.** $81, 8$	**3.** $19, 3$	**4.** $14, 2$	**5.** $24, 5$
6. $57, 7$	**7.** $40, 4$	**8.** $80, 10$	**9.** $21, 6$	**10.** $56, 9$
11. $87, 3$	**12.** $90, 5$	**13.** $95, 10$	**14.** $84, 6$	**15.** $69, 9$

Use the rules to decide whether each number is divisible by 2, 3, 5, and 10. Complete the table. Write *yes* or *no*.

	Number	Divisible by:			
		2	**3**	**5**	**10**
16.	16				
17.	85				
18.	136				
19.	260				
20.	270				

	Number	Divisible by:			
		2	**3**	**5**	**10**
21.	28				
22.	33				
23.	125				
24.	230				
25.	300				

Lesson 5.2 *(pages 152–153)*

Estimate each quotient.

1. $2\overline{)13}$	**2.** $5\overline{)16}$	**3.** $7\overline{)43}$	**4.** $8\overline{)36}$
5. $4\overline{)85}$	**6.** $9\overline{)94}$	**7.** $3\overline{)62}$	**8.** $6\overline{)132}$

9. $509 \div 5 \approx n$	**10.** $495 \div 7 \approx n$	**11.** $814 \div 9 \approx n$
12. $628 \div 7 \approx n$	**13.** $719 \div 8 \approx n$	**14.** $896 \div 9 \approx n$

Lesson 5.3 *(pages 154–155)*

Estimate. Then find the quotient.

1. $4\overline{)79}$	**2.** $5\overline{)46}$	**3.** $3\overline{)20}$	**4.** $9\overline{)80}$	**5.** $6\overline{)55}$
6. $7\overline{)51}$	**7.** $2\overline{)45}$	**8.** $8\overline{)43}$	**9.** $4\overline{)84}$	**10.** $4\overline{)44}$
11. $8\overline{)58}$	**12.** $5\overline{)76}$	**13.** $9\overline{)91}$	**14.** $7\overline{)32}$	**15.** $3\overline{)67}$

Divide. Then check each quotient.

16. $74 \div 3 = n$ **17.** $93 \div 8 = n$ **18.** $89 \div 6 = n$ **19.** $82 \div 5 = n$

20. $47 \div 8 = n$ **21.** $90 \div 4 = n$ **22.** $28 \div 6 = n$ **23.** $91 \div 7 = n$

24. $58 \div 8 = n$ **25.** $75 \div 5 = n$ **26.** $91 \div 9 = n$ **27.** $51 \div 3 = n$

Lesson 5.4 (pages 156–157)

Estimate each quotient.

1. $2\overline{)171}$ **2.** $7\overline{)263}$ **3.** $8\overline{)194}$ **4.** $7\overline{)253}$ **5.** $5\overline{)135}$

6. $9\overline{)851}$ **7.** $4\overline{)275}$ **8.** $4\overline{)351}$ **9.** $5\overline{)145}$ **10.** $6\overline{)124}$

11. $3\overline{)295}$ **12.** $9\overline{)700}$ **13.** $2\overline{)186}$ **14.** $5\overline{)361}$ **15.** $8\overline{)555}$

Divide.

16. $7\overline{)195}$ **17.** $8\overline{)608}$ **18.** $7\overline{)325}$ **19.** $5\overline{)794}$ **20.** $6\overline{)275}$

21. $4\overline{)327}$ **22.** $6\overline{)462}$ **23.** $9\overline{)315}$ **24.** $8\overline{)895}$ **25.** $3\overline{)472}$

26. $329 \div 8 = n$ **27.** $214 \div 6 = n$ **28.** $780 \div 5 = n$ **29.** $488 \div 9 = n$

30. $295 \div 6 = n$ **31.** $477 \div 8 = n$ **32.** $792 \div 7 = n$ **33.** $852 \div 9 = n$

Lesson 5.5 (pages 158–159)

Use short division to find each quotient.

1. $5\overline{)442}$ **2.** $3\overline{)854}$ **3.** $4\overline{)89}$ **4.** $5\overline{)76}$ **5.** $6\overline{)293}$

6. $8\overline{)198}$ **7.** $7\overline{)57}$ **8.** $3\overline{)945}$ **9.** $4\overline{)278}$ **10.** $7\overline{)584}$

11. $4\overline{)592}$ **12.** $6\overline{)763}$ **13.** $4\overline{)642}$ **14.** $9\overline{)212}$ **15.** $8\overline{)678}$

16. $846 \div 5 = n$ **17.** $697 \div 4 = n$ **18.** $489 \div 8 = n$ **19.** $765 \div 9 = n$

Solve.

20. What are the possible remainders if you divide by 4?

21. What are the possible remainders if you divide by 7?

22. What are the possible remainders if you divide by 6?

23. What are the possible remainders if you divide by 9?

Lesson 5.6 *(pages 160–161)*

Choose the correct operation and solve.

1. Carlos worked 7 hours on Monday, 6 hours on Tuesday, 8 hours on Wednesday, and 9 hours on Thursday. How many hours did he work in all?

2. Marty works at the Mall Flower Shop. He is planning a display of 48 plants. He wants to place the same number of plants on each of 8 shelves. How many plants will he place on each shelf?

3. The manager of a television store has 178 televisions in stock. If he sells 89 one day and 43 another day, how many televisions are left to sell?

4. Elisa sold 12 bottles of perfume at $29 each and 8 bottles of perfume at $19 each. What was the total amount of her sales?

Lesson 5.7 *(pages 164–165)*

Divide.

1. $3\overline{)60}$
2. $7\overline{)748}$
3. $5\overline{)253}$
4. $3\overline{)628}$
5. $8\overline{)835}$

6. $7\overline{)765}$
7. $3\overline{)925}$
8. $8\overline{)5,760}$
9. $5\overline{)4,152}$
10. $4\overline{)2,482}$

11. $3,000 \div 5 = n$
12. $1,817 \div 3 = n$
13. $3,675 \div 9 = n$
14. $1,418 \div 2 = n$

15. $3,640 \div 6 = n$
16. $3,481 \div 2 = n$
17. $6,020 \div 6 = n$
18. $5,490 \div 3 = n$

19. $2,025 \div 4 = n$
20. $2,100 \div 3 = n$
21. $5,745 \div 7 = n$
22. $3,002 \div 3 = n$

23. $3,405 \div 5 = n$
24. $2,960 \div 3 = n$
25. $1,609 \div 5 = n$
26. $3,659 \div 8 = n$

27. $4,283 \div 9 = n$
28. $3,562 \div 7 = n$
29. $2,520 \div 4 = n$
30. $4,523 \div 3 = n$

Lesson 5.8 *(pages 166–167)*

Estimate. Then find the quotient.

1. $2,919 \div 7 = n$
2. $7,092 \div 6 = n$
3. $14,580 \div 9 = n$

4. $62,427 \div 3 = n$
5. $29,676 \div 4 = n$
6. $81,252 \div 6 = n$

7. $71,632 \div 8 = n$
8. $53,000 \div 5 = n$
9. $15,813 \div 7 = n$

10. $63,928 \div 9 = n$
11. $67,000 \div 7 = n$
12. $23,843 \div 4 = n$

13. $34,764 \div 4 = n$
14. $73,000 \div 5 = n$
15. $42,089 \div 8 = n$

Lesson 5.9 *(pages 168–169)*

Use the table for Exercises 1–4.

1. What is the average number of tandem bicycles rented in 4 weeks?

2. Which type of vehicle averaged the greatest number of rentals in 4 weeks?

3. What is the average number of mopeds rented in 4 weeks?

June Vehicle Rentals			
	Bicycles	Tandem Bicycles	Mopeds
Week 1	98	35	49
Week 2	79	41	67
Week 3	64	45	63
Week 4	59	39	69

4. Which type of vehicle averaged the greatest number of rentals in the last two weeks?

Find the average.

5. 87; 11; 19

6. 34; 160; 85; 53

7. 160; 121; 151

8. 320; 294; 265; 301

9. 723; 859; 1,124

10. 3,121; 3,040; 2,998

11. 32; 25; 30; 28; 35

12. 1,121; 1,087; 1,095

13. 52; 34; 62; 23; 71; 52

14. 36; 113; 29; 18; 54

15. 4,212; 3,953; 958

16. 18; 42; 17; 31; 7; 23

Lesson 5.10 *(pages 170–171)*

Work backward and solve.

1. Bowler John Pezzin holds the record for the most strikes in a row. If you take the number of strikes, subtract 3, add 15, and then subtract 6, the result is 39. How many strikes is the record?

2. Because he was traded in the middle of a season, Ross Lansberry played more than 78 hockey games in a 78-game season. If you take the number of games he played, subtract 40, add 7, and then subtract 3, the result is 46. How many games did Ross Lansberry play?

3. Kirk went to the grocery store and bought apples for $1.29, bread for $0.99, and 3 cans of juice for $0.79 each. He was given $5.35 in change. How much money did he give the cashier?

4. Darla deposited $25.50 in her savings account one week. The next week she deposited $32.75. If her total savings increased to $456.90, how much was in Darla's account before she made the two deposits?

CHAPTER 6

Lesson 6.1 *(pages 180–181)*

Find the quotient.

1. $40 \div 20 = n$
2. $100 \div 10 = n$
3. $320 \div 40 = n$

4. $480 \div 60 = n$
5. $2{,}700 \div 90 = n$
6. $25{,}000 \div 50 = n$

7. $20\overline{)20}$
8. $10\overline{)70}$
9. $7\overline{)70}$
10. $30\overline{)600}$

11. $20\overline{)400}$
12. $30\overline{)180}$
13. $70\overline{)420}$
14. $90\overline{)810}$

15. $60\overline{)3{,}600}$
16. $20\overline{)8{,}000}$
17. $50\overline{)3{,}500}$
18. $30\overline{)30{,}000}$

Lesson 6.2 *(pages 182–183)*

Write two pairs of compatible numbers for each. Give two possible estimates.

1. $214 \div 35 \approx n$
2. $490 \div 77 \approx n$
3. $176 \div 27 \approx n$

4. $353 \div 57 \approx n$
5. $1{,}192 \div 28 \approx n$
6. $4{,}192 \div 77 \approx n$

Estimate the quotient.

7. $18\overline{)203}$
8. $23\overline{)217}$
9. $42\overline{)827}$
10. $46\overline{)519}$

11. $29\overline{)192}$
12. $37\overline{)856}$
13. $82\overline{)396}$
14. $11\overline{)743}$

15. $46\overline{)483}$
16. $92\overline{)789}$
17. $34\overline{)265}$
18. $21\overline{)189}$

Lesson 6.3 *(pages 184–185)*

Divide. Check with multiplication.

1. $15\overline{)46}$
2. $41\overline{)57}$
3. $21\overline{)93}$
4. $16\overline{)37}$

5. $32\overline{)82}$
6. $22\overline{)74}$
7. $19\overline{)49}$
8. $23\overline{)97}$

9. $80 \div 14 = n$
10. $54 \div 23 = n$
11. $76 \div 12 = n$

12. $75 \div 17 = n$
13. $64 \div 13 = n$
14. $98 \div 16 = n$

15. $87 \div 14 = n$
16. $74 \div 12 = n$
17. $95 \div 15 = n$

Lesson 6.4 *(pages 186–187)*

Choose the correct estimate to use in the quotient. Write **a** or **b**.

1. $16\overline{)298}$ a. 20   b. 10   6. $23\overline{)610}$ a. 30   b. 40

2. $48\overline{)176}$ a. 2   b. 3   7. $82\overline{)318}$ a. 5   b. 4

3. $35\overline{)314}$ a. 8   b. 7   8. $71\overline{)349}$ a. 4   b. 5

4. $23\overline{)160}$ a. 6   b. 7   9. $52\overline{)411}$ a. 8   b. 9

5. $41\overline{)290}$ a. 7   b. 6   10. $59\overline{)477}$ a. 7   b. 8

Divide.

11. $11\overline{)63}$ 12. $14\overline{)76}$ 13. $23\overline{)60}$ 14. $52\overline{)482}$

15. $74\overline{)449}$ 16. $34\overline{)256}$ 17. $79\overline{)239}$ 18. $84\overline{)342}$

Lesson 6.5 *(pages 188–189)*

Estimate. Then find the quotient.

1. $42\overline{)938}$ 2. $52\overline{)851}$ 3. $16\overline{)763}$ 4. $38\overline{)892}$

Find the quotient.

5. $78\overline{)957}$ 6. $40\overline{)873}$ 7. $39\overline{)897}$ 8. $17\overline{)357}$

9. $21\overline{)532}$ 10. $56\overline{)712}$ 11. $28\overline{)576}$ 12. $63\overline{)748}$

13. $30\overline{)938}$ 14. $48\overline{)495}$ 15. $54\overline{)973}$ 16. $78\overline{)712}$

17. $939 \div 44 = n$ 18. $589 \div 28 = n$ 19. $267 \div 34 = n$

Lesson 6.6 *(pages 190–191)*

Tell whether an exact answer is needed. Solve.

1. A teacher ordered a kit for $57.60, microscope slides for $5.12, and a microscope for $298.97. She had $375.00 to spend. Did she have enough money? How much did she spend?

2. About four students can work at each science center. Estimate how many centers are needed if there are 38 students in the Science Club.

Lesson 6.7 *(pages 194–195)*

Choose the correct answer. Write **a**, **b**, or **c**.

1. $15\overline{)2{,}453}$ **a.** 153   **b.** 163 r8   **c.** 162 r8

2. $17\overline{)1{,}263}$ **a.** 74 r5   **b.** 64 r5   **c.** 75

3. $32\overline{)7{,}808}$ **a.** 245   **b.** 244   **c.** 246

4. $43\overline{)1{,}384}$ **a.** 33   **b.** 31   **c.** 32 r8

5. $33\overline{)5{,}697}$ **a.** 173   **b.** 172 r21   **c.** 173 r27

6. $27\overline{)8{,}954}$ **a.** 331   **b.** 332   **c.** 331 r17

Estimate. Then find the quotient.

7. $58\overline{)4{,}128}$ 8. $24\overline{)1{,}968}$ 9. $50\overline{)3{,}361}$ 10. $62\overline{)5{,}420}$

11. $22\overline{)1{,}631}$ 12. $21\overline{)1{,}327}$ 13. $31\overline{)1{,}742}$ 14. $47\overline{)3{,}359}$

Divide.

15. $82{,}736 \div 38 = n$ 16. $15{,}398 \div 93 = n$ 17. $59{,}099 \div 64 = n$

18. $67{,}032 \div 39 = n$ 19. $19{,}047 \div 85 = n$ 20. $63{,}019 \div 54 = n$

21. $72{,}097 \div 45 = n$ 22. $13{,}946 \div 78 = n$ 23. $58{,}215 \div 93 = n$

Lesson 6.8 *(pages 196–197)*

Divide.

1. $20\overline{)400}$ 2. $14\overline{)420}$ 3. $17\overline{)685}$ 4. $19\overline{)2{,}098}$

5. $18\overline{)3{,}080}$ 6. $13\overline{)6{,}552}$ 7. $18\overline{)5{,}526}$ 8. $13\overline{)7{,}838}$

9. $3{,}131 \div 31 = n$ 10. $5{,}382 \div 26 = n$ 11. $3{,}888 \div 36 = n$

12. $13{,}150 \div 36 = n$ 13. $23{,}410 \div 57 = n$ 14. $37{,}050 \div 61 = n$

15. $14{,}649 \div 47 = n$ 16. $56{,}094 \div 34 = n$ 17. $48{,}201 \div 93 = n$

18. $19{,}040 \div 42 = n$ 19. $89{,}405 \div 31 = n$ 20. $53{,}200 \div 62 = n$

21. $12{,}090 \div 22 = n$ 22. $56{,}002 \div 91 = n$ 23. $18{,}004 \div 19 = n$

Find the quotient.

24. $34{,}921 \div 18 = n$ **25.** $27{,}090 \div 36 = n$ **26.** $50{,}325 \div 74 = n$

27. $40{,}029 \div 29 = n$ **28.** $60{,}387 \div 92 = n$ **29.** $89{,}048 \div 53 = n$

30. $30{,}847 \div 48 = n$ **31.** $59{,}048 \div 57 = n$ **32.** $47{,}408 \div 81 = n$

33. $49{,}028 \div 63 = n$ **34.** $71{,}049 \div 41 = n$ **35.** $40{,}913 \div 66 = n$

Lesson 6.9 (pages 198–199)

Use a calculator to divide. Then find the remainder.

1. $17\overline{)48{,}192}$ **2.** $81\overline{)62{,}109}$ **3.** $15\overline{)75{,}623}$ **4.** $43\overline{)29{,}815}$

5. $43\overline{)30{,}628}$ **6.** $29\overline{)62{,}517}$ **7.** $91\overline{)43{,}218}$ **8.** $21\overline{)64{,}582}$

9. $14{,}261 \div 14 = n$ **10.** $79{,}216 \div 58 = n$ **11.** $46{,}987 \div 39 = n$

12. $36{,}257 \div 17 = n$ **13.** $37{,}842 \div 36 = n$ **14.** $48{,}634 \div 56 = n$

15. $53{,}845 \div 52 = n$ **16.** $42{,}946 \div 63 = n$ **17.** $98{,}024 \div 43 = n$

18. $66{,}029 \div 14 = n$ **19.** $77{,}215 \div 79 = n$ **20.** $88{,}358 \div 51 = n$

21. $41{,}806 \div 25 = n$ **22.** $52{,}934 \div 84 = n$ **23.** $35{,}914 \div 19 = n$

24. $59{,}882 \div 86 = n$ **25.** $23{,}841 \div 21 = n$ **26.** $12{,}054 \div 35 = n$

Lesson 6.10 (pages 200–201)

Choose a strategy and solve.

1. On her birthday, Annie received $10 from her grandparents, $10 from an aunt, and $15 from her parents. She now has $70. How much money did Annie have before her birthday?

2. The sum of the ages of a mother and a daughter is 50. The difference between their ages is 22 years. How old is the mother?

3. The total number of reporters and photographers who work at the *Daily Herald* is 30. There are 12 more reporters than photographers. How many reporters work at the *Daily Herald*?

4. A zookeeper cleans the bear cage on August 2, 9, and 16. If the same pattern of cleaning continues, what is the next date the zookeeper will clean the bear cage?

CHAPTER 7

Lesson 7.1 *(pages 210–211)*

Tell which sample group would better predict the choice of fifth graders. Defend your answer.

Soccer Team Sample Group	
Favorite Sport	
Sport	**Number of Students**
Football	10
Soccer	24
Gymnastics	3
Tennis	8

Random Sample Group	
Favorite Sport	
Sport	**Number of Students**
Football	25
Soccer	9
Gymnastics	10
Tennis	6

Lesson 7.2 *(pages 212–213)*

Find the range, mean, median, and mode.

1. 67, 23, 129, 83, 83

2. 40, 50, 22, 68, 40, 35, 60

3. 85, 40, 131, 94, 85

4. 43, 60, 88, 72, 55, 88, 77

5. 18, 25, 15, 29, 18

6. 103, 109, 113, 110, 110

7. $196, $181, $196

8. 48, 72, 48, 83, 49

9. 496, 321, 480, 496, 397

10. $86, $93, $73, $42, $86

Lesson 7.3 *(pages 214–215)*

Use the pictograph for Exercises 1–7.

1. Which month had the most rainfall?

2. How much rain fell in April?

3. How much rain fell in July?

4. Which months had the same amount of rain?

5. How much more rain fell in April than in January?

6. How much more rain fell in July than in October?

7. How many symbols would represent 7 in. of rain?

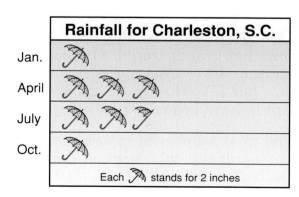

Lesson 7.4 *(pages 216–217)*

Use the bar graph for Exercises 1–6.

1. In which years were there more than 50 inches of snow?

2. In which years were there fewer than 50 inches of snow?

3. How many inches of snow fell in 1987?

4. How many more inches of snow fell in 1982 than in 1977?

5. How many inches of snow fell in 1967 and 1972 altogether?

6. How much more snow fell in 1967 than in 1972?

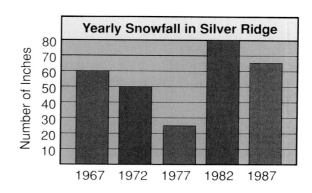

Lesson 7.5 *(pages 218–219)*

Choose the most reasonable scale for the set of data.
Write **a**, **b**, or **c**.

Favorite Pets	
Pet	**Number of Students**
Fish	10
Dog	35
Cat	40
Bird	5

a. 100 80 60 40 20 0

b. 50 45 40 35 30 25 20 15 10 5 0

c. 10 9 8 7 6 5 4 3 2 1 0

Lesson 7.6 *(pages 220–221)*

Choose a strategy and solve.

1. There are 450 report cards to distribute to fifth graders. If one teacher can give 30 students their report cards every 15 minutes, how long will it take her to distribute all of them?

2. The Art Club has orders for 300 ceramic vases. If the club can make 15 vases in one day, how many days will it take to fill the orders?

Lesson 7.7 (pages 224–225)

Use the line graph for Exercises 1–5.

1. For which months did the high temperatures differ by 1°?

2. For which months did the high temperature increase from 24°C to 28°C?

3. What is the normal high temperature for the month of April?

4. For which month is the high temperature 14°C?

5. What is the normal high temperature for the month of June?

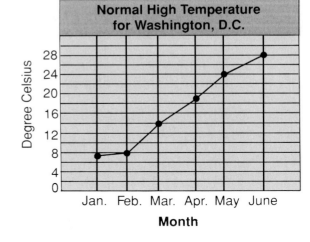

Lesson 7.8 (pages 226–227)

Use the data in the table for Exercises 1–4.

1. If you make a line graph of the data, what will the intervals be in the scale on the vertical axis?

2. What should the label be on the horizontal axis?

3. Which months had the same amount of rainfall?

4. Would the line on the graph go up or down?

Average Monthly Rainfall For Seattle, Washington	
Month	Rainfall in cm
January	14
February	12
March	9
April	6
May	4
June	4

Lesson 7.9 (pages 228–229)

Use the circle graph for Exercises 1–3.

1. How many students are in Mrs. Flanagan's class?

2. How does the part of the class that chose to read compare to the part of the class that chose to watch a movie?

3. How would you change the graph if 7 of the students who chose to watch a movie decided to play a game?

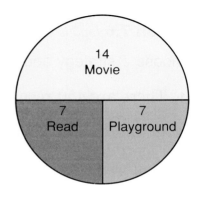

Survey Results of
Mrs. Flanagan's Class

Lesson 7.10 (pages 230–231)

Choose a type of graph for Exercises 1–7. Explain your choice.

1. monthly budget divided into different expenses

2. height development of a plant for a science project

3. amount of rainfall for the year in a certain city

4. types of sports preferred by the students in your class

5. amount of money earned by different classes from the bake sale

6. population growth in a certain city

7. number of trees in a national park

Lesson 7.11 (pages 232–233)

Organize the information in a table. Use logical reasoning to solve.

1. Megan, Chico, Loas, and Roberta belong to the Reading Club. Megan likes to read nonfiction. Roberta does not like biographies. Loas likes poetry, and one of the students reads mysteries. List the kind of book each student enjoys reading.

2. Tisha, Janel, and Bruce are signing up for after-school activities. One signs up for band, one for science club, and one for the track team. Tisha does not like to run, and Bruce does not like to run and does not play an instrument. Who signed up for each activity?

Lesson 7.12 (pages 234–235)

Name the ordered pair for each building.

1. Hotel
2. Restaurant
3. Television Store
4. Hardware Store
5. Food Store
6. Train Station
7. Bank
8. Post Office
9. Record Store
10. Bus Station
11. School
12. Clothing Store

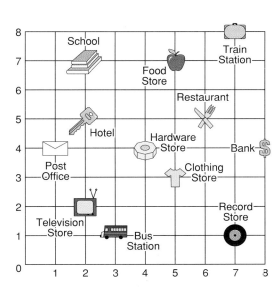

CHAPTER 8

Lesson 8.1 (pages 244–245)

Multiply each number by 10, 100, and 1,000.

1. 0.6 **2.** 4.2 **3.** 1.79 **4.** 0.23 **5.** 51.6

6. 21.64 **7.** 0.519 **8.** 1.654 **9.** 0.073 **10.** 39.083

Find each product.

11. $10 \times 0.5 = n$ **12.** $100 \times 0.8 = n$ **13.** $100 \times 5.3 = n$

14. $100 \times 36.82 = n$ **15.** $1,000 \times 0.76 = n$ **16.** $1,000 \times 0.097 = n$

17. $100 \times 8.976 = n$ **18.** $10 \times 59.29 = n$ **19.** $1,000 \times 36.907 = n$

Lesson 8.2 (pages 246–247)

Estimate each product.

1. $\begin{array}{r} 6.7 \\ \times\ 12 \\ \hline \end{array}$ **2.** $\begin{array}{r} 4.2 \\ \times\ 48 \\ \hline \end{array}$ **3.** $\begin{array}{r} 9.8 \\ \times\ 42 \\ \hline \end{array}$ **4.** $\begin{array}{r} 2.5 \\ \times\ 25 \\ \hline \end{array}$ **5.** $\begin{array}{r} 1.8 \\ \times\ 97 \\ \hline \end{array}$

6. $\begin{array}{r} 7.4 \\ \times\ 28 \\ \hline \end{array}$ **7.** $\begin{array}{r} 9.65 \\ \times\ 42 \\ \hline \end{array}$ **8.** $\begin{array}{r} 5.33 \\ \times\ 29 \\ \hline \end{array}$ **9.** $\begin{array}{r} 2.94 \\ \times\ 19 \\ \hline \end{array}$ **10.** $\begin{array}{r} 7.03 \\ \times\ 11 \\ \hline \end{array}$

11. $2.9 \times 92 \approx n$ **12.** $6.57 \times 72 \approx n$ **13.** $36.2 \times 81 \approx n$

14. $92 \times 4.76 \approx n$ **15.** $7.31 \times 48 \approx n$ **16.** $8.4 \times 49 \approx n$

Lesson 8.3 (pages 248–249)

Use a graph-paper model to find each product.

1. $0.4 \times 0.8 = n$ **2.** $0.5 \times 0.5 = n$ **3.** $0.3 \times 0.6 = n$

Use multiplication to find each product.

4. $0.8 \times 0.7 = n$ **5.** $0.6 \times 0.5 = n$ **6.** $0.2 \times 0.9 = n$

7. $0.4 \times 0.9 = n$ **8.** $0.7 \times 0.9 = n$ **9.** $0.4 \times 0.6 = n$

10. $0.6 \times 0.6 = n$ **11.** $0.5 \times 0.9 = n$ **12.** $0.7 \times 0.6 = n$

13. $0.8 \times 0.6 = n$ **14.** $0.6 \times 0.9 = n$ **15.** $0.9 \times 0.9 = n$

Lesson 8.4 *(pages 250–251)*

Place the decimal point in the product.

1.	6.3	2.	$2.19	3.	$1.95	4.	5.19	5.	27.45
	× 4		× 6		× 15		× 32		× 23
	252		$1314		$2925		16608		63135

Estimate. Then find the product.

6.	1.8	7.	4.2	8.	2.1	9.	3.19	10.	$43.29
	× 2		× 7		× 9		× 22		× 4

11.	$73.99	12.	0.673	13.	5.62	14.	6.714	15.	$619.29
	× 13		× 17		× 61		× 58		× 26

Lesson 8.5 *(pages 252–253)*

Estimate. Then find the product.

1.	1.7	2.	0.8	3.	6.7	4.	6.35	5.	3.41
	×0.9		×0.6		×9.1		× 7.4		× 6.8

6.	63.9	7.	25.8	8.	19.97	9.	573.1	10.	209.47
	× 7.5		×0.46		× 3.2		× 0.64		× 3.6

11. $0.5 \times 0.9 = n$　　　　**12.** $6.7 \times 3.2 = n$　　　　**13.** $815.6 \times 8.6 = n$

Lesson 8.6 *(pages 254–255)*

Copy each exercise. Place the decimal point in each product.
Write zeros if they are needed.

1.	0.09	2.	0.28	3.	0.1	4.	4.2	5.	0.324
	× 0.3		× 0.5		×0.7		×3.6		× 57
	0027		014		007		1512		18468

Find the product.

6.	0.07	7.	15.7	8.	0.002	9.	4.36	10.	7.285
	× 0.9		×0.36		× 49		× 7.2		× 9

11. $5.67 \times 29.6 = n$　　　　**12.** $1.78 \times 0.6 = n$　　　　**13.** $396 \times 0.89 = n$

14. $0.03 \times 0.9 = n$　　　　**15.** $0.94 \times 0.1 = n$　　　　**16.** $27 \times 0.003 = n$

Lesson 8.7 *(pages 256–257)*

Choose a method of computation and solve.

1. The Akido family spent $5.95 each for 2 adult movie tickets and $3.50 for each of 3 children's tickets. They also spent $19.78 on snacks and $3.98 on parking. About how much did the Akido family spend?

2. The Akido family went out to dinner. Mr. Akido's meal cost $13.95, and Mrs. Akido's meal cost $16.95. Each of the 3 children ordered a buffet that cost $9.95. If they gave the cashier $100.00, how much money is left from their $100.00?

Lesson 8.8 *(pages 260–261)*

Divide each number by 10, 100, and 1,000.

1. 34
2. 109
3. 496
4. 2,924
5. 16,523

6. 63,214
7. 39,880
8. 54,080
9. 23,712
10. 19,030

Divide.

11. $7.2 \div 10 = n$
12. $64 \div 10 = n$
13. $137 \div 100 = n$

14. $16.5 \div 100 = n$
15. $674 \div 100 = n$
16. $463 \div 1{,}000 = n$

17. Adam wants to save $650.00 for his summer vacation. If he has 10 months left to save, how much should he save each month?

18. Adam began saving for his vacation by counting a jar of pennies he had saved. He counted 2,094 pennies. How much money does he have in dollars and cents?

Lesson 8.9 *(pages 262–263)*

Divide. Use base-ten blocks to model each problem. Then record.

1. $6.82 \div 2 = n$
2. $2.76 \div 3 = n$
3. $7.56 \div 6 = n$

4. $10.25 \div 5 = n$
5. $5.20 \div 8 = n$
6. $1.53 \div 3 = n$

7. $6.24 \div 4 = n$
8. $8.75 \div 7 = n$
9. $6.75 \div 5 = n$

10. $7.84 \div 4 = n$
11. $8.73 \div 3 = n$
12. $9.68 \div 8 = n$

13. $14.98 \div 7 = n$
14. $9.25 \div 5 = n$
15. $16.02 \div 2 = n$

Lesson 8.10 *(pages 264–265)*

Estimate the cost for one item.

1. 3 pairs of socks for $8.88

2. 5 pounds of bananas for $2.45

3. 4 tennis lessons for $29.96

4. 1 dozen muffins for $10.68

5. 6 rolls of film for $12.90

6. 5 pencils for $0.95

7. 5 apples for $2.55

8. 7 balloons for $15.75

9. 2 pizzas for $19.99

10. 4 bottles of juice for $3.89

Find the quotient.

11. $4\overline{)7.6}$ 12. $5\overline{)3.0}$ 13. $7\overline{)0.42}$ 14. $8\overline{)5.6}$ 15. $4\overline{)4.16}$

16. $7\overline{)19.6}$ 17. $12\overline{)2.4}$ 18. $9\overline{)22.86}$ 19. $3\overline{)44.55}$ 20. $4\overline{)70.88}$

21. $48\overline{)599.04}$ 22. $39\overline{)304.2}$ 23. $16\overline{)9.44}$ 24. $87\overline{)94.83}$ 25. $11\overline{)807.4}$

26. $3\overline{)799.02}$ 27. $8\overline{)208.4}$ 28. $6\overline{)709.8}$ 29. $4\overline{)54.08}$ 30. $20\overline{)650.20}$

Solve.

31. A human heart pumps 42.3 liters of blood in 9 minutes. How many liters per minute is this?

32. The heart of a cocker spaniel pumps 10.4 liters of blood in 5 minutes. How many liters of blood per minute is this?

Lesson 8.11 *(pages 266–267)*

List the relevant information and solve.

1. Beginning aerial performers train for 7 months before their first performance. They earn $3,000 for each month that they work. Experienced aerial performers earn $14,000 for each month that they work. How much more do experienced aerial performers earn than beginning performers?

2. The red unit of the Hiho Circus has 250 members. It traveled 187 miles from New York City to Baltimore. Then it traveled 246 miles from Baltimore to Pittsburgh. How many miles did the red unit travel in all?

CHAPTER 9

Lesson 9.1 *(pages 276–277)*

Write the fraction for the part that is shaded.

1.

2.

3.

4.

Draw two pictures for each fraction. Show part of a whole with one picture and part of a group with the other picture.

5. $\dfrac{4}{6}$

6. $\dfrac{4}{5}$

7. $\dfrac{3}{7}$

8. $\dfrac{2}{3}$

Lesson 9.2 *(pages 278–279)*

Write two equivalent fractions for each pair of pictures.

1.

2.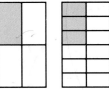

3.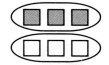

Draw two pictures to find an equivalent fraction.

4. $\dfrac{6}{20}$

5. $\dfrac{9}{18}$

6. $\dfrac{4}{5}$

7. $\dfrac{15}{25}$

8. $\dfrac{4}{16}$

Lesson 9.3 *(pages 280–281)*

Find the missing numerator or denominator.

1. $\dfrac{3}{5} = \dfrac{\blacksquare}{10}$

2. $\dfrac{1}{2} = \dfrac{\blacksquare}{8}$

3. $\dfrac{2}{3} = \dfrac{6}{\blacksquare}$

Which fraction is *not* equivalent to the given fraction?
Write **a**, **b**, or **c**.

4. $\dfrac{4}{5}$ **a.** $\dfrac{8}{10}$ **b.** $\dfrac{6}{12}$ **c.** $\dfrac{12}{15}$

5. $\dfrac{6}{8}$ **a.** $\dfrac{7}{9}$ **b.** $\dfrac{3}{4}$ **c.** $\dfrac{12}{16}$

6. $\dfrac{2}{3}$ **a.** $\dfrac{4}{6}$ **b.** $\dfrac{6}{9}$ **c.** $\dfrac{4}{9}$

7. $\dfrac{10}{15}$ **a.** $\dfrac{2}{3}$ **b.** $\dfrac{2}{5}$ **c.** $\dfrac{40}{60}$

Lesson 9.4 (pages 282–283)

Choose a strategy and solve.

1. Misha's necklace has 25 beads. The first bead is red, the second is blue, and the third is white. If this pattern continues, what color is the last bead?

2. Suppose there are 9 necklaces in a circular display. If a customer examines every fourth necklace, will all the necklaces be examined before the customer examines the first necklace again?

3. Amy's necklace has 4 beads. The red bead comes after the yellow bead. The green bead comes before the yellow bead. The blue bead comes between the green bead and the yellow bead. Which bead comes first?

4. You want to design a bracelet to wear with your necklace. The bracelet will have 10 beads. You have 4 purple beads, 4 yellow beads, and 4 gold beads. If you start the pattern as one yellow, one purple, and one gold, what color bead will be the last? What beads will be left?

Lesson 9.5 (pages 286–287)

Write *prime* or *composite* for each number.

1. 14	2. 7	3. 24	4. 17	5. 22
6. 2	7. 13	8. 15	9. 3	10. 51
11. 27	12. 10	13. 53	14. 19	15. 18
16. 25	17. 11	18. 91	19. 75	20. 29

Lesson 9.6 (pages 288–289)

List the factors of each number.

1. 9	2. 20	3. 15	4. 30	5. 27
6. 33	7. 48	8. 18	9. 8	10. 13
11. 45	12. 6	13. 39	14. 66	15. 21

List the factors of each number. Write the greatest common factor for each pair of numbers.

16. 10, 20	17. 12, 16	18. 18, 21	19. 15, 25
20. 27, 36	21. 9, 18	22. 16, 24	23. 7, 63
24. 8, 10	25. 6, 9	26. 12, 20	27. 5, 15

Lesson 9.7 *(pages 290–291)*

Tell whether the fraction is in simplest form. Write *yes* or *no*.

1. $\dfrac{8}{12}$
2. $\dfrac{3}{5}$
3. $\dfrac{7}{11}$
4. $\dfrac{14}{16}$
5. $\dfrac{5}{20}$

Write in simplest form.

6. $\dfrac{8}{12}$
7. $\dfrac{14}{16}$
8. $\dfrac{4}{10}$
9. $\dfrac{10}{15}$
10. $\dfrac{10}{20}$

11. $\dfrac{16}{32}$
12. $\dfrac{6}{9}$
13. $\dfrac{24}{27}$
14. $\dfrac{18}{32}$
15. $\dfrac{8}{16}$

16. $\dfrac{6}{8}$
17. $\dfrac{12}{16}$
18. $\dfrac{15}{45}$
19. $\dfrac{12}{30}$
20. $\dfrac{15}{60}$

21. $\dfrac{18}{40}$
22. $\dfrac{20}{24}$
23. $\dfrac{28}{42}$
24. $\dfrac{3}{12}$
25. $\dfrac{10}{35}$

Lesson 9.8 *(pages 292–293)*

Find the least common multiple.

1. $2, 3$
2. $3, 4$
3. $4, 5$
4. $5, 8$
5. $6, 7$

6. $6, 8$
7. $10, 25$
8. $12, 20$
9. $10, 15$
10. $8, 12$

11. $20, 50$
12. $12, 15$
13. $30, 45$
14. $15, 25$
15. $20, 16$

16. $16, 40$
17. $10, 14$
18. $24, 9$
19. $12, 18$
20. $12, 28$

Lesson 9.9 *(pages 294–295)*

Compare. Write $<$, $>$, or $=$ for ●.

1. $\dfrac{2}{5}$ ● $\dfrac{7}{8}$
2. $\dfrac{1}{2}$ ● $\dfrac{3}{4}$
3. $\dfrac{5}{6}$ ● $\dfrac{3}{4}$
4. $\dfrac{2}{3}$ ● $\dfrac{5}{9}$

5. $\dfrac{2}{3}$ ● $\dfrac{9}{15}$
6. $\dfrac{1}{5}$ ● $\dfrac{1}{3}$
7. $\dfrac{7}{10}$ ● $\dfrac{8}{15}$
8. $\dfrac{3}{4}$ ● $\dfrac{4}{5}$

9. $\dfrac{1}{2}$ ● $\dfrac{4}{8}$
10. $\dfrac{3}{4}$ ● $\dfrac{1}{9}$
11. $\dfrac{2}{3}$ ● $\dfrac{4}{6}$
12. $\dfrac{3}{7}$ ● $\dfrac{2}{5}$

Lesson 9.10 *(pages 296–297)*

Write in order from least to greatest.

1. $\dfrac{1}{2}, \dfrac{1}{4}, \dfrac{1}{3}$
2. $\dfrac{4}{9}, \dfrac{1}{3}, \dfrac{3}{6}$
3. $\dfrac{2}{3}, \dfrac{1}{9}, \dfrac{5}{6}$

Write in order from greatest to least.

4. $\dfrac{2}{5}, \dfrac{3}{10}, \dfrac{9}{15}$
5. $\dfrac{3}{6}, \dfrac{8}{12}, \dfrac{1}{3}$
6. $\dfrac{2}{7}, \dfrac{5}{14}, \dfrac{1}{2}$

Lesson 9.11 *(pages 298–300)*

Write a whole number or a mixed number for each picture.

1.

2.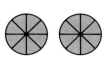

3.

4.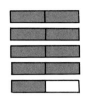

Rename each as a mixed number or a whole number.

5. $\dfrac{6}{5}$ 6. $\dfrac{11}{5}$ 7. $\dfrac{11}{8}$ 8. $\dfrac{15}{3}$

9. $\dfrac{5}{2}$ 10. $\dfrac{11}{3}$ 11. $\dfrac{13}{5}$ 12. $\dfrac{20}{4}$

13. $\dfrac{7}{6}$ 14. $\dfrac{22}{7}$ 15. $\dfrac{32}{8}$ 16. $\dfrac{17}{4}$

Rename each as a fraction.

17. $1\dfrac{5}{8}$ 18. $3\dfrac{5}{6}$ 19. $6\dfrac{3}{4}$ 20. $4\dfrac{2}{3}$ 21. $6\dfrac{3}{5}$

22. $2\dfrac{1}{5}$ 23. $4\dfrac{1}{2}$ 24. $8\dfrac{1}{3}$ 25. $5\dfrac{1}{4}$ 26. $4\dfrac{4}{7}$

Arrange in order from least to greatest.

27. $4\dfrac{2}{3}; \ 4\dfrac{5}{9}; \ 4\dfrac{1}{3}$

28. $3\dfrac{4}{6}; \ 3\dfrac{1}{3}; \ 3\dfrac{5}{18}$

Lesson 9.12 *(pages 302–303)*

Draw a picture and solve.

The 24 students in Mr. Sojo's class and the 24 students in Mrs. Olsen's class were asked to name their favorite kind of music.

1. Which class has more students who like country?

2. How many students in each class like rock?

3. How many students in each class like classical music?

4. How many students in each class like jazz?

Favorite Type of Music		
Type of Music	Mr. Sojo's Class	Mrs. Olsen's Class
Rock	$\dfrac{5}{6}$	$\dfrac{5}{8}$
Country	$\dfrac{1}{12}$	▪
Classical	$\dfrac{1}{24}$	$\dfrac{1}{6}$
Jazz	$\dfrac{1}{24}$	$\dfrac{1}{12}$

5. Is country or classical music more popular in Mr. Sojo's class?

CHAPTER 10

Lesson 10.1 *(pages 312–313)*

Estimate the sum or difference.

1. $\dfrac{2}{5}$
   $+\dfrac{4}{10}$

2. $\dfrac{7}{12}$
   $-\dfrac{1}{6}$

3. $\dfrac{5}{6}$
   $+\dfrac{8}{9}$

4. $\dfrac{8}{14}$
   $-\dfrac{1}{13}$

5. $\dfrac{5}{7}$
   $+\dfrac{13}{14}$

6. $\dfrac{17}{18}$
   $-\dfrac{2}{5}$

7. $\dfrac{2}{3} - \dfrac{4}{6} \approx n$

8. $\dfrac{3}{5} + \dfrac{6}{10} \approx n$

9. $\dfrac{13}{14} - \dfrac{3}{5} \approx n$

Lesson 10.2 *(pages 314–315)*

Write an addition or subtraction sentence for each drawing.

1.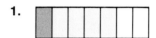

2.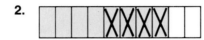

3.

Use mental math to find the sum or difference. Write the answer in simplest form.

4. $\dfrac{3}{6}$
   $+\dfrac{2}{6}$

5. $\dfrac{5}{6}$
   $-\dfrac{1}{6}$

6. $\dfrac{1}{3}$
   $+\dfrac{2}{3}$

7. $\dfrac{2}{12}$
   $+\dfrac{9}{12}$

8. $\dfrac{8}{15}$
   $-\dfrac{3}{15}$

9. $\dfrac{26}{48}$
   $-\dfrac{19}{48}$

10. $\dfrac{7}{9}$
    $+\dfrac{1}{9}$

11. $\dfrac{9}{11}$
    $-\dfrac{3}{11}$

12. $\dfrac{5}{8}$
    $+\dfrac{3}{8}$

13. $\dfrac{3}{4}$
    $-\dfrac{1}{4}$

Lesson 10.3 *(pages 316–317)*

Tell whether one denominator is a multiple of the other. Write *yes* or *no*.

1. $\dfrac{2}{5}, \dfrac{3}{15}$

2. $\dfrac{1}{6}, \dfrac{5}{13}$

3. $\dfrac{1}{2}, \dfrac{5}{8}$

4. $\dfrac{1}{3}, \dfrac{3}{5}$

5. $\dfrac{5}{8}, \dfrac{1}{16}$

Lesson 10.4 *(pages 318–319)*

Find the least common multiple.

1. $2, 5$

2. $3, 7$

3. $2, 6$

4. $3, 5$

Find the least common denominator.

5. $\dfrac{1}{2}, \dfrac{3}{10}$

6. $\dfrac{3}{4}, \dfrac{5}{6}$

7. $\dfrac{1}{2}, \dfrac{5}{9}$

8. $\dfrac{1}{6}, \dfrac{3}{12}$

Lesson 10.5 (pages 320–321)

Add or subtract. Write the answer in simplest form.

1. $\dfrac{2}{3}$
$+\dfrac{1}{4}$

2. $\dfrac{1}{2}$
$-\dfrac{1}{4}$

3. $\dfrac{5}{6}$
$-\dfrac{2}{3}$

4. $\dfrac{1}{2}$
$+\dfrac{2}{5}$

5. $\dfrac{3}{5}$
$-\dfrac{1}{3}$

6. $\dfrac{3}{5}$
$+\dfrac{3}{8}$

7. $\dfrac{1}{4}$
$-\dfrac{1}{8}$

8. $\dfrac{9}{16}$
$+\dfrac{1}{4}$

9. $\dfrac{1}{2}$
$-\dfrac{3}{8}$

10. $\dfrac{7}{12}$
$+\dfrac{3}{8}$

Lesson 10.6 (pages 322–323)

Use fraction squares to find the sum.

1. $4\dfrac{3}{5}$
$+2\dfrac{4}{5}$

2. $1\dfrac{7}{8}$
$+3\dfrac{5}{8}$

3. $6\dfrac{1}{2}$
$+1\dfrac{5}{8}$

4. $2\dfrac{5}{9}$
$+4\dfrac{2}{3}$

5. $6\dfrac{4}{5}$
$+3\dfrac{1}{3}$

Tell whether you need to rename the sum. Write *yes* or *no*.

6. $2\dfrac{2}{3}$
$+5\dfrac{5}{6}$

7. $1\dfrac{1}{10}$
$+2\dfrac{3}{5}$

8. $8\dfrac{1}{4}$
$+2\dfrac{5}{12}$

9. $1\dfrac{4}{9}$
$+3\dfrac{2}{3}$

10. $6\dfrac{9}{15}$
$+1\dfrac{3}{5}$

Lesson 10.7 (pages 324–325)

Use fraction circles to find the difference. Write the answer in simplest form.

1. $9\dfrac{1}{4}$
$-2\dfrac{3}{4}$

2. $3\dfrac{1}{3}$
$-1\dfrac{2}{3}$

3. $6\dfrac{3}{5}$
$-4\dfrac{4}{5}$

4. $4\dfrac{2}{7}$
$-3\dfrac{5}{7}$

5. $11\dfrac{5}{9}$
$-\;4\dfrac{7}{9}$

Tell whether you need to rename. Write *yes* or *no*.

6. $3\dfrac{3}{8}$
$-1\dfrac{7}{8}$

7. $6\dfrac{1}{3}$
$-4\dfrac{2}{3}$

8. $8\dfrac{4}{5}$
$-4\dfrac{1}{5}$

9. $5\dfrac{3}{4}$
$-1\dfrac{1}{4}$

10. $10\dfrac{1}{8}$
$-\;3\dfrac{5}{8}$

Lesson 10.8 (pages 326–327)

Add or subtract. Write the answer in simplest form.

1. $3\frac{3}{4}$
    $+1\frac{3}{4}$

2. $3\frac{1}{5}$
    $-2\frac{2}{3}$

3. $8\frac{7}{10}$
    $+3\frac{5}{6}$

4. $8\frac{3}{7}$
    $-7\frac{1}{2}$

5. $6\frac{5}{8}$
    $-2\frac{1}{2}$

6. $7\frac{2}{3}$
    $-5\frac{3}{4}$

7. $4\frac{3}{10}$
    $-2\frac{1}{2}$

8. $4\frac{3}{4}$
    $+2\frac{2}{3}$

9. $8\frac{1}{4}$
    $-5\frac{3}{6}$

10. $1\frac{9}{10}$
    $+6\frac{4}{5}$

Lesson 10.9 (pages 328–329)

Use the diagram to make a table of the chorus members for
Exercises 1–2.

1. What fraction of the chorus
   is made up of altos?

2. Which group makes up the greater
   fractional part of the chorus,
   alto or tenor?

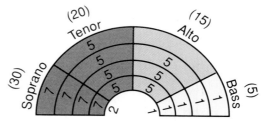

Chorus Members

Lesson 10.10 (pages 332–333)

Multiply. Write the product as a whole or mixed number.

1. $\frac{2}{3} \times 4 = n$

2. $7 \times \frac{4}{6} = n$

3. $5 \times \frac{5}{8} = n$

4. $9 \times \frac{2}{4} = n$

5. $6 \times \frac{3}{5} = n$

6. $8 \times \frac{4}{6} = n$

7. $\frac{3}{4} \times 8 = n$

8. $3 \times \frac{5}{6} = n$

Lesson 10.11 (pages 334–335)

Multiply. Write the answer in simplest form.

1. $\frac{3}{5} \times \frac{2}{3} = n$

2. $\frac{5}{6} \times \frac{3}{4} = n$

3. $\frac{3}{9} \times \frac{1}{2} = n$

4. $\frac{3}{4} \times \frac{1}{9} = n$

5. $\frac{5}{9} \times \frac{3}{5} = n$

6. $\frac{6}{7} \times \frac{1}{2} = n$

7. $\frac{4}{5} \times \frac{2}{10} = n$

8. $\frac{1}{2} \times \frac{4}{9} = n$

9. $\frac{2}{3} \times \frac{3}{6} = n$

10. $\frac{7}{8} \times \frac{2}{5} = n$

11. $\frac{3}{5} \times \frac{4}{7} = n$

12. $\frac{2}{3} \times \frac{3}{10} = n$

13. $\frac{7}{8} \times \frac{5}{7} = n$

14. $\frac{1}{10} \times \frac{5}{6} = n$

15. $\frac{1}{8} \times \frac{4}{7} = n$

16. $\frac{2}{3} \times \frac{3}{8} = n$

Lesson 10.12 *(pages 336–337)*

Draw fraction squares to help you find each product.

1. $3\frac{2}{3} \times \frac{5}{6} = n$

2. $\frac{2}{5} \times 5\frac{1}{2} = n$

3. $2\frac{1}{6} \times \frac{3}{4} = n$

4. $5\frac{1}{3} \times \frac{3}{7} = n$

5. $4\frac{1}{4} \times \frac{2}{3} = n$

6. $\frac{2}{5} \times 5\frac{5}{6} = n$

7. $\frac{3}{4} \times 4\frac{1}{4} = n$

8. $3\frac{1}{2} \times \frac{3}{4} = n$

9. $1\frac{1}{3} \times \frac{1}{3} = n$

10. $\frac{3}{5} \times 6\frac{1}{3} = n$

11. $\frac{3}{4} \times 2\frac{2}{3} = n$

12. $\frac{7}{8} \times 7\frac{1}{4} = n$

Lesson 10.13 *(pages 338–339)*

Complete.

1. How many fives are in twenty-five?

2. How many twos are in sixteen?

3. How many sevens are in thirty-five?

4. How many fours are in thirty-six?

Write a division number sentence for each picture.

5.

6.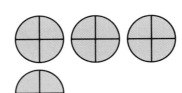

7.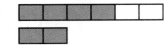

Use your rule for dividing fractions with like denominators.

8. $\frac{7}{2} \div \frac{1}{2} = n$

9. $\frac{10}{3} \div \frac{2}{3} = n$

10. $\frac{7}{8} \div \frac{1}{8} = n$

11. $\frac{28}{9} \div \frac{4}{9} = n$

12. $\frac{48}{4} \div \frac{3}{4} = n$

13. $\frac{48}{8} \div \frac{3}{8} = n$

14. $\frac{18}{3} \div \frac{2}{3} = n$

15. $\frac{20}{6} \div \frac{5}{6} = n$

16. $\frac{24}{3} \div \frac{2}{3} = n$

Lesson 10.14 *(pages 340–341)*

Make a diagram and solve.

1. Of the plants in Josie's garden, $\frac{1}{10}$ are rosebushes, $\frac{1}{2}$ are daisies, and $\frac{2}{5}$ are lilies. There are 3 rose bushes. How many lilies are planted?

2. Of the plants in Jamie's garden, $\frac{1}{4}$ are tomatoes, $\frac{1}{2}$ are lettuce, $\frac{1}{8}$ are cabbage, and $\frac{1}{8}$ are squash. There are 3 cabbage plants. How many vegetable plants were planted in all?

CHAPTER 11

Lesson 11.1 *(pages 350–351)*

Choose the most reasonable unit of measure.
Write *mm, cm, m,* or *km.*

1. the length of a room

2. the height of an apartment building

3. the thickness of a penny

4. the distance between Miami and Dallas

5. the length of a pencil

6. the length of the Mississippi River

Lesson 11.2 *(pages 352–353)*

Write the measure to the nearest cm and then write a more precise measure.

1.

2.

Measure each side of the rectangle to the nearest cm.
Add the measurements to find the perimeter.

3.

4.

Use a metric ruler. Draw a line to show each length.

5. 15 cm

6. 38 mm

7. 1 dm

8. 112 mm

Lesson 11.3 *(pages 354–355)*

Choose the more reasonable unit of measure. Write *mL* or *L.*

1. a jug of apple juice

2. a bottle of shampoo

3. a glass of milk

4. a can of paint

Lesson 11.4 *(pages 356–357)*

Choose the most reasonable unit. Write *kg, g,* or *mg.*

1.

2.

3.

Lesson 11.5 *(pages 358–359)*

Choose the smaller unit of measure. Write **a** or **b**.

1. a. meter
   b. centimeter

2. a. kilogram
   b. milligram

3. a. milliliter
   b. liter

Choose the larger unit of measure. Write **a** or **b**.

4. a. kilometer
   b. meter

5. a. centimeter
   b. decimeter

6. a. kilogram
   b. gram

Use the place-value chart on page 358. Change each measurement to the base unit.

7. 7 dm

8. 5 mL

9. 10 g

10. 4 mm

11. 8 cm

12. 14 mg

13. 2 mL

14. 50 mg

Lesson 11.6 *(pages 360–361)*

Write *multiply* or *divide* for each exercise. Then solve.

1. 4.3 cm = ▉ mm

2. 60 mm = ▉ cm

3. 3.2 m = ▉ cm

4. 14 L = ▉ mL

5. 15,000 mL = ▉ L

6. 16,000 mg = ▉ g

Lesson 11.7 *(pages 362–363)*

Use the starting temperature on each thermometer to find the new temperature.

1. 17° warmer

2. 6° colder

3. 41° warmer

4. 11° colder

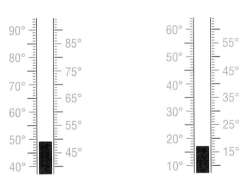
Fahrenheit

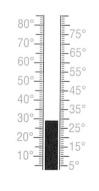
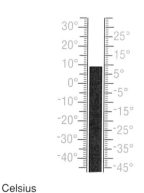
Celsius

Copy and complete the table. Use the thermometers on page 362.

Starting Temperature	80°F	**6.** ▉	9°C	64°C
Change in Temperature	fell 32°	rose 14°	fell 12°	**8.** ▉
Final Temperature	**5.** ▉	74°F	**7.** ▉	37°C

Lesson 11.8 *(pages 364–365)*

Solve.

1. Myung drank 500 mL of water in the morning, 500 mL in the afternoon, and another 500 mL in the evening. She estimates she drank 15 liters of water. Is this reasonable? Explain.

2. Sam needs to triple a recipe for beef stew. It calls for 1 lb of beef, 4 cups of stock, and 2 cups of chopped vegetables. Sam estimates he will need 12 quarts of stock. Is this reasonable? Explain.

Lesson 11.9 *(pages 368–369)*

Using an inch ruler, measure each line segment as precisely as you can.

1. ─────────────

2. ───────────────────

3. ──────────────────────────────

Draw a line segment to the given length.

4. $2\frac{7}{8}$ in.

5. $1\frac{5}{16}$ in.

6. $5\frac{1}{2}$ in.

7. $3\frac{3}{4}$ in.

Lesson 11.10 *(pages 370–371)*

Complete.

1. $2\,\text{ft} = \blacksquare\,\text{in.}$

2. $1{,}760\,\text{yd} = \blacksquare\,\text{ft}$

3. $10\,\text{yd} = \blacksquare\,\text{ft}$

4. $36\,\text{in.} = \blacksquare\,\text{yd}$

5. $6\,\text{ft} = \blacksquare\,\text{in.}$

6. $4\,\text{mi} = \blacksquare\,\text{ft}$

Add or subtract.

7. $10\,\text{ft}\ \ 9\,\text{in.}$
   $-\ \ 8\,\text{ft}\,11\,\text{in.}$

8. $6\,\text{yd}\,2\,\text{ft}$
   $+1\,\text{yd}\,2\,\text{ft}$

9. $9\,\text{ft}\ \ 6\,\text{in.}$
   $-3\,\text{ft}\,10\,\text{in.}$

10. $3\,\text{ft}\ \ 8\,\text{in.}$
    $+7\,\text{ft}\,11\,\text{in.}$

Lesson 11.11 *(pages 372–373)*

Write *multiply* or *divide*. Then complete.

1. $5\,\text{gal} = \blacksquare\,\text{qt}$

2. $3\,\text{T} = \blacksquare\,\text{lb}$

3. $6\,\text{pt} = \blacksquare\,\text{c}$

4. $24\,\text{c} = \blacksquare\,\text{fl oz}$

5. $10\,\text{qt} = \blacksquare\,\text{gal}$

6. $144\,\text{oz} = \blacksquare\,\text{lb}$

7. $18\,\text{c} = \blacksquare\,\text{pt}$

8. $6\frac{1}{2}\,\text{T} = \blacksquare\,\text{lb}$

9. $22\,\text{pt} = \blacksquare\,\text{qt}$

Lesson 11.12 (pages 374–375)

Complete.

1. 2 days = ■ hr
2. 3 min = ■ sec
3. 6 wk = ■ days

4. 240 sec = ■ min
5. 49 days = ■ wk
6. 730 days = ■ yr

7. $\frac{3}{4}$ yr = ■ mo
8. $1\frac{1}{2}$ days = ■ hr
9. 210 min = ■ hr

10. 2 yr = ■ days
11. 96 hr = ■ days
12. 60 mo = ■ yr

13. 156 wk = ■ yr
14. 11 min = ■ sec
15. 5 hr = ■ min

16. 3 hr 15 min = ■ min
17. 160 hr = ■ days ■ hr

Lesson 11.13 (pages 376–377)

Compute the time when each event began or ended.

1. The train left at 4:20 P.M.. and arrived 32 min later.

2. Lunch was served at 12:45 P.M. and took 50 min to prepare.

Add or subtract.

3.   3 hr 25 min
  $+2$ hr 50 min

4.   10 min 45 sec
  $-$ 3 min 23 sec

5.   4 hr 15 min
  -1 hr 45 min

6.   6 hr 10 min
  -4 hr 35 min

7.   3 min 29 sec
  $+5$ min 43 sec

8.   14 hr 50 min
  $+10$ hr 25 min

9.   7 min 45 sec
  -3 min 50 sec

10.   2 hr 25 min
  -1 hr 40 min

11.   8 min 35 sec
  $+5$ min 55 sec

Lesson 11.14 (pages 378–379)

Use the schedule for Exercises 1–3.

1. At what time does Flight 57 arrive in Los Angeles?

2. At what time does Flight 413 leave Sacramento?

3. Joe has an important meeting at 2:00 P.M. in Los Angeles. What is the latest flight he can take?

To Los Angeles		
Leave from Sacramento	Arrive	Flight No.
6:35 A.M.	7:45 A.M.	41
8:25 A.M.	9:28 A.M.	43
1:15 P.M.	2:18 P.M.	413
5:20 P.M.	6:27 P.M.	57

CHAPTER 12

Lesson 12.1 *(pages 388–389)*

Find the perimeter of each figure.

1.   2 cm   2 cm

2 cm   2 cm

2 cm

2.   48 mm   59 mm

34 mm

3.   6 cm

3 cm   3 cm

6 cm

4.   47 mm

45 mm   36 mm

62 mm

5.   6 cm

4 cm

8 cm 1 cm   5 cm   1 cm

6.   26 mm

24 mm

26 mm

44 mm

20 mm

52 mm

Lesson 12.2 *(pages 390–391)*

Find the perimeter of each figure.

1.   6 m

2.   9 ft

2 ft

3.   16 mm

6 mm   10 mm

8 mm   8 mm

8 mm

4.   20 cm

8 cm

5.   4 in.

6 in.   6 in.

10 in.

6.   5 m

Find the missing length in each figure.

7.   ?

4 m

Perimeter = 30 m

8.   ?

Perimeter = 32 ft

9.   ?

10 cm   10 cm

7 cm

Perimeter = 40 cm

10.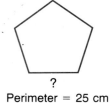

?

Perimeter = 25 cm

11.   6 cm   ?

3 cm

Perimeter = 15 cm

12.   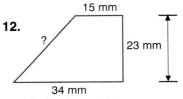   15 mm

?   23 mm

34 mm

Perimeter = 102 mm

Lesson 12.3 *(pages 392–393)*

Find the circumference. Round to the nearest tenth.

1.
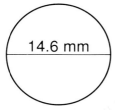
14.6 mm

2.
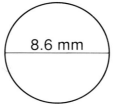
8.6 mm

3.
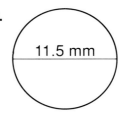
11.5 mm

Find the diameter. Round to the nearest tenth.

4. $C = 72.9 \, \text{mm}$

5. $C = 28.2 \, \text{cm}$

6. $C = 124.9 \, \text{in.}$

7. $C = 69.8 \, \text{cm}$

8. $C = 87.6 \, \text{in.}$

9. $C = 172.5 \, \text{cm}$

Lesson 12.4 *(pages 394–395)*

Find each area. Each square equals 1 cm².

1.
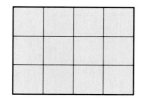

2.
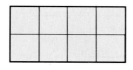

3.
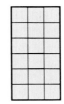

Use the formula to find the area of each rectangle.

4.
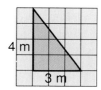
11 in.
3 in.

5.
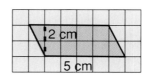
12 mm
8 mm

6.
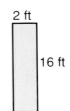
2 ft
16 ft

Lesson 12.5 *(pages 396–397)*

Find the area of each figure.

1.
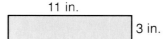
4 m
3 m

2.
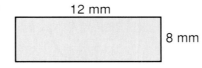
2 cm
5 cm

3.
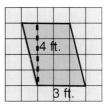
4 ft.
3 ft.

4. Triangle:
   $b = 7 \, \text{m}$
   $h = 3.5 \, \text{m}$

5. Rectangle:
   $b = 14 \, \text{in.}$
   $h = 33 \, \text{in.}$

6. Triangle:
   $b = 2.7 \, \text{cm}$
   $h = 9.4 \, \text{cm}$

Lesson 12.6 *(pages 398–399)*

Choose a strategy and solve.

1. Billy has 64 ft of square bricks to border an outdoor patio. He wants a rectangular patio with the greatest possible area. What dimensions should the patio have?

2. Misha has 36 ft of fringe. She wants to trim the edges on the largest possible rectangular tablecloth. What dimensions should the tablecloth have?

3. Monty has 32 ft of wood to use as a border for his flower bed. He wants to have a rectangular bed with the greatest possible area. What dimensions should the bed have?

4. Meredith wants to plant a rectangular garden with an area of 18 ft². She has 18 ft of fencing to put around the garden. What dimensions should her garden have?

Lesson 12.7 *(pages 402–403)*

Find the area of each complex figure.

1.
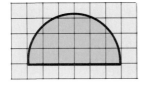
4 m
6 m
2.5 m
1.5 m

2.
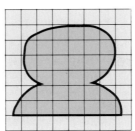
2 mm
6 mm
5 mm
6 mm

3.
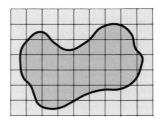
7 in.
2 in.
2 in.
12 in.

Estimate the area of each curved figure. Each unit equals 1 cm².

4.

5.

6.
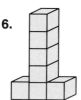

Lesson 12.8 *(pages 404–405)*

Use what you know about hidden cubes to find the number of cubes used to build each figure.

1.

2.
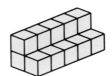

3.

4.

5.

6.

Lesson 12.9 *(pages 406–407)*

Use cubes to find the number of all the possible rectangular prisms.

1. 6 cubes

2. 10 cubes

3. 20 cubes

Guess which rectangular prism has the greater volume. Use connecting cubes to find the volume of each prism in cubic centimeters.

4.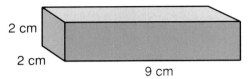

5.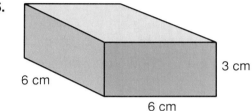

Lesson 12.10 *(pages 408–409)*

Find the volume of each.

1. $l = 6$ mm
$w = 2$ mm
$h = 1$ mm

2. $l = 10$ ft
$w = 4$ ft
$h = 2$ ft

3. $l = 0.7$ km
$w = 1.1$ km
$h = 0.4$ km

4. $l = 29$ in.
$w = 14$ in.
$h = 7$ in.

5. $l = 7$ yd
$w = 7$ yd
$h = 7$ yd

6. $l = 52$ mm
$w = 38$ mm
$h = 10$ mm

7. $l = 42$ in.
$w = 21$ in.
$h = 5$ in.

8. $l = 7$ cm
$w = 6$ cm
$h = 2$ cm

Lesson 12.11 *(pages 410–411)*

Choose the most reasonable measure. Write **a, b,** or **c.**

1. cupboard

a. 12 ft^3

b. 12 in.^{3}

c. 12 yd^3

2. cereal box

a. $4,000$ mm^3

b. $4,000$ cm^3

c. $4,000$ m^3

3. television set

a. $1,500$ in.^{3}

b. $1,500$ ft^3

c. $1,500$ yd^3

Lesson 12.12 *(pages 412–413)*

Use a formula and solve.

1. Mr. Mayo wants to cover his driveway with gravel. It is 15 yd long and 5 yd wide. What is the measure of the area he wants to cover with gravel?

2. The length of a school playground is 105 m, and the width is 74 m. If the school wants to build a fence around the playground, how much fencing will be needed?

CHAPTER 13

Lesson 13.1 *(pages 422–423)*

Write each ratio in three ways.

1. cardinals to blue jays   2. penguins to flamingos   3. eagles to nests

Write a fraction to show each ratio.

4. 3 to 4   5. 1 to 5   6. 7:10   7. 6 to 3

8. 10 to 13   9. 9 to 4   10. 4:9   11. 8 to 1

12. 143:100   13. 180:5   14. 50:200   15. 4:9

Lesson 13.2 *(pages 424–425)*

Tell whether the ratios are equivalent. Write *yes* or *no*.

1. $\frac{3}{4}$ and $\frac{9}{12}$ 2. $\frac{5}{12}$ and $\frac{7}{14}$ 3. $\frac{1}{2}$ and $\frac{15}{30}$

4. $\frac{4}{15}$ and $\frac{20}{75}$ 5. $\frac{8}{7}$ and $\frac{16}{21}$ 6. $\frac{2}{15}$ and $\frac{10}{50}$

7. $\frac{3}{15}$ and $\frac{6}{30}$ 8. $\frac{4}{8}$ and $\frac{11}{22}$ 9. $\frac{1}{5}$ and $\frac{4}{10}$

Write two ratios that are equivalent to the given ratio.

10. 6:14   11. 7:10   12. 1:4   13. $\frac{2}{3}$ 14. 1 to 3

Solve.

15. The ratio of scenic backdrops to solid-color backdrops in Lisa's studio is 2 to 5. If she has 4 scenic backdrops, how many solid-color backdrops does she have?

16. The ratio of setting changes to light-meter readings is 1 to 12. Lisa took 24 light-meter readings. How many setting changes did she make?

17. Lisa can make 3 slides for every 5 pictures she develops. If she develops 30 pictures, how many slides can she make?

18. The ratio of individual poses to group poses is 3 to 2. If Lisa takes 24 group poses, how many individual poses did she take?

Lesson 13.3 *(pages 426–427)*

Use the scale drawing for Exercises 1–12.

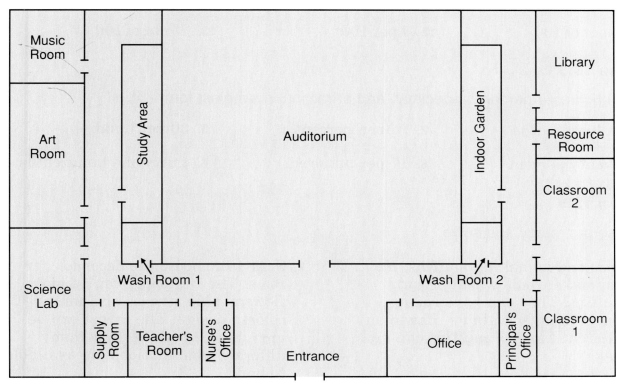

Scale: 1 cm = 4 m

Measure the drawing. Find the dimensions of these rooms.

1. Teachers' Room
2. Classroom 1
3. Art Room
4. Principal's Office
5. Study Area
6. Science Lab
7. Washroom 1
8. Resource Room
9. Auditorium
10. Nurse's Office
11. Classroom 2
12. Music Room

Lesson 13.4 *(pages 428–429)*

Write the percent that tells what part is shaded.

1.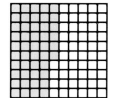
2.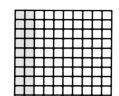
3.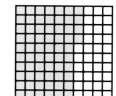
4.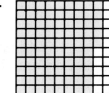

Write the percent for each ratio.

5. 6 out of 100

6. 3 out of 100

7. 24 out of 100

8. 63 per 100

9. 2 per 100

10. 55 per 100

11. 50 out of 100

12. 1 per 100

13. 75 out of 100

Lesson 13.5 *(pages 430–431)*

Write each as a percent, a decimal, and a fraction in simplest form.

1. six hundredths

2. fifteen percent

3. 30 per hundred

4. seventy percent

5. 17 per hundred

6. thirty-one hundredths

Lesson 13.6 *(pages 432–433)*

Choose a strategy and solve.

1. Desmond is making muffins. He can make whole wheat or corn muffins. They can have raisins, blueberries, or walnuts. How many different kinds of muffins can he make?

2. Suki will choose the decor for her room. The wallpaper can be pink flowers, blue stripes, or a multi-colored design. The carpet can be gray, blue, or white. How many different combinations are available to her?

Lesson 13.7 *(pages 436–437)*

Use the spinner for Exercises 1–6.

1. How many sections does the spinner have?

2. What are the possible outcomes of spinning the spinner?

3. What is the probability of landing on red? on brown? on blue?

4. What is the probability of *not* landing on green?

5. What is the probability of *not* landing on red?

6. What is the probability of landing on green or blue?

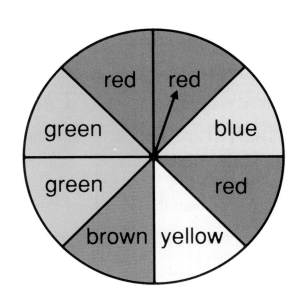

Lesson 13.8 *(pages 438–439)*

Write a fraction for the probability of picking each kind of fruit.

1. an orange
2. a banana
3. a pear
4. an apple
5. a plum
6. not an orange
7. an orange or a plum
8. not an apple
9. not a plum
10. an apple or an orange

Use the spinner for Exercises 11–16.

11. What are the possible outcomes of spinning the spinner?

12. On which number(s) is the spinner most likely to land?

13. What is the probability of the spinner landing on 2?

14. What is the probability of the spinner landing on 5?

15. What is the probability of the spinner landing on an odd number?

16. What is the probability of the spinner landing on an even number?

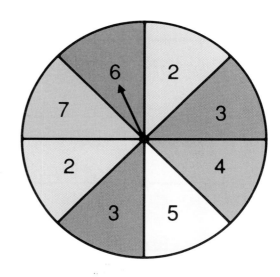

Lesson 13.9 *(pages 440–441)*

Write a problem that each program could simulate.

1. A computer program generates the digits 1–4 at random 75 times.

2. A computer program generates the digits 4–9 at random 25 times.

Use the results of one computer run to find the probability of a coin landing on heads or tails when tossed 100 times.

3. A computer program generated these possibilites for coin tosses. Which event occurred more often, heads or tails?

Toss the Coin 100 Times
HTTTTTTTHHTHHHHHTHTTHTTHHT
HHHTHHTTTHHHHHHTHTHHHHTHHHT
THTHHTTTHHTTHHHTHTTTTHHHHTHT
THTTHTHTHTTHTTTHTTHTHTHHHHHT

The Learning Resources can be traced, colored, and cut out. These resources can be used as tools to help you understand math concepts and solve problems.

Number Lines

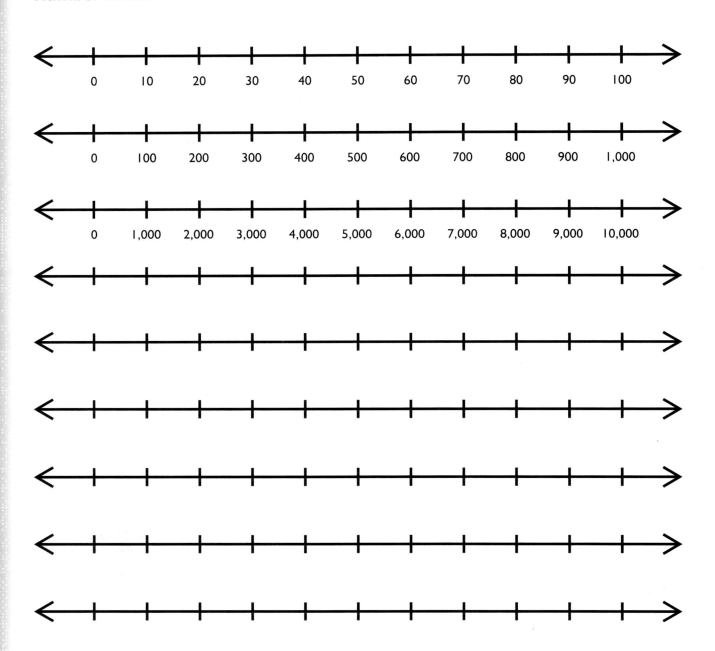

Regular Polygons

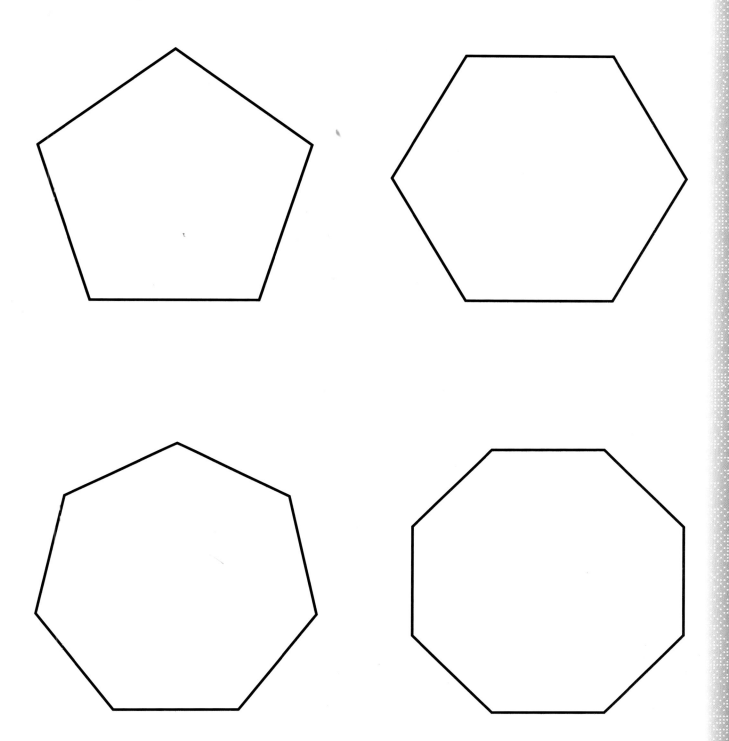

Triangles

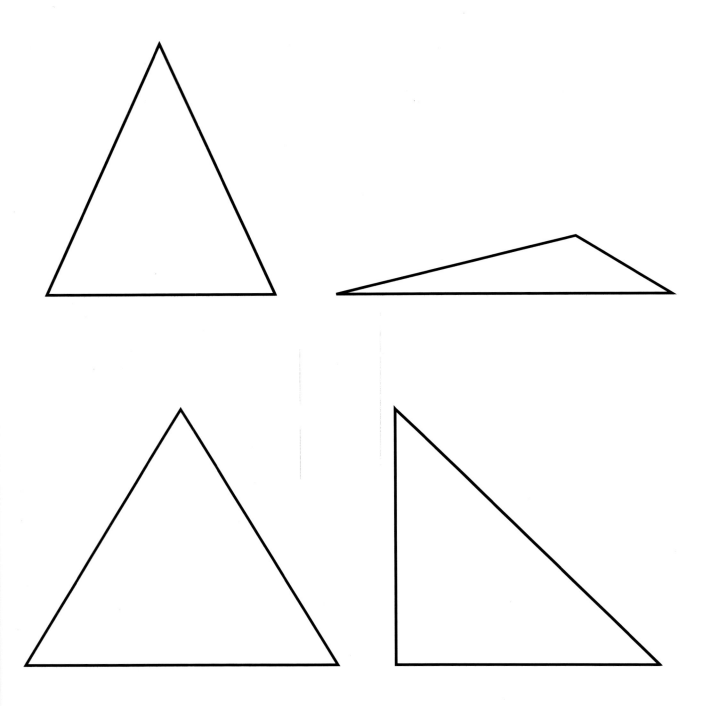

Geostrips

The number on each strip represents the distance (in cm) between the end holes.

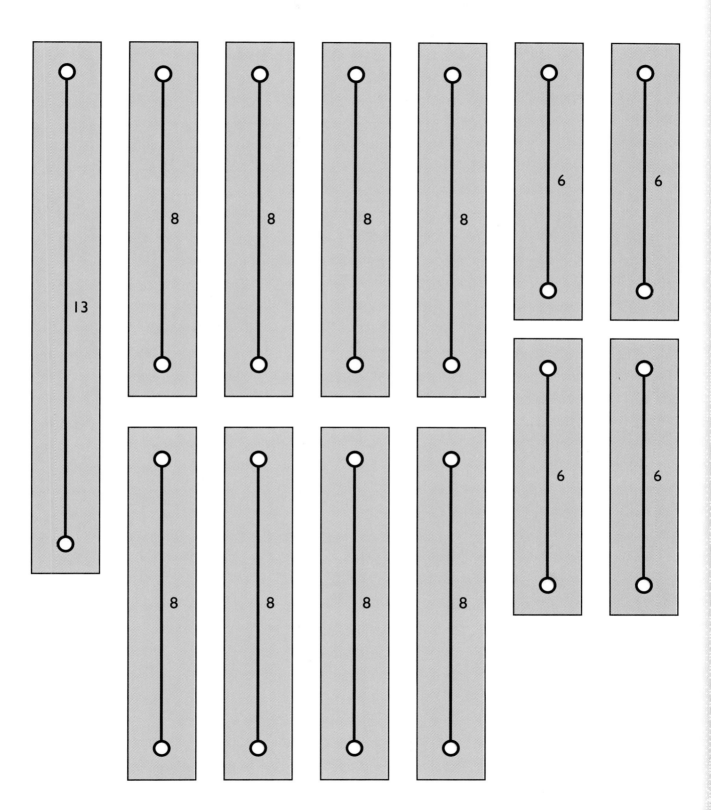

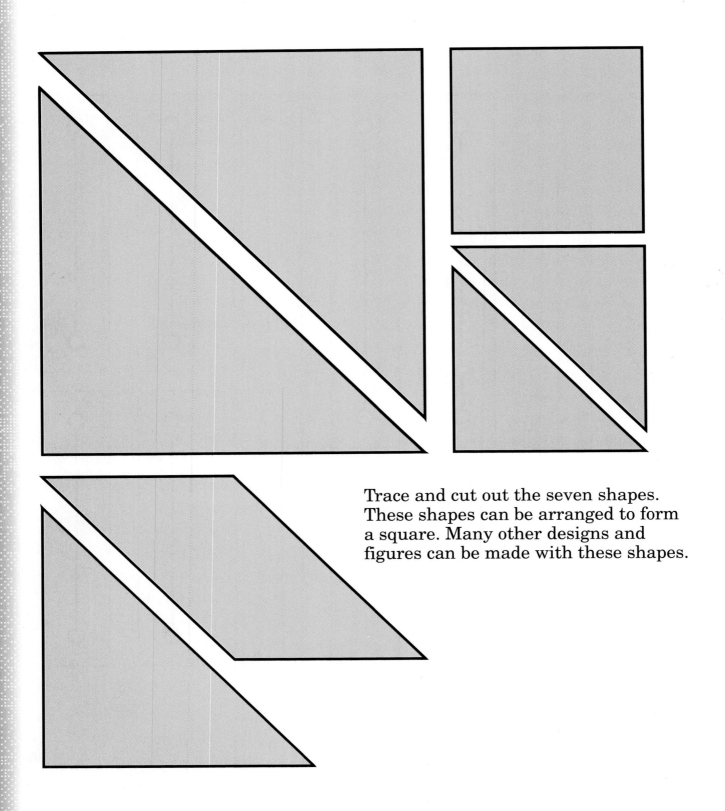

Trace and cut out the seven shapes. These shapes can be arranged to form a square. Many other designs and figures can be made with these shapes.

Solid Geometric Shape

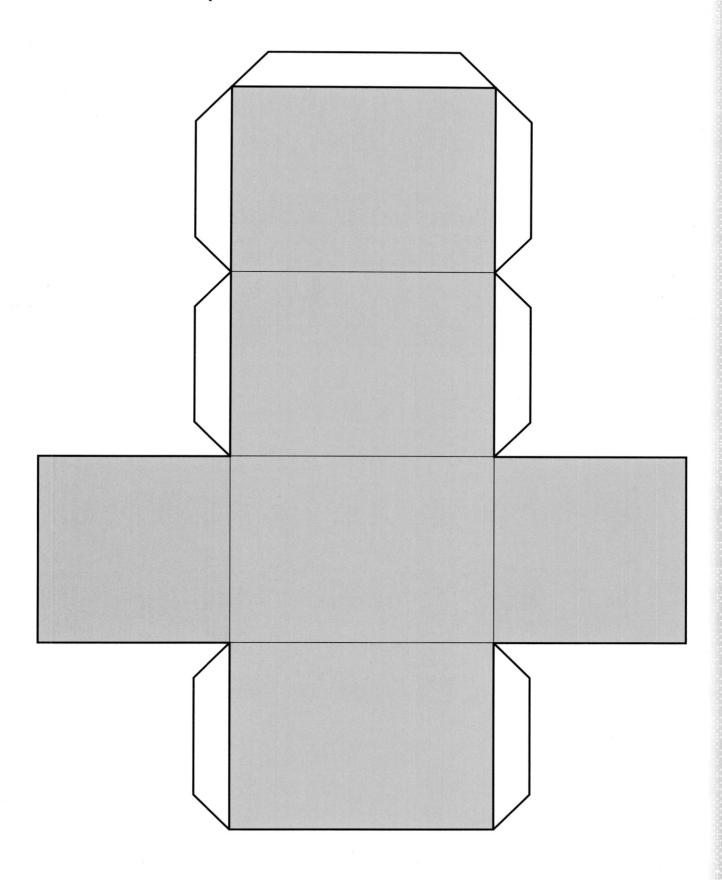

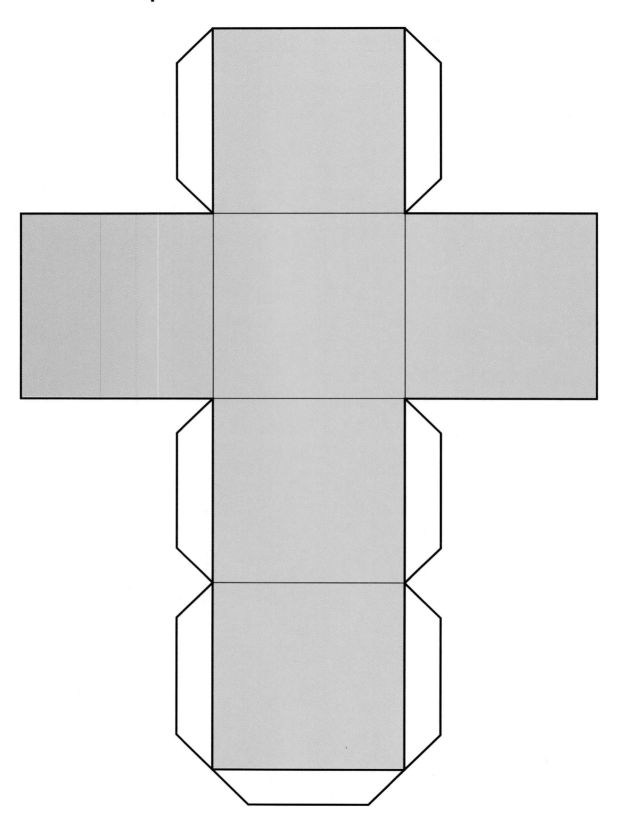

Solid Geometric Shape

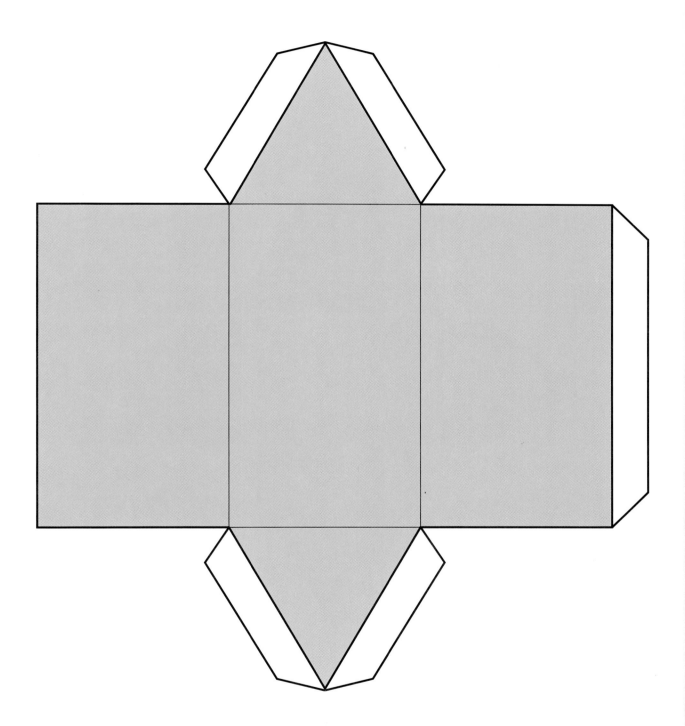

Solid Geometric Shape

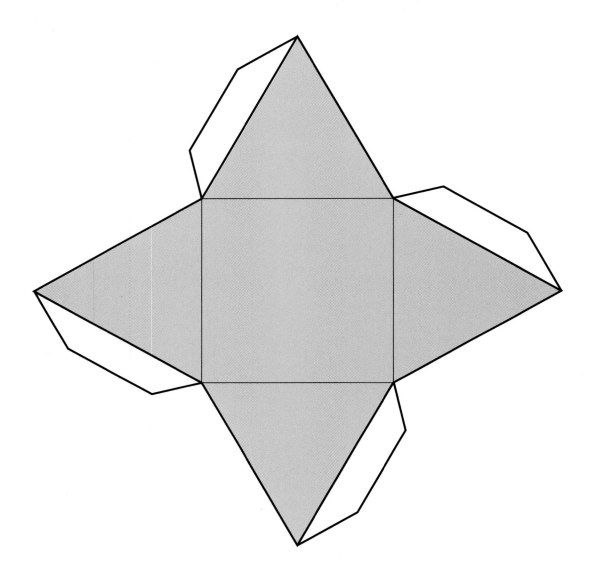

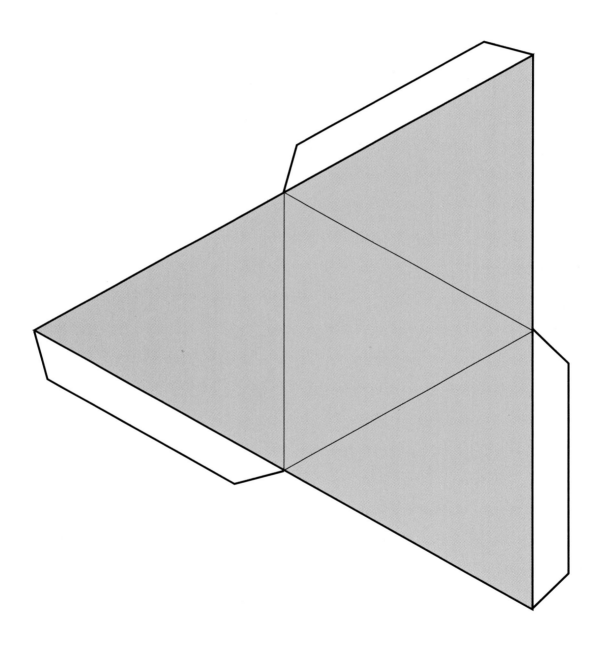

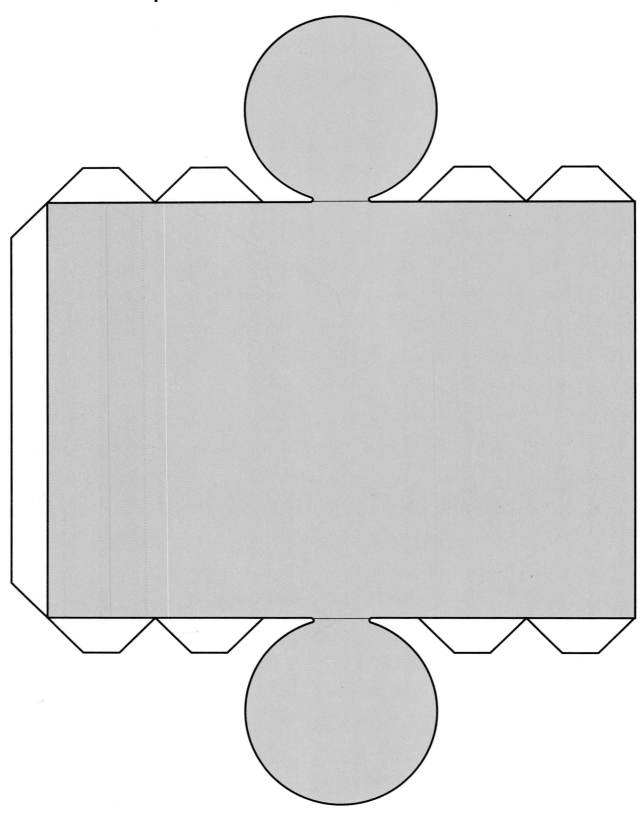

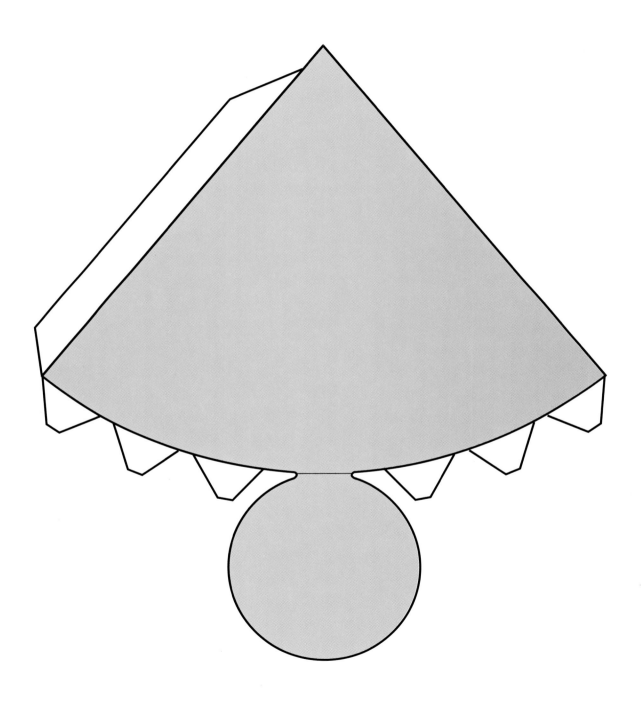

Fraction Circles

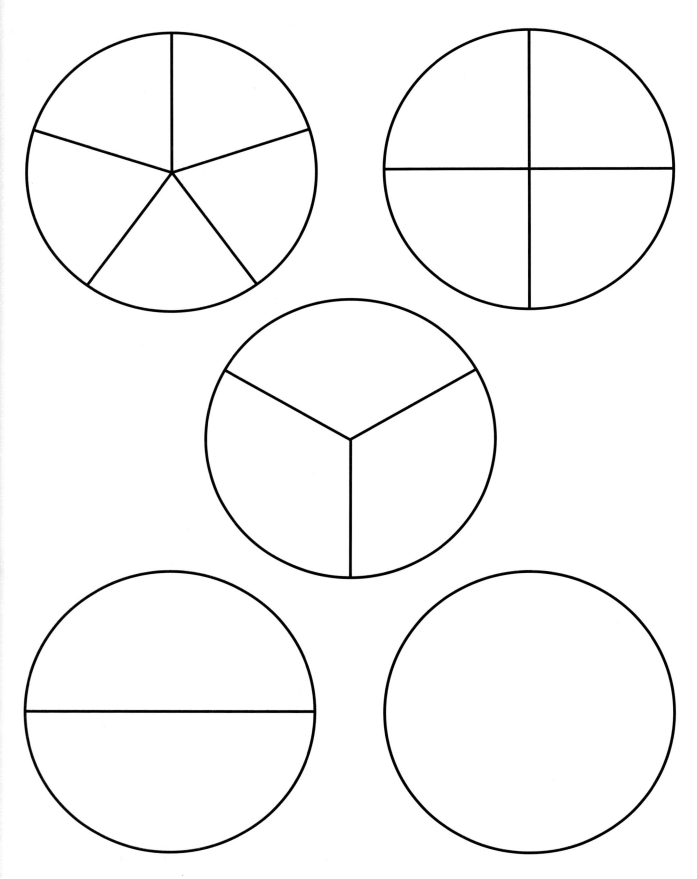

Fraction Circles

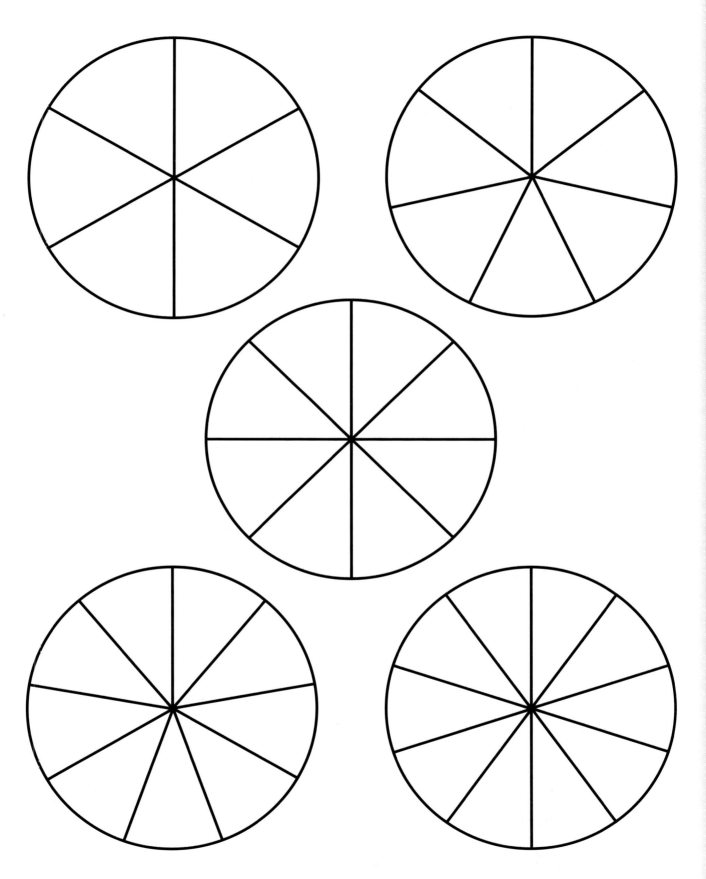

Fraction Bars

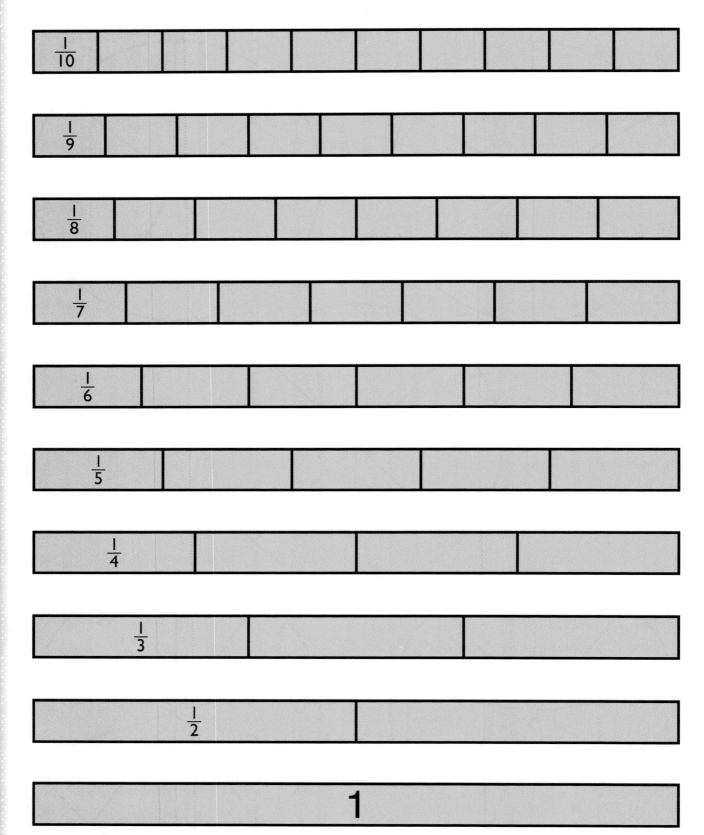

Weighing Device

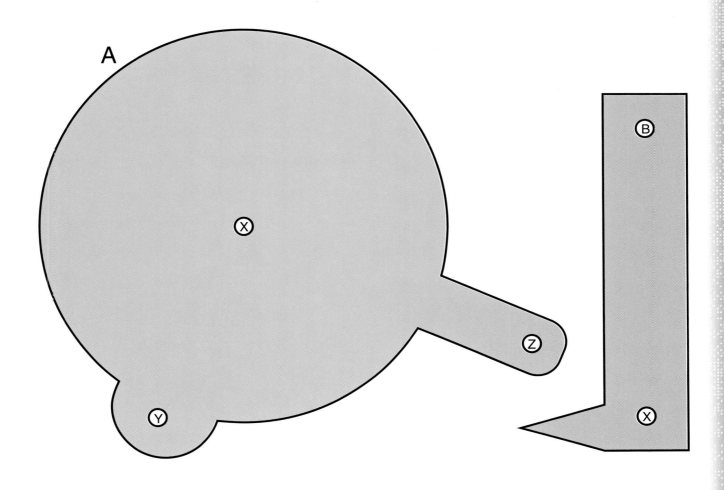

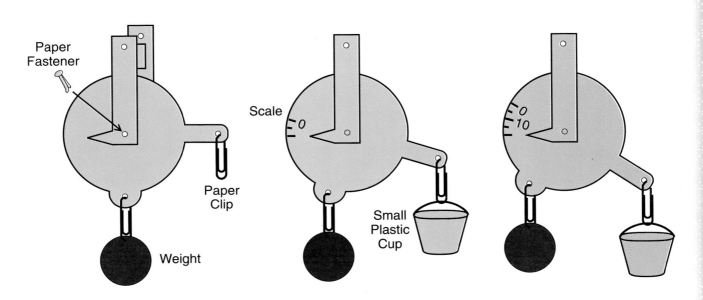

Table of Measures

METRIC	CUSTOMARY

Length

1,000 millimeters (mm) = 1 meter (m)   12 inches (in.) = 1 foot (ft)
100 centimeters (cm) = 1 meter   36 in., or 3 ft = 1 yard (yd)
10 decimeters (dm) = 1 meter   5,280 ft, or 1,760 yd = 1 mile (mi)
1 kilometer (km) = 1,000 meters

Capacity

1,000 milliliters (mL) = 1 liter (L)   1 tablespoon (tbsp) = 3 teaspoons (tsp)
250 milliliters = 1 metric cup   8 fluid ounces (fl oz) = 1 cup (c)
2 c = 1 pint (pt)
2 pt = 1 quart (qt)
4 qt = 1 gallon (gal)

Mass/Weight

1,000 milligrams (mg) = 1 gram (g)   16 ounces (oz) = 1 pound (lb)
1,000 grams = 1 kilogram (kg)   2,000 lb = 1 ton (T)

Time

60 seconds (sec) = 1 minute (min)   52 weeks = 1 year (yr)
60 minutes = 1 hour (hr)   12 months (mo) = 1 year
24 hours = 1 day   365 days = 1 year
7 days = 1 week (wk)   366 days = 1 leap year

Formulas

Perimeter of rectangle $P = (2 \times l) + (2 \times w)$ Area of Rectangle $A = l \times w$

Perimeter of square $P = 4 \times s$ Area of Triangle $A = \frac{1}{2} \times b \times h$

Circumference $C = \pi \times d$ Volume of prism $V = l \times w \times h$

Symbols

$=$	is equal to	$\overline{AB}$	line segment AB
$>$	is greater than	$\angle ABC$	angle ABC
$<$	is less than	$\triangle ABC$	triangle ABC
10^4	ten to the fourth power	π	pi (3.14)
$\approx$	is approximately equal to	$°$	degree
1:3	ratio of 1 to 3	$°C$	degree Celsius
$\overrightarrow{AB}$	ray AB	$°F$	degree Fahrenheit
$\overleftrightarrow{AB}$	line AB	(2,3)	ordered pair 2,3

Glossary

acute angle   An angle that has a measure less than 90° *(page 112)*

angle   A figure formed by two rays that meet at a common endpoint *(page 112)*

area   The number of square units needed to cover a surface *(page 394)*

Associative Property of Addition   The property which states that when adding three or more addends, any two of the addends can be joined, and the remaining addends may then be added to their sum without changing the total sum *(page 58)*
>   *Example:* $(7 + 5) + 6 = 7 + (5 + 6)$
> $\qquad\qquad 12 + 6 = 7 + 11$
> $\qquad\qquad\quad 18 = 18$

Associative Property of Multiplication   The property which states that when multiplying three or more factors, any two of the factors can be multiplied, and the remaining factors may then be multiplied without changing the total product *(page 76)*
>   *Example:* $(3 \times 4) \times 5 = 3 \times (4 \times 5)$
> $\qquad\qquad 12 \times 5 = 3 \times 20$
> $\qquad\qquad\quad 60 = 60$

average   The number found by dividing the sum of a set of numbers by the number of addends *(page 168)*

B

bar graph   A graph which uses bars of different heights or lengths to show and compare information *(page 230)*

base   A side of a polygon or a face of a solid figure by which the figure is measured or named *(page 136)*
>   *Example:*

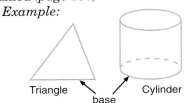

Triangle   Cylinder
base

base   A number used as a repeated factor *(page 3)*
>   *Example:* $10^3 = 10 \times 10 \times 10$
>   The base is 10. It is used as a factor three times.

C

capacity   The amount of liquid a container can hold *(page 354)*

category   A type of information in a data base, such as names or phone numbers *(page 462)*

cell   In a spreadsheet, a block area in which data or formulas can be entered; located by an address consisting of a letter and a number *(page 458)*

centimeter (cm)   A unit of length in the metric system
>   0.01 meter = 1 centimeter *(page 350)*

chord   A line segment with endpoints on a circle *(page 135)*
>   *Example:*

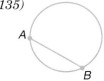

circle   A flat, round shape that has all points the same distance from the center point *(page 134)*

circle graph   A graph in the shape of a circle that shows fractions, percents, or parts of a whole *(page 230)*

circumference   The distance around a circle *(page 392)*
>   *Example:*

circumference

closed figure   An outline of a shape that begins and ends at the same point *(page 116)*

clustering   A method used in estimation when several addends are close to the same number that is easy to compute mentally *(page 55)*

common factor   A number that is a factor of two or more numbers *(page 288)*
   Example: The common factors of 6 and 12 are 1, 2, 3, and 6.

common multiple   A number that is a multiple of two or more numbers *(page 292)*
   Example: A common multiple of 2, 3, 4, and 6 is 24.

Commutative Property of Addition   The property which states that when the order of two addends is changed, the sum is the same *(page 58)*
   Example: $6 + 4 = 4 + 6$
   $\qquad\qquad 10 = 10$

Commutative Property of Multiplication   The property which states that when the order of two factors is changed, the product is the same *(page 76)*
   Example: $5 \times 7 = 7 \times 5$
   $\qquad\qquad 35 = 35$

compatible numbers   Pairs of numbers that are easy to compute mentally *(page 152)*

composite numbers   Numbers that have more than two factors *(page 287)*
   Example: 6 is a composite number since its factors are 1, 2, 3, and 6.

cone   A solid figure that has a flat, round base *(page 138)*

congruent figures   Figures that have the same size and shape *(page 130)*

coordinates   The two numbers in an ordered pair *(page 234)*

cube   A solid figure with six congruent square faces *(page 136)*

cup (c)   A customary unit for measuring capacity
   8 fluid ounces = 1 cup *(page 372)*

cylinder   A solid figure with two faces that are parallel, congruent circles *(page 138)*

data   Information, such as text, formulas, or numbers, that can be organized, sorted, collected, or used in calculations *(page 12)*

data base   A computer program used to organize, sort, and find the kind of information that is normally kept in a list or on file cards *(page 462)*

decimal   A number that uses place value and a decimal point to show values less than one, such as tenths, hundredths, and so on *(page 16)*

decimeter (dm)   A unit of length in the metric system
   10 centimeters = 1 decimeter *(page 350)*

degree (°)   A unit for measuring angles and for measuring temperature *(page 114)*

degree Celsius (°C)   A metric unit for measuring temperature *(page 362)*

degree Fahrenheit (°F)   A unit of the customary system for measuring temperature *(page 362)*

diameter   A line segment that passes through the center of a circle and has its endpoints on the circle *(page 135)*
   Example:

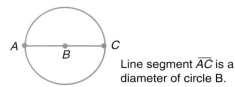

Line segment $\overline{AC}$ is a diameter of circle B.

Distributive Property of Multiplication   The property which states that multiplying a sum by a number is the same as multiplying each addend by the number and then adding the products *(page 83)*
   Example: $3 \times (4 + 2) = (3 \times 4) + (3 \times 2)$
   $\qquad\qquad\quad 3 \times 6 = 12 + 6$
   $\qquad\qquad\qquad\quad 18 = 18$

dividend   The number that is to be divided in a division problem *(page 150)*
   Example: $3\overline{)18}$
   The dividend is 18.

divisible   A number is divisible by another number if the result of the division is a whole number and the remainder is zero *(page 150)*
   Example: 18 is divisible by 3.

divisor   The number that divides the dividend *(page 150)*
   Example: $3\overline{)18}$
   The divisor is 3.

document   A file, or a group of information, that is stored on a disk or in a computer's hard drive, used by a computer program *(page 456)*

equally likely   Outcomes that have the same chance of occurring *(page 436)*

equilateral triangle   A triangle with three congruent sides *(page 118)*

equivalent decimals   Decimals that name the same number or amount *(page 62)*
Example: 0.5 = 0.50 = 0.500

equivalent fractions   Fractions that name the same number or amount *(page 279)*
Example: $\frac{3}{4} = \frac{6}{8}$

equivalent ratios   Ratios that name the same comparisons *(page 424)*

estimate   An answer close to the exact answer, found by rounding, using front-end digits, or by using compatible numbers *(pages 40, 46)*

expanded form   A way to write numbers by showing the value of each digit *(page 4)*
Example: 635 = 600 + 30 + 5 or
(6 × 100) + (3 × 10) + (5 × 1) or
$(6 \times 10^2) + (3 \times 10^1) + (5 \times 10^0)$

exponent   A number that tells how many times the base is used as a factor *(page 3)*
Example: $10^3 = 10 \times 10 \times 10$

face   A flat surface of a solid figure *(page 136)*

factor   A number multiplied by another number to find a product *(page 92)*

field   A type of information in a data base, such as names or phone numbers *(page 462)*

file   The electronic form of information stored together as a group on a disk or on a computer's hard drive *(page 457)*

flip   A move that involves turning a figure across a line of symmetry *(page 130)*
Example:

fluid ounce (fl oz)   A customary unit for measuring capacity *(page 372)*

foot (ft)   A unit of length in the customary system
12 inches = 1 foot *(page 368)*

formula   In a spreadsheet, a set of instructions that tells the computer to calculate a total or to perform a task *(page 458)*

fraction   A number that names part of a whole or part of a group *(page 276)*
Example:

$\frac{1}{3}$ of the region $\frac{1}{3}$ of the group of
is shaded.   pencils is circled.

frequency table   A chart used to show how many times each item of data occurs *(page 210)*

front-end estimation   A method using only the front-end digits to estimate sums, differences, products, and quotients *(page 40)*

gallon (gal)   A customary unit for measuring capacity
4 quarts = 1 gallon *(page 372)*

gram (g)   A unit of mass in the metric system
1,000 milligrams = 1 gram *(page 356)*

graphics   Art or designs made using the computer *(page 448)*

greatest common factor (GCF)   The greatest factor a pair of numbers have in common *(page 289)*
Example: 6 is the GCF of 18 and 30.

horizontal axis   The bottom line of a graph *(page 224)*

inch (in.)   A unit of length in the customary system *(page 368)*
Example:

1 inch

intersecting lines   Two lines that cross at exactly one point *(page 109)*
   Example:

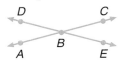

interval   The number of units between equally spaced lines on a graph *(page 214)*

inverse operations   Opposite operations that undo each other; addition and subtraction or multiplication and division are inverse operations *(page 38)*

isosceles triangle   A triangle with at least two congruent sides and two congruent angles *(page 118)*
   Example:

kilogram (kg)   A unit of mass in the metric system
   1,000 grams = 1 kilogram *(page 356)*

kilometer (km)   A unit of length in the metric system
   1,000 meters = 1 kilometer *(page 350)*

least common denominator (LCD)   The smallest common multiple of two or more denominators *(page 319)*
   Example: The LCD for $\frac{1}{4}$ and $\frac{5}{6}$ is 12.

least common multiple (LCM)   The smallest number other than zero that is a multiple of two or more given numbers *(page 292)*
   Example: The LCM of 6 and 9 is 18.

like fractions   Fractions that have a common denominator *(page 317)*
   Example: $\frac{2}{5}$ and $\frac{3}{5}$

line   A straight path extending in both directions with no endpoints *(page 108)*
   Example:

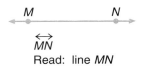
Read: line *MN*

line graph   A graph in which lines are used to show how something changes over a period of time *(page 230)*

line of symmetry   A line that divides a figure so that the two parts of the figure are congruent *(page 128)*

line segment   Part of a line with two endpoints *(page 108)*
   Example:

Read: line segment *MN*

liter (L)   A unit for measuring capacity in the metric system
   1,000 milliliters = 1 liter *(page 354)*

LOGO   A computer language used primarily to draw graphic designs *(page 450)*

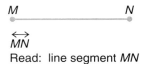

mass   The measure of the quantity of matter of an object *(page 356)*

mean   The number found by dividing the sum of a set of numbers by the number of addends, or the average *(pages 168, 212)*

median   The middle number in a ordered series of numbers *(page 212)*
   Example: The median of 1, 3, 4, 6, 7 is 4.

memory keys   Keys on a calculator that store and recall numbers from memory *(page 199)*

meter (m)   A unit of length in the metric system
   100 centimeters = 1 meter *(page 350)*

metric system   A measurement system that uses meter as the measure of length; liter as the measure of capacity; gram as the measure of mass; and degree Celsius as the unit of temperature *(page 358)*

mile (mi) A unit of length in the customary system
    5,280 feet = 1 mile *(page 368)*

milliliter (mL) A unit for measuring capacity in the metric system
    0.001 L = 1 milliliter *(page 354)*

mixed number A number that is made up of a whole number and a fraction or a whole number and a decimal *(page 299)*
    Example: $2\frac{1}{2}$, or 2.5

mode The number that occurs most often in a list of data *(page 212)*
    Example: The mode of 1, 3, 4, 4, 6 is 4.

multiple A number that is the product of a given number and another whole number *(page 78)*
    Example: Multiples of 3 are 3, 6, 9, 12, 15, . . .

number line A line with equally spaced points named by numbers *(page 10)*

obtuse angle An angle that has a measure greater than 90° and less than 180° *(page 112)*

open figure A set of points that does not completely enclose a region in the same plane *(page 116)*

ordered pair A pair of numbers used to locate a point on a grid; the first number tells the left-right position and the second number tells the up-down position *(page 234)*

ounce (oz) A unit for measuring weight in the customary system *(page 372)*

outcome A possible result in a probability experiment *(page 436)*

parallel lines Lines in a plane that stay exactly the same distance apart *(page 109)*
    Example:

parallelogram A quadrilateral with opposite sides parallel and congruent *(page 123)*

partial products Products that are added together in a multiplication problem to get the final product *(page 94)*

percent A ratio of some number to 100 *(page 429)*

perimeter The distance around a figure *(page 388)*

period Each group of three digits in a number *(page 6)*
    Example: 3,420,071
       The periods are 420 and 071.

perpendicular lines Two lines that intersect to form right angles *(page 109)*
    Example:

pi (π) The ratio of the circumference of a circle to the length of its diameter *(page 393)*
    π ≈ 3.14

pictograph A graph that uses pictures to show and compare information *(page 230)*

pint (pt) A customary unit for measuring capacity
    2 cups = 1 pint *(page 372)*

plane A flat surface that extends without end in all directions *(page 108)*

plane figure A closed figure that lies on a flat surface *(page 116)*

point An exact location in space *(page 108)*

pound (lb) A customary unit for measuring weight
    16 ounces = 1 pound *(page 372)*

prime numbers Numbers that have only two factors, 1 and the number itself *(page 287)*
    Examples: 5, 7, 11, 13, 17, and 19 are all prime numbers.

prism A solid figure whose ends are congruent, parallel polygons, and whose sides are rectangles *(page 136)*
    Examples:

Rectangular Prism   Triangular Prism

probability The chance of an event happening *(page 437)*

procedure A set of commands that directs the computer what to do *(page 450)*

Property of One for Multiplication The property which states that the product of any number and 1 is the number *(page 76)*
    Examples: $5 \times 1 = 5$
              $16 \times 1 = 16$

pyramid A solid figure with a base that is a polygon and three or more faces that are triangles with a common vertex *(page 137)*
    Examples:

Triangular Pyramid   Rectangular Pyramid

quadrilateral A four-sided polygon *(page 122)*

quart (qt) A customary unit for measuring capacity
    2 pints = 1 quart *(page 372)*

quotient The answer in a division problem *(page 150)*
    Example:
$$3\overline{)27} \quad \frac{9}{}$$
    The quotient is 9.

radius A line segment with one endpoint at the center of a circle and the other endpoint on the circle *(page 135)*
    Example:

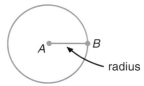

random A method of selection in which each person or item in a group has an equal chance of being chosen *(page 210)*

range A method used in estimation in which a number is rounded high and low; the difference between the greatest and least numbers in a set of data *(pages 41, 212)*

ratio A comparison of two numbers *(page 423)*

ray A part of a line that begins at one endpoint and extends forever in only one direction *(page 112)*
    Example:

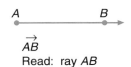

$\overrightarrow{AB}$
Read: ray *AB*

record In a data base, information for one particular person or item *(page 462)*
    Example: Joe Rossi, 950 Paces Circle,
        Jackson, MS (555) 555-1200

rectangle A parallelogram with four right angles *(page 123)*

rectangular prism A solid figure in which the parallel bases are rectangles *(page 136)*

recursion The ability of a procedure to repeat a set of commands by calling itself *(page 454)*

regular polygon A polygon with sides congruent and all angles congruent *(page 117)*
    Example:

rhombus A parallelogram with four congruent sides whose opposite angles are congruent *(page 123)*
    Example:

right angle An angle that forms a square corner and measures 90° *(page 112)*

right triangle A triangle with one right angle *(page 120)*
    Example:

round To express a number to the nearest thousandth, hundredth, tenth, one, ten, hundred, thousand, and so on *(page 10)*
> *Examples:* 473 rounded to the nearest hundred is 500.
> 37.85 rounded to the nearest tenth is 37.9.

sample group A number of people or items chosen to be representative of a larger group *(page 210)*

scale The unit length on a line compared with the number it stands for; a ratio that compares the distance on a map with an actual distance *(pages 216, 427)*

scalene triangle A triangle with three unequal angles and whose sides are not congruent *(page 118)*
> *Example:*

short division A short form of division where you multiply and subtract mentally and write the remainders in the dividend *(page 158)*

similar figures Figures that have the same shape but may not have the same size *(page 132)*
> *Example:*

simplest form A fraction that has 1 as the greatest common factor of the numerator and denominator *(page 290)*

slide The movement of a geometric figure to a new position without turning or flipping it *(page 130)*
> *Example:*

sorting A method by which the computer organizes or orders information *(page 460)*

spreadsheet A computer program that organizes information in rows and columns and makes calculations with numbers and formulas *(page 458)*

square A rectangle with four right angles and four congruent sides *(page 123)*

standard form A way to write numbers using the digits 0–9, with each digit having a place value *(page 4)*

survey To ask questions to find the most frequent choice of a group *(page 211)*

tablespoon (tbsp) A customary unit for measuring capacity
> 3 teaspoons = 1 tablespoon *(page H102)*

tessellation An arrangement of geometric figures that cover a flat surface without leaving gaps and without overlapping *(page 308)*

ton (T) A customary unit for measuring weight
> 2,000 pounds = 1 ton *(page 372)*

trapezoid A quadrilateral with only one pair of sides parallel *(page 123)*
> *Example:*

tree diagram An organized list *(page 430)*
> *Example:*

coin toss < heads / tails

triangle A polygon with three line segments *(page 118)*

turn A move that involves rotating a figure around a point *(page 130)*
> *Example:*

turtle The triangle in the computer language LOGO that is directed to draw graphic designs *(page 450)*

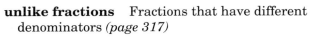

unlike fractions Fractions that have different denominators *(page 317)*

Example: $\frac{3}{4}$ and $\frac{2}{3}$

variable In LOGO, a name by a colon (:) which substitutes a numeric value *(page 450)*

Venn diagram A diagram that uses geometric shapes to show relationships *(page 225)*

vertex The point at which two rays of an angle, two sides of a polygon, or three or more edges of a solid figure meet *(page 112)*

vertical axis The left side of a graph *(page 224)*

volume The measure of space inside a solid figure *(page 406)*

word processor A computer program used to write text, such as letters, reports, word problems, or memos *(page 456)*

yard (yd) A unit of length in the customary system
3 feet = 1 yard *(page 368)*

Zero Property for Addition The property which states that the sum of zero and any number is that number *(page 58)*
Examples: $9 + 0 = 9$
$0 + 12 = 12$

Zero Property for Multiplication The property which states that the product of zero and any number is zero *(page 76)*
Examples: $13 \times 0 = 0$
$0 \times 7 = 0$

ndex

**Have fun
solving these
brain teasers!**

▶ **As you learn
▶ new things this year,
▶ you will be able
▶ to solve problems
▶ that might have
▶ stumped you at first.
▶ So, keep trying!**

These brainteasers don't stump me!

Even if you are not a coin collector, you handle coins almost every day. Find out how much you really know about coins.

Tell whether the president on each of these United States coins faces left or right.

1. penny
2. nickel
3. dime
4. quarter

Don't peek!

5. Grandpa Pegrim collects old coins. He decided to give some of his coins to his grandson Tony. He gave Tony three coins in the first month, four coins in the second month, six coins in the third month, and nine coins in the fourth month.

If Tony's grandpa continues to give him coins at the same rate, how many coins will Tony receive in the twelfth month? Explain how you got your answer.

MONEY

movers

In these puzzles it is where you move your money that counts.

1. Arrange ten pennies as shown in the diagram. Remove the least number of pennies possible so that no equilateral triangle of any size remains.

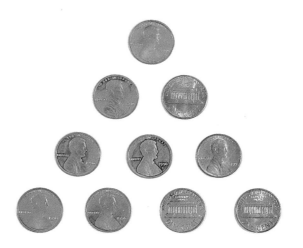

2. Trace the three squares shown at the right. Place four different coins in Square A as shown.

In as few moves as possible, move the four coins from Square A to Square C according to these rules. What is the least number of moves?

 **Rules**

- Stack the coins from largest on the bottom to smallest on top (quarter, nickel, penny, dime).

- Move only the coin on the top of a stack.

- Move only one coin at a time.

- Coins may be placed on Square B.

- Do not place a larger coin on top of a smaller coin.

- The coins must end up stacked on Square C in the same order as they were stacked on Square A.

Sum HIGH

The object of this puzzle is to find the greatest possible sum. Try to solve it yourself, or find a friend to help you!

- Copy the grid onto your own paper.

- Write each of the numbers 1–9 in a different square on the grid.

- Perform the computations in each row and column.

- Be sure to multiply and divide first, then add and subtract.

- Record each answer to the right of the row or below the column.

- Each answer must be a whole number or a fraction.

- Add all of the answers. The object is to get the greatest sum possible.

Sum: _____

CALENDAR *fun*

**These puzzles use time to help you pass time.
Can you figure out how these number
puzzles work?**

1. Choose any number.
2. Add the number of days in November.
3. Multiply by the number of days in a school week.
4. Subtract the number of years in a century.
5. Double the answer.
6. Delete the zero in the ones place.
7. Subtract your original number.

The answer should be 10.

1. Write the number of the month in which you were born.
2. Add the number of months in a year.
3. Multiply by 25.
4. Subtract 228.
5. Multiply by the number of weeks in a month.
6. Add your age.
7. Subtract 288.

The answer should be the month in which you were born followed by your age.

1. Choose a number.
2. Multiply by the number of days in a week.
3. Add the number of months in a quarter of a year.
4. Multiply by the number of days in a weekend.
5. Double your original number and subtract.
6. Divide by the number of months in one half year.
7. Subtract 1.

The answer should be twice your original number.

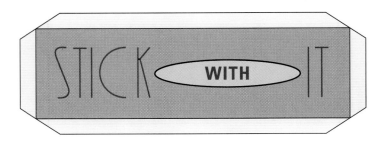

STICK WITH IT

You may find it helpful to use
toothpicks or other thin sticks
to solve these puzzles.

1. Move only one
toothpick to make
a perfect square.

HINT: A square
is not always
a square.

2. Now that you have
the right idea,
move only one
toothpick to make
another perfect
square.

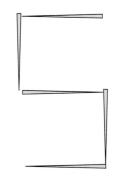

3. The tic-tac-toe
grid contains
12 toothpicks. Move
only 3 toothpicks
to make three
identical squares.

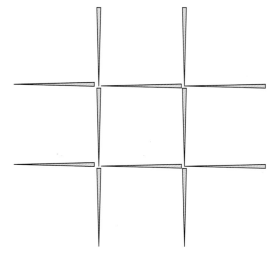

Aha!

1. **Trace the two squares onto your own paper.**

Draw four straight lines to make ten identical squares.

HINT: Two of the new squares will be outside the original squares.

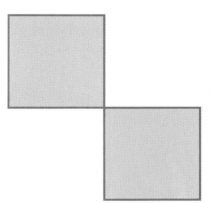

2. **Trace the figure below onto your own paper. Draw three straight lines to make 21 triangles.**

HINT: The lines can extend outside the figure.

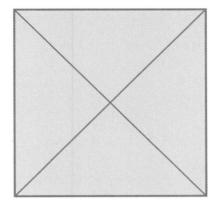

M7

Sometimes you need to see many possibilities to solve a puzzle.

Peak Park has walking paths that form many different triangles.
How many different triangles can you walk around?
List the triangles, using the letters given.

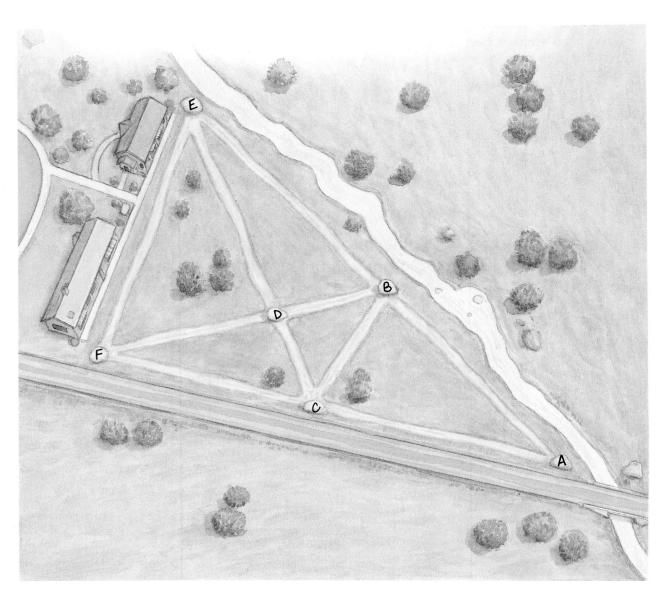

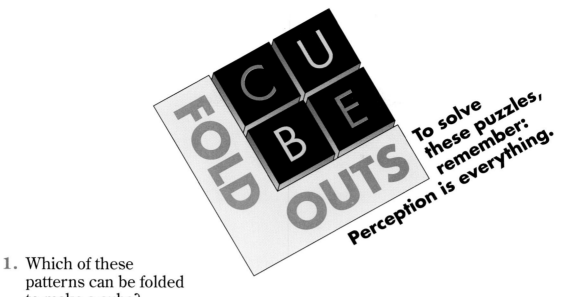

CUBE FOLD OUTS

To solve these puzzles, remember: Perception is everything.

1. Which of these patterns can be folded to make a cube?

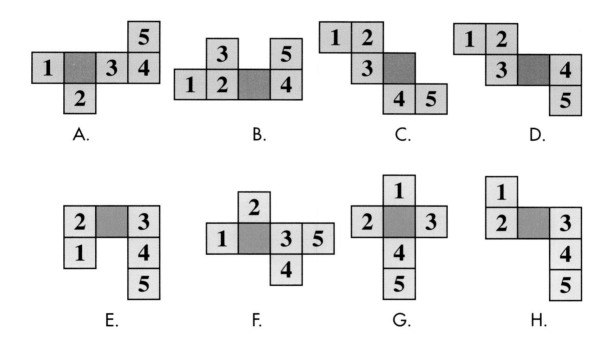

2. Refer to each of the patterns you chose. Think of the shaded face as the bottom of the cube. For each cube, what is the number of the face that would be on top?

In the stack of blocks,
T, E, and *N* in the word *TEN*
can be used to complete the word
in each row of the stack.
Each of the letters *T, E,* and *N*
must be used in each of the rows.
Any of the letters can be used
more than once in each row.
Write each completed word on your own paper.

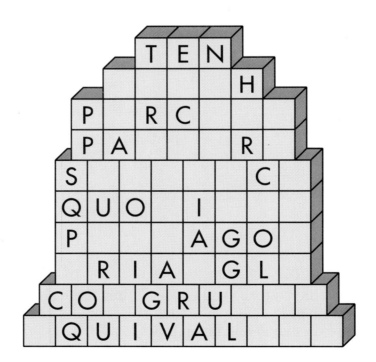

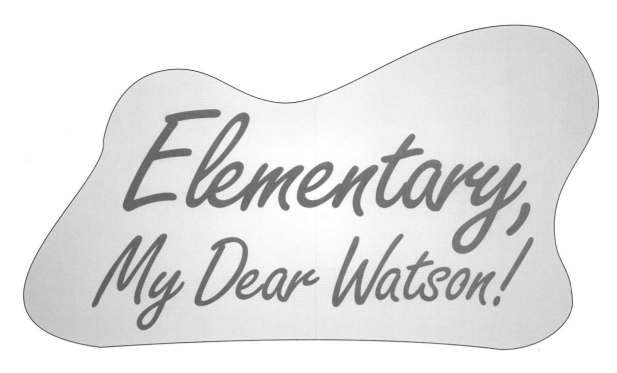

Elementary, My Dear Watson!

Are you a good word detective?
Conduct a word search, and find those fugitive
units of measure.

The table contains the customary and metric units of measure listed.
Copy the table onto graph paper. Fill in each space with the given letter.
Search the table for each word in the list. Circle the hidden words in your table.
You may read the words forward, backward, or diagonally.

C	U	P	C	E	R	U	O	H	E
S	E	C	O	N	D	F	A	C	A
M	I	N	U	T	E	N	N	N	E
L	R	E	T	E	M	O	L	I	K
E	P	I	T	I	L	T	L	E	H
C	O	G	R	A	M	E	T	E	R
N	U	Y	A	R	D	E	L	I	M
U	N	G	U	P	I	N	T	L	M
O	D	E	Q	E	L	I	T	E	R
M	I	L	L	I	L	I	T	E	R

CENTIMETER
CUP
FEET
GRAM
HOUR
INCH
KILOMETER
LITER
METER
MILE
MILLILITER
MINUTE
OUNCE
PINT
POUND
QUART
SECOND
TON
YARD

TIME Traveler

**Draw clock faces on your own paper.
For each time after 7:10 A.M., draw the hands on
a different clock face.**

1. I sat down to eat breakfast 15 minutes later.

2. I left for school 25 minutes later.

3. I arrived at school 20 minutes later.

4. I sat down in my classroom 20 minutes later.

5. I ate lunch 3 hours 15 minutes later.

6. Class began again 40 minutes later.

7. Music class started 1 hour 5 minutes later.

8. School ended 45 minutes later.

9. I got home 20 minutes later.

10. I finished my homework 1 hour 15 minutes later.

11. I went to sleep 5 hours 10 minutes later.

This clock shows that I got up at 7:10 A.M.
Use the clock to help you
find the time of each event
in my school day.

How many hours and minutes was I awake that day?

Repeat SHAPE

**When copies of a repeat shape are
laid next to each other,
a similar, but larger, shape is made.**

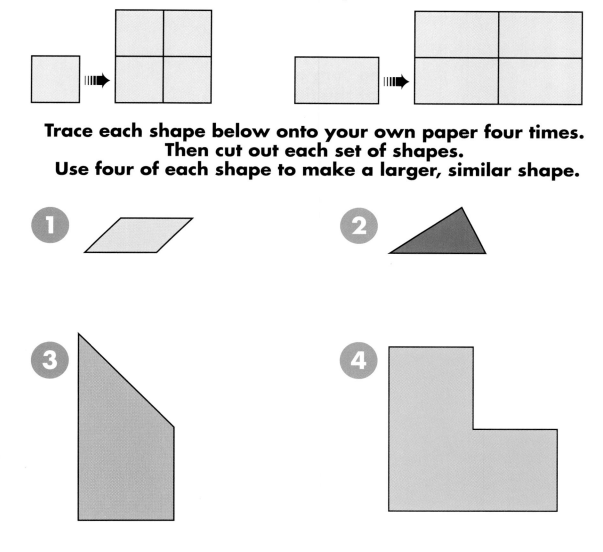

Example A   Example B

**Trace each shape below onto your own paper four times.
Then cut out each set of shapes.
Use four of each shape to make a larger, similar shape.**

1

2

3

4

HAT TRICKS

Others will tip their hats to you when you show them the secrets of these hat trick puzzles.

1. Copy this figure onto your own paper. Write the numbers 1–9 in the circles so that the sum on each of the three sides is the same.

2. Copy this figure onto your own paper. Place the numbers 1–9 in the circles so that the sums of the four numbers on each side of the triangle are equal.

No number may be used more than once.

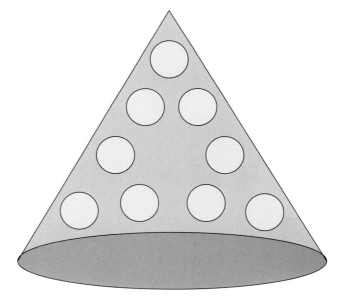

Arithmetic

Pyramids are built one stone at a time.
Complete each pyramid by finding the missing numbers.
In these pyramids addition is used to find
the number in the top stone.

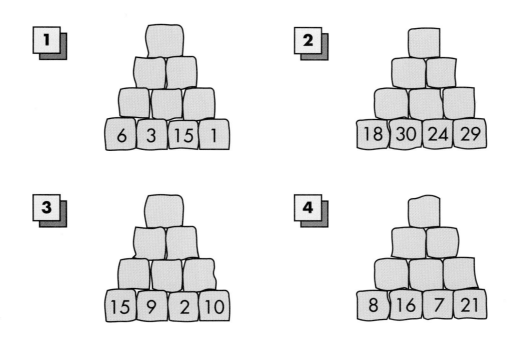

1

6 3 15 1

2

18 30 24 29

3

15 9 2 10

4

8 16 7 21

Complete each pyramid by finding the missing numbers.
In these pyramids subtraction is used to find each missing number.

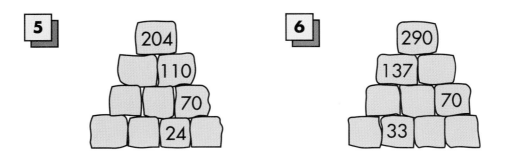

5

204
110
70
24

6

290
137
70
33

Sidewalk of STARS

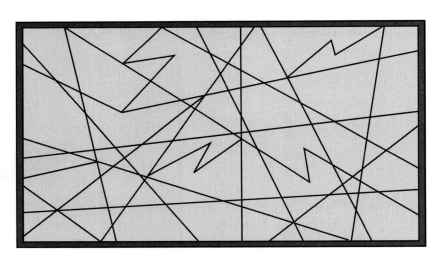

Perhaps you have noticed the cracks in a sidewalk when you used them as game boundaries or when you tried not to step on them. Sometimes interesting shapes are formed by the cracks. Examine the cracks in this section of sidewalk. How many five-pointed stars can you find?

I solved every problem! Did you?